The Martyrdom of Man

The Outcast

The Veil Of Isis;
or, Mysteries of the Druids

by
William Winwood Reade

Printed on acid free ANSI archival quality paper.
ISBN: 978-1-78139-518-9

Contents

THE VEIL OF ISIS;
OR, MYSTERIES OF THE DRUIDS

"By the bright circle of the golden sun,
By the bright courses of the errant moon,
By the dread potency of every star,
In the mysterious Zodiac's burning girth,
By each and all of these supernal signs,
We do adjure thee, with this trusty blade
To guard yon central oak, whose holy stem,
Involves the spirit of high Taranis:
Be this thy charge."

    -MASON

Dedication

TO EMILY

As those presents are always the most fashionable, and sometimes the most valued, which cannot be used, I give you this book, which you will not be able to read, but which, perhaps, you will kindly preserve in memory of its writer.

An author can pay no higher compliment to a friend than to dedicate to her a work upon which he has spent much labor and anxiety. This effort of a young man to redeem a mistake, perhaps a fault, in his literary life, deserves to be sealed with your name, for it is you who have repeatedly urged him to the task, and presided over it like a guardian angel, with kind and consoling words.

Book The First. Darkness

THERE is no study so saddening, and none so sublime as that of the early religions of mankind. To trace back the worship of God to its simple origin, and to mark the gradual process of those degrading superstitions, and unhallowed rites which darkened, and finally extinguished His presence in the ancient world.

At first men enjoyed the blessings of nature as children do, without inquiring into causes. It was sufficient for them that the earth gave them herbs, that the trees bore them fruit, that the stream quenched their thirst. They were happy, and every moment though unconsciously they offered a prayer of gratitude to Him whom as yet they did not know.

And then a system of theology arose amongst them vague and indefinite, as the waters of the boundless sea. They taught each other that the sun, and the earth, the moon, and the stars were moved and illumined by a Great Soul which was the source of all life, which caused the birds to sing, the brooks to murmur, and the sea to heave. It was a sacred Fire which shone in the firmament, and in mighty flames. It was a strange Being which animated the, souls of men, and which when the bodies died, returned to itself again.

They silently adored this Great Soul in the beginning, and spoke of Him with reverence, and sometimes raised their eyes timidly to His glittering dwelling-place on high.

And soon they learned to pray. When those whom they loved lay dying, they uttered wild lamentations, and flung their arms despairingly towards the mysterious Soul; for in times of trouble the human mind so imbecile, so helpless, clings to something that is stronger than itself.

As yet they worshipped only the sun, the moon, and the stars-and not as Gods but as visions of that Divine Essence, which alone ruled and pervaded the earth, the sky, and the sea.

They adored Him kneeling, with their hands clasped, and their eyes raised. They offered Him no sacrifices, they built Him no temples; they were content to offer Him their hearts which were full of awe, in His own temple which was full of grandeur. And it is said that there are yet some barbarous islands where men have no churches nor ceremonies, and where they worship God, reflected in the work of His thousand hands.

But they were not long content with this simple service. Prayer which had first been an inspiration fell into a system, and men already grown wicked prayed the Deity to give them abundance of wild beast's skins, and to destroy their enemies.

They ascended eminences, as if hoping that thus being nearer God, He would prefer their prayers to those of their rivals. Such is the origin of that superstitious reverence for high places which was universal throughout the whole of the heathen world.

Then Orpheus was born. And he invented instruments which to his touch and to his lips, gave forth notes of surpassing sweetness, and with these melodies he enticed the wondering savages into the recesses of the forest, and there taught them precepts of obedience to the great Soul, and of loving-kindness towards each other in harmonious words.

So they devoted groves and forests to the worship of the Deity.

There were men who had watched Orpheus, and who had seen and envied his power over the herd who surrounded him. They resolved to imitate him, and having studied these barbarians, they banded together, and called themselves their priests. Religion -is divine, but its ministers are men. And alas! sometimes they are demons with the faces and wings of angels.

The simplicity of men, and the cunning of their priests has destroyed or corrupted all the religions of the world.

These priests taught the people to sacrifice the choicest herbs and flowers. They taught them formulas of prayer, and bade them make so many obeisances to the sun, and to worship those flowers which opened their leaves when he rose, and which closed them as he set.

They composed a language of symbols which was perhaps necessary, since letters had not been invented, but which perplexed the people and perverted them from the worship of the one God.

Thus the sun and moon were worshipped as emblems of God, and fire as an emblem of the sun, water as an emblem of the moon.

The serpent was to be worshipped also as an emblem of wisdom and eternal youth, since it renews its skin every year, and thus periodically casts off all symptoms of old age.

And the bull, most vigorous of animals, and whose horns resemble those of the crescent moon.

The priests observed the avidity with which the barbarians adored these symbols, and increased them. To worship the visible is a disease of the soul inherent to all mankind, and the disease which these men could have healed they pandered to.

It is true that the first generation of men might have looked upon these merely as the empty symbols of a Divine Being, but it is also certain that in time the vulgar forgot the God in the emblem, and worshipped that which their fathers had only honored. Egypt was the fountain-head of these idolatries, and it was in Egypt that the priests first applied real attributes to the sun, and to the moon whom they called his wife.

It may perhaps interest you to listen to the first fable of the world.

From the midst of chaos was born Osiris, and at his birth a voice was heard proclaiming-*"The ruler of all the earth is born."*

From the same dark and troubled-womb were born Isis the Queen of Light, and Typhon the Spirit of Darkness.

This Osiris traveled over the whole world, and civilized its inhabitants, and taught them the art of agriculture. But on his return to Egypt the jealous Typhon laid a stratagem for him, and in the midst of a banquet had him shut up in a chest which exactly fitted his body. He was nailed down in his prison, which cast into the Nile floated down to the sea by the

Taitic mouth, which even in the time of Plutarch was never mentioned by an Egyptian but with marks of detestation.

When Isis learnt these sad new she cut off a lock of her hair, and put on her mourning robes, and wandered through the whole country in search of the chest which contained the dead body of her husband.

At length she learnt that the chest had been carried by the waves to the shore of Byblos, and had there lodged in the branches of a tamarisk bush, which quickly shot up and became a large and beautiful tree, growing round the chest so that it could not be seen.

The king of the country amazed at the vast size the tree had so speedily acquired, ordered it to be cut down to be hewn into a pillar to support the roof of his palace-the chest being still concealed in the trunk.

The voice which had spoken from Heaven at the birth of Osiris made known these things to poor Isis, who went to the shore of Byblos and sat down silently by a fountain to weep. The damsels of the queen met her and accosted her, and the queen appointed her to be nurse to her child. And Isis fed the infant with her finger instead of with her breast, and put him every night into fire to render him immortal, while transforming herself into a swallow she hovered round the pillar which was her husband's tomb, and bemoaned her unhappy fate.

It happened that the queen thus discovered her, and shrieked when she saw her child surrounded by flames. By that cry she broke the charm and deprived him of immortality.

By that cry Isis was summoned back to her goddess-form, and stood before the awe-struck queen shining with light and diffusing sweet fragrances around.

She cut open the pillar, and took the coffin with her, and opened it in a desert. There she embraced the cold corpse of Osiris, and wept bitterly.

She returned to Egypt and hid the coffin in a remote place: but Typhon, hunting by moonlight, chanced to find it, and divided the corpse into fourteen pieces. Again Isis set out on her weary search throughout the whole land, sailing over the fenny parts in a boat made of papyrus. She recovered all the fragments except one which had been thrown into the sea. Each of these she buried in the place where she found it, which explains why in Egypt there are so many tombs of Osiris.

And instead of the limb which was lost, she gave the *phallus* to the Egyptians-the disgusting worship of which was thence carried into Italy, into Greece, and into all the countries of the East.

When Isis died, she was buried in a grove near Memphis. Over her grave was raised a statue covered from head to foot with a black veil. And underneath was engraved these divine words:

I am all that has been, that is, that shall be, and none among mortals has yet dared to raise my veil.

Beneath this veil are concealed all the mysteries and learning of the past. A young scholar, his fingers covered with the dust of venerable folios, his eyes weary and reddened by nightly toil will now attempt to lift a corner of this mysterious and sacred covering.

These two Deities, Isis and Osiris were the parents of all the Gods and Godesses of the Heathens, or were indeed those Gods themselves worshipped under different names. The fable itself was received into the mythologies of the Hindoos and the Romans. Sira is said to have mutilated Brahma as Typhon did Osiris, and Venus to have lamented her slain Adonis, as Isis wept for her husband-god.

As yet the sun and moon alone were worshipped under these two names. And as we have seen, besides these twin beneficial spirits, men who had begun to recognize sin in their hearts had created an Evil One who struggled with the power of light, and fought with them for the souls of men.

It is natural for man to fabricate something that is worse than himself. Even in the theology of the American Indians which is the purest of the modem world, there is found a Mahitou or dark Spirit.

Osiris or the sun was now worshipped throughout the whole world, though under different names. He wag the Mithra of the Persians, the Brahma of India, the Baal or Adonis of the Phoenicians, the Apollo of the Greeks, the Odin Of Scandinavia, the Hu of the Britons, and the Baiwe of the Laplanders.

Isis also received the names of Islene, Ceres, Rhea, Venus, Vesta, Cybele, Niobe, Melissa--Nehalennia in the North; Isi with the Indians; Puzza among the Chinese; and Ceridwen among the ancient Britons.

The Egyptians were sublime philosophers who had dictated theology to the world. And in Chaldcea arose the first astrologers who watched the heavenly bodies with curiosity as well as with awe, and who made divine discoveries, and who called themselves *The Interpreters of God.*

To each star they gave a name, and to each day in the year they gave a star.

And the Greeks and Romans who were poets, wreathed these names into legends. Each name was a person, each person was a god.

From these stories of the stars originated the angels of the Jews, the genii of the Arabs, the heroes of the Greeks, and the saints of the Romish Church.

Now corruption grew upon corruption, and superstition flung a black and hideous veil over the doctrines of religion. A religion is lost as soon as it loses its simplicity: truth has no mysteries: it is deceit alone that lurks in obscurity.

Men multiplied God into a thousand names, and created Him always in their own image. Him, too, whom they had once deemed unworthy of any temple less noble than the floor of the earth and the vast dome of the sky, they worshipped in caves, and then in temples which were made of the trunks of trees rudely sculptured, and ranged in rows to imitate groves, and with other trunks placed upon them traversely.

Such were the first buildings of worship erected by man from no reverence for the Deity, but to display that which they doubtless conceived to be a stupendous effort in art.

It may not be needless to remind some of my readers that a superior being must view the elegant temples of the Romans, the gorgeous pagodas of India, and our own Gothic cathedrals with feelings similar to those with which we contemplate the rude efforts of the early heathens, who deemed God unworthy of the fruits and flowers which he himself had made, and offered to him the entrails of beasts, and the hearts of human beings.

We may compare an ancient and fallen religion to the ship of the Argonauts, which the Greeks desiring to preserve to posterity, repairing in so many different ways, that at length there did not remain a fragment of that vessel which had born to Colchis the conqueror of the Golden Fleece.

Let us pass over a lapse of years, and then contemplate the condition of these nations in whom religion had been first born. We find the Egyptians adoring the most common of plants, the most contemptible of beasts, the most hideous of reptiles. The solemnity and pomp of their absurd ceremonies held them up to the ridicule of the whole world.

Clemens of Alexandria describes one of their temples:--(Pœdag. lib. iii).--

"The walls shine with gold and silver, and with amber, and sparkle with the gems of India and Ethiopia: and the recesses are concealed by splendid curtains. But if you enter the penetralia, and inquire for the image of God for whose sake the fane was built; one of the Pastophori, or some other attendant on the temple approaches with a solemn and mysterious face, and putting aside the veil suffers you to obtain a glimpse of the divinity. There you behold a snake, a crocodile, or a cat, or some other beast, a fitter inhabitant of a cavern, or a bog than of a temple."

The priests of Egypt, always impostors, but once so celebrated, had now degenerated into a race of jugglers.

Also the Chaldœans lived upon the fame of their fathers, and upon their own base trickeries.

The Brachmans or Brahmins, those priests of India, once so virtuous and so wise-ah! they too had fallen. Once they had forbidden the shedding of so much as an insects blood: one day in the year alone, at the feast of Jagam, they were authorized to sacrifice the flesh of a beast, and from this many had refrained from attending, unable- to conquer their feelings of abhorrence.

But now they had learnt from the fierce Scythians and from the Phoenicians who traded on their coasts to sacrifice the wife upon her husbands pyre--to appease the gentle Brahmah with the blood of men.

Now the angels who had presided over them became savage demons, who scourged them on to cruel penances, nay to life-times of suffering and famine.

In the sacred groves where once the Brachman Fathers had taught their precepts of love, men emaciated, careworn, dying, wandered sadly, waiting for death as tortured prisoners wait for their liberty.

But worse still, these wicked priests sought through the land for the most beautiful young women, and trained them to dance in the temples, and to entice the devotees to their arms with lustful attitudes and languishing looks, and with their voices which mingled harmoniously with the golden bells suspended on their feet. They sang hymns to the Gods in public, and in private enriched the treasuries of the pagoda with their infamous earnings. Thus a pure and simple religion was debased by the avarice and lewdness of its priests: till the temples became a den of thieves: till prostitution sat enthroned upon the altars of the Gods.

Greece and Rome buried in sloth and luxury did not escape the general contamination. The emblem of generation which Isis had bestowed upon the Egyptians, and which they had held in abstract reverence, had now obtained a prominent place in the festivals of these nations as did the Lingam in those of the Hindoos. It was openly paraded in processions in the streets: it was worn by Roman nations in bracelets upon their arms.

The sacred festivals and mysteries which they had received from the Egyptians, and for which the women had been wont to prepare themselves by continence, and the men by fasting, were now mere vehicles for depravities of the lowest kind. Men were permitted to join the women in their worship of Bacchus, of Adonis, of the Bona Dea, and even of Priapus, and so dissolute did the Dionusia become, that the civil powers were compelled to interfere with those of religion, and the Bacchanalia were abolished by a decree of the Roman senate.

And the Jews, the chosen people of God, had not their religion changed? had not God, weary with their sins, yielded them to captivity, scourged them with sorrow, menaced them with curses?

They worshipped Baal-peor, the Priapus of Assyria, they sacrificed their children to Moloch: they had dancing-girls in the holy temple.

I will not go deeper into particulars so degrading to human nature. I will rather invite you to follow me to a corner of the world where, at least for many ages religion was preserved in its pristine purity, and whose priests, through a barbarous soldiery, were received as martyrs in heaven before they had learned to be knaves upon earth.

It was an isolated spot unknown to the world in the earlier ages of vice. It is now a kingdom renowned for its power and for its luxuries from hemisphere to hemisphere.

It was encircled by the blue waters of the German and Atlantic Seas, and abounded in the choicest gifts of nature.

It was called *The White Island* from those cliffs which still frown so coldly upon Gaul, and *The Land of Green Hills* from its verdant mountains. Come with me to its shores, and I will show you its priests in their white robes, and its warriors in the blue paint of war, and its virgins with their long and glossy yellow hair.

But first I will lead you back into the past, and relate to you why this land was called Albion, and why Britain.

Book The Second. Aborigines

I. Albion

AS travelers, who have lost their way by night, gaze ever towards the east for the first rays of light and hope, so we who grope in the darkness of antiquity must direct our eyes to the land of the rising sun, whence learning and life itself first sprang.

Listen then to a romance of the East.

Danaus, King of Greece, had fifty sons, whom he married to the fifty daughters of his brother Ægistus, King of Egypt. But soon these women thirsted for dominion, and conspired secretly to slay their husbands and to rule in their steads. But the youngest and the most beautiful had a tender heart, which crept from her lips in words of warning to her father and her spouse. Then they were all seized and set adrift in ships upon the sea, which after many storms bore them in safety to a large and uninhabited island.

Here they staid and named it Albion, after Albina their eldest sister, and here they maintained themselves by the chase, killing the deer and the boars, and wild bulls, and large birds which they found in the forests with arrows and bolts, and bowstrings, and snares and pitfalls.

And while filled with meat and drink, and with lustful thoughts, they lay sleeping on the ground covered with the skins of wild beasts, dark brooding spirits swept towards them from the sky, and encircled them with their shadowy arms, and intoxicated them with their flaming breath

By these were born huge and hideous giants which soon bore others, till they filled the whole land with a strange and fierce crew.

II. Britain

MEANWHILE Troy had fallen: the wanderings of Eneas were past: and Ascanius had died leaving behind him his son Silvius.

The son of Silvius loved a maid, who became pregnant. Then the wise men and women of the land were sent for, and all those who knew songs of magic art. They cast. their lots and found sorrowful spells: that a child would be born through whom both his father and mother would suffer death: that through their death he would be driven from the land, and after a long time would be crowned with honor.

His mother died as she gave him to the world, and the child, whom they named Brutus, when he had become a youth, shot his father through the breast a-hunting the deer.

His kindred banished him from the land, and he sailed sadly over the sea-streams into Greece where he headed an insurrection against Pandrasus the king, and with such success that the king offered him all his ships, and treasures, and Imogen his only daughter if he would consent to seek another kingdom.

So Brutus, with his followers, like Eneas of old, sailed forth upon the waters in search of a new land.

After two days and two nights the sea became blue: the wild waves were hushed: they came to a desolate island: its inhabitants had been slain by the pirates: the timid deer coursed over its wasted shores.

But they found there a marble temple, and within the fair and beautiful image of Diana.

Brutus with twelve wise men, and with Gerion, his priest, entered the temple while his followers remained without. He bore a vessel of red gold in his hand: it was filled with wine and with the milk of a white hind which he had killed. Having kindled a fire by the altar, he walked around it nine times. He called to the goddess beloved of his heart: he kissed the altar and poured the wine and milk upon the fire.

"Lady Diana! loved Diana! High Diana!" he cried. "Help me in my need. Teach me whither I may go and wherein I may dwell. And there I will make thee a lofty dwelling and honor thee with great worship.

Then he spread the hide of the white hind upon the altar, and kneeling upon it fell asleep. In his dreams he beheld Diana floating towards him with sweet smiles. She laid her hands like a wreath of flowers upon his head, saying:

Beyond Gaul in the west thou shall find a winsome land: therein thou shalt prosper. Therein is fowl: there is fish: there dwell fair deer: there is wood: there is water: there is much desert: grim giants dwell in the land. It is called *Albion*.

For thirty days and thirty nights they sailed past Africa and over the lake of Silvius, and over the lake of Philisteus: by Ruscikadan they took the sea, and by the mountain country of Azare. They fought with the pirates, and gained from them such treasures that there was not a man in the fleet who did not wear gold and pall. And by the pillars of Hercules they were encompassed by mermen who sing songs so sweet that mariners will rest slothfully on their oars, and listen to them for days without wearying of their songs to hear--these impeded them much with their wicked crafts, but they escaped them safely.

In a peaceful sea, and among the playing fish they came to Dartmouth in Totnes. There the ships bit the sands, and with merry hearts the warriors went ashore.

It happened after many days that Brutus and his people were celebrating holy writs, with meat, with drink, and with merry glee sounds: with silver and with gold: with horses and with vestments.

Twenty strong giants descended the hills: trees were their clubs: in the centre of their foreheads was a single eye vivid as the blue ice. They hurled huge stones and slew five hundred of the Trojans. But soon the fierce steel arrows of the Trojans whistled through the air, and blood began to spurt from their monstrous sides. They tried to fly; but those darts followed them swift and revengeful, as birds of prey winged with the dark feathers of death.

Nineteen were slain and Geog-magog, their leader was brought bound before Brutus, who ordered a wrestling match to be held between the giant and Corineus, a chieftain of his army.

A mighty crowd gathered upon the downs by the sea-cliff.

Corineus and the giant advanced towards each other, they yoked their arms and stood breast to breast. Their eyes gushed blood, their teeth gnashed like wild boars, their bones cracked. Now their faces were black and swollen, now red and flaming with rage. Geog-magog thrust Corineus off his breast and drawing him back broke three of his ribs with his mighty hand. But Corineus was not overcome, he hugged the giant grimly to his waist, and grasping him by the girdle swung him over the cliff upon the rocks below.

Which spot is called "Geog-magog's leap" to this day. And to Corineus, the conqueror, was given a dukedom, which was thence called Corinee and thence Cornwall.

Brutus having conquered the giant off-spring of the treacherous sisters, built a New Troy, and erected temples to the great Diana, and caused her to be worshipped throughout the land.

Which was named *Britain* after Brutus, the first man who set foot upon its shores.

III. Analysis

FABLES are seldom actual impostures. They are usually truths disguised in gaudy or grotesque garments, but so disguised that the most profound philosophers are often at a loss how to separate the tinsel from the gold.

But even when they remain insolvable enigmas, they are, at least, to be preferred to the etymological eurekas and tedious conjectures with which antiquarians clog the pages of history, and which are equally false and less poetical.

My fable of Albion is derived from the ancient chronicles of Hugh de Genesis, an historiographer now almost forgotten, and is gravely advanced by John Hardyng, in his uncouth rhymes, as the source of that desire for sovereignty which he affirms to be a peculiarity of his own countrywomen.

The story of Brû or Brutus was first published by Geoffrey of Monmouth, and was generally supposed to have been a monkish fabrication, till it was discovered in the historical poems of Tyssilia, a Welsh bard.

It is worthy of remark that the boys of Wales still amuse themselves by cutting out seven enclosures in the sward, which they call the City of Troy, and dance round and between them as if in imitation of the revolution of the planets.

In a poem by Taliesin, the Ossian of Wales, called The Appeasing, of Lhudd, a passage occurs, of which this is a literal translation:

"A numerous race, fierce, they are said to have been,
Were thy original colonists, Britain, first of isles,
Natives of a country in Asia, and the city of Gafiz
Said to have been a skilful people, but the district is unknown
Which was mother to these children, warlike adventurers on the sea;
Clad in their long dress, who could equal them?
Their skill is celebrated, they were the dread of Europe."

This is strong evidence in favor of the Phœnicians, at that time the pirate-scourges of the sea, but in the Welsh triads, or traditional chronicles, we read that--

*"The first of the three chieftains who established the colony was Hu, the Mighty, who came with the original settlers. They came over the Hazy Sea from the summer country, which is called*Deffrobani, *that is where* Constinoblys *now stands."*--Triad 4.

It maybe possible to reconcile these contradictions of history in its simplest state, to which I might add a hundred from later writers.

We learn fromJosephus that the Scythians, were called *Magogæi* by the Greeks, and it is probable that these (who certainly did migrate to Britain at a remote period) were the real aborigines, and the race alluded to in the fourth Triad. That then the warlike race of Taliesin also migrated from another region of the East, and that their battles with the Scythians gave rise to the fables of Brutus and Magog; for it was a practice, common enough with illiterate nations, to express heroes in their war-tales by the images of giants.

This superstition is somewhat borne out by the assertion of Tacitus and other classical writers, that at the time of Cæsar's invasion, there were three distinct races in Britain, especially contrasting-the red-haired, large-limbed, and blue-eyed Celts of the North, with the Silures of Devon, Cornwall, and the Cassiterides or Scilly Isles, who had swarthy faces and dark curly hair, like the Iberi of Spain.

But let us pass on from such dateless periods of guess-work, to that in which *The White Island* first obtained notice from those philosophers, and poets, and historians, whom now we revere and almost deify.

IV. Description

THE north of the island was inhabited by wild hordes of savages, who lived upon the bark of trees, and upon the precarious produce of the chase; went naked, and sheltered themselves from the weather under the cover of the woods, or in the mountain caves.

The midland tribes were entirely pastoral. They lived upon the flesh and milk which their flocks afforded them, and clothed themselves in their skins.

While the inhabitants of the south, who had been polished by intercourse with strangers, were acquainted with many of the arts of civilization, and were ruled by a priesthood which was second to none in the world for its learning and experience.

They manured their ground with marl, and sowed corn, which they stored in thatched houses, and from which they took as much as was necessary for the day and having dried the ears, beat the grain out, bruised it, and baked it into bread.

They ate little of this bread at their banquets, but great quantities of flesh, which they either boiled in water, or broiled upon the coals, or roasted upon spits. They drank ale or metheglin, a liquor made of milk and honey, and sat upon the skins of wolves or dogs.

They lived in small houses built in a circular form, thatched with rushes into the shape of a cone; an aperture being left by which the smoke might escape.

Their dress was of their own manufacture. A square mantle covered a vest and trousers, or a deeply-plaited tunic of braided cloth; the waist was encircled by a belt, rings adorned the second finger of each hand, and a chain of iron or brass was suspended from the neck. These mantles, at first the only covering of the Britons, were of one color, with long hair on the outside, and were fastened upon the breast by a clasp, with the poorer classes by a thorn.

The heads were covered with caps made of rushes, and their feet with sandals of untanned skin; specimens of which are still to be met with-of the former in Wales, of the latter in the Shetland Isles.

The women wore tunics, wrought and interwoven with various colors, over which was a loose robe of coarser make, secured with brazen buckles. They let their hair flow at freedom, and dyed it yellow like the ladies of ancient Rome; and they wore chains of massive gold about their necks, bracelets upon their arms, rings upon their fingers.

They were skilled in the art of weaving, in which, however, the Gauls had obtained a still greater proficience. The most valuable of their cloths were manufactured of fine wool of different tints, woven chequer-wise, so as to fall into small squares of various colors. They also made a kind of cloth, which, without spinning or weaving, was, when worked up with vinegar, so hard and impenetrable, that it would turn the edge of the sharpest sword.

They were equally famous for their linen, and sail-cloths constituted a great part of their trade.

When they had finished the linen in, the loom, they had this curious method of bleaching it:

The flax having been whitened before it was sent to the loom, the unspun yarn was placed in a mortar where it was pounded and beaten into water; it was then sent to the weaver, and when it was received from him made into cloth, it was laid upon a large smooth stone, and beaten with broad-headed cudgels, the juice of poppies being mingled with the water.

For scouring cloths, they used a soap invented by themselves, which they made from the fat of animals and the ashes of certain vegetables.

Distinct from these southern tribes, were the inhabitants of the Cassiterides, who wore long black garments, and beards falling on each side of their mouths like wings, and who are described by Pliny as "carrying staves with three serpents curling round like Furies in a tragedy."

It is probable that the nudity of the northern nations did not proceed from mere barbarous ignorance. We know that savages are first induced to wear clothing, not from shame, but from vanity; and it was this passion which restrained them from wearing the skins of beasts, or the gaudy clothes of their civilized neighbors.

For it was their custom to adorn their bodies with various figures by a tedious and painful process. At an early age, the outlines of animals were impressed with a pointed instrument into the skin; a strong infusion of *woad*, (a Gallic herb from which a blue dye was extracted) was rubbed into the punctures, and the figures expanding with the growth of the body retained their original appearance. Like the South-Sea Islanders they esteemed that to be a decoration which we consider a disfigurement, and these tatooings (which were used by the Thracicans and by the ancient inhabitants of Constantinople, and which were forbidden by Moses, *Levit. xix. 28.*) were only displayed by Southern races as a kind of war-paint.

Like the Gauls, who endeavored to make their bright red hair rough and bristly not for ornament, but as a terror to their enemies, these Britons on the day of battle flung off their clothes, and with swords girded to their naked sides, and spear in hand, marched with joyful cries against their enemies.

Also upon certain festivals they, with their wives and children, daubed themselves from head to foot with the blue dye of the woad and danced in circles bowing to the altar.

But the Picts, or painted men, as the Romans named them, colored themselves with the juice of green grass.

Hunting was their favorite exercise and sport, and Britain which was then filled with vast swamps and forests afforded them a variety of game.

The elephant and the rhinoceros, the moose-deer, the tiger and other beasts now only known in Eastern climes, and mammoth creatures that have since disappeared from the face of the earth made the ground tremble beneath their stately tread. The brown bear preyed upon their cattle, and slept in the hollow oaks which they revered. The hyenas yelped by night, and prowled round the fold of the shepherd. The beaver fished in their streams, and built its earthen towns upon their banks. And hundreds of wolves, united by the keen frosts of winter, gathered round the rude habitations of men and howled from fierce hunger, rolling their horrible green eyes and gnashing their white teeth.

Their seas abounded with fish, but since they held water sacred they would not, injure its inhabitants for they believed them to be spirits.

I will now consider the primeval state of trade in Britain, now the greatest commercial country in the world.

It was periodically visited by the Phœnicians, a crafty and enterprising nation whose commerce embraced the whole of the known world, from the frozen borders of Scythia to the burning coasts of Africa and Hindostan; whose vessels like the Spanish galleons and our own East Indiamen of old were equipped equally for trade or war; who robbed the weak with their drawn swords, and the strong with their cunning arts; who traded with Arabia for spices and precious stones; with Damascus for the Mesopotamian white wool, and for wine of Aleppo, a beverage so costly that it was drunk by kings alone: with Judœa for fruits of the soil, corn, grape-honey, oil and balm; with Armenia for mules and chariot-horses, flocks and herds; with the shores of the Baltic for amber; with Spain for minerals; with the Euxine for tunny-fish; with India for the cinnamon of Ceylon, for cotton garments and for steel which sold in Arabia for twice its weight in gold, and of which the Damascus blades so celebrated in the middle ages were made.

It was not long before they discovered the lead and tin mines of Cornwall and the Cassiterides, which would appear (from several flint-headed tools called *celts* lately discovered within them) to have been worked by the Britons themselves.

And as they were wont to exchange the pottery of Athens for the ivory of Africa, and live Jews for the gold and jewels of the Greeks, so they bartered salt, earthenware and brazen trinkets with the Britons for tin, lead, and the skins of wild beasts.

It was the policy of the Phœnicians (in which they were afterwards imitated by the Dutch) to preserve their commercial secrets with the greatest jealousy, and to resort to extremes in order to protect their interests. Although they had supplied tin and amber for several years to the Greeks, Herodotus, who had visited Tyre, could only obtain very vague accounts as to the countries from which they had been obtained, and on making inquiries respecting cinnamon and frankincense, was explicitly informed that the first was procured by stratagem from the nests of birds built upon inaccessible crags, and the latter from a tree guarded by winged serpents.

There-is also the story of the master of a Phœnician trader from Cadiz to the Cassiterides, who finding himself followed by a Roman ship ran his own vessel ashore preferring death to discovery. The Romans were also shipwrecked, and were drowned, but the patriot escaped to tell his tale at Tyre, and to receive from a grateful state the value of his cargo and an additional reward.

In spite of these precautions, either by accident, or by the treachery of some renegade Phœnician, or from the colony of Phocians at Marseilles, the Greeks discovered the secret about three hundred years before the Christian era.

Thus monopoly being ended, the commerce of the Britons was extended. and improved, and after the descent of the Romans they exported not only tin and lead, but also gold, silver, iron, corn, cattle, slaves hunting-dogs, pearls, and those wicker baskets which Martial has immortalized in his epigrams.

It also appears that chalk was an article of their trade, by this inscription which was found with many others near Zeland, A. D. 1647-

DEAE NEHALENNIAE
OB MERCES RECTE CONSER
VATAS SECVND SILVANVS
NEGO X TOR CRETARIVS
BRITANNICIANUS
V. S. L. M.

To the Goddess Nehalennia
For his goods well preserved
Secundus Silvanus
A chalk merchant
Of Britain
Willingly performed his merited vow.

Before describing the religion and superstitions of our earliest ancestors, which will bring me to the real purpose of this book, I will add a few remarks upon their manners and peculiarities.

Curiosity, which is certainly the chief characteristic of all barbarous and semi-barbarous nations, was possessed by the Celts in so extraordinary a degree that they would compel travelers to stop, even against their wills, and make them tell some news, and deliver an opinion upon the current events of the day. They would also crowd round the merchants in towns with the same kind of inquiries.

But the great failing of these Celts was their hastiness and ferocity. Not content with pitched battles against their enemies abroad, they were always ready to fight duels with their friends at home. In fact, the end of a British feast was always the beginning of a fray; two warriors would rise and fight each other with such *sang-froid* that Athenœus wrote in astonishment, *Mortem pro joco habent*, "They turn death into a joke;" and it was from these spectacles that the Romans conceived and executed the idea of gladiatorial entertainments.

They feared nothing these brave men. They sang as they marched to battle, and perhaps to death. They shot arrows at the heavens when it thundered; they laughed as they saw their own hearts' blood gushing forth.

And yet they were plain and simple in their manners; open and generous, docile and grateful, strangers to low cunning and deceit, so hospitable that they hailed the arrival of each fresh guest with joy and festivities, so warm-hearted that they were never more pleased than when they could bestow a kindness.

Their code of morals, like those of civilized nations, had its little contradictions; they account it disgraceful to steal, but honorable to rob, and though they observed the strictest chastity, they did not blush to live promiscuously in communities of twelve.

This extraordinary custom induced Caesar to assert that they enjoyed each other's wives in common; but in this he is borne out by no other authorities, and, indeed, there are many instances of this kind among barbarous nations, who love, apparently, to hide their real purity with a gross and filthy enamel.

Richard of Circencester (probably alluding to Bath the *aquæ solis* of the ancients) mentions, however, some salt and warm springs used by the ancient Britons, from which were formed hot baths suited to all ages, with distinct places for the two sexes; a refinement which was unknown in Lacedœmon.

And Procopius writes:--

"So highly rated is chastity among these barbarians, that if even the bare mention of marriage occurs without its completion, the maiden seems to lose her fair fame."

Having thus briefly sketched the condition and employments of the early Britons-- having proved that our ancestors were brave, and that their daughters were virtuous, I will now show you those wise and potent men of whom these poor barbarians were but the disciples and the slaves.

Book The Third. The Druids

I. Origin

ALTHOUGH the term Druid is local, their religion was of deep root, and a distant origin. It was of equal antiquity with those of the Persian Magi, the Chaldees of Assyria, and the Brachmans of Hindostan.

It resembled them so closely in its sublime precepts, in its consoling promises, as to leave no doubt that these nations, living so widely apart, were all of the same stock and the same religion-that of Noah, and the children of men before the flood.

They worshiped but one God, and erected to him altars of earth, or unhewn stone, and prayed to him in the open air; and believed in a heaven, in a hell, and in the immortality of the soul.

It is strange that these offsprings of the patriarchs should also be corrupted from the same sources, and should thus still preserve a resemblance to one another in the minor tenets of their polluted creeds.

Those pupils of the Egyptian priests, the Phœnicians, or Canaanites, who had taught the Israelites to sacrifice human beings, and to pass their children through the fire to Moloch, infused the same bloodthirsty precepts among the Druids. As the Indian wife was burnt upon her husband's pyre, so, on the corpses of the Celtic lords, were consumed their children, their slaves, and their horses.

And, like the other nations of antiquity, as I shall presently prove, the Druids worshipped the heavenly bodies, and also trees, and water, and mountains, and the signs of the serpent, the bull and the cross.

The doctrine of the transmigration of souls which formed a leading theory on the system of the Brachmans, of the Druids, and afterwards of the Pythagoreans was obtained, through the Phœnicians, from Egypt, the fatherland of heathen mythology.

It cannot be denied that they also honored inferior deities, to whom they gave the names of Hu and Ceridwen, Hesus Taranis, Belenus, Ogmius, and the attributes of Osiris and Isis (or Zeus and Venus) Bacchus, Mercury, Apollo, and Hercules.

From the sandy plains of Egypt to the icebergs of Scandinavia, the whole world has rung with the exploits of Hercules, that invincible god, who but appeared in the world to deliver mankind from monsters and from tyrants.

He -was really a Phoenician *harokel*, or merchant, an enterprising mariner, and the discoverer of the tin mines of the Cassiterides. He it was who first sailed through the Straits of Gibraltar, which, to this day, are called *The Pillars of Hercules*: who built the first ship: who discovered the mariner's compass, and the loadstone, or *lapes Heractius.*

It is gratifying to learn that his twelve labors were, in reality, twelve useful discoveries, and that he had not been deified for killing a wild beast and cleaning out stables.

As the Chaldeans, who were astronomers, made Hercules an astronomer; and as the Greeks and Romans, who were warriors, made him a hero of battles; so the Druids, who were orators, named him *Ogmius*, or the Power of Eloquence, and represented him as an old man followed by a multitude, whom he led by slender and almost invisible golden chains fastened from his lips to their ears.

As far as we can learn, however, the Druids paid honors, rather than adoration to their deities, as the Jews revered their arch-angels, but reserved their worship for Jehovah.

And, like the God of the Jews, of the Chaldees, of the Hindoos, and of the Christians, this Deity of the Druids had three attributes within himself, and each attribute was a god.

Let those learn who cavil at the mysterious doctrine of the Trinity, that it was not invented by the Christians, but only by them restored from times of the holiest antiquity into which it had descended from heaven itself.

Although the Druids performed idolatrous ceremonies to the stars, to the elements, to hills, and to trees, there is a maxim still preserved among the Welsh mountaineers, which shows that in Britain the Supreme Being was never so thoroughly forgotten and degraded as he had been in those lands to which he first gave life.

It is one of those sublime expressions which can be but faintly rendered in a foreign language.

"*Nid dim oxd duw: nid duw ond dim.*" God cannot be matter; what is not matter must be God."

II. Power

THIS priesthood flourished in Gaul and in Britain, and in the islands which encircled them.

In whichever country they may first have struck root we at least know that the British Druids were the most famous, and that it was a custom in the time of Julius Cæsar for the Gallic students to cross the British channel to study in the seminaries of the sister island.

But by that time, Druidism had begun to wane in Gaul, and to be deprived of many of its privileges by the growing intelligence of the secular power.

It is generally acknowledged that there were no Druids in Germany, though Keysler has stoutly contested this belief and has cited an ancient tradition to the effect that they had Druidic colleges in the days of Hermio, a German Prince.

The learned Selden relates that some centuries ago in a monastery upon the borders of Vaitland, in Germany, were found six old statues which being exposed to view, Conradus Celtes, who was present, was of opinion that they were figures of ancient Druids. They were seven feet in height, bare-footed, their heads covered with a Greek hood, a scrip by their sides and a beard descending from their nostrils plaited out in two divisions to the middle; in their hands a book and a Diogenes staff five feet in length; their features stern and morose; their eyes lowered to the ground.

Such evidence is mere food for conjecture. Of the ancient German priests we only know that they resembled the Druids, and the medicine-men of the American aborigines in being doctors as well as priests.

The Druids possessed remarkable powers and immunities. Like the Levites, the Hebrews, and the Egyptian priests they were exempted from taxes and from military service. They also annually elected the magistrates of cities: they educated all children of whatever station, not permitting their parents to receive them till they were fourteen years of age. Thus the Druids were regarded as the real fathers of the people.

The Persian Magi were entrusted with the education of their sovereign; but in Britain the kings were not only brought up by the Druids, but also relieved. by them of all but the odium and ceremonies of sovereignty.

These terrible priests formed the councils of the state, and declared peace or war as they pleased. The poor slave whom they seated on a throne, and whom they permitted to wear robes more gorgeous even than their own was surrounded, not by his noblemen, but by Druids. He was a prisoner in his court, and his jailors were inexorable, for they were priests.

There was a Chief Druid to advise him, a bard to sing to him, a *sennechai*, or chronicler, to register his action in the Greek character, and a physician to attend to his health, and to cure or kill him as the state required.

All the priests in Britain and all the physicians, all the judges and all the learned men, all the pleaders in courts of law and all the musicians belonged to the order of the Druids. It can easily be conceived then that their power was not only vast but absolute.

It may naturally excite surprise that a nation should remain so barbarous and illiterate as the Britons undoubtedly were, when ruled by an order of men so polished and so learned.

But these wise men of the West were no less learned in human hearts than in the triplet verses, and oral of their. fathers. They imbibed with eagerness the heathen rites of the Phœnician Cabiri, and studied to involve their doctrines and their ceremonies in the deepest mystery. They knew that it is almost impossible to bring women and the vulgar herd of mankind to piety and virtue by the unadorned dictates of reason. They knew the admiration which uneducated minds have always for those things which they cannot understand. They knew that to retain their own sway they must preserve these barren minds in their abject ignorance and superstition.

In all things, therefore, they endeavored to draw a line between themselves and the mass. In their habits, in their demeanor, in their very dress.

They wore long robes which descended to the heel, while that of others came only to the knee; their hair was short and their beards long, while the Britons wore but moustaches on their upper lips, and their hair generally long.

Instead of sandals they wore wooden shoes of a pentagonal shape, and carried in their hands a white wand called *slatan drui' eachd*, or magic wand, and certain mystical ornaments around their necks and upon their breasts.

It was seldom that anyone was found hardy enough to rebel against their power. For such was reserve a terrible punishment. It was called *Excommunication*.

Originating among the Hebrews, and descending from the Druids into the Roman Catholic Church. It was one of the most horrible that it is possible to conceive. At the dead of night, the unhappy culprit was seized and dragged before a solemn tribunal, while torches, painted black, gave a ghastly light, and a low hymn, like a solemn murmur, was chanted as he approached.

Clad in a white robe, the Arch-Druid would rise, and before the assembly of brother-Druids and awestricken warriors would pronounce a curse, frightful as a death warrant, upon the trembling sinner. Then they would strip his feet, and he must walk with them bare for the remainder of his days; and would clothe him in black and mournful garments, which he must never change.

Then the poor wretch would wander through the woods, feeding on berries and the roots of trees, shunned by all as if he had been tainted by the plague, and looking to death as a salvation from such cruel miseries.

And when he died, none dared to weep for him; they buried him only that they might trample on his grave. Even after death, so sang the sacred bards, his torments were not ended; he was borne to those regions of eternal darkness, frost, and snow, which, infested with lions, wolves, and serpents, formed the Celtic hell, or *Ifurin*.

These Druids were despots; and yea they must have exercised their power wisely and temperately to have retained so long their dominion over a rude and warlike race.

There can be little doubt that their revenues were considerable, though we have no direct means of ascertaining this as a fact. However, we know that it was customary for a victorious army to offer up the chief of its spoils to the gods; that those who consulted the oracles did not attend them empty-handed, and that the sale of charms and medicinal herbs was a constant trade among them.

Although all comprehended under the one term DRUID, there were, in reality, three distinct sects comprised within the order.

First, the Druids or Derwydd, properly so called. These were the sublime and intellectual philosophers who directed the machineries of the state and the priesthood, and presided over the dark mysteries of the consecrated groves.

Their name was derived from *derw* (pronounced *derroo*) Celtic for oak, and *ydd*, a common termination of nouns in that language, equivalent to the *or* or *er* in governor, reader, &c., in ours.

The Bards or Bardd from *Bar*, a branch, or, the top.

It was their province to sing the praises of horses in the warrior's feasts, to chant the sacred hymns like the musician's among the Levites, and to register genealogies and historical events.

The Ovades or Ovydd, (derived from *ov*, raw, pure, and *ydd*, above explained) were the noviciates, who, under the supervision of the Druids, studied the properties of nature, and offered up the sacrifices upon the altar.

Thus it appears that Derwydd, Bardd, and Ovydd, were emblematical names of the three orders of Druidism.

The Derwydd was the trunk and support of the whole; the Bardd the ramification from that trunk arranged in beautiful foliage; and the Ovydd was the young shoot, which, growing up, ensured a prospect of permanency to the sacred grove.

The whole body was ruled by an Arch-Druid elected by lot from those senior brethren who were the most learned and the best born.

At Llamdan in Anglesea, there are still vestiges of *Trér Dryw* the Arch-Druid's mansion, *Boadrudau* the abode of the inferior ones, *Bod-owyr* the abode of the ovades, and *Trér-Beirdd* the hamlet of the bards.

Let us now consider these orders under their respective denominations-Derwydd, Bardd, Ovyd; and under their separate vocations, as philosophers musicians, and priests.

III. The Derwydd, Or Philosophers

DRUIDISM was a religion of philosophy; its high-priests were men of learning and science.

Under the head of the Ovydd, I shall describe their initiatory and sacrificial rites, and shall now merely consider their acquirements, as instructors, as mathematicians, as law-givers and as physicians.

Ammianus Marcellinus informs us that the Druids dwelt together in fraternities, and indeed it is scarcely possible that they could have lectured in almost every kind of philosophy and preserved their arcana from the vulgar, unless they had been accustomed to live in some kind of convent or college.

They were too wise, however, to immure themselves wholly in one corner of the land, where they would have exercised no more influence upon the nation than the Heads and Fellows of our present universities. While some lived the lives of hermits in caves and in hollow oaks within the dark recesses of the holy forests; while others lived peaceably in their college-home, teaching the bardic verses to children, to the young nobles, and to the students who came to them from a strange country across the sea, there were others who led an active and turbulent existence at court in the councils of the state and in the halls of nobles.

In Gaul, the chief seminaries of the Druids was in the country of the Carnutes between Chartres and Dreux, to which at one time scholars resorted in such numbers that they were obliged to build other academies in various parts of the land, vestiges of which exist to this day, and of which the ancient College of Guienne is said to be one.

When their power began to totter in their own country, the young Druids resorted to Mona, now Anglesea, in which was the great British university, and in which there is a spot called*Myrfyrion*, the seat of studies.

The Druidic precepts were all in verses, which amounted to 20,000 in number, and which it was forbidden to write. Consequently a long course of preparatory study was required, and some spent so much as twenty years in a state of probation.

These verses were in rhyme, which the Druids invented to assist the memory, and in a triplet form from the veneration which was paid to the number three by all the nations of antiquity.

In this the Jews resembled the Druids, for although they had received the written law of Moses, there was a certain code of precept among them which was taught by mouth alone, and in which those who were the most learned were elevated to the Rabbi.

The mode of teaching by memory was also practised by the Egyptians and by Lycurgus, who esteemed it better to imprint his laws on the minds of the Spartan citizens than to engrave them upon tablets. So, too, were Numa's sacred writing buried with him by his orders, in compliance perhaps with the opinions of his friend Pythagoras who, as well as Socrates, left nothing behind him committed to writing.

It was Socrates, in fact, who compared written doctrines to pictures of animals which resemble life, but which when you question them can give you no reply.

But we who love the past have to lament this system. When Cambyses destroyed the temples of Egypt, when the disciples of Pythagoras died in the Meta-pontine tumults, all their mysteries and all their learning died with them.

So also the secrets of the Magi, the Orpheans and the Cabiri perished with their institutions, and it is owing to this law of the Druids that we have only the meagre evidence of ancient authors and the obscure emblems of the Welsh Bards, and the faint vestiges of their mighty monuments to teach us concerning the powers and direction of their philosophy.

There can be no doubt that they were profoundly learned. For ordinary purposes of writing, and in the keeping of their accounts on the Alexandrian method, they used the ancient Greek character of which Cadmus, a Phœnician, and Timagines, a Druid, were said to have been the inventors and to have imported into Greece.

This is a fac-simile of their alphabet as preserved in the *Thesaurus Muratori*. Vol IV. 2093.

ΑΒΓΔΕϜΗΓΚ ⴼΜΝΟΓΡϚΤΥ

Both in the universities of the Hebrews, which existed from the earliest times, and in those of the Brachmans it was not permitted to study philosophy and the sciences, except so far as they might assist the student in the perusal and comprehension of the sacred writings. But a more liberal system existed among the Druids, who were skilled in all the arts and in foreign languages.

For instance, there was Abaris, a Druid and a native of the Shetland Isles who traveled into Greece, where he formed a friendship with Pythagoras and where his learning, his politeness, his shrewdness, and expedition in business, and above all, the ease and elegance with which he spoke the Athenian tongue, and which (so said the orator Himerius) would have made one believe that he had been brought up in the academy or the Lycceum, created for him as great a sensation as that which was afterwards made by the admirable Crichton among the learned doctors of Paris.

It can easily be proved that the science of astronomy was not unknown to the Druids. One of their temples in the island of Lewis in the Hebrides, bears evident signs of their skill in the science. Every stone in the temple is placed astronomically. The circle consists of twelve equistant obelisks denoting the twelve signs of the zodiac. The four cardinal points of the compass are marked by lines of obelisks running out from the circle, and at each point subdivided into four more. The range of obelisks from north, and exactly facing the south is double, being two parallel rows each consisting of nineteen stones. A large stone in the centre of the circle, thirteen feet high, and of the perfect shape of a ship's rudder would seem as a symbol of their knowledge of astronomy being made subservient to navigation, and the Celtic word for star, ruth-iul, "a-guide-to-direct-the-course," proves such to have been the case.

This is supposed to have been the winged temple which Erastosthenes says that Apollo had among the Hyperboreans--a name which the Greeks applied to all nations dwelling north of the Pillars of Hercules.

But what is still more extraordinary, Hecateus makes mention that the inhabitants of a certain Hyperborian island, little less than Sicily, and over against Celtiberia--a description answering exactly to that of Britain--could bring the moon so near them as to show the mountains and rocks, and other appearances upon its surface.

According to Strabo and Bochart, glass was a discovery of the Phoenicians and a staple commodity of their trade, but we have some ground for believing that our philosophers bestowed rather than borrowed this invention.

Pieces of glass and crystal have been found in the cairns, as if in honor to those who invented it; the process of vitrifying the very walls of their houses, which is still to be seen in the Highlands prove that they possessed the art in the gross; and the Gaelic name for glass is not of foreign but of Celtic extraction, being *glasine* and derived from *glas-theine*, glued or brightened by fire.

We have many wonderful proofs of the skill in mechanics. The *clacha-brath*, or rocking-stones, were spherical stones of an enormous size, and were raised upon other flat stones into which they inserted a small prominence fitting the cavity so exactly, and so concealed by loose stones lying around it, that nobody could discern the artifice. Thus these globes were balanced so that the slightest touch would make them vibrate, while anything of greater weight pressing against the side of the cavity rendered them immovable.

In Iona, the last asylum of the Caledonian Druids, many of these *clacha-brath* (one of which is mentioned in Ptolemy Hephestion's History, Lib. iii. cap 3.) were to be found at the beginning of this century, and although the superstitious natives defaced them and turned them over into the sea, they considered it necessary to have something of the kind in their stead, and have substituted for them rough stone balls which they call by the same name.

In Stonehenge, too, we find an example of that oriental mechanism which is displayed so stupendously in the pyramids of Egypt. Here stones of thirty or forty tons that must have been a draught for a herd of oxen, have been carried the distance of sixteen computed miles and raised to a vast height, and placed in their beds with such ease that their very mortises were made to tally.

The temples of Abury in Wiltshire, and of Carnac in Brittany, though less perfect, are even more prodigious monuments of art.

It is scarcely to be wondered at that the Druids should be acquainted with the properties of gunpowder, since we know that it was used in the mysteries of Isis, in the temple of Delphi, and by the old Chinese philosophers.

Lucan in his description of a grove near Marseilles, writes:--"There is a report that the grove is often shaken and strangely moved, and that dreadful sounds are heard from its caverns; and that it is sometimes in a blaze without being consumed."

In Ossian's poem of *Dargo the son of the Druid of Bet*, similar phenomenon are mentioned, and while the Celtic word lightning is *De'lanach*, "the flash or flame of God," they had another word which expresses a flash that is quick and sudden as lightning--*Druilanach*, "the flame of the Druids."

It would have been fortunate for mankind had the monks of the middle ages displayed the wisdom of these ancient priests in concealing from fools and madmen so dangerous an art.

All such knowledge was carefully retained within the holy circle of their dark caves and forests and which the initiated were bound by a solemn oath never to reveal.

I will now consider the Druids of active life-the preachers, the law-givers, and the physicians.

On the seventh day, like the first patriarchs, they preached to the warriors and their wives from small round eminences, several of which yet remain in different parts of Britain.

Their doctrines were delivered with a surpassing eloquence and in triplet verses, many specimens which are to be found in the Welsh poetry but of which these two only have been preserved by the classical authors.

The first in Pomponius Mela.

> "Ut forent ad bella meliores,
> Æternas esse animas,
> Vitamque alteram ad manes."

> "To act bravely in war,
> That souls are immortal,
> And there is another life after death."

The second in Diogenes Laertius.

> ξεξειν Θεους
>
> ηαι μηδεν ηαηον δςαν
>
> ηαι ανδςειαν ασηειν

"To worship the Gods,
And to do no evil,
And to exercise fortitude."

Once every year a public assembly of the nation was held in Mona at the residence of the Arch-Druid, and there silence was no less rigidly imposed than in the councils of the Rabbi and the Brachmans. If any one interrupted the orator, a large piece of his robe was cut off--if after that he offended, he was punished with death. To enforce Punctuality, like the Cigonii of Pliny, they had the cruel custom of cutting to pieces the one who came last. Their laws, like their religious precepts, were at first esteemed too sacred to be committed to writing-the first written laws being those of Dyrnwal Moelmud, King of Britain, about 440 B. c. and called the Moelmutian laws; for these were substituted the Mercian code or the laws of Martia, Queen of England, which was afterwards adopted by King Alfred and translated by him into Saxon.

The Manksmen also ascribe to the Druids those excellent laws by which the Isle of Man has always been governed.

The Magistrates of Britain were but tools of the Druids, appointed by them and educated by them also; for it was a law in Britain that no one might hold office who had not been educated by the Druids.

The Druids held annual assizes in different parts of Britain (for instance at the monument called *Long Meg and her Daughters* in Cumberland and at the *Valley of Stones* in Cornwall) as Samuel visited Bethel and Gilgal once a year to dispense justice.

There they heard appeals from the minor courts, and investigated the more intricate cases, which sometimes they were obliged to settle by ordeal. The rocking-stones which I have just described, and the walking barefoot through a fire which they lighted on the summit of some holy hill and called *Samb'in*, or the fire of peace, were their two chief methods of testing the innocence of the criminal, and in which they were imitated by the less ingenious and perhaps less conscientious judges of later days.

For previous to the ordeal which they named *Gabha Bheil*, or "the trial of Beil," the Druids used every endeavor to discover the real merits of the case, in order that they might decide upon the verdict of Heaven--that is to say, which side of the stone they should press, or whether they should anoint his feet with that oil which the Hindoo priests use in their religious festivals, and which enables the barefoot to pass over the burning wood unscathed.

We may smile at another profanity of the Druids who constituted themselves judges not only of the body but of the soul.

But as Mohammed inspired his soldiers with sublime courage by promising Paradise to those who found a death-bed upon the corpses of their foes, so the very superstitions, the very frauds of these noble Druids tended to elevate the hearts of men towards their God, and to make them lead virtuous lives that they might merit the sweet fields of *Fla'innis*, the heaven of their tribe.

Never before since the world, has such vast power as the Druids possessed been wielded with such purity, such temperance, such discretion.

When a man died a platter of earth and salt was placed upon his breast, as is still the custom in Wales and in the North of Britain.

The earth an emblem of incorruptibility of the body--the salt an emblem of the incorruptibility of the soul.

A kind of court was then assembled round the corpse, and by the evidence of those with whom he had been best acquainted, it was decided with what funeral rites he should be honored.

If he had distinguished himself as a warrior, or as man of science, it was recorded in the death-song; a cairn or pile of sacred stones was raised over him, and his arms and tools or other symbols of his profession were buried with him.

If his life had been honorable, and if he had obeyed the three grand articles of religion, the bard sang his *requiem* on the harp, whose beautiful music alone was a pass-port to heaven.

It is a charming idea, is it not? The soul lingering for the first strain which might release it from the cold corpse, and mingle with its silent ascent to God.

Read how the heroes of Ossian longed for this funereal hymn without which their souls, pale and sad as those which haunted the banks of the Styx, were doomed to wander through the mists of some dreary fen.

When this hymn had been sung, the friends and relatives of the deceased made great rejoicings, and this it was that originated those sombre merry-makings so peculiar to the Scotch and Irish funerals.

In the philosophy of medicine, the Derwydd were no less skilled than in sciences and letters. They knew that by means of this divine art they would possess the hearts as well as the minds of men, and obtain not only the awe of the ignorant but also the love of those whose lives they had preserved.

Their sovereign remedy was the missoldine or mistletoe of the oak which, in Wales, still bears its ancient name of *Oll-iach*, or all-heal, with those of *Pren-awr*, the celestial tree, and *Uchelwydd*, the lofty shrub.

When the winter has come and the giant of the forest is deserted by its leaves and extends its withered arms to the sky, a divine hand sheds upon it from heaven a mysterious seed, and a delicate green plant sprouts from the bark, and thus is born while all around is dying and decayed.

We need not wonder that the mistletoe should be revered as a heaven-born plant, and as a type of God's promise and consolation to those who were fainting on death's threshold in the winter of old age.

When the new year approached, the Druids beset themselves to discover this plant upon an oak, on which tree it grows less frequently than upon the ash-crab or apple tree. Having succeeded, and as soon as the moon was six days old, they marched by night with great solemnity towards the spot, inviting all to join their procession with these words: *The New Year is at hand: let us gather the mistletoe.*

First marched the Ovades in their green sacrificial robes leading two milk-white bullocks. Next came the bards singing the praises of the Mighty Essence, in raiment blue as the heavens to which their hymn ascended. Then a herald clothed in white with two wings drooping down on each side of his head, and a branch of vervain in his hand encircled by two serpents. He was followed by three Derwydd--one of whom carried the sacrificial bread--another a vase of water-and the third a white wand. Lastly, the Arch-Druid, distinguished by the tuft or tassel to his cap, by the bands hanging from his throat, by the sceptre in his hand and by the golden crescent on his breast, surrounded by the whole body of the Derwydd and humbly followed by the noblest warriors of the land.

An altar of rough stones was erected under the oak, and the Arch-Druid, having sacramentally distributed the bread and wine, would climb the tree, cut the mistletoe with a golden knife, wrap it in a pure white cloth, slay and sacrifice the bullocks, and pray to God to remove his curse from barren women, and to permit their medicines to serve as antidotes for poisons and charms from all misfortunes.

They used the mistletoe as an ingredient in almost all their medicines, and a powder was made from the berries for cases of sterility.

It is a strong purgative well suited to the lusty constitutions of the ancient Britons, but, like bleeding, too powerful a remedy for modern ailments.

With all the herbs which they used for medicine, there were certain mummeries to be observed while they were gathered, which however were not without their object-first in enhancing the faith of the vulgar by exciting their superstitions-and also in case of failure that the patient might be reproached for blundering instead of a physician.

The vervain was to be gathered at the rise of the dog-star, neither sun nor moon shining at the time; it was to be dug tip with an iron instrument and to be waved aloft in the air, the left hand only being used.

The leaves, stalks and flowers were dried separately in the shade and were used for the bites of serpents, infused in wine.

The *samulos* which grew in damp places was to be gathered by a person fasting-without looking behind him-and with his left hand. It was laid into troughs and cisterns where cattle drank, and when bruised was a cure for various distempers.

The *selago*, a kind of hedge hyssop, was a charm as well as a medicine. He who gathered it was to be clothed in white-to bathe his feet in running water-to offer a sacrifice of bread and wine-and then with his right hand covered by the skirt of his robe, and with a brazen hook to dig it up by the roots and wrap it in a white cloth.

Prominent among the juggleries of the Druids, stands the serpent's egg--the *ovus anguinum* of Pliny--the *glein neidr* of the ancient Britons-the *adderstone* of modern folk-lore.

It was supposed to have been formed by a multitude of serpents close entwined together, and by the frothy saliva that proceeded from their throats. When it was made, it was raised up in the air by their combined hissing, and to render it efficacious it was to be caught in a clean white cloth before it could fall to the ground-for in Druidism that which touched the ground was polluted. He who performed this ingenious task was obliged to mount a swift horse, and to ride away at full speed pursued by the serpents from whom he was not safe till he had crossed a river.

The Druids tested its virtue by encasing it in gold, and throwing it into a river. If it swam against the stream it would render it possessor superior to his adversaries in all disputes, and obtain for him the friendship of great men.

The implicit belief placed in this fable is curiously exemplified by the fact of a Roman Knight of the Vocontii, while pleading his own cause in a law suit was discovered with one of these charms in his breast and was put to death upon the spot.

Their reverence for the serpent's egg has its origin in their mythology. Like the Phœnicians and Egyptians, they represented the creation by the figure of an egg coming out of a serpent's mouth, and it was doubtless the excessive credulity of the barbarians which tempted them to invent the above fable that they might obtain high prices for these amulets, many of which have been discovered in Druidic barrows, and are still to be met with in the Highlands, where a belief in their power has not yet subsided; for it is no uncommon thing when a distemper rages among men or beasts, for the *Glass-physician* to be sent for from as great a distance as fifty miles.

These eggs are made of some kind of glass or earth glazed over, and are sometimes blue, green, or white, and sometimes variegated with all these colors intermixed.

For mental disorders and some physical complaints they used to prescribe pilgrimages to certain wells, always situated at a distance from the patient, and the waters of which were to be drunk and bathed in. With these ablutions, sacred as those of the Musselmen, were mingled religious ceremonies with a view to remind them of the presence of that God who alone could relieve them from their infirmities. After reaching the wells, they bathed thrice-that mysterious number-and walked three times round the well, *deis'iul,* in the same direction as the course of the sun, also turning and bowing from East to West.

These journeys were generally performed before harvest, at which time the modern Arabs go through a series of severe purgings, and when English laborers, twenty years ago, used systematically to go to the market town to be bled.

The season of the year--the exercise--the mineral in the water-above all the strong faith of the patients effected so many real cures that in time it became a custom (still observed in Scotland with the well of Strathfillan and in many parts of Ireland) for all who were afflicted with any disorder to perform an annual pilgrimage to these holy wells.

Caithbaid, an Irish historian, speaks of the Druid Trosdan who discovered an antidote for poisoned arrows, and there are many instances on record of the medicinal triumphs of the Druids.

They were more anxious to prevent disease than to cure them, and issued many maxims relating to the care of the body, as wise as those which appertained to the soul were divine.

Of these I will give you one which should be written in letters of Gold.

Bi gu sugach geanmnaidh mocher' each.

"Cheerfulness, temperance and early rising.

IV. The Bardd, Or Musicians

AS there were musicians among the Levites, and priests among the Phœnicians who chanted bare-foot and in white surplices the sacred hymns, so there were bards among the Druids.

Who were divided into three classes.

I. The *Fer-Laoi,* or Hymnists, who sang the essence and immortality of the soul; the works of nature; the course of the celestial bodies; with the order and harmony of the spheres.

II. The *Senachies* who sang the fabulous histories of their ancestors in rude stanzas, and who with letters cut from the bark of trees inscribed passing events and became the historians of their nation.

The *Fer-Dan* who were accustomed to wander through the country, or to be numbered in the retinues of kings and nobles, who not only sang enconiums upon the great warriors of the age, but who wrote satires upon the prevailing vices, worthy of a Juvenal or a Horace.

I can best give the reader some idea of the style and power of their conceptions, by quoting some of their axioms which have descended to us traditionally.

They are in the form of Triads, of which the subjects are, language-fancy and invention-the design of poetry-the nature of just thinking-rules of arrangement-method of description--*e.g.*

The three qualifications of poetry--endowment of genius, judgment from experience, and happiness of mind.

The three foundations of judgment--bold design, frequent practice, and frequent mistakes.

The three foundations of learning--seeing much, studying much, and suffering much.

The three foundations of happiness--a suffering with contentment, a hope that it will come, and a belief that it will be.

The three foundations of thought--perspicuity, amplitude, and preciseness.

The three canons of perspicuity--the word that is necessary, the quantity that is necessary, and the manner that is necessary.

The three canons of amplitude--appropriate thought, variety of thought and requisite thought.

How full of wisdom and experience! what sublime ideas in a few brief words!

These poets were held in high honor by the Britons, for among a barbarous people musicians are angels who bring to them a language from the other world, and who alone can soften their iron hearts and fill their bold blue eyes with gentle tears.

There is an old British law commanding that all should be made freedmen of slaves who were of these three professions. A scholar learned. in the languages--a bard--or a smith. When once the smith had entered a smithy, or the scholar had been polled, or the bard had composed a song, they could never more be deprived of their freedom.

Their ordinary dress was brown, but in religious ceremonies they wore ecclesiastical ornaments called *Bardd-gwewll*, which was an azure robe with a cowl to it-a costume afterwards adopted by the lay monks of Bardsey Island (the burial-place of Myrrddin or Merlin) and was by them called *Cyliau Duorn*, or black cowls; it was then borrowed by the Gauls and is still worn by the Capuchin friars.

Blue which is an emblem of the high heavens and the beautiful sea had always been a favorite color with the ancient Britons, and is still used as a toilet paint by the ladies of Egypt and Tartary. Blue rosettes are the insignia of our students in the twin universities, and for the old Welsh proverb. *Y gwer las ni chyll mói liu*, -True blue keeps its hue," one of our proverbial expressions may be traced.

The harp, or lyre, invented by the Celts had four or five strings, or thongs made of an ox's hide, and was usually played upon with a plectrum made of the jaw-bone of a goat. But we have reason to believe that it was the instrument invented by Tubal which formed the model of the Welsh harps.

Although the Greeks (whom the learned Egyptians nicknamed "children," and who were the most vain-glorious people upon the earth) claimed the harp as, an invention of their ancient poets, Juvenal in his third satire acknowledges that both the Romans and the Greeks received it from the Hebrews. This queen of instruments is hallowed to our remembrance by many passages in the Bible. It was from the harp that David before Saul drew such enchanting strains that the monarch's heart was melted and the dark frown left his brow. It was on their harps that the poor Jewish captives were desired to play, on their harps which swayed above them on the branches of the willow trees while the waters of Babylon sobbed past beneath their feet.

And it was the harp which St. John beheld in the white hands of the angels as they stood upon the sea of glass mingled with fire, singing the song of Moses, the servant of God, and the song of the lamb. The trunks of these harps were polished and in the shape of a heart; they were embraced between the breast and the arm; their strings were of glossy hair. In Palestine they were made from the wood of the Cedars of Lebanon; in Britain of *Pren-masarn*, or the sycamore.

In their construction, the same mysterious regard was paid to the number three. Their shape was triangular; their strings were three in number, and their turning keys had three arms.

In later times the Irish, who believe that they are descended from David, obtained an European fame for their skill in the making of this instrument. Dante mentions the circumstance, and the harp is still a mint-mark upon Irish coin.

The Bards from what we can learn of them, neither debased their art to calumny nor to adulation, but were in every way as worthy of our admiration as those profound philosophers to whom alone they were inferior.

We learn that, (unlike the artists of later times) they were peculiarly temperate, and that in order to inure themselves to habits of abstinence they would have all kinds of delicacies spread out as if for a banquet, and upon which having feasted their eyes for some time they would order to be removed.

Also that they did their utmost to stay those civil wars which were the bane of Britain, and that often when two fierce armies had stood fronting each other in array of battle, their swords drawn, their spears pointing to the foe and waiting but for the signal from their chieftains to begin the conflict, the Bards had stepped in between and had touched their harps with such harmony, and so persuaded them with sweet thrilling verses, that suddenly, on either side soldiers had dropped their arms and forgotten the fierce resentment which had been raging in their breasts.

V. The Ovades, Or Noviciates

IN writing of the Derwydd, or Philosophers, I have written also of the high priests, or magicians for *magnus* is but another name for priest, and in the Chinese and various hieroglyphical languages, the same sign represents a magician and a priest.

I have now to describe the lower order of *sacrificers* who, under the direction of their masters, slew the victims upon the altar, and poured out the sacramental wine.

The Ovades were usually dressed in white, while their sacerdotal robes were of green, an ancient emblem of innocence and youth, still retained in our language, but debased and vulgarized into slang.

They are generally represented with chaplets of oak-leaves on their brows, and their eyes modestly fixed on the ground.

Having been carefully trained in the Druidic seminaries, their memory being stored with the holy triads, and with the outward ceremonies of their religion, they were prepared for initiation into the sublime mysteries of Druidism.

During a period of probation, the Ovade was closely watched; eyes, to him invisible, were ever upon him, noting his actions and his very looks, searching into his heart for its motive, and into his soul for its abilities.

He was then subjected to a trial so painful to the body, so terrible to the mind, that many lost their senses for ever, and others crawled back to the daylight pale and emaciated, as men who had grown old in prison.

These initiations took place in caves, one of which still exists in Denbighshire. We have also some reason to believe that the catacombs of Egypt and those artificial excavations which are to be found in many parts of Persia and Hindostan were constructed for the same purpose.

The Ovade received several wounds from a man who opposed his entrance with a drawn sword. He was then led blind-folded through the winding alleys of the cave which was also a labyrinth. This was intended to represent the toilsome wanderings of the soul in the mazes of ignorance and vice.

Presently the ground would begin to rock beneath his feet; strange sounds disturbed the midnight silence. Thunder crashed upon him like the fall of, an avalanche, flashes of green lightning flickered through the cave displaying to his view hideous spectres arrayed against the walls.

Then lighted only by these fearful fires a strange procession marched past him, and a hymn in honor of the Eternal Truth was solemnly chanted by unseen tongues.

Here the profounder mysteries commenced. He was admitted through the North Gate or that of Cancer, where he was forced to pass through a fierce fire. Thence he was hurried to the Southern Gate or that of Capricorn, where he was plunged into a flood, and from which he was only released when life was at its last gasp.

Then he was beaten with rods for two days, and buried up to his neck in snow.

This was the baptism of fire, of water, and of blood.

Now arrived on the verge of death, an icy chill seizes his limbs; a cold dew bathes his brow, his faculties fail him; his eyes close; he is about to faint, to expire, when a strain of music, sweet as the distant murmur of the holy brooks, consoling as an angel's voice, bids him to rise and to live for the honor of his God.

Two doors with a sound like the fluttering of wings are thrown open before him. A divine light bursts upon him, he sees plains shining with flowers open around him.

Then a golden serpent is placed in his bosom as a sign of his regeneration, and he is adorned with a mystic zone upon which are engraved twelve mysterious signs; a tiara is placed upon his head; his form naked and shivering is clothed in a purple tunic studded with innumerable stars; a crozier is placed in his hand. He is a king; for he is initiated; for he is a Druid.

VI. Rites And Ceremonies

A RELATION of the duties of the Ovades as sacrificers will naturally lead us into a description of the ceremonies of the priesthood, of their altars, their temples and their objects of worship or veneration.

The *clachan*, or stone temples of the Druids were round like those of the Chinese, the primitive Greeks, the Jews, and their copyists the Templars. This shape was adopted because it was typical of eternity, and also of the solar light--the word *circus* being derived from the Phœnician *cir* or *cur*, the Sun.

Like those of the Thracians they were open at the roof, for the Druids deemed it impious to attempt to enclose within a house that God, whose shrine was the universe.

There were two celebrated temples of the Druids, Abury in Wiltshire, and Carnac in Brittany, which were built in the form of a serpent.

There is scarcely a spot in the world in which the serpent has not received the prayers and praises of men. At first an emblem of the sun's light and power, it is worshipped in lands where the sun is not recognized as a Deity, for instance on the coasts of Guinea where the negroes curse him every morning as he rises, because he scorches them at noon.

The winged serpent was a symbol of the Gods of Egypt, Phœnicia, China, Persia, and Hindostan. The Tartar princes still carry the image of a serpent upon a spear as their military standard. Almost all the Runic inscriptions found upon tombs are engraved upon the sculptured forms of serpents. In the temple of the Bona Dea, serpents were tamed and consecrated. In the mysteries of Bacchus, women used to carry serpents in their hands and twined around their brows, and with horrible screams cry, *Eva! Eva!* In the great temple of Mexico, the captives taken in war and sacrificed to the sun, had wooden collars in the shape of a serpent put round their necks. And water-snakes are to this day held sacred by the natives of the Friendly Isles.

It was not only worshipped as a symbol of light, of wisdom and of health, personified under the name of God, but also as an organ of divination. Serpents formed the instruments of the Egyptian enchanters, the *fetich* of the Hottentots, and the girdles of the medicine-men of the North American Indians. The Norwegians, too, of the present day, when hunting will often load their guns with serpents to make them fortunate.

The serpent must have obtained this world-wide worship from its beauty, and its wisdom. Subtle in heart beyond all the beasts of the field; rapid and mysterious in its wary footless movements, to which the ancients were wont to resemble the aerial progress of the Gods; above all its eyes so bright, so lovely, so weird in their powers of facinations, no wonder that it should excite the awe and admiration of superstitious barbarians.

And they believed it immortal, for every year they saw it cast its skin, wrinkled and withered with age, and when they tried to kill it they found that it retained life with miraculous pertinacity.

Finally it was the brazen serpent elevated upon a cross that Moses erected in the wilderness, and upon which all who gazes were saved from death; and it was this serpent which Jewish and Christian writers have agreed in asserting to be a type of the Messiah.

The *cromleachs* were the altars of the Druids, and were so called from a Hebrew word signifying, "to bow," and from the bowing of the worshippers who believed them to be guarded by spirits.

They were constructed of a large flat stone placed upon two rough pillars. These stones were always unhewn, for by the Druidic law it was ordained that no axe should touch the sacred stones, a precept which very strangely coincides with the Mosaic law. "*Thou shall not build an altar of hewn stones.*" Exod. xx, 25.

These *cromleachs* were also sepulchres, as is testified by the number of urns and human bones that have been discovered beneath some few of them. It is probable that their *clachan* were used for the same purpose, as the Egyptian mummies were interred in the catacombs of the pyramids, and as we bury bodies in the vaults of our churches.

We generally find them situated on hills or mountains, which prove that the Druids entertained the same reverence for high places as the nations of the East, and even the Scandinavians, for we read in the *Erybygga-Saga* that when Thoralf established his colony in the promontory of Thorsness in Iceland he erected an eminence called *Helgafels*, the Holy Mount, upon which none might look till they had made their ablutions under pain of death.

And sometimes by the side of a lake or running stream, for water was held holy by the Druids, and they were even wont to propitiate its deities, by offering it presents.

There was a Druidic temple at Toulouse, on the borders of a lake into which the Druids threw large quantities of gold, and in which Capion, a Roman knight, and his followers miserably perished in an attempt to recover it. So, *Aurum Tolosanum*, "Gold from Toulouse," became a bye-word among the Romans to express any accident or misfortune.

In the islands surrounding Britain and Gaul, especially in the Channel Islands where they are called *Pouquelays*, these altars are very common. Islands were held sacred for some reason by the ancients.

They were often erected within the recesses of the sacred grove beneath the shadow of an oak.

This, the fairest and strongest of trees has been revered as a symbol of God by almost all the nations of heathendom, and by the Jewish Patriarchs.

It was underneath the oaks of Mamre that Abraham dwelt a long time, and where he erected an altar to God, and where he received the three angels.

It was underneath an oak that Jacob hid the idols of his children, for oaks were held sacred and inviolable. (Judges II. 5. 6.)

From the Scriptures, too, we learn that it was worshipped by the Pagans who corrupted the Hebrews (Hosea. IV. v. 13. Ezekiah VI. 13. Isaiah I. v. 29.)

Homer mentions people entering into compacts under oaks as places of security. The Grecians had their vocal oaks at Dodona. The Arcadians believed that stirring the waters of a fountain with an oaken bough would bring rain. The Sclavonians worshipped oaks which they enclosed in a consecrated court.

The Romans consecrated the oak to Jupiter their Supreme God, as they consecrated the myrtle to Venus, the laurel to Apollo, the pine to Cybele, the poplar to Hercules, wheat-ears to Ceres, the olive to Minerva, fruits to Pomona, rose-trees to the river nymphs, and hay to poor Vertumnus whose power and merits could obtain him nothing better.

The Hindoos who had no oaks revered the Banian tree.

When an oak died, the Druids stripped off its bark, &c., shaped it reverently into the form of a pillar, a pyramid, or a cross, and still continued to worship it as an emblem of their God.

Besides the *clanchan* and *cromleach* there are many stone monuments remaining in various parts of Gaul and Britain, which bear the. Druid stamp in their rudeness and simplicity.

These were sometimes trophies of victory, sometimes memorials of gratitude, sometimes images of God.

When erected they were anointed with rose-oil, as Jacob anointed the first stone monument on record -that which he raised at Bethel in memory of his dream.

The custom of raising plain stone pillars for idolatrous purposes was afterwards adopted by the Pagans and forbidden by the Mosaic law (Lev. XXVI. 1.)

Mercury, Apollo, Neptune and Hercules were worshipped under the form of a square stone. A large black stone was the emblem of Buddha among the Hindoos, and of Manah Theus-Ceres in Arabia. The Paphians worshipped their Venus under the form of a white pyramid, the Thebans their Bacchus under that of a pillar, the Scandinavians their Odin under that of a cube, the Siamese their Sommonacodum under that of a black pyramid.

And in the temple of the Sun at Cuzco, in Peru, was a stone column in the shape of a cone, which was worshipped as an emblem of the Deity.

Every one has heard of the Stone of Memnon in Egypt, which was said to speak at sun-rise, and the remains of which are covered with inscriptions by Greek and Latin travelers bearing testimony to the fact.

There is a story in Giraldus Cambrensis which proves that the Druids had the same superstition. In his time, a large flat stone ten feet long, six feet wide, and one foot thick served as a bridge over the river Alun at St. David's, in Pembrokeshire. It was called in British *Lech Larar*, "the speaking stone," and it was a tradition that if a dead body was carried over the stone it would speak, and that with the struggle of the voice it would crack in the middle, and that then the chink would close.

Keysler informs us that the Northern nations believed their stone deities to be inhabited by fairies or demons, and adduces an instance from the *Holmveria Saga* of Norway.

"Indridus going out of his house lay in wait for his enemy Thorstenus, who was wont to go to the temple of his God at such a particular time. Thorstenus came and, entering the temple before sun-rise, prostrated himself before the stone-deity and offered his devotion. Indridus standing by heard the stone speak, and pronounce Thorstenus' doom in these words:

> Tu huc
> Ultima vice
> Morti vicinis pedibus
> Terram calcasti;
> Certè enim antequam
> Sol splendeat,
> Animosus Indridus
> Odium tibi rependet.

> Heedless of thy approaching fate
> Thou treadst this holy ground;
> Last step of life! thy guilty breast
> Ere Phœbus gilds the ruddy East,
>   Must expiate
>   Thy murderous hate
>   Deep piere'd with crimson wound.

To fire, also, as an emblem of the sun, the Druids paid peculiar reverence.

Indeed fire would appear to have been the chosen element of God. In the form of a flaming bush He appeared to Moses. On Mount Sinai His presence was denoted by torrents of flame, and in the form of fire he preceded the little band of Israelites by night, through the dreary wilderness, which is perhaps the origin of the custom of the Arabians who always carry fire in front of their caravans.

All the great nations had their holy fires which were never suffered to die. In the temple of the Gaditanian Hercules at Tyre, in the Temple of Vesta at Rome, among the Brachmans, the Jews, and the Persians were these immortal fires which might not be desecrated by the breath of men, and which might be fed with peeled wood alone. So also the American savages when they have gained a victory, would light fires and dance round them.

The Druids thus conducted their worship of the holy element. Having stripped the bark off dry wood they poured oil of roses upon it, and lighted it by rubbing sticks together, which is said to have been an invention of the Phœnicians.

To this they prayed at certain times, and whoever dared to blow the fire with his mouth, or to throw dirt or dead beasts into it they punished with death.

They had circular temples consecrated to their never-dying fires; into these the priests entered every day, and reverently fed the fire and prayed to it for a whole hour, holding branches of vervain in their hands and crowned with tiaras which hung down in flaps on each side of their faces covering their cheeks and lips.

They also kindled the Beltein, or fire of the rock on May-eve to welcome the sun after his travels behind the clouds and tempests of the dark months. On that night all other fires were extinguished, and all repaired to the holy mount to pay their annual tribute to the Druids.

Then were held solemn rites, and men and beasts, and even goblets of wine were passed through the purifying flames. After which the fires were all relighted, (each from the sacred fire) and general festivity prevailed.

In Cornwall there are *Karn-Gollowa*, the Cairn of Lights, and *Karn-Leskyz*, the Cairn of Burnings which names proves that the fiendish rites of Moloch and Baal were really observed with all their impious cruelty in the island of Britain.

From these same blood-thirsty Phœnicians who had taught the Israelites to sin, the Druids learnt to pollute their altars with human blood, and to assert that nothing was so pleasing to God as the murder of a man.

In the golden age, men's hearts softened and elevated by gratitude towards their Maker offered him the choicest herbs and the sweetest flowers of the soil.

But in the age of iron, when men had learnt to tremble at their own thoughts, to know that they were thieves, and liars, and murderers, they felt that there was need of expiation.

To appease the God whom they still believed to be merciful, they offered Him *Blood*.

They offered Him the blood of animals.

And then they offered Him the most innocent and beautiful of His creations--beautiful virgins and chaste youths--their eldest sons, their youngest daughters.

Do you disbelieve me? read as I have read all the great writers of the past, and then you will shudder as I have shuddered at such terrible wickedness in man.

Read Manetho, Sanchionatho, Herodotus, Pausanias, Josephus, Philo the Jew, Diodorus of Sicily, Strabo, Cicero, Cæsar, Macrobius, Pliny, Titus Livius, Lucan, and most of the Greek and Latin-poets.

Read the books of Leviticus, Deuteronomy, the judges, Kings, the 105th Psalm, the Prophesies of Isaiah, Jeremiah, Ezekiel, and many of the old fathers, and there you will find that the Egyptians, the Israelites, the Arabs, the Cathaginians, the Athenians, Spartans and Ionians, the Romans, the Scythians, the Albanians, the Germans, Iberians and Gauls had adopted this cruel custom, which like the practice of magic had risen in Phœnicia, and had spread like a plague over the whole world.

The Egyptians sacrificed every year a young and beautiful virgin, whom arrayed in rich robes, they flung into the Nile. They also offered up men with red hair at the shrine of Osiris.

The Spartans whipped boys to death in sight of their parents before starting upon an expedition. The natives of the Tauric Chersonesus hospitably sacrificed to Diana all the strangers whom chance threw upon their coast. The Cimbri ripped their victims open, and divined from their smoking entrails. The Norwegians used to beat their brains out with an axe, the Icelanders by dashing them against a stone. The Scythians cut off the shoulder and arm, and flinging them in the air drew omens from the manner in which they fell upon the pile. The Romans and Persians buried them alive.

This mania for blood was universal. Even Themistocles, the deliverer of Greece, had once sacrificed three youths.

The ancient Peruvians, when one of their nation was dangerously ill, sacrificed his eldest son or youngest daughter to the solar deity, entreating him to spare the father's life. And periodically at their religious festivals they murdered children and virgins, drowning them and then sacrificing them.

And the ancient Mexicans forced their victims to lie down upon a pyramidical stone, and tearing out their hearts, lifted them smoking towards the sun.

I might continue this long and disgusting catalogue of religious crimes, but let us return to the Druids, who at least only sacrificed human beings in some great and peculiar crisis.

The word sacrifice means an *offering of the cake*, and there can be no doubt that those thin broad cakes of the ancient Britons, which, with a libation of flour, milk, eggs, and herbs, or milk, dew and acorns are still superstitiously offered in the north of Britain, formed the usual sacrifice.

They also offered the boar, and it is not improbable that the hare, hen and goose which they were forbidden to eat, but which Cæsar informs us that they reared *causa voluptatis*, were used for sacrificial purposes.

The human victims were selected from criminals or prisoners of war. In lack of these they were chosen by lot, and it sometimes happened that Curtius-like they offered themselves up for their country.

Such a one was led into a sacred forest watered by running streams. In the centre, a circular space surrounded by grey and gigantic stones. Then the birds ceased to sing, the wind was hushed; and the trees around extended their spectral arms which were soon to be sprinkled with human blood.

Then the victim would sing the Song of Death.

The Druid would approach, arrayed in his judicial robes. He was dressed in white; the serpent's egg encased in gold was on his bosom; round his neck was the collar of judgment which would strangle him who delivered an unjust sentence; on his finger was the ring of divination; in his hand was a glittering blade.

They would crown the victim with oak leaves in sombre mockery. They would scatter branches of the oak upon the altar.

The voices of the blue-robed Bards would chant a solemn dirge, their harps would tone forth sinister notes.

Pale and stern the Druid would approach, his knife uplifted in the air.

He would stab him in the back. With mournful music on his lips he would fall weltering in blood, and in the throes of death.

The diviners would draw round, and would calmly augur from his struggles.

After which, fresh oak-leaves would be cast upon the blood-polluted altar, and a death feast would be held near the corpse of the sacrificed.

VII. Priestesses

THE Druids had many rites of divination--from the entrails of their victims--from the flight of birds--from the waves of the sea--from the bubbling of wells-and from the neighing of white horses.

By the number of criminals causes in the year they formed an estimate of the scarcity or plenty of the year to come.

They also used divining rods, which they cut in the shape of twigs from an apple tree which bore fruit, and having distinguished them from each other by certain marks, threw them promiscuously upon a white garment. Then the Diviner would take up each billet or stick three times, and draw an interpretation from the marks before imprinted on them.

The ordering of these divinations were usually placed in the hands of women who formed an order of Sibylls among these ancient prophets.

It has been the belief of every age that women are more frequently blessed with the gifts of inspiration, and that the mists of the future hang less darkly before their eyes than before those of men.

And thus it was that women were admitted to those holy privileges which none others could obtain except with the learning and struggles of a lifetime, thus it was that even the commonest women was admitted to that shrine from which the boldest warriors were excluded.

There is, however, a tradition that at one period both in Gaul and Britain, the women were supreme, that they ruled the councils of state, that they led the armies of war. That the Druids by degrees supplanted them, and obtained the power for themselves. But to propitiate these women who had the blood of Albina in their veins, they admitted them into their order, and gave them the title of Druidesses.

They were eventually formed into three classes.

I. Those who performed the servile offices about the temple, and the persons of the Druids, and who were not separated from their families.

II. Those who assisted the Druids in their religious services, and who, though separated from their husbands, were permitted to visit them occasionally.

III. A mysterious sisterhood who dwelt in strict chastity and seclusion, and who formed the oracles of Britain.

Such is the origin of Christian mummeries. In all important events the Britons repaired to their dwelling. Not even a marriage was consummated among them without consulting the Druidess, and her *purin*, the seic seona of the Irish, viz., five stones thrown up and caught on the back of the hand, and from which she divined.

There are several instances recorded in classical history of predictions from these priestesses which came true.

Alexander Severus had just set out upon an expedition when he was met by a Druidess, "Go on, my Lord," she said aloud to him as he passed, "but beware of your soldiers."

He was assassinated by his soldiers in that same campaign.

My next example is still more peculiar. When Dioclesian was a private soldier he had a Druidess for hostess, who found him every day reckoning up his accounts with a military exactitude to which the army in those days was a stranger.

"You are niggardly," she said.

"Yes," he answered, "but when I become an Emperor I will be generous."

"You have said no jest," replied the priestess, for you will be Emperor when you have killed a wild boar--*cum aprum occideris.*"

In our language this prophecy loses its point, for there is a play upon the Latin word which cannot be translated. *Aper* means both the name of a man and a wild beast, and thus the prediction was wrapped in that wise ambiguity which has been the characteristic of all human prophecy.

Dioclesian, whose ambition gave him faith, was much perplexed with the double meaning of the word, but hunted assiduously till he had killed so many wild boars, that he began to fear he had taken the word in its wrong acceptation.

So he slew Aper, his stepfather, the assassin of Numerianus, and shortly afterwards sat upon the imperial throne.

In marble, as well as in ink, there are memorials of the sect of Druidesses. The following inscription was discovered at Metz in Normandy:

SILVANO

SACR

ET NYMPHIS LOCI

APETE DRUIS

ANTISTITA

SOMNO MONITA.

Of Druidic oracles we know only of one at Kildare in Ireland; of one at Toulouse which ceased when Christianity was introduced there by St. Saturnins; of one at Polignac dedicated to Apollo, or Belenus, or Baal; and most celebrated of all that in the island of Sena (now Sain) at the mouth of the River Loire.

This island was inhabited by seven young women who were beautiful as angels, and furious as demons.

They were married but their husbands might never visit them. The foot of man was not permitted to set foot upon their isle.

When the mantle of night had began to descend upon the earth, seven dusky forms might be seen gliding to the shore, and springing into their wicker boats, which were covered with the skins of beasts, would row across to the main-land, and fondle with their husbands, and smile upon them as if with the sweet innocence of youth.

But when the streaks of light began to glimmer in the East, like restless spirits summoned back to their daylight prison, strange fires would gleam from their eyes, and they would tear themselves from their husband's arms.

To them came the sailors who fished and traded on the seas, and entreated them for fair winds. But as they came and as they spoke, they shuddered at the sight of these women whose faces were distorted by inspiration, whose voices seemed to be full of blood.

When Christianity began to prevail in the north, it was believed that these women, by culling certain herbs at various periods of the moon, transformed themselves into winged and raging beasts, and attacking such as were baptized and regenerated by the blood of Jesus Christ, killed them without the visible force of arms, opened their bodies, tore out their hearts and devoured them; then substituting wood or straw for the heart, made the bodies live on as before and returned through the clouds to their island-home.

It is certain that they devoted themselves chiefly to the service of the Moon, who was said to exercise a peculiar influence over storms and diseases-the first of which they pretended to predict, the latter to cure.

They worshipped her under the name of Kêd or Ceridwen, the northern name for the Egyptian Isis.

They consecrated a herb to her, called *Belinuncia*, in the poisonous sap of which they dipped their arrows to render them as deadly as those malignant rays of the moon, which can shed both death and madness upon men.

It was one of their rites to procure a virgin and to strip her naked, as an emblem of the moon in an unclouded sky. Then they sought for the wondrous *selago* or golden herb. She who pressed it with her foot slept, and heard the language of animals. If she touched it with iron, the sky grew dark and a misfortune fell upon a world. When they had found it, the virgin traced a circle round it, and covering her hand in a white linen cloth which had never been before used, rooted it out with a point of her little finger--a symbol of the crescent moon. Then they washed it in a running spring, and having gathered green branches plunged into a river and splashed the virgin, who was thus supposed to resemble the moon clouded with vapors. When they retired, the virgin walked backwards that the moon might not return upon its path in the plain of the heavens.

They had another rite which procured them a name as infamous and as terrible as that of the Sirens of the South, who were really Canaanite priestesses that lured men to their island with melodious strains, and destroyed them as a sacrifice to their Gods.

They had a covered temple in imitation probably of the two magnificent buildings which the Greek colonists had erected at Massilia. This it was their custom annually to unroof, and to renew the covering before the sun set by their united labors.

And if any woman dropt or lost the burden that she was carrying, she was immediately torn to pieces by these savage creatures, who daubed their faces and their white bosoms with their victim's blood, and carried her limbs round the temple with wild and exulting yells.

It was this custom which founded the story told at Athens and at Rome, that in an island of the Northern seas there were virgins who devoted themselves to the service of Bacchus, and who celebrated orgies similar to those of Samothrace.

For in those plays, performed in honor of Dionusus, there was always a representation of a man torn limb from limb. And in the Island of Chios, as in Sena, this drama was enacted to the life.

Book The Fourth. The Destruction Of The Druids

I. The Destruction Of The Druids

ON the South coast of Britain the people were thronging by hundreds to the sea-shore. It was to see a vessel which was sailing past, and which had come from some strange country across the seas.

Its prow was adorned with a swan's head and neck made of bronze. Below the prow and projecting a little above the keel was a brazen beak, which was called the *rostrum* and which had been invented by the Tyrrhenian Pisœus for breaking the sides of the enemy's ships.

The stern was elevated and adorned with the figure of a God. There seated, they could distinguish the prominent figure of a man who paddled a huge broad-bladed oar backwards and forwards in the water, and with which he appeared to guide the vessel.

There were two masts made of fire-wood from the forests of Scandinavia, and a triangular sail suspended from each, inflated by the wind.

The sides of this vessel presented an extraordinary sight. Three banks of rowers, raised above each other, were plying their oars which swung in leather thongs, and which surrounded the ship with creamy foam, and which dashed the transparent spray high in the air.

The Britons perched upon the rocks, or in their little wicker boats, continued to watch this ship till it had disappeared, and then returned to their homes to relate this incident to their wives with Celtic garrulity.

It remained to them an enigma, till they received intelligence from the merchants of the main that the ship was a Roman trireme, or war galley; that its commander was Caius Volusenus, and that he had been sent by Julius Cæsar the Divine, to explore the coasts of that country upon which he meditated an invasion.

In fact, it was this great general who, aspiring to outvie the conquests of Pompey, had determined to subdue this island of Britain, which was then only known to the world. by some vague and exaggerated reports of the ferocity of its inhabitants, the perils of its seas, the darkness of its sky, and the marvelous beauty of its pearls.

However, the remoteness of the country with the difficulty and danger of the enterprise were those obstacles which form the stepping-stones to greatness; while the precious stones and metals with which it was said to abound, served to excite the cupidity of his soldiers whose souls were less open to those glorious passions which elevated that of their commander.

The brigands and pirates (that is to say the invaders) of those days even, considered it necessary to invent a paltry excuse for some act of lawless oppression; and Cæsar before he attacked the freedom and properties of a nation, affirmed that it was in revenge for the assistance which a small tribe of Britons had rendered to his enemies the Gauls.

The Britons terrified by this report, sent ambassadors to Rome. Cæsar received them kindly, and sent Commius, a Roman to whom he had given land in Gaul, as his ambassador in return.

The Britains violated the law of nations and put Commius in prison. Cæsar invaded Britain.

Then the groves of the Druids resounded with the cries of victims, and blood flowed from the knife of the sacrificer. Then the huge image of a bull made of wicker-work was erected, and filled with animals and men, was set on fire, while the drums and cymbals of the priests drowned those piteous cries which strange to say was thought ill-omened to bear.

Then the Bards who before had sung the blessings of peace, and who had parted armies in their fierce strife, sang the war-hymns of their ancestors, and fired every heart with fortitude and emulation.

On the 26th of August, in the year 55 B.C., at about ten o'clock in the forenoon, Cæsar reached the British coasts, where he found the hills covered with armed men.

He sailed along the coast till he came to that low sandy plain on which the town of Deal Dow stands. It was there that he intended to land, and there that the Britons, perceiving the prows of his vessels turned towards the shore, crowded with horse, foot and chariots to repel him.

The water was too shallow to admit of the galleys approaching close to land. The Romans had therefore to wade through the sea under a cloud of arrows, and fighting with waves as well as with men. Thus they were thrown into disorder, and the waters were reddened with their blood. But Cæsar had commanded the rowing-boats to approach, in which were erected slings with divers instruments of war, and which darted over the water like sharks springing to their prey.

The Britons had begun to yield, but were rallying their courage as they saw that the Romans were fearing those waves which bore past on their dark bosoms the corpses of their comrades. When the standard-bearer of the tenth legion invoked the gods and cried:-- "Follow me, if you do not wish me to lose my standard among the foe; but if I lose my life, I shall have done my duty to Rome, and to my general."

The brave man sprang into the sea, with the brazen eagle held aloft, and his bright sword flashing in his hand. The whole legion followed him, and after a long contest obtained a victory which had the Romans possessed cavalry to pursue their routed enemy, would have been as sanguinary as it was glorious and decisive.

From that epoch indeed, Britain may be considered as a Roman state, and its after history as merely the history of its insurrections.

Under Julius Cæsar, the rebellion of Cassebilanus compelled him to make a second expedition against Britain.

Augustus threatened to invade their island if the Britons continued to refuse to pay taxes. Intimidated by his menaces, they sent ambassadors to Rome who implored the pardon of the Emperor, and brought him large gifts, and swore fealty to him in the temple of Mars.

The Britons broke their oath under the reign of Caligula, who made grand preparations for an invasion of the island, but who preferred leading his army against the ocean which he had conquered in this manner.

Having drawn up all his men in battle array upon the seashore, he caused the *balistas*, or slings, and other instruments of war to be ranged before them; he then sailed in a war-galley some little distance into the sea, returned, ordered his trumpeters to sound the charge, and the soldiers to fill their helmets with the shells from the beach, which he stored as the trophies of a conquered enemy in the Capitol. Having commended the courage of his soldiers and rewarded them profusely, he erected a tower upon the spot as if to prevent the nation from forgetting that Cæsar was a madman.

This display of imbecility naturally strengthened the Britons in their resolution to pay no taxes, and to re-assert their freedom.

When Claudius Cæsar came to the throne, he determined (partly on the advice of Bericus, a British outlaw) to invade this rebellious state.

Aulus Plautius, was placed at the head of a large army, and after several fierce engagements returned to Rome where he was rewarded with an ovation.

Ostorius was sent to Britain in the same reign to quell an insurrection, and also returned successful, bringing with him Caractacus, its leader, as prisoner.

In the reign of the blood-thirsty Nero, Suetonius was appointed Governor of Britain. For two whole years he made war upon the refractory Britons with great success, subduing fresh tribes and establishing garrisons.

But he had long perceived that there was an influence working against him, which was all the more powerful because it was concealed. It was that of the Druids, who still possessed an extraordinary sway over the minds of British warriors, and who animated them with promises of paradise to the defence of their country and their homes.

He discovered that the chief stronghold of the craft was the island of Mona, now Anglesea. It was to Mona that the British chieftains resorted as an oracle, to learn their destinies and to receive the encouragements of those whom they revered. It was to Mona that the wounded were borne, and were placed under the gentle care of those physicians who knew the secret properties of all herbs and flowers. It was to Mona that the Derwydd, weary with warfare had withdrawn, and for which they had deserted their magnificent seat at Abury, and their circular temple in Salisbury plain.

This island is reported to have been one of the fortunate islands sung of by the Grecian poets, as the Elysian fields. It was watered by clear streams it was clothed with fair meadows like a soft green mantle; it was full of oaken groves sacred to the Gods, from which it was called *Ynys Dewyll* the dark and shadowy island.

It was in the year A.D. 61, that Suetonius resolved to invade this delicious retreat, and to carry the sword into the palace of the Arch-Druid, into the seminary of the Bardic Muse.

He forded the narrow channel which divides the isle from the main-land with his cavalry, while his infantry crossed over in flat-bottomed boats, called *scaphæ*, and by which we learn that they landed near Llamdan where there is a place called *Pant yr yscraphie* to this day.

As the Romans landed, they were petrified by the horrible sight which awaited them.

It was night, and the British army dusky and grim, stood arrayed against them. Women clad in dark and mournful garments, and carrying torches in their hands like the furies of hell, were running up and down the ranks uttering loud wailing cries, while the Druids kneeling before them with hands raised to heaven, made the air resound with frightful imprecations.

At some distance behind them, in the obscurity of a neighboring grove, twinkled innumerable fires.

In these the Roman prisoners were to be burnt alive.

At first, horror-struck, they remained motionless: it was only when their generals exhorted them not to fear a crowd of women and priests, and when a flight of arrows from the Britons assured them that they had really flesh and blood foes to contend with, that they could be brought to advance to the charge with their usual valor and precision.

That night the Druids were burnt in the flames which they themselves had lighted.

But there were many who escaped into the recesses of the sacred groves, or by boat to the neighboring isles. These only waited for an opportunity to excite the Britons to fresh struggles for their freedom, and such an opportunity was soon afforded.

Prasutagus, King of the Iceni, having died, left the half of his property to Cæsar and half to his daughters. This which had been done to obtain the favor of the Romans had an opposite effect. His kingdom and palace were plundered and destroyed, his daughters ravished, his queen beaten like a slave.

The Britons driven to despair by these outrages took arms under Boadicea, the widow of Prasutagus.

Then the image of victory which the Romans had erected, fell down without any apparent cause and backwards as if it would give place to its enemies. And certain women, distempered with fury, went singing by way of prophecy that destruction was at hand. And strange sounds were heard in the council house of the Romans, and their theatre echoed with hideous howlings, and a bleeding sword was seen in the sky, and a spectre in the arm of the sea, and the ocean was reddened as if with blood, and the shape of men's bodies were left in the sand at the ebb of the tide.

The Britons won several battles, and cruelly massacred all the Romans that they took captive without distinction either of age or sex.

It was already sung by the Bards who accompanied the army with their three-stringed harps that Britain was free.

But Suetonius with his formidable fourteenth legion was as yet unconquered.

With ten thousand men he occupied a strong possession in a pass at the head of an open plain, with a thick wood behind for purposes of retreat and ambush.

Here were drawn up the Roman cavalry, armed after the Greek fashion with spears and bucklers, and the infantry in due order of battle--the *velites* with javelin and target-the *hastali* with their shields and Spanish swords, and coats of mail--and the *triarii* with their pikes.

The British army numbered 230,000 men, which was divided into their infantry, their cavalry, and their war-chariots. The infantry also was divided into three nations, which were subdivided into family tribes resembling the Highland clans.

Those of the South were habited like the Belgic Gauls in woolen tunics thickly woven with coarse harsh wool; their legs and thighs covered with close garments, called *Brachæ*. They wore also helmets of brass, adorned with figures of birds or beasts rudely carved; iron breastplates, protruding with hooks; a long sword hanging obliquely across their thighs; a shield ornamented with figures; and a huge dart whose shaft was of iron, a cubit in length and as broad as two hands put together.

The inland nations were clothed in the skins of beasts and armed with spears and bucklers.

The Caledonians went naked, armed only with long broad pointless swords, and short spears with round balls of brass at the end, with which they used to make a noise before battle to frighten the horses of the enemy.

These Northern nations were of all the most resolute and troublesome enemies of Rome; for they could sleep on bogs covered with water, and live upon the barks and roots of trees, and possessed a peculiar kind of meat, a morsel of which no larger than a bean could protect them for days from hunger and thirst.

The cavalry were mounted upon small but hardy and mettlesome horses, which they managed with great dexterity. Their arms were the same as those of the infantry, for they would often dismount from their horses and fight on foot.

Their war-chariots were adorned with beautiful carvings, and were guided by the flower of the nobility. They were furnished with enormous hooks and scythes, which spread death around as they were driven at terrific speed through the ranks of the foe.

The plain was surrounded by carts and wagons in which, according to the Celtic custom, were placed the wives and daughters of the warriors who animated them with their cries, and who tended the wounded that were brought to them from the field of blood.

In the midst of this army there was a woman standing in a chariot, clothed in a mantle, with a gold chain round her neck, her face grave and stern, her yellow hair falling to the ground.

It was Queen Boadicea, who with her two daughters by her side, had come to die or to be revenged.

With a royal dignity sublime in its shamelessness she showed them her body covered with sore and ignoble stripes; with a trembling hand she pointed to her two daughters disgraced and defiled; with a loud and fierce voice she reminded them of their victories, and prayed to God to complete their work of vengeance.

"Ye Britons, she cried, are wont to fight under the conduct of a woman, but now I ask ye not to follow me because I am descended from illustrious ancestors, nor because my kingdom has been stolen from me. I ask ye to avenge me as a simple woman who has been whipped with rods, and whose daughters have been ravished before her eyes. These Romans are insatiable, they respect neither the age of our fathers, nor the virginity of our daughters. They tax our bodies; they tax our very corpses. And what are they? They are not men. They bathe in tepid water, live on dressed meats, drink undiluted wine, anoint themselves with spikenard and repose luxuriously. They are far inferior to us. Dread them not. They must have shade and shelter, pounded corn, wine and oil, or they perish. While to us every herb and root is food, every juice is oil, every stream wine, every tree a house. Come then, remember your past victories, remember the causes of this war, and you will understand that the day is come when you must either conquer or die. Such at least shall be a woman's lot; let those live who desire to remain slaves." So saying, she loosed a hare as an omen of victory from her bosom, and the Britons with wild shouts advanced upon their foe.

Suetonius cheered his veterans with a few emphatic words, and showed them with contempt the wild and disorderly multitude which poured confusedly towards them. He bid the trumpets sound and the troops advance.

Then arose a terrible struggle--a nation fighting for its freedom--an army fighting for its fame.

Alas! that sea of blood, that dreadful apparition, those figures in the sand were omens of Britain's downfall. Four-score thousand of its proudest warriors were slain; their wives and daughters were butchered, and Boadicea overcome with sorrow and disgrace, destroyed herself with poison.

Thus ends the reign of the Druids; the priest-kings of the North. Thus they were stripped of their crowns, and their sceptres, and their regal robes, and compelled to fly to the islands of the Irish channel and the German Sea, where they dwelt in hollow oaks and in little round stone houses, many of which still remain and are held in reverence by the simple islanders.

In Gaul the work of destruction had been completed even prior to the time of Suetonius. This beautiful religion had been proscribed by Tiberius ostensibly because it permitted human sacrifices, really because it possessed a dangerous power. This prohibition had been afterwards enforced by Claudius, and the Druids were massacred by the Romans wherever they were to be found. The priestesses of Sena were burnt by one of the ancient Dukes of Brittany.

Yet it is difficult to subroot an ancient religion by imperial edicts. The minds of men though prone to novelty will frequently return fondly to their first faiths, as the hearts of maidens creep back to former and almost forgotten loves.

In the fifth century, Druidism sprang back to life under the mighty Merlin, whose prophecies became so famous throughout Gaul and Britain, and who forms so conspicuous a character in the Arthurian romances.

But these wee drops of the *elixir vitæ*, which could only animate the corpse for a brief space--which but gave vigor to the frame, and light to the eyes, as a lamp apparently extinguished will burst into flame ere it dies out for ever.

We find many decrees of Roman emperors, and canons of Christian councils in the sixth, seventh and eighth centuries against Druidism, and in the day of King Canute, the Dane, a law was made against the worship of the sun and moon, mountains, lakes, trees and rivers.

It is possible to discover many vestiges of the Druids and their religion in our times, and many peculiar analogies between their superstitions and those of other nations and of other priests.

Having related how this order of Priests emanated from the Patriarchs; how they received their idolatrous and ceremonial usuages from the Phœnicians; how they obtained a supreme power in those two countries which ere now have struggled for the possession of the world; how they were attacked and annihilated by the Roman soldiers, I shall leap over a chasm of centuries, and trace their faint footsteps in our homes, in our churches and in our household words.

Book The Fifth. Vestiges Of Druidism

I. In The Ceremonies Of The Church Of Rome

THERE is no religion so pure and simple, and yet so mystic and divine as the religion of the Christians. What need is there of arguments to prove that it is derived from heaven, for what mortal mind could have conceived so grand and touching a principle, as that of a God who filled with love and pity could descend from His throne of bliss and honor to save from destruction this one poor star, this one faint mote in the vastness of His firmament.

To twelve men the dear Jesus left his precepts and commands. From the children of these men and of their disciples sprang a noble flock who, like their great Master, suffered harsh words and cruel torments, and death itself in a holy cause.

When God rewarded them by shedding peace upon the church from without, dissensions from within played Satan's work with her chastity and her love. Swords were then drawn for the first time by Christians against each other--swords which never thence till now have been for a moment sheathed. The Christian religion is divided into three established churches, the Church of Rome, the Church of Greece, and the Church of England. Besides these, there are sects whose origins have been abuse upon the one hand, and ambition upon the other hand, and whose very titles it would occupy pages to enumerate.

Between the vulgar members of these three churches burns a heathenish and diabolical hatred. Its root is jealousy. Each church affects to be the only ladder to heaven, and damns all such souls as refuse to ascend by them.

They are barbarians and place themselves in the same scale with the tribe of the Cherokee Indians, who firmly believe that the Black Hawks will not be admitted to the pleasures of the happy hunting grounds because they are not Cherokees.

Between the doctrines and ceremonies of the Greek and Romish Churches, there are but a few delicate and unimportant distinctions. Yet the Patriarch of the Church, every Holy Thursday, solemnly excommunicates the Pope and all his followers.

The Church of England, and the Church of Rome worship the same Christ. Between these two churches, as between two armies, is waged a scandalous, vituperative war, and each fresh convert is a battle won.

The Romish Church was sullied by many abuses, which authorized a schism and a separation among its members. Since many of those plague-spots still remain, it is right that this separation should continue. But a dark and dangerous heresy has long been creeping silently into the heart of our religion, and converting its ministers into false vipers who, warmed and cherished by the bosom of this gentle church, use their increasing strength in darting black poison through all her veins.

They wish to transmit to our church those papist emblems and imagery, those ceremonies and customs which are harmless in themselves, but which by nourishing superstition elevate the dangerous power of the priests.

We can at present be proud of our priesthood. They constitute a body of pious, honorable, hardworking men. It is because they can exercise no undue power. Give them supreme power, and they will be Neros who will fasten us with iron chains, and murder us if we disobey them.

The priesthood of the Druids stands almost alone in the history of the past. It was directed by men, with minds elevated by philosophy and learned in the human heart. But read the religious history of other nations, and you will discover how frightfully the power of the priests has been abused.

The priests invented a thousand Gods; the priests told a thousand lies; the priests instituted a thousand absurd and horrible customs. Who first taught nations to be idolaters, to be murderers but the priests. Who instituted the festival of the juggernaut, the Inquisition, the massacre of St. Bartholomew, but the priests.

Calvin, a priest of the Reformation, ordered his victims to be burnt with green wood--a truly Christian refinement of cruelty!

Aaron, a priest, manufactured a golden calf and taught the Jews to insult their God. And it was Caiaphas, a high priest, who committed that murder of which the more virtuous heathen Pilate washed his hands.

Look everywhere, look everywhere, and you will see the priests reeking with gore. They have converted popular and happy nations into deserts, and have made our beautiful world into a slaughter house drenched with blood and tears.

Englishmen! they are planting images, they are performing ceremonies in your houses of worship which you find it impossible to understand. They are hidden from your eyes by a dark veil; it is the veil of a Pagan goddess; it is the veil of Isis.

I would not raise this veil, and disclose the heathen origin of emblems and ceremonies which so many sanctify and revere, were it not to answer some good purpose.

I write then in the hope that the church may be preserved in its simplicity--and its priesthood in that honor and integrity which now, as a body, they possess to an extent unequalled in any instance that the priest-history of the past or the present can afford. It is indeed seldom that an English clergyman becomes a wolf clothed in lamb-skin, and preys upon his flock under words and looks of religion.

But we know that power presents temptations, which minds fortified only by three years education at a college are often unable to resist.

Before letters were invented, symbols were necessary to form a language; and it is still an argument of the Greek and Romish Churches that pictures and images are the books of those who cannot read.

They say also that since man is not a disembodied spirit like the angels, it is also impossible that he can worship the Deity with his heart alone. And it cannot be denied that dim and shadowy lights, sweet perfumes, majestic processions and strains of music will elevate the soul towards God and prepare the mind to receive heavenly and sublime impressions.

Without objecting to the use of such aids to devotion, I wish to guard people from attaching a peculiar sanctity to the bare aids in themselves, which is nothing less than idolatry. This I can best prevent by showing them how they first came into a Christian Church. And in doing so, I shall depart little from the original design of this chapter which is to investigate the vestiges of Druidism in the ceremonies of the Roman Catholic Religion.

Not only the ceremonies, but also the officers and many of the doctrines of the Church of Rome may be traced to heathen sources.

The Pope of Rome exactly resembles the Secular High-Priest of ancient Rome, and in Latin his title is the same--*Pontifex Maximus*. The office was probably an imitation of that of the Arch-Druid, who, as I have described, had supreme power over secular as well as ecclesiastical affairs, and who was surrounded by a Senate of the Chief Druids, as the Pontifex Maximus was by *Flamines*, and the Pope by Cardinals.

The distinguishing sign of the *flamen* was a HAT; and "the cardinal's hat" is a European proverb.

The Arch-Druid held his foot to be kissed on certain occasions by the common people. Julius Cæsar who had observed this custom, on being made Pontifex Maximus, compelled Pompey to do the same; in this he was followed by Caligula and Heliogabalus, whom the Pope also has wisely imitated.

The tonsure of the Romish priests is the same as that of the priests of Isis whose heads were shaved, a practice forbidden by God: (*Levit. xx. 1. Ezek xliv.* 20).

Their celibacy is also heathenish. Origen when emasculated himself, only imitated the Hierophantes of Athens who drank an infusion of hemlock to render themselves impotent. St. Francis who, when tempted with carnality, would throw himself naked on the snow making balls which he applied to his body calling them his maid and his wife, did but copy Diogenes who lived in a tub-a cloak, his covering--a wallet, his kitchen--the palm of his hand, his bottle and cup; who in the searching heat of summer would lie naked on the hot gravel, and in the harshest frost would embrace stone statues covered with snow.

Plato, Pythagoras, Heraclitus, Democritus and Zeno, the prince of Stoics, imposed celibacy upon their disciples. The priests of Cybele, the Megabyzes of Ephesus and the priests of Egypt maintained the vow of chastity. Eneas (*Æneid lib vi.*) in passing through the infernal regions saw no priests there but such as had passed their lives in celibacy.

It need not be proved that there were many hermits and orders of monks among the heathen. Even the begging friars of the Romish church are not original. There was a tribe of lazy mendicant priests among the heathens, against whom Cicero wrote in his Book of Laws, who used to travel from house to house with sacks on their backs, and which were gradually filled with eatables by the superstition of their hosts.

Pythagoras established an order of nuns over whom he placed his daughter. The Roman vestals were nuns who took a vow of chastity, and who, like Christian nuns that we have heard of, were punished with death if they disgraced it.

There was a sisterhood of Druidesses at Kildare in Ireland, whose office it was, like the Roman Vestals, to preserve a holy fire ever burning. They devoted themselves to the service of Bright, the Goddess of Poetry, of Physics, and of Smiths, and who is spoken of in the old Irish MSS. as the *Presiding Care*. When Druidism was abolished, these priestesses became Christian nuns, and Brighit became St. Bridget, the tutelary saint of Ireland. The fire was still preserved in honor of this Christian saint, and though extinguished once by the Archbishop of London, was relighted and only finally extinguished at the suppression of the monasteries in the reign of King Henry the Eighth.

The dress and ornaments of the Romish priest are borrowed from the heathens. The Phœnician priests wore surplices. Lambskin was worn by the Persian priests. The *pelt*, which the canons wear with the fur outward, is a memorial of the custom of the early heathens, who having killed the beasts for sacrifice, flayed them and taking the skins put them over their head with the fur outwards. On the *saccos*, or episcopal garment of the Russian bishops are suspended small silver bells, which were also worn on the robes of the priests of Persia and of the High-Priest of the Jews.

The *crosier*, or pastoral staff of the Pope was also used by the Druids, and answers to the *lituus* of the Roman augurs and the *hieralpha* of the Hindoos.

The Arch-Druid wore bands precisely resembling those which the Romish and English clergy wear now, and which a short time ago the students of our universities were compelled to wear in their public examinations.

Votive offerings and pilgrimages are known by all to be of Pagan extraction.

The fasts, penances and self-tortures of the Romish priests find a parallel among the Yogees or Gymnosophists of India, who wandered about the world naked as they had been born, sometimes standing on one leg on the burning sands--passing weeks without nourishment, years without repose--exposed to the sun, to the rain, to the wind--standing with their arms crossed above their heads till the sinews shrank and their flesh withered away--fixing their eyes upon the burning sun till their moisture was seared and their light extinguished.

When a Brahmin became a grandfather he gave up the management of his affairs to his son, and quitted the city for the desert, the company of men for eternal solitude. He dressed in the bark of trees; he was not permitted to wear linen nor to cut his nails. He bathed nine times a day; he read and meditated ever on the Holy Vedas. At night alone he slept, and then on the bare ground. In the summer months he sat in the full blaze of the sun, surrounded by four fires; in the four months of rain, he dwelt in a stage raised above the water by four poles but unroofed; during the four winter months he sat all night in the cold water.

And always performing the fast of Chanderayan.

Soon his spirits would sink, and tired of life he was allowed to commit suicide, which was considered the sure passport to heaven. Some burn themselves, some drowned themselves, some flung themselves from precipices, and some walked, walked, walked till they dropped down dead.

The fast of Chanderayan consisted in eating one mouthful a day, and increasing a mouthful every day for a month, and then decreasing a mouthful every day for the same length of time. A tribe of the Egyptian priests fasted perpetually, abstaining from eggs which they considered liquid meat, and from milk which they esteemed a kind of blood.

The members of the Greek Church are more scrupulous than those of Rome, for they will not eat eggs or fish when fasting.

The religious rites of the Romish Church are closely assimilated to those of the heathens.

In the *Dibaradané* or offering-of-fire, the officiating Brahmin always rang a small bell. Also the women-of-the-idol, the dancing girls of the Indian pagodas had golden bells attached to their feet.

The wax tapers which are constantly kept burning in Roman Catholic churches remind us of the practice of most of the ancient nations who preserved fires continually burning in their temples; for instance in the pagodas of the Brahmins; in the sanctuaries of Jupiter Ammon; in the Druidic temple at Kildare; in the Capitol at Rome; and in the temple of the Gaditanian Hercules at Tyre.

The Egyptians used lamps in the celebration of their religious services. They had one festival which they called *The Feast of Lamps*, which they used to celebrate by sailing down the Nile to the temple of Isis at Sais by torchlight. Those who were unable to attend, lighted the lamps, which were small cups filled with salt and oil, and a lighted wick floated within.

It is curious that this Pagan observance should be still preserved by the Papists. A few years ago I was in the house of a Roman Catholic at vesper time. "I cannot attend vespers to-day," he said, "so I do this." And he fetched a glass saucer which was filled with oil, and lighted a wick which was floating in the midst. After some few minutes the light died out, "Now," said he, "vespers are over."

The Persians used a kind of holy water which was named *zor*. But it is needless to produce such instances. Water, as a principle of generation, and as one of the four elements was revered by all heathendom. The very *aspersoire* or sacred water-pot which the ancient Romans. used for their temple, may be found among the implements of their successors.

Their turnings and genuflexions are copied from the *deisuls* of the Druids. The Druidic religious dances which were performed in a circle, in imitation of the revolution of the heavenly bodies, are preserved to posterity by the cardinals who advance to the Pope in a circle, by the Turkish dervishes, and by the French and English peasantry in various rural dances.

The heathens were not without their liturgies.

The Persians used a long form of prayer for the ceremony of marriage, and the use of the ring on the third finger of the left hand was known to a the ancients as Tertullian himself admits. In the Greek Church of Russia the couple are crowned with garlands which are removed on the eighth day. This, an ancient Roman observance, is not a traditional superstition of the Russians, but a ceremony authorized by their religion, and a service in their liturgy. The veil which our brides wear is also a remnant of ancient Rome.

--Dudum sedet illa parato
Flammeolo.--*Juv. Sat.* X.

As is also the superstition among Papist that it is unlucky to marry in the month of May. Ovid records it in a distich.

Nec viduæ tœdis eadem nec virginis apta
Tempora. Quæ nupsit non diuturna fuit.
Hac quoque de causâ si te proverbia tangunt
Mense malas Maio nubere vulgus ait.

Our funeral practice of throwing three handfuls of earth on the coffin, and saying : *earth to earth, ashes to ashes, dust to dust*, was in use among the ancient Egyptians, and our mutes resemble the hired mourners of all the ancient nations.

The Vedas are full of exorcisms against those evil spirits which, as the Hindoos supposed, crowded about the sacrifice and impeded the religious rites. There are forms of exorcism used by Romish priests, and in the first liturgy of Edward VI, there was a form of exorcism in the baptismal service which since has been erased.

The Romans used to consecrate their temples, when first built, with prayers and sacrifices, and sprinklings of holy water.

The mass is acknowledged by the Catholic priests to be a sacrificial service, and the host made of wheat flour is an exact imitation of the consecrated cakes which were used by the heathens.

The ancient Persians carried their infants to the temple a few days after they were born, and presented them to the priest who stood before the holy fire in the presence of the burning sun. He took the child and plunged it into a vase full of water for the purification of its soul. After which it was anointed, received the sign of the cross, and was fed with milk and honey.

Such is the origin of infant baptism, of the font, and of the ceremony of signing the forehead with the figure of the cross-none of which are derived from God or from His Holy Scriptures.

When the child had arrived at the age of fifteen years, the priest invested him with the robe called *Sudra* and with the girdle, and initiated him into the mysteries of their religion.

This is plainly the same as the Christian confirmation, before which the church does not permit us to receive the sacrament.

We first hear of the sacramental offering of bread and wine as used by Melchisedek. I have described it among the ceremonies of Druidism. Among the Hebrews it was called *qum* whence our word "communion."

I have now to consider the great symbol of the Christian religion--the cross. Were it regarded as a mere emblem of our Lord's suffering I should be silent upon the matter; but since it is an object of actual idolatry in the Roman Catholic church, and threatens to become the same in our own, I must endeavor to correct the abuse by exposing its Pagan origin.

This cross which the Roman Catholics worship on Good Friday by taking off their shoes and approaching it on their knees, and reverently kissing it, was once as common a symbol among Pagans as the circle, the serpent or the bull.

In Ezekiel, IX. 4-6, we read that God directed the six destroyers to kill all whom they found in the city of Jerusalem, except those on whose forehead the Taw was inscribed. This letter Taw is the last in the Hebrew alphabet, and according to its ancient method of writing, exactly resembles a cross, as St. Jerome remarked 1400 years ago.

The *crux ansata* of the Egyptians, according to Ruffinus and Sozomen, was hieroglyphic, and imparted the time that was to come.

The ♂ was a phallic emblem in Egypt. Thereby also the Syrians and Phoenicians represented the planet Venus. On some of the early coins of the latter nation, we find the cross attached to a chaplet of beads placed in a circle so as to form a rosary, such as the

Lamas of Thibet and China, the Hindoos and the Roman Catholics now tell over as they pray.

On a Phœnician medal discovered by Dr. Clarke in the ruins of Citium, are inscribed the cross, the rosary and the lamb.

⚕℘† were the monograms of Osiris, Venus and Jupiter Ammon.

ㅏㄱ of the Scandinavian Teutates or Tuisco.

The Vaishnavas of India mark one of their idols with crosses, thus ⚕ and with triangles ✡.

On the Egyptian monuments in the British Museum may be seen the mystic cross in great numbers of places, and upon the breast of one of the mummies in the Museum of the London University is a cross exactly in this shape.

The two principal pagodas of India, those of Benares and Mathura are built in the form of a cross. The Mexican temples are built in the form of a cross and face the four cardinal points.

Crosses have been discovered on the Scandinavian "Mark" stones in the Scottish Isles, and there are many ancient monuments in Great Britain which, but for the cross engraved upon them, would be considered Druidical.

That the Druids, like the aborigines of America and the ancient conjurers of Lapland, revered the form of the cross can hardly be doubted. *Schedius de Mor. Germ.* informs us that it was their custom to seek studiously for an oak tree large and handsome, growing up with two principal arms in the form of a cross beside the main stem. If the two horizontal arms were not sufficiently adapted to the figure, they fastened a cross beams to it. Then they consecrated it by cutting upon the right branch in fair characters the word *Hesus*, upon the middle stem, the word *Taranis*, upon the left branch *Belenus*, and over them the word *Thaw*.

The tree so inscribed, they would make their Kebla like the Jewish Jerusalem, the Turk's Mecca, and the Christian's altar to which they would direct their faces when they prayed.

I can best explain the adoration of this symbol by deriving it from that constellation *The Southern Cross*, which appears only in tropical skies and which perhaps the heathens, attracted by its beauty, learned to worship, as they worshipped the sun for its God like grandeur, and the moon for its beneficent light. The idolatry of the Roman Catholics is not confined to emblems. They have deified martyrs and other holy men, and render them a worship that is only due to God.

It is true that they draw a distinction between the adoration which they pay to God, and the homage which they pay to Saints, calling the one in the language of the schools *Latria*, from γατ̔εια worship due to God only, and the latter *Dulia*, from δουλεια an inferior kind of worship. But this distinction is too delicate for the illiterate to understand.

A plurality of Gods I have shown to be one of the abuses of ancient heathenism. In this abuse, they have been imitated by the modern idolaters of Rome, not only in the abstract but in the concrete: there is not only assimilation, but a reproduction.

The Romans ridiculed the Gods of Egypt whom they themselves adored but under different names. They burnt Serapis, Anubis, and Isis; they revered Pluto, Mercury and Ceres.

So the Roman Catholics while pretending to abjure the Gods of heathenism have actually adopted many of them.

The petty divinities of the Pagans were deified men, and were intercessors with Osiris, Zeus or Jupiter, as the canonized saints of the Catholic Church are with the God of the Christians.

The Chaldees divided the year into twelve months with an angel over each month. The saints perform the same office in the Romish Calendar, and in several of the Greek churches there are twelve pictures for the twelve months representing the twelve principal saints.

The *divi*, or inferior Gods of the Romans worked miracles; altars were erected in their honor with lights continually burning before them; their relics were worshipped; convents were formed of religious men and women who took the name of *divus* or inferior God, to whom they devoted themselves, such as the Quirinals from Quirinus or Romulus; the Martiales from Mars; the Vulcanates from Vulcan. So also the Augustines from Augustine; the Franciscans from Francis; the Dominicans from Dominic.

The Roman *divi* were tutelary Gods over various vocations--as Neptune over mariners--Pan over shepherds--Pales over husbandmen--Flora over courtezans--Diana over huntsmen. So the seamen, among Catholics, pray to St. Nicholas--the shepherds to St. Windoline--the husbandmen to St. John the Baptist--the courtezans to St. Magdalene--and the huntsmen to St. Hubert.

The saints too have received the equipage of the *divi*. To St. Wolfgang, the hatchet or hook of Saturn--to Moses, the horns of Jupiter Ammon--to St. Peter, the keys of Janus.

In the same way as the Pagans worshipped these *divi* but stigmatized them--Apollo as a rake, Mercury as an arrant thief, and Venus as a courtezan; there are things recorded by pious Catholics themselves of those Popes which are infallible and of saints which are said to be in heaven, quite as little to their credit.

Minutius Felix jeers the Pagans for the vile drudgery they have put upon their Gods. "Sometimes," says he, "Hercules is set to empty dung; Apollo turns cow-herd to Ametus; Neptune hires himself to Laomedon as bricklayer to build up the walls of Troy, and is cheated out of his wages."

So among the glorious miracles of the Holy Virgin, we find that she descends from heaven to bleed a young man in the arm; to take the place of a naughty abbess who has eloped with a monk; to mend the gown of St. Thomas of Canterbury who had torn it on a nail, and to wipe the sweat off the faces of the monks of Chevraux whilst they were at work.

But as I have said before, there has been something more than imitation. There has been adoption. The Roman Catholics have canonized several of the pagan gods. Bacchus, the God of topers, has become St. Baccus, a worshipful saint of the perennial calendar; and Brighit, the Goddess of the Druids, St. Bridget, a patron saint of Ireland.

The most distinguishing feature of the Roman Catholic religion is the idolatrous worship of the Virgin Mary. It is idolatrous, for to this woman whom it is palpable from Scripture that Christ treated as a being inferior to himself, are rendered prayers and honors as numerous and high as those which are rendered to Him, and in all instances they are placed upon a level with each other.

They have made her immaculate, although she was the wife of a carpenter, and although the. brethren of Jesus are more than once mentioned in the gospels.

And as there was no mention made in Scripture of her death, they inferred that, like Enoch and Elijah and her Holy Son, she had been taken up into Heaven. Upon this bare conjecture, the doctrine was assiduously inculcated into the minds of the ignorant, and a service was introduced into the liturgy called "The Assumption of the Virgin Mary."

Bonaventura who was canonized a saint, and who is spoken of by his brother-catholics as the Seraphic Doctor, wrote a book called "The Imitation of the Virgin Mary," after St. Thomas-a-Kempis' well-known work, in which he exhorts all faithful catholic; to pray to the Virgin Mary by whose intercession their souls may be saved.

In the Psalter which St. Bonaventura edited, he changes in each of the 150 Psalms the word Lord or God, for that of Lady or Mary, interspersing in some much of his own composition, and adding the Gloria Patri to each.

For instance in the 148th Psalm-(*page 491 of the Psalter*).

"Praise our Lady of Heaven, glorify her in the highest. Praise her all ye men and cattle, ye birds of the heaven and fishes of the sea. Praise her sun and moon, ye stars and circles of the planets. Praise her Cherubin and Seraphin, thrones and dominions and powers. Praise her all ye legions of angels. Praise her all ye orders of spirits on high.

"Let everything that hath breath praise our Lady."

Theophilus Raynaud, a Jesuit of Lyons, in his work entitled *Diptycha Mariana* thus writes:--

"The torrents of Heaven and the fountains of the great deep, I would rather open than close in homage of the Virgin. *And if her son Jesus has omitted anything, as to the pre-eminence of the exaltation of his own mother*, I a servant, I a slave, not indeed with effect, but with affection would delight in filling it up."

Again:--

"In like manner are her feet to be blessed with which she carried the Lord, the womb in which she carried him, the heart whence she courageously believed in him and fervently loved him, the breasts with which she gave him suck, the hands with which she nourished him, the mouth and tongue with which she gave to him the happy kisses of our redemption, the nostrils with which she smelled the sweet-smelling fragrance of his humanity, the ears with which she listened with delight to his eloquence, the eyes with which she devoutly looked upon him, the body and soul which Christ consecrated in her with every benediction. And these most sacred members must be saluted and blessed with all devotion, so that separate salutations must be addressed to the several members separately, namely, *Hail Mary!* two to the feet, one to the womb, one to the heart, two to the breasts, two to the hands, two to the mouth and tongue, two to the lips, two to the nostrils, two to the ears, two to the eyes, two to the soul and body. And thus in all there are twenty salutations which after the manner of a daily payment with separate and an equal number of kneelings, if it can be done before her image or altar, are to be paid to the glorious Virgin according to that psalm, (144). Every day will I give thanks unto thee and praise THY name for ever and ever."

In the following extract from a little work published at Dublin, 1836, and entitled "*The Little Testament of the Holy Virgin,*" God and the Virgin are placed upon an equality.

"Mary! sacred name under which no one should despair. Mary! sacred name often assaulted but always victorious. Mary! it shall be my life, my strength, my comfort. Every day shall I invoke it and the divine name of Jesus. The Son shall awake the recollection of the mother, and the mother that of the son. *Jesus and Mary!* this is what my heart shall say at my last hour if my tongue cannot. I shall hear them on my death-bed, they shall be wafted on my expiring breath, and I with them to see THEM, know THEM, bless and love THEM for eternity. Amen."

But she is sometimes made even greater than God.

"My soul," says the blessed Eric Suzon, is in the hands of Mary, so that if the judge wishes to condemn me, the sentence must pass through this clement Queen, and she knows how to prevent its execution."

It even became a custom at one time in their church to date the Christian era not from the birth of the Christ, but from the virgin mother of God. See Emanuel Acosta's Acts of the Jesuits in the East. Dilingæ. 1571. *Ad annum usque a Deipara Virgine,* 1568.

The question now naturally arises, why does the Virgin Mary receive this worship and these honors which are only due to God.

You will be surprised when I tell you that this also is a remnant of heathenism.

In all nations, long before the Christian era, a female with a child in her arms had been worshipped. Among the Egyptians it was Isis, among the Etruscans it was Venus, among the Phrygians it was Atys.

In fact as Isis was the original of the Proserpine, the Venus, the Diana, the Juno, the Maia and the Cere of ancient Rome, so she was the original of the Virgin Mary of the Roman Catholic Church.

In Montfaucon we find several plates of Isis giving suck to the boy Horus.

In the year 1747, a Mithraic monument was found at Oxford--a female nursing an infant-which Dr. Stukeley proved to be a representation of the Goddess of the Year nursing the God Day.

It is indeed not improbable that Oxford with its seven hills, its river Isis, and the bull in its coat of arms had been established by priests who, like the Druids, were acquainted with Egyptian lore.

An ancient Etruscan monument was discovered at Rome, the precise model of those pictures of the Madonna and her child so common in Italy and throughout the world.

In many churches on the continent, the Virgin Mary is represented with a lily or lotus in her hand. This plant was sacred to Isis, and was held in reverence by the priests of Egypt and of India.

Isis was the wife of Osiris, as the moon was called the wife of the sun.

In the hymn of the Assumption, the Virgin is entreated "to calm the rage of her heavenly husband."

The month of May was sacred to Isis.

It is called by the Papists "*Mary's month.*"

Venus, the Isis of the Romans, was born from the foam of the sea.

In the form of prayer called *Litaniæ Lauritanæ*, there are more than forty addresses to the Virgin, invoking her as the star of the sea, as the mystical rose, and by a variety of other heathen epithets.

In another prayer she is named *amica stella, naufragis,* and in Sanval's Historie des Antiquités de Paris, *étoile eclantante de la mer.*

The chief title of Venus was *Regina Cæloium.*

And the Holy Virgin is repeatedly invoked in the Romish liturgy as the Queen of Heaven.

Finally, on the 25th of March the ancient Phrygians devoted a festival to the mother of the Gods, which very day still bears among Catholics and their Protestant imitators the name of Lady's Day.

All this does not impeach one iota or tittle of the truth of Christianity. I do not say that the Christians invented a personage, and called her the Virgin Mary. I merely prove that the Roman Catholics pay those idolatrous tributes to the Virgin Mary which their ancestors rendered to Isis in Egypt, or to Venus in Rome, and that they represent her in the same manner.

For instance, in the pictures of the Madonna and the Child, we see the Virgin's head encircled by a crescent halo of light, and the child's by many luminous rays.

The one is a symbol of the new moon sacred to Isis, the latter an imitation of the radiance of the sun of whom Horus was the offspring.

The spires and towers of our churches are also imitated from the pyramids and obelisks of antiquity. These were erected as emblems of the sun's beams which fall pyramidically upon the earth.

Many of the heathen festivals are still celebrated by Christians. In the liturgy of the Greek Church there is a ritual named "The Benediction of the Waters." A wooden temple, richly gilt and hung round with sacred pictures, is erected upon the Neva at St. Petersburg when it is frozen, and a procession is formed by the clerks, the deacons, the priests and the bishops dressed in their richest robes, and bearing the tapers and the sacred pictures, and the service is read within the temple.

This is not unlike "The Feast of Lamps" before described, which the Egyptians partly celebrated on the Nile, a river which in one of the prayers of the Greek Church is called "The Monarch of the Floods."

The conception of the Virgin Mary is represented on the same day (the 2nd of February) as that of the miraculous conception of Juno by the ancient Romans. This, says the author of the Perennial Calendar, is a remarkable coincidence.

It is also a remarkable coincidence that the Feast of All-Saints, which is celebrated by the Roman Catholics on the 2nd of November and which retains its place in the Protestant calendar, should have been on the same day as the *Festum dei Mortis* of the Romans, and should still be annually kept by the Buddhists of Thibet, and by the natives of South America and as a Druidic custom by the rustic classes of Ireland.

It is also a remarkable coincidence that the Romans should have had their *Prosipernalia*, or Feast of Candles or Candlemass in February-their *Palelia*, or shepherd's feast on Midsummer Day which is sacred to St. John the Baptist, and that the Romish Carnival should be held at the same time as the ancient Saturnalia, and should resemble so closely those orgies which were of a masquerade character.

Thus we see that the Roman Catholics have been in the habit of celebrating Christian festivals upon days which were held sacred by the heathens. Whether this was from mere slavish imitation, or from a fondness for old associations, or from a desire to sanctify those days unhallowed by paganism it is impossible to say.

One of the most extraordinary examples of this custom is to be found in our grand festival of Christmas.

All will allow, I think, that there is no evidence to prove that the twenty-fifth of December was the actual day upon which Christ was born. And that He really arose on Easter Day can scarcely be believed, since the fixing of that day was not arranged among the early Christians till after swords as well as words had been used in the conflict, and several fierce battles had been fought.

I hope that I shall not weaken the genial feelings with which Christmas Day, that holiday of the year, is greeted by the nation if I expose the real origin of the festival. But that I feel sure is impossible. It would need something more than a few facts from old books to blot out all those happy associations which crowd around that glorious festival, which though it may be celebrated on the wrong day is kept in the right manner.

I may, however, show those Christians who worship the letter and not the spirit, who attach more sanctity to the day than to the festival, who set their children over grave books and who forbid them to laugh on that day when there is a smile even on the poor man's lips, I may show those word-mongers, those silly Puritans, those harsh blunderers in religion what honor they have paid to heathenism all their lives.

The festival of the twenty-fifth of December, which we call Christmas, was observed by the Druids on that day by lighting great fires on the tops of hills. The festival was repeated on the twelfth day afterwards, which we call old Christmas Day.

And even now there are certain rites performed under the sacred mistletoe on Christmas Day which certainly have little to do with Christianity.

The Jews also celebrated a festival on the twenty-fifth of December which -they called Ϡως or the feast of light, and which Josephus believed to have been instituted by Judas Maccabaeus.

The twenty-fifth of December too was the birthday of the God Mithra, and it was an old custom of the heathens to celebrate the birthdays of their Gods.

And now I will explain when this day was first established as the birthday of Christ. The Cœnobite monks finding that in their monasteries (most of which were pagan seminaries built before the Christian era) a day had been from time immemorial dedicated to the God Sol as his birthday, and that he bore the name of *Lord*--this *Lord* they conceived must be their Lord, and after many disputes the twenty-fifth of December was established as the anniversary of Christ, and so the Druidic festival of the winter solstice became a Christian ceremony.

The origin of *Sunday* is very similar; but while the heathen festival of Christmas has received a Christian name, this has retained its Pagan appellation.

Such was the abhorrence which the early Christians felt for their persecutors, the Jews, that they were wont to reject all that was Jewish, as the first Puritans rejected all that was Romish without considering its intrinsic merits.

God had ordained the seventh day for man's rest and recreation. He had given forth that edict from Mount Sinai not to the Israelites only, but to the whole world. But since the Jews faithfully kept this commandment, the Christians hated the Sabbath and took a step which was wholly unauthorized by their Master, or by any of his Apostles. They changed the day.

They called this new day the Lord's Day, or the Day-of-the-Sun.

The word *Lord* is heathen, and is equivalent to Baal in Chaldee and to Adonis in Phoenician. It first crept into the Scripture thus:

The Jews, in obedience to the law "thou shalt not take the name of Jehovah thy God in vain," never wrote or spoke His name except on the most solemn occasions. And the first translators to avoid the frequent repetition of the word, first used this hieroglyphic 𝔒𝔓 and afterwards the term which the Pagans applied to their God Sol, which in Greek was πυθιος in Latin *dominus*, in Celtic *adon*, in Hebrew *adoni*.

Now the Persians set apart every month four of these Lord's days or lesser festivals to the Sun. On these days, they had more solemn service in their temples than on other days, reading portions of their sacred books and preaching morality.

But the most curious point of resemblance is that on these days alone they prayed *standing*. And in the sixteenth canon of the Council of Nice to kneel in prayer on Sundays is forbidden.

Constantine, after pretending to be converted to Christianity, ordered the day *Domini invicti Solis* to be set apart for the celebration of peculiar mysteries in honor of the great god Sol.

The early Christians were accused by the heathens of worshipping the sun, and Justin, as if loathing the very name of the Jewish Sabbath, preferred writing of it μεθα τον ηλις the day-of-the-sun.

Since it would be now almost impossible to restore our weekly day of rest to that day which God thought fit to appoint, and which man thought fit to alter, I may be blamed for having made these disclosures which certainly do not redound to the honor of our religion.

But I have had my reason. It is to show the folly of those who go word-mongering, to make triumphant comparisons between the Day-of-the-sun as observed by Christians, and God's Sabbath as observed by Jews; who bring out their religion, their consciences, their bibles, their sternest faces and their best clothes upon this day, and who believe or seem to believe that God sleeps all the week, and that if they go to church on Sunday they succeed in deceiving him.

It is not at this hour or at that hour that God is to be worshipped. Lip-services resemble the treacherous kisses of a Judas, and the heart does not naturally aspire towards heaven at the striking of a clock or at the ringing of a church bell.

Before concluding this chapter, I should wish to exculpate myself from the supposition that I have written in an unjust spirit against the members of the Roman Catholic Church.

I know that they can boast of many devout disciples-of many enterprising missionaries-of many conscientious priests. I know that they are not now more foolish and bigoted than the members of the Protestant churches, as in former times the murderers of St. Bartholomew were no worse than the cruel Calvin, nor Bloody Mary than James the First. In those days a remnant of the horrible custom of human sacrifice was preserved by all alike. They martyred those of the same religion as themselves but not of the same sect, burning them, drowning them, tearing them limb from limb like the Pagans of old, as offerings to a kind and gracious God.

It is true that the Roman Catholics were the most ruthless in barbarity and the most ingenious in torture, but it was because they possessed the most power.

I know that Roman Catholic priests do not really worship those images of the saints to which they bend their knees. But though they are not idolaters themselves, it cannot be denied that they have taught their disciples to be idolaters.

I do not suppose that men of genius or even of education ever yet were, or ever could be image worshippers.

Listen to these words of the Emperor Julian, written in an age that is supposed to have been enslaved in idolatry :

"The statues of the gods, the altars that are raised to them, and the holy fires that are burnt in their honor have been instituted by our fathers as signs and emblems of the presence of the Gods, not that we should regard them as Gods, but that we should honor the Gods in them."

I might quote fifty other passages to prove that in all idolatrous nations the priests and philosophers, though affecting to be image-worshippers, have in their hearts scorned those pieces of wood and stone to which their dupes so devoutly kneeled.

In papistry, there are as many dupes and as much idolatry as ever existed in Egypt, in Italy, or in Greece.

Witness a Roman Catholic service, and you will see heads bowed before stone-images and prayers, murmured not in mere reverence but in actual adoration.

Study the doctrine of Transubstantiation. Is not that an instance of the emblem being forgotten in the God?

These abuses are melancholy to contemplate, for these alone it is which hold two Christian churches asunder. These with the Platonic dogma of purgatory upon which no man can decide, and upon which therefore it is foolish for man to contend.

English priests beware how you nurse idolatry; for those who do so, enchain not only others but themselves.

In the reign of Peter the Great, a law was passed by a synod of the Greek Church in Russia enacting that the use of pictures in churches was contrary to the principles in Christianity, and that all such should be removed from places of worship.

The Emperor sanctioned this law, but feared to put it into execution lest it should cause a general insurrection.

Superstition, born of Satan, fed and fostered by priests, like a hideous cuttle-fish has cast its white and slimy arms around the Harlot of Babylon, and. has bedaubed her with its black blood. Now she loves this blood and knows not that it defiles her; she loves these embraces and knows not that they enslave her. But some day aspiring to be free, she will attempt to rise from her grave of sand and foul weeds; and then seizing her in its horrible arms, that demon who so long has triumphed over her will sink with her forever beneath the waves.

II. In The Emblems Of Freemasonry

THERE is a divine and hidden science whose origin can only be discovered by the wavering lights of tradition, whose doctrines and purposes are enveloped in sacred mysteries.

It is now degenerated into a society of gluttons and wine-bibbers, who yawn while their Masters expound to them those emblems which have excited the wonder of the greatest philosophers of the past, and who deem that the richest gem of freemasonry, is the banquet which closes the labor of the Lodge.

And yet this order can boast of some learned and intellectual men, who endeavor to find the key to the hidden language of symbols, and who appreciate at its true value the high honors which the initiated are permitted to enjoy.

In spite of the abuses with which it has been degraded, in spite of the sneers with which the ignorant revile it, this institution still possesses much that is holy and sublime.

No feelings can be compared with those which a young man feels when, attired in strange array, blind-folded, the dagger pointed to his naked left breast, he is led through the mystic labyrinth, whose intricate ways are emblematical of the toilsome wanderings of his soul.

The strains of solemn music-the mysterious words-the low knock at the portal--the sudden blaze of light--and the strange sight which await his eyes feeble and fluttering from their long imprisonment.

What awe he feels, as kneeling on his right knee, his left hand placed upon the Book of the Law, encircled by the Masters in their robes of office, and the two white wands held over his head in the form of a cross, he takes the oath of secrecy and faith, "to hail, conceal and never reveal the hidden mysteries of the fellowship" to which he is now admitted.

And what pride flushes in his heart when the secret signs and key-words are imparted to him, and when the white apron, a badge more glorious than the fabled Golden Fleece, or the Roman Eagle is tied round his waist.

Surrounded by all those signs and symbols by which the ancient nations were wont to express the power and presence of God, the Mason's Lodge resembles a scene of enchantment in the midst of this wilderness which we call the world. And those who are thus assembled together in mystic robes, seem spirits of another age, who have returned to hold their hidden meetings once more in the catacombs of the Egyptian pyramids, or in the cavern-temple sacred to Mithra, or in the subterranean labyrinths of the holy Druids.

The brethren seated in a circle, one of the Masters arises and advances to the midst. He relates to them a tradition of the origin of their craft.

"After the sun had descended down the seventh age from Adam before the flood of Noah, there was born unto Methusael, the son of Mehujael, a man called Lamach who took unto himself two wives. the name of the one was Adah, of the other Zillah. Now Adah his first wife, bare two sons--the one named Jabel and the other Jubal. Jabal was the inventor of geometry and the first who built houses of stone and timber, and Jubal was the inventor of music and harmony. Zillah, his second wife, bare Tubal Cain, the instructor of every artificer in brass and iron, and a daughter called Naamah who was the founder of the weaver's craft.

"All these had knowledge from above, that the Almighty would take vengeance for sin either by fire or by water, so great was the wickedness of the world. So they reasoned among themselves how they might preserve the knowledge of the sciences which they had found, and Jabal said that there were two different kinds of stone of such virtue that one would not burn and the other would not sink--the one called *marble* and the other *latres*. They then agreed to write all the science that they had found upon these stones.

"After the destruction of the world, these two pillars were discovered by Hermes, the son of Shem. Then the craft of masonry began to flourish, and Nimrod was one of the earliest patrons of the art. Abraham, the son of Jerah, was skilled in the seven sciences and taught the Egyptians the science of grammar. Euclid was his pupil, and instructed them in the art of making mighty walls and ditches to preserve their houses from the inundations of the Nile, and by geometry measured out the land, and divided it into partitions so that each man might ascertain his own property. And he it was who gave masonry the name of geometry.

"In his days, it came to pass that the sovereign and lords of the realm had gotten many sons unlawfully by other men's wives, insomuch that the land was grievously burdened with them. A council was called but no reasonable remedy was proposed. The king then ordered a proclamation to be made throughout his realms, that high rewards would be given to any man who would devise a proper method for maintaining the children. Euclid dispelled the difficulty. He thus addressed the king: 'My noble sovereign, if I may have order and government of these lord's sons, I will teach them the seven liberal sciences, whereby they may live honestly like gentlemen, provided that you will grant me power over them by virtue of your royal commission.'

"This request was immediately complied with, and Euclid established a Lodge of Masons."

This tale is curious as being the earliest account of an educational institution.

There are various traditions of minor interest relating to the patriarchal ages and to the wanderings of the Israelites in the wilderness.

The Freemasons claim descent from that body of builders who, some from Phœnicia, and some from India, came to Jerusalem to erect the temple of Solomon. They also assert that these masons were governed by the same laws, and united by the same ties as those of the modern order, and in the initiation of a Master-mason the following tradition is related respecting the death of the Phœnician Hiram Abiff, the master architect who directed the building of the temple:

"There were fifteen fellow-craftsmen, who finding that the temple was almost finished, and that they had not received the master's word because their time was not come, agreed to extort it from their master, the skilful Hiram Abiff, on the first opportunity, that they might pass for masters in other countries and have masters' wages. Twelve recanted and the other three determined to carry out the plot. Their names were Jubela, Jubelo, and Jubelum. These three crafts knowing that it was always the master's custom at twelve at noon, when the men were called off to refreshment, to go into the *sanctum sanctorum* to pray to the true and living God--they placed themselves at the three entrances to the temple, viz., at the west, south and east doors. There was no entrance in the north, because thence the sun darts no rays. Thus they waited while he made his prayer to the Lord, to have the word or grip as he came out, or his life. So Hiram came to the east door, and Jubela demanded the master's word. Hiram told him he did not receive it in such a manner but he must wait, and time and a little patience would bring him to it, for it was not in his power to deliver it except the three Grand Masters were together, viz: Solomon, King of Israel, Hiram, King of Tyre, and Hiram Abiff.

"Jubela struck him across the throat with a 24-inch gauge. He fled thence to the south door where he was accosted in the same manner by Jubelo to whom he gave a similar answer, and who gave him a blow with a square upon his left breast. Hiram reeled but recovered himself, and flew to the west door where Jubelum gave him a heavy blow upon the head with a common gavel or setting maul which proved his death.

"After this they carried him out of the west door and hid him in a heap of rubbish till it was twelve at night, when they found means to bury him in a handsome grave, six feet east and west, and six feet in height.

"When Hiram was missed, King Solomon made great inquiry after him, and not hearing anything of him supposed him to be dead. The twelve crafts that had recanted hearing the said report, and their consciences pricking them, went and informed King Solomon with white aprons and gloves as tokens of their innocence. King Solomon forthwith sent them in search of the three murderers who had absconded, and they agreed to make the pursuit in four parties, three going north, three south, three east, and three west.

"As one of these parties traveled down to the sea of Joppa, one of them sitting himself down to rest by the side of a rock, heard the following lamentations proceed from a cleft within:--

"'O that I had my throat cut across, and my tongue torn out by the root, and buried in the sands of the sea at low water a cable length from the shore, where the tide doth regularly ebb and flow twice in the course of the twenty-four hours, than that I had been concerned in the death of our master Hiram.'

And then another voice:

"'Oh! that I had my heart torn from under my naked left breast, and given to the vultures of the air as a prey, rather than I had been concerned in the death of so good a master.'

"'But oh!' cried Jubelum. I struck him harder than you both, for I killed him. Oh! that I had had my body severed in two, one part carried to the south, and the other to the north, my bowels burnt to ashes and scattered before the four winds of the earth, rather than I had been concerned in the death of our master Hiram.'

"The brother that heard these sorrowful lamentations hailed the other two, and they went into the cleft of the rock and took them and bound them, and brought them before King Solomon, when they owned what had passed, and what they had done, and did not desire to live, therefore King Solomon ordered their own sentences to be executed upon them, saying, 'They have signed their own deaths, and let it be upon them as they have said.'

"'Jubela was taken out, and his throat cut across, and his tongue torn out by the root, and buried in the sands of the sea at low water, a cable length from the shore, where the tide did regularly ebb and flow twice in the course of the twenty-four hours.

"Jubelo's heart was torn from under his naked left breast, and was given to the vultures of the air as a prey.

"Jubelum's body was severed in two, one part was carried to the north, the other to the south, his bowels were burnt to ashes and scattered to the four winds of the earth."

The real secret of Freemasonry, viz., its origin and purport, as yet remain an enigma and will probably ever remain so.

There are some authors who have fixed the source of this sacred and mysterious fountain within the oaken groves of the extinguished order of the Druids.

Who assert that when Druidism was proscribed, its priests adopted various disguises and carried their learning into various professions. Some became school-masters and taught science to the youth of Britain, as they had once done in the forest seminaries of Mona. Some fortune-tellers, the parents of the tribes of gypsies who still retain a kind of brotherhood united by oaths and secret signs, and who at one time possessed so strange an ascendancy over the minds of the vulgar.

And others who formed themselves into a community resembling, if not in their power, at least in their unanimity, that ancient body of priests who had once been the sovereigns of Britain.

At first I was inclined to believe that such was really the case, and that Freemasonry was no more than a reproduction of Druidism in the Middle Ages. On searching for materials, I met with evidence *in limine* which tended to confirm me in this conviction. There was a manuscript discovered in the Bodleian Library at Oxford in 1696, which was supposed to have been written about the year 1436. It purports to be an examination of one of the brotherhood by King Henry VI, and is allowed by all masonic writers to be genuine.

Its title is as follows: "*Certain questions with answers to the same concerning the mystery of masonry written by King, Henry the Sixth and faithfully copied by me John Leylande, antiquarian, by command of his highness.*"

I give an extract modernizing the English of the original, which, though quaint, would be unintelligible to all but antiquaries:--

"What mote it be? It is the knowledge of nature, and the power of its various operations; particularly the skill of reckoning, of weights and measures, of constructing buildings and dwellings of all kinds, and the true manner of forming all things for the use of man.

"Where did it begin ?-it began with the first men of the East, who were before the first men of the West, and coming with it, it hath brought all comforts to the wild and comfortless.

"Who brought it to the West?--the Phoenicians who, being great merchants, came first from the East into Phoenicia, for the convenience of commerce, both East and West by the Red and Mediterranean Seas.

"How came it into England?--Pythagoras, a Grecian, traveled to acquire knowledge in Egypt and in Syria, and in every other land where the Phoenicians had planted masonry; and gaining admittance into all lodges of masons, he learned much, and returned and dwelt in Grecia Magna, growing and becoming mighty wise and greatly renowned. Here he formed a great lodge at Crotona, and made many masons, some of whom traveled into France, and there made many more, from whence, in process of time, the art passed into England."

This, I need not remind the reader, is a story very similar to those current respecting the first planting of Druidism in Britain.

I also discovered as I thought, a key to the tradition of Hiram Abiff, which I have just related, viz., that it was simply the story of Osiris (killed by Typhon the Evil Spirit, buried in a coffin and found by Isis) so corrupted by modern Masons.

In the continuation of the story of Hiram, it is stated that the twelve crafts on discovering his body were unable to raise it, and that King Solomon ordered a lodge of master-masons to be summoned and said, "*I will go myself in person and try to raise the body by the master's grip or the lion's paw.*

By means of this grip the Grand-Master Hiram was raised.

Now in a figure painted on a mummy at the Austin Fryar's of *La Place des Victores*, representing the death and resurrection of Osiris, is seen an exact model of the position of the master-mason as he raises Hiram.

Jubela, Jubelo, Jubelum are merely variations from the Latin word *jubeo*, I command. The pretended assassins are represented as demanding the master's grip and word from Hiram in an imperious manner.

A more satisfactory proof of the truth of this statement is contained in an astronomical notion of the Hindoos, whose *Chrisna* is the same as the Osiris of the Egyptians.

The *Decans*, or *Elohim*, are the gods of whom it is said the Almighty created the Universe. They arranged the order of the zodiac. The *Elohim* of the summer were gods of a benevolent disposition: they made the days long, and loaded the sun's head with topaz. While *the three wretches* that presided in the winter at the extreme end of the year, hid in the realms below, were, with the constellation to which they belonged, cut off from the rest of the zodiac; and *as they were missing*, were consequently accused of bringing Chrisna into those troubles which at last ended in his death.

Even allowing these premises to be true, it does not necessarily follow that the traditionary account of the building of Solomon's Temple by masons was also allegorical.

And indeed there is so much that is purely Hebrew in ceremonial masonry, that one is almost forced to believe that the Freemasons of the present day are really descended from a body of architects, who, like the Dionysiacks of Asia Minor, were united into a fraternal association and who erected the temple of Solomon.

In these ceremonies, however, and in their emblems there is much also that is Druidic, and if Freemasonry did not emanate from Druidism, there can be no doubt that it sprang from the same origin.

I will trace out the affinity between the Masonic Order of the Present, and the Druid Order of the Past. It shall be for the reader to decide whether these Masonic usages are vestiges of Druidism, or mere points of family resemblance.

The initiations of Masons are so similar to those of the Druids, that any Mason reading my article upon the subject must have been struck by the resemblance.

The ovade wore a gold chain round his neck. And the apprentice when initiated has a silk cord, in masonic parlance a *cable-tow*, suspended from his throat. Like the ovade, the apprentice is blindfolded, and as the former was led through the mazes of a labyrinth, the latter is led backwards and forwards, and in various directions.

Thunder and lightning were counterfeited in the initiation of a Druid, and in that of the Royal Arch the Companions fire pistols, clash swords, overturn chairs, and roll cannon balls across the floor.

The tiler stands at the door with a drawn sword.

And tests of fortitude though less severe than in former times are not unknown among Masons. The following arduous trial was used in the Female Lodges of Paris:--

"A candidate for admission was usually very much excited. During a part of the ceremony she was conducted to an eminence, and told to look down at what awaited her if she faltered in her duty. Beneath her appeared a frightful abyss in which a double row of iron spikes were visible. No doubt her mind was in a chaos of fanaticism, for instead of shrinking at the sight, she exclaimed "I can encounter all," and sprang forward. At that moment a secret spring was touched, and the candidate fell not on the spikes, but on a green bed in imitation of a verdant plain. She fainted but was soon recovered by her friends, when the scene having changed she was reanimated and soothed by the sweet strains of choral music."

I have already shown, I trust conclusively, that the Druidic mysteries were founded on those of the Egyptians, and were analogous to those of Tyre, Persia and Hindostan; and that their moral doctrines and pristine simplicity of worship were those of the Hebrew Patriarchs.

It will be easy to show that those of Freemasonry, if not a mere perpetuation of the Druidic were derived from the same fountains, and that the secrets of this science and philosophy are hidden from us by the veil of Isis.

To the Egyptian candidate on his- initiation, the Hierophant displayed the holy volume of hieroglyphics which he then restored to its repository.

So when the eyes of the apprentice are first released from darkness, he beholds the volume of the sacred law.

During the Persian initiations, the doctrine was enforced ex cathedra, from the desk or pulpit. So the Grand Master sits on a throne before which the candidate kneels, pointing a dagger to his naked left breast and two white wands being crossed above his head.

On the seal of the ancient Abbey of Arbroath in Scotland, is a representation which bears a curious resemblance to the engraving on a seal used by the priests of Isis, and which

Plutarch describes in his Essay on Isis and Osiris--*a man kneeling, his hands bound, and a knife at his throat.*

In all the ancient mysteries before an aspirant could claim participation in the higher secrets of the institution, he was placed within the *pastos* or *bed*, or *coffin*, and was subjected to a confinement in darkness for a certain time.

This I have described to be practiced by the Druids. In some of their labyrinths, discovered in France, the remains of cells have been found, and there was a dark cell of probation recently standing near Maidstone, Kitt's Cotti House--from *Ked* (or Ceridwen) the British Isis, and *cotti* an ark, or chest.

So in the initiation of a Master Mason, the candidate is in some lodges buried in a coffin to represent the death of the murdered Hiram Abiff.

The grand festival of Masonry is on Midsummer Day, which was also the grand festival of the Druids.

The processional movements of the Masons as of the Druids were mostly circular.

I have already instanced the symbol by which the Jews expressed the word 'Jehovah.' This letter ❜ jod was believed by them to denote the presence of God, especially when conveyed in a circle ◉. Masons also have a word which they are not allowed to pronounce except in the presence of a full lodge, and they pay peculiar reverence to a point within a circle.

Some of the Druidic monuments are simple circles with a stone standing in the midst, and the boss in the centre of their circular shields had probably the same signification.

The Masonic Lodge, like all Pagan temples, is built due east and west. Its form is an oblong square which the ancients believed to be the shape of the world. In the west are two pillars surmounted by globes. The one on the left is called Boaz, and is supposed to represent Osiris or the sun, the other Jachin, the emblem of Isis or the moon. The floor is mosaic, and the walls are adorned with the various symbols of the craft.

The cross is one of the chief emblems in Masonry as it was in Druidism, and in all the Pagan religions. The Taw ⱶ is a badge in Royal Arch Masonry, and almost all the other varieties of the symbol are used in Masonry.

The key and the cross-keys are also mosaic symbols. They are supposed to be astronomical signs of Anubis, or the Dog-Star.

An ear-of-corn is a prominent emblem in Masonry, proving that the order did not confine their intellects and their labors to the building of houses, but devoted themselves also to agriculture.

A sprig of acacia is one of the emblems revered by the Masons, and answers to the Egyptian lotus, to the myrtle of Eleusis, to the golden branch of Virgil and to the Druidic mistletoe. It is curious that *Houzza* which Mahomet esteemed an idol--Houzza so honored in the Arabian works of Ghatfân Koreisch, Kenanah and Salem should be simply the acacia. Thence was derived the word *huzza!* in our language, which was probably at first a religious exclamation like the *Evohe!* of the Bacchantes.

The doctrines of Masonry are the most beautiful that it is possible to conceive. They breathe the simplicity of the earliest ages animated by the love of a martyred God.

76

That word which the Puritans translated "charity," but which is really "love"--love is the key-stone of the Royal Arch upon which is supported the entire system of this mystic science.

In the lectures of the French Lodges the whole duty of a Mason is summed up in this one brief sentence: "*Aimez-vous les uns les autres, instruisez-vous, secourez-vous, voilà tout noire livre, toute noire loi, toule noire science.*"

"Love one another, teach one another, help one another. That is all our doctrine, all our science, all our law."

Ah! rail against us bigoted and ignorant men, slander us curious and jealous women if you will. Those who obey the precepts of their masters, and those who listen to the truths which they inculcate can readily forgive you. It is impossible to be a good Mason without being a good man.

We have no narrow-minded prejudices; we do not debar from our society this sect or that sect; it is sufficient for us that a man worships God, no matter under what name or in what manner, and we admit him. Christians, Jews, Mahometans, Buddhists are enrolled among us, and it is in the Mason's Lodge alone that they can kneel down together without feeling hatred, without professing contempt against their brother worshippers.

III. In Rustic Folk-Lore

IT is strange with what pertinacity the ignorant retain those customs which their fathers observed, and which they hold sacred without understanding either their origin or their purpose.

It is an attribute of human nature to hallow all that belongs to the past. It is impossible to look without admiration upon a venerable building which has lived through centuries, an immortal work of art; it is natural that we should also revere those customs which have descended to us by no written laws, by no kingly proclamations, but simply from lip to ear, from father to son.

Before I enter the homes of our peasants however, come with me to the mountains of Wales where we shall find the true descendants, not only of the ancient Britons but also of the Holy Druids themselves.

I mean the Bards, or harpers, who still continue to strike melodious notes in this land of music and metheglin, and who still convey to their hearers the precepts of their great ancestors.

The Bards were always held in high reverence in Wales, and that is why they have lived so long. When the priests had been swept away by the sword of the new religion, this glorious association of musicians remained, and consented to sing praises to Jesus Christ the Redeemer, instead of to HU the pervading spirit.

Indeed it was said of Barach, who was chief Bard to Conchobhar Nessan, King of Ulster, that he described the passion of Jesus in such moving words that the king, transported with rage, drew his sword and fell to hacking and hewing the trees of the wood in which he was standing, mistaking them for Jews, and even died of the frenzy.

By studying the old Welsh laws of Howel the good king (A. D.,940), one finds some curious matter respecting the position which the Bards held at that time in the Court and country.

Y Bardd Teulu, or Court Bard (an appointment from which that of our poet-laureate probably originated) on receiving his commission, was presented by the king with a silver harp, by the queen with a gold ring. He held the eighth place at Court. He possessed his land free. At the three great festivals of the year, Christmas, Easter, and Whitsuntide, he sat at the prince's table. On these occasions, he was entitled to have the *disdain's* or steward-of-the-household's garment for his fee. In addition to these perquisites, the king found him in woolen robes, and the queen in linen, and he received a present from every maiden when she married, but nothing at the bridal feasts of women who had been married before.

At regal feasts the guests were placed in threes; a tune called *Gosteg yr Halen*, "the prelude of the salt," was sung as the salt-cellar was placed before the king, and as they were served with meats, &c., upon platters of clean grass and rushes, the harp played all the while.

When a song was called for after the feast, the *Oadeir-fardd*, or the bard who possessed the badge of-the-chair sang a hymn to the glory of God, and then another in honor of the king. After which, the *Teuluwr*, or Bard of the Hall sang upon some other subject.

If the queen wished for a song after she had retired to her apartment, the *Teuluwr*, might sing to her, but in a low voice, lest he disturb the other performers in the hall.

If a Bard desired a favor of the king, he was obliged to play one of his own compositions; if of a nobleman, three; and if of a villain, till he was exhausted.

His person was held so sacred that whoever slightly injured him was fined VI cows and CXX pence, and the murderer of a Bard was fined CXXVI cows. The worst murder in those days, like criminal conversations in the present age, only needed pecuniary atonement.

On a plundering expedition, the Bard received a large portion of the spoil. He preceded the warriors to battle, reciting a poem called *Unhenaeth Prydain*, "the glory of Britain."

An edict was issued by King Edward I. authorizing the massacre of the Bards, one of them having prophesied the liberation of Wales. The murder of the last Bard has been beautifully described by Gray in one of his poems.

Queen Elizabeth also issued a proclamation, but of a less sanguinary character against certain wandering minstrels, who appear to have been among the musicians of those days what quacks are among our modern M.D.'s. It also commissioned certain gentlemen to inquire into the various capabilities of the Welsh Bards, and to license those who were most fit to represent the musical talent of their country.

This profound question was settled at an *Eisteddfod*, or a musical meeting of the Bard who contested once a year for a silver harp. This practice which had existed from time immemorial is still continued in Wales, and the transactions of the *Aberffraw Royal Eisteddfod* were published in the year 1849.

I know little of the peculiar character of Welsh music except that it is executed mostly in B flat. Part-singing may be considered as a peculiarity of the Welsh bards. Extempore performances were common to all the ancient minstrels of the world.

A kind of extempore composition is still exercised among the Welsh peasantry, and is called *Penillion* singing. The harper being seated, plays one of his native airs while the singers stand round him and alternately compose a stanza upon any subject they please.

There are many *clerwyr*, or wandering minstrels still in Wales. Like their predecessors, they are in the habit of going from house to house, and of officiating, as our gypsy fiddlers do at all rustic festivals and weddings.

They have a curious tradition, that Madoc, a brother of one of the Kings of Wales, sailed from that country in the year 1171 A. D. and was the first European settler in Mexico. Sir Thomas Herbert who wrote a scarce book of travels in 1665, mentions it as a fact, and in Hackett's Collection of Epitaphs (1757) is this one:--

FOUND AT MEXICO.

"Madoc wyf mwydic ei wedd
lawn genan Owain Gwynedd
Ni fynnwn dir fy awydd oedd
Na da mawr ond y Moroedd."

Madoc I am-mild in countenance
Of the right line of Owen Gwynedd
I wished not for land; my bent was
For no great riches, but for the seas.

We have it on the authority of a Captain Davies, and Lieutenant Roberts of Hawcorden in Flintshire, and from a MS. entry in William Penn's journal, evidence collected by the famous Dr. Owen Pughe, that the tribes of the Illinois, Madocautes, the Padoucas and Mud Indians spoke the Welsh language.

Without entering into a useless dissertation upon this subject, I will note a curious custom in which the American Indians resemble the Welsh, viz., in the habit of carrying their canoes upon their backs from rapid to rapid. Giraldus Cambrensis informs us that the Welsh used to carry their triangular boats from river to river, which occasioned a famous dealer, named Bledherc, to say: "There is amongst us a people who when they go out in search of prey carry their horses on their backs to the place of plunder; in order to catch their prey, they leap upon their horses, and when it is taken, carry their horses home again upon their shoulders."

They worshipped the same symbols of God as the ancient British-the sun, the moon, fire, water, the serpent, the cross, &c., and in the course of this chapter I shall mention other customs common to both nations.

Among the peasantry of Great Britain and Ireland, there are observed not only those traditional customs which are meaningless because they are out of date, but actual idolatries.

It may surprise the reader that the worship of fire with which our preachers and tract-writers jeer the inhabitants of Persia, is not yet extinct among us.

Spenser says that the Irish never lighted a fire without uttering a prayer. In some parts of England it is considered unlucky for the fire to go out. They have a peculiar fuel with which they feed it during the night. The Scotch peat-fires are seldom allowed to die out.

There are three days in the year on which the worship of fire is especially observed-May-day, Midsummer Eve and Allhallow E'en.

On the first of May which is called *Beltan,* or *Beltein-Day* from the Druidic *Beltenus,* the Phœnician *Baal,* the Highland herdsmen assemble on a moor, They cut a table in the sod, of a round figure, by casting a trench in the ground of such circumference as to hold the whole company. They kindle a wood fire and dress a large caudle of eggs, butter, oatmeal and milk, taking care to be supplied with plenty of beer and whiskey as well. The rites begin with spilling some of the caudle on the ground by way of a libation; on that, every one takes a cake of oatmeal, upon which are raised nine square knobs, each dedicated to some particular being, the supposed preserver of their flocks and herbs, or to some particular animal the real destroyer of them. Each person then turns his face to the fire, breaks off a knob and flinging it over his shoulder, says: *This I give to thee, preserve thou my horses; this I give to thee, preserve thou my sheep,* and so on. After that, they use the same ceremony to the noxious animals. *This I give to thee, oh fox! spare thou my lambs! this to thee, oh hooded crow; this to thee, oh eagle!*

They then knead another cake of oatmeal which is toasted at the embers against a stone. They divide this cake into so many portions (as similar as possible to each other in size and shape) as there are persons in the company. They daub one of these portions all over with charcoal until it is quite black. They put all the bits into a bonnet and every one, blind-folded, draws. He who holds the bonnet is entitled to the last bit. Whoever draws the black morsel is the devoted person who is to be sacrificed to Baal, and is compelled to leap three times through the fire, after which they dine on the caudle.

When the feast is finished, the remains are concealed by two persons deputed for that purpose, and on the next Sunday they re-assemble and finish it.

This, you see, is a relic of the Druidic human sacrifices as well as of their fire-worship. I will give two more examples of the former.

I have noticed the custom of the Druids in great extremities of constructing a large wicker engine, of filling it with sheep, oxen and sometimes men, and setting light to it, as a mammoth sacrifice. Dr. Milner in his History of Winchester, informs us that at Dunkirk and at Douay there has existed an immemorial custom of constructing huge figures of wicker-work and canvas, and moving them about to represent a giant that was killed by their patron saint. And St. Foix, in his Essay on Paris, describes a custom which is not yet abolished in some of the small towns in France, viz., for the mayors on the Eve of St. John to put into a large basket a dozen or two cats, and to throw them into one of the festive bonfires lighted upon that occasion.

To return to May Day. In Munster and Connaught the Irish peasants drive their cattle between two fires, as if for purposes of purification. In some parts of Scotland they light a fire to feast by, and having thrown a portion of their refreshments into the flames as a propitiatory sacrifice, deck branches of mountain-ash with wreaths of flowers and heather, and walk three times round it in a procession.

Precisely the same custom is observed by the natives of America and at the same period, i.e., that of the vernal equinox.

In India there is a festival in honor of *Bhavani* (a Priapic personification of nature and fecundity), which the Hindoos commemorate by erecting a pole in the fields, and by adorning it with pendants and flowers round which the young people dance precisely the same as in England.

The Jews also keep a solar festival at the vernal equinox, on which occasion the Paschal lamb is sacrificed.

The Floridians and Mexicans erect a tree in the centre of their sacred enclosures around which they dance.

On May Eve the Cornish erect stumps of trees before their doors. On the first of the month the famous May-pole is raised, adorned with flowers and encircled by the pretty country lasses who little know of what this pole, or φαλλος is an emblem.

On Midsummer Eve an involuntary tribute is paid by the peasants of Great Britain and Ireland to the shades of their ancient priests, and to the Gods whom they worshipped, by lighting bonfires. The word bonfire, I may observe, is by some called *bonefire* because they believe (without any particular reason), that their fuel consisted of bones; by others *boon-fire*, because the wood was obtained by begging. *Utrum horum marvis accipe.*

The cooks of Newcastle lighted fires on Midsummer Day in the streets of that town; the custom is general almost all over Ireland, and as late as the year 1786, the custom of lighting fires was continued in the Druidic Temple at Bramham, near Harrowgate in Yorkshire, on the eve of the summer solstice.

In the Cornish tongue, Midsummer is called *Goluan*, which means light and rejoicing. At that season, the natives make a procession through the towns or villages with lighted torches.

The Irish dance round these fires, and sometimes fathers, taking their children in their arms, will run through the flames.

In Hindostan it is the mother who performs this office.

On all sacred days among the Druids, they resorted to their different kinds of divination, and I should tire the reader were I to enumerate half the charms and incantations which are made use of in the country on Midsummer Eve.

I have always remarked that those divinations which were probably used by priests to foretell the fate of a kingdom, or to decide upon the life or death of a human being, have now become mere methods of love prophecies with village sweethearts.

One will sow hemp-seed on Midsummer Eve, saying, *Hemp-seed I sow, hemp-seed I hoe, and he that is my true love come after me and mow.* She will then turn round, and expects to see the young man who will marry her.

Another will pick a kind of root which grows under mug-wort, and which, if pulled exactly at midnight on the Eve of St. John the Baptist and placed under her pillow, will give her a dream of her future husband.

Another will place over her head the orphine-plant, commonly called *Midsummer-men*: the bending of the leaves to the right or to the left will tell her whether her husband was true or false.

Bourne cites from the Trullan Council a species of divination, so singular, that it is impossible to read it without being reminded of the Pytheness on her tripod, or the Druidess on her seat of stone.

"On the 23rd of June, which is the Eve of St. John the Baptist, men and women were accustomed to gather together in the evening at the sea-side or in certain houses, and there adorn a girl who was her father's first-begotten child after the manner of a bride. Then they feasted and leaped after the manner of Bacchanals, and danced and shouted as they were wont to do on their holy-days; after this, they poured into a narrow-necked vessel some of the sea-water, and also put into it certain things belonging to each of them. Then as if the devil gifted the girl with the faculty of telling future things, they would enquire with a loud voice about the good or evil fortune that should attend them; upon this the girl took out of the vessel the first thing that came to hand and showed it, and gave it to the owner, who, upon receiving it, was so foolish as to imagine himself wiser, as to the good or evil fortune that should attend him."

The Druidic vervain was held in estimation on this day as we read in *Ye Popish Kingdome.*

Then doth ye joyfal feast of John ye Baptist take his turne,
When bonfiers great with lofty flame in every town doe burne,
And young men round about with maides doe dance in every streete,
With garlands wrought of mother-wort, or else with verwain sweete.

The following extract from the Calendar of the Romish Church, shows us what doings there used to be at Rome on the Eve and Day of St. John the Baptist--the Roman Pales-- the Druidic Belenus.

JUNE.
23. The Virgil of the Nativity of John the Baptist.
Spices are given at Vespers.
Fires are lighted up.
A girl with a little drum that proclaims the garland.
Boys are dressed in girl's clothes:
Carols to the liberal: imprecations against the avaricious.
Waters are swum in during the night, and are brought in vessels that hang for purposes of divination.
Fern in great estimation with the vulgar on account of its seed.
Herbs of different kinds are sought with many ceremonies.
Girl's Thistle is gathered, and a hundred crosses by the same.
24. The Nativity of John the Baptist.
Dew and new leaves in estimation.
The vulgar solstice.

It was on Hallow-E'en that the Druids used to compel their subjects to extinguish their fires, which, when the annual diies were paid, were relighted from that holy fire which burnt in the clachan of the Druids, and which never died.

Even now all fires are extinguished on HallowE'en, and a fire being made by rubbing two sticks together they are relighted from that, and from that alone.

The same custom is observed among the Cherokee Indians.

At the village of Findern in Derbyshire, the boys and girls go every year on the 2nd of November and light a number of small fires among the furze growing there, which they call Tindles. They can give no reason for so doing.

Throughout the United Kingdom there are similar divining customs observed to those which I have just described as exercised on Midsummer Eve.

There are miscellaneous vestiges of fire-worship besides those already noticed.

In Oxfordshire revels, young women will sometimes tuck their skirts (twisting them in an ingenious manner round the ankles, and holding the ends in front of them) into a very good resemblance of men's trousers, and dance round a candle placed upon the floor, concluding by leaping over it three times. The name of this dance, too coarse to be written here, as the dance is to be described, betrays its phallic origin.

Then there is the "*Dance round our coal fire*," an ancient practice of dancing round the fires in the Inns of Court, which was observed in 1733, at an entertainment at the Inner Temple Hall on Lord Chancellor Talbot's taking leave of the house, when "the Master of the Revels took the Chancellor by the hand, and he Mr. Page, who with the Judges, Sergeants and Benchers danced round the Coal Fire, according to the old ceremony three times; and all the time the ancient song with music was sung by a man in a bar gown."

Last and most singular of all the *Tinegin*, or need-fire of the Highlanders.

To defeat sorceries, certain persons appointed to do so are sent to raise the need-fire. By any small river or lake, or upon any island a circular booth of turf or stone is erected, on which a rafter of birch-tree is placed and the roof covered over. In the centre is set a perpendicular post, fixed by a wooden pin to the couple, the lower end being placed in an oblong groove on the floor, and another pole placed horizontally between the upright post and the leg of the couple into both of which the ends being tapered are inserted. This horizontal timber is called the auger, being provided with four short spokes by which it can be turned. As many men as can be collected are then set to work. Having divested themselves of all kinds of metals, they turn the pole two at a time by means of the levers, while others keep driving wedges under the upright post so as to press it against the auger, which by the friction soon becomes ignited. From this the need-fire is instantly procured, and all other fires being quenched, those that are rekindled both in dwelling houses and offices are accounted sacred, and the diseased and bewitched cattle are successively made to smell them.

This contrivance is elaborate and its description not unnaturally awkward. It is however worthy of remark that in the initiation of Freemasons all metals are taken from them.

Water was worshipped by the Druids, and was used by them for purification. The Welsh peasantry hold sacred the rain-water which lodges in the crevices of their cromleachs or altars, and the Irish proverb "To take a dip in the Shannon," would seem to show that its waters were held in the same superstitious reverence as are those of the Ganges by the natives of Hindostan.

The Druids besprinkled themselves with dew when they went to sacrifice, and it is a belief among the English lasses that those who bathe their faces in the dew on May Day morning will have beautiful complexions.

It is a belief in Oxfordshire that to cure a man bitten by a mad dog, he should be taken to the sea and dipped therein nine times.

The regard still paid, however, to wells and fountains by the peasantry is the most extraordinary feature of water-worship. In the early ages it prevailed with such strength, that the Roman Catholics fearing to combat the custom christianized it by giving the holy wells the names of popular saints, and by enjoining pilgrimages after the Pagan fashion to their shrine.

In some parts of England it is still customary to decorate these wells with boughs of trees, garlands of tulips, and other flowers placed in various fancied devices.

At one time, indeed it was the custom on Holy Thursday, after the service for the day at the church, for the clergyman and singers to pray and sing psalms at these wells.

Pilgrimages are still made by invalids among the poor Irish to wells, whose waters are supposed to possess medicinal properties under the influence of some beneficent saint.

The well of Strathfillan in Scotland is also resorted to at certain periods of the year. The water of the well of Trinity Gask in Perthshire is supposed to cure any one seized with the plague. In many parts of Wales the water used for the baptismal font is fetched from these holy wells.

Not only a reverence, but actual sacrifices are offered to some of these wells and to the saints which preside over them, or to the spirits which are supposed to inhabit them.

In a quillet, called *Gwern Degla*, near the village of Llandegla in Wales there is a small spring. The water is under the tutelage of St. Tecla and is esteemed a sovereign remedy for the falling sickness. The patient washes his limbs in the well, makes an offering into it of fourpence, walks round it three times, and thrice repeats the Lord's prayer. If a man, he sacrifices a cock; if a woman a hen. The fowl is carried in a basket first round the well, after that into the churchyard and round the church. The votary then enters the church, gets under the communion table, lies down with the Bible under his head, is covered with a cloth and rests there till break of day. When he departs, he offers sixpence and leaves the fowl in the church. If the bird dies, the cure is supposed to have been affected and the disease transferred to the devoted victim.

The custom of sticking bits of rag on thorns near these wells is inexplicable, as it is universal. Between the walls of Alten and Newton, near the foot of Rosberrye Toppinge, there is a well dedicated to St. Oswald. The neighbors have a belief that a shirt or shift taken off a sick person and thrown into the well will prognosticate his fate. If it floats the person will recover, if it sinks he will die. And to reward the saint for his intelligence, they tear a rag off the shirt and leave it hanging -on the briars thereabouts, "where" says Grose, citing a MS. in the Cotton Library, marked Julius F. vi. "*I have seen such numbers as might have made a fayre rheme in a pajermyll.*"

That the Highlanders still believe in spirits which inhabit their lakes is easily proved. In Strathspey there is a lake called *Loch nan Spiordan*, the Lake of Spirits. When its waters are agitated by the wind and its spray mounts whirling in the air, they believe that it is the anger of this spirit whom they name *Martach Shine*, or the Rider of the Storm.

The Well of St. Keyne in the parish of St. Keyne, in Cornwall, is supposed to possess a curious property which is humorously explained in the following verses

THE WELL OF ST. KEYNE.

A well there is in the west country,
And a clearer one never was seen
There is not a wife in the west country
But has heard of the Well of St. Keyne.

An oak and an elm tree stand beside,
And behind doth an ash tree grow,
And a willow from the bank above
Droops to the water below.

A traveler came to the Well of St. Keyne,
Pleasant it was to his eye;
For from cock-crow he had been traveling,
and there was not a cloud in the sky.

He drank of the water so cool and clear,
For thirsty and hot was he;
And he sat him down upon the bank,
Under the willow tree.

There came a man from a neighboring town,
At the well to fill his pail;
On the well-side he rested it,
And bade the stranger hail.

Now, art thou a bachelor, stranger? quoth he,
For an if thou hast a wife,
The happiest draught thou hast drank this day
That ever thou didst in thy life.

Or has your good woman, if one you have,
    In Cornwall ever been?
For an if she have, I'll venture my life,
She has drunk of the Well of St. Keyne.

I have left a good woman who never was here,
The stranger he made reply;
But that my draught should be better for that,
I pray thee tell me why.

St. Keyne, quoth the countryman, many a time,
Drank of this chrystal well;
And before the angel summoned her,
She laid on the water a spell.

If the husband, (of this gifted well),
Shall drink before his wife,
A happy man thenceforth is he,
For he shall be master for life.

But if the wife should drink of it first,
God help the husband then!
The stranger stooped to the well of St. Keyne,
And drank of its waters again.

You drank of the well I warrant betimes?
He to the countryman said,
But the countryman smiled as the stranger spoke,
And sheepishly shook his head.

I hastened as soon as the wedding was done.
And left my wife in the porch,

But i'faith I found her wiser than me,
For she took a bottle to church.

I must not omit to mention a method of divination by water, which is practiced at Madern Well in the parish of Madern, and at the well of St. Ennys, in the parish of Sancred, Cornwall. At a certain period of the year, moon or day, come the uneasy, impatient and superstitious, and by dropping pins or pebbles into the water, and by shaking the ground round the spring so as to raise bubbles from the bottom, endeavor to predict the future. This practice is not indigenous to Britain. The Castalian fountain in Greece was supposed to be of a prophetic nature. By dipping a mirror into a well the Patræans received, as they supposed, omens of ensuing sickness or health from the figures portrayed upon its surface. In Laconia, they cast into a lake, sacred to Juno, three stones, and drew prognostications from the several turns which they made in sinking.

I will translate at length a pretty French story which I have met with, and which will adorn as well as illustrate the present subject:--

THE LEGEND OF THE PIN.

In the West of France the pin is endowed with a fabulous power, which is not without a certain interest. One of its supposed attributes is the power of attracting lovers to her who possess it, after it has been used in the toilet of a bride. Consequently it is a curious sight in La Vendeé or Les Deux-Sèvres, to see all the peasant girls anxiously placing a pin in the bride's dress: the number being often so considerable that she is forced to have a pin - cushion attached to her waist-band to receive all the prickly charms. At night, on the threshold of the bridal chamber, she is surrounded by her companions, each one easily seizing upon the charmed pin, which is kept as a sacred relic.

In Brittany the pin is regarded as the guardian of chastity, a mute witness which will one day stand forth to applaud or condemn in the following manner:--

Some days before the wedding, the betrothed leads his future bride to the edge of some mysterious current of water, and taking one of her pins drops it into the water. If it swims, the girl's innocence is incontestable--if on the contrary it sinks to the bottom, it is considered the judgment of heaven; it is an accusation which no evidence can overcome. But as the peasant girls in Brittany never use any pins heavier than the long blackthorn, which they find in the hedges, the severity of the tribunal is not very formidable.

On the 7th of December, a young peasant mounted on a strong cob, full of hope and gaiety, was seen urging his way towards Morlaix with a handsome girl of twenty on a pillion behind him, her arm tenderly clasping his waist. It was easy to see in their happy faces that they were two lovers, and from the direction which they took, that they were going on a pilgrimage to try the charm of the pin at the fountain of St. Douet. Jean's father was one of the richest land-holders in the neighborhood, but above all the young ladies round him, he had chosen Margaret, whose sole wealth consisted in her beauty and virtue.

Through all the glades of the wood with wild thyme and violets beneath their horses feet, they journeyed on till they came to a wild and deserted plain, whence they plunged once more into the dark forests of Finisterre filled with Druidical memories. It might have been those sombre shades which saddened them for a moment, but it was only for a moment. jean feared not the trial, for he loved Margaret, and believed her to be an angel. And Margaret feared it not, for she knew that she was innocent.

Now they were close to the sacred fountain, which burst through the crevices of a rock overgrown with moss into a natural bason, and thence like a thread of silver through the forest.

They dismounted, and Margaret, kneeling down, prayed fervently for some moments. Then rising, she gave her left hand to her lover, and full of confidence, advanced toward the well. Alas! she had too much faith in the virtue of the legend. Instead of a thorn pin, she took from a neckerchief one with a silver head which he had given her. He pressed her fingers affectionately as he took it from her hand and dropped it into the well. It disappeared instantaneously. Margaret sank to the ground with a heart-broken groan.

He raised her and placed her on his horse, but he did not speak to her, he did not caress her. In mournful silence he walked by her side. Her arm could no longer embrace him. She was not his Margaret now. She was a guilty wretch who had dared to tempt the judgment of God.

He placed her down at her father's door, and stooping he kissed her on the forehead. It was a silent adieu he was bidding her; it was his last kiss -it was the kiss of death.

Next morning her corpse was found underneath his window. There were no marks of violence upon her body; the wound was in her heart; she had died a victim to a destestable superstition.

To the element of air we do not find our peasants pay any particular homage, unless the well-known practice of sailors of whistling for the wind in a dead calm, and of the Cornish laborers when engaged in winnowing may be regarded as such.

But the worship of the heavenly bodies has not yet died out among us' The astrologists of the middle ages were but copyists of the ancient Chaldeans, and the lower classes to this day draw omens from meteors and falling stars. General Vallancey, by the way, records a curious instance in his *Collectanea de rebus Hibernicis*, of an Irish peasant who could neither read nor write but who could calculate eclipses.

When we consider how universal and how prominent was the worship of the sun in the world, it is almost surprising that we do not find more vestiges of this idolatry. There are some few however.

It was once a custom of the vulgar to rise early on Easter Day to see the sun dance, for they fancied that the reflection of its beams played or danced upon the waters of any spring or lake they might look into.

In the British Apollo, fol. Lond. 1708, vol. i. No. 40, we read:

> Q. Old wives, Phœbus, say
> That on Easter day,
> To the music o'the spheres you do caper,
> If the fact, sir, be true,
> Pray let's the cause know,
> When you have any room in your paper.
>
> A. The old wives get merry,
> With spic'd ale or sherry,
> On Easter, which makes them romance
> And whilst in a rout,

Their brains whirl about,
They fancy we caper and dance.

The sun shining on the bride as she goes to church is a good omen. The cloudy rising of the sun is a presage of misfortune. The Highlanders, when they approach a well to drink, walk round it from east to west, sometimes thrice.

The Orkney fishermen, on going to sea, would think themselves in imminent peril, were they by accident to turn their boat in opposition to the sun's course; and I have seen many well-educated people seriously discomfited if the cards from the pack, the balls from the pool-basket, or the decanters at the dining-table had not been sent round *as the sun goes*.

All the ancient dances were in imitation of the revolutions of the heavenly bodies, and were used in religious worship. Such were the circular dances of the Druids--the slower and statelier movements of the Greek strophe--the dances of the Cabiri or Phoenician priests, the devotional dances of the Turkish dervishes, the Hindoo *Raas Jattra* or dance-of-the-circle, and the war dances of the American and other savage nations round their camp-fires, lodges, or triumphal poles.

Such also is the Round About, or Cheshire Round, which is referred to by Goldsmith in his Vicar of Wakefield, and which is not yet extinct in England.

But the best instance of sun-worship is found in the fires lighted by the common Irish on Midsummer's Eve, and which they tell you candidly are burnt *"in honor of the sun."*

The fires which the Scotch Highlanders light on May Day are to welcome back the sun after his long pilgrimage in the frosts and darkness of winter.

Crantz in his History of Greenland, informs us that the natives of that country observe a similar festival to testify their joy at the re-appearance of the sun, and the consequent renewal of the hunting season.

In matters of divination, the moon is supposed by the vulgar to possess a peculiar power. She was supposed to exercise an influence not only over the tides of the sea, and over the minds of men, but also over the future, in weather, cookery, and physic.

When the moon is encircled by a halo, or is involved in a mist, when she is called "greasy," it portends rain--when she is sharp horned, windy weather. It is also a general belief among all classes that as the weather is at the new moon, so it will continue during the whole month.

In many of the old almanacs and books of husbandry, it is directed to kill hogs when the moon is increasing, and the bacon will prove the better, in boiling; to shear sheep at the moon's increase; to fell hand-timber from the full to the change; to fell frith, coppice, and fuel at the first quarter; to geld cattle when the moon is in Aries, Sagittarius, or Capricorn.

In *The Husbandman's Practice, or Prognostication for ever*, the reader is advised "To purge with electuaries the moon in Cancer, with pills the moone in Pisces, with potions the moone in Virgo," and in another place, "To set, sow seeds, graft, and plant, the moone being in Taurus, Virgo or Capricorn, and all kinds of corne in Cancer, to graft in March, at the moone's increase, she being in Taurus or Capricorn."

Werenfels in his Dissertation on Superstition, speaking of a superstitious man, writes, "He will have his hair cut either when the moon is in Leo, that his locks may stare like the lion's shag, or in Aries that they may stare like a ram's horn. Whatever he would have to grow he sets about when she is in the increase; for whatever he would have made less he chooses her wane. When the moon is in Taurus, he can never be persuaded to take physic, lest that animal which chews its cud should make him cast it up again; and if at any time he has a mind to be admitted to the presence of a prince, he will wait till the moon is in conjunction with the sun, for 'tis then the society of an inferior with a superior is salutary and successful."

The islanders of Sky will not dig peats (which is their only fuel) in the increase of the moon, believing that they are less moist, and will burn more clearly if cut in the wane.

In the parishes of Kirkwall and St. Ola, Orkney, none marry or kill cattle in the wane.

In Angus it is believed that if a child be put from the breast during the waning of the moon, it will decay all the time that the moon continues to wane. I will mention two more instances of divination, one from Thomas Hodge's *Incarnate Divells*, viz., "That when the moone appeareth in the springtime, the one horn spotted and hidden with a blacke and great cloude from the first day of her apparition to the fourth day after, it is some signe of tempests and troubles in the aire the summer after."

When the new moon appears with the old moon in her arms, or in other words when that part of the moon which is covered by the shadow of the earth is seen through it, it is considered not only an omen of bad weather, but also of misfortune, as we learn from the following stanza in the ballad of *Sir Patrick Spence*:

> Late, late yestreen
> I saw the new moone
> Wi'the auld moone in her arme;
> And I feir, I feir, my deir master,
> That we will come to harm.

One might enumerate examples of this kind to volumes, and I fear I have already passed the limits of human endurance; I must, however, write a few words upon the subject of moon-worship.

The feminine appellation is traditionally derived from the fable of Isis, who was entitled the wife of the sun. The superstition of the man-in-the-moon, is supposed to have originated in the account given in the Book of Numbers, XV. 32 *et seq.* of a man punished with death for gathering sticks on the Sabbath Day, though why, it is difficult to explain. In Ritson's Ancient Songs we read, "The man-in-the-moon is represented leaning upon a fork, on which he carries a bush of thorn, because it was for 'pycchynde stake' on a Sunday that he is reported to have been thus confined." And in Midsummer Night's Dream, one of the actors says, "All I have to say is to tell you that the lantern is the moon, I the man-in-the-moon, this thorn bush my thorn bush, and this dog my dog." *Vide* also Tempest, act. ii. sc. 2.

The new moon still continues to be idolatrously worshipped by the vulgar of many countries.

On the night of the new moon, the Jews assemble to pray to God under the names of the Creator of the planets, and the restorer of the moon.

The Madingoe Tribe of African Indians whisper a short prayer with their hands held before their face; they then spit upon their hands and religiously anoint their faces with the same.

At the end of the Mahometan Feast of Rhamadan (which closely resembles the Romish Carnival) the priests await the reappearance of the moon, and salute her with clapping of hands, beating of drums and firing of muskets.

In the 65th Canon of the 6th council of Constantinople, A. D. 680, is the following interdiction: "Those bone-fires that are kindled by certaine people on new moones before their shops and houses, over which also they are most foolishly and ridiculously to leape by a certaine antient custom, we command them from henceforth to cease. Whoever therefore shall do any such thing, if he be a clergyman let him be deposed-if a layman let him be excommunicated."

No bonfires are now lit in honor of the new moon, but the common Irish on beholding her for the first time cross themselves, saying:

May thou leave us as safe as thou hast found us.

English peasants often salute the new moon, saying: "There is the new moon, God bless her," usually seating themselves on a stile as they do so.

They also believe that a new moon seen over the right shoulder is lucky, over the left shoulder unlucky, and straight before good luck to the end of the moon.

That if they look straight at the new moon (or a shooting star) when they first see it, and wish for something, their wish will be fulfilled before the end of the year.

The peasant girls, in some parts of England, when they see the new moon in the new year, take their stocking off from one foot and run to the next stile; when they get there, they look between the great toe and the next, and expect to find a hair which will be the color of their lover's.

In Yorkshire, it is common enough for an inquisitive maid to go out into a field till she finds a stone fast in the earth, to kneel upon this with naked knees and looking up at the new moon to say:

All hail, new moon, all hail to thee,
I prithee, good moon, reveal to me
This night, who shall my true love be,
Who he is, and what he wears,
And what he does all months and years.

She then retires backwards till she comes to a stile, and goes to bed directly without speaking a word.

The Irish believe that eclipses of the moon are effected by witchcraft, and this occasions me to narrate a curious custom of the ancient Peruvians who were the Egyptians of the New World.

When the moon became eclipsed, they imagined that she was ill and would fall down and crush the world. Accordingly as soon as the eclipse commenced, they made a noise with cornets and drums, and tying dogs to trees beat them till they howled in order to awake the fainting moon who is said to love these animals, for Diana and Nehalenna are seldom represented without a dog by their side.

Since we find in a book, called Osborne's Advice to his Son, p. 79, that "the Irish and Welch during eclipses ran about beating kettles and pans, thinking their clamor and vexations available to the assistance of the higher orbes," it is probable that they made use of the same canine resources as the natives of Peru, and that such is the origin of the Irish proverb that "*dogs will bark at the moon.*"

Having thus considered the worship of the elements and of the heavenly bodies extant among us, let us pass on to those minor idolatries which are still retained among the lower orders.

There is no religious custom of the Russians so celebrated as that of presenting each other with eggs dyed and stained, saying, "Christ is risen." To which the other replies "He is indeed," and they exchange kisses.

An egg was the Egyptian emblem of the universe, and it was from the Egyptians that all the Pagan nations, and afterwards the Greek Christians derived this ceremony. They are used also by the Roman Catholics and by the Jews in their Paschal festival.

It is probable that it was also a Druidic ceremony, for it prevails in Cumberland and many other counties of England. On Easter Monday and Tuesday the inhabitants assemble in the meadows, the children provided with hard boiled eggs, colored or ornamented in various ways, some being dyed with logwood or cochineal; others tinged with the juice of herbs and broom-flowers; others stained by being boiled in shreds of parti-colored riband; and others covered with gilding. They roll them along the ground, or toss them in the air till they break when they eat them-a part of the ceremony which they probably understand the best. They are called *pace-eggs* or *paste-eggs*, probably corrupted from *pasche*.

This reminds us of the strange fable of the serpent's egg. As I mentioned in an earlier chapter many of these eggs or adder-stones are preserved with great reverence in the Highlands. There are also some traditions upon this subject which are worth narrating.

Monsieur Chorier in his *Histoire de Dauphiné* informs us that in the divers parts of that county, especially near the mountain of Rochelle on the borders of Savoy, serpents congregate from the 15th of June to the 15th of August for purposes of generation. The place which they have occupied after they have gone, is covered with a sticky white foam which is indescribably disgusting to behold.

Camden relates that in most parts of Wales and throughout Scotland and Cornwall, it is an opinion of the vulgar that about Midsummer Eve the snakes meet together in companies, and that by joining heads together and hissing, a kind of bubble is formed which the rest by continual hissing blow on till it quite passes through the body, when it immediately hardens and resembles a glass ring which will make its finder prosperous in all his undertakings. The rings thus generated are called *gleinu madroeth*, or snake stones. They are small glass amulets commonly about half as wide as our finger rings, but much thicker, of a green color usually though sometimes blue and waved with red and white.

Careu in his *Survey of Cornwall* says that its inhabitants believe that snakes breathing upon a hazel wand produce a stone ring of a blue color, in which there appears the yellow figure of a snake, and that beasts which have been bit by a mad dog or poisoned, if given some water to drink wherein this stone has been infused, will perfectly recover.

The following custom is evidently a dramatic representation of the rape of the serpent's egg à la Pliny:

On Easter Monday, in Normandy, the common people congregate *à la motte de Pougard* which they surround. They place at the foot a basket containing a hundred eggs, the number of the stones of the temple of Aubury. A man takes the eggs and places them singly on the top of the tumulus, and then descends in the same manner to return them to the basket. While this is doing, another man runs to a village half a league off, and if he can return before the last egg is restored to the basket, he gains a barrel of cider as a prize, which he empties with the co-operation of his friends, and a Bacchanalian dance round the tumulus ends the proceedings.

Serpent-worship is almost extinct, if not entirely so; . and the belief of the lower orders in Ireland that St. Patrick expelled all the snakes and other reptiles from the island is perhaps derived from his having extinguished their adorers.

However, it is considered unlucky in England to kill the harmless green snake; and there is a superstition almost universally present, that it will not die till the setting of that sun, of which it was an emblem.

Its tenacity of life is indeed something marvelous. Mr. Payne Knight, in his work on Phallic worship, (which I read at the British Museum, but which is somewhat absurdly excluded from the catalogue) states that he has seen the heart of an adder throb for some moments after it had been completely taken from the body, and even renew its beatings ten minutes afterwards when dipped in hot water.

Many of our ladies wear bracelets in the shape of a snake, as did the Egyptian dames of old. The lower orders believe that a serpent's skin will extract thorns, and its fat is sold to London chemists at five shillings a pound for its medicinal properties.

Most curious of all, is the superstition that by eating snakes one may grow young, and of which the three following passages are illustrations.

"A gentlewoman told an ancient bachelor, who looked very young, that she thought he had eaten a snake. No mistress, (he said) it is because I never meddled with any snakes which maketh me look so young. "--*Holy State*, 1642, p. 36.

> He hath left off o' late to feed on snakes,
> His beard's turned white again.

> *Massinger*, Old Law. Act V. Sc. 1.

> He is your loving brother, sir, and will tell nobody
> But all he meets, that you have eat a snake,
> And are grown young, gamesome, and rampant.

> *Ibid*, Elder Brother, Act IV., Sc- 4-

Of stone worship there are still many vestiges. In a little island near Skye is a chapel dedicated to St. Columbus; on an altar is a round blue stone which is always moist. Fishermen, detained by contrary winds, bathe this stone in water, expecting thereby to obtain favorable winds; it is likewise applied to the sides of people troubled with stitches, and it is held so holy, that decisive oaths are sworn upon it.

There is a stone in the parish of Madren, Cornwall, through which many persons are wont to creep for pains in the back and limbs, and through which children are drawn for the rickets. In the North, children are drawn through a hole cut in the *Groaning Cheese*, a huge stone, on the day they are christened.

To go into the cleft of a rock was an ancient method of penitence and purification. It may be remembered that in the tradition of Hiram Abiff, the assassins were found concealed in a hollow rock, in which they were lamenting their crime.

To sleep on stones on particular nights is a cure for lameness with our peasants, though perhaps a hazardous one, especially if the disease originated from rheumatism.

A Druidic monument of great historical interest is to be seen under the coronation chair in Westminster Abbey. Originally called *Liag-fial*, the Fatal Stone, by others *Cloch na cineamhna* or the Stone of Fortune, it was that upon which the Kings of Ireland used to be inaugurated, and which, being enclosed in a wooden chair, was, by the ingenuity of the Druids, made to emit a sound under the rightful candidate, and mute under a man of bad title. It was superstitiously sent to confirm the Irish colony in Scotland, and it continued at Scone as the coronation of the Scotch Kings, from the commencement of the Christian Era till 1300 A. D.,when Edward I. imported it into England. It is still a superstition in the Highlands that those who lay their hands against the Druids' stones will not prosper.

Many of these monuments are approached with great reverence by the natives of Scotland and the Isles, especially the *Tighe nan Druidhneach* in the Isle of Skye, little arched, round stone buildings capable of holding one, where the contemplative Druid sat when his oak could not shelter him from the weather. The common people never pass these without walking round them three times from east to west.

In Chartres, which teems with Druidic vestiges, a curious specimen of stone worship remains. At the close of service in the cathedral, no one leaves the church without kneeling and saying a short prayer before a small pillar or stone--without polish, base or capital-- placed in a niche, and much worn on one side by the kisses of the devout. This stone is rumored to be of high antiquity, even earlier than the establishment of Christianity--for many centuries to have remained in a crypt of the cathedral where lamps were constantly burning--but the stairs having been much worn on one side by the great resort of pilgrims to the spot, the stone had been removed from its original site, to avoid the expenses of repairs. It was said to be a miraculous stone, and that its miracles were performed at the intercession of the Virgin Mary.

There is a certain reverence paid by the peasantry to those caves in which the Druids held their initiatory rites. Many of them are said to be inhabited by spirits, and there is one in the neighborhood of Dunskey, Scotland, which is held in peculiar veneration. At the change of the moon it is usual to bring even from a great distance infirm persons, and particularly rickety children whom they supposed bewitched, to bathe in a stream which flows from the hill, and then to dry them in the cave.

As among the Druids it is still customary to place a platter of salt and earth upon the breast of the corpse in many parts of Britain. Salt was held in great reverence by the Eastern nations as an emblem of incorruptibility. So among us to spill salt is considered unlucky; it was only the other day that I saw a talented and well educated lady overwhelmed with consternation at this mishap, but with admirable presence of mind she flung a pinch over her left shoulder and so recovered her self-possession.

Hare was forbidden to the ancient Britons by their religion, and to this day the Cornish eat it with reluctance. Boadicea also augured from the running of a hare; and a hare that runs across a path (to any one but a sportsman, or rather a pot-hunter) is an omen of ill- luck.

The onion was an emblem of the deity among the Egyptians, perhaps also among the Druids, for it is a custom in some parts of England for girls to divine by it, as Barnaby Googe in his translation of Naogeorgus' Popish Kingdome informs us.

In these same days young wanton gyrles that meete for marriage be,
Doe search to know the names of them that shall their husbands bee;
Four onyons, five, or eight, they take, and make in every one
Such names as they do fancie most, and best to think upon,
Thus nere the chimney them they set, and that same Onyon then
That firste doth sproute, doth surely bear the name of their good man.

In matters of dress, there are not many traces of the Druids and the ancient Britons to be found.

The caps of rushes, however, which they wore tied at the top and twisted into a band at the bottom, may still be seen upon the heads of children in Wales and some parts of England. In Shetland, the ancient sandals of untanned skins are worn, and also, by fishermen in cold weather, the Druidic wooden shoes. I could not discover their real origin during my visit there: some said they had been imported by the Dutch, others that the Dutch had borrowed the idea from them; but in any case these wooden shoes, the sabots of the lower orders of France, are derived from the Druids.

The best instance of dress however, is the Highland plaid, which was the very garment worn by the Druid Abaris, on his visit to Athens, and which is an extraordinary example of savage conservatism. From the *breachan* of the Gauls and Britons, is derived our word *breeches* and also that inelegant but necessary article of clothing.

Upon the subject of words I will also remark that our word *fortnight* or fourteen nights, is derived from the Druidic habit of counting time by nights instead of days; and the word *dizzy* from their *deisul*, or circular dance, (in Hebrew *dizzel*). I could give a multitude more, but *ohe! jam satis est.*

A very curious memorial of Druidism in the very bosom of victorious Christianity was discovered a few years ago by the well-known French Antiquary, M. Hersart de la Villemarqué. It is a fragment of Latin poetry which all the children in the parish of Nizon, Canton de Pont-Aven, are taught to sing at school and in church. The original poetry is almost the same as its Latin adaptation, except that in the latter various biblical allusions have been slipped in.

I will give the first strophe of the original, then its translation in the French of M. Villemarqué which is too good for me to meddle with, and then the Latin hymn as sung by the children

ANN DROUIZ.

Daik mab gwerm Drouiz; ore;
Daik petra fell d'id-dei
Petra ganinn-me d'id-de.

AR MAP

Kan d'in euz a eur raun,
Ken a ouffenn breman.

LE DRUIDE.

Tout beau enfant blanc du Druide, tout beau réponds-moi; que veux-tu? te chanterai-je?

L'ENFANT.

Chante-moi la division du nombre un jusqu'à ce que je l'apprenne aujourd'hui.

LE DRUIDE.

Pas de division pour le nombre un, la nécessitéuni que; la mort père de la douleur; rien avant, rien après. Tout beau, &c.

L'ENFANT.

Chante-moi la division du nombre deux, &c.

LE DRUIDE.

Deux bœufs attelés à une coque; ils tirent, ils vont expirer--Voyez la merveille!

Pas de division, &c.

L'ENFANT.

Chante-moi la division du nombre trois, &c.

LE DRUIDE.

Il y a trois parties dans le monde; trois commencements et trois fins pour l'homme, comme pour le chêne; trois cêlestes, royaumes de Merlin; fruits d'or, fleurs brillantes, petits enfants qui rient.
Deux bœufs, &c.
Pas de division, &c.

The christianized version in Latin is as follows:

L'ENFANT.

Dic mihi quid unus,
Dic mihi quid unus.

LE MAITRE.

Unus est Deus,
Qui regnat in Cœlis.

L'ENFANT.

Dic mihi quid duo.
Dic mihi quid duo.

LE MAITRE.

Duo testamenta,
Unus est Deus,
Qui regnat in Cœlis.

L'ENFANT.

Dic mihi qui sunt tres
Dic mihi que sunt tres.

LE MAITRE.

Tres sunt patriarchæ,
Duo sunt testamenta;
Unus est deus,
Qui regnat in Cœlis.

Both of these dialogues are continued to the number twelve. In the Druidic version containing precepts on theology, cosmogony, chronology, astronomy, geography, magic, medicine and history. The Latin version teaching that there is one God, two testaments, three prophets, four evangelists, five books of Moses, six pitchers at the marriage of Cana, seven sacraments, eight beatitudes, nine choirs of angels, ten commandments, eleven stars which appeared to Joseph, and twelve apostles.

The resemblance of style and precept throughout is very striking, and a discovery which I have made of the same nature renders it still more surprising.

There is a peculiar song of the Oxfordshire peasants, the meaning of which had often perplexed me and which of course those who sung it were the least able to explain.

It is sung in this manner. One of them begins:--

I will sing you my one O!

To which the rest sing in chorus.

What is your one O!

And he sings.

One is all alone,
And ever doth remam so.

The song continues to the number twelve, each verse repeated after each as in the original versions above. Most of these verses are local corruptions, and it is probable that in some parts of England a purer version is retained. However, since the first refers to the One Deity, the second to "two white boys clothed in green," the fourth to "four gospel preachers," the seventh to the "seven stars," &c., there can be no doubt as to its origin.

There is so superstitious a reverence paid by the lower orders in many parts of Britain to bees, that one is almost inclined to suppose that they also were held sacred by the Druids.

The Cornishmen consider bees too sacred to be bought. In other counties, on the death of their proprietor, a ceremonious announcement of the fact is made to them and a piece of funeral cake presented to them. It is believed that were this omitted they would fly away. In Lithuania a similar practice prevails.

There is no clue to this, except in the circumstance that *the bee-hive* is one of the emblems of Freemasonry, and like many other Druidic and Masonic symbols, *e.g.* the seven stars, the cross-keys, &c., a favorite tavern sign. For instance the one at Abingdon, under which is written the following jocose distich:

Within this hive were all alive,
Good liquor makes us funny,

> So if your dry, come in and try,
> The flavor of our honey.

From the apple-tree the Druids were wont to cut their divining rods. And to this tree at Christmas, in Devon, Cornwall and other counties a curious ceremony is paid. The farmer and his laborers soak cakes in cider, and place them on the trenches of an apple tree, and sprinkling the tree repeat the following incantation :

> Here's to thee, old apple tree!
> Whence thou mayst bud, and whence thou mayest blow.
> Hats full! Caps full?
> Bushel, bushel, sacks full!
> And my pockets full too! Huzza!

After which they dance round the tree and get drunk on the cider which remains. They believe that if they did not do this the tree would not bear.

I have now to consider the vestiges of mistletoe-worship extant among the descendants of the Druids.

On Christmas Eve it was lately the custom at York to carry mistletoe to the high altar of the Cathedral, and to proclaim a public and universal liberty, pardon and freedom to all sorts of inferior and even wicked people at the gates of the city towards the four quarters of heaven.

The mistletoe was considered of great medicinal virtue by Sir John Coldbatch for epilepsy and other convulsive disorders. The mistletoe of the oak is used by the common people for wind ruptures in children.

Like the *houzza!* of the East, the mistletoe would seem to have a religious exclamation, as I judge from finding it so often the refrain to old French songs, especially this one :

> O gué la bonne adventure, O gué.

And in one celebrated English ballad:

> O the mistletoe bough! and O the mistletoe bough!

It is still a custom in many parts of France for children to run down the street on New Year's Day, and to rap the doors crying "*Au gui l'an né*, or *Au gui, l'an neuf.*"

In the island of Sein, there is a mistletoe feast which it is believed has been perpetuated by the Bas Breton *tailors* who, strange to say, have been formed from time immemorial into a fine association. They are poets, musicians and wizards who never contract marriages with strangers, and who have a language of their own, called *lueache* which they will not speak in the presence of foreigners.

At this feast there is a procession. An altar covered with green boughs is erected in the centre of a circular space of ground. Thence they start, and thither marching round the island return. Two fiddlers form the vanguard; they are followed by children carrying bill-hooks and oak-branches, and leading an ox and a horse covered with flowers. After them a huge crowd which stops at intervals crying *Gui-na-né voilà le Gui.*

There is one more mistletoe custom which I had almost forgotten. Let us imagine ourselves in the hall of some old-fashioned country mansion. Let it be Christmas- night, and at that hour when merriment and wine has flushed every face, and glowed into every heart.

And now I will paint to you a young maiden who embraced in the arms of her lover is whirled round the hall, her eyes sparkling, her white bosom heaving and her little feet scarce seeming to touch the floor. They pause for a moment. An old lady with an arch twinkle in her eye whispers something to her partner, he nods and smiles; she blushes and turns her eyes, pretending not to hear.

They join the dance again, when suddenly he stays her in the centre of the hall. Above their heads droops down a beautiful plant with pale white berries and leaves of a delicate green. He stoops and gives her *the kiss-under-the-mistletoe.* All laugh and follow his example till the scene vies the revels of the ancient Bacchanals.

It is this picture which awakes me from a reverie into which I have long been buried. Reader! you have sought with me for the first germs of religion in the chaos of youthful Time; you have dived with me into those mysteries which the Veil of Isis held secret from our sight; you have sojourned with me among the tombs of the past, and trod upon the dust of a fallen World.

Let us now return from these caverns of learning to the glorious day-light of the Present, and to the enjoyments, of a real existence.

THE MARTYRDOM OF MAN

Author's Preface

In 1862-3 I made a tour in Western Africa, and afterwards desired to revisit that strange country with the view of opening up new ground and of studying religion and morality among the natives. I was, however, unable to bear a second time the great expenses of African travel, and had almost given up the hope of becoming an explorer when I was introduced by Mr. Bates, the well known Amazon traveller and Secretary of the Royal Geographical Society, to one of its Associates, Mr. Andrew Swanzy, who had long desired to do something in the cause of African discovery. He placed unlimited means at my disposal, and left me free to choose my own route. I travelled in Africa for two years (1868-70) and made a journey which is mentioned in the test. The narrative of my travels will be published in due course; I allude to them now in order to show that I have had some personal experience of savages. I wish also to take the first opportunity of thanking Mr. Swanzy for his assistance, which was given not only in the most generous but also in the most graceful manner.

With respect to the present work, I began it intending to prove that "Negroland" or Inner Africa is not cut off from the main-stream of events, as writers of philosophical history have always maintained, but connected by means of Islam with the lands of the East; and also that it has, by means of the slave-trade, powerfully influenced the moral history of Europe and the political history of the United States. But I was gradually led from writing the history of Africa into writing the history of the world. I could not describe the Negroland of ancient times without describing Egypt and Carthage. From Egypt I was drawn to Asia and to Greece; from Carthage I was drawn to Rome. That is the first chapter.

Next, having to relate the progress of the Mohammedans in Central Africa, it was necessary for me to explain the nature and origin of Islam, but that religion cannot be understood without a previous study of Christianity and of Judaism, and those religions cannot be understood without a study of religion among savages. That is the second chapter.

Thirdly, I sketched the history of the slave-trade, which took me back to the discoveries of the Portuguese, the glories of Venetian commerce, the revival of the arts, the Dark Ages, and the invasion of the Germans. Thus finding that my outline of universal history was almost complete, I determined in the last chapter to give a brief summary of the whole, filling up the parts omitted, and adding to it the materials of another work suggested several years ago by The Origin of Species.

One of my reasons for revisiting Africa was to collect materials for this work, which I had intended to call The Origin of Mind. However, Mr. Darwin's Descent of Man has left little for me to say respecting the birth and infancy of the faculties and affections. I therefore merely follow in his footsteps, not from blind veneration for a great master, but because I find that his conclusions are confirmed by the phenomena of savage life.

On certain minor points I venture to dissent from Mr. Darwin's views, as I shall show in my personal narrative, and there is probably much in this work of which Mr. Darwin will disapprove. He must therefore not be made responsible for all the opinions of his disciple.

I had intended to give my authorities in full with notes and elucidations, but am prevented from doing so by want of space, this volume being already larger than it should be. I wish therefore to impress upon the reader that there is scarcely anything in this work which I can claim as my own. I have taken not only facts and ideas, but phrases and even paragraphs, from other writers. I cannot pay all my debts in full, but I must at least do myself the pleasure of mentioning those authors who have been my chief guides. On Egypt they are Wilkinson, Herodotus (Rawlinson's edition), Bunsen; Ethiopia or Abyssinia, Bruce, Baker, Lepsius; Carthage, Heeren (African Nations), Niebuhr, ommsen; East Africa, Vincent (Periplus), Guillain, Hakluyt Society's Publications; Moslem Africa (Central), Park, Caillie, Denham and Clapperton, Lander, Barth, Ibn Batuta, Leo Africanus; Guinea and South Africa, Azurara, Barros, Major, Hakluyt, Purchas, Livingstone; Assyria, Sir H. Rawlinson, Layard; India, Max Muller, Weber; Persia, Heeren (Asiatic Nations); Central Asia, Burnes, Wolff, Vambery; Arabia, Niebuhr, Caussin de Perceval,

Sprenger, Deutsch, Muir, Burckhardt, Burton, Palgrave; Palestine, Dean Stanley, Renan, Dollinger, Spinoza, Robinson, Neander; Greece, Grote, O. Muller, Curtius, Heeren, Lewes, Taine, About, Becker (Charicles); Rome, Gibbon, Macaulay, Becker (Gallus); Dark Ages, Hallam, Guizot, Robertson, Prescott, Irving; Philosophy of History, Herder, Buckle Comte, Lecky, Mill, Draper; Science, Darwin, Lyell, Herbert, Spencer, Huxley, Tyndall, Chambers (Vestiges of Creation), Wallace, Tylor, and Lubbock. All of the works of the above named authors deserve to be carefully read by the students of universal history, and in them he will find references to the original authorities, and to all writers of importance on the various subjects treated of in this work.

As for my religious sentiments, they are expressed in opposition to the advice and wishes of several literary friends, and of the publisher, who have urged me to alter certain passages which they do not like, and which they believe will provoke against me the anger of the public. Now, as a literary workman I am thankful to be guided by the knowledge of experts, and I bow to the decisions of the great public, for whom alone I write, whom alone I care to please, and in whose broad unbiased judgment I place implicit trust. But in the matter of religion I listen to no remonstrance; I acknowledge no decision save that of the divine monitor within me. My conscience is my adviser, my audience, and my judge. It bade me write as I have written, without evasion, without disguise; it bids me to go on as I have begun, whatever the result may be. If therefore my religious opinions should be condemned, without a single exception, by every reader of the book, it will not make me regret having expressed them, and it will not prevent me from expressing then again. It is my earnest and sincere conviction that those opinions are not only true, but also that they tend to elevate and purify the mind. One thing at all events I know--that it has done me good to write this book, and therefore I do not think that it can injure those by whom it will be read.

Chapter I. War

Egypt

The land of Egypt is six hundred miles long, and is bounded by two ranges of naked limestone hills which sometimes approach and sometimes retire from each other, leaving between them an average breadth of seven miles. On the north they widen and disappear, giving place to a marshy meadow plain which extends to the Mediterranean coast. On the south they are no longer of limestone, but of granite; they narrow to a point; they close in till they almost touch; and through the mountain gate thus formed the river Nile leaps with a roar into the valley, and runs north towards the sea.

In the winter and spring it rolls a languid stream through a dry and dusty plain. But in the summer an extraordinary thing happens. The river grows troubled and swift; it turns red as blood, and then green; it rises, it swells, till at length, overflowing its banks, it covers the adjoining lands to the base of the hills on either side. The whole valley becomes a lake from which the villages rise like islands, for they are built on artificial mounds.

This catastrophe was welcomed by the Egyptians with religious gratitude and noisy mirth. When their fields had entirely disappeared they thanked the gods and kept their harvest-home. The tax gatherers measured the water as if it were grain, and announced what the crops and the budget of the next year would be. Gay barges with painted sails conveyed the merry husbandmen from village to village and from fair to fair. It was then that they had their boat tournaments, their wrestling matches, their bouts at single-stick and other athletic sports. It was then that the thimble-riggers and jack-puddings, blind harpers and nigger minstrels from Central Africa, amused the holiday-hearted crowd. It was then that the old people sat over draughts and dice-box in the cosy shade, while the boys played at mora, or at pitch and toss, and the girls at a game of ball, with forfeits for the one who missed a catch. It was then that the house-father bought new dolls for the children, and amulets or gold ear-rings or necklaces of porcelain bugles for the wife. It was then that the market stalls abounded with joints of beef and venison, and with geese hanging down in long rows, and with chickens hatched by thousands under heaps of dung. Salted quails, smoked fish, date sweetmeats, doura cakes, and cheese; leeks, garlic cucumbers, and onions; lotus seeds mashed in milk, roasted stalks of papyrus, jars of barley beer and palm wine, with many other kinds of food, were sold in unusual plenty at that festive time.

It was then also that the white-robed priests, bearing the image of a god and singing hymns, marched with solemn procession to the waterside, and cast in a sacrifice of gold. For the water which had thus risen was their life. Egypt is by nature a rainless desert which the Nile and the Nile only, converts into a garden every year.

Far, far away in the distant regions of the south, in the deep heart of Africa, lie two inland seas. These are the headwaters of the Nile; its sources are in the sky. For the clouds, laden with waters collected out of many seas, sail to the African equator, and there pour down a ten months' rain. This ocean of falling water is received on a region sloping towards the north, and is conveyed by a thousand channels to the vast rocky cisterns which form the Speke and Baker Lakes. [Lakes Victoria and Albert] They, filled and bursting, cast forth the Nile, and drive it from them through a terrible and thirsty land. The hot air lies on the stream and laps it as it flows. The parched soil swallows it with open pores, but ton after ton of water is supplied from the gigantic reservoirs behind, and so it is enabled to cross that vast desert which spreads from the latitude of Lake Tchad to the borders of the Mediterranean Sea.

The existence of the Nile is due to the Nyanza Lakes alone, but the inundation of the river has a distinct and separate cause. In that phenomenon the lakes are not concerned.

Between the Nile and the mouth of the Arabian Gulf are situated the highlands of Abyssinia, rising many thousand feet above the level of the sea, and intercepting the clouds of the Indian Ocean in their flight towards the north. From these mountains, as soon as the rainy season has set in, two great rivers come thundering down their dried-up beds, and rush into the Nile. The main stream is now forced impetuously along; in the Nubian desert its swelling waters are held in between walls of rock; as soon as it reaches the low lying lands of Egypt it naturally overflows.

The Abyssinian tributaries do even more than this. The waters of the White Nile are transparent and pure; but the Atbara and Blue Nile bring down from their native land a black silt which the flood strews over the whole valley as a kind of top-dressing or manure. On that rich and unctuous mud, as soon as the waters have retired, the natives cast their seed. Then their labours are completed; no changes of weather need afterwards be feared; no anxious looks are turned towards the sky; sunshine only is required to fulfil the crop, and in Egypt the sun is never covered by a cloud.

Thus, were it not for the White Nile, the Abyssinian rivers would be drunk up by the desert; and were it not for the Abyssinian rivers, the White Nile would be a barren stream. The river is created by the rains of the equator; the land by the tropical rains condensed in one spot by the Abyssinian mountain pile.

In that fair Egyptian valley, fattened by a foreign soil, brightened by eternal sunshine, watered by terrestrial rain, the natives were able to obtain a year's food in return for a few days' toil, and so were provided with that wealth of time which is essential for a nation's growth.

A people can never rise from low estate as long as they are engrossed in the painful struggle for daily bread. On the other hand, leisure alone is not sufficient to effect the self-promotion of men. The savage of the primeval forest burns down a few trees every year; his women raise an easy crop from the ashes which mingle with the soil. He basks all day in the sunshine, or prostrates himself in his canoe with his arms behind his head and a fishing-line tied to his big toe. When the meat-hunger comes upon him he takes up bow and arrow and goes for a few days into the bush. His life is one long torpor, with spasms of activity. Century follows century, but he does not change. Again, the shepherd tribes roam from pasture to pasture; their flocks and herds yield them food and dress and "houses of hair," as they call their tents. They have little work to do; their time is almost entirely their own. They pass long hours in slow conversation, in gazing at the heavens, in the sensuous, passive oriental reverie. The intellectual capacities of such men are by no means to be despised, as those who have lived among them are aware. They are skilful interpreters of nature's language and of the human heart; they compose beautiful poems; their religion is simple and sublime; yet time passes on, and they do not advance. The Arab sheikh of the present day lives precisely as Abraham did three thousand years ago; the Tartars of Central Asia are the Scythians whom Herodotus described.

It is the first and indispensable condition of human progress that a people shall be married to a single land; that they shall wander no more from one region to another, but remain fixed and faithful to their soil. Then, if the Earth-wife be fruitful, she will bear them children by hundreds and by thousands; and then calamity will come and teach them by torture to invent.

The Egyptians were islanders, cut off from the rest of the world by sand and sea. They were rooted in their valley; they lived entirely upon its fruits, and happily these fruits sometimes failed. Had they always been able to obtain enough to eat, they would have remained always in the semi-savage state.

It may appear strange that Egypt should have suffered from famine, for there was no country in the ancient world where food was so abundant and so cheap. Not only did the land produce enormous crops of corn; the ditches and hollows which were filled by the overflowing Nile supplied a harvest of wholesome and nourishing aquatic plants, and on the borders of the desert thick groves of date-palms, which love a neutral soil, embowered the villages, and formed live granaries of fruit.

But however plentiful food may be in any country, the population of that country, as Malthus discovered, will outstrip it in the long run. If food is unusually cheap, population will increase at an unusually rapid rate, and there is not limit to its ratio of increase--no limit, that is to say, except disease and death. On the other hand, there is a limit to the amount of food that can be raised, for the basis of food is land, and land is a fixed quantity. Unless some discovery is made by means of which provisions may be manufactured with as much facility as children, the whole earth will some day be placed in the same predicament as the island in which we live, which has outgrown its food-producing power, and is preserved from starvation only by means of foreign corn.

At the time we speak of, Egypt was irrigated by the Nile in a natural and therefore imperfect manner. Certain tracts were overflooded; others were left completely dry. The valley was filled with people to the brim. When it was a good Nile, every ear of corn, every bunch of dates, every papyrus stalk and lotus root was pre-engaged. There was no waste and no surplus store. But sometimes a bad Nile came.

The bread of the people depended on the amount of inundation, and that depended on the tropical rains, which vary more than is usually supposed. If the rainfall in the Abyssinian highlands happened to be slight, the river could not pay its full tribute of earth and water to the valley below; and if the rainfall was unusually severe, houses were swept away, cattle were drowned, and the water, instead of returning at the usual time, became stagnant on the fields. In either case famine and pestilence invariably ensued. The plenty of ordinary years, like a baited trap, had produced a luxuriance of human life, and the massacre was proportionally severe. Encompassed by the wilderness, the unfortunate natives were unable to escape. They died in heaps; the valley resembled a field of battle; each village became a charnel-house; skeletons sat grinning at street corners, and the winds clattered among dead men's bones. A few survivors lingered miserably through the year, browsing on the thorny shrubs of the desert, and sharing with the vultures their horrible repast.

"God made all men equal" is a fine sounding phrase, and has also done good service in its day, but it is not a scientific fact. On the contrary, there is nothing so certain as the natural inequality of men. Those who outlive hardships and sufferings which fall on all alike owe their existence to some superiority, not only of body but of mind. It will easily be conceived that among such superior-minded men there would be some who, stimulated by the memory of that which was past and by the fear of that which might return, would strain to the utmost their ingenuity to control and guide the fickle river which had hitherto sported with their lives.

We shall not attempt to trace out their inventions step by step. Humble in its beginnings, slow in its improvements, the art or science of hydraulics was finally mastered by the Egyptians. They devised a system of dikes, reservoirs, and lock-canals, by means of which the excessive waters of a violent Nile were turned from the fields and stored up to supply the wants of a dry year. Thus also the precious fluid was conveyed to tracts of land lying above the level of the river, and was distributed over the whole valley with such precision that each lot or farm received a just and equal share. Next, as the inundation destroyed all landmarks, surveying became a necessary art in order to settle the disputes which broke out every year. And, as the rising of the waters was more and more carefully observed, it was found that its beginning coincided with certain aspects of the stars. This led to the study of astronomy and the discovery of the solar year. Agriculture became a mathematical art. It was ascertained that so many feet of water would yield so many quarters of corn, and thus, before a single seed was sown, they could count up the harvest as correctly as if it had been already gathered in.

A natural consequence of all this was the separation of the inventor class, who became at first the counsellors and afterwards the rulers of the people. But while the men of mind were battling with the forces of Nature, a contest of another kind was also going on. Those who dwell on the rich banks of a river flowing through desert lands are always liable to be attacked by the wandering shepherd hordes who resort to the waterside in summer, when the wilderness pasture is dried up. There is nothing such tribes desire better than to conquer the corn-growing people of the river lands, and to make them pay a tribute of grain when the crops are taken in. The Egyptians, as soon as they had won their harvests from the flood, were obliged to defend them against the robbers of the desert, and out of such wars arose a military caste. These allied themselves with the intellectual caste, who were also priests, for among the primitive nations religion and science were invariably combined. In this manner the bravest and wisest of the Egyptians rose above the vulgar crowd, and the nation was divided into two great classes, the rulers and the ruled.

Then oppression continued the work which war and famine had begun. The priests announced, and the armies executed, the divine decrees. The people were reduced to servitude. The soldiers discovered the gold and emerald mines of the adjoining hills, and filled their dark recesses with chained slaves and savage overseers. They became invaders;

they explored distant lands with the spear. Communications with Syria and the fragrant countries at the mouth of the Red Sea, first opened by means of war, were continued by means of commerce. Foreign produce became an element of Egyptian life. The privileged classes found it necessary to be rich. Formerly the priests had merely salted the bodies of the dead; now a fashionable corpse must be embalmed, at an expense of two hundred and fifty pounds, with asphalt from the Dead Sea and spices from the Somali groves; costly incense must be burnt on the altars of the gods; aristocratic heads must recline on ivory stools; fine ladies must glitter with gold ornaments and precious stones, and must be served by waiting-maids and pages with woolly hair and velvety black skins. War and agriculture were no longer sufficient to supply these patrician wants. It was no longer sufficient that the people should feed on dates and the coarse doura-bread, while the wheat which they raised was sold by their masters for gewgaws and perfumes. Manufactures were established; slaves laboured at a thousand looms; the linen goods of Egypt became celebrated throughout the world. Laboratories were opened; remarkable discoveries were made. The Egyptian priests distilled brandy and sweet waters. They used the blow-pipe, and were far advanced in the chemical processes of art. They fabricated glass mosaics, and counterfeited precious stones and porcelain of exquisite transparency and delicately blended hues. With the fruits of these inventions they adorned their daily life, and attracted into Egypt the riches of other lands.

Thus, when Nature selects a people to endow them with glory and with wealth, her first proceeding is to massacre their bodies, her second to debauch their minds. She begins with famine, pestilence and war; next, force and rapacity above, chains and slavery below. She uses evil as the raw material of good; though her aim is always noble, her earliest means are base and cruel. But as soon as a certain point is reached she washes her black and bloody hands, and uses agents of a higher kind. Having converted the animal instinct of self-defence into the ravenous lust of wealth and power, that also she transforms into ambition of a pure and lofty kind. At first knowledge is sought only for the things which it will buy-- the daily bread indispensable to life, and those trinkets of body and mind which vanity demands. Yet those low desires do not always and entirely possess the human soul. Wisdom is like the heiress of the novel who is at first courted only for her wealth, but whom the fortune-hunter learns afterwards to love for herself alone.

At first sight there seems little in the arts and sciences of Egypt which cannot be traced to the enlightened selfishness of the priestly caste. For in the earlier times it was necessary for the priests to labour unceasingly to preserve the power which they had usurped. It was necessary to overawe not only the people who worked in the fields, but their own dangerous allies, the military class; to make religion not only mysterious but magnificent; not only to predict the precise hour of the rising of the waters, or the eclipses of the moon, but also to adopt and nurture the fine arts, to dazzle the public with temples, monuments, and paintings. Above all, it was necessary to prepare a system of government which should keep the labouring classes in subjection and yet stimulate them to labour indefatigably for the state; which should strip them of all the rewards of industry and yet keep that industry alive. Expediency will therefore account for much that the Egyptian intellect produced, but it certainly will not account for all. The invention of hieroglyphics is alone sufficient to prove that higher motives were at work than mere political calculation and the appetite of gold. For writing was an invention which at no time could have added in a palpable manner to the wealth or power of the upper classes, and which yet could not have been finished to a system without a vast expenditure of time and toil. It could not have been the work of a single man, but of several men labouring in the same direction, and in its early beginnings must have appeared as unpractical, as truly scientific to them, as the study of solar chemistry and the observation of the double stars to us. Besides, the intense and faithful labour which is conspicuous in all the Egyptian works of art could only have been inspired by that enthusiasm which belongs to noble minds.

We may fairly presume that Egypt once possessed its chivalry of the intellect, its heroic age, and that the violent activity of thought generated by the love of life and developed by the love of power was raised to its full zenith by the passion for art and science, for the beautiful and the true.

At first the Nile valley was divided into a number of independent states, each possessing its own corporation of priests and soldiers, its own laws and system of taxation, its own tutelary god and shrine, but each a member of one body, united by the belief in one religion, and assembling from time to time to worship the national gods in an appointed place. There, according to general agreement ratified by solemn oaths, all feuds were suspended, all weapons laid aside. There also, under the shelter of the sanctuary, property was secure, and the surplus commodities of the various districts could be conveniently interchanged. In such a place, frequented by vast crowds of pilgrims and traders, a great city would naturally arise, and such it seems probable was the origin of Thebes.

But Egypt, which possesses a simple undivided form, and which is nourished by one great arterial stream, appears destined to be surmounted by a single head, and we perceive in the dim dawn of history a revolution taking place, and Menes, the Egyptian Charlemagne, founding an empire upon the ruins of local governments, and inspiring the various tribes with the sentiment of nationality. Thebes remained the sacred city, but a new capital, Memphis, was built at the other end of the valley, not far from the spot where Cairo now stands.

By degrees the Egyptian empire assumed a consolidated form. A regular constitution was established and a ritual prescribed. The classes were organised in a more effective manner, and were not at first too strictly fixed. All were at liberty to intermarry, excepting only the swineherds, who were regarded as unclean. The system of government became masterly, and the servitude of the people became complete. Designs of imperial magnitude were accomplished, some of them gigantic but useless, mere exploits of naked human strength, others structures of true grandeur and utility. The valley was adorned with splendid monuments and temples; colossal statues were erected, which rose above the houses like the towers and spires of our cathedral towns. An army of labourers was employed against the Nile. The course of the mighty stream was altered; its waters were snatched from its bosom and stored up in Lake Moeris, an artificial basin hollowed out of an extensive swamp, and thence were conducted by a system of canals into the neighbouring desert, which they changed to smiling fields. For the Sahara can always be revived. It is barren only because it receives no rain.

The Empire consisted of three estates--the Monarch, the Army, and the Church. There were in theory no limits to the power of the king. His authority was derived directly from the gods. He was called "the Sun"; he was the head of the religion and the state; he was the supreme judge and lawgiver; he commanded the army and led it to war. But in reality his power was controlled and reduced to mere pageantry by a parliament of priests. He was elected by the military class, but as soon as he was crowned he was initiated into the mysteries and subjected to the severe discipline of the holy order. No slave or hireling might approach his person: the lords in waiting, with the state parasol and the ostrich-feather fans, were princes of the blood; his other attendants were invariably priests. The royal time was filled and measured by routine: laws were laid down in the holy books for the order and nature of the king's occupations. At daybreak he examined and dispatched his correspondence; he then put on his robes and attended divine service in the temple. Extracts were read from those holy books which contained the sayings and actions of distinguished men, and these were followed by a sermon from the High Priest. He extolled the virtues of the reigning sovereign, but criticised severely the lives of those who had preceded him--a post-mortem examination to which the king knew that he would be subjected in his turn.

He was forbidden to commit any kind of excess: he was restricted to a plain diet of veal and goose, and to a measured quantity of wine. The laws hung over him day and night; they governed his public and private action: they followed him even to the recesses of his chamber, and appointed a set time for the embraces of his queen. He could not punish a single person except in accordance with the code; the judges took oath before the king that they would disobey the king if he ordered them to do anything contrary to law. The ministry were responsible for the actions of their master, and they guarded their own safety. They made it impossible for him to forfeit that reverence and affection which the ignorant and the religious always entertain for their anointed king. He was adored as a god when living, and when he died he was mourned by the whole nation as if each man had lost a well-beloved child. During seventy-two days the temples were closed; lamentations filled the air; and the people fasted, abstaining from flesh and wine, cooked food, ointments, baths, and the company of their wives. The Army appears to have been severely disciplined. To run twenty miles before breakfast was part of the ordinary drill. The amusements of the soldiers were athletic sports and martial games. Yet they were not merely fighting men. They were also farmers. Each warrior received from the state twelve acres of choice land; these gave him a solid interest in the prosperity of the fatherland and in the maintenance of civil peace.

The most powerful of the three estates was undoubtedly the Church. In the priesthood were included not only the ministers of religion, but also the whole civil service and the liberal professions. Priests were the royal chroniclers and keepers of the records, the engravers of inscriptions, physicians of the sick and embalmers of the dead, lawyers and lawgivers, sculptors and musicians. Most of the skilled labour of the country was under their control. In their hands were the linen manufactories and the quarries between the Cataracts. Even those posts in the Army which required a knowledge of arithmetic and penmanship were supplied by them: every general was attended by young priest scribes, with papyrus rolls in their hands and reed pencils behind their ears. The clergy preserved the monopoly of the arts which they had invented; the whole intellectual life of Egypt was in them. It was they who, with the nilometers, took the measure of the waters, and proclaimed good harvests to the people or bade them prepare for hungry days. It was they who studied the diseases of the country, compiled a pharmacopoeia, and invented the signs which are used in our prescriptions at the present day. It was they who judged the living and the dead, who enacted laws which extended beyond the grave, who issued passports to paradise, or condemned to eternal infamy the memories of men that were no more.

Their power was immense, but it was exercised with justice and discretion: they issued admirable laws, and taught the people to obey them by the example of their own humble, self-denying lives.

Under the tutelage of these pious and enlightened men, the Egyptians became a prosperous and also a highly moral people. The monumental paintings reveal their whole life, but we read in them no brutal or licentious scenes. Their great rivals, the Assyrians, even at a later period, were accustomed to impale and flay alive their prisoners of war. The Egyptians granted honours to those who fought gallantly against them. The penalty for the murder of a slave was death; this law exists without parallel in the dark slavery annals both of ancient and of modern times. The pardoning power in cases of capital offence was a cherished prerogative of royalty with them as with us; and with them, also as with us, when a pregnant woman was condemned to death the execution was postponed until after the birth of the guiltless child. It is a sure criterion of the civilisation of ancient Egypt that the soldiers did not carry arms except on duty, and that the private citizens did not carry them at all. Women were treated with much regard. They were allowed to join their husbands in the sacrifices to the gods; the bodies of man and wife were united in the tomb. When a party was given the guests were received by the host and hostess seated side by side in a large armchair. In the paintings their mutual affection is portrayed. Their fond manners, their gestures of endearment, the caresses which they lavish on their children, form sweet and touching scenes of domestic life.

Crimes could not be compounded, as in so many other ancient lands, by the payment of a fine. The man who witnessed a crime without attempting to prevent it was punished as partaker. The civil laws were administered in such a manner that the poor could have recourse to them as well as the rich. The judges received large salaries that they might be placed above the temptation of bribery, and might never disgrace the image of Truth which they wore round their necks suspended on a golden chain.

But most powerful of all, to preserve the morality of the people by giving a tangible force to public opinion, and by impeaching those sins against society which no legal code can touch, was that sublime police institution the "Trial of the Dead."

When the corpse had been brought back from the embalming house it was encased in a sycamore coffin covered with flowers, placed in a sledge, and drawn by oxen to the sacred lake. The hearse was followed by the relations of the deceased, the men unshorn and casting dust upon their heads, the women beating their breasts and singing mournful hymns. On the banks of the lake sat forty-two judges in the shape of a crescent; a great crowd was assembled; in the water floated a canoe, and within it stood Charon the ferryman, awaiting the sentence of the chief judge. On the other side of the lake lay a sandy plain, and beyond it a range of long, low hills, in which might be discerned the black mouths of the caverns of the dead.

It was in the power of any man to step forward and accuse the departed before the body could be borne across. If the charge was held to be proved, the body was denied burial in the consecrated ground, and the crowd silently dispersed. If a verdict of not guilty was returned, the accuser suffered the penalty of the crime alleged, and the ceremony took its course. The relatives began to sing with praises the biography of the deceased; they sang in what manner he had been brought up from a child till he came to man's estate, how pious he had been towards the gods, how righteous he had been towards men. And if this was true, if the man's life had indeed been good, the crowd joined in chorus, clapping their hands, and sang back in return that he would be received into the glory of the just. Then the coffin was laid in the canoe, the silent ferryman plied his oar, a priest read the service of the dead, and the body was deposited in the cemetery caves. If he was a man of rank he was laid in a chamber of his own, and the sacred artists painted on the walls an illustrated catalogue of his possessions, the principal occupations of his life, and scenes of the society in which he moved. For the priests taught that, since life is short and death is long, man's dwelling-house is but a lodging, and his eternal habitation is the tomb. Thus the family vault of the Egyptian was his picture gallery, and thus the manners and customs of this singular people have, like their bodies, been preserved through long ages by means of religious art.

There are also still existing on the walls of the temples, and in the grotto tombs, grand historical paintings which illuminate the terse chronicles engraved upon the granite. Among these may be remarked one subject in particular which appears to have been a favourite with the artist and the public, for it again and again recurs. The Egyptians, distinguished always by their smooth faces and shaven heads, are pursuing an enemy with long beards and flowing robes, who are surrounded by flocks and herds. The Egyptians here show no mercy; they appear alive with fury and revenge. Sometimes the victor is depicted with a scornful air, his foot placed upon the neck of a prostrate foe; sometimes he is piercing the body through and through with a spear. Certain sandals have also been discovered in which the figure of the same enemy is painted on the inner sole, so that the foot trod upon the portrait when the sandal was put on.

Those bearded men had inflicted on Egypt long years of dreadful disaster and disgrace. They were the Bedouins of the Arabian peninsula, a pastoral race who wandered eternally in a burning land, each tribe or clan within an orbit of its own. When they met they fought, the women uttering savage cries and cursing their husbands if they retreated from the foe. Accustomed to struggle to the death for a handful of withered grass or for a little muddy water at the bottom of a well, what a rich harvest must Egypt have appeared to them! In order to obtain it they were able to suspend all feuds, to take an oath of alliance, and to unite into a single horde. They descended upon their prey and seized it at the first swoop. There does not appear to have been even one great battle, and this can be explained if, as is probable enough, the Egyptians before that invasion had never seen a horse.

The Arab horse, or rather mare, lived in her master's tent and supped from the calabash of milk, and lay down to sleep with the other members of the family. She was the playmate of the children; on her the cruel, the savage Bedouin lavished the one tender feeling of his heart. He treasured up in his mind her pedigree as carefully as his own; he composed songs in honour of his beloved steed--his friend, his companion, his ally. He sang to her of the gazelles which they had hunted down, and of the battles which they had fought together--for the Arab horse was essentially a beast of war. When the signal was given for the charge, when the rider, loudly yelling, couched his spear, she snorted and panted and bounded in the air. With tail raised and spreading to the wind, with neck beautifully arched, mane flapping, red nostrils dilating, and eyes glaring, she rushed like an arrow into the midst of the melee. Though covered with wounds, she would never turn restive or try to escape, but if her master was compelled to take to flight she would carry him till she dropped down dead.

It is quite possible that when the mounted army appeared in the river plain the inhabitants were paralysed with fright, and believed them to be fabulous animals, winged men. Be that as it may, the conquest was speedy and complete; the imperial Memphis was taken, Egypt was enslaved, and the king and his family and court were compelled to seek a new home across the sandy seas.

On the south side of the Nubian desert was the land of Ethiopia, the modern Sudan, which had been conquered by the Egyptians, and which they used as an emporium in their caravan trade with Central Africa and the shores of the Red Sea. But it could be reached only by means of a journey which is not without danger at the present day, and which must have been inexpressibly arduous at a time when the camel had not been introduced.

The Nile, it is true, flows through this desert, and joins Ethiopia to Egypt with a silver chain. But from the time of its leaving the Sudan until it reaches the black granite gate which marks the Egyptian frontier, it is confined within a narrow, crooked, hollow way. Navigation is impossible, for its bed is continually broken up by rocks and the stream is walled in; it cannot overflow its banks. The reign of the Sahara is uninterrupted, undisturbed. On all sides is the desert, the brown, shining desert, the implacable waste. Above is a ball of fire ascending and descending in a steel blue sky; below, a dry and scorching sea which the wind ripples into gloomy waves. The air is a cloud which rains fire, for it is dim with perpetual dust--each molecule a spark. The eye is pained and dazzled; it can find no rest. The ear is startled; it can find no sound. In the soft and yielding sand the footstep perishes unheard; nothing murmurs, nothing rustles, nothing sings. This silence is terrible, for it conveys the idea of death, and all know that in the desert death is not far off. When the elements become active they assume peculiar and portentous forms. If the wind blows hard a strange storm arises; the atmosphere is pervaded by a dull and lurid glare; pillars of sand spring up as if by magic, and whirl round and round in a ghastly and fantastic dance. Then a mountain appearing on the horizon spreads upward in the sky, and a darkness more dark than night falls suddenly upon the earth. To those who gasp with swelled tongues and blackened lips in the last agonies of thirst, the mirage, like a mocking stream, exhibits lakes of transparent water and shady trees. But the wells of this desert are scanty, and the waters found in them are salt.

The fugitives concealed the images of the gods, and taking with them the sacred animals, embarked upon their voyage of suffering and woe. After many weary days they again sighted land; they arrived on the shores of Ethiopia, the country of the blacks. Once more their eyes were refreshed with green pastures; once more they listened to the rustling of the palms, and drank the sweet waters of the Nile. Yet soon they discovered that it was not their own dear river, it was not their own beloved land. In Egypt Nature was a gentle handmaid; here she was a cruel and capricious queen. The sky flashed and bellowed against them; the rain fell in torrents, and battered down the houses of the Ethiopians--wretched huts like hay-ricks, round in body with a cone-shaped roof, built of grass and mud. The lowlands changed beneath the flood, not into meadows of flowers and fields of waving corn, but into a pestilential morass. At the rising of the dog-star came a terrible fly which drove even the wild beasts from the river banks and destroyed all flocks and herds. At that evil season the Egyptian colonists were forced to migrate to the forests of the interior, which were filled with savage tribes. Here were the Troglodytes who lived under ground. An ointment was their only dress; their language resembled the hissing of serpents and the whistling of bats. Every month they indulged in a carouse; every month they opened the veins of their sheep and drank of the warm and gurgling blood as if it had been delicious wine. They made merry when they buried their dead, and, roaring with laughter, cast stones upon the corpse until it was concealed from view. Here were the root-eaters, the twig-eaters and the seed-eaters, who lived entirely on such wretched kinds of food. Here were the elephant-eaters, who, sitting on the tops of trees like birds, watched the roads, and when they had sighted a herd crept after it, and hovered round it till the sleepy hour of noon arrived. Then they selected a victim, stole up to it snake-like from behind, hamstrung the enormous creature with a dexterous cut from a sharp sword, and as it lay helpless on the ground feasted upon morsels of its live and palpitating flesh. Here were the locust-eaters, whose harvest was a passing swarm, for they lit a smoky fire underneath, which made the insects fall like withered leaves; they roasted them, pounded them, and made them into cakes with salt. The fish-eaters dwelt by the coral-line borders of the Red Sea; they lived in wigwams thatched with seaweed, with ribs of whales for the rafters and the walls. The richest men were those who possessed the largest bones. There was no fresh water near the shore where they hunted for their food. At stated times they went in herds like cattle to the distant river-side, and singing to one another discordant songs, lay flat on their bellies and drank till they were gorged.

Such was the land to which the Pharaohs were exiled. In the meantime the Bedouins established a dynasty which ruled a considerable time, and is known as that of the Hyksos or Shepherd Kings.

But those barbarians were not domiciled in Egypt. They could not breathe inside houses, and could not understand how the walls remained upright. The camp was their true fatherland. They lived aloof from the Egyptians; they did not ally themselves with the country gods; they did not teach the people whom they had conquered to regard them as the successors of the Pharaohs. Their art of government began and ended with the collection of a tax. The Shepherd Kings were associated in the minds of the Egyptian fellahin, not with their ancient and revered religion, not with the laws by which they were still governed under their local chiefs, but only with the tribute of corn which was extorted from them every harvest by the whip. The idea of revolution was always present in their minds. Misfortune bestowed upon them the ferocious virtues of the desert, while the vice of cities crept into the Bedouin camp. The invaders became corrupted by luxurious indolence and sensual excess, till at length a descendant of the Pharaohs raised an army in Ethiopia and invaded Egypt. The uprising was general, and the Arabs were driven back into their own harsh and meagre land.

The period which followed the Restoration is the most brilliant in Egyptian history. The expulsion of the Bedouins excited an enthusiasm which could not be contained within the narrow valley of the Nile. Egypt became not only an independent but a conquering power. Her armies overran Asia to the shores of the Euxine and of the Caspian Sea. Her fleets swept over the Indian Ocean to the mud-stained shallows at the Indus mouth. On the monuments we may read the proud annals of those campaigns. We see the Egyptian army, with its companies of archers shooting from the ear like the Englishmen of old; we see their squadrons of light and heavy chariots of war, which skilfully skirmished or heavily charged the dense masses of the foe; we see their remarkable engines for besieging fortified towns, their scaling ladders, their movable towers, and their shield-covered rams. We see the Pharaoh returning in triumph, his car drawn by captive kings, and a long procession of prisoners bearing the productions of their respective lands. The nature and variety of those trophies sufficiently prove how wide and distant the Egyptian conquests must have been, for among the animals that figure in the triumph are the brown bear, the baboon, the Indian elephant, and the giraffe. Among the prisoners are negroes of the Sudan in aprons of bulls' hides, or in wild-beast skins with the tails hanging down behind. They carry ebony, ivory, and gold; their chiefs are adorned with leopard robes and ostrich feathers, as they are at the present day. We see also men from some cold country of the North, with blue eyes and yellow hair, wearing light dresses and long-fingered gloves, while others clothed like Indians are bearing beautiful vases, rich stuffs, and strings of precious stones.

When the kings came back from their campaigns, they built temples of the yellow and rose-tinted sandstone, with obelisks of green granite and long avenues of sphinxes, to commemorate their victories and immortalise their names. They employed prisoners of war to erect these memorials of war; it became the fashion to boast that a great structure had been raised without a single Egyptian being doomed to work. By means of these victories the servitude of the lower classes was mitigated for a time, and the wealth of the upper classes was enormously increased. The conquests it is true, were not permanent; they were merely raids on a large scale. But in very ancient times, when seclusion and suspicion formed the foreign policy of states, and when national intercourse was scarcely known, invasion was often the pioneer of trade. The wealth of Egypt was not derived from military spoil--which soon dissolves, however large it may appear--but from the new markets opened for her linen goods.

It is certain that the riches contained in the country were immense. The house of an Egyptian gentleman was furnished in an elegant and costly style. The cabinets, tables, and chairs were beautifully carved, and were made entirely of foreign woods--of ebony from Ethiopia, of a kind of mahogany from India, of deal from Syria, or of cedar from the heights of Lebanon. The walls and ceilings were painted in gorgeous patterns similar to those which are now woven into carpets. Every sitting room was adorned with a vase of perfumes, a flower-stand, and an altar for unburnt offerings. The house was usually one storey high, but the roof was itself an apartment, sometimes covered, but always open at the sides. There the house-master would ascent in the evening to breathe the cool wind, and to watch the city waking into life when the heat was past. The streets swarmed and hummed with men; the river was covered with gilded gondolas gliding by. And when the sudden night had fallen, lamps flashed and danced below; from the house-yards came sounds of laughter and the tinkling of castanets; from the stream came the wailing music of the boatmen and the soft splashing of the lazy oar.

The Egyptian grandee had also his villa or country house. Its large walled garden was watered by a canal communicating with the Nile. One side of the canal was laid out in a walk shaded by trees--the leafy sycamore, the acacia with its yellow blossoms, and the doum or Theban palm. In the centre of the garden was a vineyard, the branches being trained over trellis-work so as to form a boudoir of green leaves, with clusters of red grapes glowing like pictures on the walls. Beyond the vineyard, at the further end of the garden, stood a summer house or kiosk; in front of it a pond which was covered with the broad leaves and blue flowers of the lotus, and in which waterfowl played. It was also stocked with fish which the owner amused himself by spearing: or sometimes he angled for them as he sat on his camp-stool. Adjoining this garden were the stables and coach-houses, and a large park in which gazelles were preserved for coursing. The Egyptian gentry were ardent lovers of the chase. They killed wild ducks with throw-sticks, made use of decoys, and trained cats to retrieve. They harpooned hippopotami in the Nile; they went out hunting in the desert with lions trained like dogs. They were enthusiastic pigeon fanciers, and had many different breeds of dogs. Their social enjoyments were not unlike our own. Young

114

ladies in Egypt had no croquet, but the gentle sport of archery was known among them. They had also boating parties on the Nile, and water picnics beneath the shady foliage of the Egyptian bean. They gave dinners, to which, as in all civilised countries, the fair sex were invited. The guests arrived for the most part in palanquins, but the young men of fashion drove up to the door in their cabs, and usually arrived rather late. Each guest was received by a cluster of servants, who took off his sandals, gave him water to wash his hands, anointed and perfumed him, presented him with a bouquet, and offered him some raw cabbage to increase his appetite for wine, a glass of which was taken before dinner--the sherry and bitters of antiquity.

The gentlemen wore wigs and false beards, and their hands were loaded with rings. The ladies wore their own hair plaited in a most elaborate manner, the result of many hours between their little bronze mirrors and the skilful fingers of their slaves. Their eyelashes were pencilled with the antimonial powder, their finger-nails tinged with the henna's golden juice--fashions older than the Pyramids which still govern the women of the East.

The guests met in the dining-room, and grace was said before they sat down. They were crowned with garlands of the lotus, the violet, and the rose--the florists of Egypt were afterwards famous in Rome. A band of musicians played during the repast on the harp, the lyre, the flute, and the guitar. Some of the servants carried round glass decanters of wine encircled with flowers, and various dishes upon trays. Others fanned the porous earth-jars which contained the almond-flavoured water of the Nile. Others burnt Arabian incense or flakes of sweet-scented wood to perfume the air. Others changed the garlands of the guests as soon as they began to fade. Between the courses dwarfs and deformed persons skipped about before the company with marvellous antics and contortions; jugglers and gymnasts exhibited many extraordinary feats; girls jumped through hoops, tossed several balls into the air after the manner of the East, and performed dances after the manner of the West. Strange as it may appear, the pirouette was known to the Egyptians three thousand years ago, and stranger still, their ballet-girls danced it in lighter clothing than is worn by those who now grace the operatic boards. At the beginning of the repast a mummy, richly painted and gilded, was carried round by a servant, who showed it to each guest in turn and said, "Look on this, drink and enjoy thyself, for such as it is now, so thou shalt be when thou art dead." So solemn an injunction was not disregarded, and the dinner often ended as might be expected from the manner in which it was begun. The Hogarths of the period have painted the young dandy being carried home by his footman without his wig, while the lady in her own apartment is showing unmistakable signs of the same disorder.

But we must leave these pleasant strolls in the bypaths of history and return to the broad and beaten road. The vast wealth and soft luxury of the New Empire undermined its strength. It became apparent to the Egyptians themselves that the nation was enervated and corrupt, a swollen, pampered body from which all energy and vigour had for ever fled. A certain Pharaoh commanded a curse to be inscribed in one of the temples against the name of Menes, who had first seduced the Egyptians from the wholesome simplicity of early times. Filled with a spirit of prophecy, the king foresaw his country's ruin, which indeed was near at hand, for though he himself was buried in peace, his son and successor was compelled to hide in the marshes from a foreign foe.

To the same cause may be traced the ruin and the fall, not only of Egypt, but of all the powers of the ancient world; of Nineveh and Babylon and Persia; of the Macedonian kingdom and the Western Empire. As soon as those nations became rich they began to decay. If this were the fifth century, and we were writing history in the silent and melancholy streets of Rome, we should probably propound a theory entirely false, yet justified at that time by the universal experience of mankind. We should declare that nations are mortal like the individuals of which they are composed; that wealth is the poison, luxury the disease, which shortens their existence and dooms them to an early death. We should point to the gigantic ruins around--to that vast and mouldering body from which the soul had fled--moralise about Lucullus and his thrushes, recount the enormous sums that had been paid for a dress, a table or a child, and assure our Gothic pupils that national life and health are only to be preserved by contented poverty and simple fare.

But what has been the history of those barbarians? In the Dark Ages there was no luxury in Europe. It was a miserable continent inhabited by robbers, fetishmen, and slaves. Even the Italians of the eleventh century wore clothes of unlined leather, and had no taste except for horses and for shining arms, no pride except that of building strong towers for their lairs. Man and wife grabbled for their supper from the same plate, while a squalid boy stood by them with a torch to light their greasy fingers to their mouths. Then the India trade was opened; the New World was discovered; Europe became rich, luxurious, and enlightened. The sunshine of wealth began first to beam upon the costs of the Mediterranean Sea, and gradually spread towards the North. In the England of Elizabeth it was declared from the pulpit that the introduction of forks would demoralise the people and provoke divine wrath. But in spite of sermons and sumptuary laws, Italian luxuries continued to pour in, and national prosperity continued to increase. At the present day the income of a nation affords a fair criterion of its intellect and also of its strength. It may safely be asserted that the art of war will soon be reduced to a simple question of expenditure and credit, and that the largest purse will be the strongest arm. As for luxury, a small tradesman at the present day is more luxurious than a king in ancient times. It has been wisely and wittily remarked that Augustus Caesar had neither glass panes to his windows nor a shirt to his back, and the luxury of the Roman senators may without exaggeration be compared with that of the West Indian creoles in the eighteenth century. The gentleman and his lady glittered with jewels; the table and sideboard blazed with plate; but the house itself was little better than a barn, and the attendants a crowd of dirty, half-naked slaves who jostled the guests as they performed the service of the table, and sat down in the verandah over the remnants of the soup before they would condescend to go to the kitchen for the fish.

In the modern world we find luxury the harbinger of progress, in the ancient world the omen of decline. But how can this be? Nature does not contradict herself; the laws which govern the movements of society are as regular and unchangeable as those which govern the movements of the stars.

Wealth is in reality as indispensable to mankind for purposes of growth as water to the soil. It is not the fault of the water if its natural circulation is interfered with, if certain portions of the land are drowned while others are left completely dry. Wealth in all countries of the ancient world was artificially confined to a certain class. More than half the area of the Greek and Roman world was shut off by slavery from the fertilising stream. This single fact is sufficient to explain how that old civilisation, in some respects so splendid, was yet so one-sided and incomplete.

But the civilisation of Egypt was less developed still, for that country was enthralled by institutions from which Greece and Rome, happily for them, were free.

116

It has been shown that the instinct for self-preservation, the struggle for bare life against hostile nature, first aroused the mental activity of the Egyptian priests, while the constant attacks of the desert tribes developed the martial energies of the military men. Next, the ambition of power produced an equally good effect. The priests invented, the warriors campaigned; mines were opened, manufactories were founded; a system of foreign commerce was established; sloth was abolished by whip and chain; the lower classes were saddled, the upper classes were spurred; the nation careered gallantly along. Finally, chivalrous ardour, intellectual passion, inspired heart and brain; war was loved for glory's sake; the philosopher sought only to discover, the artist to perfect.

And then there came a race of men who, like those that inherit great estates, had no incentive to continue the work which had been so splendidly begun. In one generation the genius of Egypt slumbered, in the next it died. Its painters and sculptors were no longer possessed of that fruitful faculty with which kindred spirits contemplate each other's works; which not only takes, but gives; which produces from whatever it receives; which embraces to wrestle, and wrestles to embrace; which is sometimes sympathy, sometimes jealousy, sometimes hatred, sometimes love, but which always causes the heart to flutter, and the face to flush, and the mind to swell with the desire to rival and surpass; which is sometimes as the emulative awe with which Michaelangelo surveyed the dome that yet gladdens the eyes of those who sit on the height of fair Fiesole, or who wander afar off in silver Arno's vale; which is sometimes as that rapture of admiring wrath which incited the genius of Byron when his great rival was pouring forth masterpiece on masterpiece with invention more varied, though perhaps less lofty, and with fancy more luxuriant even than his own.

The creative period passed away, and the critical age set in. Instead of working, the artists were content to talk. Their admiration was sterile, yet still it was discerning. But the next period was lower still. It was that of blind worship and indiscriminating awe. The past became sacred, and all that it had produced, good and bad, was reverenced alike. This kind of idolatry invariably springs up in that interval of languor and reaction which succeeds an epoch of production. In the mind-history of every land there is a time when slavish imitation is inculcated as a duty, and novelty regarded as a crime. But in Egypt the arts and sciences were entangled with religion. The result will easily be guessed. Egypt stood still, and theology turned her into stone. Conventionality was admired, then enforced. The development of the mind was arrested; it was forbidden to do any new thing.

In primitive times it is perhaps expedient that rational knowledge should be united with religion. It is only by means of superstition that a rude people can be induced to support, and a robber soldiery to respect, an intellectual class. But after a certain time this alliance must be ended, or harm will surely come. The boy must leave the apartments of the women when he arrives at a certain age. Theology is an excellent nurse, but a bad mistress for grown-up minds. The essence of religion is inertia; the essence of science is change. It is the function of the one to preserve, it is the function of the other to improve. If, as in Egypt, they are firmly chained together, either science will advance, in which case the religion will be altered, or the religion will preserve its purity, and science will congeal.

The religious ideas of the Egyptians became associated with a certain style. It was enacted that the human figure should be drawn always in the same manner, with the same colours, contour, and proportions. Thus the artist was degraded to an artisan, and originality was strangled in its birth.

The physicians were compelled to prescribe for their patients according to the rules set down in the standard works. If they adopted a treatment of their own and the patient did not recover, they were put to death. Thus even in desperate cases heroic remedies could not be tried, and experiment, the first condition of discovery, was disallowed.

A censorship of literature was not required, for literature in the proper sense of the term did not exist. Writing, it is true, was widely spread. Cattle, clothes, and workmen's tools were marked with the owners' names. The walls of the temples were covered and adorned with that beautiful picture character, more like drawing than writing, which cold delight the eyes of those who were unable to penetrate its sense. Hieroglyphics may be found on everything in Egypt, from the colossal statue to the amulet and gem. But the art was practised only by the priests, as the painted history plainly declares. No books are to be seen in the furniture of houses; no female is depicted in the act of reading; the papyrus scroll and pencil never appear except in connection with some official act.

The library at Thebes was much admired. It had a blue ceiling speckled with golden stars. Allegorical pictures of a religious character and portraits of the sacred animals were painted on the walls. Above the door were inscribed these words, "The Balsam of the Soul." Yet this magnificent building contained merely a collection of prayer books and ancient hymns, some astronomical almanacs, some works on religious philosophy, medicine, music, and geometry, and the historical archives, which were probably little else than a register of the names of kings, with the dates of certain inventions and a scanty outline of events.

Even these books, so few in number, were not open to all the members of the learned class. They were the manuals of the various departments or professions, and each profession stood apart; each profession was even sub-divided within itself. In medicine and surgery there were no general practitioners. There were oculists, aurists, dentists, doctors of the head, doctors of the stomach, etc., and each was forbidden to invade the territory of his colleagues. This specialist arrangement has been highly praised, but it has nothing in common with that which has arisen in modern times.

It is one of the first axioms of medical science that no one is competent to treat the disease of a single organ unless he is competent to treat the diseases of the whole frame. The folly of dividing the diseases of such organs as the head and stomach, between which the most intimate sympathy exists, is evident even to the unlearned. But the whole structure is united by delicate white threads, and by innumerable pipes of blood. It is scarcely possible for any complaint to influence one part alone. The Egyptian, however, was marked off like a chess board into little squares, and whenever the pain made a move a fresh doctor had to be called in.

This arrangement was part of a system founded on an excellent principle, but carried to absurd excess. It is needless to explain that division of labour is highly potent in developing skill and economising time. It is also clearly of advantage that in an early stage of society the son should follow the occupation of the father. It is possible that hereditary skill or tastes come into play; it is certain that apprenticeship at home is more natural and more efficient than apprenticeship abroad. The father will take more pains to teach, the boy will take more pains to learn, than will be the case when master and pupil are strangers to each other.

The founders of Egyptian civilisation were acquainted with these facts. Hence they established customs which their successors petrified into unchanging laws. They did it no doubt with the best of motives. They adored the grand and noble wisdom of their fathers; whatever came from them must be cherished and preserved. They must not presume to depart from the guidance of those god-like men. They must paint as they painted, physic as they physicked, pray as they prayed. The separation of classes which they had made must be rendered rigid and eternal.

And so the arts and sciences were ordered to stand still, and society was divided and sub-divided into functions and professions, trades and crafts. Every man was doomed to follow the occupation of his father, to marry within his own class, to die as he was born. Hope was torn out of the human life. Egypt was no longer a nation, but an assemblage of torpid castes isolated from one another and breeding in and in. It was no longer a body animated by the same heart, fed by the same blood, but an automaton neatly pieced together, of which the head was the priesthood, the arms were the army, and the feet the working-class. In quiescence it was a perfect image of the living form, but a touch came from without, and the arms broke asunder at the joints and fell upon the ground.

The colony founded in the Sudan by the exiled Pharaohs became after the restoration an important province. When the new empire began to decline a governor-general rebelled, and the kingdom of Ethiopia was established. It was a medley dominion composed of brown men and black men, shepherds and savages, half-caste Egyptians, Arabs, Berbers, and negroes, ruled over by a king and a college of priests. It was enriched by annual slave hunts into the Black Country, and by the caravan trade in ivory, gold dust, and gum. It also received East India goods and Arabian produce through its ports on the Red Sea. Meroe, its capital, attained the reputation of a great city; it possessed its temples and its pyramids like those of Egypt, but on a smaller scale. The Ethiopian empire in its best days might have comprised the modern Egyptian provinces of Kordofan and Sennaar, with the mountain kingdom of Abyssinia as it existed under Theodore. Of all the classical countries it was the most romantic and the most remote. It was situated, according to the Greeks, on the extreme limits of the world; its inhabitants were the most just of men, and Jupiter dined with them twice a year. They bathed in the waters of a violet-scented spring which endowed them with long life, noble bodies, and glossy skins. They chained their prisoners with golden fetters; they had bows which none but themselves could bend. It is at least certain that Ethiopia took its place among the powers of the ancient world. It is mentioned in the Jewish records and in the Assyrian cuneiform inscriptions.

So far had Egypt fallen that now it was conquered by its ancient province. Sabaco of Ethiopia seized the throne and sat upon it many years. But he was frightened by a dream; he believed that a misfortune impended over him in Egypt. He abdicated in haste and fled back to his native land.

His departure was followed by uproar and confusion, a complete disruption of Egyptian society, usurpation, and civil war.

But why should this have been? Sabaco was an Egyptian by descent, though his blood had been darkened on the female side. He had governed in the Egyptian manner. He had abolished capital punishment, but in no other way had altered the ancient laws. He had improved the public works. He had taken the country rather as a native usurper than as a foreign foe. His reign was merely a change of dynasty, and Egyptian history is numbered by dynasties as English history is numbered by kings.

But indirectly the Ethiopian conquest had prepared a revolution. Between the two services, the Army and the Church, there had existed a constant and perhaps wholesome rivalry since the days of Menes, the first king. It was a victory of the warrior class which established the regal power. It was a victory of the priests which assigned to themselves the right hand, to the officers the left hand, of the sovereign when seated on his throne. It was an evident compromise between the two that the king should be elected from the army, and that he should be ordained as soon as he was crowned. During the brilliant campaigns of the Restoration the military had been in power, but a long period of inaction had intervened since then. The discipline of the soldiers was relaxed; their dignity was lowered; they no longer tilled their own land--that was done by foreign slaves. Their rivals possessed the affection and reverence of the common people, while these soldiers, who had never seen a battle, were detested as idle drones who lived upon what they had not earned. Under the new dynasty their position became insecure. In Ethiopia there was no military caste. The army of Sabaco had been levied from the pastoral tribes on the outskirts of the desert, from the Abyssinian mountaineers and the negroes of the river plain. The king of Ethiopia was a priest, elected by his peers. He therefore regarded the soldier aristocracy with no friendly eye. He did not formally invade their prescriptive rights, but he must have disarmed them or in some way have taken out their sting. For as soon as he was gone the priests were able to form an alliance with the people, and to place one of their own caste upon the throne. This king deprived the soldiers of their lands, and the triumph of the hierarchy was complete.

But in such a country as Egypt Disestablishment is a dangerous thing. During long centuries the people had been taught to associate innovation with impiety. That venerable structure the Egyptian constitution had been raised by no human hands. As the gods had appointed certain animals to swim in the water, and others to fly in the air, and others to move upon the earth, so they had decreed that one man should be a priest, and that another should be a soldier, and that another should till the ground. There are times when every man feels discontented with his lot. But it is evident that if men were able to change their occupation whenever they chose, there would be a continual passing to and fro. Nobody would have patience to learn a trade; nobody would settle down in life. In a short time the land would become a desert, and society would be dissolved. To provide against this the gods had ordained that each man should do his duty in that state of life into which he had been called, and woe be to him that disobeys the gods! Their laws are eternal and can never change. Their vengeance is speedy and can never fail.

Such, no doubt, was the teaching of the Egyptian Church, and now the Church had shown it to be false. The revolution had been begun, and, as usually happens, it could not be made to stop half way. As soon as the first precedent was unloosed, down came the whole fabric with a crash. The priest-king Sethos reigned in peace, but as soon as he died the central government succumbed; the old local interests which had been lying dormant for ages raised their heads; the empire broke up into twelve states, each governed by a petty king.

We now approach the event which first brought Egypt into contact with the European world. Psammiticus, one of the twelve princes, received as his allotment the swampy district which adjoined the sea-coast and the mouths of the Nile. His fortune, as we shall see, was made by this position.

120

The commerce of Egypt had hitherto been conducted entirely by means of caravans. From Arabia Felix came a long train of camels laden with the gums of that aromatic land, and with the more precious produce of countries far beyond--with the pearls of the Persian Gulf and the carpets of Babylon, the pepper and ginger of Malagar, the shawls of Kashmir, the cinnamon of Ceylon, the fine muslins of Bengal, the calicoes of Coromandel, the nutmegs and camphor and cloves of the Indian Archipelago, and even silk and musk from the distant Chinese shores. From Syria came other caravans with the balm of Gilead, so precious in medicine, asphalt from the Dead Sea for embalming, cedar from Lebanon, and enormous quantities of wine and olive oil in earthen jars. Meroe contributed the spices of the Somali country, ebony, ivory, ostrich feathers, slaves, and gold in twisted rings; the four latter products were also imported direct from Darfour, and by another route which connected Egypt through Fezzan with Carthage, Morocco, and the regions beyond the desert in the neighbourhood of Timbuktu. In return, the beautiful glass wares of the Egyptians and other artistic manufactures were exported to Hindustan; the linen goods of Memphis were carried into the very heart of Africa as Manchester goods are now; and then, as now, a girdle of beads was the essential part of an African young lady's dress.

On the side of the Mediterranean Egypt was a closed land, and this Chinese policy had not been adopted from superstitious motives. The first ships which sailed that sea were pirates who had kidnapped and plundered the dwellers on the coast. The government had therefore in self-defence placed a garrison at Rhacotis harbour, with orders to kill or enslave any stranger who should land. When the Phoenicians from pirates had become merchants they were allowed to trade with Egypt by way of the land, and with this they were content. It was left for another people to open up the trade by sea.

Ionia was the fairest province of Asiatic Greece. It lay opposite to Athens, its motherland. The same soft blue waters, the same fragrant breezes caressed their shores by turn. It was celebrated by the poets as one of the gardens of the world. There the black soil granted a rich harvest and the fruit hung heavily on the branches. It was the birth-place of poetry, of history, of philosophy, and of art. It was there that the Homeric poems were composed. It was there that men first cast off the chains of authority and sought in Nature the materials of a creed.

It was, however, as a seafaring and commercial people that the Ionians first obtained renown. They served on board Phoenician vessels and laboured in the dockyards of Tyre and Sidon until they learnt how to build the "sea-horses" for themselves, and how to navigate by that small but constant star which the Tyrians had discovered in the constellation of the Little Bear. They took to the sea on their own account, and in Egypt they found a good market. The wine and oil of Palestine, which the Phoenicians imported, were expensive luxuries; the lower classes drank only the fermented sap of the palm-tree and barley beer, and had only castor oil, with which they rubbed their bodies, but with which, for obvious reasons, they could not cook their food. The Ionians were able to sell red wine and sweet oil at a much lower price, for in the first place they had vineyards and olive groves of their own, and secondly such bulky wares could be brought by sea more cheaply than by land.

The Greeks first appeared on the Egyptian coast as pirates clad in bronze, next as smugglers, welcomed by the people, but in opposition to the laws, and lastly as allies and honoured friends. They took advantage of the confusion which followed the departure of Sabaco to push up the Nile with thirty vessels, each of fifty oars, and established factories upon its banks. They negotiated with Psammiticus, who ascertained that their country produced not only oil but men. He ordered a cargo, and transports arrived with troops. Europeans for the first time entered the valley of the Nile. Their gallantry and discipline were irresistible, and the empire of the Pharaohs was restored. But now commenced a new regime. There succeeded to the throne a series of kings who were not related to the ancient Pharaohs, who were not always men of noble birth, who were not even good Egyptians. They were called Phil-Hellenes, or Lovers of the Greeks. Of these Psammiticus was the founder and the first. He moved Egypt towards the sea. He placed his capital near the mouth of the river, that the Greek ships might anchor beneath its walls. This new city of Sais, being distant from the quarries, was built of bricks from the black mud of the Nile, but it was adorned with spoils from the forsaken Memphis. Chapels, obelisks, and sphinxes were brought down on rafts. There was also a kind of Renaissance under the new kings; for a short time the arts again became alive. Psammiticus retained the soldiers who had fought his battles, and sent children to the camp to be taught Greek. Hence rose a class who acted as brokers, interpreters, and ciceroni to the travellers who soon crowded into Egypt. The king encouraged such visits, and gave safe-conducts to those who desired to pass into the interior.

All this was a cause of deep offence to the people of the land. They regarded their country as a temple, and all strangers as impure. And now they saw men whose swords had been reddened with Egyptian blood swaggering as conquerors through the streets, pointing with derision at the sacred animals, eating things strangled and unclean. The warriors were those who suffered most. As a caste they still survived, but all their power and prestige were gone. In battle the foreigners were assigned the post of honour--the right wing. In times of peace the foreigners were the favourite regiments--the household troops, the Guards. While the royals lived merrily at Sais crowned with garlands of the papyrus, and revelling at banquets to the music of the flute, the native troops were stationed on the hot and dismal frontiers of the desert; year followed year, and they were not relieved. Such a state of things was no longer to be borne. One king had robbed them of their lands, and now another had robbed them of their honour. They were no longer soldiers, they were slaves; they determined to leave the country in which they were despised, and to seek a better fortune in the Sudan. In number two hundred thousand, they gathered themselves together and began their march.

They were soon overtaken by envoys from the king, who had no desire to lose an army. The soldiers were entreated to return and not to desert their fatherland. They cried out, beating their shields and shaking their spears, that they would soon get another fatherland. Then the messengers began to speak of their wives and little ones at home. Would they leave them also, and go wifeless and childless to a savage land? But one of the soldiers explained, with a coarse gesture, that they had the means of producing families wherever they might go. This ended the conference. Psammiticus pursued them with his Ionians, but could not overtake them. In the wastes of Nubia there may yet be seen a colossal statue, on the right leg of which is an inscription in Greek announcing that it was there they gave up the chase. The Egyptian soldiers arrived at Meroe in safety; the king presented them with a province which had rebelled. They drove out the men, married the women, and did much to civilise the native tribes. In the meantime Psammiticus and his successors opened wider and wider the gloomy portals of the land. The town of Naucratis was set apart, like Canton, for the foreign trade. Nine independent Greek cities had their separate establishments within that town, and their magistrates and consuls, who administered their respective laws. The merchants met in the Hellenion, which was half temple, half exchange, to transact their business and offer sacrifices to the gods. Naucratis was in all respects a European town. There the garlic-chewing sailors, when they came on shore, could enjoy a holiday in the true Greek style. They could stroll in the market-place, where the money-changers sat before their tables and the wine merchants ran about with sample flasks under their arms, and where garlands of flowers, strange-looking fish, and heaps of purple dates were set out for sale. They could resort to the barbers' shops and gather the gossip of the day, or to taverns where quail fighting was always going on. Nor were the chief ornaments of sea-port society wanting to grace the scene. No Egyptian girl, as Herodotus discovered, would kiss a Greek. But certain benevolent and enterprising men had imported a number of Heterae or "lady-friends," the most famous of whom was Rhodopis, "the rosy-faced," with whom Sappho's brother fell in love, and whom the poetess lampooned.

The foreign policy of Egypt was now completely changed. A long period of seclusion had followed the conquests of the new empire. But the battle-pieces of the ancient time still glowed upon the temple walls. With their vivid colours and animated scenes they seemed to incite the modern Pharaohs to heroic deeds. The throne was surrounded by warlike and restless men. It was determined that Egypt should become a naval power. For this, timber was indispensable, and the forests of Lebanon must be seized. War was carried to the continent. Syria was reduced. A garrison was planted on the banks of the Euphrates. A navy was erected in the Mediterranean Sea, and the Tyrians were defeated in a great sea-battle. The Suez Canal was opened for the first time, and an exploring expedition circumnavigated Africa.

Yet, for all that and all that, the Egyptian people were not content. The victories won by mercenary troops excited little patriotic pride, and the least reverse occasioned the most gloomy forebodings, the most serious discontent. The Egyptians indeed had good cause to be alarmed--the Phil-Hellenes were playing at a dangerous game. Times had changed since Sesostris overran Asia. A great power had arisen on the banks of the Tigris; a greater power still on the banks of the Euphrates. They had narrowly escaped Sennacherib when Nineveh was in its glory, and now Babylon had arisen and Nebuchadnezzar had drawn the sword. For a long time Chaldea and Egypt fought over Syria, their battle-ground and their prey. At last came the decisive day of Carchemish. The Phoenicians, the Syrians, and the Jews obtained new masters; the Egyptians were driven out of Asia.

Yet even then the kings were not cured of their taste for war. An expedition was sent against Cyrene, a Greek kingdom on the northern coast of Africa. It was unsuccessful, and the sullen disaffection which had so long smouldered burst forth into flame. The king was killed, and Amasis, a man of the people, was placed upon the throne.

This monarch did not go to war, and he contrived to favour the Greeks without offending the prejudices of his fellow-countrymen. He was, however, a true Phil-Hellene; he encircled himself with a bodyguard of Greeks; he married a princess of Cyrene; he gave a handsome subscription to the fund for rebuilding the temple at Delphi; he extended the commerce of Egypt and improved its manufactures. The liberal policy in trade which he pursued had the most satisfactory results. Never had Egypt been so rich as she was then. But she was defenceless; she had lost her arms. It is probable that under Amasis she was a vassal of Babylon, paying tribute every year; and now a time was coming when gold could no longer purchase repose, when the horrified people would see their temples stripped, their idols dashed to pieces, their sacred animals murdered, their priests scourged, and the embalmed body of their king snatched from its last resting-place and flung upon the flames.

A vast wilderness extends from the centre of Africa to the jungles of Bengal. It consists of rugged mountain and of sandy wastes; it is traversed by three river basins or valley plains.

In its centre is the basin of the Tigris and Euphrates. On its east is the basin of the Indus; on its west is the basin of the Nile. Each of these river systems is enclosed by deserts. The whole region may be pictured to the mind as a broad yellow field with three green streaks running north and south.

Egypt, Babylonia, and India proper, or the Punjab, are the primeval countries of the ancient world. In these three desert-bound, river-watered valleys we find, in the earliest dawn of history, civilisation growing wild. Each in a similar manner had been fostered and tortured by Nature into progress; in each existed a people skilled in the management of land, acquainted with manufactures, and possessing some knowledge of practical science and of art. The civilisation of India was the youngest of the three, yet Egypt and Chaldea were commercially its vassals and dependents. India offered for sale articles not elsewhere to be found--the shining warts of the oyster; glass-like stones dug up out of the bowels of the earth, or gathered in the beds of dried-up brooks; linen which was plucked as a blossom from a tree, and manufactured into cloth as white as snow; transparent fabrics, webs of woven wind which when laid on the dewy grass melted from the eyes; above all, those glistening, glossy threads stolen from the body of a caterpillar, beautiful as the wings of the moth into which that caterpillar is afterwards transformed.

Neither the Indians, the Chaldeans, nor the Egyptians were in the habit of travelling beyond the confines of their own valleys. They resembled islanders, and they had no ships. But the intermediate seas were navigated by the wandering shepherd tribes, who sometimes pastured their flocks by the waters of the Indus, sometimes by the waters of the Nile. It was by their means that the trade between the river lands was carried on. They possessed the camels and other beasts of burden requisite for the transport of goods. Their numbers and their warlike habits, their intimate acquaintance with the watering-places and seasons of the desert, enabled them to carry the goods in safety through a dangerous land, while the regular profits they derived from the trade, and the oaths by which they were bound, induced them to act fairly to those by whom they were employed. At a later period the Chinese, who were once a great naval people, and who claim the discovery of the New World, doubled Cape Comorin in their huge junks, and sailed up the western coasts of India into the Persian Gulf, and along the coast of Arabia to the mouth of the Red Sea. It as probably from them that the arts of shipbuilding and navigation were acquired by the Arabs of Yemen and the Indians of Guzerat, who then made it their business to supply Babylon and Egypt and Eastern Africa with India goods. At a later period still these India goods were carried by the Phoenicians to the coasts of Europe, and acorn-eating savages were awakened to industry and ambition. India, as a "land of desire," has contributed much to the development of man. On the routes of the India caravan, as on the banks of navigable rivers, arose great and wealthy cities, which perished when the route was changed. Open the book of universal history at what period we may, it is always the India trade which is the cause of internal industry and foreign negotiation.

The intercourse between the Indians, Chaldeans, and Egyptians was often interrupted by wars, which recurred like epidemics, and which like epidemics closely resembled one another. The roving tribes of the sandy deserts, the pastoral mountains, or the elevated steppe-plateaux pressed by some mysterious impulse--a famine, an enemy in their rear, or the ambition of a single man--swept down upon the plains of the Tigris and Euphrates, and thence spread their conquests right and left. Sometimes they merely encamped, and the natives recovered their independence. But more frequently they adopted the manners of the conquered people, and flung themselves into luxury with the same ardour which they had displayed in war. This luxury was not based on refinement but on sensuality, and it soon made them indolent and weak. Sooner or later they suffered the fate which their fathers had inflicted, and a new race of invaders poured over the empire, to be supplanted in their turn when their time was come.

Invasions of this nature were on the whole beneficial to the human race. The mingling of a young, powerful people with the wise but somewhat weary nations of the plains produced an excellent effect. And since the conquerors adopted the luxury of the conquered, they were obliged to adopt the same measure for supplying the foreign goods--for luxury means always something from abroad. As soon as the first shock was over the trade routes were again opened, and perhaps extended, by the brand-new energies of the barbarian kings.

Western Asia

Babylonia or Chaldea, the alluvial country which occupies the lower course of the Euphrates, was undoubtedly the original abode of civilisation in Western Asia. But it was on the banks of the Tigris that the first great empire arose--the first at least of which we know. For who can tell how many cities, undreamt of by historians, lie buried beneath the Assyrian plains? And Nineveh itself may have been built from some dead metropolis, as Babylon bricks were used in the building of Baghdad. Recorded history is a thing of yesterday--the narrative of modern man. There is, however, a science of history; by this we are enabled to restore in faint outline the unwritten past, and by this we are assured that whatever the names and number of the forgotten empires may have been, they merely repeated one another. In describing the empire of Nineveh we describe them all.

The Assyrian empire covered a great deal of ground. The kingdom of Troy was one of its fiefs. Its rule was sometimes extended to the islands of the Grecian sea. Babylon was its subject. It stretched far away into Asia. But the conquered provinces were loosely governed, or rather no attempt was made to govern them at all. Phoenicia was allowed to remain a federation of republics. Israel, Judah, and Damascus were allowed to continue their angry bickerings and petty wars. The relations between the conquered rulers and their subjects were left untouched. Their laws, their manners, and their religion were in no way changed. It was merely required that the vassal kings or senates should acknowledge the Emperor of Nineveh as their suzerain or lord, that they should send him a certain tribute every year, and that they should furnish a certain contingent of troops when he went to war.

As long as a vigorous and dreaded king sat upon the throne this simple machinery worked well enough. Every year the tributes, with certain forms of homage and with complimentary presents of curiosities and artisans, were brought to the metropolis. But whenever an imperial calamity of any kind occurred--an unsuccessful foreign war, the death or even sickness of the reigning prince--the tributes were withheld. Then the emperor set to work to subdue the provinces again. But this time the conquered were treated not as enemies only but as traitors. The vassal king and his advisers were tortured to death, the cities were razed to the ground, and the rebels were transplanted by thousands to another land--an effectual method of destroying their patriotism or religion of the soil. The Syrian expeditions of Sennacherib were provoked by the contumacy of Judah and of Israel. The kingdom of Israel was blotted out, but a camp plague broke up the Assyrian army before Jerusalem, and not long afterwards the empire crumbled away. All the vassal nations became free, and for a short time Nineveh stood alone, naked but unattacked. Then there was war in every direction, and when it was over the city was a heap of charred ruins, and three great kingdoms took its place.

The first kingdom was that of the Medes, who had set the example of rebellion, and by whom Nineveh had been destroyed. They inhabited the highland regions bordering on the Tigris, Ecbatana was their capital. They were renowned for their luxury, and especially for their robes of flowing silk. Their priests were called Magi, and formed a separate tribe or caste; they were dressed in white, lived only on vegetables, slept on beds of leaves, worshipped the sun and the element of fire, as symbols of the deity, and followed the precepts of Zoroaster. The empire of the Medes was bounded on the west by the Tigris. They inherited the Assyrian provinces in Central Asia, the boundaries of which are not precisely known.

The civilisation of Nineveh had been derived from Babylon, a city famous for its rings and gems, which were beautifully engraved, its carpets in which the figures of fabulous animals were interwoven, its magnifying glasses, its sun-dials, and its literature printed in cuneiform characters on clay tablets, which were then baked in the oven. Many hundreds of these have lately been deciphered, and are found to consist chiefly of military dispatches, law papers, royal game-books, observatory reports, agricultural treatises, and religious documents. In the partition of Assyria Babylon obtained Mesopotamia, or "the Land between the Rivers," and Syria, including Phoenicia and Palestine. Nebuchadnezzar was the founder of the Empire; he routed the Egyptians, he destroyed Jerusalem, transplanted the Jews on account of their rebellion, and reduced Tyre after a memorable siege. He built a new Babylon as Augustus built a new Rome, and the city became one of the wonders of the world. It was a vast fortified district, five or six times the area of London, interspersed with parks and gardens and fields, and enclosed by walls on which six chariots could be driven side by side. Its position in a flat country made it resemble in the distance a mountain with trees waving at the top. These were the "hanging gardens," a grove of large trees planted on the square surface of a gigantic tower, and ingeniously watered from below. Nebuchadnezzar erected this extraordinary structure to please his wife, who came from the highlands of Media, and who, weary of the interminable plains, coveted meadows on mountain tops such as her native land contained. The Euphrates ran through the centre of the city, and was crossed by a stone bridge which was a marvel for its time. But more wonderful still, there was a kind of Thames Tunnel passing underneath the river, and connecting palaces on either side. The city was united to its provinces by roads and fortified posts; rafts inflated with skins, and reed boats pitched over with bitumen, floated down the river with timber from the mountains of Armenia and stones for the purposes of building. A canal large enough for ships to ascend was dug from Babylon to the Persian Gulf, and on its banks were innumerable machines for raising the water and spreading it upon the soil.

The third kingdom was that of the Lydians, a people in manners and appearance resembling the Greeks. They did not consider themselves behind the rest of the world. They boasted that they had invented dice, coin, and the art of shop-keeping, and also that the famous Etruscan state was a colony of theirs. They inhabited Asia Minor, a sterile, rugged tableland, but possessing a western coast enriched by nature and covered with the prosperous cities of the Asiatic Greeks. Hitherto Ionia had never been subdued, but the cities were too jealous of one another to combine, and Croesus was able to conquer them one by one. This was the man whose wealth is still celebrated in a proverb--he obtained his gold from the washings of a sandy stream. Croesus admired the Greeks; he was the first of the lion-hunters, and invited all the men of the day to visit him at Sardis, where he had the pleasure of hearing Aesop tell some of his own fables. He was anxious that his capital should form part of the grand tour which had already become the fashion of the Greek philosophers, and that they should be able to say when they returned home that they had not only seen the pyramids of Egypt and the ruins of Troy, but also the treasure-house of Croesus. When he received a visit from one of these sages in cloak and beard he would show him his heaps of gold and silver, and ask him whether, in all his travels, he had ever seen a happier man--to which question he did not always receive a very courteous reply.

After long wars, peace was established between the Babylonians, the Lydians, and the Medes on a lasting and secure foundation. The royal families were united by marriage; alliances, defensive and offensive, were made and ratified on oath. Egypt was no longer able to invade, and there was a period of delicious calm in that stormy Asiatic world, broken only by the plaintive voices of the poor Jewish captives who sat by the waters of Babylon and sang of the Holy City that was no more.

In the twinkling of an eye all this was changed. A band of hardy mountaineers rushed out of the recesses of Persia and swept like a wind across the plains. They were dressed in leather from top to toe; they had never tasted fruit or wine; they had never seen a market; they knew not how to buy or sell. They were taught only three things--to ride on horseback, to hurl the javelin, and to speak the truth.

The Persians

All Asia was covered with blood and flames. The allied kingdoms fell at once. India and Egypt were soon afterwards added to this empire, the greatest that the world had ever seen. The Persians used to boast that they ruled from the land of uninhabitable heat to the land of uninhabitable cold; that their dominion began in regions where the sun frizzled the hair and blackened the faces of the natives, and ended in a land where the air was filled with snow like feathers and the earth was hard as stone. The Persian empire was in reality bounded by the deserts which divided Egypt from Ethiopia on the south and from Carthage on the west; by the desert which divided the Punjab from Bengal; by the steppes which lay on the other side of the Jaxartes; by the Mediterranean, the Caspian, and the Black Sea.

Darius, the third emperor, invented a system of provincial government which, though imperfect when viewed by the wisdom of modern times, was far superior to any that had preceded it in Asia. He appointed satraps or pashas to administer the conquered provinces. Each of these viceroys received with his commission a map of his province engraved on brass. He was at once the civil governor and commander of the troops, but his power was checked and supervised by a secretary or clerk of the accounts, and the province was visited by royal commissioners once a year. The troops in each province were of two kinds; some garrisoned the cities; others, for the most part cavalry, lived, like the Roman legions, always in a camp; it was their office to keep down brigands, and to convey the royal treasure from place to place. The troops were subsisted by the conquered people; this formed part of the tribute, and was collected at the point of the sword. There was also a fixed tax in money and in kind, which was received by the clerk of the accounts and dispatched to the capital every year. The Great King still preserved in his habits something of the nomad chief. He wintered at Babylon, but in the summer the heat was terrible in that region; the citizens retired to their cellars, and the king went to Susa, which was situated on the hills, or to Ecbatana, the ancient capital of the Medes, or to Persepolis, the true hearth and home of the Persian race. When he approached one of these cities the magi came forth to meet him, dressed all in white and singing hymns. The road was strewn with myrtle boughs and roses, and silver altars with blazing frankincense were placed by the wayside.

His palaces were built of precious woods, but the naked wood was never permitted to be seen: the walls were covered with golden plates, the roof with silver tiles. The courts were adorned with white, green, and blue hangings, fastened with cords of fine linen to pillars of marble by silver rings. The gardens were filled with rare and exotic plants; from the cold bosom of the snow-white stone fountains sprang upwards, sparkling in the air; birds of gorgeous plumage flashed from tree to tree, resembling flowers where they perched. And as the sun sank low in the heavens and the shadows on the earth grew deep, the voice of the nightingale was heard in the thicket, and the low cooing of the dove. Sounds of laughter proceeded from the house; lattices were opened; ponderous doors swung back, and out poured a troop of houris which a Persian poet alone would venture to describe. For there might be seen the fair Circassian, with cheeks like the apple in its rosy bloom; and the Abyssinian damsel, with warm brown skin and voluptuous drowsy eyes; the Hindu girl, with lithe and undulating form and fingers which seemed created to caress; the Syrian, with aquiline and haughty look; the Greek with features brightened by intellect and vivacity; and the home-born beauty prepared expressly for the harem, with a complexion as white as the milk on which she had been fed, and a face in form and expression resembling the full moon.

All these dear charmers belonged to the king, and no doubt he often wished half of them away. For if he felt a serious passion rising in his breast, etiquette compelled him to put it down. Inconstancy was enjoined on him by law. He was subjected to a rotation of kisses by the regulated science of the harem. Ceremony interdicted affection and caprice. He suffered from unvarying variety and the monotony of eternal change. The whole empire belonged to him, and all its inhabitants were his slaves. If he happened to be struck to the heart by a look cast from under a pair of black-edged eyelids, if he became enamoured of a high-bosomed virgin, with a form like the oriental willow, he had only to say the word; she was at once taken to the apartments of the women, and her parents received the congratulations of their friends. But then he was not allowed to see his beloved for a twelve-month: six months she must be prepared with the oil of myrrh, six months with the sweet odours, before she was sufficiently purified and perfumed to receive the august embraces of the king, and to soothe a passion which meanwhile had ample time to cool.

The Great King slept on a splendid couch, overspread by a vine of branching gold, with clusters of rubies representing grapes. He wore a dress of purple and white, with scarlet trousers, a girdle like that of a woman, and a high tiara encircled by a sky-blue turban. He lived in a prison of rich metal and dazzling stone. Around him stood the courtiers with their hands wrapped in their robes, and covering their mouths lest he should be polluted by their base-born breath. Those who desired to speak to his majesty prostrated themselves before him on the ground. If any one entered uncalled, a hundred sabres gleamed in the air, and unless the king stretched out his sceptre the intruder would be killed.

An army sat down to dinner in the palace every day, and every day a herd of oxen was killed for them to eat. These were only the household troops. But when the Great King went to war, the provinces sent in their contingents, and then might be seen, as in some great exhibition, a collection of warriors from the four quarters of the earth. Then might be seen the Immortals, or Persian life-guards; their arms were of gold and silver, their standards were of silk. Then might be seen the heavy-armed Egyptian troops, with long wooden shields reaching to the ground; the Greeks from Ionia, with crested helmets and breastplates of bronze; the fur-clad Tartars of the steppes, who "raised hair" like the Red Indians, a people probably belonging to the same race; the Ethiopians of Africa, with fleecy locks, clad in the skins of lions and armed with throw-sticks and with stakes, the points of which had been hardened in the fire, or tipped with horn or stone; the Berbers in their four-horse chariots; the camel cavalry of Arabia, each camel being mounted by two archers sitting back to back, and thus prepared for the enemy on either side; the wild horsemen of the Persian hills who caught the enemy with their lassos; the black-skinned but straight-haired aborigines of India, with their bows of the bamboo and their shields made of the skins of cranes; and above all the Hindus, dressed in white muslin and seated on the necks of elephants, which were clothed in Indian steel and which looked like moving mountains with snakes for hands. Towers were erected on their backs, in which sat bowmen, who shot down the foe with unerring aim, while the elephants were taught to charge, to trample down the opposing ranks in heaps, and to take up armed men in their trunks and hand them to their riders. Sometimes huge scythes were fastened to their trunks, and they mowed down regiments as they marched along. The army was also attended by packs of enormous blood-hounds to hunt the fugitives when a victory had been gained, and by falcons which were trained to fly at the eyes of the enemy to baffle them, or even blind them as they were fighting.

When this enormous army began to march it devoured the whole land over which it passed. At night the camp-fires reddened the sky as if a great city was in flames. In the morning, a little after daybreak, a trumpet sounded, and the image of the sun, cased in crystal and made of burnished gold, was raised on the top of the king's pavilion, which was built of wood, covered with cashmere shawls, and supported on silver poles. As soon as the ball caught the first rays of the rising sun the march began. First went the chariot with the altar and the sacred fire, drawn by eight milk-white horses driven by charioteers, who walked by the side with golden wands. The chariot was followed by a horse of extraordinary magnitude, which was called the "Charger of the Sun." The king followed with the ten thousand Immortals, and with his wives in covered carriages drawn by mules, or in cages upon camels. Then came the army without order or precision, and there rose a dust which resembled a white cloud, and which could be seen across the plain for miles. The enemy, when this cloud drew near, could distinguish within it the gleaming of brazen armour, and they could hear the sound of the lash, which was always part of the military music of the Persians. When a battle was fought, the king took his seat on a golden throne, surrounded by his secretaries, who took notes during the engagement and recorded every word which fell from the royal lips.

This army was frequently required by the Persians. They were a restless people, always lusting after war. Vast as their empire was, it was not large enough for them. The courtiers used to assure an enterprising monarch that he was greater than all the kings that were dead, and greater than those that were yet unborn; that it was his mission to extend the Persian territory as far as God's heaven reached, in order that the sun might shine on no land beyond their borders. Hyperbole apart, it was the aim and desire of the kings to annex the plains of Southern Russia, and so to make the Black Sea a lake in the interior of Persia; and to conquer Greece, the only land in Europe which really merited their arms. In both these attempts they completely failed. The Russian Tartars, who had no fixed abode and whose houses were on wheels, decoyed the Persian army far into the interior, eluded it in pursuit, harassed and almost destroyed it in retreat. The Greeks defeated them in pitched battles on Greek soil, and defeated their fleets in Greek waters.

This contest, which lasted many years, to the Greeks was a matter of life and death, but it was merely an episode in Persian history. The defeats of Plataea and Salamis caused the Great King much annoyance, and cost him a shred of land and sea. But they did not directly affect the prosperity of his empire. What was the loss of a few thousand slaves, and of a few hundred Phoenician and Egyptian and Ionian ships, to him? Indirectly, indeed, it decided the fate of Persia by developing the power of the Greeks, but ruined in any case that empire must have been, like all others of its kind. The causes of its fall must be sought for within and not without. In the natural course of events it would have become the prey of some people like the Parthian highlanders or the wandering Turks. The Greek wars had this result; the empire was conquered at an earlier period than would otherwise have been the case, and it was conquered by a European instead of an Asiatic power.

The Greeks

There is no problem in history so interesting as the unparalleled development of Greece. How was it that so small a country could exert so remarkable an influence on the course of events and on the intellectual progress of mankind? The Greeks, as the science of language clearly proves, belonged to the same race as the Persians themselves. Many centuries before history begins a people migrated from the highlands of Central Asia and overspread Europe on the one side, on the other side Hindustan. Celts and Germans, Russians and Poles, Romans and Greeks, Persians and Hindus, all sprang from the loins of a shepherd tribe inhabiting the tableland of the sources of the Oxus and Jaxartes, and are quite distinct from the Assyrians, the Arabs, and Phoenicians, whose ancestors descended into the plains of Western Asia from the tableland of the sources of the Tigris and Euphrates. It is also inferred from the evidence of language that at some remote period the Egyptians belonged to the same stock as the mountaineers of Armenia, the Chinese to the same stock as the highlanders of Central Asia, and that at a period still more remote the Turanian or Chinese Tartar, the Aryan or Indo-European, and the Semitic races and languages were one. Upon this last point philologists are not agreed, though the balance of authority is in favour of the view expressed. But as regards the descent of the English and Hindus from the same tribe of Asiatic mountaineers, that is now as much a fact of history as the common descent of the English and the Normans from the same race of pirates on the Baltic shores. The Celts migrated first into Europe; they were followed by the Graeco-Italian people, and then by the German-Slavonians, the Persians and Hindus remaining longest in their primeval homes. The great difference between the various breeds of the Indo-European race is partly due to their intermixture with the natives of the countries which they colonised and conquered. In India the Aryans found a black race which yet exist in the hills and jungles of that country, and who yet speak languages of their own which have nothing in common with the noble Sanskrit. Europe was inhabited by a people of Tartar origin who still exist as the Basques of the Pyrenees, and as the Finns and Lapps of Scandinavia. It is probable that these people also were intruders of comparatively recent date, and that a yet more primeval race existed on the gloomy banks of the Danube and the Rhine, in huts built on stakes in the shallow waters of the Swiss lakes, and in the mountain caverns of France and Spain. The Aryans, who migrated into India, certainly intermarried with the blacks, and there can be no reasonable doubt that the Celts who first migrated into Europe took the wives as well as the lands of the natives. The aborigines were therefore largely absorbed by the Celts, to the detriment of that race, before the arrival of the Germans, whose blood remained comparatively pure.

We may freely use the doctrine of intermarriage to explain the difference in colour between the sepoy and his officer. We may apply it--though with less confidence--to explain the difference in character and aspect between the Irish and the English, but we do not think that the doctrine will help us much towards expounding the genius of Greece. And if the superiority of that people was not dependent in any way on race distinction, inherent or acquired, it must have been in some way connected with locality and other incidents of life.

A glance at the map is sufficient to explain how it was that Greece became civilised before the other European lands. It is nearest to those countries in which civilisation first arose. It is the borderland of East and West. The western coast of Asia and the eastern coast of Greece lie side by side; the sea between them is narrow, with the islands like stepping-stones across a brook. On the other hand, a mountain wall extends in the form of an arc from the Adriatic to the Black Sea and shuts off Europe from Greece, which is thus compelled to grow towards Asia as a tree grows towards the light. Its coasts are indented in a peculiar manner by the sea. Deep bays and snug coves, forming hospitable ports, abound. The character of the Aegean is mild and humane; its atmosphere is clear and favourable for those who navigate by the eye from island to island and from point to point. The purple shell-fish, so much in request with the Phoenicians for their manufactures, was found upon the coasts of Greece. A trade was opened up between the two lands, and with trade there came arithmetic and letters to assist the trade, and from these a desire on the part of the Greeks for more luxury and more knowledge. All this was natural enough. But how was it that whatever came into the hands of the Greeks was used merely as raw material--that whatever they touched was transmuted into gold? How was it that Asia was only their dame's school, and that they discovered the higher branches of knowledge for themselves? How was it that they who were taught by the Babylonians to divide the day into twelve hours afterwards exalted astronomy to the rank of an exact science? How was it that they who received from Egypt the canon of proportions and the first ideas of the portraiture of the human form, afterwards soared into the regions of the ideal, and created in marble a beauty more exquisite than can be found on earth--a vision, as it were, of some unknown yet not unimagined world?

The mountains of Greece are disposed in a peculiar manner, so as to enclose extensive tracts of land which assume the appearance of large basins or circular hollows, level as the ocean and consisting of rich alluvial soil through which rise steep insulated rocks. The plain subsisted a numerous population; the rock became the Acropolis or citadel of the chief town, and the mountains were barriers against invasion. Other districts were parcelled out by water in the same manner; their frontiers were swift streaming rivers or estuaries of the sea. Each of these cantons became an independent city-state, and the natives of each canton became warmly attached to their fatherland. Nature had given them ramparts which they knew how to use. They defended with obstinacy the river and the pass; if those were forced the citadel became a place of refuge and resistance, and if the worst came to the worst they could escape to inaccessible mountain caves.

Each of these states possessed a constitution of its own, and each was home-made and differed slightly from the rest. It may be imagined what a variety of ideas must have risen in the process of their manufacture. The laws were debated in a general assembly of the citizens; each community within itself was full of intellectual activity.

Self-development and independence are too often accompanied by isolation, and nations, like individuals, become torpid when they retire from the world. But this was not the case with Greece. Though its people were divided into separate states, they all spoke the same language and worshipped the same gods, and there existed certain institutions which at appointed times assembled them together as a nation.

Greece is a country which possesses the most extraordinary climate in the world. Within two degrees of latitude it ranges from the beech to the palm. In the morning the traveller may be shivering in a snow-storm, and viewing a winter landscape of naked trees; in the afternoon he may be sweltering beneath a tropical sun, with oleanders blooming around him and oranges shining in the green foliage like balls of gold. From this variety of climate resulted a variety of produce which stimulated the natives to barter and exchange. A central spot was chosen as the market-place, and it was made, for the common protection, a sanctuary of Apollo. The people, when they met for the purposes of trade, performed at the same time religious rites, and also amused themselves, in the rude manner of the age, with boxing, wrestling, running races, and throwing the spear; or they listened to the minstrels, who sang the ballads of ancient times, and to the prophets or inspired politicians, who chanted predictions in hexameters. That sanctuary became in time the famous oracle of Delphi, and those sports expanded into the Olympian Games. To the great fair came Greeks from all parts of the land, and when chariot races were introduced it became necessary to make good roads from state to state, and to build bridges across the streams. The administration of the sanctuary, the laws and regulations of the games, and the management of the public fund subscribed for the expenses of the fair, could only be arranged by means of a national council composed of deputies from all the states. This congress was called the Amphictyonic League, which, soon extending its powers, enacted national laws, and as a supreme court of arbitration decided all questions that arose between state and state.

At Olympia the inhabitants of the coast displayed the scarlet cloth and the rich trinkets which they had obtained from Phoenician ships. At Olympia those who had been kidnapped into slavery, and had afterwards been ransomed by their friends at home, related to an eager crowd the wonders which they had seen in the enchanted regions of the East.

And then throughout all Greece there was an inward stirring and a hankering after the unknown, and a desire to achieve great deeds. It began with the expedition of Jason--an exploring voyage to the Black Sea; it culminated in the siege of Troy.

132

In such countries as the Grecian states, where the area is small, the community flourishing, and the frontier inexorably defined, the law of population operates with unusual force. The mountain walls of the Greek cantons, like the deserts which surrounded Egypt, not only kept out the enemy but also kept in the natives; they were not only fortresses but prisons. In order to exist, the Greeks were obliged to cultivate every inch of soil. But when this had been done the population still continued to increase, and now the land could no longer be increased. In those early days they had no manufactures, mines, or foreign commerce by means of which they could supply themselves, as we do, with food from other lands. In such an emergency the government, if it acts at all, has only two methods to pursue. It must either strangle or bleed the population; it must organise infanticide or emigration.

The first method was practised to some extent, but happily the last was now within their power. The Trojan war had made them acquainted with the Asiatic coast, and overcrowded states began to send forth colonies by public act. The emigrants consisted chiefly, as may be supposed, of the poor, the dangerous, and the discontented classes. They took with them no women; they went forth, like the buccaneers, sword in hand. They swooped down on the Ionian coast--there was at that time no power in Asia Minor which was able to resist them. They obtained wives, sometimes by force, sometimes by peaceable arrangement with the natives. In course of time the coast of Asia Minor was lined with rich and flourishing towns. The mother country continued to pour forth colonies, and colonies also founded colonies. The Greeks sailed and settled in every direction. They braved the dark mists and the inclement seasons of the Black Sea, and took up their abode among a people whose faces were almost concealed in furs, who dwelt at the mouths of great rivers and cultivated boundless plains of wheat. This wheat the Greeks exported to the mother country, with barrels of the salted tunny-fish, and the gold of Ural, and even the rich products of the Oriental trade which were brought across Asia from India or China by the waters of the Oxus to the Aral Sea, from the Aral to the Caspian Sea by land, from the Caspian to the Black Sea by the Volga and the Don.

But where Italy dipped her arched and lovely foot in the blue waters of an untroubled sea, beneath the blue roof of an unclouded sky--where the flowers never perished, where eternal summer smiled, where mere existence was voluptuous and life itself a sensual joy-- there the Greek cities clustered richly together--cities shining with marble and built in fairy forms, before them the deep tranquil harbour, behind them violet valleys, myrtle groves, and green lakes of waving corn.

When a bank of emigrants went forth they took with them fire kindled on the city hearth. Although each colony was independent, it regarded with reverence the mother state, and all considered themselves with pride not foreigners but Greeks; for Greece was not a country but a people; wherever the Greek language was spoken, that was Greece.

They all spoke the same grand and harmonious language--although the dialects might differ; they had the same bible, for Homer was in all their hearts, and the memory of their youthful glory was associated in their minds with the union of Greek warriors beneath the walls of Troy. The chief colonial states were represented at the meetings of the Amphictyonic League, and any Greek from the Crimea to Marseilles might contend at the Olympian Games with the full rights of a Spartan or Athenian, a privilege which the Great King could by no means have obtained.

The intense enthusiasm which was excited by the Olympian Games was the chief cause of the remarkable development of Greece. The man who won the olive garland on that celebrated course was famous for ever afterwards. His statue was erected in the public hall at Delphi; he was received by his native city with all the honours of a formal triumph; he was not allowed to enter by the gates--a part of the city wall was beaten down. The city itself became during five years the talk of Greece, and wherever its people travelled they were welcomed with congratulations and esteem.

The passion for praise is innate in the human mind. It is only natural that throughout the whole Greek world a spirit of eager rivalry and emulation should prevail. In every city was established a gymnasium where crowds of young men exercised themselves naked. This institution was originally intended for those only who were in training for the Olympian Games, but afterwards it became a part of daily life, and the Greeks went to the gymnasium with the same regularity as the Romans went to the bath.

At first the national prizes were only for athletes, but at a later period the principle of competition was extended to books and musical compositions, paintings and statues. There was also a competition in rich and elegant display. The carriages and retinues which were exhibited upon the course excited a desire to obtain wealth, and gave a useful impulse to foreign commerce, manufactures, and mining operations.

The Greek world was composed of municipal aristocracies--societies of gentlemen living in towns, with their farms in the neighbourhood, and having all their work done for them by slaves. They themselves had nothing to do but to cultivate their bodies by exercise in the gymnasium, and their minds by conversation in the market-place. They lived out of doors while their wives remained shut up at home. In Greece a lady could only enter society by adopting a mode of life which in England usually facilitates her exit. The Greeks spent little money on their wives, their houses, or their food: the rich men were expected to give dramatic entertainments, and to contribute a company or a man-of-war for the protection of the city. The market-place was the Greek club. There the merchants talked their business--the labours of the desk were then unknown. The philosopher instructed his pupils under the shade of a plane-tree, or strolling up and down a garden path. Mingling with the song of the cicada from the boughs might be heard the chipping of the chisel from the workshop of the sculptor, and the laughter and shouts from the gymnasium. And sometimes the tinkle of a harp would be heard; a crowd would be collected, and a rhapsodist would recite a scene from the Iliad, every word of which his audience knew by heart, as an audience at Naples or Milan knows every bar of the opera which is about to be performed. Sometimes a citizen would announce that his guest, who had just arrived from the sea of Azov or the Pillars of Hercules, would read a paper on the manners and customs of the barbarians. It was in the city that the book was first read and the statue exhibited--the rehearsal and the private view; it was in Olympia that they were published to the nation. When the public murmured in delight around a picture of Xeuxis or a statue of Praxiteles, when they thundered in applause to an ode by Pindar or a lecture by Herodotus, how many hundreds of young men must have gone home with burning brows and throbbing hearts, devoured by the love of fame! And when we consider that though the geographical Greece is a small country, the true Greece--that is to say, the land inhabited by the Greeks--was in reality a large country; when we consider with what an immense number of ideas they must have been brought in contact on the shores of the Black Sea, in Asia Minor, in Southern Italy, in Southern France, in Egypt, and in Northern Africa; when we consider that, owing to those noble contests of Olympia, city was every contending against city, and within the city man against man, there is surely no longer anything mysterious in the exceptional development of that people.

Education in Greece was not a monopoly; it was the precious privilege of all the free. The business of religion was divided among three classes. The priests were merely the sacrificers and guardians of the sanctuary; they were elected, like the mayors of our towns, by their fellow citizens for a limited time only, and without their being withdrawn from the business of ordinary life. The poets revealed the nature, and portrayed the character, and related the biography of the gods. The philosophers undertook the education of the young, and were also the teachers and preachers of morality. If a man wished to obtain the favour of the gods, or to take divine advice, he went to a priest; if he desired to turn his mind to another, though scarcely a better world, he took up his Homer or his Hesiod; and if he suffered from sickness or mental affliction he sent for a philosopher.

It will presently be shown that the philosophers invaded the territory of the poets, who were defended by the government and by the mob, and that a religious persecution was the result. But the fine arts were free; and the custom which came into vogue of erecting statues to the gods, to the victors of the games, and to other illustrious men favoured the progress of sculpture, which was also aided by the manners of the land. The gymnasium was a school of art. The eyes of the sculptor revelled on the naked form--not purchased, as in London, at eighteenpence an hour, but visible in marvellous perfection at all times and in every pose. Thus ever present to the eye of the artist, it was ever present to his brain, and flowed forth from his fingers in lovely forms. As art was fed by nature, so nature was fed by art. The Greek women placed statues of Apollo or Narcissus in their bedrooms, that they might bear children as beautiful as those on whom they gazed. Such children they prayed the gods to give them, for the Greeks loved beauty to distraction, and regarded ugliness as sin. They had exhibitions of beauty at which prizes were given by celebrated artists who were appointed to the judgment-seat. There were towns in which the most beautiful men were elected to the priesthood. There were connoisseurs who formed companies of soldiers composed exclusively of comely young men, and who could plead for the life of a beautiful youth amidst the wrath and confusion of the battlefield.

The Persian wars gave a mighty impulse to the intellect of Greece. Indeed, before that period Greek art had been uncouth; it was then that the Age of Marble really began, and that Phidias moulded the ideas of Homer into noble forms. It was then that Athens, having commanded the Greeks in the War of Independence, retained the supremacy and became the centre of the nation. Athens had died for Greece; it had been burnt by the Persians to the ground, and from those glorious ashes arose the Athens of history--the City of the Violet Crown. To Athens were summoned the great artists: to Athens came every young man who had talent and ambition: to Athens every Greek who could afford it sent his boys to school. The Academy was planted with wide-spreading plane-trees and olive groves, laid out in walks with fountains, and surrounded by a wall. A theatre was built entirely of masts which had been taken from the enemy. A splendid harbour was constructed--a harbour which was in itself a town. All that fancy could create, all that money could command, was lavished upon the city and its environs--the very milestones on the roads were works of art.

The Persians assisted the growth of Greece, not only by those invasions which had favoured the union, aroused the ardour, multiplied the desires, and ennobled the ambition of the Greek people, but also by their own conquests. Their failure in Europe and their success in Asia were equally profitable to the Greeks. Trade and travel were much facilitated by their extensive rule. A government postal service had been established: royal couriers might by seen every day galloping at full speed along the splendid roads which united the provinces of the Punjab and Afghanistan and Bokhara on one side of the Euphrates, and of Asia Minor, Syria and Egypt on the other side of that river, with the imperial palaces at Babylon, Susa, Ecbatana, and Persepolis. Caravanserais were fitted up for the reception of travellers in lonely places where no other houses were to be found. Troops of mounted police patrolled the roads. In desert tracts thousands of earthen jars, filled with water and planted up to their necks in sand, supplied the want of wells. The old system of national isolation and closed ports was battered down. The Greeks were no longer forbidden to enter the Phoenician ports, or compelled to trade exclusively at one Egyptian town. Greek merchants were able to join in the caravan trade of Central Asia, and to traffic on the shores of the Indian Ocean. Philosophers, taking with them a venture of oil to pay expenses, could now visit the learned countries of the East with more profit than had previously been the case. Since that country was deprived of its independence, the priests were inclined to encourage the cultivated curiosity of their new scholars.

Egypt from the earliest times had been the university of Greece. It had been visited, according to tradition, by Orpheus and Homer: there Solon had studied law-making, there the rules and principles of the Pythagorean order had been obtained, there Thales had taken lessons in geometry, there Democritus had laughed and Xenophanes had sneered. And now every intellectual Greek made the voyage to that country; it was regarded as a part of education, as a pilgrimage to the cradle-land of their mythology. To us Egypt is a land of surpassing interest, but nevertheless merely a charnel-house, a museum, a valley of ruins and dry bones. The Greeks saw it alive. They saw with their own eyes the solemn and absurd rites of the temple--the cat solemnly enthroned, the tame crocodiles being fed, ibis mummies being packed up in red jars, scribes carving the animal language upon the granite. They wandered in the mazes of the Labyrinth: they gazed on the mighty Sphinx couched on the yellow sands with a temple between its paws: they entered the great hall of Carnac, filled with columns like a forest and paved with acres of solid stone. In that country Herodotus resided several years and took notes on his wooden tablets of everything that he saw, ascertained the existence of the Niger, made inquiries about the sources of the Nile, collated the traditions of the priests of Memphis with those of Thebes. To Egypt came the divine Plato, and drank long and deeply of its ancient lore. The house in which he lived at Heliopolis was afterwards shown to travellers--it was one of the sights of Egypt in Strabo's day. There are some who ascribe the whole civilisation of Greece, and the rapid growth of Greek literature, to the free trade which existed between the two lands. Greece imported all its paper from Egypt, and without paper there would have been few books. The skins of animals were too rare, and their preparation too expensive, to permit the growth of a literature for the people.

Gradually the Greeks become dispersed over the whole Asiatic world, and such was the influence of their superiority that countries in which they had no political power adopted much of their culture and their manners. They surpassed the inhabitants of Asia as much in the arts of war as in those of peace. They served as mercenaries in every land; wherever the kettledrum was beaten they assembled in crowds.

It soon became evident to keen observers that the Greeks were destined to inherit the Persian world. That vast empire was beginning to decay. The character of the ruling people had completely changed. It is said that the Lombards of the fourth generation were terrified when they looked at the portraits of their savage ancestors who, with their hair shaved behind and hanging down over their mouths in front, had issued from the dark forests of Central Europe, and had streamed down from the Alps upon the green Italian plains. The Persians soon ceased to be the rude and simple mountaineers who had scratched their heads with wonder at the sight of a silk dress, and who had been unable to understand the object of changing one thing for another. It was remarked that no people adopted more readily the customs of other nations. Whenever they heard of a new luxury they made it their own. They soon became distinguished for that exquisite and refined politeness which they retain at the present day; their language cast off its guttural sounds and became melodious to the ear. Time went on, and their old virtues entirely departed. They made use of gloves and umbrellas when they walked out in the sun; they no longer hunted except in battues, slaughtering without danger or fatigue the lean, mangy creatures of the parks. They painted their faces and pencilled their eyebrows and wore bracelets and collars, and dined on a variety of entrees, tasting a little here and a little there, drank deep, yawned half the day in their harems, and had valets de chambre to help them out of bed. Their actions were like water, and their words were like the wind. Once a Persian's right hand had been a pledge which was never broken; now no one could rely on his most solemn oath.

A country in which polygamy prevails can never enjoy a well-ordered constitution. There is always an uncertainty about succession. The kingdom does not descend by rule to the eldest son, but to the son of the favourite wife; it is not determined beforehand by a national law, constant and unchangeable, given forth from the throne and ratified by the estates; it may be decided suddenly and at any moment in that hour when men are weak and yielding, women sovereign and strong--when right is often strangled by a fond embrace and reason kissed to sleep by rosy lips. The fatal "Yes"! is uttered and cannot be revoked. The heir is appointed and an injustice has been done. But the rival mother has yet a hope--the appointed heir may die. Then the seraglio becomes a nursery of treason; the harem administration is stirred by dark whispers; the cabinet of women and eunuchs is cajoled and bribed. A crime is committed and is revenged. The whole palace smells of blood. The king trembles on his throne. He himself is never safe; he is always encircled by soldiers; he never sleeps twice in the same place; his dinner is served in sealed trays; a man stands at his left hand who tastes from the cup before he dares to raise it to his lips.

The satrap form of government is far superior to that of vassal kings. As long as the system of inspection is kept up there is no comparison between the two. But if once the satrapies are allowed to become hereditary there is no difference between the two. In the latter days of the Persian empire the satraps were no longer supervised by royal visitors and clerks of the accounts. Each of these viceroys had his bodyguard of Persians and his army of mercenary Greeks. Sometimes they fought against each other; sometimes they even contested for the throne. As for the subject nations, they were by no means idle; revolts broke out in all directions. Egypt enjoyed a long interlude of independence, though afterwards she was again reduced to servitude. The Indians appear to have shaken themselves free, and to have attained the position of allies. Many provinces still recognised the emperor as their suzerain and lord, but did not pay him any tribute. When he travelled from Susa to Persepolis he had to go through a rocky pass where he paid a toll. The king of Persia could not enter Persia proper without buying the permission of a little shepherd tribe.

A remarkable event now occurred. A pretender to the throne hired a Greek army, led it to Babylon, and defeated the Great King at the gates of his palace. The empire was won, but the pretender had fallen in the battle; his Persian adherents went over to the other side; the Greeks were left without a commander and without a cause. They were in the heart of Asia, cut off from their home by swift streaming rivers and burning plains of sand. They were only ten thousand strong, yet in spite of their desperate condition they cut their way back to the sea. That glorious victory, that still more glorious retreat, exposed the true state of affairs to public view, and it became known all over Greece that the Persian empire could be overcome.

But Greece unhappily was subject to vices and abuses of its own, and was not in a position to take advantage of the weakness of its neighbour.

The intellectual achievements of the Greeks have been magnificently praised. And when we consider what the world was when they found it, and what it was when they left it, when we review their productions in connection with the time and the circumstances under which they were composed, we are forced to acknowledge that it would be difficult to exaggerate their excellence. But the splendour of their just renown must not blind us to their moral defects, and to their exceeding narrowness as politicians.

In the arts and letters they were one nation, and their jealousy of one another only served to stimulate their inventiveness and industry. But in politics this envious spirit had a very different effect; it divided them, it weakened them; the Ionian cities were enslaved again and again because they could not combine. And one reason of their not being able to combine was this: they never trusted one another. It was their inveterate dishonesty, their want of faith, their disregards for the sanctity of oaths, their hankering after money, which had much to do with their disunion even in the face of danger. There are some who desire to persuade us that the Greeks whom the Romans described were entirely a different race from the Greeks of the Persian wars. But an unprejudiced study of original authorities gives no support to such a theory. From the pirates to the orators, from the heroic and treacherous Ulysses to the patriotic and venal Demosthenes, we find almost all their best men tainted with the same disease. Polybius complains that the Greek statesmen would never keep their hands out of the till. In Xenophon's Retreat of the Ten Thousand a little banter is exchanged between a Spartan and an Athenian which illustrates the state of public opinion in Greece. They have come to a country where it is necessary to rob the natives in order to provide themselves with food. The Athenian says that, as the Spartans are taught to steal, now is the time for them to show that they have profited by their education. The Spartan replies that the Athenians will no doubt be able to do their share, as the Athenians appoint their best men to govern the state, and their best men are invariably thieves. The same kind of pleasantry, no doubt, goes on in Greece at the present day; to rob a foreigner in the mountains, or to filch the money from the public chest, are looked upon in that country as "little affairs" which are not disgraceful so long as they are not found out. But the modern Greeks are degenerate in every way. The ancient Greeks surpassed them not only in sculpture and in metaphysics but also in duplicity. With their fine phrases and rhetorical expressions, they have even swindled history, and obtained a vast amount of admiration under false pretences.

The narrowness of the Greeks was not less strongly marked. When Athens obtained the supremacy a wise and just policy might have formed the Greeks into a nation. But Pericles had no sympathies beyond the city walls: he was a good Athenian but a bad Greek.

He removed the federal treasury from Delphi to Athens, where it was speedily emptied on the public works. Since Athens had now become the university and capital of Greece, it appears not unjust that it should have been beautiful at the expense of Greece. But it must be remembered that the Athenians considered themselves the only pure Greeks, and no Athenian was allowed to marry a Greek who was not also an Athenian. Heavy taxes were laid on the allies, and were not spent entirely on works of art. Besides the money that was purloined by government officials, large sums were distributed among the citizens of Athens as payment for attending the law courts, the parliament, and the theatre. It was also ordered that all cases of importance would be tried at Athens, and judicial decisions then as now were looked upon at Athens as saleable articles belonging to the court. The Greeks soon discovered that the Athenians were harder masters than the Persians. They began to envy the fate of the Ionian cities, whose municipal rights were undisturbed. They rose up against their tyrant; long wars ensued; and finally the ships of Athens were burnt and its walls beaten down to the music of flutes. Then Sparta became supreme, also tyrannised, and also fell; and then Thebes followed its example, till at last all the states of Greece were so exhausted that the ambition of supremacy died away, and each city cared only for its own life.

The jealousy and distrust which prevented the union of the Greeks, and the constant wars in which they were engaged, sufficiently explain how it was that they did not conquer Persian, and by this time Persia had discovered how to conquer them. When Xerxes was on his famous march he was told by a Greek that if he chose to bribe the orators of Greece he could do with that country what he pleased, but that he would never conquer it by force. This method of making war was now adopted by the king. When Agesilaus the Spartan had already begun the conquest of the Persian empire, ten thousand golden coins marked with the effigy of a bowman were sent to the demagogues of Athens, Corinth, and Thebes. Those cities at once made war upon Sparta, and Agesilaus was recalled--driven out of Asia, as he used to say, by ten thousand of the king's archers. In this manner the Greek orators, who were often very eloquent men but who never refused a bribe, kept their country continually at war, till at last it was in such an enfeebled state that the Persian had no longer anything to fear, and even used his influence in making peace. The land which might have been the mistress of the East passed under the protection of an empire in its decay.

It was now that a new power sprang into life. Macedonia was a hilly country on the northern boundaries of Greece; a Greek colony having settled there in ancient times, the reigning house and the language of the courts were Hellenic; the mass of the people were barbarians. It was an old head placed on young shoulders--the intellect of the Greek united with the strength and sinews of wild and courageous mountaineers.

The celebrated Philip, when a young man, had passed some time in Greece; he had seen what could be done with money in that country; he conjectured what might be done if the money were sustained by arms. When he became king of Macedon, he made himself president of the Greek confederation, obtaining by force and skilful address, by bribery and intrigue, the position which Athens and Sparta had once possessed. He was preparing to conquer Persia and to avenge the ancient wrongs of Greece when he was murdered, and Alexander, like Frederick the Great, inherited an army disciplined to perfection and the great design for which that army had been prepared.

Alexander reduced and garrisoned the rebellious Greeks, passed over into Asia Minor, defeated a Persian army at the Granicus, marched along the Ionian coast, and crossed over the snowy range of Taurus, which the Persians neglected to defend. He heard that the Great King was behind him with his army entangled in the mountains. He went back, won the battle of Issus, and took prisoner the mother and wife and daughter of Darius. He passed into Syria and laid siege to Tyre, the Cherbourg of the Persians, and took it after several months; this gave him possession of the Mediterranean Sea. He passed down the Syrian coast, crossed the desert--a three days' journey--which separates Palestine from Egypt, received the submission of that satrapy and made arrangements for its administration, visited the oracle of Jupiter Ammon in The Sahara, and returned to Tyre. Thence making a long detour to avoid the sandy deserts of Arabia, he entered the plains of Mesopotami, inhabited only by the ostrich and the wild ass, and marched towards the ruins of Nineveh, near which he fought his third and last great battle with the Persians. He proceeded to Babylon, which at once opened its vast gates. He restored the Chaldean priesthood and the old idolatry of Belus. He took Susa, Ecbatana, and Persepolis, the other three palatial cities, reducing the highlanders who had so long levied blackmail on the Persian monarchs. He pursued Darius to the moist, forest-covered shores of the Caspian Sea, and inflicted a terrible death on the assassins of that ill-fated king. The Persian histories relate that Alexander discovered Darius apparently dead upon the ground. He alighted from his horse; he raised his enemy's head upon his knees; he shed tears and kissed the expiring monarch who opened his eyes and said, "The world has a thousand doors through which its tenants continually enter and pass away." "I swear to you," cried Alexander, "I never wished a day like this. I desired not to see your royal head in the dust, nor that blood should stain these cheeks." The legend is a fiction, but it illustrates the character of Alexander. Such legends are not related of Genghis Khan or of Tamerlane by the people whom they conquered.

Alexander now marched by way of Mushed, Herat, and the reedy shores of Lake Zurrah to Kandahar and Kabul. He entered that delightful land in which the magpies fluttering from tree to tree, and the white daisies shining in the meadow grass, reminded the soldiers of their home. Turning again towards the north, he climbed over the lofty back of the Hindu Kush, where the people are kept inside their houses half the year by snow, and descended into the province of Bactria, a land of low, waving hills, destitute of trees and covered only with a dry kind of grass. But as he passed on, crossing the muddy waters of the Oxus, he arrived at the oases of Bokhara and Samarkand, regions of garden-land with smiling orchards of fruit trees and poplars rustling their silvery leaves. Finally he reached the banks of the Jaxartes, the frontier of the Persian empire. Beyond that river was an ocean of salt and sandy plains, inhabited by wild Tartar or Turkish tribes who boasted that they reposed beneath the shade neither of a tree nor of a king, who lived by rapine like beasts of prey, and whose wives rode forth to attack a passing caravan if their husbands happened to be robbing elsewhere--a practice which gave rise to the romantic stories of the Amazons. These people came down to the banks of the river near Khojend and challenged Alexander to come across and fight. He inflated the soldiers' tents, which were made of skins, formed them into rafts, paddled across and gave the Tartars as much as they desired. He returned to Afghanistan and marched through the western passes into the open plains of the Punjab, where perhaps at some future day hordes of drilled Mongols and Hindu sepoys will fight under Russian and English officers for the empire of the Asiatic world. He built a fleet on the Indus, sailed down it to its mouth, and dispatched his general Nearchus to the Persian

Gulf by sea, while he himself marched back through the terrific deserts which separate Persian from the Indus.

So ended Alexander's journey of conquest, which was marked not only by heaps of bones on battlefields and by the blackened ashes of ruined towns, but also by cities and colonies which he planted as he passed. The memory of that extraordinary man has never perished in the East. The Turkomans still speak of his deeds of war as if they had been performed a few years ago. In the tea booths of Bokhara it is yet the custom to read aloud the biography in verse of Secunder Rooni--by some believed to be a prophet, by others one of the believing genii. There are still existing chiefs in the valleys of the Oxus and the Indus who claim to be heirs of his royal person, and tribes who boast that their ancestors were soldiers of his army, and who refuse to give their children in marriage to those who are not of the same descent.

He returned to Babylon, and there found ambassadors from all parts of the world waiting to offer him the homage of their masters. His success was incredible; it had not met with a single check. The only men who had ever given him cause to be alarmed were his own countrymen and soldiers, but these also he had mastered by his skill and strength of mind.

The Macedonians

The Macedonians had expected that he would adhere to the constitution and customs of their own country, which gave the king small power in time of peace and allowed full liberty and even licence of speech on the part of the nobles round the throne. But Alexander now considered himself not king of Macedonia but emperor of Asia, and successor of Darius, the King of Kings. They had supposed that he would give them the continent to plunder as a carcass; that they would have nothing to do but plunder and enjoy. There were disappointed and alarmed when they found that he was reappointing Persian gentlemen as satraps, everywhere treating the conquered people with indulgence, everywhere levying native troops. They were disgusted and alarmed when they saw him put on the tiara of the Great King, and the woman's girdle, and the white and purple robe, and they burst into fierce wrath when he ordered that the ceremony of prostration should be performed in his presence as it had been in that of the Persian king.

In all this they saw only the presumption of a man intoxicated by success. But Alexander knew well that he could only govern an empire so immense by securing the allegiance of the Persian nobles; he knew that they would not respect him unless they were made to humble themselves before him after the manner of their country, and this they certainly would not do unless his own officers did the same. He therefore attempted to obtain the prostration of the Macedonians, and alleged as a pretext for so extraordinary a demand the oracle of Ammon--that he was the son of Jove.

It is possible, indeed, that he believed this himself, for his vanity amounted to madness. He could not endure a candid word, and was subject under wine and contradiction to fits of ungovernable rage. At Samarkand he murdered Clitus, who had insulted him grossly but who was his friend and associate, and who had saved his life. It was a drunken action, and his repentance was as violent as his wrath. For Alexander was a man of extremes: his magnanimity and his cruelty were without bounds. If he forgave it was right royally; if he punished he pounded to the dust and scattered to the winds. Yet with all his faults it is certain that he had some conception of the art of governing a great empire. Mr. Grote complains that "he had none of that sense of correlative right and obligation which characterised the free Greeks," but Mr. Grote describes Alexander too much from the Athenian point of view. In all municipalities, in all aristocratic bodies, in all corporate assemblies, in all robber communities, in all savage families or clans, the privileged members have a sense of correlative right and obligation. The real question is, how far and to what extent this feeling prevails outside the little circle of selfish reciprocity and mutual admiration. The Athenians did not include their slaves in their ideas of correlative right and obligation; nor their prisoners of war, when they passed a public decree to cut off all their thumbs, so that they might not be able to handle the pike, but might still be able to handle the oar; nor their allies, when they took their money and spent it all upon themselves. Alexander committed some criminal and despotic acts, but it was his noble idea to blot out the word "barbarian" from the vocabulary of the Greeks, and to amalgamate them with the Persians.

Mr. Grote declares that Alexander intended to make Greece Persian, not Persia Greek. Alexander certainly intended to make Greece a satrapy, as it was afterwards made a Roman province. And where would have been the loss? The independence of the various Greek cities had at one time assisted the progress of the nation. But that time was past. Of late they had made use of their freedom only to indulge in civil war. All that was worthy of being preserved in Greece was its language and its culture, and to that Alexander was not indifferent. He sent thirty thousand Persian boys to school, and so laid the foundations of the sovereignty of Greek ideas. He behaved towards the conquered people not as a robber but as a sovereign. The wisdom of his policy is clearly proved by the praises of the Oriental writers and by the blame of the Greeks, who looked upon barbarians as a people destined by nature to be slaves. But had Alexander governed Persia as they desired, the land would have been in a continual state of insurrection, and it would have been impossible for him, even had he lived, to have undertaken new designs.

The story that he wept because there were no more worlds for him to conquer would seem to imply that after the conquest of the Persian empire there was nothing left for him in the way of war but to go out savage-hunting in the forests of Europe, the steppes of Tartary, or the deserts of Central Africa. However, there still remained a number of powerful and attractive states, even if we place China entirely aside as a land which could not be touched by the stream of events, however widely they might overflow.

Alexander no doubt often reflected to himself that after all he had only walked in the footsteps of other men. It was the genius of his father which had given him possession of Greece; it was the genius of the Persians which had planted the Asia that he had gathered. It is true that he had conquered the Persian empire more thoroughly than the Persians had ever been able to conquer it themselves. He had not left behind him a single rock fortress or forest den uncarried, a single tribe untamed. Yet still he had not been able to pass the frontiers which they had fixed. He had once attempted to do so and had failed. When he had reached the eastern river of the Punjab, or "Land of the Five Streams," he stood on the brink of the empire with the Himalayas on his left and before him a wide expanse of sand. Beyond that desert was a country which the Persians had never reached. There a river as mighty as the Indus took its course towards the sea through a land of surpassing beauty and enormous wealth. There ruled a king who rode on a white elephant, and who wore a mail coat composed entirely of precious stone; whose wives slept on a thousand silken mattresses and a thousand golden beds. The imagination of Alexander was inflamed by these glowing tales. He yearned to discover a new world, to descend upon a distant and unknown people like a god, to enter the land of diamonds and rubies, of gleaming and transparent robes--the India of the Indies, the romantic, and half-fabulous Bengal. But the soldiers were weary of collecting plunder which they could not carry, and refused to march. Alexander spent three days in his tent in an agony of anger and distress. He established garrisons on the banks of the Indus; there could be little doubt that some day or other he would resume his lost design.

There was one country which had sent him no ambassadors. It was Arabia Felix, situated at the mouth of the Red Sea, abounding in forests of those tearful trees which shed a yellow, fragrant gum grateful to the gods, burnt in their honour on all the altars of the world. Arabia was also enriched by the monopoly of the trade between Egypt and the coast of Malabar. It was filled with rich cities. It had never paid tribute to the Persians. On the land side it was protected by deserts and by wandering hordes who drank from hidden wells. But it could easily be approached by sea.

On the opposite side of the Arabian gulf lay Ethiopia, reputed to be the native land of gold, but chiefly attractive to a vain-glorious and emulative man from the fact that a Persian emperor had attempted its conquest and had failed. There was also Carthage, the great republic of the West, and there were rich silver-mines in Spain.

And can it be supposed that Alexander would remain content when he had not yet made the circuit of the Grecian world? Was there not Sicily, which Athens had attempted to conquer, and in vain? Rome had not yet become great, but the Italian city-states were already famed in war. Alexander's uncle had invaded that country and had been beaten back. He declared that Alexander had fallen on the chamber of the women and he on the chamber of the men. This sarcasm followed the conqueror into Central Asia, and was flung in his teeth by Clitus on that night of drunkenness and blood, every incident of which must have been continually present to his mind.

We might therefore fairly infer, even if we had no evidence to guide us, that Alexander did not consider his career accomplished. But in point of fact we do know that he had given orders to fit out a thousand ships-of-war; that he intended one fleet to attack Arabia from the Mediterranean Sea. He had already arranged a plan for connecting Egypt with his North African possession that were to be, and had he lived a few years longer the features of the world might have been changed. The Italians were unconquerable if united, but there was at that time no supreme city to unite them as they were afterwards united against Pyrrhus. It is at least not impossible that Alexander might have conquered Italy; that the peninsula might have become a land of independent cultivated cities like the Venice and Genoa and Florence of the Middle Ages; that Greek might have been established as the reigning language, and Latin remained a rustic dialect and finally died away. It is at all events certain that in a few more years Alexander would have made Carthage Greek, and that event alone would have profoundly influenced the career of Rome.

However, this was not to be. Alexander went out in a boat among the marshes in the neighbourhood of Babylon and caught a fever, the first symptoms of which appeared after a banquet which had been kept up all the night and the whole of the following day. At that time the Arabian expedition was prepared, and Nearchus the admiral was under sailing orders. Day after day the king continued to send for his officers to give orders, and to converse about his future plans. But the fever gradually increased, and while yet in the possession of his sense he was deprived of the power of speech. The physicians announced that there was no longer any hope.

And then were forgotten all the crimes and follies of which he had been guilty--his assumption of the honours of a god, the murder of his bosom friend. The Macedonian soldiers came in to him weeping to bid him the last farewell. He sat up and saluted them man by man as they marched past his bedside. When this last duty had been discharged he threw back his weary frame. He expired on the evening of the next day.

The night, the dark, murky night, came on. None dared light a lamp; the fires were extinguished. By the glimmering of the stars and the faint beams of the horned moon, the young nobles of the household were seen wandering like maniacs through the town. On the roofs of their houses the Babylonians stood grave and silent, with folded hands and eyes turned towards heaven as if awaiting a supernatural event. High aloft in the air the trees of the hanging gardens waved their moaning boughs, and the daughters of Babylon sang the dirge of the dead. In that sorrowful hour the conquerors could not be distinguished from the conquered; the Persians lamented their just and merciful master; the Macedonians their greatest, bravest king. In an apartment of the palace an aged woman was lying on the ground; her hair was torn and dishevelled; a golden crown had fallen from her head. "Ah! Who will now protect my girls?" she said. Then, veiling her face and turning from her grand-daughters, who wept at her feet, she stubbornly refused both food and light. She who had survived Darius was unable to survive Alexander. In famine and darkness she sat, and on the fifth day she died.

Alexander's body lay cold and stiff. The Egyptian and Chaldean embalmers were commanded to do their work. Yet long they gazed upon that awful corpse before they could venture to touch it with their hands. Placed in a golden coffin, shrouded in a bed of fragrant herbs, it remained two years at Babylon, and was then carried to Egypt to be buried in the oasis of Ammon. But Ptolemy stopped it on the road, and interred it at Alexandria in a magnificent temple, which he built for the purpose and surrounded with groves for the celebration of funereal rites and military games. Long afterwards, when the dominion of the Macedonians had passed away, there came Roman emperors who gazed upon that tomb with reverence and awe. The golden coffin had been sold by a degenerate Ptolemy, and had been changed for one of glass through which the body could be seen. Augustus placed upon it a nosegay and crown. Septimus Severus had the coffin sealed up in a vault. Then came the savage Caracalla, who had massacred half Alexandria because he did not like the town. He ordered the vault to be opened and the coffin to be exposed, and all feared that some act of sacrilege would be committed. But those august remains could touch the better feelings which existed even in a monster's heart. He took off his purple robe, his imperial ornaments, all that he had of value on his person, and laid them reverently upon the tomb.

The empire of Alexander was partitioned into three great kingdoms--that of Egypt and Cyrene, that of Macedonia, including Greece, and that of Asia, the capital of which was at first on the banks of the Euphrates, but was afterwards unwisely transferred to Antioch. In these three kingdoms, and in their numerous dependencies, Greek became the language of government and trade. It was spoken all over the world--on the shores of Malabar, in the harbours of Ceylon, among the Abyssinian mountains, in distant Mozambique. The shepherds of the Tartar steppes loved to listen to recitations of Greek poetry, and Greek tragedies were performed to Brahmin "houses" by the waters of the Indus. The history of the Greeks of Inner Asia, however soon comes to an end. Sandracottus, the Rajah of Bengal, conquered the Greek province of the Punjab. The rise of the Parthian power cut off the Greek kingdom of Bokhara from the Western world, and it was destroyed, according to the Chinese historians, by a powerful horde of Tartars a hundred and thirty years after its foundation.

Alexandria

We can now return to African soil, and we find that a city of incomparable splendour has arisen, founded by Alexander and bearing his name. For as he was on his way to the oasis of Ammon, travelling along the sea-coast, he came to a place a little west of the Nile's mouth where an island close to the shore, and the peculiar formation of the land, formed a natural harbour, while a little way inland was a large lagoon communicating with the Nile. A few houses were scattered about, and this, he was told, was the village of Rhacotis, where in the old days the Pharaohs stationed a garrison to prevent the Greek pirates from coming on shore. He saw that the spot was well adapted for a city, and with his usual impetuosity went to work at once to mark it out. When he returned from the oasis, the building of the city had begun, and in a few years it had become the residence of Ptolemy and the capital of Egypt.

It filled up the space between the sea and the lagoon. On the one side its harbour was filled with ships which came from Italy and Greece and the lands of the Atlantic with amber, timber, tin, wine, and oil. On the other side were the cargo boats that came from the Nile with the precious stones, the spices, and the beautiful fabrics of the East. The island on which stood the famous lighthouse was connected with the mainland by means of a gigantic mole furnished with drawbridges and forts. It is on this mole that the modern city stands--the site of the old Alexandria is sand.

When Ptolemy the First, one of Alexander's generals, mounted the throne he applied himself with much caution and dexterity to that difficult problem the government of Egypt. Had the Greeks been the first conquerors of the country, it is doubtful whether the wisest policy would have kept its natives quiet and content. For they were like the Jews, a proud, ignorant, narrow-minded, religious race who looked upon themselves as the chosen people of the gods, and upon all foreigners as unclean things. But they had been taught wisdom by misfortune; they had felt the bitterness of an Oriental yoke; the feet of the Persians had been placed upon their necks. On the other hand, the Greeks had lived for centuries among them, and had assisted them in all their revolts against the Persian king. During their interlude of independence the towns had been garrisoned partly by Egyptian and partly by Greek soldiers: the two nations had grown accustomed to each other. Persia had finally re-enslaved them, and Alexander had been welcomed as the saviour of their country. The golden chain of the Pharaohs was broken. It was impossible to restore the line of ancient kings. The Egyptians therefore cheerfully submitted to the Ptolemies, who reciprocated this kindly feeling to the full. They patronised the Egyptian religion, they built many temples in the ancient style, they went to the city of Memphis to be crowned, they sacrificed to the Nile at the rising of the waters, and they assumed the divine titles of the Pharaohs. The priests were content, and in Egypt the people were always guided by the priests. The Rosetta Stone, that remarkable monument which, with its inscription in Greek, in the Egyptian vernacular, and in the sacred hieroglyphics, has afforded the means of deciphering the mysterious language of the Nile, was a memorial of gratitude from the Egyptian priests to a Greek king, to whom in return for favours conferred they erected an image and a golden shrine.

But while the Ptolemies were Pharaohs to the Egyptians, they were Greeks to the colonists of Alexandria, and they founded or favoured that school of thought upon which modern science is established.

There is a great enterprise in which men have always been unconsciously engaged, but which they will pursue with method as a vocation and an art, and which they will devoutly adopt as a religious faith as soon as they realise its glory. It is the conquest of the planet on which we dwell, the destruction or domestication of the savage forces by which we are tormented and enslaved. An episode of this war occurring in ancient Egypt has been described; the war itself began with the rise of our ancestors into the human state, and when, drawing fire from wood or stone, they made it serve them night and day the first great victory was won. But we can conquer Nature only by obeying her laws, and in order to obey those laws we must first learn what they are.

Storms and tides, thunder and lightning and eclipse, the movements of the heavenly bodies, the changing aspects of the earth, were among all ancient people regarded as divine phenomena. In the Greek world there was no despotic caste, but the people clung fondly to their faith, and the study of Nature, which began in Ionia, was at first regarded with abhorrence and dismay. The popular religion was supported by the genius of Homer. The Iliad and the Odyssey were regarded not only as epic poems but as sacred writ; even the geography had been inspired. However, when the Greeks began to travel, the old legends could no longer be received. It was soon discovered that the places visited by Ulysses did not exist, that there was no River Ocean which ran round the earth, and that the earth was not shaped like a round saucer with the oracle of Delphi in its centre. The Egyptians laughed in the faces of the Greeks, and called them children when they talked of their gods of yesterday, and so well did their pupils profit by their lesson that they soon laughed at the Egyptians for believing in the gods at all. Xenophanes declaimed against the Egyptian myth of an earth-walking, dying resuscitated god. He said that if Osiris was a man they should not worship him, and that if he was a god they need not lament his sufferings. This remarkable man was the Voltaire of Greece; there had been free-thinkers before his time, but they had reserved their opinions for their disciples.

Xenophanes declared that the truth should be made known to all. He lived, like Voltaire, to a great age; he poured forth a multitude of controversial works; he made it his business to attack Homer, and reviled him bitterly for having endowed the gods of his poems with the passions and propensities of men; he denied the old theory of the Golden Age, and maintained that civilisation was the work of time and of man's own toil. His views were no doubt distasteful to the vulgar crowd by whom he was surrounded, and even to cultivated and imaginative minds which were sunk in sentimental idolatry, blinded by the splendour of the Homeric poems. He was, however, in no way interfered with; religious persecution was unknown in the Greek world except at Athens. In that city free thought was especially unpopular because it was imported from abroad. It was the doctrine of those talented Ionians who streamed into Athens after the Persian wars. When one of these philosophers announced, in his open-air sermon in the market-place, that the sun which the common people believed to be alive--the bountiful god Helios which shone both on mortals and immortals--was nothing but a mass of red-hot iron; when he declared that

146

those celestial spirits the stars were only revolving stones; when he asserted that Jupiter, and Venus and Apollo, Mars, Juno, and Minerva, were mere creatures of the poet's fancy, and that if they really existed they ought to be despised; when he said that over all there reigned, not blind Fate, but a supreme, all seeing Mind, great wrath was excited among the people. A prophet went about uttering oracles in a shrill voice, and procured the passing of a decree that all who denied the religion of the city or who philosophised in matters appertaining to the gods should be indicted as state criminals. This law was soon put in force. Damon and Anaxagoras were banished; Aspasia was impeached for blasphemy, and the tears of Pericles alone saved her; Socrates was put to death; Plato was obliged to reserve pure reason for a chosen few, and to adulterate it with revelation for the generality of his disciples; Aristotle fled from Athens for his life, and became the tutor of Alexander. Alexander had a passion for the Iliad. His edition had been corrected by Aristotle; he kept it in a precious casket which he had taken from the Persian king, and it was afterwards known as the "edition of the casket." When he invaded Asia he landed on the plains of Troy, that he might see the ruins of that celebrated town and hang a garland upon the tomb of Achilles. But it was not poetry alone that he esteemed; he had imbibed his master's universal tastes. When staying at Ephesus he used to spend hours in the studio of Apelles, sitting down among the boys who ground colours for the great painter. He delighted in everything that was new and rare. He invented exploration. He gave a large sum of money to Aristotle to assist him in composing the history of animals, and employed a number of men to collect for him in Asia. He sent him a copy of the astronomical records of the Babylonians, although by that time they had quarrelled--like Dionysius and Plato, Frederick and Voltaire. It is taken for granted that Alexander was the one to blame, as if philosophers were immaculate and private tutors never in the wrong.

The Ptolemies were not unworthy followers of Alexander. They established the Museum, which was a kind of college, with a hall where the professors dined together, with corridors for promenading lectures, and a theatre for scholastic festivals and public disputation. Attached to it also was the Botanical Garden, filled with medicinal and exotic plants; a menagerie of wild beasts and rare birds; and the famous Library, where 700,000 volumes were arranged on cedar shelves, and where hundreds of clerks were continually at work copying from scroll to scroll, gluing the separate strips of papyrus together, smoothing with pumice-stone and blackening the edges, writing the titles on red labels, and fastening ivory tops on the sticks round which the rolls were wrapped.

All the eminent men of the day were invited to take up their abode at the Museum, and persons were dispatched into all countries to collect books. It was dangerous to bring original manuscripts into Egypt--they were at once seized and copied, the originals being retained. The city of Athens lent the autograph editions of its dramatists to one of the Ptolemies, and saw them no more. It was even said that philosophers were sometimes detained in the same manner.

Soon after the wars of Alexander, the "barbarians" were seized with a desire to make known to their conquerors the history of their native lands. Berosus, a priest of Babylon, compiled a history of Chaldea; Menander, and Phoenician, a history of Tyre; and Manetho wrote in Greek, but from Egyptian sources, a history which Egyptology has confirmed. It was at the Museum also that the Old Testament was translated under royal patronage into Greek, and at the same time the Zoroastrian Bible or Zend-Avesta.

There was some good work done at the Museum. Among works of imagination the pastorals of Theocritus have alone obtained the approbation of posterity. But it was in Alexandria that the immortal works of the preceding ages were edited and arranged, and it was there that language was first studied for itself, and that lexicons and grammars were first compiled. It was only in the Museum that anatomists could sometimes obtain the corpse of a criminal to dissect; elsewhere they were forced to content themselves with monkeys. There Eratosthenes, the "Inspector of the Earth," elevated geography to a science, and Euclid produced that work which, as Macaulay would say, "every schoolboy knows." There the stars were carefully catalogued and mapped, and chemical experiments were made. Expeditions were sent to Abyssinia to ascertain the cause of the inundation of the Nile. The Greek intellect had hitherto despised the realities of life: it had been considered by Plato unworthy of a mathematician to apply his knowledge to so vulgar a business as mechanics. But this notion was corrected at Alexandria by the practical tendencies of Egyptian science. The Suez Canal was reopened, and Archimedes taught the Alexandrians to apply his famous screw to the irrigation of their fields. These Egyptian pumps, as they were then called, were afterwards used by the Romans to pump out the water from their silver-mines in Spain.

No doubt most of the Museum professors were pitiful "Graeculi"-- narrow-minded pedants such as are always to be found where patronage exists, parasites of great libraries who spend their lives in learning the wrong things. No doubt much of the astronomy was astrological, much of the medicine was magical, much of the geography was mythical, and much of the chemistry was alchemical--for they had already begun to attempt the transmutation of metals and to search for the elixir vitae and the philosopher's stone. No doubt physics were much too metaphysical, in spite of the example which Aristotle had given of founding philosophy on experiment and fact; and the alliance between science and labour, which is the true secret of modern civilisation, could be but faintly carried out in a land which was under the fatal ban of slavery. Yet with all this it should be remembered that from Alexandria came the science which the Arabs restored to Europe, with some additions, after the Crusades. It was in Alexandria that were composed those works which enabled Copernicus to lay the keystone of astronomy, and which emboldened Columbus to sail across the Western seas.

The history of the nation under the Ptolemies resembles its history under the Phil-Hellenes, Egypt and Asia were again rivals, and again contested for the vineyards of Palestine and the forests of Lebanon. Alexander had organised a brigade of elephants for his army of the Indus, and these animals were afterwards invariably used by the Greeks in war. Pyrrhus took them to Italy, and the Carthaginians adopted the idea from him. The elephants of the Asiatic Greeks were brought from Hindustan. The Ptolemies, like the Carthaginians, had elephant forests at their own doors. Shooting-boxes were built on the shores of the Red Sea: elephant hunting became a royal sport. The younger members of the herd were entrapped in large pits, or driven into enclosures cunningly contrived; were then tamed by starvation, shipped off to Egypt, and drilled into beasts of war. On the field of battle the African elephants, distinguished by their huge, flapping ears and their convex brows, fought against the elephants of India, twisting their trunks together and endeavouring to gore one another with their tusks. The Indian species is unanimously described as the larger animal and the better soldier of the two.

The third Ptolemy made two brilliant campaigns. In one he overran Greek Asia and brought back the sacred images and vessels which had been carried off by the Persians centuries before; in the other he made an Abyssinian expedition resembling the achievement of Napier. He landed his troops in Annesley Bay, which he selected as his base of operations, and completely subdued the mountaineers of the plateau, carrying the Egyptian arms, as he boasted, where the Pharaohs themselves had never been. But the policy of the Ptolemies was on the whole a policy of peace. Their wars were chiefly waged for the purpose of obtaining timber for their fleet, and of keeping open their commercial routes. They encouraged manufactures and trade, and it was afterwards observed that Alexandria was the most industrious city in the world. "Idle people were there unknown. Some were employed in the blowing of glass, others in the weaving of linen, others in the manufacture of the Papyrus. Even the blind and the lame had occupations suited to their condition."

The glorious reigns of the three first Ptolemies extended over nearly a century, and then Egypt began again to decline. Such must always be the case where a despotic government prevails, and where everything depends on the taste and temper of a single man. As long as a good king sits upon the throne all is well. A gallant service, an intellectual production, merit of every kind is recognised at once. Corrupt tax-gatherers and judges are swiftly punished. The enemies of the people are the enemies of the king. His palace is a court of justice always open to his children; he will not refuse a petition from the meanest hand. But sooner or later in the natural course of events the sceptre is handed to a weak and vicious prince, who empties the treasury of its accumulated wealth; who plunders the courtiers, allowing them to indemnify themselves at the expense of those that are beneath them; who dies, leaving behind him a legacy of wickedness which his successors are forced to accept. Oppression has now become a custom, and custom is the tyrant of kings. In Egypt the prosperity of the land depended entirely on the government. Unless the public works were kept in good order half the land was wasted, half the revenue was lost, half the inhabitants perished of starvation. But the dikes could not be repaired and the screw pumps could not be worked without expense, and so if the treasury was empty the inland revenue ceased to flow in. The king could still live in luxury on the receipts of the foreign trade, but the life of the people was devoured, and the ruin of the country was at hand. The Ptolemies became invariably tyrants and debauchees--perhaps the incestuous marriages practised in that family had something to do with the degeneration of the race. The Greeks of Alexandria became half Orientals, and were regarded by their brethren of Europe with aversion and contempt. One by one the possessions of Egypt abroad were lost. The condition of the land became deplorable. The empire which had excited the envy of the world became deficient in agriculture, and was fed by foreign corn. Alexandria glittered with wealth which it was no longer able to defend. The Greeks of Asia began to fix their eyes on the corrupt and prostrate land. Armies gathered on the horizon like dark clouds; then was seen the flashing of arms; then was heard the rattling of distant drums. The reigning Ptolemy had but one resource. In that same year a great battle had been fought, a great empire had fallen on the African soil. For the first time in history the sun was seen rising in the West. Towards the West, ambassadors from Egypt went forth with silks and spices and precious stones. They returned bringing with them an ivory chair, a coarse garment of purple, and a quantity of copper coin. These humble presents were received in a delirium of joy. The Roman Senate accorded its protection, and Alexandria was saved. But its independence was forfeited, its individuality became extinct. Here endeth the history of Egypt. Let us travel to another shore.

There was a time when the waters of the Mediterranean were silent and bare; when nothing disturbed the solitude of that blue and tideless sea but the weed which floated on its surface and the gull which touched it with its wing.

A tribe of Canaanites, or people of the plain, driven hard by their foes, fled over the Lebanon and took possession of a narrow strip of land shut off by itself between the mountains and the sea.

The Phoenicians

The agricultural resources of the little country were soon outgrown, and the Phoenicians were forced to gather a harvest from the water. They invented the fishing-line and net, and when the fish could no longer be caught from the shore they had to follow them out to sea or starve. They hollowed trunks of trees with axe and fire into canoes; they bound logs of wood together to form a raft, with a bush stuck in it for a sail. The Lebanon mountains supplied them with timber; in time they discovered how to make boats with keels, and to sheathe them with copper, which also they found in their mountains. From those heights of Lebanon the island of Cyprus could plainly be seen, and the current assisted them across. They colonised the island; it supplied them with pitch, timber, copper, and hemp--everything that was required in the architecture of a ship. With smacks and cutters they followed the tunny-fish in their migrations; they discovered villages on other coasts, pillaged them, and carried off their inhabitants as slaves. Some of these, when they had learnt the language, offered to pay a ransom for their release; the arrangement was accomplished under oath, and presents as tokens of goodwill were afterwards exchanged. Each party was pleased to obtain something which his own country did not produce, and thus arose a system of barter and exchange.

The Phoenicians from fishermen became pirates, and from pirates traders: from simple traders they became also manufacturers. Purple was always the fashionable colour in the East, and they discovered two kinds of shell-fish which yielded a handsome dye. One species was found on rocks, the other under water. These shells they collected by means of divers and pointer dogs. When the supply on their own coast was exhausted they obtained them from foreign coasts, and as the shell yielded but a small quantity of fluid, and therefore was inconvenient to transport, they preferred to extract the dyeing material on the spot where the shells were found. This led to the establishment of factories abroad, and permanent settlements were made. Obtaining wool from the Arabs and other shepherd tribes, they manufactured woven goods and dyed them with such skill that they found a ready market in Babylonia and Egypt. In this manner they purchased from those countries the produce and manufactures of the East, and these they sold at a great profit to the inhabitants of Europe.

When they sailed along the shores of that savage continent and came to a place where they intended to trade, they lighted a fire to attract the natives, pitched tents on shore, and held a six days' fair, exhibiting in their bazaar the toys and trinkets manufactured at Tyre expressly for their naked customers, with purple robes and works of art in tinted ivory and gold for those who, like the Greeks, were more advanced. At the end of the week they went

150

away, sometimes kidnapping a few women and children to "fill up." But in the best trading localities the factory system prevailed, and their establishments were planted in the Grecian Archipelago and in Greece itself, on the marshy shores of the Black Sea, in Italy, in Sicily, on the African coast and in Spain.

Then, becoming bolder and more skilful, they would no longer be imprisoned within the lake-like waters of the land-locked sea. They sailed out through the Straits of Gibraltar and beheld the awful phenomenon of tides. They sailed on the left hand to Morocco for ivory and gold dust, on the right hand for amber and tin to the ice-creeks of the Baltic and the foaming waters of the British Isles. They also opened up an inland trade. They were the first to overcome the exclusiveness of Egypt, and were permitted to settle in Memphis itself. Their quarter was called the Syrian camp; it was built round a grove and chapel sacred to Astarte. Their caravan routes extended in every direction towards the treasure countries of the East. Wandering Arabs were their sailors, and camels were their ships. They made voyages by sand, more dangerous than those by sea, to Babylon through Palmyra or Tadmor on the skirts of the desert; to Arabia Felix and the market city of Petra; and to Gerrha, a city built entirely of salt on the rainless shores of the Persian Gulf.

Phoenicia itself was a narrow, undulating plain about a hundred miles in length, and at the most not more than a morning's ride in breadth. It was walled in by the mountains on the north and east. To those who sailed along its coast it appeared to be one great city interspersed with gardens and fields. On the lower slopes of the hills beyond gleamed the green vineyard patches and the villas of the merchants. The offing was whitened with sails, and in every harbour was a grove of masts. But it was Tyre which of all the cities was the queen. It covered an island which lay at anchor off the shore. The Greek poet Nonnus has prettily described the mingling around it of the sylvan and marine. "The sailor furrows the sea with his oar," he says, "and the ploughman the soil; the lowing of oxen and the singing of birds answer the deep roar of the main; the wood nymph under the tall trees hears the voice of the sea-nymph calling to her from the waves; the breeze from the Lebanon, while it cools the rustic at his midday labour, speeds the mariner who is outward bound."

These Canaanitish men are fairly entitled to our gratitude and esteem, for they taught our intellectual ancestors to read and write. Wherever a factory trade is carried on it is found convenient to employ natives as subordinate agents and clerks. And thus it was that the Greeks received the rudiments of education. That the alphabet was invented by the Phoenicians is improbable in the extreme, but it is certain that they introduced it into Europe. They were intent only on making money, it is true; they were not a literary or artistic people; they spread knowledge by accident like birds dropping seeds. But they were gallant, hardy, enterprising men. Those were true heroes who first sailed through the sea-valley of Gibraltar into the vast ocean and breasted its enormous waves. Their unceasing activity kept the world alive. They offered to every country something which it did not possess. They roused the savage Briton from his torpor with a rag of scarlet cloth, and stirred him to sweat in the dark bowels of the earth. They brought to the satiated Indian prince the luscious wines of Syria and the Grecian amber-gatherers of the Baltic mud to the nutmeg-growers of the equatorial groves, from the mulberry plantations of the Celestial Empire to the tin-mines of Cornwall and the silver-mines of Spain, emulation was excited, new wants were created, and whole nations were stimulated to industry by the agency of the Phoenicians.

Shipbuilding and navigation were their inventions, and for a long time were entirely in their hands. Phoenician shipwrights were employed to build the fleet of Sennacherib: Phoenician mariners were employed by Necho to sail round Africa. But they could not forever monopolise the sea. The Greeks built ships on the Phoenician model, and soon showed their masters that kidnapping and piracy was a game at which two could play. The merchant kings who possessed the whole commercial world were too wise to stake their prosperity on a single province. They had no wish to tempt a siege of Tyre which might resemble the siege of Troy. They quickly retired from Greece and its islands, and the western coast of Asia Minor and the margin of the Black Sea. They allowed the Greeks to take the foot of Italy and the eastern half of Sicily, and did not molest their isolated colonies of Cyrene in Africa and Marseilles in Southern Gaul.

But in spite of all their prudence and precautions, the Greeks supplanted them entirely. The Phoenicians, like the Jews, were vassals of necessity and by position: they lived half-way between two empires. They found it cheaper to pay tribute than to go to war, and submitted to the emperor of Syria for the time being, sending their money with equal indifference to Nineveh or Memphis.

But when the empire was disputed, as in the days of Nebuchadnezzar and of Necho, they were compelled to choose a side. Like the Jews, they chose the wrong one, and the old Tyre and Jerusalem were demolished at the same time.

From that day the Phoenicians began to go down the hill, and under the Persians their ships and sailors were forced to do service in the royal navy. This was the hardest kind of tribute that they could be made to pay, for it deprived them not only of their profits but of the means by which those profits were obtained. In the Macedonian war they went wrong again; they chose the side of the Persians although they had so often rebelled against them and Tyre was severely handled by its conqueror. But it was the foundation of Alexandria which ruined the Phoenician cities, as it ruined Athens. Form that time Athens ceased to be commercial and became a university. Tyre also ceased to be commercial, but remained a celebrated manufactory. Under the Roman empire it enjoyed the monopoly of the sacred purple, which was afterwards adopted by the popes. It prospered under the caliphs; its manufactories in the Middle Ages were conducted by the Jews; but it fell before the artillery of the Turks to rise no more. The secret of the famous dye was lost, and the Vatican changed the colour of its robes.

But while Phoenicia was declining in the East its great colony, Carthage, was rising in the West. This city had been founded by malcontents from Tyre. But they kindly cherished the memories of their motherland, and, like the Pilgrim Fathers, always spoke of the country which had cast them forth as "Home." And after a time all the old wrongs were forgotten, all angry feelings died away. Every year the Carthaginians sent to the national temple a tenth part of their revenues as a free-will offering. During the great Persian wars, when on all sides empires and kingdoms were falling to the ground, the Phoenicians refused to lend their fleet to the Great King to make war upon Carthage. When Tyre was besieged by Alexander the nobles sent their wives and children to Carthage, where they were tenderly received.

The Africa of the ancients--the modern Barbary--lies between the Sahara and the Mediterranean Sea. It is protected from the ever-encroaching waves of the sandy ocean by the Atlas range. In its western parts this mountain wall is high and broad and covered with eternal snow. It becomes lower as it runs towards the east, also drawing nearer to the sea, and dwindles and dwindles till finally it disappears, leaving a wide, unprotected region between Barbary and Egypt. Over this the Sahara flows, forming a desert barrier tract to all intents and purposes itself a sea, dividing the two lands from each other as completely as the Mediterranean divides Italy and Greece. This land of North Africa is in reality a part of Spain; the Atlas is the southern boundary of Europe. Grey cork-trees clothe the lower sides of those magnificent mountains; their summits are covered with pines, among which the cross-bill flutters, and in which the European bear may still be found. The flora of the range, as Dr. Hooker has lately shown, is of a Spanish type; the Straits of Gibraltar is merely an accident; there is nothing in Morocco to distinguish it from Andalusia. The African animals which are there found are desert-haunting species--the antelope and gazelle, the lion, the jackal, the hyena, [spelt hyaena in original text] and certain species of the monkey tribe; and these might easily have found their way across the Sahara from oasis to oasis. It is true that in the Carthaginian days the elephant abounded in the forests of the Atlas, and it could not have come across from central Africa, for the Sahara, before it was a desert, was a sea. It is probable that the elephant of Barbary belonged to the same species as the small elephant of Europe, the bones of which have been discovered in Malta and in certain caves of Spain, and that it outlived the European kind on account of its isolated position in the Atlas, which was thinly inhabited by savage tribes. But it did not long withstand the power of the Romans. Pliny mentions that in his time the forests of Morocco were being ransacked for ivory, and Isidore of Seville, in the seventh century observes that "there are no longer any elephants in Mauritania."

In Morocco the Phoenicians were settled only on the coast. The Regency of Tunis and part of Algeria is the scene on which the tragedy of Carthage was performed.

In that part of Africa the habitable country must be divided into three regions; first a corn region, lying between the Atlas and the sea, exceedingly fertile but narrow in extent; secondly the Atlas itself, with its timber stores and elephant preserves; and thirdly a plateau region of poor sandy soil, affording a meagre pasture, interspersed with orchards of date-trees, abounding in ostriches, lions, and gazelles, and gradually fading away into the desert.

Africa belonged to a race of man whom we shall call Berbers or Moors, but who were known as the ancients under many names, and who still exist as the Kabyles or Algeria, the Shilluhs of the Atlas, and the Tuaricks or tawny Moors of the Sahara. Their habits depended on the locality in which they dwelt. Those who lived in the Tell or region of the coast cultivated the soil and lived in towns, some of which appear to have been of considerable size. Those who inhabited the plateau region led a free Bedouin life, wandering from place to place with flocks and herds, and camping under oblong huts which the Romans compared to boats turned upside down. In holes and caverns of the mountains dwelt a miserable black race, apparently the aborigines of the country, and represented to this day by the Rock Tibboos. They were also found on the outskirts of the desert, and were hunted by the Berbers in four-horse chariots, caught alive, and taken to the Carthage market to be sold.

The Phoenician settlements were at first independent of one another, but Carthage gradually obtained the supremacy as Tyre had obtained it in Phoenicia. The position of Utica towards Carthage was precisely that of Sidon towards Tyre. It was the more ancient city of the two, and it preserved a certain kind of position without actual power. Carthage and Utica, like Tyre and Sidon, were at one time always spoken of together.

The Carthaginians began by paying a quit-rent or custom to the natives, but that did not last very long; they made war, and exacted tribute from the original possessors of the soil. When Carthage suffered from over-population, colonies were dispatched out west along the coast, and down south into the interior. These colonies were more on the Roman than the Greek pattern; the emigrants built cities and intermarried freely with the Berbers, for there was no difference of colour between them, and little difference of race. In course of time the whole of the habitable region was subdued; the Tyrian factory became a mighty empire. Many of the roving tribes were broken in; the others were driven into the desert or into wild Morocco. A line of fortified posts and block-houses protected the cultivated land. The desire to obtain red cloth and amber and blue beads secured the allegiance of many unconquerable desert tribes, and by their means, although the camel had not yet been introduced, a trade was opened up between Carthage and Timbuktu. Negro slaves, bearing tusks of ivory on their shoulders and tied to one another so as to form a chain of flesh and blood, were driven across the terrible desert--a caravan of death, the route of which was marked by bones bleaching in the sun. Gold dust also was brought over from those regions of the Niger, and the Carthaginian traders reached the same land by sea. For they were not content, like the Tyrians, to trade only on the Morocco coast as far as Mogadore. By good fortune there has been preserved the log-book of an expedition which sailed to the wood-covered shores of Guinea; saw the hills covered with fire, as they always are in the dry season when the grass is being burnt; heard the music of the natives in the night; and brought home the skins of three chimpanzees which they probably killed near Sierra Leone.

When Phoenicia died, Carthage inherited its settlements on the coasts of Sicily and Spain and on the adjoining isles. Not only were these islands valuable possessions in themselves--Malta as a cotton plantation, Elba as an iron-mine, Majorca and Minorca as a recruiting ground for slingers; they were also useful as naval stations to preserve the monopoly of the Western waters.

The foreign policy of Carthage was very different from that of the motherland. The Phoenicians had maintained an army of mercenaries, but had used them only to protect their country from the robber kings of Damascus and Jerusalem. They had many ships of war, but had used them only to convoy their round-bellied ships of trade and to keep off the attacks of the Greek and Etruscan pirates. Their settlements were merely fortified factories; they made no attempt to reduce the natives of the land. If their settlements grew into colonies, they let them go. But Carthage founded many colonies and never lost a single one. Situated among them, and possessing a large fleet, she was able both to punish and protect. She defended them in time of war; she controlled them in time of peace.

A policy of concession had not saved the Phoenicians from the Greeks, and now these same Greeks were settling in the West and displaying immense activity. The Carthaginians saw that they must resist or be ruined, and they went to war as a matter of business. They first put down the Etruscan rovers, in which undertaking they were assisted by the events which occurred on the Italian main. They next put a stop to the spread of the Greek power in Africa itself.

Half-way between Algeria and Egypt, in the midst of the dividing sea of sand, is a coast oasis formed by a tableland of sufficient height to condense the vapours which float over from the sea, and to chill them into rain. There was a hole in the sky above it, as the natives used to say. To this island-tract came a band of Greeks directed thither by the oracle at Delphi, where geography was studied as a part of the system. They established a city and called it Cyrene.

The land was remarkably fertile, and afforded them three harvests in the course of the year. One was gathered on the coast meadows, which were watered by the streams that flowed down from the hills; a second on the hill-sides; a third on the surface of the plateau, [spelt pleateau in the original text] which was about two thousand feet above the level of the sea. Cyrenaica produced the silphium, or asafoetida, which, like the balm of Gilead, was one of the specifics of antiquity, and which is really a medicine of value. It was found in many parts of the world--for instance, in certain districts of Asia Minor, and on the summit of the Hindu Kush. But the asafoetida of Cyrene was the most esteemed. Its juice, when dried, was worth its weight in gold; its leaves fattened cattle and cured them of all diseases.

Some singular pits or chasms existed in the lower part of the Cyrene hills. Their sides were perpendicular walls of rock: it appeared impossible to descend to the bottom of the precipice, and yet, when the traveller peeped over the brink, he saw to his astonishment that the abyss beneath had been sown with herbs and corn. Hence rose the legend of the Gardens of the Hesperides.

Cyrene was renowned as the second medical school of the Greek world. It produced a noted free-thinker, who was a companion of Socrates and the founder of a school. It was also famous for its barbs, which won more than one prize in the chariot races of the Grecian games. It obtained the honour of more than one Pindaric ode. But owing to internal dissension it never became great. It was conquered by Persia, it submitted to Alexander, and Carthage speedily checked its growth towards the west by taking the desert which lay between them, and which it then garrisoned with nomad tribes.

The Carthaginians hitherto had never paid tribute, and they had never suffered a serious reverse. Alcibiades talked much of invading them when he had done with Sicily, and the young men of his set were at one time always drawing plans of Carthage in the dust of the market-place at Athens; but the Sicilian expedition failed. The affection of the Tyrians preserved them from Cambyses. Alexander opportunely died. Pyrrhus in Sicily began to collect ships to sail across, but he who tried to take up Italy with one hand and Carthage with the other, and who also excited the enmity of the Sicilian Greeks, was not a very dangerous foe. Agathocles of Syracuse invaded Africa, but it was the action of a desperate and defeated man and bore no result.

Sicily was long the battlefield of the Carthaginians, and ultimately proved their ruin. Its western side belonged to them: its eastern side was held by a number of independent Greek cities which were often at war with one another. Of these Syracuse was the most important: its ambition was the same as that of Carthage--to conquer the whole island, and then to extend its rule over the flourishing Greek towns on the south Italian coast. Hence followed wars generation after generation, till at length the Carthaginians obtained the upper hand. Already they were looking on the island as their own when a new power stepped upon the scene.

The ancient Tuscans or Etruscans had a language and certain arts peculiar to themselves, and Northern Italy was occupied by Celtic Gauls. But the greater part of the peninsula was inhabited by a people akin to the Greeks, though differing much from them in character, dwelling in city-states, using a form of the Phoenician alphabet, and educating their children in public schools. The Greek cities on the coast diffused a certain amount of culture through the land.

A rabble of outlaws and runaway slaves banded together, built a town, fortified it strongly, and offered it as an asylum to all fugitives. To Rome fled the over-beaten slave, the thief with his booty, the murdered with blood-red hands. This city of refuge became a war-town--to use an African phrase--its citizens alternately fought and farmed; it became the dread and torment of the neighbourhood. However, it contained no women, and it was hoped that in course of time the generation of robbers would die out. The Romans offered their hands and hearts to the daughters of a neighbouring Sabine city. The Sabines declined, and told them that they had better make their city an asylum for runaway women. The Romans took the Sabine girls by force; a war ensued, but the relationship had been established; the women reconciled their fathers to their husbands, and the tribes were united in the same city.

The hospitality which Rome had offered in its early days in order to sustain its life became a custom and a policy. The Romans possessed the art of converting their conquered enemies into allies, and this was done by means of concessions which cities of respectable origin would have been too proud to make.

Their military career was very different from that of the Persians, who swept over the continent in a few months. The Romans spent three centuries in establishing their rule within a circle of a hundred miles round the city. Whatever they won by the sword they secured by the plough. After every successful war they demanded a tract of land, and on this they planted a colony of Roman farmers. The municipal governments of the conquered cities were left undisturbed. The Romans aimed to establish, at least in appearance, a federation of states, a united Italy. At the time of the first Punic War this design had nearly been accomplished. Wild tribes of Celtic shepherds still roamed over the rich plains at the foot of the Alps, but the Italian boroughs had acknowledged the supremacy of Rome. The Greek cities on the southern coast had, a few years before, called over Pyrrhus, King of Epirus, a soldier of fortune and the first general of the day. But the legion broke the Macedonian phalanx, and the broadsword vanquished the Macedonian spear. The Greek cities were no longer independent except in name. Pyrrhus returned to Greece, and prophesied of Sicily, as he left its shores, that it would become the arena of the Punic and the Roman arms.

In the last war that was ever waged between the Syracusans and the Carthaginians, the former had employed some mercenary troops belonging to the Mamertines, an Italian tribe. When the war was ended these soldiers were paid off and began to march home. They passed through the Greek town of Messina on their road, were hospitably received by the citizens, and provided with quarters for the night. In the middle of the night they rose up and massacred the men, married the widows, and settled down as rulers of Messina, each soldier beneath another man's vine and fig-tree. A Roman regiment stationed at Rhegium, a Greek town on the Italian side of the straits, heard of this exploit, considered it an excellent idea, and did the same. The Romans marched upon Rhegium, took it by storm, and executed four hundred of the soldiers in the Forum. The king of Syracuse, who held the same position in eastern Sicily as did Rome on the peninsula, marched against Messina. The Mamertine bandits became alarmed; one party sent to the Carthaginians for assistance; another party sent to Rome, declaring that they were kinsmen and desired to enter the Italian league.

156

The Roman Senate rejected this request on account of its "manifest absurdity." They had just punished their soldiers for imitating the Mamertines; how then could they interfere with the punishment of the Mamertines? But in Rome the people possessed the sovereign power of making peace or war. There was a scarcity of money at that time; a raid on Sicily would yield plunder, and troops were accordingly ordered to Messina. For the first time Romans went outside Italy--the vanguard of an army which subdued the world. The Carthaginians were already in Messina: the Romans drove them out, and the war began. The Syracusans were defeated in the first battle, and then went over to the Roman side. It became a war between Asiatics and Europeans.

Carthage and Rome

The two great republics were already well acquainted with each other. In the apartment of the Aediles in the Capitol was preserved a commercial treaty between Carthage and Rome, inscribed on tables of brass in old Latin; in the time of Polybius it could scarcely be understood, for it had been drawn up twenty eight years before Xerxes invaded Greece. When Pyrrhus invaded Italy the Carthaginians had taken the Roman side, for the Greeks were their hereditary enemies. There were Carthaginian shops in the streets of Rome, a city in beauty and splendour far inferior to Carthage, which was called the metropolis of the Western world. The Romans were a people of warriors and small farmers, quaint in their habits and simple in their tastes. Some Carthaginian ambassadors were much amused at the odd fashion of their banquets, where the guests sang old ballads in turn while the piper played, and they discovered that there was only one service of plate in Rome, and that each senator borrowed it when he gave a dinner. Yet there were already signs that Rome was inhabited by a giant race. The vast aqueducts had been constructed; the tunnel-like sewers had been hollowed out; the streets were paved with smooth and massive slabs. There were many temples and statues to be seen; each temple was the monument of a great victory; each statue was the memorial of a hero who had died for Rome.

The Carthaginian army was composed entirely of mercenary troops. Africa, Spain and Gaul were their recruiting grounds, an inexhaustible treasury of warriors as long as the money lasted which they received as pay. The Berbers were a splendid Cossack cavalry; they rode without saddle or bridle, a weapon in each hand; on foot they were merely a horde or savages with elephant-hide shields, long spears, and bear-skins floating from their shoulders. The troops of Spain were the best infantry that the Carthaginians possessed; they wore a white uniform with purple facings; they fought with pointed swords. The Gauls were brave troops but were badly armed; they were naked to the waist; their cutlasses were made of soft iron and had to be straightened after every blow. The Balearic Islands supplied a regiment of slingers whose balls of hardened clay whizzed through the air like bullets, broke armour, and shot men dead. We read much of the Sacred Legion in the Sicilian wars. It was composed of young nobles, who wore dazzling white shields and breast-plates which were works of art; who even in the camp never drank except from goblets of silver and of gold. But this corps had apparently become extinct, and the Carthaginians only officered their troops, who they looked upon as ammunition, and to whom their orders were delivered through interpreters. The various regiments of the Carthaginian army had therefore nothing in common with one another or with those by whom they were led. They rushed to battle in confusion, "with sounds, discordant as their various tribes," and with no higher feeling than the hope of plunder or the excitement which the act of fighting arouses in the brave soldier.

In Rome the army was the nation: no citizen could take office unless he had served in ten campaigns. All spoke the same language, all were inspired by the same ambition. The officers were often small farmers like the men, but this civil equality produced no ill effects; the discipline was most severe. It was a maxim that the soldier should fear his officer more than he feared his foe. The drill was unremitting; when they were in winter quarters they erected sheds in which the soldiers fenced with swords cased in leather with buttons at the point and hurled javelins, also buttoned, at one another. These foils were double the weight of the weapons that were actually used. When the day's march was over they took pick-axe and spade, and built their camp like a town with a twelve-foot stockade around it, and a ditch twelve feet deep and twelve feet broad. When the red mantle was hung before the general's tent each soldier said to himself, "Perhaps to-day I may win the golden crown." Laughing and jesting they rubbed their limbs with oil, and took out of their cases the bright helmets and the polished shields which they used only on the battle-day. As they stood ready to advance upon the foe, the general would address them in a vigorous speech; he would tell them that the greatest honour which could befall a Roman was to die for his country on the field, and that glorious was the sorrow, enviable the woe of the matron who gave a husband or a son to Rome. Then the trumpets pealed, and the soldiers charged, first firing a volley of javelins and then coming to close quarters with the solid steel. The chief fault of the Roman military system at that time was in the arrangement of the chief command. There were two commanders-in-chief, possessing equal powers, and it sometimes happened that they were both present on the same spot, that they commanded on alternate days, and that their tactics differed. They were appointed only for the year, and when the term drew near its end a consul would often fight a battle at a disadvantage, or negotiate a premature peace, that he might prevent his successor from reaping the fruits of his twelve month's toil. The Carthaginian generals had thereby an advantage, but they also were liable to be recalled when too successful by the jealous and distrustful government at home.

The wealth of Carthage was much greater than that of Rome, but her method of making war was more costly, and a great deal of money was stolen and wasted by the men in power. In Carthage the highest offices of state were openly bought from a greedy and dangerous populace, just as in Pompey's time tables were set out in the streets of Rome at which candidates for office paid the people for their votes. But at this time bribery was a capital offence at Rome. It was a happy period in Roman history, the interlude between two aristocracies. There had been a time when a system of hereditary castes prevailed; when the plebeians were excluded from all share in the public lands and the higher offices of state; when they were often chained in the dungeons of the nobles, and marked with scars upon their backs: when Romans drew swords on Romans and the tents of the people whitened the Sacred Hill. But the Licinian Laws were carried; the orders were reconciled; plebeian consuls were elected; and two centuries of prosperity, harmony, and victory prepared Rome for the prodigious contest in which she was now engaged.

To her subject people Carthage acted as a tyrant. She had even deprived the old Phoenician cities of their liberty of trade. She would not allow them to build walls for fear they should rebel, loaded them with heavy burdens grievous to be borne, treated the colonial provinces as conquered lands, and sent decayed nobles as governors to wring out of the people all they could. If the enemies of Carthage invaded Africa they would meet with no resistance except from Carthage herself, and they would be joined by thousands of Berbers who longed to be revenged on their oppressors. But if the enemies of Rome invaded Italy they would find everywhere walled cities ready to defend their liberties and having liberties to defend. No tribute was taken by Rome from her allies except that of military service, which service was rewarded with a share of the harvest that the war brought in.

The Carthaginians were at a greater distance from the seat of war than the Romans, who had only to sail across a narrow strait. However, this was counterbalanced by the superiority of the Punic fleet. At that time the Carthaginians were completely masters of the sea; they boasted that no man could wash his hands in the salt water without their permission. The Romans had not a single decked vessel, and in order to transport their troops across the straits they were obliged to borrow triremes from the Italian-Greeks. But their marvellous resolution and the absolute necessities of the case overmastered their deficiencies and their singular dislike of the sea. The wreck of a Carthaginian man-of-war served them as a model; they ranged benches along the beach and drilled sailors who had just come from the plough's tail to the service of the oar. The vessels were rudely built and the men clumsy at their work, and, when the hostile fleets first met, the Carthaginians burst into loud guffaws. Without taking order of battle they flew down upon the Romans, the admiral leading the van in a seven-decker that had belonged to Pyrrhus. On they went, each ship in a bed of creamy foam, flags flying, trumpets blowing, and the negroes singing and clanking their chains as they laboured at the oar. But presently they perceived some odd-looking machines on the forecastles of the Roman ships; they had never seen such things before, and this made them hesitate a little. But when they saw in what a lubberly fashion the ships were worked their confidence returned; they dashed in among the Roman vessels, which they tried to rip up with their aquiline prows. As soon as they came to close quarters the machines fell down upon them with a crash, tore open their decks, and grappled them tightly in their iron jaws, forming at the same time a gangway over which the Roman soldiers poured. The sea fight was made a land fight, and only a few ships with beaks all bent and broken succeeded in making their escape. They entered the harbour of Carthage with their bows covered with skins, the signal of defeat.

However, by means of skilful manoeuvring the invention of Duilius was made of no avail, and the Carthaginians for many years remained the masters of the sea. Twice the Roman fleet was entirely destroyed, and their treasury was now exhausted. But the undaunted people fitted out a fleet by private subscription, and so rapidly was this done that the trees, as Florus said, were transformed into ships. Two hundred five-deckers were ready before the enemy knew that they had begun to build, and so the Carthaginian fleet was one day surprised by the Romans in no fighting condition, for the vessels were laden to the gunwales with corn, and only sailors were on board; the whole fleet was taken or sunk, and the war was at an end. Yet when all was added up it was found that the Romans had lost two hundred vessels more than the Carthaginians. But Rome, even without large ships, could always reinforce Sicily, while the Carthaginians, without a full fleet, were completely cut off from the seat of war, and they were unable to rebuild in the manner of the Romans.

The war in Sicily had been a drawn game. Hamilcar Barca, although unconquered, received orders to negotiate for peace. The Romans demanded a large indemnity to pay for the expenses of the war, and took the Sicilian settlements which Carthage had held for four hundred years.

Peace was made, and the mercenary troops were sent back to Carthage. Their pay was in arrear, and there was no money left. Matters were so badly managed that the soldiers were allowed to retain their arms. They burst into mutiny, ravaged the country, and besieged the capital. The veterans of Hamilcar could only be conquered by Hamilcar himself. He saved Carthage, but the struggle was severe. Venerable senators, ladies of gentle birth, innocent children, had fallen into the hands of the brutal mutineers, and had been crucified, torn to pieces, tortured to death in a hundred ways. During those awful orgies of Spendius and Matho, the Roman war had almost been forgotten; the disasters over which men had mourned became by comparison happiness and peace. The destruction of the fleet was viewed as a slight calamity when death was howling at the city gates. At last Hamilcar triumphed, and the rebels were cast to the elephants, who kneaded their bodies with their feet and gored them with their tusks; and Carthage, exhausted, faint from loss of blood, attempted to repose.

But all was not yet over. The troops that were stationed in Sardinia rebelled, and Hamilcar prepared to sail with an armament against them.

The Romans had acted in the noblest manner towards the Carthaginians during the civil war. The Italian merchants had been allowed to supply Carthage with provisions, and had been forbidden to communicate with the rebels. When the Sardinian troops mutinied they offered the island to Rome; the city of Utica had also offered itself to Rome, but the Senate had refused both applications. And now all of a sudden, as if possessed by an evil spirit, they pretended that the Carthaginian armament had been prepared against Rome, and declared war. When Carthage, in the last stage of misery and prostration, prayed for peace in the name of all the pitiful gods, it was granted. But Rome had been put to some expense on account of this intended war; they must therefore pay an additional indemnity, and surrender Corsica and Sardinia. Poor Carthage was made to bite the dust indeed.

Hamilcar Barca was appointed commander-in-chief. He was the favourite of the people. He had to the last remained unconquered in Sicily. He had saved the city from the mutineers. His honour was unstained, his patriotism was pure.

In that hour of calamity and shame, when the city was hung with black, when the spacious docks were empty and bare, when there was woe in every face and the memory of death in every house, faction was forced to be silent, and the people were permitted to be heard, and those who loved their country more than their party rejoiced to see a Man at the head of affairs. But Hamilcar knew well that he was hated by the leaders of the government, the politicians by profession, those men who had devoured the gold which was the very heart of Carthage, and had brought upon her by their dishonesty this last distressing war; those men who by their miserable suspicions and intrigues had ever deprived their best generals of their commands as soon as they began to succeed, and appointed generals whom they--and the enemy--had no cause to fear. To him was entrusted by the patriots the office of regenerating Carthage. But how was it to be done? Without money he was powerless; without money he could not keep his army together; without money he could not even retain his command. He had been given it by the people, but the people were accustomed to be bribed. Gold they must have from the men in power; if he had none to give they would go to those who had. His enemies he knew would be able to employ the state revenues against him. What could he do? Where was the money to be found? He saw before him nothing but defeat, disgrace, and even an ignominious death--for in Carthage they sometimes crucified their generals. Often he thought that it would be better to give up public life, to abandon the corrupt and ruined city, and to sail to those sweet islands which the Carthaginians had discovered in the Atlantic Sea. There the earth was always verdant, the sky was always pure. No fiery sirocco blew, and no cold rain fell in that delicious land. Odoriferous balm dripped from the branches of the trees; canary birds sang among the leaves; streams of silver water rippled downwards to the sea. There Nature was a calm and gentle mother: there the turmoils of the world might be forgotten; there the weary heart might be at rest.

Yet how could he desert his fatherland in its affliction? To him the nation turned its sorrowful eyes; on him the people called as men call upon their gods. At this feet lay the poor, torn, and wounded Carthage--the Carthage once so beautiful and so strong, the Carthage who had fed him from her full breast with riches and with power, the Carthage who had made him what he was. And should he, who had never turned his back upon her enemies, desert her now?

Then a glorious idea flashed in upon his brain. He saw a way of restoring Carthage to her ancient glory, of making her stronger than she had ever been, of making her a match for Rome. He announced to the senate that he intended to take the army to Tangiers to reduce a native tribe which had caused some trouble in the neighbourhood. He quickly made all arrangements for the march. A few vessels had been prepared for the expedition to Sardinia. These were commanded by his brother, and he ordered that they should be sailed along the coast side by side with the army as it marched. It might have appeared strange to some persons that he should require ships to make war against a tribe of Moors on land. But there was no fear of his enemies suspecting his design. It was so strange and wild that when it had been actually accomplished they could scarcely believe that it was real.

The night before he marched he went to the Great Temple to offer the sacrifice of propitiation and entreaty. He took with him his son, a boy nine years of age. When the libations and other rites were ended and the victim lay divided on the altar, he ordered the attendants to withdraw. He remained alone with his son.

The temple of Baal was a magnificent building supported by enormous columns, covered with gold, or formed of a glass-like substance which began to glitter and sparkle in a curious manner as the night came on. Around the temple walls were idols representing the Phoenician gods; prominent among them was the hideous statue of Moloch, with its downward-sloping hands and the fiery furnace at its feet. There also might be seen beautiful Greek statues, trophies of the Sicilian Wars--especially the Diana which the Carthaginians had taken from Segesta, which was afterwards restored to that city by the Romans, which Verres placed in his celebrated gallery and Cicero in his celebrated speech. There also might be seen the famous brazen bull which an Athenian invented for the amusement of Phalaris. Human beings were put inside, a fire was lit underneath, and the throat was so contrived that the shrieks and groans of the victims made the bull bellow as if he was alive. The first experiment was made by King Phalaris upon the artist, and the last by the people upon King Phalaris.

Hamilcar caressed his son and asked him if he would like to go to the war; when the boy said yes, and showed much delight, Hamilcar took his little hands and placed them upon the altar, and made him swear that he would hate the Romans to his dying day. Long years afterwards, when that boy was an exile in a foreign land--the most glorious, the most unfortunate of men--he was accused by his royal host of secretly intriguing with the Romans. He then related this circumstance, and asked if it was likely that he would ever be a friend to Rome.

Hamilcar marched. The politicians supposed that he was merely engaged in a third-rate war, and were quite easy in their minds. But one day there came a courier from Tangiers. He brought tidings which plunged the whole city in a tumult of wonder and excitement. The three great streets which led to the market-place were filled with streaming crowds. A multitude collected round the city hall, in which sat the senators anxiously deliberating. Women appeared on the roofs of the houses and bent eagerly over the parapets, while men ran along bawling out the news. Hamilcar Barca had gone clean off. He was no longer in Africa. He had crossed the sea. The Tangier expedition was a trick. He had taken the army right over into Spain, and was fighting with the native chiefs who had always been the friends and allies of Carthage.

By a strange fortuity, Spain was the Peru of the ancient world. The horrors of the mines in South America, the sufferings of the Indians, were copied, so to speak, from the early history of the people who inflicted them. When the Phoenicians first entered the harbours of Andalusia they found themselves in a land where silver was used as iron. They loaded their vessel with the precious metal to the water's edge, cast away their wooden lead-weighted anchor, and substituted a lump of pure silver in its stead. Afterwards factories were established, arrangements were made with the chiefs for the supply of labour, and the mining was conducted on scientific principles. The Carthaginians succeeded the Phoenicians, and remained, like them, only on the coast.

It was Hamilcar's design to conquer the whole country, to exact tribute from the inhabitants, to create a Spanish army. His success was splendid and complete. The peninsula of Spain became almost entirely a Punic province. Hamilcar built a city which he called New Carthage--the Carthagena of modern times--and discovered in its neighbourhood rich mines of silver-lead which have lately been reopened. He acquired a private fortune, formed a native army, fed his party at Carthage, and enriched the treasury of the state. He administered the province nine years, and then dying, was succeeded by his brother, who, after governing or reigning a few years, also died. Hannibal, the son of Hamilcar, became Viceroy of Spain.

It appears strange that Rome should so tamely have allowed the Carthaginians to take Spain. The truth was that the Romans just then had enough to do to look after their own affairs. The Gauls of Lombardy had furiously attacked the Italian cities, and had called to their aid the Gauls who lived beyond the Alps. Before the Romans had beaten off the barbarians the conquest in Spain had been accomplished. The Romans therefore accepted the fact, and contented themselves with a treaty by which the government of Carthage pledged itself not to pass beyond the Ebro.

But Hannibal cared nothing about treaties made at Carthage. As Hamilcar without orders had invaded Spain, so he without orders invaded Italy. The expedition of the Gauls had shown him that it was possible to cross the Alps, and he chose that extraordinary route. The Roman army was about to embark for Spain, which it was supposed would be the seat or war, when the news arrived that Hannibal had alighted in Italy with elephants and cavalry, like a man descending from the clouds.

If wars were always decided by individual exploits and pitched battles, Hannibal would have conquered Italy. He defeated the Romans so often and so thoroughly that at last they found it their best policy not to fight with him at all. He could do nothing then but sweep over the country with his Cossack cavalry, plunder, and destroy. It was impossible for him to take Rome, which was protected by walls strong as rocks and by rocks steep as walls. When he did march on Rome, encamping within three miles of the city and raising a panic during an afternoon, it was done merely as a ruse to draw away the Roman army from the siege of Capua. But it did not have even that effect. The army before Capua remained where it was, and another army appeared as if by magic to defend the city. Rome appeared to be inexhaustible, and so in reality it was.

Hannibal knew well that Italy could be conquered only by Italians. So great a general could never have supposed that with a handful of cavalry he could subdue a country which had a million armed men to bring into the field. He had taken it for granted that if he could gain some success at first he would be joined by the subject cities. But in spite of his great victories they remained true to Rome. Nothing shows so clearly the immense resources of the Italian Republic as that second Punic War. Hannibal was in their country, but they employed against him only a portion of their troops. A second army was in Sicily waging war against his Greek allies; a third army was in Spain, attacking his operations at the base, pulling Carthage out of Europe by the roots. Added to which, it was now the Romans who ruled the sea. When Scipio had taken New Carthage and conquered Spain, he crossed over into Africa, and Hannibal was of necessity recalled. He met on the field of Zama a general whose genius was little inferior to his own, and who possessed an infinitely better army. Hannibal lost the day, and the fate of Carthage was decided. It was not the battle which did that; it was the nature and constitution of the state. In itself the battle of Zama was not a more ruinous defeat than the battle of Cannae. But Carthage was made of different stuff from that of Rome. How could a war between those two people have ended otherwise than as it did? Rome was an armed nation fighting in Italy for hearth and home, in Africa for glory and revenge. Carthage was a city of merchants, who paid men to fight for them, and whose army was dissolved as soon as the exchequer was exhausted. Rome could fight to its last man; Carthage could fight only to its last dollar. At the beginning of both wars the Carthaginians did wonders, but as they became poor they became feeble; their strength dribbled out with their gold; the refusal of Alexandria to negotiate a loan perhaps injured them more deeply than the victory of Scipio.

The fall of the Carthaginian empire is not a matter for regret. Outside the walls of the city existed hopeless slavery on the part of the subject, shameless extortion on the part of the officials. Throughout Africa Carthage was never named without a curse. In the time of the mercenary war the Moorish women, taking oath to keep nothing back, stripped off their gold ornaments and brought them all to the men who were resisting their oppressors. That city, that Carthage, fed like a vulture upon the land. A corrupt and grasping aristocracy, a corrupt and turbulent populace, divided between them the prey. The Carthaginian customs were barbarous in the extreme. When a battle had been won they sacrificed their handsomest prisoners to the gods; when a battle had been lost the children of their noblest families were cast into the furnace. Their Asiatic character was strongly marked. They were a people false and sweet-worded, effeminate and cruel, tyrannical and servile, devout and licentious, merciless in triumph, faint-hearted in danger, divinely heroic in despair.

Let us therefore admit that, as an imperial city, Carthage merited her fate. But henceforth we must regard her from a different point of view. In order to obtain peace she had given up her colonies abroad, her provinces at home, her vessels and elephants of war. The empire was reduced to a municipality. Nothing was left but the city and a piece of ground. The merchant princes took off their crowns and went back into the glass and purple business. It was only as a town of manufacture and trade that Carthage continued to exist, and as such her existence was of unmixed service to the world.

Hannibal was made prime minister, and at once set to work to reform the constitution. The aristocratic party informed the Romans that he was secretly stirring up the people to war. The Romans demanded that he should be surrendered; he escaped to the court of Antiochus, the Greek king in Asia Minor, and there he did attempt to raise war against Rome. The senate were justified in expelling him from Carthage, for he was really a dangerous man. But the persecution to which he was afterwards subjected was not very creditable to their good fame. Driven from place to place, he at last took refuge in Bithynia, on the desolate shores of the Black Sea, and a Roman consul, who wished to obtain some notoriety by taking home the great Carthaginian as a show, commanded the prince under whose protection he was living to give him up. When Hannibal heard of this he took poison, saying, "Let me deliver the Romans from their cares and anxieties since they think it too tedious and too dangerous to wait for the death of a poor, hated old man." The news of this occurrence excited anger in Rome, but it was the presage of a greater crime which was soon to be committed in the Roman name.

There was a Berber chief named Masinissa who had been deprived of his estates, and who during the war had rendered important services to Rome. He was made king of Numidia, and it was stipulated in the treaty that the Carthaginians should restore the lands and cities which had belonged to him and to his ancestors. The lands which they had taken from him were accordingly surrendered, and then Masinissa sent in a claim for certain lands which he said had been taken from his ancestors. The wording of the treaty was ambiguous. He might easily declare that the whole of the sea-coast had belonged to his family in ancient times, and who could disprove the evidence of a tradition? He made no secret of his design; it was to drive the Phoenician strangers out of Africa and to reign at Carthage in their stead. He soon showed that he was worthy to be called the King of Numidia and the Friend of Rome. He drilled his bandits into soldiers; he taught his wandering shepherds to till the ground. He made his capital, Constantine, a great city; he opened schools in which the sons of native chiefs were taught to read and write in the Punic tongue. He allied himself with the powers of Morocco and the Atlas. He reminded the Berbers that it was to them the soil belonged, that the Phoenicians were intruders who had come with presents in their hands and with promises in their mouths, declaring that they had met with trouble in their own country, and praying for a place where they might repose from the weary sea. Their fathers had trusted them; their fathers had been bitterly deceived. By force and by fraud the Carthaginians had taken all the lands which they possessed; they had stolen the ground on which their city stood.

In the meantime Rome advanced into the East. As soon as the battle of Zama had been fought Alexandria demanded her protection. This brought the Romans into contact with the Graeco-Asiatic world; they found it in much the same condition as the English found Hindustan, and they conquered it in much the same manner.

Time went on. The generation of Hannibal had almost become extinct. In Carthage war had become a tradition of the past. The business of that city was again as flourishing as it had ever been. Again ships sailed to the coasts of Cornwall and Guinea; again the streets were lined with the workshops of industrious artisans. Such is the vis medicatrix, the restoring power of a widely extended commerce, combined with active manufactures and the skilful management of soil, that the city soon regained its ancient wealth. The Romans had imposed an enormous indemnity which was to be paid off by instalments extending over a series of years. The Carthaginians paid it off at once.

But in the midst of all their prosperity and happiness there were grave and anxious hearts. They saw ever before them the menacing figure of Masinissa. The very slowness of his movements was portentous. He was in all things deliberate, gradual, and calm. From time to time he demanded a tract of land; if it was not given up at once he took it by force. Then, waiting as if to digest it, he left them for a while in peace.

They were bound by treaty not to make war against the Friend of Rome. They therefore petitioned the Senate that commissioners should be sent and the boundary definitely settled. But the Senate had no desire that Carthage should be left in peace. The commissioners were instructed to report in such a manner that Masinissa might be encouraged to continue his depredations. They brought back astonishing accounts of the magnificence and activity of the African metropolis; and among these commissioners there was one man who never ceased to declare that the country was in danger, and who never rose to speak in the House without saying before he sat down: "And it is my opinion, fathers, that Carthage must be destroyed."

Cato the censor has been called the last of the old Romans. That class of patriot farmers had been extinguished by Hannibal's invasion. In order to live during the long war they had been obliged to borrow money on their lands. When the war was over the prices of everything rose to an unnatural height; the farmers could not recover themselves, and the Roman law of debt was severe. They were ejected by thousands--it was the favourite method to turn the women and children out of doors while the poor man was working in the fields. Italy was converted into a plantation; slaves in chains tilled the land. No change was made in the letter of the constitution, but the commonwealth ceased to exist. Society was now composed of the nobles, the money-merchants or city men, and a mob like that of Carthage, which lived on saleable votes, sometimes raging for agrarian laws, and which was afterwards fed at government expense like a wild beast every day.

At this time a few refined and intellectual men began to cultivate a taste for Greek literature and the fine arts. They collected libraries, and adorned them with busts of celebrated men and with antiques of Corinthian bronze. Crowds of imitators soon arose, and the conquests in the East awakened new ideas. In the days of old the Romans had been content to decorate their door-posts with trophies obtained in single combat, and their halls with the waxen portraits of their ancestors. The only spoils which they could then display were flocks and herds, wagons of rude structure, and heaps of spears and helmets. But now the arts of Greece and the riches of Asia adorned the triumphs of their generals, and the reign of taste and luxury commenced. A race of dandies appeared who wore semi-transparent robes, and who were always passing their hands in an affected manner through their hair--who lounged with the languor of the Sybarite, and spoke with the lisp of Alcibiades. The wives of senators and bankers became genteel, kept a herd of ladies' maids, passed hours before their full-length silver mirrors, bathed in asses' milk, rouged their cheeks and dyed their hair, never went out except in palanquins, gabbled Greek phrases, and called their slaves by Greek names even when they happened to be of Latin birth. The houses of the great were paved with mosaic floors, and the painted walls were works of art: sideboards were covered with gold and silver plate, with vessels of amber and of the tinted Alexandrine glass. The bathrooms were of marble, with the water issuing from silver tubes.

New amusements were invented, and new customs began to reign. An academy was established, in which five hundred boys and girls were taught castanet dances of anything but a decorous kind. The dinner hour was made later, and instead of sitting at table they adopted the style of lying down to eat on sofas inlaid with tortoiseshell and gold. It was chiefly in the luxuries of the cuisine that the Romans exhibited their wealth. Prodigious prices were paid for a good Greek cook. Every patrician villa was a castle of gastronomical delight: it was provided with its salt-water tank for fish and oysters, and an aviary which was filled with field-fares, ortolans, nightingales, and thrushes; a white dove-cot, like a tower, stood beside the house, and beneath it was a dark dungeon for fattening the birds; there was also a poultry ground, with pea-fowl, guinea-fowl, and pink feathered flamingoes imported from the East, while an orchard of fig-trees, honey-apples, and other fruits, and a garden in which the trees of cypress and yew were clipped into fantastic shapes, conferred an aspect of rural beauty on the scene. The hills round the Bay of Naples were covered with these villas; and to that charming region it became the fashion to resort at a certain season of the year. In such places gambling, drinking, and lovemaking shook off all restraints. Black-eyed soubrettes tripped perpetually about with billets-doux in Greek; the rattle of the ivory dice-box could be heard in the streets, like the click of billiard balls in the Parisian boulevards; and many a boat with purple sails and with garlands of roses twined round its mast floated softly along the water, laughter and sweet music sounding from the prow.

Happily for Cato's peace of mind, he died before the casino with its cachucha--or cancan, or whatever it might have been--was introduced, and before the fashions of Asia had been added to those of Greece. But he lived long enough to see the Graeco-maniacs triumphant. In earlier and happier days he had been able to expel two philosophers from Rome, but now he saw them swarming in the streets with their ragged cloaks and greasy beards, and everywhere obtaining seats as domestic chaplains at the tables of the rich. He could now do no more than protest in his bitter and extravagant style against the corruption of the age. He prophesied that as soon as Rome had thoroughly imbibed the Greek philosophy she would lose the empire of the world; he declared that Socrates was a prating, seditious fellow who well deserved his fate; and he warned his son to beware of the Greek physicians, for the Greeks had laid a plot to kill all the Romans, and the doctors had been deputed to put it into execution with their medicines.

Cato was a man of an iron body which was covered with honourable scars, a loud, harsh voice, greenish-grey eyes, foxy hair, and enormous teeth resembling tusks. His face was so hideous and forbidding that, according to one of the hundred epigrams that were composed against him, he would wander for ever on the banks of the Styx, for hell itself would be afraid to let him in. He was distinguished as a general, as an orator, and as an author, but he pretended that it was his chief ambition to be considered a good farmer. He lived in a little cottage on his Sabine estate, and went in the morning to practise as an advocate in the neighbouring town. When he came home he stripped to the skin and worked in the fields with his slaves, drinking as they did the vinegar-water or the thin, sour wine. In the evening he used to boil the turnips for his supper while his wife made the bread. Although he cared so little about external things, if he gave an entertainment and the slaves had not cooked it or waited to his liking, he used to chastise them with leather thongs. It was one of his maxims to sell his slaves when they grew old--the worst cruelty that a slave-owner can commit. "For my part," says Plutarch, "I should never have the heart to sell an ox that had grown old in my service, still less my aged slave."

Cato's old-fashioned virtue paid very well. He gratified his personal antipathies and obtained the character of the people's friend. He was always impeaching the great men of his country, and was himself impeached nearly fifty times. The man who sets up as being much better than his age is always to be suspected, and Cato is perhaps the best specimen of the rugged hypocrite and austere charlatan that history can produce. This censor of morals bred slaves for sale. He made laws against usury and then turned usurer himself. He was always preaching about the vanity of riches, and wrote an excellent work on the best way of getting rich. He degraded a Roman knight for kissing his wife in the day-time in the presence of his daughter, and he himself, while he was living under his daughter-in-law's roof, bestowed his favours on one of the servant girls of the establishment, and allowed her to be impudent to her young mistress. "Old age," he once said to a grey-headed debauchee, "has deformities enough of its own. Do not add to it the deformity of vice." At the time of the amorous affair above mentioned Cato was nearly eighty years of age.

On the other hand, he was a most faithful servant to his country; he was a truly religious man, and his god was the Commonwealth of Rome. Nor was he destitute of the domestic virtues, though sadly deficient in that respect. He used to say that those who beat their wives and children laid their sacrilegious hands on the holiest things in the world. He educated his son himself, taught him to box, to ride, and to swim, and wrote out for him a history of Rome in large pothook characters, that he might become acquainted at an early age with the great actions of the ancient Romans. He was as careful in what he said before the child as if he had been in the presence of the vestal virgins.

This Cato was the man on whom rests chiefly the guilt of the murder which we must now relate. In public and in private, by direct denunciation, by skilful innuendo, by appealing to the fears of some and to the interests of others, he laboured incessantly towards his end. Once, after he had made a speech against Carthage in the senate, he shook the skirt of his robe as if by accident, and some African figs fell upon the ground. When all had looked and wondered at their size and beauty he observed that the place where they grew was only three days' sail from Rome.

It is possible that Cato was sincere in his alarms, for he was one of the few survivors of the second Punic War. He had felt the arm of Carthage in its strength. He could remember that day when even Romans had turned pale; when the old men covered their faces with their mantles; when the young men clambered on the walls; when the women ran wailing round the temples of the gods, praying for protection and sweeping the shrines with their hair; when a cry went forth that Hannibal was at the gates; when a panic seized the city; when the people, collecting on the roofs, flung tiles at Roman soldiers, believing them to be the enemy already in the town; when all over the Campagna could be seen the smoke of ricks and farmhouses mounting in the air, and the wild Berber horsemen driving herds of cattle to the Punic camp.

Besides, it was his theory that the annihilation of foreign powers was the building up of Rome. He used to boast that in his Peninsular campaign he had demolished a Spanish town a day. There were in the Senate many enlightened men who denied that the prosperity of

167

Rome could be assisted by the destruction of trading cities, and Carthage was defended by the Scipio party. But the influence of the banker class was employed on Cato's side. They wanted every penny that was spent in the Mediterranean world to pass through their books. Carthage and Corinth were rival firms which it was to their profit to destroy. These money-mongers possessed great power in the senate and the state, and at last they carried the day. It was privately resolved that Carthage should be attacked as soon as an opportunity occurred.

Thus in Africa and in Italy Masinissa and Cato prepared the minds of men for the deed of blood. It was as if the Furies of the slaughtered dead had entered the bodies of those two old men and kept them alive beyond their natural term. Cato had done his share. It was now Masinissa's turn. As soon as he was assured that he would be supported by the Romans, he struck again and again the wretched people, who were afraid to resist and yet who soon saw that it would be folly to submit. It was evident that Rome would not interfere. If Masinissa was not checked he would strip them of their cornfields; he would starve them to death. The war party at last prevailed; the city was fortified and armed. Masinissa descended on their villas, their gardens, and their farms. Driven to despair, the Carthaginians went forth to defend the crops which their own hands had sown. A great battle was fought, and Masinissa was victorious.

On a hill near the battlefield sat a young Roman officer, Scipio Aemilianus, a relative of the man who had defeated Hannibal. He had been sent over from Spain for a squadron of elephants, and arrived in Masinissa's camp at this interesting crisis. The news of the battle was soon despatched by him to Rome. The treaty had now been broken, and the Senate declared war.

The Carthaginians fell into an agony of alarm. They were now so broken down that a vassal of Rome could defeat them in the open field. What had they to expect in a war with Rome? Ambassadors were at once dispatched with full powers to obtain peace--peace at any price--from the terrible Republic. The envoys presented themselves before the Senate; they offered the submission of the Carthaginians, who formally disowned the act of war, who had put the two leaders of the war-party to death, and who desired nothing but the alliance and goodwill of Rome. The answer which they received was this: "Since the Carthaginians are so well advised, the senate returns them their country, their laws, their sepulchres, their liberties, and their estates, if they will surrender three hundred sons of their senators as hostages, and obey the orders of the consuls."

The Roman army had already disembarked. When the consuls landed on the coast no resistance was made. They demanded provisions. Then the city gates were opened, and long trains of bullocks and mules laden with corn were driven to the Roman camp. The hostages were demanded. Then the senators brought forth their children and gave them to the city; the city gave them to the Romans; the Romans placed them on board the galleys, which at once spread their sails and departed from the coast. The roofs of the palaces of Carthage were crowded with women who watched these receding sails with straining eyes and outstretched arms. Never more would they see their beloved ones. Yet they would not perhaps have grieved so much at the children leaving Carthage had they known what was to come.

The city gates again opened. The Senate sent its council to the Roman camp. A company of venerable men clad in purple, with golden chains, presented themselves at headquarters and requested to know what were the "orders of the consuls." They were told that Carthage must disarm. They returned to the city and at once sent out to the camp all their fleet material and artillery, all the military stores in the public magazines, and all the arms that could be found in the possession of private individuals. Three thousand catapults and two hundred thousand sets of armour were given up.

They again came out to the camp. The military council was assembled to receive them. The old men saluted the Roman ensigns, and bowed low to the consuls, placing their hands upon their breasts. The orders of the consuls, they said, had been obeyed. Was there anything more that their lords had to command?

The senior consul rose up and said that there was something more. He was instructed by the Roman Senate to inform the senators of Carthage that the city must be destroyed, but that in accordance with the promise of the Roman Senate their country, their laws, their sepulchres, their liberties, and their estates would be preserved, and they might build another city. Only it must be without walls, and at a distance of at least ten miles from the sea.

The Carthaginians cast themselves upon the ground, and the whole assembly fell into confusion. The consul explained that he could exercise no choice: he had received his orders, and they must be carried out. He requested them to return and apprise their fellow-townsmen. Some of the senators remained in the Roman camp; others ventured to go back. When they drew near the city the people came running out to meet them, and asked them the news. They answered only by weeping and beating their foreheads, and stretching out their hands and calling on the gods. They went on to the senate house; the members were summoned; an enormous crowd gathered in the market-place. Presently the doors opened; the senators came forth, and the orders of the consuls were announced.

And then there rose in the air a fierce, despairing shriek, a yell of agony and rage. The mob rushed through the city and tore limb from limb the Italians who were living in the town. With one voice it was resolved that the city should be defended to the last. They would not so tamely give up their beautiful Carthage, their dear and venerable home beside the sea. If it was to be burnt to ashes, their ashes should be mingled with it, and their enemies' as well.

All the slaves were set free. Old and young, rich and poor, worked together day and night forging arms. The public buildings were pulled down to procure timber and metal. The women cut off their hair to make strings for the catapults. A humble message was sent in true Oriental style to the consul, praying for a little time. Days passed, and Carthage gave no signs of life. Tired of waiting, the consul marched towards the city, which he expected to enter like an open village. He found, to his horror, the gates closed, and the battlements bristling with artillery.

Carthage was strongly fortified, and it was held by men who had abandoned hope. The siege lasted more than three years. Cato did not live to see his darling wish fulfilled. Masinissa also died while the siege was going on, and bitter was his end. The policy of the Romans had been death to all his hopes. His dream of a great African empire was dissolved. He sullenly refused to co-operate with the Romans--it was his Carthage which they had decreed should be levelled to the ground.

There was a time when it seemed as if the great city would prove itself to be impregnable; the siege was conducted with small skill or vigour by the Roman generals. More than one reputation found its grave before the walls of Carthage. But when Scipio

Aemilianus obtained the command, he at once displayed the genius of his house. Perceiving that it would be impossible to subdue the city as long as smuggling traders could run into the port with provisions, he constructed a stone mole across the mouth of the harbour. Having thus cut off the city from the sea, he pitched his camp on the neck of the isthmus-- for Carthage was built on a peninsula--and so cut it off completely from the land. For the first time in the siege the blockade was complete: the city was enclosed in a stone and iron cage. The Carthaginians in their fury brought forth the prisoners whom they had taken in their sallies, and hurled them headlong from the walls. There were many in the city who protested against this outrage. They were denounced as traitors; a reign of terror commenced; the men of the moderate party were crucified in the streets. The hideous idol of Moloch found victims in that day; children were placed on its outstretched and downward-sloping hands and rolled off them into the fiery furnace which was burning at its feet. Nor were there wanting patriots who sacrificed themselves upon the altars that the gods might have compassion upon those who survived. But among these pestilence and famine had begun to work, and the sentinels could scarcely stand to their duty on the walls. Gangs of robbers went from house to house and tortured people to make them give up their food; mothers fed upon their children; a terrible disease broke out; corpses lay scattered in the streets; men who were burying the dead fell dead upon them; others dug their own graves and lay down in them to die; houses in which all had perished were used as public sepulchres, and were quickly filled.

And then, as if the birds of the air had carried the news, it became known all over Northern Africa that Carthage was about to fall. And then from the dark and dismal corners of the land, from the wasted frontiers of the desert, from the snow lairs, and caverns of the Atlas, there came creeping and crawling to the coast the most abject of the human race--black, naked, withered beings, their bodies covered with red paint, their hair cut in strange fashions, their language composed of muttering and whistling sounds. By day they prowled round the camp and fought with the dogs for the offal and the bones. If they found a skin they roasted it on ashes and danced round it in glee, wriggling their bodies and uttering abominable cries. When the feast was over they cowered together on their hams, and fixed their gloating eyes upon the city, and expanded their blubber lips, and showed their white fangs.

At last the day came. The harbour walls were carried by assault, and the Roman soldiers pressed into the narrow streets which led down to the water side. The houses were six or seven storeys high, and each house was a fortress which had to be stormed. Lean and haggard creatures, with eyes of flame, defended their homesteads from room to room, onwards, upwards, to the death struggle on the broad, flat roof.

Day followed day, and still that horrible music did not cease--the shouts and songs of the besiegers, the yells and shrieks of the besieged, the moans of the wounded, the feeble cries of children divided by the sword. Night followed night, and still the deadly work went on; there was no sleep and no darkness; the Romans lighted houses that they might see to kill.

Six days passed thus, and only the citadel was left. It was a steep rock in the middle of the town; a temple of the God of Healing crowned its summit.

The rock was covered with people, who could be seen extending their arms to heaven and uniting with one another in the last embrace. Their piteous lamentations, like the cries of wounded animals, ascended in the air, and behind the iron circle which enclosed them could be heard the crackling of the fire and the dull boom of falling beams.

The soldiers were weary with smiting: they were filled with blood. Nine-tenths of the inhabitants had been already killed. The people on the rock were offered their lives; they descended with bare hands and passed under the yoke. Some of them ended their days in prison; the greater part were sold as slaves.

But in the temple on the summit of the rocky hill nine hundred Roman deserters, for whom there could be no pardon, stood at bay. The trumpets sounded; the soldiers, clashing their bucklers with their swords and uttering the war-cry alala! alala! Advanced to the attack. Of a sudden the sea of steel recoiled, the standards reeled; a long tongue of flame sprang forth upon them through the temple door. The deserters had set the building on fire that they might escape the ignominious death of martial law.

A man dressed in purple rushed out of the temple with an olive branch in his hand. This was Hasdrubal, the commander-in-chief, and the Robespierre of the reign of terror. His life was given him; he would do for the triumph. And as he bowed the knee before the consul a woman appeared on the roof of the temple with two children in her arms. She poured forth some scornful words upon her husband, and then plunged with her children into the flames.

Carthage burned seventeen days before it was entirely consumed. Then the plough was passed over the soil to put an end in legal form to the existence of the city. House might never again be built, corn might never again be sown, upon the ground where it had stood. A hundred years afterwards Julius Caesar founded another Carthage and planted a Roman colony therein. But it was not built upon the same spot. The old site remained accursed; it was a browsing ground for cattle, a field of blood. When recently the remains of the city walls were disinterred they were found to be covered with a layer of ashes from four to five feet deep. Filled with half-charred pieces of wood, fragments of iron, and projectiles.

The possessions of the Carthaginians were formed into a Roman province which was called Africa. The governor resided at Utica, which with the other old Phoenician towns received municipal rights, but paid a fixed stipend to the state exchequer. The territory of Carthage itself became Roman domain land, and was let on lease. Italian merchants flocked to Utica in great numbers and reopened the inland trade, but the famous sea trade was not revived. The Britons of Cornwall might in vain gather on high places and strain their eyes towards the west. The ships which had brought them beads and purple cloth would come again no more.

A descendant of Masinissa, who inherited his genius, defied the Roman power in a long war. He was finally conquered by Sylla and Marius, caught, and carried off to Rome. Apparelled in barbaric splendour, he was paraded through the streets. But when the triumph was over his guards rushed upon him and struggled for the finery in which he had been dressed. They tore the rings from his ears with such force that the flesh came away; they cast him naked into a dungeon under ground. "O Romans, you give me a cold bath!" were the last words of the valiant Jugurtha.

The next Numidian prince who appeared at a triumph was the young Juba, who had taken the side of Pompey against Caesar. "It proved to be a happy captivity for him," says Plutarch, "for from a barbarous and unlettered Numidian he became an historian worthy to be numbered amongst the learned men of Greece."

171

When the empire became established the kingdoms of Numidia, of Cyrene, and of Egypt were swept away. Africa was divided into seven fruitful provinces ranging along the coast from Tripoli to Tangiers. Egypt was made a province, with the tropical line for its southern frontier. The oasis of Cyrene, with its fields of asafoetida, was a middle station between the two. But still the history of Northern Africa and the history of Egypt remain distinct. The Roman empire, though held together for a time by strong and skilful hands, was divided by customs and modes of thought arising out of language into the Greek and Latin worlds. In the countries which had been civilised by the Romans Latin had been introduced. In the countries which before the Roman conquest had been conquered by Alexander, the Greek language maintained its ground. Greece, Macedonia, Asia Minor, Syria, Egypt, and Cyrene belonged to the Greek world; Italy Gaul, Spain, and Africa belonged to the Latin world. Greek was never spoken in Roman Carthage except by a few merchants and learned men. Latin was never spoken in Alexandria except in the law courts and at Government House. Whenever there was a partition of the empire Egypt was assigned to one emperor, Carthage to the other. In the Church history of Africa the same phenomenon may be observed. The Church of Africa was the daughter of the Church of Rome, and was chiefly occupied with questions of discipline and law. The Church of Egypt was essentially a Greek church; it was occupied entirely with definitions of the undefinable and solutions of problems in theology.

In one respect, however, the histories of Egypt and Africa are the same. They were both of them cornfields, and both of them were ruined by the Romans. In the early days of the empire there was a noble reform in provincial affairs resembling that which Clive accomplished in British India when he visited that country for the last time. There was then an end to that tyrant of prey who under the republic had contrived in a few years to extort an enormous fortune from his proconsulate, and who was often accompanied by a wife more rapacious than himself; who returned to Rome with herds of slaves and cargoes of bullion and of works of art. Governors were appointed with fixed salaries; the Roman law was everywhere introduced; vast sums of money were expended on the public works.

Unhappily this did not last. Rome was devoured by a population of mean whites, the result of foreign slavery, which invariably degrades labour. This vast rabble was maintained by the state; rations of bread and oil were served out to it every day. When the evil time came and the exchequer was exhausted, the governors of Africa and Egypt were required to send the usual quantity of grain all the same, and to obtain their percentage as best they could. They were transformed into satraps or pashas. The great landowners were accused of conspiracy, and their estates escheated to the crown. The agriculturists were reduced to serfdom. There might be a scarcity of food in Africa, but there must be none in Rome. Every year were to be seen the huge ships lying in the harbours of Alexandria and Carthage, and the mountains of corn piled high upon the quays. When the seat of empire was transferred to the Bosphorus the evil became greater still. Each province was forced to do double work. There was now a populace in Constantinople which was fed entirely by Egypt, and Africa supported the populace of Rome. While the Egyptian fellah and the Moorish peasant were labouring in the fields, the sturdy beggars of Byzantium and Rome were amusing themselves at the circus or basking on marble in the sun.

But Africa was not only a plantation of corn and oil for their imperial majesties the Italian lazzaroni. It also contained the preserves of Rome. The lion was a royal beast; it was licensed to feed upon the flock of the shepherds, and upon the shepherd himself if it preferred him. The unfortunate Moor could not defend his life without a violation of the game laws, which were quite as ferocious as the lion. It will easily be imagined that the Roman rule was not agreeable to the native population. They had fallen beneath a power compared with which that of the Carthaginians was feeble and kind; which possessed the strength of civilisation without its mercy. But when that power began to decline they lifted up their heads and joined the foreign invaders as soon as they appeared, as their fathers had joined the Romans in the ancient days.

These invaders were the Vandals, a tribe of Germans from the North who had conquered Spain and who, now pouring over the Gibraltar Straits, took Carthage and ruled there a hundred years. The Romans struggled hard to regain their cornfields, and the old duel of Rome and Carthage was resumed. This time it was Carthage that was triumphant. It repelled the Romans when they invaded Africa. It became a naval power, scoured the Mediterranean, re-conquered Sicily and Sardinia, plundered the shores of Italy, and encamped beneath the mouldering walls of Rome. The gates of the city were opened, and the bishop of Rome, attended by his clergy, came forth in solemn procession to offer the submission of Rome, and to pray for mercy to the churches and their captives. Doubtless in that army of Germans and Moors by whom they were received there were men of Phoenician descent who had read in history of a similar scene. Rome was more fortunate than ancient Carthage: the city was sacked, but it was not destroyed. Not long afterwards it was taken by the Goths. Kings dressed in furs sat opposite each other on the thrones of Carthage and of Rome.

The Emperor of the East sent the celebrated Belisarius against the Carthaginian Vandals, who had become corrupted by luxury and whom he speedily subdued. Thus Africa was restored to Rome, but it was a Greek speaking Rome, and the citizens of Carthage still felt themselves to be under foreign rule. Besides, the war had reduced the country to a wilderness. One might travel for days without meeting a human being in those fair coast lands which had once been filled with olive groves, and vineyards, and fields of waving corn. The savage Berber tribes pressed more and more fiercely on the cultivated territory which still remained. It is probable that if the Arabs had not come the Moors would have driven the Byzantines out of the land, or at least have forced them to remain as prisoners behind their walls.

With the invasion of the Arabs the proper history of Africa begins. It is now that we are able for the first time to leave the coasts of the Mediterranean and the banks of the Nile, and to penetrate into that vast and mysterious world of which the ancient geographers had but a faint and incorrect idea.

It is evident enough from the facts which have been adduced in the foregoing sketch that Egypt and Carthage contributed much to human progress--Egypt by instructing Greece, Carthage by drawing forth Rome to the conquest of the world.

But these countries did little for Africa itself. The ambition of Egypt was with good reason turned towards Asia, that of Carthage towards Europe. The influence of Carthage on the regions of the Niger was similar to that of Egypt on the negro regions of the Nile. In each case it became the fashion for the native chiefs to wear Egyptian linen or the Tyrian purple, and to decorate their wives with beads which are often discovered by the negroes of the present day in ancient and forgotten graves. Elephants were hunted and gold pits were dug in Central Africa, that these luxuries might be procured; but the chief article of export was the slave, and this commodity was obtained by means of war. The negroes have often been accused of rejecting the civilisation of the Egyptians and Carthaginians, but they were never brought into contact with those people. The intercourse between them was conducted by the intermediate Berber tribes.

Those Berber tribes who inhabited the regions adjoining Egypt and Cyrene appear to have been in some degree improved. But they were a roving people, and civilisation can never ripen under tents. Something, however, was accomplished among those who were settled in cities or the regions of the coast. That the Berber race possesses a remarkable capacity for culture has been amply proved. It is probable that Terence was a Moor. It is certain that Juba, whose works have been unfortunately lost, was of unmixed Berber blood. Reading and writing were common among them, and they used a character of their own. When the Romans took Carthage they gave the public library and archives to the Berber chiefs. At one time it seemed as if Barbary was destined to become a civilised province after the pattern of Spain and Gaul. Numidian princes adopted the culture of the Greeks, and Juba was placed on his ancestral throne that he might tame his wild subjects into Roman citizens. But this movement soon perished, and the Moorish chiefs fell back into their bandit life.

Roman Africa

The African Church has obtained imperishable fame. In the days of suffering it brought forth martyrs whose fiery ardour and serene endurance have never been surpassed. In the days of victory it brought forth minds by whose imperial writings thousands of cultivated men have been enslaved. But this church was for the most part confined to the walled cities on the coast, to the farming villages in which the Punic speech was still preserved, and to a few Moorish tribes who lived under Roman rule. In the days of St. Augustine Christianity was in its zenith, and St. Augustine complains that there were hundreds of Berber chiefs who had never heard the name of Christ. Even in Roman Africa the triumph of Christianity was not complete. In Carthage itself Astarte and Moloch were still adored, and a bare-footed monk could not show himself in the streets without being pelted by the populace. At a later date the Moorish tribes became an heretical and hostile sect; the religious persecutions of the Arian Vandals were succeeded by the persecutions of the Byzantine Greeks. Christianity was divided and almost dead when the Arabs appeared, and the Church which had withstood ten imperial persecutions succumbed to the tax which the conquerors imposed on "the people of the book."

The Arabs

The failure of Christianity in Africa was owing to the imperfection of the Roman conquest. Their occupation was of a purely military kind, and it did not embrace an extensive area. The Romans were entirely distinct from the natives in manners and ideas. It was natural that the Berbers should reject the religion of a people whose language they did not understand, whose tyranny they detested, and whose power most of them defied. But the Arabs were accustomed to deserts; they did not settle, like the Romans and the Carthaginians, on the coast; they covered the whole land; they penetrated into the recesses of the Atlas; they pursued their enemies into the depths of the Sahara. But they also mingled persuasion with force. They believed that the Berbers were Arabs like themselves, and invited them as kinsmen to accept the mission of the prophet. They married the daughters of the land; they gathered round their standards the warriors whom they had defeated, and led them to the glorious conquest of Spain. The two peoples became one; the language and religion of the Arabs were accepted by the Moors.

With this event the biography of ancient Africa is closed, and the history of Asiatic Africa begins. But I have in this work a twofold story to unfold. I have to describe the Dark Continent: to show in what way it is connected with universal history; what it has received and what it has contributed to the development of man. And I have also to sketch in broad outline the human history itself. This task has been forced upon me in the course of my inquiries. It is impossible to measure a tributary and to estimate its value with precision except by comparing it with the other affluents, and by carefully mapping the main stream. In writing a history of Africa I am compelled to write the history of the world, in order that Africa's true position may be defined.

And now, passing to the general questions discussed in this chapter, it will be observed that war is the chief agent of civilisation in the period which I have attempted to portray. It was war which drove the Egyptians into those frightful deserts in the midst of which their Happy Valley was discovered. It was war which under the Persians opened lands which had been either closed against foreigners or jealously held ajar. It was war which colonised Syria and Asia Minor with Greek ideas, and which planted in Alexandria the experimental philosophy which will win for us in time the dominion of the earth. It was war which united the Greek and Latin worlds into a splendid harmony of empire. And when that ancient world had been overcome by languor and had fallen into Oriental sleep; when nothing was taught in the schools which had not been taught a hundred years before; when the rapacity of tyrants had extinguished the ambition of the rich and the industry of the poor; when the Church also had become inert, and roused itself only to be cruel--then again came war across the Rhine and the Danube and the Alps, and laid the foundations of European life among the ruins of the Latin world. In the same manner Asia awoke as if by magic, and won back from Europe the lands which she had lost. But this latter conquest, though effected by means of war, was preserved by means of religion, an element of history which must be analysed with scientific care. In the next chapter I shall explain the origin of the religious sentiment and theory in savage life. I shall sketch the early career of the three great Semitic creeds and the characters of three men--Moses, Jesus, and Mohammed--who, whatever may have been their faults, are entitled to the eternal gratitude of the human race. Then, resuming the history of Africa, I shall follow the course of Islam over the Great Desert into the Sudan, and shall describe its progress in that country by means of the sword and of the school, something of which I have seen and studied under both forms.

Chapter II. Religion

The Natural History of Religion

When the poet invokes in his splendid frenzy the shining spheres of heaven, the murmuring fountains, and the rushing streams; when he calls upon the earth to hearken, and bids the wild sea listen to his song; when he communes with the sweet secluded valleys and the haughty-headed hills as if those inanimate objects were alive, as if those masses of brute matter were endowed with sense and thought, we do not smile, we do not sneer, we do not reason, but we feel. A secret chord is touched within us: a slumbering sympathy is awakened into life. Who has not felt an impulse of hatred, and perhaps expressed it in a senseless curse, against a fiery stroke of sunlight or a sudden gust of wind? Who has not felt a pang of pity for a flower torn and trampled in the dust, a shell dashed to fragments by the waves? Such emotions or ideas last only for a moment; they do not belong to us; they are the fossil fancies of a bygone age; they are a heritage of thought from the childhood of our race. For there was a time when they possessed the human mind. There was a time when the phrases of modern poetry were the facts of ordinary life. There was a time when man lived in fellowship with nature, believing that all things which moved or changed had minds and bodies kindred to his own.

To those primeval people the sun was a great being who brightened them in his pleasure and who scorched then in his wrath. The earth was a sleeping monster: sometimes it rose a little and turned itself in bed. They walked upon its back when living; they were put into its belly when they died. Fire was a savage animal which bit when it was touched. The birds and beasts were foreigners possessing languages and customs of their own. The plants were dumb creatures with characters good or bad, sometimes gloomy in aspect, malignant in their fruit, sometimes dispensing wholesome food and pleasant shade.

These various forms of nature they treated precisely as if they had been men. They sometimes adorned a handsome tree with bracelets like a girl; they offered up prayers to the fruit trees, and made them presents to coax them to a liberal return. They forbade the destruction of certain animals which they revered on account of their wisdom, or feared on account of their fierceness, or valued on account of their utility. They submitted to the tyranny of the more formidable beasts of prey, never venturing to attack them for fear the nation or species should retaliate, but making them propitiatory gifts. In the same manner they offered sacrifices to avert the fury of the elements, or in gratitude for blessings which had been bestowed. But often a courageous people, when invaded, would go to war, not only with the tiger and the bear but with powers which to them were not less human-like and real. They would cut with their swords at the hot wind of the desert, hurl their spears into the swollen river, stab the earth, flog the sea, shoot their arrows at the flashing clouds, and build up towers to carry heaven by assault.

But when through the operation of the law of growth the intellectual faculties of men become improved, they begin to observe their own nature, and in course of time a curious discovery is made. They ascertain that there is something which resides within them entirely independent and distinct from the body in which it is contained. They perceive that it is this mind, or soul, or genius, or spirit, which thinks and desires and decides. It commands the body as the chief commands the slave. While the body is asleep it is busy weaving thoughts in the sleeper's brain, or wanders into other lands and converses with people whom he, while awake, has never seen. They hear words of wisdom issuing from the toothless mouth of a decrepit old man. It is evident that this soul does not grow old, and therefore it does not die. The body, it is clear, is only a garment which is in time destroyed, and then where does its inmate go?

When a loved one has been taken she haunts the memory of him who weeps till the image imprinted on the heart is reflected on the curtain of the eye. Her vision appears not when he is quite asleep, as in an ordinary dream, but as he is passing into sleep. He meets her in the twilight land which divides the world of darkness from the world of day. He sees her form distinctly; he clasps it in his arms; he hears the accents of her sweet and gentle voice; he feels the pressure of her lips upon his own. He awakes, and the illusion is dispelled; yet with some it is so complete that they firmly believe it was a spirit whom they saw.

Among savages it is not love which can thus excite the imagination and deceive the sense, but reverence and fear. The great chief is dead. His vision appears in a half-waking dream: it threatens and it speaks. The dreamer believes that the form and the voice are real, and therefore he believes that the great chief still exists. It is thus that the grand idea is born. There is life after death. When the house or garment of the body is destroyed the soul wanders forth into the air. Like the wind it is unseen; like the wind it can be soft and kind; like the wind it can be terrible and cruel. The savage then believes that the pains of sickness are inflicted by the hand which so often inflicted pain upon him when it was in the flesh, and he also believes that in battle the departed warrior is still fighting with unseen weapons at the head of his own clan. In order to obtain the goodwill of the father-spirit, prayers are offered up to him and food is placed beside his grave. He is, in fact, still recognised as king, and to such phantom monarchs the distinctive title of god is assigned. Each chief is deified and worshipped when he dies. The offerings and prayers are established by rule; the reigning chief becomes the family priest; he pretends to receive communications from the dead, and issues laws in their name. The deeds of valour which the chiefs performed in their lifetime are set to song; their biographies descend from generation to generation, changing in their course, and thus a regular religion and mythology are formed.

It is the nature of man to reason from himself outwards. The savage now ascribes to the various forms of matter souls or spirits such as he imagines that he has discovered in himself. The food which he places at the grave has a soul or essence, and it is this which is eaten by the spirit of the dead, while the body of the food remains unchanged. The river is not mere water which may dry up and perish, but there dwells within it a soul which never dies; and so with everything that lives and moves, from the blade of grass which shivers in the wind to the star which slowly moves across the sky. But as men become more and more capable of general ideas, of classing facts into systems and of arranging phenomena into

177

groups, they believe in a god of the forests, a god of the waters, and a god of the sky, instead of ascribing a separate god to every tree, to every river, and to every star. Nature is placed under the dominion of a federation of deities. In some cases the ancestor gods are identified with these; in others their worship is kept distinct. The trees and the animals, which were once worshipped for themselves from love or fear, are now supposed to be objects of affection to the gods, and are held sacred for their sake.

These gods are looked upon as kings. Their characters are human, and are reflected from the minds of those who have created them. Whatever the arithmetical arrangement of the gods may be--single or triune, dual or plural--they are in all countries and in all times made by man in his own image. In the plural period some of the gods are good and some are bad, just as there are good and evil kings. The wicked gods can be softened by flattery and presents, the good ones can be made fierce by neglect. The wicked gods obtain the largest offerings and the longest prayers, just as in despotic countries the wicked kings obtain the most liberal presents--which are merely taxes in disguise.

The savage has been led by indigestion and by dreams to believe in the existence of the soul after death--or, using simpler language, to believe in ghosts. At first these souls or ghosts have no fixed abode; they live among the graves. At a later period the savage invents a world to which the ghosts depart and in which they reside. It is situated underground. In that world the ghosts live precisely as they lived on earth. There is no retribution and no reward for the actions of the earthly life; that life is merely continued in another region of the world. Death is in fact regarded as a migration in which, as in all migrations, the emigrants preserve their relative positions. When a man of importance dies his family furnish him with an outfit of slaves and wives, and pack up in his grave his arms and ornaments and clothes, that he may make his appearance in the under-world in a manner befitting his rank and fortune. It is believed that the souls of the clothes, as well as of the persons sacrificed, accompany him there, and it is sometimes believed that all the clothes which he has worn in his life will then have their resurrection day.

The under-world and the upper-world are governed by the same gods or unseen kings. Man's life in the upper-world is short: his life in the under-world is long. But as regards the existence of the worlds themselves, both are eternal, without beginning and without end. This idea is not a creation of the ripened intellect, as is usually supposed. It is a product of limited experience, and expression of a seeming fact. The savage did not see the world begin; therefore it had no beginning. He has not seen it grow older; therefore it will have no end.

The two worlds adjoin each other, and the frontier between them is very faintly marked. The gods often dress themselves in flesh and blood and visit the earth to do evil or to do good--to make love to women, to torment their enemies, to converse with their favourites and friends. On the other hand there are men who possess the power of leaving their bodies in their beds and of passing into the other world to obtain divine poisons which they malignantly employ. The ghosts of the dead often come and sit by their old firesides and eat what is set apart for them. Sometimes a departed spirit will re-enter the family, assuming a body which resembles in its features the one he previously wore. Distinguished heroes and prophets are often supposed to be hybrids or mulattoes, the result of a union between a woman and a god. Sometimes it is believed that a god has come down on earth out of love for a certain nation, to offer himself up as a sacrifice, and so to quench the blood-thirst of some sullen and revengeful god who has that nation in his

178

power. Sometimes a savage people believe that their kings are gods who have deigned to take upon them a perishable body for a time, and there are countries in which a still more remarkable superstition prevails. The royal body even is immortal. The king never eats, never sleeps, and never dies. This kind of monarch is visible only to his priests. When the people wish to present a petition he gives them audience seated behind a curtain, from beneath which he thrusts out his foot in token of assent. When he dies he is secretly buried by the priests, and a new puppet is elected in his stead.

The savage lives in a strange world, a world of special providences and divine interpositions, not happening at long intervals and for some great end, but every day and almost at every hour. A pain, a dream, a sensation of any kind, a stroke of good or bad luck--whatever, in short, does not proceed from man, whatever we ascribe, for want of a better word, to chance--is by him ascribed to the direct interference of the gods. He knows nothing about the laws of nature. Death itself is not a natural event. Sooner or later men make the gods angry and are killed.

It is difficult for those who have not lived among savages perfectly to realise their faith. When told that his gods do not exist the savage merely laughs in mild wonder at such an extraordinary observation being made. It seems quite natural to him that his gods should be as his parents and grandparents have described; he believes as he breathes, without an effort; he feels that what he has been taught is true. His creed is in harmony with his intellect, and cannot be changed until his intellect is changed. If a god in a dream, or through the priests, has made him a promise and the promise is broken, he does not on that account doubt the existence of the god. He merely supposes that the god has told a lie. Nor does it seem strange to him that a god should tell a lie. His god is only a gigantic man, a sensual, despotic king who orders his subjects to give him the first fruits of the fields, the firstlings of the flock, virgins for his harem, human bodies for his cannibal repasts. As for himself, he is the slave of that god or king; he prays, that is to say, he begs; he sings hymns, that is to say, he flatters; he sacrifices, that is to say, he pays tribute, chiefly out of fear, but partly in the hope of getting something better in return--long life, riches, and fruitful wives. He is usually afraid to say of the gods what he thinks, or even to utter their real name. But sometimes he gives vent to the hatred which is burning in his heart. Writhing on a bed of sickness, he heaps curses on the god who he declares is "eating his inside"; and when he is converted prematurely to a higher creed his god is still to him the invisible but human king. "O Allah!" a Somali woman was heard to say, "O Allah! May thy teeth ache like mine! O Allah! May thy gums be sore as mine!" That Christian monarch the late King Peppel once exclaimed, when he thought of his approaching end, that if he could see God he would kill him at once because he made men die.

The arithmetical arrangement of the gods depends entirely upon the intellectual faculties of the people concerned. In the period of thing-worship, as it may be termed, every brook, tree, hill, and star is itself a living creature, benevolent or malignant, asleep or awake. In the next stage every object and phenomenon is inhabited or presided over by a genius or spirit, and with some nations the virtues and the vices are also endowed with personality. As the reasoning powers of men expand their gods diminish in number and rule over larger areas, till finally it is perceived that there is unity in nature, that everything which exists is a part of one harmonious whole. It is then asserted that one being manufactured the world and rules over it supreme. But at first the Great Being is distant and indifferent, "a god sitting outside the universe"; and the old gods become viceroys to whom he has deputed the government of the world. They are afterwards degraded to the rank of messengers or angels, and it is believed that God is everywhere present; that he fills the earth and sky; that from him directly proceeds both the evil and the good. In some systems of belief, however, he is believed to be the author of good alone, and the dominion of evil is assigned to a rebellious angel or a rival god.

So far as we have gone at present, there has been no question of morality. All doctrines relating to the creation of the world, the government of man by superior being, and his destiny after death, are conjectures which have been given out as facts, handed down with many adornments by tradition, and accepted by posterity as "revealed religion." They are theories more or less rational which uncivilised men have devised in order to explain the facts of life, and which civilised men believe that they believe. These doctrines are not in themselves of any moral value. It is of no consequence, morally speaking, whether a man believes that the world has been made by one god or by twenty. A savage is not of necessity a better man because he believes that he lives under the dominion of invisible tyrants who will compel him some day or other to migrate to another land.

There is a moral sentiment in the human breast which, like intelligence, is born of obscure instincts, and which gradually becomes developed. Since the gods of men are the reflected images of men, it is evident that as men become developed in morality the character of their gods will also be improved. The king of a savage land punishes only offences against himself and his dependents. But when that people become more civilised the king is regarded as the representative of public law. In the same manner the gods of a savage people demand nothing from their subjects but taxes and homage. They punish only heresy, which is equivalent to treason; blasphemy, which is equivalent to insult; and the withholding of tribute and adoration, which is equivalent to rebellion. And these are the offences which even among civilised nations the gods are supposed to punish most severely. But the civilised gods also require that men shall act justly to one another. They are still despots, for they order men to flatter them and to give them money. But they are not mere selfish despots; they will reward those who do good, they will punish those who do evil to their fellow-men.

That vice should be sometimes triumphant and virtue sometimes in distress creates no difficulty to the savage mind. If a good man meets with misfortune it is supposed that he is being punished for the sins of an ancestor or a relation. In a certain stage of barbarism society is composed not of individuals but of families. If a murder is committed the avengers of blood kill the first man they meet belonging to the guilty clan. If the life cannot be obtained in that generation the feud passes on, for the family never dies. It is considered just and proper that children should be punished for the sins of their fathers unto the third and fourth generation.

In a higher state of society this family system disappears; individualism becomes established. And as soon as this point is reached the human mind takes a vast stride. It is discovered that the moral government of this world is defective, and it is supposed that poetical justice will be administered in the next. The doctrine of rewards and punishments in a future state comes into vogue. The world of ghosts is now divided into two compartments. One is the abode of malignant spirits, the kingdom of darkness and of pain to which are condemned the blasphemers and the rebels, the murderers and the thieves. The other is the habitation of the gods, the kingdom of joy and light, to which angels welcome the obedient and the good. They are dressed in white robes and adorned with golden crowns; they dwell eternally in the royal presence, gazing upon his lustrous countenance and singing his praises in chorus round the throne.

To the active European mind such a prospect is not by any means inviting; but heaven was invented in the East, and in the East to be a courtier has always been regarded as the supreme felicity. The feelings of men towards their god in the period at which we have now arrived are precisely those of an Eastern subject towards his king. The Oriental king is the lord of all the land; his subjects are his children and his slaves. The man who is doomed to death kisses the fatal firman and submits with reverence to his fate. The man who is robbed by the king of all that he has earned will fold his hands and say "The king gave and the king taketh away. Blessed be the name of the king!" The man who lives in a distant province, who knows the king only by means of the taxes which are collected in his name, will snatch up his arms if he hears that his sacred person is in danger, and will defend him as he defends his children and his home. He will sacrifice his life for one whom he has never seen, and who has never done him anything but harm.

This kind of devotion is called loyalty when exhibited towards a king, piety when exhibited towards a god. But in either case the sentiment is precisely the same. It cannot be too often repeated that god is only a special name for king; that religion is a form of government, its precepts a code of laws; that priests are gatherers of divine taxes, officers of divine police; that men resort to churches to fall on their knees and to sing hymns from the same servile propensity which makes the Oriental delight in prostrating himself before the throne; that the noble enthusiasm which inspires men to devote themselves to the service of their god, and to suffer death rather than deny his name, is identical with the devotion of the faithful subject who, to serve his royal master, gives up his fortune or his life without the faintest prospect of reward. The religious sentiment, about which so much has been said, has nothing distinctive in itself. Love and fear, self-denial and devotion, existed before those phantoms were created which men call gods, and men have merely applied to invisible kings the sentiments which they had previously felt towards their earthly kings. If they are a people in a savage state they hate both kings and gods within their hearts, and obey them only out of fear. If they are a people in a higher state love is mingled with their fear, producing an affectionate awe which in itself is pleasing to the mind. That the worship of the unseen king should survive the worship of the earthly king is natural enough, but even that will not endure for ever; the time is coming when the crowned idea will be cast aside and the despotic shadow disappear.

By thus translating, or by re-translating, god into king, piety into loyalty, and so on; by bearing in mind that the gods were not abstract ideas to our ancestors as they are to us, but bona fide men differing only from men on earth in their invisibility and other magic powers; by noting that the moral disposition of a god is an image of the moral sense of those who worship him--their beau-ideal of what a king should be; by observing that the number and arrangement of the gods depend exclusively on the intellectual faculties of the people concerned, on their knowledge of nature, and perhaps to some extent on the political forms of government under which they live: above all by remembering that there is a gradual development in supernatural ideas, the student of comparative religion will be able to sift and classify with ease and clearness dense masses of mythology. But he must understand that the various stages overlap. Just as sailing vessels and four-horse coaches are still used in this age of steam, and as stone implements were still to be found in use long after the age of iron had set in, so in the early period of god-belief thing-worship still to a certain extent endured. In a treaty between Hannibal and Philip of Macedonia which Polybius preserved, the contracting parties take oath with one another "n the presence of Jupiter, Juno, and Apollo; in the presence of the deity of the Carthaginians and of Hercules and of Iolaus; in the presence of Mars, Triton, and Neptune; in the presence of all the gods who are with us in the camp; and of the sun, the moon, and the earth; the rivers, the lakes, and the waters." In the time of Socrates the Athenians regarded the sun as an individual. Alexander, according to Arian, sacrificed not only to the gods of the sea but "the sea itself was honoured with is munificence." Even in Job, the purest of all monotheistic works, the stars are supposed to be live creatures which sing around the heavenly throne.

Again, in those countries where two distinct classes of men exist, the one intellectual and learned, the other illiterate and degraded, there will be in reality two religions, though nominally there may be only one. Among the ancient Sabaeans the one class adored spirits who inhabited the stars, the other class adored the stars themselves. Among the worshippers of fire that element to one class was merely an emblem, to the other an actual person. Wherever idols or images are used the same phenomenon occurs. These idols are intended by the priests as aids to devotion, as books for those who cannot read. But the savage believes that his god inhabits the image, or even regards the image as itself a god. His feelings towards it are those of a child towards her doll. She knows that it is filled with sawdust and made of painted wood, and yet she loves it as if it were alive. Such is precisely the illusion of the savage, for he possesses the imagination of a child. He talks to his idol fondly and washes its face with oil or rum, beats it if it will not give him what he asks, and hides it in his waistcloth if he is going to do something which he does not wish it to see.

There is one other point which it is necessary to observe. A god's moral disposition, his ideas of right and wrong, are those of the people by whom he is created. Wandering tribes do not as a rule consider it wrong to rob outside the circle of their clan: their god is therefore a robber like themselves. If they settle in a fertile country, pass into the agricultural state, build towns, and become peaceful citizens with property of their own they change their views respecting theft, and accordingly their god forbids it in his laws. But it sometimes happens that the sayings and doings of the tent-god are preserved in writings which are accepted as revelation by the people of a later and better age. Then may be observed the curious and by no means pleasing spectacle of a people outgrowing their religion, and believing that their god performed actions which would be punished with the gallows if they were done by men.

The mind of an ordinary man is in so imperfect a condition that it requires a creed--that is to say, a theory concerning the unknown and the unknowable in which it may place its deluded faith and be at rest. But whatever the creed may be, it should be one which is on a level with the intellect, and which inquiry will strengthen not destroy.

As for minds of the highest order, they must ever remain in suspension of judgement and in doubt. Not only do they reflect the absurd traditions of the Jews, but also the most ingenious attempts which have been made to explain on rational and moral grounds the origin and purpose of the universe. Intense and long-continued labour reveals to them this alone, that there are regions of thought so subtle and so sublime that the human mine is unable therein to expand its wings, to exercise its strength. But there is a wide speculative field in which man is permitted to toil with the hope of rich reward, in which observation and experience can supply materials to his imagination and his reason. In this field two great discoveries have been already made. First, that there is a unity of plan in nature, that the universe resembles a body in which all the limbs and organs are connected with one another; and second, that all phenomena, physical and moral, are subject to laws as invariable as those which regulate the rising and setting of the sun. It is in reality as foolish to pray for rain or a fair wind as it would be to pray that the sun should set in the middle of the day. It is as foolish to pray for the healing of a disease or for daily bread as it is to pray for rain or a fair wind. It is as foolish to pray for a pure heart or for mental repose as it is to pray for help in sickness or misfortune. All the events which occur upon the earth result from law: even those actions which are entirely dependent on the caprices of the memory or the impulse of the passions are shown by statistics to be, when taken in the gross entirely independent of the human will. As a single atom man is an enigma: as a whole he is a mathematical problem. As an individual he is a free agent, as a species the offspring of necessity.

The unity of the universe is a scientific fact. To assert that it is the operation of a single mind is a conjecture based upon analogy, and analogy may be a deceptive guide. It is the most reasonable guess that can be made, but still it is no more than a guess, and it is one by which nothing after all is really gained. It tells us that the earth rests upon the tortoise: it does not tell us on what the tortoise rests. God issued the laws which manufactured the universe and which rule it in its growth. But who made God? Theologians declare that he made himself, materialists declare that matter made itself, and both utter barren phrases, idle words. The whole subject is beyond the powers of the human intellect in its present state. All that we can ascertain is this: that we are governed by physical laws which it is our duty as scholars of Nature to investigate, and by moral laws which it is our duty as citizens of Nature to obey.

The dogma of a single deity who created the heavens and the earth may therefore be regarded as an imperfect method of expressing an undoubted truth. Of all religious creeds it is the least objectionable from a scientific point of view. Yet it was not a Greek who first discovered or invented the one god, but the wild Bedouin of the desert. At first sight this appears a very extraordinary fact. How, in a matter which depended entirely upon the intellect, could these barbarians have preceded the Greeks, so far their superiors in every other respect? The anomaly, however, can be easily explained. In the first theological epoch every object and every phenomenon of Nature was supposed to be a creature, in the second epoch the dwelling or expression of a god. It is evident that the more numerous the objects and phenomena, the more numerous would be the gods, the more difficult it would be to unravel Nature, to detect the connection between phenomena, to discover the unity which underlies them all. In Greece there is a remarkable variety of climate and contour; hills, groves, and streams diversify the scene; rugged, snow-covered peaks and warm coast lands with waving palms lie side by side. But in the land of the Bedouins, Nature may be seen in the nude. The sky is uncovered; the earth is stripped and bare. It is as difficult for the inhabitants of such a country to believe that there are many gods as for the people of such a land as Greece to believe that there is only one. The earth and the wells and some uncouth stones, the sun, the moon, and the stars are almost the only materials of superstition that the Bedouin can employ; and that they were so employed we know. Stone worship and star idolatry, with the adoration of ancestral shades, prevailed within Arabia in ancient times, and even now are not extinct. "The servant of the sun" was one of the titles of their ancient kings. Certain honours are yet paid to the morning star. But in that country the one-god belief was always that of the higher class of minds, at least within historic time; it is therefore not incorrect to term it the Arabian creed. We shall now proceed to show in what manner that belief, having mingled with foreign elements, became a national religion, and how from that religion sprang two other religions which overspread the world.

Long after the building of the Pyramids, but before the dawn of Greek and Roman life, a Bedouin sheikh named Abraham, accompanied by his nephew Lot, migrated from the plains which lie between the Tigris and Euphrates, crossed over the Syro-Arabian desert, and entered Canaan, a country about the size of Wales lying below Phoenicia between the desert and the Mediterranean Sea. They found it inhabited by a people of farmers and vine-dressers, living in walled cities and subsisting on the produce of the soil. But only a portion of the country was under cultivation: they discovered wide pastoral regions unoccupied by men, and wandered at their pleasure from pasture to pasture and from plain to plain. Their flocks and herds were nourished to the full, and multiplied so fast that the Malthusian Law came into force; the herdsmen of Abraham and Lot began to struggle for existence; the land could no longer bear them both. It was therefore agreed that each should select a region for himself. A similar arrangement was repeated more than once in the lifetime of the patriarch. When his illegitimate sons grew up to man's estate he gave them cattle and sent them off in the direction of the east.

At certain seasons of the year he encamped beneath the walls of cities, and exchanged the wool of his flocks for flour, oil, and wine. He established friendships with the native kings, and joined them in their wars. He was honoured by them as a prince, for he could bring three hundred armed slaves into the field, and his circle of tents might fairly be regarded as a town. Before their canvas doors sat the women spinning wool and singing the Mesopotamian airs, while the aged patriarch in the Great Tent, which served as the forum and the guesthouse, measured out the rations for the day, gave orders to the young men about the stock, and sat in judgment on the cases which were brought before him, as king and father to decide.

He bought from the people of the land a field and a cave, in which he buried his wife and in which he was afterwards himself interred. He was succeeded by Isaac as head of the family. Esau and Jacob, the two sons of Isaac, appear to have been equally powerful and rich.

The Israelites

Up to this time the children of Abraham were Bedouin Arabs--nothing more. They worshipped Eloah or Allah, sometimes erecting to him a rude altar on which they sacrificed a ram or kid; sometimes a stone pillar on which they poured a drink, and then smeared it with oil to his honour and glory. Sometimes they planted a sacred tree. The life which they led was precisely that of the wandering Arabs who pasture their flocks on the outskirts of Palestine at the present day. Not only Ishmael, but also Lot, Esau, and various Abrahamites of lesser note became the fathers of Arabian tribes. The Beni-Israel did not differ in manners and religion from the Beni-Ishmael and Beni-Esau, and Beni-Lot. It was the settlement of the clan in a foreign country, the influence of foreign institutions, which made the Israelites a peculiar people. It was the sale of the shepherd boy--at first a house-slave, then a prisoner, then a favourite of the Pharaoh--which created a destiny for the House of Jacob, separated it from the Arab tribes, and educated it into a nationality. When Joseph became a great man he obtained permission to send for his father and his brethren. The clan of seventy persons, with their women and their slaves, came across the desert by the route of the Syrian caravan. The old Arab, in his coarse woollen gown and with his staff in his hand, was ushered into the royal presence. He gave the king his blessing in the solemn manner of the East, and after a short conversation was dismissed with a splendid gift of land. When Jacob died his embalmed corpse was carried up to Canaan with an Egyptian escort and buried in the cave which Abraham had bought. Joseph had married the daughter of a priest of Heliopolis, but his two sons did not become Egyptians; they were formally admitted into the family by Jacob himself before he died.

When Joseph also died the connection between the Israelites and the court came to an end. They led the life of shepherds in the fertile pasturelands which had been bestowed upon them by the king. In course of time the twelve families expanded into twelve tribes, and the tribe itself became a nation. The government of Memphis observed the rapid increase of this people with alarm. The Israelites belonged to the same race as the hated Hyksos or Shepherd Kings. With their long beards and flowing robes they reminded the Egyptians of the old oppressors. It was argued that the Bedouins might again invade Egypt, and in that case the Israelites would take their side. By way of precaution the Israelites were treated as prisoners of war, disarmed, and employed on the public works. And as they still continued to increase it was ordered that all their male children should be killed. It was doubtless the intention of the government to marry the girls as they grew up to Egyptians, and so to exterminate the race.

One day the king's daughter, as she went down with her girls to the Nile to bathe, found a Hebrew child exposed on the waters in obedience to the new decree. She adopted the boy and gave him an Egyptian name. He was educated as a priest, and became a member of the University of Heliopolis. But although his face was shaved and he wore the surplice, Moses remained a Hebrew in his heart. He was so overcome by passion when he saw an Egyptian ill-using an Israelite that he killed the man upon the spot. The crime became known: there was a hue and cry; he escaped to the peninsula of Sinai, and entered the family of an Arab sheikh.

The peninsula of Sinai lies clasped between two arms of the Red Sea. It is a wilderness of mountains covered with a thin, almost transparent coating of vegetation which serves as pasture to the Bedouin flocks. There is one spot only--the oasis of Feiran--where the traveller can tread on black, soft earth and hear the warbling of birds among the trees, which stand so thickly together that he is obliged as he walks to part the branches from his face. The peninsula had not escaped the Egyptian arms; tablets may yet be seen on which are recorded in paintings and hieroglyphics five thousand years old the victories of the Pharaohs over the people of the land. They also worked mines of copper in the mountains, and heaps of slag still remain. But most curious of all are the Sinaitic inscriptions, as they are called--figures of animals rudely scrawled on the upright surface of the black rocks and mysterious sentences in an undeciphered tongue.

Among the hills which crown the high plateau there is one which at that time was called the Mount of God. It was holy ground to the Egyptians, and also to the Arabs, who ascended it as pilgrims and drew off their sandals when they reached the top. Nor is it strange that Sinai should have excited reverence and dread; it is indeed a weird and awful land. Vast and stern stand the mountains, with their five granite peaks pointing to the sky; avalanches like those of the Alps, but of sand, not of snow, rush down their naked sides with a clear and tinkling sound resembling convent bells; a peculiar property resides in the air; the human voice can be heard at a surprising distance, and swells out into a reverberating roar; and sometimes there rises from among the hills a dull booming sound like the distant firing of heavy guns.

Let us attempt to realise what Moses must have felt when he was driven out of Egypt into such a harsh and rugged land. Imagine this man, the adopted son of a royal personage, the initiated priest, sometimes turning the astrolabe towards the sky, perusing the papyrus scroll, or watching the crucible and the alembic; sometimes at the great metropolis enjoying the busy turmoil of the street, the splendid pageants of the court, reclining in a carpeted gondola or staying with a noble at his country house. In a moment all is changed. He is alone on the mountain-side, a shepherd's crook in his hand. He is a man dwelling in a tent; he is married to the daughter of a barbarian; his career is at an end. Never more will he enter that palace where once he was received with honour, where now his name is uttered only with contempt. Never more will he discourse with grave and learned men in the peaceful college gardens, beneath the willows that hang over the Fountain of the Sun. Never more will he see the people of his tribe whom he loves so dearly, and for whom he endures this miserable fate. They will suffer, but he will not see them; they will mourn, but he will not hear them--or only in his dreams. In his dreams he hears them and sees them, alas, too well. He hears the whistling of the lash and the convulsive sobs and groans. He sees the poor slaves toiling in the field, their hands brown with the clammy clay. He sees the daughters of Israel carried off to the harem with struggling arms and streaming hair, and then--O lamentable sight!--the chamber of the woman in labour--the seated shuddering, writhing form--the mother struggling against maternity--the tortured one dreading her release--for the king's officer is standing by the door, and as soon as the male child is born its life is at an end.

The Arabs with whom he was living were also children of Abraham, and they related to him legends of the ancient days. They told him of the patriarchs who lay buried in Canaan with their wives; they told him of Eloah, whom his fathers had adored. Then, as one who returns to a long lost home, the Egyptian priest returned to the simple faith of the desert, to the God of Abraham, of Isaac, and of Jacob. As he wandered on the mountain heights he looked to the west and he saw a desert: beyond it lay Egypt, the house of captivity, the land of bondage. He looked to the east and he saw a desert: beyond it lay Canaan, the home of his ancestors, a land of peace and soon to be a land of hope. For now new ideas rose tumultuously within him. He began to see visions and to dream dreams. He heard voices and beheld no form; he saw trees which blazed with fire and yet were not consumed. He became a prophet; he entered the ecstatic state.

Meanwhile the king had died; a new Pharaoh had mounted on the throne; Moses was able to return to Egypt and to carry out the great design which he had formed. He announced to the elders of the people, to the heads of houses and the sheikhs of tribes, that Eloah, the God of Abraham, had appeared to him in Sinai and had revealed his true name-- it was Jehovah--and had sent him to Egypt to bring away his people, to carry them to Canaan. The elders believed in his mission and accepted him as their chief. He went to Pharaoh and delivered the message of Jehovah: the king received it as he would have received the message of an Arab chief--gods were plentiful in Egypt. But whenever a public calamity occurred Moses declared that Jehovah was its author, and there were Egyptians who said that their own gods were angry with them for detaining a people who were irreligious, filthy in their habits, and affected with unpleasant diseases of the skin. The king gave them permission to go and offer a sacrifice to their desert god. The Israelites stole away, taking with them the mummy of Joseph and some jewellery belonging to their masters. Guides marched in front bearing a lighted apparatus like that which was used in Alexander's camp, which gave a pillar of smoke by day and a flame by night. Moses led them by way of Suez into Asia, and then along the weed-strewn, shell-strewn shore of the Red Sea to the wilderness of Sinai and the Mount of God. There with many solemn and imposing rites he delivered laws which he said had been issued to him from the clouds. He assembled the elders to represent the people, and drew up a contract between them and Jehovah. It was agreed that they should obey the laws of Jehovah, and pay the taxes which he might impose, while he engaged on his part to protect them from danger in their march through the desert and to give them possession of the Promised Land. An ark or chest of acacia-wood was made in the Egyptian style, and the agreement was deposited therein with the ten fundamental laws which Moses had engraved on stone. A tent of dyed skins was prepared and fitted with church furniture by voluntary subscription, partly out of stolen goods. This became the temple of the people and the residence of Jehovah, who left his own dwelling above the vaulted sky that he might be able to protect them on the way. Moses appointed his brother Aaron and his sons to serve as priests; they wore the surplice, but to distinguish them from Egyptian priests they were ordered not to shave their heads. The men of Levi, to which tribe Moses himself belonged, were set apart for the service of the sacred tent. They were in reality his bodyguard, and by their means he put down a mutiny at Sinai, slaughtering three thousand men.

When thus the nation had been organised the march began. At daybreak two silver trumpets were blown, the tents were struck, the tribes assembled under their respective banners, and the men who bore the ark went first with the guides to show the road and to choose an encampment for the night. The Israelites crossed a stony desert, suffering much on the way. Water was scarce; they had no provisions, and were forced to subsist on manna or angel's bread, a gummy substance which exudes from a desert shrub and is a pleasant syrup and a mild purge, but not a nourishing article of food.

As they drew near the land of Canaan the trees of the desert, the palm and the acacia, disappeared. But the earth became carpeted with green plants and spotted with red anemones like drops of blood. Here and there might be seen a patch of corn, and at last in the distance rounded hills with trees standing against the sky. They encamped, and a man from each tribe was deputed to spy the land. In six weeks they returned bringing with them a load of grapes. Two scouts only were in favour of invasion. The other ten declared that the land was a good land, as the fruits showed--a land flowing with milk and honey; but the people were like giants; their cities were walled and very great; the Israelites were as grasshoppers in comparison, and would not be able to prevail against them.

This opinion was undoubtedly correct. The children of Israel were a rabble of field slaves who had never taken a weapon in their hands. The business before them was by no means to their taste, and it was not what Moses had led them to expect. He had agreed on the part of Jehovah to give them a land. They had expected to find it unoccupied and prepared for their reception like a new house. They did not require a prophet to inform them that a country should be theirs if they were strong enough to take it by the sword, and this it was clear they could not do. So they poured forth the vials of their anger and their grief. They lifted up their voice and cried; they wept all the night. Would to God they had died in the wilderness! Would to God they had died in Egypt! Jehovah had brought them there that they might fall by the sword, and that their wives and little ones might be a prey. They would choose another captain; they would go back to Egypt. Joshua and Caleb, the two scouts who had recommended invasion, tried to cheer them up, and were nearly stoned to death for their pains. Next day the people of Canaan marched out against them: a skirmish took place and the Israelites were defeated. They went back to the desert, and wandered forty years in the shepherd or Bedouin state.

And then there was an end of that miserable race who were always whining under hardship, hankering after the fleshpots of the old slave life. In their stead rose up a new generation--genuine children of the desert-- who could live on a few dates soaked in butter and a mouthful of milk a day; who were practised from their childhood in predatory wars; to whom rapine was a business, and massacre a sport. The conquest of Canaan was an idea which they had imbibed at their mothers' breasts, and they were now quite ready for the work. Moses before his death drew up a second agreement between Jehovah and the people. It was to the same effect as the covenant of Sinai. Loyalty and taxes were demanded by Jehovah; long life, success in war, and fruitful crops were promised in return. Within this contract was included a code of laws which Moses had enacted from time to time, in addition to the ten commandments; and this second agreement was binding not only on those who were present but on their posterity as well.

Moses died; Joshua was made commander-in-chief, and the Israelites began their march of war. This time they approached the land not from the south but from the east.

The river Jordan rises in the Lebanon mountains, half way between Tyre and Damascus; it runs due south, and ends its curling, twisting course in the dismal waters of the Dead Sea. Its basin belongs to the desert, for it does not overflow its banks.

Along the coast of the Mediterranean Sea, parallel to the valley of the Jordan, lies a fertile strip of land without good harbours, but otherwise resembling Phoenicia, from which it is divided by two large promontories, the Tyrian Ladder and the White Cape.

And thirdly, between the naked valley of the Jordan and this corn-producing line of coast there rises a tableland of limestone formation, honeycombed with caves, watered by running streams of no great size, and intersected by ravines and also by flat, extensive valley plains.

The coast belonged to the Philistines, the basin of the Jordan and the pastoral regions on the south to roving Arab tribes; the tableland was inhabited by farmers whose towns and villages were always perched on the tops of hills, and who cultivated the vine on terraces, each vineyard being guarded by a watch tower and a wall; the valley plains were inhabited by Canaanites or lowlanders, who possessed cavalry and iron chariots of war.

The Israelites differed from other Bedouin tribes in one respect--they were not mounted, and they were unable to stand their ground against the horsemen of the plain. The Philistines, a warlike people probably of the Aryan race, also retained their independence. The conquests of the Israelites were confined to the land of the south, the Jordan valley and the mountain regions, though even in the highlands the conquest under Joshua was not complete.

However, the greater part of Palestine was taken and partitioned among the Israelitish tribes. Some of these inclined to the pastoral and others to the agricultural condition, and each was governed by its own sheikh. During four hundred years Ephraim remained the dominant tribe, and with Ephraim the high priest took up his abode. At a place called Shiloh there was erected an enclosure of low stone walls over which the sacred tent was drawn. This was the oracle establishment, or House of God, to which all the tribes resorted three times a year to celebrate the holy feasts with prayer and sacrifice, and psalmody, and the sacred dance.

The Levites had no political power and no share in civil life, but they had cities of their own, and they also travelled about like mendicant friars from place to place performing certain functions of religion, and supported by the alms of the devout.

It was owing to these two institutions, the oracle and the monkish order, that the nationality of Israel was preserved. Yet though it escaped extinction it did not retain its unity and strength. So far from extending their conquests, after their first inroad under Joshua the Israelites constantly lost ground. They were divided into twelve petty states, always jealous of one another and often engaged in civil war. The natives took advantage of these dissensions, and subdued them one by one. Now and then a hero would arise, rouse them to a war of independence, and rule over them as judge for a few years. Then again they would fall apart, and again be conquered, sometimes paying tribute as vassals, sometimes hiding in the mountain caves. However, at last there came a change. The temporal and spiritual powers, united in the hands of Moses, were divided at his death. Joshua became the general of Jehovah; the high priest became his grand vizier. Joshua could do nothing of importance without consulting the high priest, who read the commands of the Divine Sheikh in the light and play of Urim and Thummim, the oracular shining stones. On the other hand, the high priest could not issue laws; he could only give decisions and replies. But now a Nazarite or servant of the Church, named Samuel, usurped the office, or at all events the powers, of high priest which belonged to the family of Aaron, and also obtained the dignity of president or judge. He professed to be the recipient of private instructions from Jehovah, issued laws in his name, and went round on circuit judging the twelve tribes.

In his old age he delegated this office to his sons, who gave false judgments and took bribes. The elders of the people came to Samuel and asked him to appoint them a king.

Samuel had established a papacy, intending to make it hereditary in his house, and now the evil conduct of his sons frustrated all his hopes. He protested in the name of Jehovah against this change in the constitution; he appealed to his own blameless life; he drew a vivid picture of the horrors of despotism; but in vain. The people persisted in their demand; they were at that time in the vassal state, and their liege lords, the Philistines, did not permit them to have smiths lest they should make weapons and rebel. Samuel himself had united the tribes, and had inspired them with the sentiments of nationality. They yearned to be free, and they observed that they lost battles because their enemies were better officered than themselves. They saw that they needed a military chief who would himself lead them to the charge, instead of sacrificing a sucking lamb or kneeling on a neighbouring hill with his hands up in the air.

Samuel, still protesting, elected Saul to the royal office. The young man was gladly accepted by the people on account of his personal beauty, and as he belonged to the poorest family of the poorest tribe in Israel, Samuel hoped that he would be able to preserve the real power in his own hands. But it so happened that Saul was not only a brave soldier and a good general; he was also at times a "god-intoxicated man," and did not require a third person to bring him the instructions of Jehovah. He made himself the head of the Church, as well as of the state, and Samuel was compelled to retire into private life. It is for this reason that Saul's character has been so bitterly attacked by the priest-historians of the Jews. For what after all are the crimes of which he was guilty? He administered the battle-offering himself, and he spared the life of a man whom Samuel had commanded him to kill as a human sacrifice to Jehovah. Saul was by no means faultless, but his character was pure as snow when compared with that of his successor. David was undoubtedly the greater general of the two, yet it was Saul who laid the foundations of the Jewish kingdom. It was Saul who conquered the Philistines and won freedom for the nation with no better weapons than their mattocks and their axes and their sharpened goads. Saul's persecution of David is the worst stain upon his life, yet if it is true that David had been in Saul's lifetime privately anointed king, he was guilty of treason and deserved to die. But that story of the anointing might have been invented afterwards to justify his succession to the throne.

At first David took refuge with the Philistines and fought against his own countrymen. Next he turned brigand, and was joined by all the criminals and outlaws of the land. The cave of Adullam was his lair, whence he sallied forth to levy blackmail on the rich farmers and graziers of the neighbourhood, cutting their throats when they refused to pay. At the same time, he was a very religious man, and never went on a plundering expedition without consulting a little image which revealed to him the orders and wishes of Jehovah, just as the Bedouins always pray to Allah before they commit a crime, and thank him for his assistance when it has been successfully performed.

Saul was succeeded by his son Ishbosheth, who was accepted by eleven tribes. But David, supported by his own tribe and by his band of well-trained robbers, defied the nation and made war upon his lawful king. He had not the shadow of a claim; however, with the help of treason and assassination he finally obtained the crown. His military genius had then full scope. He took Jerusalem, a pagan stronghold which during four hundred years had maintained its independence. He conquered the coast of the Philistines, the plains of Canaan, the great city of Damascus, and the tribes of the desert far and near. He garrisoned Arabia Petraea. He ruled from Euphrates to the Red Sea.

This man after God's own heart had a well-stocked harem, and the usual intrigues took place. He disinherited his eldest son and left the kingdom to the son of his favourite wife--a woman for whom he had committed a crime which had offended the not over-delicate Jehovah. The nation seemed taken by surprise, and Solomon, in order to preserve the undivided affections of his people, at once killed his brother and his party--a coronation ceremony not uncommon in the East.

The wisdom of Solomon has become proverbial. But whatever his intellectual attainments may have been, he did not possess that kind of wisdom which alone is worthy of a king. He did not attempt to make his monarchy enduring, his people prosperous and content. He was a true Oriental sultan, sleek and sensual, luxurious and magnificent, short-sighted and unscrupulous, cutting down the tree to eat the fruit. The capital of a despot is always favoured, and with the citizens of Jerusalem he was popular enough. They were in a measure his guests and companions, the inmates of his house. They saw their city encircled with enormous walls, and paved with slabs of black and shining stone. Their eyes were dazzled and their vanity delighted with the splendid buildings which he raised--the ivory palace, the cedar palace, and the temple. The pilgrims who thronged to the sanctuary from all quarters of the land, and the travellers who came for the purposes of trade, brought wealth into the city. Foreign commerce was a court monopoly, but the city was a part of the court. Outside the city walls, however, or at least beyond the circle of the city lands, it was a very different affair. The rural districts were severely taxed, especially those at a distance from the capital. The tribes of Israel, which but a few years before had been on terms of complete equality among themselves, were now trampled underfoot by this upstart of the House of Judah. The tribe of Ephraim, which had so long enjoyed supremacy, became restless beneath the yoke. While Solomon yet reigned the standard of revolt was raised; as soon as he died this empire of a day dissolved. Damascus became again an independent state. The Arabs cut the road to the Red Sea. The king of Egypt, who had probably been Solomon's liege lord, dispatched an army to fetch away the treasures of the temple and the palace. The ten tribes seceded, and two distinct kingdoms were established.

The ten tribes of Israel, or the Kingdom of the North, extended over the lands of Samaria and Galilee. Its capital was Shechem, its sanctuary Mount Gerizim.

The Jews

Judah and Benjamin, the royal tribes, occupied the highlands of Judea. Jerusalem was their capital; its temple was their sanctuary, and the Levites, whom the Israelites had discarded, were their priests. It is needless to relate the wars which were almost incessantly being waged between these two miserable kingdoms. When the empire of the Tigris took the place of Egypt as suzerain of Syria both Israel and Judah sent their tribute to Nineveh; and as the cuneiform history relates, both of them afterwards rebelled. Sennacherib marched against them and carried off the ten tribes into captivity. Judea was more mountainous, and on that account more difficult to conquer than the land of the North. The Jews, as they may now be called, defended themselves stoutly, and a camp plague broke up the army before Jerusalem. By this occurrence Egypt also was preserved from conquest. At that time Sethos, the priest, was king, and the soldiers, whose lands he had taken, refused to fight. Both the Egyptians and the Jews ascribed their escape to a miracle performed by their respective gods.

Great events now took place. The Assyrian empire fell to pieces, and Nineveh was destroyed. The Medes inherited its power on the east of the Euphrates; the Chaldeans inherited its power on the west. Egypt under the Phil-Hellenes was again spreading into Asia, and a terrific duel took place between the two powers. The Jews managed so well that when the Egyptian star was in the ascendant they took the side of Babylon; and when the Babylonians had won the battle of Carchemish the Jews intrigued with the fallen nation. Nebuchadnezzar gave them repeated warnings, but at last his patience was exhausted and he levelled the rebellious city to the ground. Some of the citizens escaped to Egypt; the aristocracy and priesthood were carried off to Babylon; the peasants alone were left to cultivate the soil.

At Babylon there was a collection of captive kings, each of whom was assigned his daily allowance and his throne. In this palace of shadows the unfortunate Jehoiachin ended his days. But the Jewish people were not treated as captives or as slaves, and they soon began to thrive.

When the ten tribes seceded they virtually abandoned their religion. They withdrew from the temple which they had once acknowledged as the dwelling of Jehovah; they had no hereditary priesthood; they had no holy books; and so as soon as they ceased to possess a country they ceased to exist as a race. But the Jews preserved their nationality intact.

Moses had been an Egyptian priest, and the unity of God was a fundamental article of that religion. The unity of God was also the tenet of the more intelligent Arabs of the desert. Whether therefore we regard that great man as an Egyptian or as an Arab, it can scarcely be doubted that the views which he held of the Deity were as truly unitarian as those of Mohammed and Abdul-Wahhab. It is, however, quite certain that to the people whom he led Jehovah was merely an invisible Bedouin chief who travelled with them in a tent, who walked about the camp at night and wanted it kept clean, who manoeuvred the troops in battle, who delighted in massacres and human sacrifice, who murdered people in sudden fits of rage, who changed his mind, who enjoyed petty larceny and employed angels to tell lies--who, in short, possessed all the vices of the Arab character. He also possessed their ideal virtues, for he prohibited immorality and commanded them to be hospitable to the stranger, to be charitable to the poor, and to treat with kindness the domestic beast and the captive wife.

It was impossible for Moses to raise their minds to a nobler conception of the Deity; it would have been as easy to make them see Roman noses when they looked into a mirror. He therefore made use of their superstition in order to rule them for their own good, and descended to trumpetings and fire-tricks which chamber moralists may condemn with virtuous indignation, but which those who have known what it is to command a savage mob will not be inclined to criticise severely.

When the settlement in Canaan took place the course of events gave rise to a theory about Jehovah which not only the Israelites held but also the Philistines. It was believed that he was a mountain god and could not fight on level ground. He was unlike the pagan gods in one respect, namely, that he ordered his people to destroy the groves and idols of his rivals, and threatened to punish them if they worshipped any god but him. However, as might be supposed, although the Israelites were very loyal on the mountains, they worshipped other gods when they fought upon the plains. Whenever they won a battle they sang a song in honour of Jehovah and declared that he was "a man of war," but when they lost a battle they supposed that Baal or Dagon had trodden Jehovah under foot. The result of this was a mixed religion: they worshipped Jehovah, but they worshipped other gods as well. Solomon declared when he opened the temple that Jehovah filled the sky, that there were no other gods but he. But this was merely Oriental flattery. Solomon must have believed that there were other gods because he worshipped other gods.

His temple was in fact a Pantheon, and altars were raised on the Mount of Olives to Moloch and Astarte. After the reign of Solomon, however, the Jews became a civilised people; a literary class arose. Jerusalem, situated on the highway between the Euphrates and the Nile, obtained a place in the Asiatic world. The minds of the citizens became elevated and refined, and that reflection of their minds which they called Jehovah assumed a pure and noble form: he was recognised as the one God, the Creator of the world.

During all these years Moses had been forgotten, but now his code of laws (so runs the legend) was discovered in a corner of the temple, and laws of a higher kind adapted to a civilised people were issued under his name. The idols were broken, the foreign priests were expelled. It was in the midst of this great religious revival that Jerusalem was destroyed, and it may well be that the law which forbade the Jews to render homage to a foreign king was the chief cause of their contumacy and their dispersal. It was certainly the cause of all their

192

subsequent calamities: it was their loyalty to Jehovah which provoked the destruction of the city by the Romans: it was their fidelity to the law which brought down upon them all the curses of the law.

The reformation in the first period had been by no means complete: there had been many relapses and backslidings, and they therefore readily believed that the captivity was a judgment upon them for their sins. By the waters of Babylon they repented with bitter tears; in a strange land they returned to the god of their fathers and never deserted him again. Henceforth religion was their patriotism. Education became general: divine worship was organised: schools and synagogues were established wherever Jews were to be found.

And soon they were to be found in all the cities of the Eastern world. They had no land, and therefore adopted commerce as their pursuit; they became a trading and a travelling people, and the financial abilities which they displayed obtained them employment in the households and treasuries of kings.

The dispersion of the Jews must be dated from this period and not from the second destruction of the city. When Cyrus conquered Babylon he restored to the Jews their golden candlesticks and holy vessels, allowed them to return home, and rendered them assistance partly from religious sympathy--for the Jews made him believe that his coming had been predicted by their prophets--and partly from motives of policy. Palestine was the key to Egypt, against which Cyrus had designs, and it was wise to plant in Palestine a people on whom he could rely. But not all the Jews availed themselves of his decree. The merchants and officials who were now making their fortunes by the waters of Babylon were not inclined to return to the modest farmer life of Judea. Their piety was warm and sincere, but it was no longer combined with a passion for the soil. They began to regard Jerusalem as the Mohammedans regard Mecca. The people who did return were chiefly the fanatics, the clergy, and the paupers. The harvest, as we shall find was worthy of the seed.

Beneath the Persian yoke the Jews of Judea were content, and paid their tribute with fidelity. They could do so without scruple, for they identified Ormuzd with Jehovah, took lessons in theology from the doctors of the Zend-Avesta, and recognised the Great King as God's viceroy on earth. But when the Persian empire was broken up Palestine was again tossed upon the waves. The Greek kings of Alexandria and Antioch repeated the wars of Nebuchadnezzar and Necho. Again Egypt was worsted, and Syria became a province of the Graeco-Asiatic empire. The government encouraged emigration into the newly conquered lands, and soon Palestine was covered with Greek towns and filled with Greek settlers. Judea alone remained like an island in the flood. European culture was detested by the doctors of the law, who inflicted the same penalty for learning Greek as for eating pork. They therefore resisted the spread of civilisation, and Jerusalem was closed against the Greeks.

In the Hellenic world toleration was the universal rule. An oracle at Delphi had expressed the opinion of all when it declared that the proper religion for each man was the religion of his fatherland. Governments, therefore, did not interfere with the religious opinions of the people, but on the other hand the religious opinions of the people did not interfere with their civil duties. We allow the inhabitants of the holy city of Benares to celebrate the rites of their pilgrimage in their own manner, and to torture themselves in moderation, but we should at once begin what they would call a religious persecution if they were to purify the town by destroying the shops of the beef-butchers and other institutions which are an abomination in their eyes. Antiochus Epiphanes was by nature a humane and enlightened prince; he attempted to Europeanise Jerusalem; he could do this only by abolishing the Jewish laws; he could abolish their laws only by destroying their religion; and thus he was gradually drawn into barbarous and useless crimes of which he afterwards repented, but which have gained him the reputation of a Nero.

At first, however, it appeared as if he would succeed. The aristocratic party of Jerusalem were won over to the cause. A gymnasium was erected, and Jews with artificial foreskins appeared naked in the arena. Riots broke out. Then royal edicts were issued forbidding circumcision, and keeping of the Sabbath, and the use of the law. A pagan altar was set up in the Holy of Holies, and swine were sacrificed upon it to the Olympian Jove. The riots increased. Then a Greek regiment garrisoned the city; all new-born children that were found to be circumcised were hurled with their mothers from the walls; altar pork was offered as a test of loyalty to the elders of the Church, and those who refused to eat were put to death with tortures too horrible to be described. And now the Jews no longer raised riots: they rebelled. The empire was at that time in a state of weakness and disorder, and under the gallant Maccabees the independence of Judea was achieved. Yet it is only in adversity that the Jews can be admired. As soon as they obtained the power of self-government they showed themselves unworthy to possess it, and in the midst of a civil war they were enveloped by the Roman power, which had extended them its protection in the period of the Maccabees. The Senate placed Herod the great, an Arab price, upon the throne.

Herod was a man of the world, and his policy resembled that of the Ptolemies in Egypt. He built the Temple at Jerusalem and a theatre at Caesarea, in which city he preferred to dwell. The kingdom at his death was divided between his three sons: they were merely rajahs under the rule of Rome, and the one who governed Judea having been removed for misbehaviour, that country was attached to the pro-consulate of Syria. A lieutenant-governor was appointed to reside in the turbulent district to collect the revenues and maintain order. The position of the first commandant whom Russia sends to garrison Bokhara will resemble that of the procurator who took up his winter quarters at Jerusalem.

Those Jews of Judea, those Hebrews of the Hebrews, regarded all the Gentiles as enemies of God; they considered it a sin to live abroad, or to speak a foreign language, or to rub their limbs with foreign oil. Of all the trees, the Lord had chosen but one vine; and of all the flowers but one lily; and of all the birds but one dove; and of all the cattle but one lamb; and of all the builded cities only Sion; and among all the multitude of peoples he had elected the Jews as a peculiar treasure, and had made them a nation of priests and holy men. For their sake God had made the world. On their account alone empires rose and fell. Babylon had triumphed because God was angry with his people; Babylon had fallen because he had forgiven them. It may be imagined that it was not easy to govern such a race. They acknowledged no king but Jehovah, no laws but the precepts of their holy books. In paying tribute they yielded to absolute necessity, but the tax-gatherers were looked upon as unclean creatures; no respectable men would eat with them or pray with them; their evidence was not accepted in the courts of justice.

Their own government consisted of a Sanhedrin or Council of Elders, presided over by the High Priest. They had power to administer their own laws, but could not inflict the punishment of death without the permission of the procurator. All persons of consideration devoted themselves to the study of the law. Hebrew had become a dead language, and some learning was therefore requisite for the exercise of this profession, which was not the prerogative of a single class. It was a rabbinical axiom that the crown of the kingdom was deposited in Judah, and the crown of the priesthood in the seed of Aaron, but that the crown of the law was common to all Israel. Those who gained distinction as expounders of the sacred books were saluted with the title of rabbi, and were called scribes and doctors of the law. The people were ruled by the scribes, but the scribes were recruited from the people. It was not an idle caste--an established Church--but an order which was filled and refilled with the pious, the earnest, and the ambitious members of the nation.

There were two great religious sects which were also political parties, as must always be the case where law and religion are combined. The Sadducees were the rich, the indolent, and the passive aristocrats; they were the descendants of those who had belonged to the Greek party in the reign of Antiochus, and it was said that they themselves were tainted with the Greek philosophy. They professed, however, to belong to the conservative Scripture and original Mosaic school. As the Protestants reject the traditions of the ancient Church, some of which have doubtless descended viva voce from apostolic times, so all traditions, good and bad, were rejected by the Sadducees. As Protestants always inquire respecting a custom or doctrine, "Is it in the Bible?" so the Sadducees would accept nothing that could not be shown them in the law. They did not believe in heaven and hell because there was nothing about heaven and hell in the books of Moses. The morality which their doctors preached was cold and pure, and adapted only for enlightened minds. They taught that men should be virtuous without the fear of punishment and without the hope of reward, and that such virtue alone is of any worth.

The Pharisees were mostly persons of low birth. They were the prominent representatives of the popular belief, zealots in patriotism as well as in religion--the teaching, the preaching, and the proselytising party. Among them were to be found two kinds of men. Those Puritans of the Commonwealth with lank hair and sour visage and upturned eyes, who wore sombre garments, sniffled through their noses, and garnished their discourse with Scripture texts, were an exact reproduction, so far as the difference of place and period would allow, of certain Jerusalem Pharisees who veiled their faces when they went abroad lest they should behold a woman or some unclean thing; who strained the water which they drank for fear they should swallow the forbidden gnat; who gave alms to the sound of trumpet, and uttered long prayers in a loud voice; who wore texts embroidered on their robes and bound upon their brows; who followed minutely the observances of the ceremonial law; who added to it with their traditions; who lengthened the hours and deepened the gloom of the Sabbath day, and increased the taxes which it had been ordered should be paid upon the altar.

On the other hand, there had been among the Puritans many men of pure and gentle lives, and a similar class existed among the Pharisees. The good Pharisee, says the Talmud, is he who obeys the law because he loves the Lord. They addressed their god by the name of "Father" when they prayed. "Do unto others as you would be done by" was an adage often on their lips. That is the law, they said; all the rest is mere commentary. To the Pharisees belonged all that was best and all that was worst in the Hebrew religious life.

The traditions of the Pharisees related partly to ceremonial matters which in the written law were already diffuse and intricate enough. But it must also be remembered that without traditions the Hebrew theology was barbarous and incomplete. Before the captivity the doctrine of rewards and punishments in a future state had not been known. The Sheol of the Jews was a land of shades in which there was neither joy nor sorrow, in which all ghosts or souls dwelt promiscuously together. When the Jews came in contact with the Persian priests they were made acquainted with the heaven and hell of the Zend-Avesta. It is probable, indeed, that without foreign assistance they would in time have developed a similar doctrine for themselves. Already in the Psalms and Book of Job are signs that the Hebrew mind was in a transition state. When Ezekiel declared that the son should not be responsible for the iniquity of the father nor the father for the iniquity of the son, that the righteousness of the righteous should be upon him, and that the wickedness of the wicked should be upon him, he was preparing the way for a new system of ideas in regard to retribution. But as it was, the Jews were indebted to the Zend-Avesta for their traditional theory of a future life, and they also adopted the Persian ideas of the resurrection of the body, the rivalry of the evil spirit, and the approaching destruction and renovation of the world.

The Satan of Job is not a rebellious angel, still less a contending god: he is merely a mischievous and malignant sprite. But the Satan of the restored Jews was a powerful prince who went about like a roaring lion, and to whom this world belonged. He was copied from Ahriman, the God of Darkness, who was ever contending with Ormuzd, the God of Light. The Persians believed that Ormuzd would finally triumph, and that a prophet would be sent to announce the gospel or good tidings of his approaching victory. Terrible calamities would then take place; the stars would fall down from heaven; the earth itself would be destroyed. After which it would come forth new from the hands of the Creator; a kind of Millennium would be established; there would be one law, one language, and one government for men, and universal peace would reign.

This theory became blended in the Jewish minds with certain expectations of their own. In the days of captivity their prophets had predicted that a Messiah or anointed king would be sent, that the kingdom of David would be restored, and that Jerusalem would become the headquarters of God on earth. All the nations would come to Jerusalem to keep the feast of tabernacles and to worship God. Those who did not come should have no rain; and as the Egyptians could do without rain, if they did not come they should have the plague. The Jewish people would become one vast priesthood, and all nations would pay them tithe. Their seed would inherit the Gentiles. They would suck the milk of the Gentiles. They would eat the riches of the Gentiles. These same unfortunate Gentiles would be their ploughmen and their vine-dressers. Bowing down would come those that afflicted Jerusalem, and would lick the dust off her feet. Strangers would build up her walls, and kings would minister unto her. Many people and strong nations would come to see the Lord of Hosts in Jerusalem. Ten men in that day would lay hold of the skirt of a Jew saying, "We will go with you, for we have heard that God is with you." It was an idea worthy of the Jews that they should keep the Creator to themselves in Jerusalem, and make their fortunes out of the monopoly.

In the meantime these prophecies had not been fulfilled, and the Jews were in daily expectation of the Messiah--as they are still, and as they are likely to be for some time to come. It was the belief of the vulgar that this Messiah would be a man belonging to the family of David, who would liberate them from the Romans and become their king; so they were always on the watch, and whenever a remarkable man appeared they concluded that he was the son of David, the Holy One of Israel, and were ready at once to proclaim him king and to burst into rebellion. This illusion gave rise to repeated riots or revolts, and at last brought about the destruction of the city.

But among the higher class of minds the expectation of the Messiah, though not less ardent, was of a more spiritual kind. They believed that the Messiah was that prophet, often called the Son of Man who would be send by God to proclaim the defeat of Satan and the renovation of the world. They interpreted the prophets after a manner of their own: the kingdom foretold was the kingdom of heaven, and the new Jerusalem was not a Jerusalem on earth but a celestial city built of precious stones and watered by the Stream of Life.

Such were the hopes of the Jews. The whole nation trembled with excitement and suspense; the mob of Judea awaiting the Messiah or king who should lead them to the conquest of the world; the more noble-minded Jews of Palestine, and especially the foreign Jews, awaiting the Messiah or Son of Man who should proclaim the approach of the most terrible of all events. There were many pious men and women who withdrew entirely from the cares of ordinary life, and passed their days in watching and in prayer.

The Neo-Jewish or Persian-Hebrew religion, with its sublime theory of a single god, with its clearly defined doctrine of rewards and punishments, with its one grand duty of faith or allegiance to a divine king, was so attractive to the mind on account of its simplicity that it could not fail to conquer the discordant and jarring creeds of the pagan world as soon as it should be propagated in the right manner. There is a kind of natural selection in religion; the creed which is best adapted to the mental world will invariably prevail, and the mental world is being gradually prepared for the reception of higher and higher forms of religious life. At this period Europe was ready for the reception of the one-god species of belief, but it existed only in the Jewish area, and was there confined by artificial checks. The Jews held the doctrine that none but Jews could be saved, and most of them looked forward to the eternal torture of Greek and Roman souls with equanimity, if not with satisfaction. They were not in the least desirous to redeem them; they hoarded up their religion as they did their money, and considered it a heritage, a patrimony, a kind of entailed estate. There were some Jews in foreign parts who esteemed it a work of piety to bring the Gentiles to a knowledge of the true God, and as it was one of the popular amusements of the Romans to attend the service at the synagogue a convert was occasionally made. But such cases were very rare, for in order to embrace the Jewish religion it was necessary to undergo a dangerous operation and to abstain from eating with the pagans--in short, to become a Jew. It was therefore indispensable for the success of the Hebrew religion that it should be divested of its local customs. But however much the Pharisees and Sadducees might differ on matters of tradition, they were perfectly agreed on this point, that the ceremonial laws were necessary for salvation. These laws could never be given up by Jews unless they first became heretics, and this was what eventually occurred. A schism arose among the Jews: the sectarians were defeated and expelled. Foiled in their first object, they cast aside the law of Moses and offered the Hebrew religion without the Hebrew ceremonies to the Greek and Roman world. We shall now sketch the character of the man who prepared the way for this remarkable event.

It was a custom in Israel for the members of each family to meet together once a year that they might celebrate a sacred feast. A lamb roasted whole was placed upon the table, and a cup of wine was filled. Then the eldest son said, "Father, what is the meaning of this feast?" And the father replied that it was held in memory of the sufferings of their ancestors, and of the mercy of the Lord their God. For while they were weeping and bleeding in the land of Egypt there came his voice unto Moses and said that each father of a family should select a lamb without blemish from his flock, and should kill it on the tenth day of the month Abib, at the time of the setting of the sun; and should put the blood in a basin, and should take a sprig of hyssop and sprinkle the door-posts and lintel with the blood; and should then roast the lamb and eat it with unleavened bread and bitter herbs. They should eat it as if in haste, each one standing with his loins girt, his sandals on his feet, and his staff in his hand. That night the angel of the Lord slew the first born of the Egyptians, and that night Israel was delivered from her bonds.

When the father had thus spoken the lamb was eaten, and four cups of wine were drunk, and the family sang a hymn. At this beautiful and solemn festival all persons of the same kin endeavoured to meet together, and Hebrew pilgrims from all parts of the world journeyed to Jerusalem. When they came within sight of the Holy City and saw the Temple shining in the distance like a mountain of snow, some clamoured with cries of joy, some uttered low and painful sobs. Drawing closer together, they advanced towards the gates singing the Psalms of David, and offering up prayers for the restoration of Israel.

At this time the subscriptions from the various churches abroad were brought to Jerusalem, and were carried to the Temple treasury in solemn state; and at this time also the citizens of Jerusalem witnessed a procession which they did not like so well. A company of Roman soldiers escorted the lieutenant-governor, who came up from Caesarea for the festival that he might give out the vestments of the High Priest, which, being the insignia of government, the Romans kept under lock and key.

It was the nineteenth year of the reign of Tiberius Caesar. Pontius Pilate had taken up his quarters in the city, and the time of the Passover was at hand. Not only Jerusalem, but also the neighbouring villages, were filled with pilgrims, and many were obliged to encamp in tents outside the walls.

It happened one day that a sound of shouting was heard; the men ran up to the roofs of their houses, and the maidens peeped through their latticed windows. A young man mounted on a donkey was riding towards the city. A crowd streamed out to meet him, and a crowd followed him behind. The people cast their mantles on the road before him, and also covered it with green boughs. He rode through the city gates straight to the Temple, dismounted, and entered the holy building.

In the outer courts there was a kind of bazaar in connection with the Temple worship. Pure white lambs, pigeons, and other animals of the requisite age and appearance were there sold, and money merchants, sitting at their tables, changed the foreign coin with which the pilgrims were provided. The young man at once proceeded to upset the tables and to drive their astonished owners from the Temple, while the crowd shouted and the little gamins, who were not the least active in the riot, cried out, "Hurrah for the son of David!" Then people suffering from diseases were brought to him, and he laid his hands upon them and told them to have faith and they would be healed. When strangers inquired the meaning of this disturbance they were told that it was Joshua--or--as the Greek Jews called him, Jesus--the Prophet of Nazareth. It was believed by the common people that he was the Messiah. But the Pharisees did not acknowledge his mission. For Jesus belonged to Galilee, and the natives of that country spoke a vile patois, and their orthodoxy was in bad repute. "Out of Galilee," said the Pharisees with scorn, "out of Galilee there cometh no prophet."

All persons of imaginative minds know what it is to be startled by a thought; they know how ideas flash into the mind as if from without, and what physical excitement they can at times produce. They also know what it is to be possessed by a presentiment, a deep, overpowering conviction of things to come. They know how often such presentiments are true, and also how often they are false.

The Prophets

The prophet or seer is a man of strong imaginative powers which have not been calmed by education. The ideas which occur to his mind often present themselves to his eyes and ears in corresponding sights and sounds. As one in a dream he hears voices and sees forms; his whole mien is that of a man who is possessed; his face sometimes becomes transfigured and appears to glow with light; but usually the symptoms are of a more painful kind, such as foaming of the mouth, writhing of the limbs, and a bubbling ebullition of the voice. He is sometimes seized by these violent ideas against his will. But he can to a certain extent produce them by long fasting and by long prayer, or in other words by the continued concentration of the mind upon a single point; by music, dancing, and fumigations. The disease is contagious, as is shown by the anecdote of Saul among the prophets, and similar scenes have been frequently witnessed by travellers in the East.

Prophets have existed in all countries and at all times, but the gift becomes rare in the same proportion as people learn to read and write. Second sight in the Highlands disappeared before the school, and so it has been in other lands. Prophets were numerous in ancient Greece. In the Homeric period they opposed the royal power and constituted another authority by the grace of God. Herodotus alludes to men who went about prophesying in hexameters. Thucydides says that while the Peloponnesians were ravaging the lands of Athens there were prophets within the city uttering all kinds of oracles, some for going out and some for remaining in. It was a prophet who obtained the passing of that law under which Socrates was afterwards condemned to death. In Greece, Egypt, and in Israel the priests adopted and localised the prophetic power. The oracles of Amon, Delphi, and Shiloh bore the same relation to individual prophets as an Established Church to itinerant preachers. Syria was especially fertile in prophets. Marius kept a Syrian prophetess named Martha, who attended him in all his campaigns. It matters nothing what the Syrian religion might be; the same phenomenon again and again recurs. Balaam was a prophet before Israel was established. Then came the prophets of the Jews, and they again have been succeeded by the Christian cave saint and the Moslem dervish, whom the Arabs have always regarded with equal veneration. But it was among the Jews from the time of Samuel to the captivity that prophets or dervishes were most abundant. They were then as plentiful as politicians--and politicians in fact they were, and prophesied against each other. Some would be for peace and some would be for war: some were partisans of Egypt, others were partisans of Babylon. The prophetic ideas differ in no respect from those of ordinary men except in the sublime or ridiculous effect which they produce on the prophetic mind and body. Sometimes the predictions of the Jewish prophets were fulfilled, and sometimes they were not. To use the Greek phrase, their oracles were often of base metal, and in such a case the unfortunate dervish was jeered at as a false prophet, and would in his turn reproach the Lord for having made him a fool before men.

The Jewish prophet was an extraordinary being. He was something more and something less than a man. He spoke like an angel; he acted like a beast. As soon as he received his mission he ceased to wash. He often retired to the mountains, where he might be seen skipping from rock to rock like a goat; or he wandered in the desert with a leather girdle round his loins, eating roots and wild honey, or sometimes browsing on grass and flowers. He always adapted his actions to the idea which he desired to convey. He not only taught in parables but performed them. For instance, Isaiah walked naked through the streets to show that the Lord would strip Jerusalem, and make her bare. Ezekiel cut off his hair and beard and weighed it in the scales: a third part he burnt with fire, a third part he strewed about with a knife, and a third part he scattered to the wind. This was also intended to illustrate the calamities which would befall the Jews. Moreover he wore a rotten girdle as a sign that their city would decay, and buttered his bread in a manner we would rather not describe, as a sign that they would eat defiled bread among the Gentiles. Jeremiah wore a wooden yoke as a sign that they should be taken into captivity. As a sign that the Jews were guilty of wantonness in worshipping idols, Hosea cohabited three years with a woman of the town; and as a sign that they committed adultery in turning from the Lord their God, he went and lived with another man's wife.

Such is the ludicrous side of Jewish prophecy; yet it has also its serious and noble side. The prophets were always the tribunes of the people, the protectors of the poor. As the tyrant revelled in his palace on the taxes extorted from industrious peasants, a strange figure would descend from the mountains and, stalking to the throne, would stretch forth a lean and swarthy arm and denounce him in the name of Jehovah, and bid him repent, or the Lord's wrath should fall upon him and dogs should drink his blood. In the first period of the Jewish life the prophets exercised these functions of censor and of tribune, and preached loyalty to the god who had brought them up out of Egypt with a strong hand. They were also intensely fanatical, and published Jehovah's wrath not only against the king who was guilty of idolatry and vice, but also against the king who took a census, or imported horses, or made treaties of friendship with his neighbours. In the second period the prophets declared the unity of God and exposed the folly of idol-worship. They did even more than this. They opposed the ceremonial law, and preached the religion of the heart. They declared that God did not care for their Sabbaths and their festivals, and their new moons, and their prayers and church services and ablutions, and their sacrifices of meat and oil and of incense from Arabia and of the sweet cane from a far country. "Cease to do evil," said they; "learn to do well; relieve the oppressed; judge the fatherless; plead for the widow." It is certain that the doctrines of the great prophets were heretical. Jeremiah flatly declared that in the day that God brought them from the land of Egypt he did not command them concerning burnt offerings or sacrifices, and this statement would be of historical value if prophets always spoke the truth.

They were bitter adversaries of the kings and priests, and the consolers of the oppressed. "The Lord hath appointed me," says one whose oracles have been edited with those of Isaiah, but whose period was later and whose true name is not known, "the Lord hath appointed me to preach good tidings unto the meek; he that sent me to bind up the broken-hearted, to proclaim liberty to the captives, to give unto them that mourn beauty for ashes, the oil of joy for lamentation, the garment of praise for the spirit of heaviness."

The aristocracy who lived by the altar did not receive these attacks in a spirit of submission. There was a law ascribed to Moses--like all the other Jewish laws, but undoubtedly enacted by the priest party under the kings--that false prophets should be put to death; and though it was dangerous to touch prophets on account of the people, who were always on their side, they were frequently subjected to persecution. Urijah fled from

King Jehoiakim to Egypt; armed men were sent after him; he was arrested, brought back and killed. Zachariah was stoned to death in the courts of the Temple. Jeremiah was formally tried and was acquitted, but he had a narrow escape: he was led, as he remarked, like a sheep to the slaughter. At another time he was imprisoned; at another time he was let down by ropes into a dry well; and there is a tradition that he was stoned to death by the Jews in Egypt after all. The nominal Isaiah chants the requiem of such a martyr in a poem of exquisite beauty and grandeur. The prophet is described as one of hideous appearance, so that people hid their faces from him. "His visage was marred more than any man, and his form more than the sons of men." The people rejected his mission and refused to acknowledge him as a prophet. "He was despised and rejected of men, a man of sorrows and acquainted with grief." He was arraigned on a charge of false prophecy; he made no defence, and he was put to death. "He was oppressed and afflicted, yet he opened not his mouth: he was brought as a lamb to the slaughter, and as a sheep before her shearers is dumb, so he opened not his mouth. He was taken from the prison to the judgment; he was cut off from the land of the living." It was believed by the Jews that the death of such a man was accepted by God as a human sacrifice, an atonement for the sins of the people, just as the priest in the olden time heaped the sins of the people on the scapegoat and sent him out into the wilderness. "He bare the sins of many, and made intercession for the transgressors. The Lord hath laid on him the iniquity of us all. Surely he hath borne our griefs and hath carried our sorrows. His soul was made an offering for sin. He was wounded for our transgressions, he was bruised for our iniquities, and with his stripes we are healed."

There are many worthy people who think it a very extraordinary thing that this poem can be used almost word for word to describe the rejected mission and martyrdom of Jesus. But as the Hebrew prophets resembled one another, and were tried before the same tribunal under the same law, the coincidence is not surprising. A poetical description, in vague and general terms, of the rebellion of the English people and the execution of Charles the First would apply equally well to the rebellion of the French people and the execution of the Louis the Sixteenth.

The Character of Jesus

The Prophet of Nazareth did not differ in temperament and character from the noble prophets of the ancient period. He preached, as they did, the religion of the heart; he attacked, as they did, the ceremonial laws; he offered, as they did, consolation to the poor; he poured forth, as they did, invectives against the rulers and the rich. But his predictions were entirely different from theirs, for he lived, theologically speaking, in another world. The old prophets could only urge men to do good that the Lord might make them prosperous on earth, or at the most that they might obtain an everlasting name. They could only promise to the people the restoration of Jerusalem and the good things of the Gentiles; the reconciliation of Judah and Ephraim, and the gathering of the dispersed. The morality which Jesus preached was also supported by promises and threats, but by promises and threats of a more exalted kind: it was also based upon self-interest, but upon self-interest applied to a future life. For this he was indebted to the age in which he lived. He was superior as a prophet to Isaiah, as Newton as an astronomer was superior to Kepler, Kepler to Copernicus, Copernicus to Ptolemy, Ptolemy to Hipparchus, and Hipparchus to the unknown Egyptian or Chaldean priest who first began to register eclipses and to catalogue the stars. Jesus was a carpenter by trade, and was urged by a prophetic call to leave his workshop and to go forth into the world, preaching the gospel which he had received. The current fancies respecting the approaching destruction of the world, the conquest of the Evil Power, and the reign of God had fermented in his mind, and had made him the subject of a remarkable hallucination. He believed that he was the promised Messiah or Son of Man, who would be sent to prepare the world for the kingdom of God, and who would be appointed to judge the souls of men and to reign over them on earth. He was a man of the people, a rustic and an artisan: he was also an imitator of the ancient prophets, whose works he studied and whose words were always on his lips. Thus he was led as man and prophet to take the part of the poor. He sympathised deeply with the outcasts, the afflicted, and the oppressed. To children and to women; to all who suffered and shed tears; to all from whom men turned with loathing and contempt; to the girl of evil life who bemoaned her shame; to the tax-gatherer who crouched before his God in humility and woe; to the sorrowful in spirit and the weak in heart; to the weary and the heavy laden, Jesus appeared as a shining angel with words sweet as the honeycomb and bright as the golden day. He laid his hands on the heads of the lowly; he bade the sorrowful be of good cheer, for the day of their deliverance and their glory was at hand.

If we regard Jesus only in his relations with those whose brief and bitter lives he purified from evil and illumined with ideal joys, we might believe him to have been the perfect type of a meek and suffering saint. But his character had two sides, and we must look at both. Such is the imperfection of human nature that extreme love is counterbalanced by extreme hate; every virtue has its attendant vice, which is excited by the same stimulants, which is nourished by the same food. Martyrs and persecutors resemble one another; their minds are composed of the same materials. The man who will suffer death for his religious faith will endeavour to enforce it even unto death. In fact, if Christianity were true religious persecution would become a pious and charitable duty: if God designs to punish men for their opinions it would be an act of mercy to mankind to extinguish such opinions. By burning the bodies of those who diffuse them many souls would be saved that would otherwise be lost, and so there would be an economy of torment in the long run. It is therefore not surprising that enthusiasts should be intolerant. Jesus was not able to display the spirit of a persecutor in his deeds, but he displayed it in his words. Believing that it was in his power to condemn his fellow-creatures to eternal torture, he did so condemn by anticipation all the rich and almost all the learned men among the Jews. It was his belief that God reigned in heaven but that Satan reigned on earth. In a few years God would invade and subdue the earth. It was therefore his prayer, "Thy kingdom come; thy will be done in earth as it is in heaven." God's will was not at that time done on earth, which was in the possession of the Prince of Darkness. It was evident, therefore, that all prosperous men were favourites of Satan, and that the unfortunate were favourites of God. Those would go with their master to eternal pain: these would be rewarded by their master with eternal joy.

He did not say that Dives was bad or that Lazarus was good, but merely that Dives had received his good things on earth and Lazarus his evil things on earth, that afterwards Lazarus was rewarded and Dives tormented. Dives might have been as virtuous as the Archbishop of Canterbury, who is also clothed in fine linen and who fares sumptuously every day; Lazarus might have been as vicious as the Lambeth pauper who prowls round the palace gates, and whose mind, like his body, is full of sores. Not only the inoffensive rich were doomed by Jesus to hell-fire, but also all those who did anything to merit the esteem of their fellow-men. Even those that were happy and enjoyed life--unless it was in his own company--were lost souls. "Woe unto you that are rich," said he, "for ye have received your consolation. Woe unto you that are full, for ye shall hunger. Woe unto you that laugh now, for ye shall mourn and weep. Woe unto you when all men shall speak well of you, for so did their fathers of the false prophets." He also pronounced eternal punishment on all those who refused to join him. "He that believeth and is baptised," said he, "shall be saved. He that believeth not shall be damned."

He supposed that when the kingdom of God was established on earth he would reign over it as viceroy. Those who wished to live under him in that kingdom must renounce all the pleasures of Satan's world. They must sell their property and give the proceeds to the poor, discard all domestic ties, cultivate self-abasement, and do nothing which could possibly raise them in the esteem of other people. For they could not serve two masters: they could not be rewarded in the kingdom of this world, which was ruled by Satan, and also in the new kingdom, which would be ruled by God. If they gave a dinner they were not to ask their rich friends lest they should be asked back to dinner, and thus lose their reward. They must ask only the poor, and for that benevolent action they would be recompensed thereafter. They were not to give alms in public or to pray in public, and when they fasted, they were to pretend to feast; for if it was perceived that they were devout men and were praised for their devotion, they would lose their reward. Robbery and violence they were not to resist. If a man smote them on one cheek they were to offer him the other also; if he took their coat they were to give him their shirt; if he forced them to go with him one mile they were to go with him two. They were to love their enemies, to do good to them that did them evil. And why? Not because it was good so to do, but that they might be paid for the same with compound interest in a future state.

It might be supposed that as in the philosophy of Jesus poverty was equivalent to virtue and misery a passport to eternal bliss, sickness would be also a beatific state. But Jesus, like the other Jews, believed that disease proceeded from sin. In Palestine it was always held that a priest or a prophet was the best physician, and prayer, with the laying on of hands, the most efficacious of all medicines. Among the sins of Asa it is mentioned that, having sore feet, he went to a doctor instead of to the Lord. Jesus informed those on whom he laid his hands that their sins were forgiven them, and warned those he healed to sin no more lest a worse thing should come upon them. Such theological practitioners have always existed in the East, and exist there at the present day. A text from the Koran written on a board and washed off into a cup of water is considered God's own physic; and as the patient believes in it, and as the mind can sometimes influence the body, the disease is occasionally healed upon the spot. The exploits of the miracle doctor are exaggerated in his lifetime, and after his death it is declared that he restored sight to men that were born blind, cleansed the lepers, made the lame to walk, cured the incurable, and raised the dead to life.

In Jerusalem the scribe had succeeded to the seer. The Jews had already a proverb, "A scholar is greater than a prophet." The supernatural gift was regarded with suspicion, and if successful with the vulgar excited envy and indignation. In the East at the present day there is a permanent hostility between the Mullah, or doctor of the law, and the dervish, or illiterate "man of God." Jesus was, in point of fact, a dervish, and the learned Pharisees were not inclined to admit the authority of one who spoke a rustic patois and misplaced the aspirate, and who was no doubt, like other prophets, uncouth in his appearance and uncleanly in his garb. At Jerusalem Jesus completely failed, and this failure appears to have stung him into bitter abuse of his successful rivals the missionary Pharisees, and into the wildest extravagance of speech. He called the learned doctors a generation of vipers, whited sepulchres, and serpents; he declared that they should not escape the damnation of hell. Because they had made the washing of hands before dinner a religious ablution, Jesus, with equal bigotry, would not wash his hands at all, though people eat with the hand in the East, and dip their hands in the same dish. He told his disciples that if a man called another a fool he would be in danger of hell-fire; and whoever spoke against the Holy Ghost, it would not be forgiven him "neither in this world nor in the world to come." He said that if a man had done anything wrong with his hand or his eye, it were better for him to cut off his guilty hand, or to pluck out his guilty eye, rather than to go with this whole body into hell. He cursed a fig-tree because it bore no fruit, although it was not the season of fruit--an action as rational as that of Xerxes, who flogged the sea. He retorted to those who accused him of breaking the Sabbath that he was above the Sabbath.

It is evident that a man who talked in such a manner--who believed that it was in his power to abrogate the laws of the land, to forgive sins, to bestow eternal happiness upon his friends, and to send all those who differed from him to everlasting flames--would lay himself open to a charge of blasphemy, and it is also evident that the "generation of vipers" would not hesitate to take advantage of the circumstance. But whatever share personal enmity might have had in the charges that were made against him, he was lawfully condemned according to Bible law. He declared in open court that they would see him descending in the clouds at the right hand of the power of God. The High Priest tore his robes in horror; false prophecy and blasphemy had been uttered to his face.

The Christians

After the execution of Jesus his disciples did not return to Galilee: they waited at Jerusalem for his second coming. They believed that he had died as a human sacrifice for the sins of the people, and that he would speedily return with an army of angels to establish the kingdom of God on earth. Already in his lifetime these simple creatures had begun to dispute about the dignities which they should hold at court, and Jesus, who was not less simple than themselves, had promised that they should sit on twelve thrones judging the twelve tribes of Israel. He had assured them again and again, in the most positive language, that this event would take place in their own lifetime. "Verily, verily," he said, "there are some standing here who shall not taste of death till they see the Son of Man coming in his kingdom." They therefore remained at Jerusalem and scrupulously followed his commands. They established a community of goods, or at least gave away their superfluities to the poorer members of the Church, and had charitable arrangements for relieving the sick. They admitted proselytes with the ceremony of baptism. At the evening repast which they held together they broke bread and drank wine in a certain solemn manner, as Jesus had been wont to do, and as they especially remembered he did at the Last Supper. But in all respects they were Jews, just as Jesus himself had been a Jew. They attended divine service in the temple; they offered up the customary sacrifices; they kept the Sabbath; they abstained from forbidden meats. They held merely the one dogma that Jesus was the Messiah, and that he would return in power and glory to judge the earth.

Jerusalem was frequented at the time of the pilgrimage by thousands of Jews from the great cities of Europe, North Africa, and Asia Minor. These pilgrims were of a very different class from the fishermen of Galilee. They were Jews in religion but they were scarcely Jews in nationality. They were members of great and flourishing municipalities; they enjoyed political liberty and civil rights. They prayed in Greek and read the Bible in a Greek translation. Their doctrine was tolerant and latitudinarian. At Alexandria there was a school of Jews who had mingled the metaphysics of Plato with their own theology. Many of these Greek Jews became converted, and it is to them that Jesus owes his reputation, Christianity its existence. The Palestine Jews desired to reserve the Gospel to the Jews. They had no taste or sympathy for the Gentiles, from whom they lived entirely apart, and who were associated in their minds with the abominations of idolatry, the payment of taxes, and the persecution of Antiochus. But these same Gentiles, these poor benighted Greeks and Romans, were the compatriots and fellow-citizens of the Hellenic Jews, who therefore entertained more liberal ideas upon the subject. Two parties accordingly arose--the conservative or Jewish party, who would receive no converts except according to the custom of the orthodox Jews in such cases, and the Greek party, who agitated for complete freedom from the law of Moses. The latter were headed by Paul, an enthusiastic and ambitious man who refused to place himself under the rule of the twelve apostles, but claimed a special revelation. A conference was held at Jerusalem, and a compromise was arranged to the effect that pagan converts should not be subjected to the rite of circumcision, but that they should abstain from pork and oysters and should eat no animals which had not been killed by the knife.

But the compromise did not last. The Church diverged in discipline and dogma more and more widely from its ancient form, till in the second century the Christians of Judea, who had faithfully followed the customs and tenets of the twelve apostles, were informed that they were heretics. During that interval a new religion had arisen. Christianity had conquered paganism, and paganism had corrupted Christianity. The legends which belonged to Osiris and Apollo had been applied to the life of Jesus. The single Deity of the Jews had been exchanged for the Trinity, which the Egyptians had invented and which Plato had idealised into a philosophic system. The man who had said "Why callest thou me good? There is none good but one, that is God," had now himself been made a god--or the third part of one. The Hebrew element, however, had not been entirely cast off. With some little inconsistency, the Jewish sacred books were said to be inspired, and nearly all the injunctions contained in them were disobeyed. It was heresy to deny that the Jews were the chosen people, and it was heresy to assert that the Jews would be saved.

The Christian religion was at first spread by Jews who, either as missionaries or in the course of their ordinary avocations, made the circuit of the Mediterranean world. In all large towns there was a Ghetto or Jews' quarter, in which the traveller was received by the people of his own race. There was no regular clergy among the Jews, and it was their custom to allow, and even to invite, the stranger to preach in their synagogue. Doctrines were not strictly defined, and they listened without anger, and perhaps with some hope, to the statement that Jesus of Nazareth was the Messiah, and that he would shortly return to establish his kingdom upon earth. But when these Christians began to preach that the eating of pork was not a deadly sin, and that God was better pleased with a sprinkle than a slash, they were speedily stigmatised as heretics, and all the Jewries in the world were closed against them.

Those strange religious and commercial communities, those landless colonies which an Oriental people had established all over the world, from the Rhone and the Rhine to the Oxus and Jaxartes--which corresponded regularly among themselves, and whose members recognised each other, wherever they might be and in whatever garb, by the solemn phrase, "Hear, Israel, there is one God!"--afforded a model for the Christian churches of the early days. The primitive Christians did not indeed live together in one quarter like the Jews, but they gathered together for purposes of worship and administration in set places at appointed times. They did not establish commercial relations with the Christians in other towns, but they kept up an active social correspondence, and hospitably entertained the foreign brother who brought letters of introduction as credentials of his creed. Travelling, though not always free from danger, was unobstructed in those days: coasters sailed frequently from port to port, and the large towns were connected by paved roads with a posting-house at every six-mile stage. All inn-keepers spoke Greek: it was not necessary to learn Latin even in order to reside at Rome.

And now we return to that magnificent city which was adorned with the spoils of a hundred lands, into which streamed all the wealth, the energy, and the ambition of East and West. Ostia-on-the-Sea, where the ancient citizens had boiled their salt was now a great port in which the grain from Egypt and Carthage was stored up in huge buildings, and to which in the summer and autumn came ships from all parts of the world. The road to Rome was fifteen miles in length, and was lined with villas and with lofty tombs. Outside the city, on the neighbouring hills, were gardens open to the public; and from these hills were conducted streams, by subterranean pipes, into the town, where they were trained to run like rivulets, making everywhere a pleasant murmur, here and there reposing in artificial grottoes or dancing as fountains in the air. The streets were narrow, and the tall houses buried them in deep shade. They were lined with statues; there was a population of marble men. Flowers glittered on roofs and balconies. Vast palaces of green and white and golden tinted marble were surrounded by venerable trees. The Via Sacra was the Regent Street of Rome, and was bordered with stalls where the silks and spices of the East, the wool of Spain, the glass wares of Alexandria, the smoked fish of the Black Sea, the wines of the Greek isles, Cretan apples, Alpine cheese, the oysters of Britain, and the veined wood of the Atlas were exposed for sale. In that splendid thoroughfare a hundred languages might be heard at once, and as many costumes were displayed as if the universe had been invited to a fancy-dress ball. Sometimes a squadron of the Imperial Guard would ride by--flaxen-haired, blue-eyed Germans covered with shining steel. Then a procession of pale-faces, shaven Egyptian priests, bearing a statue of Isis and singing melancholy hymns. A Greek philosopher would next pass along with abstracted eyes and ragged cloak, followed by a boy with a pile of books. Men from the East might be seen with white turbans and flowing robes, or in sheep-skin mantles with high black caps; and perhaps beside them a tattooed Briton gaping at the shops. Then would come a palanquin with curtains half drawn, carried along at a swinging pace by sturdy Cappadocian slaves, and within it the fashionable lady with supercilious, half-closed eyes, holding a crystal ball between her hands to keep them cool. Next a senator in white and purple robe, receiving as he walked along the greetings and kisses of his friends and clients, not always of the cleanest kind.

So crowded were the streets that carriages were not allowed to pass through them in the day-time. The only vehicles that appeared were the carts employed in the public works; and as they came rolling and grinding along, bearing huge beams and blocks of stone, the driver cracked his whip and pushed people against the wall, and there was much squeezing and confusion, during which pickpockets, elegantly dressed, their hands covered with rings, were busy at their work, pretending to assist the ladies in the crowd. People from the country passed towards the market, their mules or asses laden with panniers in which purple grapes and golden fruits were piled up in profusion, and refreshed the eye, which was dazzled by the stony glare. Hawkers went about offering matches in exchange for broken glass, and the keepers of the cook-shops called out in cheerful tones, "Smoking sausages!" "Sweet boiled peas!" "Honey wine, O honey wine!" And then there was the crowd itself--the bright-eyed, dark-browed Roman people, who played in the shade at dice or mora like the old Egyptians; who lounged through the temples, which were also the museums, to look at the curiosities; or who stood in groups reading the advertisements on the walls, and the programmes which announced that on such and such a day there would be a grand performance in the circus and that all would be done in the best style. A blue awning, with white stars in imitation of the sky, would shade them from the sun; trees would be transplanted, and a forest would appear upon the stage; giraffes, zebras, elephants, lions, ostriches, stags, and wild boars would be hunted down and killed; armies of gladiators would contend; and by way of after-piece the arena would be filled with water, and a naval battle would be performed--ships, soldiers, wounds, agony, and death being admirably real.

So passed the Roman street-life day, and with the first hours of darkness the noise and the turmoil did not cease; for then the travelling carriages rattled towards the gates, and carts filled with dung--the only export of the city. The music of serenades rose softly in the air, and sounds of laughter from the tavern. The night watch made their rounds, their armour rattling as they passed. Lights were extinguished, householders put up their shutters, to which bells were fastened--for burglaries frequently occurred. And then for a time the city would be almost still. Dogs, hated by the Romans, prowled about sniffing for their food. Men or prey from the Pontine Marshes crept stealthily along the black side of the street signalling to one another with sharp whistles or hissing sounds. Sometimes torches would flash against the walls as a knot of young gallants reeled home from a debauch, breaking the noses of the street statues on their way. And at such an hour there were men and women who stole forth from their various houses, and with mantles covering their faces hastened to a lonely spot in the suburbs, and entered the mouth of a dark cave. They passed through long galleries, moist with damp and odorous of death--for coffins were ranged on either side in tiers one above the other. But soon sweet music sounded from the depths of the abyss; an open chamber came to view, and a tomb covered with flowers, laid out with a repast, encircled by men and women who were apparelled in white robes, and who sang a psalm of joy. It was in the catacombs of Rome, where the dead had been buried in the ancient times, that the Christians met to discourse on the progress of the faith; to recount the trials which they suffered in their homes; to confess to one another their sins and doubts, their carnal presumption, or their lack of faith; and also to relate their sweet visions of the night, the answers to their earnest prayers. They listened to the exhortations of their elders, and perhaps to a letter from one of the apostles. They then supped together as Jesus had supped with his disciples, and kissed one another when the love feast was concluded. At these meetings there was no distinction of rank; the high-born lady embraced the slave whom she had once scarcely regarded as a man. Humility and submission were the cardinal virtues of the early Christians; slavery had not been forbidden by the apostles because it was the doctrine of Jesus that those who were lowest in this world would be highest in the next, his theory of heaven being earth turned upside down.

Slavery therefore was esteemed a state of grace, and some Christians appear to have rejected the freeman's cap on religious grounds, for Paul exhorts such persons to become free if they can --advice which slaves do not usually require.

As time passed on, the belief of the first Christians that the end of the world was near at hand became fainter and gradually died away. It was then declared that God had favoured the earth with a respite of one thousand years. In the meantime the gospel or good tidings which the Christians announced was this. There was one God, the Creator of the world. He had long been angry with men because they were what he had made them. But he sent his only begotten son into a corner of Syria, and because his son had been murdered his wrath had been partly appeased. He would not torture to eternity all the souls that he had made; he would spare at least one in every million that were born. Peace unto earth and goodwill unto men if they would act in a certain manner; if not, fire and brimstone and the noisome pit. He was the emperor of heaven, the tyrant of the skies; the pagan gods were rebels, with whom he was at war, although he was all-powerful, and whom he allowed to seduce the souls of men although he was all-merciful. Those who joined the army of the cross might entertain some hopes of being saved; those who followed the faith of their fathers would follow their fathers to hell-fire. This creed with the early Christians was not a matter of half-belief and metaphysical debate, as it is at the present day, when Catholics and Protestants discuss hell-fire with courtesy and comfort over filberts and port wine. To those credulous and imaginative minds God was a live king, hell a place in which real bodies were burnt with real flames, which was filled with the sickening stench of roasted flesh, which resounded with agonising shrieks. They saw their fathers and mothers, their sisters and their dearest friends, hurrying onward to that fearful pit unconscious of danger, laughing and singing, lured on by the fiends whom they called the gods. They felt as we should feel were we to see a blind man walking towards a river bank. Who would have the heart to turn aside and say it was the business of the police to interfere? But what was death, a mere momentary pain, compared with tortures that would have no end? Who that could hope to save a soul by tears and supplications would remain quiescent as men do now, shrugging their shoulders and saying that it is not good taste to argue on religion, and that conversion is the office of the clergy? The Christians of that period felt more and did more than those of the present day, not because they were better men but because they believed more; and they believed more because they knew less. Doubt is the offspring of knowledge: the savage never doubts at all.

In that age the Christians believed much, and their lives were rendered beautiful by sympathy and love. The dark, deep river did not exist--it was only a fancy of the brain: yet the impulse was not less real. The heart-throb, the imploring cry, the swift leap, the trembling hand out-reached to save; the transport of delight, the ecstasy of tears, the sweet, calm joy that a man had been wrested from the jaws of death--are these less beautiful, are these less real, because it afterwards appeared that the man had been in no danger after all?

In that age every Christian was a missionary. The soldiers sought to win recruits for the heavenly host; the prisoner of war discoursed to his Persian jailer; the slave girl whispered the gospel in the ears of her mistress as she built up the mass of towered hair; there stood men in cloak and beard at street corners who, when the people, according to the manners of the day, invited them to speak, preached not the doctrines of the Painted Porch but the words of a new and strange philosophy; the young wife threw her arms round her husband's neck and made him agree to be baptised, that their souls might not be parted after death. How awful were the threats of the heavenly despot; how sweet were the promises of a life beyond the grave! The man who strove to obey the law which was written on his heart, yet often fell for want of support, was now promised a rich reward if he would persevere. The disconsolate woman whose age of beauty and triumph had passed away was taught that if she became a Christian her body in all the splendour of its youth would rise again. The poor slave who sickened from weariness of a life in which there was for him no hope, received the assurance of another life in which he would find luxury and pleasure when death released him from his woe.

Ah, sweet fallacious hopes of a barbarous and poetic age! Illusion still cherished, for mankind is yet in its romantic youth! How easy it would be to endure without repining the toils and troubles of this miserable life if indeed we could believe that when its brief period was past we should be united to those whom we have loved, to those whom death has snatched away; or whom fate has parted from us by barriers cold and deep and hopeless as the grave. If we could believe this the shortness of life would comfort us--how quickly the time flies by!--and we should welcome death. But we do not believe it, and so we cling to our tortured lives, dreading the dark nothingness, dreading the dispersal of our elements into cold, unconscious space. As drops in the ocean of water, as atoms in the ocean of air, as sparks in the ocean of fire within the earth, our minds do their appointed work and serve to build up the strength and beauty of the one great human mind which grows from century to century and from age to age, and is perhaps itself a mere molecule within some higher mind.

oon it was whispered that there was in Rome a secret society which worshipped an unknown god. Its members wore no garlands on their brows; they never entered the temples; they were governed by laws which strange and fearful oaths bound them ever to obey; their speech was not as the speech of ordinary men; they buried instead of burning the bodies of the dead; they married, they educated their children after a manner of their own. The politicians who regarded the established Church as essential to the safety of the state became alarmed. Secret societies were forbidden by law, and here was a society in which the tutelary gods of Rome were denounced as rebels and usurpers. The Christians, it is true, preached passive obedience and the divine right of kings, but they proclaimed that all men were equal before God--a dangerous doctrine in a community where more than half the men were slaves. The idle and superstitious lazzaroni did not love the gods, but they believed in them, and they feared lest the "atheists," as they called the Christians, would provoke the vengeance of the whole divine federation against the city, and that all would be involved in the common ruin. Soon there came a time when every public calamity--an epidemic, a fire, a famine, or a flood--was ascribed to the anger of the offended gods. And then arose imperial edicts, popular commotions, and the terrible street-cry of Christiani ad leones!

But the persecutions thus provoked were fitful and brief, and served only to fan the flame. For to those who believed in heaven--not as men now believe, with a slight tincture of perhaps unconscious doubt, but as men believe in things which they see and hear and feel and know--death was merely a surgical operation with the absolute certainty of consequent release from pain and of entrance into unutterable bliss. The Christians therefore encountered it with joy, and the sight of their cheerful countenances as they were being led to execution induced many to inquire what this belief might be which could thus rob death of its dreadfulness and its despair.

But the great moralists and thinkers of the empire looked coldly down upon this new religion. In their pure and noble writings they either allude to Christianity with scorn or do not allude to it at all. This circumstance has occasioned much surprise: it can, however, be easily explained. The success of Christianity among the people, and its want of success among the philosophers, were due to the same cause--the superstition of the Christian teachers.

Among the missionaries of the present day there are many men who in earnestness and self-devotion are not inferior to those of the apostolic times. Yet they almost invariably fail--they are too enlightened for their congregations. With respect to their own religion, indeed, that charge cannot be justly brought against them. Set them talking on the forbidden apple, Noah's ark, the sun standing still to facilitate murder, the donkey preaching to its master, the whale swallowing and ejecting Jonah, the miraculous conception, the water turned to wine, the fig-tree withered by a curse, and they will reason like children, or in other words they will not reason at all; they will merely repeat what they have been taught by their mammas. But when they discourse to the savage concerning his belief they use the logic of Voltaire, and deride witches and men possessed in a style which Jesus and the twelve apostles, the fathers of the Church, the popes of the Middle Ages, and Martin Luther himself would have accounted blasphemous and contrary to Scripture. Now it is impossible to persuade an adult savage that his gods do not exist, and he considers those who deny their existence to be ignorant foreigners unacquainted with the divine constitution of his country. Hence he laughs in his sleeve at all that the missionaries say. But the primitive Christians believed in gods and goddesses, satyrs and nymphs, as implicitly as the pagans themselves. They did not deny and they did not disbelieve the miracles performed in pagan temples. They allowed that the gods had great power upon earth, but asserted that they would have it only for a time; that it ceased beyond the grave; that they were rebels, and that God was the rightful king. Here then were two classes of men whose intellects were precisely on the same level. Each had a theory, and the Christian theory was the better of the two. It had definite promises and threats, and without being too high for the vulgar comprehension, it reduced the scheme of the universe to order and harmony, resembling that of the great empire under which they lived.

But to the philosophers of that period it was merely a new and noisy form of superstition. Experience has amply proved that minds of the highest order are sometimes unable to shake off the ideas which they imbibed when they were children; but to those of whom we speak Christianity was offered when their powers of reflection were matured, and it was naturally rejected with contempt. They knew that the pagan gods did not exist. Was it likely that they would sit at the feet of those who still believed in them? They had long ago abandoned the religious legends of their own country; they had shaken off the spell which Homer with his splendid poetry had laid upon their minds. Was it likely that they would believe in the old Arab traditions, or in these tales of a god who took upon him the semblance of a Jew, and suffered death upon the gallows for the redemption of mankind? They had obtained by means of intellectual research a partial perception of the great truth that events result from secondary laws. Was it likely that they would join a crew of devotees who prayed to God to make the wind blow this way or that way, to give them a dinner, or to cure them of a pain? When the Tiber overflowed its banks the pagans declared that it was owing to the wrath of the gods against the Christians: the Christians retorted that it was owing to the wrath of God against the idolaters. To a man like Pliny, who studied the phenomena with his notebook in his hand, where was the difference between the two?

In the Greek world Christianity became a system of metaphysics as abstract and abstruse as any son of Hellas could desire. But in the Latin world it was never the religion of a scholar and a gentleman. It was the creed of the uneducated people, who flung themselves into it with passion. It was something which belonged to them and to them alone. They were not acquainted with Cicero or Seneca: they had never tasted intellectual delights, for the philosophers scorned to instruct the vulgar crowd. And now the vulgar crowd found teachers who interpreted to them the Jewish books, who composed for them a magnificent literature of sermons and epistles and controversial treatises, a literature of enthusiasts and martyrs written in blood and fire. The people had no share in the politics of the empire, but now they had politics of their own. The lower orders were enfranchised; women and slaves were not excluded. The barbers gossiped theologically. Children played at church in the streets. The Christians were no longer citizens of Rome. God was their emperor, heaven was their fatherland. They despised the pleasures of this life; they were as emigrants gathered on the shore waiting for a wind to waft them to another world. They rendered unto Caesar the things that were Caesar's, for so it was written they should do. They honoured the king, for such had been the teaching of St. Paul. They regarded the emperor as God's vice-regent upon earth, and disobeyed him only when his commands were contrary to those of God. But this limitation, which it was the business of the bishops to define, made the Christians a dangerous party in the state. The Emperor Constantine, whose title was unsound, entered into alliance with this powerful corporation. He made Christianity the religion of the state and the bishops peers of the realm.

In the days of tribulation it had often been predicted that when the empire became Christian war would cease, and men would dwell in brotherhood together. The Christian religion united the slave and his master at the same table and in the same embrace. On the pavement of the basilica men of all races and of all ranks knelt side by side. If any one were in sickness and affliction it was sufficient for him to declare himself a Christian: money was at once pressed into his hands: compassionate matrons hastened to his bedside. Even at the time when the pagans regarded the new sect with most abhorrence they were forced to exclaim, "See how these Christians love one another!" It was reasonable to suppose that the victory of this religion would be the victory of love and peace. But what was the actual result? Shortly after the establishment of Christianity as a state religion there was uproar and dissension in every city of the Empire; then savage persecutions and bloody wars, until a pagan historian could observe to the polished and intellectual coterie for whom alone he wrote that now the hatred of the Christians against one another surpassed the fury of savage beasts against man.

It is evident that the virtues exhibited by those who gallantly fight against desperate odds for an idea will not be invariably displayed by those who when the idea is realised enjoy the spoil. It is evident that bishops who possess large incomes and great authority will not always possess the same qualities of mind as those spiritual peers who had no distinction to expect except that of being burnt alive. In all great movements of the mind there can be but one heroic age, and the heroic age of Christianity was past. The Church became the state concubine; Christianity lost its democratic character. The bishops who should have been the tribunes of the people became the creatures of the Crown. Their lives were not always of the most creditable kind, but their virtues were perhaps more injurious to society than their vices. The mischief was done not so much by those who intrigued for places and rioted on tithes at Constantinople as by those who, often with the best intentions, endeavoured to make all men think alike "according to the law."

It was the Christian theory that God was a king, and that he enacted laws for the government of men on earth. Those laws were contained in the Jewish books, but some of them had been repealed and some of them were exceedingly obscure. Some were to be understood in a literal sense, others were only metaphorical. Many cases might arise to which no text or precept could be with any degree of certainty applied. What then was to be done? How was God's will to be ascertained? The early Christians were taught that by means of prayer and faith their questions would be answered, their difficulties would be solved. They must pray earnestly to God for help: and the ideas which came into their heads after prayer would be emanations from the Holy Ghost.

In the first age of Christianity the Church was a republic. There was no distinction between clergymen and laymen. Each member of the congregation had a right to preach, and each consulted God on his own account. The spiritus privatus everywhere prevailed. A committee of presbyters or elders, with a bishop or chairman, administered the affairs of the community.

The second period was marked by an important change. The bishop and presbyters, though still elected by the congregation, had begun to monopolise the pulpit; the distinction of clergy and laity was already made. The bishops of various churches met together at councils or synods to discuss questions of discipline and dogma, and to pass laws, but they went as representatives of their respective congregations.

In the third period the change was more important still. The congregation might now be appropriately termed a flock; the spiritus privatus was extinct; the priests were possessed of traditions which they did not impart to the laymen; the Water of Life was kept in a sealed vessel; there was no salvation outside the Church: no man could have God for a father unless he had also the Church for a mother, as even Bossuet long afterwards declared; excommunication was a sentence of eternal death. Henceforth disputes were only between bishops and bishops, the laymen following their spiritual leaders and often using material weapons on their behalf. In the synods the bishops now met as princes of their congregations, and under the influence of the Holy Ghost [spiritu sancto suggerente] issued imperial decrees. The penalties inflicted were of the most terrible nature to those who believed that hell-fire and purgatory were at the disposal of the priesthood, while those who entertained doubts upon the subject allowed themselves to be cursed and damned with equanimity. But when the Church became united with the state, the secular arm was at its disposal, and was vigorously used.

The bishops were all of them ignorant and superstitious men, but they could not all of them think alike. And as if to ensure dissent they proceeded to define that which had never existed, and which if it had existed could never be defined. They described the topography of heaven. They dissected the godhead and expounded the miraculous conception, giving lectures on celestial impregnations and miraculous obstetrics. They not only said that 3 was 1, and that 1 was 3: they professed to explain how that curious arithmetical combination had been brought about. The indivisible had been divided and yet was not divided: it was divisible and yet it was indivisible; black was white and white was black, and yet there were not two colours, but one colour; and whoever did not believe it would be damned. In the midst of all this subtle stuff, the dregs and rinsings of the Platonic school, Arius thundered out the common-sense but heretical assertion that the Father had existed before the Son. Two great parties were at once formed. A council of bishops was convened at Nicaea to consult the Holy Ghost. The chair was taken by a man who wore a wig of many colours and a silken robe embroidered with golden thread. This was Constantine the great, patron of Christianity, Nero of the Bosphorus, murderer of his wife and son. The discussion was noisy and abusive, and the Arians lost the day. Yet the matter did not end there. Constantius took up the Arian side. Arian missionaries converted the Vandals and the Goths. Other emperors took up the Catholics, and they converted the Franks. The court was divided by spiritual eunuchs and theological intrigues: the provinces were laid waste by theological wars which lasted three hundred years. What a world of woe and desolation, what a deluge of blood, because the Greeks had a taste for metaphysics!

The Arian difference did not stand alone; every province had its own schism. Caste sympathy induced the emperors to protect the pagan aristocracy from the fury of the bishops, but the heretics belonged chiefly to the subject nationalities. The Nestorians were men of the Semitic race, the Jacobites were Egyptians, the Donatists were Berbers. Of such a nature was the treatment which these people received that they were ready at any time to join the enemies of the empire, whoever they might be. Difference of nationality occasioned difference in mode of thought. Difference in mode of thought occasioned difference in religious creed. Difference in religious creed occasioned controversy, riots and persecution. Persecution intensified distinctions of nationality. Such then was the state of religion in the Grecian world. In the West the Church, overwhelmed by the barbarians, was displaying virtues in adversity, and was laying the foundations of a majestic kingdom. But as for the East, Christianity had lived in vain. In Constantinople and in Greece it had done no good. In Asia, Barbary, and Egypt it had done harm. Its peace was apathy: its activity was war. Instead of healing the old wounds of conquest it opened them afresh. It was not enough that the peasants of the ancient race, once masters of the soil, should be crushed with taxes; a new instrument of torture was invented; their priests were taken from them; their altars were overthrown. But the day of vengeance was at hand. Soon they would enjoy, under rulers of a different religion but of the same race, that freedom of conscience which a Christian government refused.

The Byzantine empire in the seventh century included Greece and the islands, with a part of Italy. In Asia and Africa its possessions were those of the Turkish Empire before the cession of Algiers. There was a Greek viceroy of Egypt: there were Greek governors in Egypt and Asia Minor, Carthage, and Cyrene. The capital was fed with Egyptian corn and enriched by silken manufactures--for two Nestorian monks had brought the eggs of the silkworm from China in hollow canes. These eggs had been hatched under lukewarm dung, and the culture of the cocoon had been established for the first time on European soil. The eastern boundary of the empire was sometimes the Tigris, sometimes the Euphrates; the land of Mesopotamia, which lay between the rivers, was the subject of continual war between the Byzantines and the Persians.

Alexander the Great had not been long dead before the Parthians, a race of hardy mountaineers, occupied the lands to the east of the Euphrates, made themselves famous in their wars with Rome, and established a wide empire. In the third century it was broken up into petty principalities, and a private citizen who claimed to be heir-at-law of the old Persian kings headed a party, seized the crown, restored the Zoroastrian religion, and raised the empire to a state of power and magnificence scarcely inferior to that of the Great

Kings. But the Greeks were still in Asia Minor and Egypt, and it became the hereditary ambition of the Persians to drive them back into their own country. In the seventh century Chosroes the Second accomplished this idea, and restored the frontiers of Cambyses and the first Darius. He conquered Asia Minor, Syria, and Egypt. He carried his arms to Cryene, and extinguished the last glimmer of culture in that ancient colony. Heraclius, the Byzantine emperor, was in despair. While the Persians overran his provinces in Asia a horde or Cossacks threatened him in Europe. Constantinople, he feared, would soon be surrounded, and it already suffered famine from the loss of Egypt, as Rome had formerly suffered when the Vandals plundered it of Africa. He determined to migrate to Carthage, and had already prepared to depart when the Patriarch persuaded him to change his mind. He obtained peace from Persia by sending earth and water in the old style, and by promising to pay as tribute a thousand talents of gold, a thousand talents of silver, a thousand silk robes, a thousand horses, and a thousand virgins. But instead of collecting these commodities he collected an army, and suddenly dashed into the heart of Persia. Chosroes recalled his troops from the newly conquered lands, but was defeated by the Greeks, and was in his turn compelled to sue for ignominious peace. In the midst of the triumphs which Heraclius celebrated at Constantinople and Jerusalem, an obscure town on the confines of Syria was pillaged by a band of Arab horsemen, who cut in pieces some troops which advanced to its relief. This appeared a trifling event, but it was the beginning of a mighty revolution. In the last eight years of his reign Heraclius lost to the Saracens the provinces which he had recovered from the Persians.

Arabia

The peninsula of Arabia is almost as large as Hindustan, but does not contain a single navigable river. It is for the most part a sterile tableland furrowed by channels which in winter roar with violent and muddy streams, and which in summer are completely dry. In these stream-beds at a little depth below the surface there is sometimes a stratum of water which, breaking out here and there into springs, creates a habitable island in the waste. Such a fruitful wadi or oasis is sometimes extensive enough to form a town, and each town is in itself a kingdom. This stony, green-spotted land was divided into Arabia Petraea on the north and Arabia Deserta on the south. The north supplied Constantinople, and the south supplied Persia, with mercenary troops; the leaders, on receiving their pay, established courts at home, and rendered homage to their imperial masters. The princes of Arabia Deserta ruled in the name of the Chosroes. The princes of Arabia Petraea were proud to be called the lieutenants of the Caesars.

In the south-west corner of the peninsula there is a range of hills sufficiently high to intercept the passing clouds and rain them down as streams to the Indian Ocean and the Red Sea. This was the land of Yemen or Sabaea, renowned for its groves of frankincense and for the wealth of its merchant kings. Its forests in ancient times were inhabited by squalid negro tribes who lived on platforms in the trees, and whose savage stupor was ascribed to the drowsy influence of the scented air. The country was afterwards colonised by men of the Arab race, who built ships and established factories on the east coast of Africa, on the coast of Malabar, and in the island of Ceylon. They did not navigate the Red Sea, but dispatched the Indian goods, the African ivory and gold dust, and their own fragrant produce by camel caravan to Egypt or to Petra, a great market city in the north.

The Pharaohs and the Persian kings did not interfere with the merchant princes of Yemen. In the days of the Ptolemies a few Greek ships made the Indian voyage, but could not compete with the Arabs who had so long been established in the trade. But the Roman occupation of Alexandria ruined them completely. The just and moderate government of Augustus, and the demand for Oriental luxuries at Rome, excited the enterprise of the Alexandrine traders, and a Greek named Hippalus made a remarkable discovery. He observed that the winds or monsoons of the Indian Ocean regularly blew during six months from east to west and during six months from west to east. He was bold enough to do what the Phoenicians themselves had never done. He left the land and sailed right across the ocean to the Indian shore with one monsoon, returning with the next to the mouth of the Red Sea. By means of this ocean route the India voyage could be made in half the time. The goods were thereby cheapened, the demand was thereby increased, the Indian Ocean was covered with Greek vessels, a commercial revolution was created, the coasting and caravan trade of the Arabs came to an end, the Romans destroyed Aden, and Yemen withered up and remained independent only because it was obscure.

Arabia had always been a land of refuge, for in its terrible deserts security might always be found. To Arabia had fled the Priests of the Sun after the victories of Alexander and the restoration of Babylonian idolatry. To Arabia had fled thousands of Jews after the second destruction of Jerusalem. To Arabia had fled thousands of Christians who had been persecuted by pagan and still more by Christian emperors. The land was divided among independent princes--many of them were Christians and many of them were Jews. There is nothing more conducive to an enlightened scepticism, and its attendant spirit toleration, than the spectacle of various religious creeds each maintained by intelligent and pious men. A king of Arabia, Felix, in the fourth century received an embassy from the Byzantine emperor, with a request that Christians might be allowed to settle in his kingdom, and also that he would make Christianity the religion of the state. He assented to the first proposition. With reference to the second he replied "I reign over men's bodies, not over their opinions. I exact from my subjects obedience to the government; as to their religious doctrine, the judge of that is the great Creator."

But it came to pass that a king of the Jewish persuasion succeeded to the throne: he persecuted his Christian subjects and made war on Christian kings, burning houses, men, and gospels wherever he could find them. A Christian Arab made his escape, travelled to Constantinople, and, holding up a charred Testament before the throne, demanded help in the name of the Redeemer. The emperor at once prepared for war, and dispatched an envoy to his faithful ally the Negus of Abyssinia.

The old kingdom of Ethiopia had escaped Cambyses and Alexander, and had lost its independence to the Ptolemies only for a time. The Romans made an Abyssinian expedition with complete success, but withdrew from the savage country in disdain. Ethiopia was left to its own devices, which soon became of an Africanising nature. The priests kept the king shut up in his palace and when it suited their convenience sent him word, in the African style, that he must be tired and that it would be good for him to sleep; upon which he migrated to the lower world with his favourite wives and slaves. But there was once a king named Ergamenes who had improved his mind by the study of Greek philosophy, and who, when he received the message of the priests, soon gave them a proof that they were quite mistaken, and that so far from being sleepy he was wide awake. He ordered them to collect in the Golden Chapel, and then, marching in with his guards, he put them all to death. From that time Abyssinia became a military kingdom. As the princes of Numidia had used elephants after the destruction of the Carthaginian republic, so the Abyssinians used them in pageantry and war long after the days of the Ptolemies, who had first shown them how the huge beasts might be entrapped. Hindus were probably employed by the Ptolemies, as they were by the Carthaginians, for the management of the elephantine stud. In the fourth century two shipwrecked Christians converted the king and his people to the new religion--a beneficial event, for thus they were brought into connection with the Roman Empire. The Patriarch of Alexandria was the Abyssinian pope, as he is at the present day, and during all these years he has never ceased to send them their aboona or archbishop. This ecclesiastic is regarded with much reverence; he costs six thousand dollars; he is never allowed to smoke; and by way of blessing he spits upon his congregation, who believe that the episcopal virtue resides in the saliva, and not, as we think, in the fingers' ends.

Abyssinia had still its ancient seaport in Annesley Bay, and sent trading vessels to the India coast. The Byzantine emperor, having made his proposals through the Patriarch of Alexandria, and having received from the Negus a favourable reply, dispatched a fleet of transports down the Red Sea; the king filled them with his brigand troops; Yemen was invaded and subdued, and now it was the Christians who began to persecute. Another Arab prince ran off for help, and he went to the Persian king, who at first refused to take the country as a gift, saying it was too distant and too poor. However, at last he ordered the prisons to be opened, and placed all the able-bodied convicts they contained at the disposal of the prince. The Abyssinians were driven out, but they returned and re-conquered the land. Chosroes then sent a regular army with orders to kill all the men with black skins and curly hair. Thus Yemen became a Persian province, and no less than three great religions-- that of Zoroaster, that of Moses, and that of Jesus--were represented in Arabia.

Midway between Yemen and Egypt is a sandy valley two miles in length, surrounded on all sides by naked hills. No gardens or fields are to be seen; no trees except some low brushwood and the acacia of the desert. On all sides are barren and sunburnt rocks. But in the midst of this valley is a wonderful well. It is not that the water is unusually cool and sweet--connoisseurs pronounce it "heavy" to the taste--but it affords an inexhaustible supply. No matter what quantity may be drawn up, the water in the well remains always at the same height. It is probably fed by a perennial stream below.

This valley, on account of its well, was made the halting-place of the India caravans, and there the goods changed carriers--the south delivered them over to the north. As the north and south were frequently at war, the valley was hallowed with solemn oaths for the protection of the trade. A sanctuary was established; the well Zemzem became sacred; its fame spread, and it was visited from all parts of the land by the diseased and the devout. The tents of the valley tribe became a city of importance, enriched by the customs receipts and dues of protection, and by the carrier hire of the caravans. When the navigation of the Red Sea put an end to the carrying trade by land the city was deserted; its inhabitants returned to the wandering Bedouin life. In the fifth century, however, it was restored by an enterprising man, and the shrine was rebuilt. Mecca was no longer a wealthy town; it was no longer situated on one of the highways of the world; but it manufactured a celebrated leather, and sent out two caravans a year--one to Syria and one to Abyssinia. Some of the Meccans were rich men; Byzantine gold pieces and Persian copper coins circulated in abundance; the ladies dressed themselves in silk, had Chinese looking-glasses, wore shoes of perfumed leather, and made themselves odorous of musk. It was the fame of Mecca as a holy place which brought this wealth into the town. The citizens lived upon the pilgrims. However, they esteemed it a pious duty to give hospitality if it was required to the "guests of God, who came from distant cities on their lean and jaded camels, fatigued and harassed with the dirt and squalor of the way." The poor pilgrims were provided during six days with pottage of meat and bread and dates; leather cisterns filled with water were also placed at their disposal.

Mecca

During four months of the year there was a Truce of God, and the Arab tribes, suspending their hostilities, journeyed towards Mecca. As soon as they entered the Sacred Valley they put on their palmers' weeds, proceeded at once to the Caaba or house of God, walked round it naked seven times, kissed the black stone and drank of the waters of the famous well. Then a kind of Eisteddfod was held. The young men combated in martial games; poems were recited, and those which gained the prize were copied with illuminated characters and hung up on the Caaba before the golden-plated door.

There was no regular government in the holy city, no laws that could be enforced, no compulsory courts of justice, and no public treasury. The city was composed of several families or clans belonging to the tribe of the Corayshites, by whom New Mecca had been founded. Each family inhabited a cluster of houses surrounding a courtyard and well, the whole enclosed by solid walls. Each family was able to go to war and to sustain a siege. If a murder was committed the injured family took the law into its own hands; sometimes it would accept a pecuniary compensation--there was a regular tariff--but more frequently the money was refused. They had a belief that if blood was not avenged by blood a small winged insect issued from the skull of the murdered person and fled screeching through the sky. It was also a point of honour on the part of the guilty clan to protect the murderer and to adopt his cause. Thus blood feuds rose easily and died hard.

The head of the family was a despot, and enjoyed the power of life and death over the members of his own house. But he had also severe responsibilities. It was his duty to protect those who dwelt within the circle of his yard; all its inmates called him father; to all of them he owed the duties of a parent. If his son was little better than a slave, on the other hand his slave was almost equal to a son. It sometimes happened that masterless men, travellers, or outcasts required his protection. If it was granted, the stranger entered the family, and the father was accountable for his debts, delicts, and torts. The body of the delinquent might be tendered in lieu of fine or feud, but this practice was condemned by public opinion, and in all semi-savage communities public opinion has considerable power.

There was a town hall in which councils were held to discuss questions relating to the common welfare of the federated families, but the minority were not bound by the voice of the majority. If, for instance, it was decided to make war, a single family could hold aloof. In this town hall marriages were celebrated, circumcisions were performed, and young girls were invested with the dress of womanhood. It was the starting place of the militia and the caravans. It was near the Caaba and opened towards it: in Mecca the Church was closely united to the state.

Throughout all time Mecca had preserved its independence and its religion; the ancient idolatry had there a sacred home. The Meccans recognised a single creator, Allah Taala, the Most High God, who Abraham, and others before Abraham, had adored. But they believed that the stars were live beings, daughters of the Deity, who acted as intercessors on behalf of men; and to propitiate their favour idols were made to represent them. Within the Caaba or around it were also images of foreign deities and of celebrated men; a picture of Mary with the child Jesus in her lap was painted on a column, and a portrait of Abraham with a bundle of divining arrows in his hands upon the wall.

Among the Meccans there were many who regarded that idolatry with abhorrence and contempt; yet to that idolatry their town owed all that it possessed, its wealth and its glory, which extended round a crescent of a thousand miles. They were therefore obliged as good citizens to content themselves with seeking a simpler religion for themselves, and those who did protest against the Caaba gods were persuaded to silence by their families, or, if they would not be silent, were banished from the town under penalty of death if they returned.

But there rose up a man whose convictions were too strong to be hushed by the love of family or to be quelled by the fear of death. Partly owing to his age and dignified position and unblemished name, partly owing to the chivalrous nature of his patriarch or patron, he was protected against his enemies, his life was saved. Had there been a government at Mecca, he would unquestionably have been put to death, and as it was he narrowly escaped.

The Character of Mohammed

Mohammed was a poor lad subject to a nervous disease which made him at first unfit for anything except the despised occupation of the shepherd.

When he grew up he became a commercial traveller, acted as agent for a rich widow twenty-five years older than himself, and obtained her hand. They lived happily together for many years. They were both of them exceedingly religious people, and in the Ramadan, a month held sacred by the ancient Arabs, they used to live in a cave outside the town, passing the time in prayer and meditation.

The disease of his childhood returned upon him in his middle age; it affected his mind in a strange manner, and produced illusions of his senses. He thought that he was haunted, that his body was the house of an evil spirit. "I see a light," he said to his wife, "and I hear a sound. I fear that I am one of the possessed." This idea was most distressing to a pious man. He became pale and haggard; he wandered about on the hill near Mecca, crying out to God for help. More than once he drew near the edge of a cliff, and was tempted to hurl himself down and so put an end to his misery at once.

And then a new idea possessed his mind. He lived much in the open air, gazing on the stars, watching the dry ground grown green beneath the gentle rain, surveying the firmly rooted mountains and the broad expanded plain. He pondered also on the religious legends of the Jews which he had heard related on his journeys, at noonday beneath the palm-tree by the well mouth, at night by the camp fire; and as he looked and thought, the darkness was dispelled, the clouds dispersed, and the vision of God in solitary grandeur rose up within his mind. And there came upon him an impulse to speak of God; there came upon him a belief that he was a messenger of God sent on earth to restore the religion of

Abraham which the pagan Arabs had polluted with their idolatry, the Christians in making Jesus a divinity, the Jews in corrupting their holy books.

In the brain of a poet stanzas will sometimes arise fully formed without a conscious effort of the will, as once happened to Coleridge in a dream; and so into Mohammed's half-dreaming mind there flew golden-winged verses echoing to one another in harmonious sound. At the same time he heard a Voice; and sometimes he saw a human figure; and sometimes he felt a noise in his ears like the tinkling of bells, or a low, deep hum as if bees were swarming round his head. At this period of his life every chapter of the Koran was delivered in throes of pain. The paroxysm was preceded by depression of spirits; his face became clouded; his extremities turned cold; he shook like a man in an ague and called for a covering. His face assumed an expression horrible to see; the vein between his eyebrows became distended; his eyes were fixed; his head moved to and fro, as if he was conversing; and then he gave forth the oracle or sudra. Sometimes he would fall like a man intoxicated to the ground, but the ordinary conclusion of the fit was a profuse perspiration, by which he appeared to be relieved. His sufferings were at times unusually severe--he used often to speak of the three terrific sudras which had given him grey hairs.

His friends were alarmed at his state of mind. Some ascribed it to the eccentricities of poetical genius; others declared that he was possessed of an evil spirit; others said he was insane. When he began to preach against the idols of the Caaba, the practice of female infanticide, and other evil customs of the town; when he declared that there was no divine being but God, and that he was the messenger of God; when he related the ancient legends of the prophets which he said had been told him by the angel Gabriel, there was a general outburst of merriment and scorn. They said he had picked it all up from a Christian who kept a jeweller's shop in the town. They requested him to perform miracles; the poets composed comic ballads which the people sang when he began to preach; the women pointed at him with the finger; it became an amusement of the children to pelt Mohammed. This was perhaps the hardest season of his life--ridicule is the most terrible of all weapons. But his wife encouraged him to persevere, and so did the Voice, which came to him and sang: "By the brightness of the morn that rises, and by the darkness of the night that descends, thy God hath not forsaken thee, Mohammed. For know that there is a life beyond the grave, and it will be better for thee than thy present life; and thy Lord will give thee a rich reward. Did he not find thee an orphan, and did he not care for thee? Did he not find thee wandering in error, and hath he not guided thee to truth? Did he not find thee needy, and hath he not enriched thee? Wherefore oppress not the orphan, neither repulse the beggar, but declare the goodness of the Lord."

This Voice was the echo of Mohammed's conscience and the expression of his ideas. Owing to his peculiar constitution his thoughts became audible as soon as they became intense. So long as his mind remained pure, the Voice was that of a good angel; when afterwards guilty wishes entered his heart, the voice became that of Mephistopheles.

Mohammed's family did not accept his mission: his converts were at first chiefly made among the slaves. But soon these converts became so numerous among all classes that the Meccans ceased to ridicule Mohammed and began to hate him. Nor did he attempt to ingratiate himself in their affections. "He called the living fools, the dead denizens of hell-fire." The heads of families took counsel together. They went to Abu Talib, the patriarch of the house to which Mohammed belonged, and offered the price of blood, and then double the price of blood, and then a stalwart young man for Mohammed's life, and then, being always refused, went off declaring that there would be war. Abu Talib adjured Mohammed not to ruin the family. The prophet's lip quivered: he burst into tears, but he said he must go on. Abu Talib hinted that his protection might be withdrawn. Then Mohammed declared that if the sun came down on his right hand and the moon on his left he would not swerve from the work which God had given him to do. Abu Talib, finding him inflexible, assured him that his protection should never be withdrawn. In the meantime the patriarchs returned and said, "What is it that you want, Mohammed? Do you wish for riches? We will make you rich. Do you wish for honour? We will make you the mayor of the town." Mohammed replied with a chapter of the Koran. They then assembled in the town hall and entered into a solemn league and covenant to keep apart from the family of Abu Talib. It was sent to Coventry. None would buy with them nor sell with them, eat with them nor drink with them. This lasted for three years, but when as people passed by the house they heard the cries of the starving children from behind the walls, they relented and sold them grain. There was one member of the family, Abu Laheb, who withdrew from it at that juncture and became Mohammed's most inveterate foe.

Each family agreed also to punish its own Mohammedans. Many were exposed to the glow of the midday sun on the scorching gravel outside the town, and to the torments of thirst. A mulatto slave was tortured by a great stone being placed on his chest, the while he cried out continually, "There is only one God! There is only one God!" Mohammed recommended his disciples to escape to Abyssinia, "a land of righteousness, a land where none was wronged." They were kindly received by the Negus, who refused to give them up in spite of the envoys with presents of red leather who were sent to him from Mecca with that request.

During the period of the sacred months Mohammed used often to visit the encampments of the pilgrims outside the town. He announced to them his mission; he preached on the unity of God and on the terrors of the judgment-day. "God has no daughters," said he, "for how can he have daughters when he has no spouse? He begetteth not, neither is he begotten. There is none but he. O beware, ye idolators, of the time that is to come, when the sun shall be folded up, when the stars shall fall, when the mountains shall be made to pass away, when the children's hair shall grow white with anguish, when souls like locust swarms shall rise from their graves, when the girl who hath been buried alive shall be asked for what crime she was put to death, when the books shall be laid open, when every soul shall know what it hath wrought! O the striking, the striking, when men shall be scattered as moths in the wind! And then Allah shall cry to Hell, Art thou filled full? And Hell shall cry to Allah, More, give me more!"

But there followed him everywhere a squint-eyed man, fat, with flowing locks on both sides of his head, and clothed in raiment of fine Aden stuff. When Mohammed had finished his sermon he would say, "This fellow's object is to draw you away from the gods to his fanciful ideas; wherefore follow him not, O my brothers, neither listen to him." And who should this be but his uncle, Abu Laheb! Whereupon the strangers would reply, "Your own kinsmen ought to know you best. Why do they not believe you if what you say is true?" In return for these kind offices Mohammed promised his uncle that he should go down to be burned in flaming fire, and that his wife should go too, bearing a load of wood, with a cord of twisted palm fibres round her neck.

And now two great sorrows fell upon Mohammed. He lost almost at the same time his beloved wife and the noble-hearted parent of his clan. The successor of Abu Talib continued the protection, yet Mohammed felt insecure. His religion also made but small progress. The fact is that he failed at Mecca as Jesus had failed at Jerusalem. He had made a few ardent disciples who spent the day at his feet, or in reading snatches of the Koran scrawled on date leaves, shoulder-blades of sheep, camel bones, scraps of parchment, or tablets of smooth white stone. But he had not so much as shaken the ruling idolatry, which was firmly based on custom and self-interest. No doubt his disciples would in course of time have diffused his religion throughout Arabia. Islam was formed; Islam was alive; but Mohammed himself would never have witnessed its triumph had it not been for a curious accident which now occurred. The Arabs belonging to that city which was afterwards called Medina had conquered a tribe of Jews. These had consoled themselves for the bitterness of their defeat by declaring that a great prophet, the Messiah, would soon appear, and would avenge them upon all their foes. The Arabs believed them and trembled, for they stood in great dread of the book which the Jews possessed, and which they supposed to be a magical composition. So, when certain pilgrims from Medina heard Mohammed announce that he was a messenger from God, they took it for granted that he was the man, and determined to steal a march upon the Jews by securing him for themselves. At their request he sent a missionary to Medina; the townsmen were converted, and invited him to come and live among them. In a dark ravine near Mecca, at the midnight hour, his patriarch or father delivered him solemnly into their hands. Mohammed was now no longer a citizen of Mecca; he was no longer "protected"; he had changed his nationality, and he was hunted like a deer before he arrived safely in his new home.

Had Mohammed been killed in that celebrated flight he would have been classed by historians among the glorious martyrs and the gentle saints. His character before the Hegira resembled the character of Jesus. In both of them we find the same sublime insanity, compounded of loyalty to God, love for man, and inordinate self-conceit; both were subject to savage fits of wrath, and having no weapons but their tongues, consigned souls by wholesale to hell-fire. Both also humbled themselves before God, preaching the religion of the heart, led pure, unblemished lives, devoted themselves to a noble cause, and uttered maxims of charity and love at strange variance with their occasional invectives. Of the life of Jesus it is needless to speak; if he had any vices they have not been recorded. But the conduct of Mohammed at Mecca was apparently not less pure. He was married to an old woman; polygamy was a custom of the land; his passions were strong, as was afterwards too plainly shown; yet he did not take a second wife as long as his dear Khadijah was alive. He never frequented the wine-shop or looked at the dancing girls or talked abroad in the bazaars. He was more modest than a virgin behind the curtain. When he met children he would stop and pat their cheeks; he followed the bier that passed him in the street; he visited the sick; he was kind to his inferiors; he would accept the invitation of a slave to dinner; he was never the first to withdraw his hand when he shook hands; he was humble, gentle, and kind; he waited always on himself, mending his own clothes, milking his own goats; he never struck any one in his life. When once asked to curse someone he said, "I have not been sent to curse but to be a mercy to mankind." He reproached himself in the Koran for having behaved unkindly to a beggar, and so immortalised his own offence. He issued a text, "Use no violence in religion."

But this text, with many others, he afterwards expunged. When he arrived at Medina he found himself at the head of a small army, and he began to publish his gospel of the sword. Henceforth we may admire the statesman or the general; the prophet is no more. It will hence be inferred that Mohammed was hypocritical, or at least inconstant. But he was constant throughout his life to the one object which he had in view--the spread of his religion. At Mecca it could best be spread by means of the gentle virtues; he therefore ordered his disciples to abstain from violence which would only do them harm. At Medina he saw that the Caaba idolatry could not be destroyed except by force; he therefore felt it his duty to make use of force. He obeyed his conscience both at Mecca and Medina, for the conscience is merely an organ of the intellect, and is altered, improved, or vitiated according to the education which it receives and the incidents which act upon it.

And now Mohammed's glory expanded, and at the same time his virtue declined. He broke the Truce of God: he was not always true to his plighted word. As Moses forbade the Israelites to marry with the pagans and then took unto himself an Ethiopian wife, so Mohammed, broke his own marriage laws, beginning the career of a voluptuary at fifty years of age. His Koran sudras were now official manifestoes, legal regulations, delivered in an extravagant and stilted style differing much from that of his fervid oracles at Mecca. But whatever may have been his private defects, when we regard him as a ruler and lawgiver we can only wonder and admire. He established for the first time in history a united Arabia. In the moral life of his countrymen he effected a remarkable reform. He abolished drunkenness and gambling--vices to which the Arabs had been specially addicted. He abolished the practice of infanticide, and also succeeded in rendering its memory detestable. It is said that Omar, the fierce apostle of Islam, shed but one tear in his life, and that was when he remembered how in the days of darkness his child had beat the dust off his beard with her little hand as he was laying her in the grave. Polygamy and slavery he did not prohibit, but whatever laws he made respecting women and slaves were made with the view of improving their condition. He removed that facility of divorce by means of which an Arab could at any time repudiate his wife: he enacted that no Moslem should be made a slave, that the children of a slave girl by her master should be free. Instead of repining that Mohammed did no more, we have reason to be astonished that he did so much. His career is the best example that can be given of the influence of the individual in human history. That single man created the glory of his nation and spread his language over half the earth. The words which he preached to jeering crowds twelve hundred years ago are now being studied by scholars or by devotees in London and Paris and Berlin; in Mecca, where he laboured, in Medina, where he died; in Constantinople, in Cairo, in Fez, in Timbuktu, in Jerusalem, in Damascus, in Basra, in Baghdad, in Bokhara, in Kabul, in Calcutta, in Pekin; on the steppes of Central Asia, in the islands of the Indian Archipelago, in lands which are as yet unmarked upon our maps, in the oases of thirsty deserts, in obscure villages situated by unknown streams. It was Mohammed who did all this, for he uttered the book which carried the language, and he prepared the army which carried the book. His disciples and successors were not mad fanatics but resolute and sagacious men, who made shrewd friendship with the malcontent Christians among the Greeks and with the persecuted Jews in Spain, and who in a few years created an empire which extended from the Pyrenees to the Hindu Kush.

This empire, it is true, was soon divided, and soon became weak in all its parts. The Arabs could conquer, but they could not govern. Separate sovereignties or caliphates were established in Babylonia, Egypt, and Spain, while provinces such as Morocco or Bokhara frequently obtained independence by rebellion. It is needless to describe at length the history of the Caliphs and their successors--it is only the twice-told tale of the Euphrates and the Nile. The caliphs were at first Commanders of the Faithful in reality, but they were soon degraded both in Cairo and Baghdad to the position of the Roman Pope at the present time. The government was seized by the Praetorian Guards, who in Baghdad were descended from Turkish prisoners or negroes imported from Zanzibar, and in Egypt from Mamelukes or European slaves, brought in their boyhood from the wild countries surrounding the Black Sea, and trained up from tender years to the practice of arms--the sons of Christian parents, but branded with a cross on the soles of their feet that they might never cease to tread upon the emblem of their native creed.

However, by means of the Arab conquest the East was united as it had never been before. The Euphrates was no longer a line of partition between two worlds. Arab traders established their factories on both sides of the Indian Ocean and along the Asiatic shores of the Pacific. Men from all countries met at Mecca once a year. The religion of the Arabs conquered nations whom the Arabs themselves had never seen. When the Mohammedan Turks of Central Asia took Constantinople and reduced the caliphates to provinces, although the people of Mohammed were driven back to their wilderness the strength and glory of his religion was increased. In the same manner the conquest of Hindustan was an achievement of Islam in which the Arabs bore no part, and in Africa also we shall find that the Koran reigns over extensive regions which the Arabs visit only as travellers and merchants.

Once upon a time Morocco and Spain were one country, and Europe extended to the Atlas mountains, which stood upon the shores of a great salt sea. Beyond that ocean, to the south, lay the Dark Continent, surrounded on all sides by water except on the north-east, where it was joined to Asia near Aden by an isthmus. A geological revolution converted the African ocean into a sandy plain, and the straits of Bab-el-Mandeb and Gibraltar were torn open by the retreating waves. But the Sahara, though no longer under water, is still in reality a sea; the true Africa begins on its southern coast, and is entirely distinct from the European-like countries between the Mediterranean and the Atlas, and from the strip of garden land which is cast down every year in the desert by the Nile. The Black Africa or Sudan is a gigantic tableland; its sides are built of granite mountains which surround it with a parapet or brim, and which send down rivers on the outside towards the sea, on the inside into the plateau. The outside rivers are brief and swift: the inside rivers are long and sluggish in their course, winding in all directions, collecting into enormous lakes, and sometimes flowing forth through gaps in the parapet to the Sahara or the sea.

Description of Africa

A tableland is seldom so uniform and smooth as the word denotes. The African plateau is intersected by mountain ranges and ravines, juts into volcanic isolated cones, and varies much in its climate, its aspect, its productions, and its altitude above the sea. It may be divided into platforms or river basins which are true geographical provinces, and each of which should be labelled with the names of its explorers. There is the platform of Abyssinai, which belongs to Bruce; the platform of the White Nile, including the Lakes of Burton (Tanganyika), of Speke (Victoria Nyanza), and of Baker (Albert Nyanza); the platform of the Zambezi, with its lakes Nyasa and Ngami, discovered by Livingstone, the greatest of African explorers; the platform of the Congo, including the regions of Western Equatorial Africa, hitherto unexplored; the platform of South Africa (below 20° S.), which enjoys an Australian climate, and also Australian wealth in its treasure-filled mountains and its wool-abounding plains; and lastly the platform of the Niger, which deserves a place, as will be shown, in universal history. The discoverers of the Niger in its upper are Park (who first saw the Niger), Caillie, and myself: in its central and eastern parts Laing, who first reached Timbuktu; Caillie, who first returned from it; Denham, Clapperton, Lander, and Barth.

The original inhabitants of Africa were the Hottentots or Bushmen, a dwarfish race who have restless, rambling, ape-like eyes, a click in their speech, and bodies which are the wonder of anatomists. They are now found only on the South African platform, or perhaps here and there on the platform of the Congo. They have been driven southward by the negroes, as the Eskimos in America were driven north by the Red Indians and the Finns in Europe by the Celtic tribes, while the negroes themselves have yielded in some parts of Africa to Asiatic tribes, as the Celts in Gaul and Britain yielded to the Germans.

These negroes are sometimes of so deep a brown that the skin appears to be quite black; sometimes their skin is as light as a mulatto's. The average tint is a rich deep bronze. Their eyes are dark, though blue eyes are occasionally seen; their hair is black, though sometimes of rusty red, and is always of a woolly texture. To this rule there are no exceptions--it is the one constant character, the one infallible sign by which the race may be detected. Their lips are not invariably thick; their noses are frequently well formed. In physical appearance they differ widely from one another. The inhabitants of the swamps, the dark forests and the mountains are flat-nosed, long armed, and thin-calved, with mouths like mussles, broad splay feet, and projecting heels. It was for the most part from this class that the American slave markets were supplied; the negroes of the States and the West Indies represent the African in the same manner as the people of the Pontine Marshes represent the inhabitants of Italy. The negroes of South Africa stand at the opposite extreme. Enjoying an excellent climate and a wholesome supply of food, they are superior to most other people of their race. Yet it is certain that they are negroes, for they have woolly hair, and they do not differ in language or manners from the inhabitants of the other platforms. When the Portuguese first traded on the African coasts they gave the name Caffres (or pagans) to the negroes of Guinea, as well as to those of the Cape and Mozambique. It is quite an accident that the name has been retained for the latter tribes alone, yet such is the power of a name that the Caffres and negroes are universally supposed to be distinct. It is impossible, however, to draw any line between the two. Pure negroes are born on the coast of Guinea and in the interior with complexions as light, with limbs as symmetrical, and with features as near to the European standard as can be found in all Caffraria. Between the hideous being of the Nile and Niger deltas and the robust shepherds of the south, or the aristocratic chieftains of the west, there is a wide difference, no doubt but intermediate gradations exist.

There is also much variety among the negroes in respect to manners, mental condition, political government, and mode of life. Some tribes live only on the fruit of net and spear, eked out with insects and berries and shells. Property is ill defined among them; if a man makes a canoe the others use it when they please; if he builds a better house than his neighbours they pull it down. Others, though still in the hunting condition, have gardens of plantains and cassada. In this condition the headman of the village has little power, but property is secured by law. Other tribes are pastoral, and resemble the Arabs in their laws and customs; the patriarchal system prevails among them. There are regions in which the federal system prevails; many villages are leagued together; and the headmen, acting as deputies of their respective boroughs, meet in congress to debate questions of foreign policy and to enact laws. Large empires exist in the Sudan. In some of these the king is a despot who possesses a powerful bodyguard equivalent to a standing army, a court with its regulations of etiquette, and a well-ordered system of patronage and surveillance. In others he is merely an instrument in the hands of priests or military nobles, and is kept concealed, giving audience from behind a curtain to excite the veneration of the vulgar. There are also thousands of large walled cities resembling those of Europe in the Middle Ages, or of ancient Greece, or of Italy before the supremacy of Rome, encircled by pastures and by arable estates, and by farming villages to which the citizens repair at harvest-time to superintend the labour of their slaves. But such cities, with their villeggiatura, their municipal government, their agora or forum, their fortified houses, their feuds and street frays of Capulet and Montague, are not indigenous in Africa; their existence is comparatively modern and is due to the influence of religion.

An African village (old style) is usually a street of huts, with walls like hurdles, and the thatch projecting so that its owner may sit beneath it in sun or rain. The door is low--one has to crawl in order to go in. There are no windows. The house is a single room. In its midst burns a fire which is never suffered to go out, for it is a light in darkness, a servant, a companion, and a guardian angel; it purifies the miasmatic air. The roof and walls are smoke-dried but clean; in one corner is a pile of wood neatly cut up into billets, and in another is a large earthen jar filled with water on which floats a gourd or calabash, a vegetable bowl. Spears, bows, quivers, and nets hang from pegs upon the walls. Let us suppose that it is night; four or five black forms are lying in a circle with their feet toward the fire, and two dogs with pricked-up ears creep close to the ashes which are becoming grey and cold.

The day dawns; a dim light appears through the crevices and crannies of the walls. The sleepers rise and roll up their mats, which are their beds, and place on one side the round logs of wood which are their pillows. The man takes down his bow and arrows from the wall, fastens wooden rattles round his dogs' necks, and goes out into the bush. The women replenish the fire, and lift up an inverted basket whence sally forth a hen and her chickens which make at once for the open door to find their daily bread for themselves outside. The women take hoes and go to the plantation, or they take pitchers to fill at the brook. They wear round the waist, before and behind, two little aprons made from a certain bark, soaked and beaten until it is as flexible as leather. Every man has a plantation of these cloth-trees round his hut. The unmarried girls wear no clothes at all, but they are allowed to decorate themselves with bracelets and anklets of iron, flowers in their ears, necklaces of red berries like coral, girdles of white shells, hair oiled and padded out with the chignon, and sometimes white ashes along the parting.

The ladies fill their pitchers and take their morning bath, discussing the merits or demerits of their husbands. The air is damp and cold, and the trees and grass are heavy with dew; but presently the sun begins to shine, the dewdrops fall heavy and large as drops of rain; the birds chirp; the flowers expand their drowsy leaves and receive the morning calls of butterflies and bees. The forest begins to buzz and hum like a great factory awaking to its work.

When the sun is high, boys come from the bush with vegetable bottles frothing over with palm wine. The cellar of the African, and his glass and china shop, and his clothing warehouse, are in the trees. In the midst of the village is a kind of shed, a roof supported on bare poles. It is the palaver-house, in which at this hour the old men sit and debate the affairs of state or decide lawsuits, each orator holding a spear when he is speaking, and planting it in the ground before him as he resumes his seat. Oratory is the African's one fine art. His delivery is fluent; his harangues, though diffuse, are adorned with phrases of wild poetry. That building is also the club house of the elders, and there, when business is over, they pass the heat of the day, seated on logs which are smooth and shiny from use. At the hour of noon their wives or children bring them palm wine, and present it on their knees, clapping their hands in a token of respect. And then all is still; it is the hour of silence and tranquillity, the hour which the Portuguese call "the calm." The sun sits enthroned on the summit of the sky; its white light is poured upon the earth; the straw thatch shines like snow. The forest is silent; all nature sleeps.

Then down, down, down sinks the sun, and its rays shoot slantwise through the trees. The hunters return, and their friends run out and greet them as if they had been gone for years, murmuring to them in a kind of baby language, calling them by their names of love, shaking their right hands, caressing their faces, patting them upon their breasts, embracing them in all ways except with the lips--for the kiss is unknown among the Africans. And so they toy and babble and laugh with one another till the sun turns red, and the air turns dusky, and the giant trees cast deep shadows across the street. Strange perfumes arise from the earth; fireflies sparkle; grey parrots come forth from the forest, and fly screaming round intending to roost in the neighbourhood of man. The women bring their husbands the gourd dish of boiled plantains or bush yams, made hot with red pepper, seasoned with fish or venison sauce. And when this simple meal is ended, boom! boom! Goes the big drum; the sweet reed flute pipes forth; the girls and lads begin to sing. In a broad, clean-swept place they gather together, jumping up and down with glee; the young men form in one row, the women in another, and dance in two long lines, retreating and advancing with graceful undulations of their bodies and arms waving in the air. And now there is a squealing, wailing, unearthly sound, and out of the wood, with a hop, skip, and jump, comes Mumbo Jumbo, a hideous mask on his face and a scourge in his hand. Woe to the wife who would not cook her husband's dinner, or who gave him saucy words, for Mumbo Jumbo is the censor of female morals. Well the guilty ones know him as they run screaming to their huts. Then again the dance goes on, and if there is a moon it does not cease throughout the night.

Such is the picturesque part of savage life. But it is not savage life--it merely lies upon the surface as paint lies upon the skin. Let us take a walk through that same village on another day. Here in a hut is a young man with one leg in the stocks, and with his right hand bound to his neck by a cord. The palm wine, and the midnight dance, and the furtive caresses of Asua overpowered his discretion; he was detected, and now he is "put in log." If his relations do not pay the fine he will be sold as a slave; or if there is no demand for slaves in that country he will be killed. His friends reprove him for trying to steal what the husband was willing to sell; and might he not have guessed that Asua was a decoy?

Another day the palaver-house has the aspect of a Crockford's. An old man who is one of the village grandees is spinning nuts for high stakes, and has drunk too much to see that he is overmatched. He loses his mats, his weapons, his goats, his fowls, his plantation, his house, his slaves whom he took prisoners in his young and warlike days, his wives, his children, and his aged mother who fed him at her breast--all are lost, all are gone. And then, with flushed eyes and trembling hand, he begins to gamble for himself. He stakes his right leg and loses it. He may not move it until he has won it back or until it is redeemed. He loses both legs; he stakes his body and loses that also, and becomes a bond-servant, or is sold as a slave.

Let us give another scene. A young man of family has died; the whole village is convulsed with grief and fear. It does not appear natural to them that a man should die before he has grown old. Some malignant power is at work among them. Is it an evil spirit whom they have unwittingly offended and who is taking its revenge, or is it a witch? The great fetish-man has been sent for, and soon he arrives, followed by his disciples. He wears a cap waving with feathers and a parti-coloured garment covered with charms--horns of gazelles, shells of snails, and a piece of leopard's liver wrapped up in the leaves of a poison-giving tree. His face is stained with the white juice from a dead man's brain. He rings an iron bell as he enters the town, and at the same time the drum begins to beat. The drum has its language, so that those who are distant from the village understand what it is saying. With short, lively sounds it summons to the dance; it thunders forth the alarm of fire or war, loudly and quickly with no interval between the beats; and now it tolls the hour of judgment and the day of death. The fetish-man examines the dead man and says it is the work of a witch. He casts lots with knotted cords; he mutters incantations; he passes round the villagers and points out the guilty person, who is usually some old woman whom popular opinion has previously suspected and is ready to condemn. She is, however, allowed the benefit of an ordeal: a gourd filled with the "red water" is given her to drink. If she is innocent it acts as an emetic; if she is guilty it makes her fall senseless to the ground. She is then put to death with a variety of tortures--burnt alive or torn limb from limb; tied on the beach at low water to be drowned by the rising tide; rubbed with honey and laid out in the sun; or buried in an ant-hill, the most horrible death of all.

These examples are sufficient to show that the life of the savage is not a happy one, and the existence of each clan or tribe is precarious in the extreme. They are like the wild animals, engaged from day to night in seeking food, and ever watchful against the foes by whom they are surrounded. The men who go out hunting, the girls who go with their pitchers to the village brook, are never sure that they will return, for there is always war with some neighbouring village, and their method of making war is by ambuscade. But besides these real and ordinary dangers, the savage believes himself to be encompassed by evil spirits who may at any moment spring upon him in the guise of a leopard, or cast down upon him the dead branch of a tree. In order to propitiate these invisible beings, his life is entangled with intricate rites; it is turned this way and that way as oracles are delivered or as omens appear. It is impossible to describe, or even to imagine, the tremulous condition of the savage mind, yet the traveller can see from their aspect and manners that they dwell in a state of never-ceasing dread.

Let us now suppose that a hundred years have passed, and let us visit the village again. The place itself and the whole country around have been transformed. The forest has disappeared, and in its stead are fields covered with the glossy blades of the young rice, with the tall red-tufted maize, with the millet and the Guinea corn, with the yellow flowers of the tobacco plant growing in wide fields, and with large shrubberies of cotton, the snowy wool peeping forth from the expanding leaves. Before us stands a great town surrounded by walls of red clay flanked by towers, and with heavy wooden gates. Day dawns, and the women come forth to the brook decorously dressed in blue cotton robes passed over the hair as a hood. Men ride forth on horseback, wearing white turbans and swords suspended on their right shoulders by a crimson sash. They are the unmixed descendants of the forest savage; their faces are those of pure negroes, but the expression is not the same. Their manners are grave and composed; they salute one another, saying in the Arabic "Peace be with you." The palaver-house or town hall is also the mosque; the parliamentary debates and the law trials which are there held have all the dignity of a religious service; they are opened with prayer, and the name of the creator is often solemnly invoked by the orator or advocate, while all the elders touch their foreheads with their hands and murmur in response, Amina! Amina! (Amen! Amen!). The town is pervaded by a bovine smell, sweet to the nostrils of those who have travelled long in the beefless lands of the people of the forest. Sounds of industry may also be heard--not only the clinking of the blacksmith's hammer, but also the rattling of the loom, the thumping of the cloth-maker, and the song of the cordwainer as he sits cross-legged making saddles or shoes. The women, with bow and distaff and spindle, are turning the soft tree-wool into thread; the work in the fields is done by slaves. The elders smoke or take snuff in their verandahs, and sometimes study a page of the Koran. When the evening draws on there is no sound of flute and drum. A bonfire of brushwood is lighted in the market-place, and the boys of the town collect around it with wooden boards in their hands, and bawl their lessons, swaying their bodies to and fro, by which movement they imagine the memory is assisted. Then rises a long, loud, harmonious cry, "Come to prayers, come to prayers! Come to security! God is great! He liveth and he dieth not! Come to prayers! O thou Bountiful!"

La ilah illa Allah: Mohammed Rasul Allah. Alahu Akbaru. Alahu Akbar.

Such towns as these may be less interesting to the traveller than the pagan villages--he finds them merely a second-hand copy of Eastern life. But though they are not so picturesque, their inhabitants are happier and better men. Violent and dishonest deeds are no longer arranged by pecuniary compensation. Husbands can no longer set wife-traps for their friends; adultery is treated as a criminal offence. Men can no longer squander away their relations at the gaming table, and stake their own bodies on a throw. Men can no longer be tempted to vice and crime under the influence of palm wine. Women can no longer be married by a great chief in herds, and treated like beasts of burden and like slaves. Each wife has an equal part of her husband's love by law; it is not permitted to forsake and degrade the old wife for the sake of the young. Each wife has her own house, and the husband may not enter until he has knocked at the door and received the answer, Bismillah! [In the name of God!] Every boy is taught to read and write in Arabic, which is the religious and official language in the Sudan, as Latin was in Europe in the Middle Ages; he also writes his own language with the Arabic character, as we write ours with the Roman letter. In such countries the policy of isolation is at an end; they are open to all the Moslems in the world, and are thus connected with the lands of the East. Here there is a remarkable change, and one that deserves a place in history. It is a movement the more interesting since it is still actively going on. The Mohammedan religion has already overspread a region of Negroland as large as Europe. It is firmly established not only in the Africa of the Mediterranean and the Nile and in the oases of the Sahara, but also throughout that part of the continent which we have termed the platform of the Niger.

In 1797 Mungo Park discovered the Niger in the heart of Africa, at a point where it is as broad as the Thames at Westminster; in 1817 Rene Caillie crossed it at a point considerably higher up; in 1822 Major Laing attempted to reach it by striking inland from

Sierra Leone, but was forced by the natives to return when he was only fifty miles distant from the river; and in 1869 I made the same attempt, was turned back at the same place, but made a fresh expedition, and reached the river at a higher point than Caillie and Park. But my success also was incomplete, for native wars made it impossible for me to reach the source, though it was near at hand; and that still remains a splendid prize for one who will walk in my footsteps as I walked in those of Laing. The source of the Niger, as given in the maps; was fixed by Laing from native information which I ascertained to be correct. There is no doubt that this river rises in the backwoods of Sierra Leone, at a distance of only two hundred miles from the coast. It runs for some time as a foaming hill-torrent bearing obscure and barbarous names, and at the point where I found it glides into the broad, calm breast of the plateau, and receives its illustrious name of the Joliba, or Great River.

It flows north-east, and enters the Sahara as if intending, like the Nile, to pour its waters into the Mediterranean Sea. But suddenly it turns towards the east, so that Herodotus, who heard of it when he was at Memphis, supposed that it joined the Nile; and such was the prevailing opinion not only among the Greeks but also among the Arabs in the Middle Ages. They did not know that the eccentric river again wheels round, flows towards the sea near which it rose, passes through the latitude of its birth, and, having thus described three quarters of a circle, debouches by many mouths into the Bight of Benin. So singular a course might well baffle the speculations of geographers and the investigations of explorers. The people who dwell on the banks of the river do not know where it ends. I was told by some that it went to Mecca, by others that it went to Jerusalem. Mungo Park's own theory was ludicrously incorrect--he believed that the Congo was its mouth. Others declared that it never reached the sea at all. It was Lander who discovered the mouth of the Niger, at one time as mysterious as the sources of the Nile, and so established the hypothesis which Reichard had advanced and which Mannert had declared to be "contrary to nature."

The Niger platform or basin is flat, with here and there a line of rolling hills containing gold. The vegetation consists of high, coarse grass and trees of small stature, except on the banks of streams, where they grow to a larger size. The palm-oil tree is not found on this plateau, but the shea-butter or tallow tree abounds in natural plantations which will some day prove a source of enormous wealth. As the river flows on, these trees disappear; the plains widen and are smoothed out, and the country assumes the character of the Sahara.

The negroes who inhabited the platform of the Niger lived chiefly on the banks of the river, subsisting on lotus root and fish. Like all savages, they were jealous and distrustful; their intercourse was that of war. But nature, by means of a curious contrivance, has rendered it impossible for men to remain eternally apart. Common salt is one of the mineral constituents of the human body, and savages, who live chiefly on vegetable food, are dependent upon it for their life. In Africa children may be seen sucking it like sugar. "Come and eat with us today," says the hospitable African; "we are going to have salt for dinner." It is not in all countries that this mineral food is to be found, but the saltless lands in the Sudan contain gold dust, ivory, and slaves, and so a system of barter is arranged, and isolated tribes are brought into contact with one another.

The two great magazines are the desert and the ocean. At the present day the white, powdery English salt is carried on donkeys and slaves to the upper waters of the Niger, and is driving back the crystalline salt of the Sahara. In the ancient days the salt of the plateau came entirely from the mines of Bilma and Toudeyni, in the desert, which were occupied and worked by negro tribes. But at a period far remote, before the foundations of Carthage were laid, a Berber nation, now called the Tuaricks, overspread the desert and conquered the oases and the mines. This terrible people are yet the scourge of the peaceful farmer and the passing caravan. They camp in leather tents; they are armed with lance and sword, and with shields on which is painted the image of a cross. The Arabs call them "the muffled ones," for their mouths and noses are covered with a bandage, sometimes black, sometimes white, above which sit in deep sockets, like ant-lions in their pits, a pair of dark, cruel, sinister looking eyes. They levy tolls on all travellers, and murder those who have the reputation of unusual wealth--as they did Miss Tinne, whose iron water tanks they imagined to be filled with gold. When they poured down on the Sahara they were soon attracted by the rich pastures and alluvial plains of the black country. In course of time their raids were converted into conquests, and they established a line of kingdoms from the Niger to the Nile, in the borderland between the Sahara and the parallel 10° N. Timbuktu, Haoussa, Bornu, Bagirmi, Waday, Darfur, and Kordofan were the names of these kingdoms; in all of them Islam is now the religion of the state; all of them belong to the Asiatic world.

The Tuaricks of the Sudan were merely the ruling castes, and were much darkened by harem blood, but they communicated freely with their brethren of the desert, who had dealings with the Berbers beyond the Atlas. When the Andalusia of the Arabs became a polite civilised land crowds of ingenious artisans, descended from the old Roman craftsmen or from the Greek emigrants, or from their Arab apprentices, took architecture over to North Africa. The city of Morocco was filled with magnificent palaces and mosques; it became the metropolis of an independent kingdom; it was called the Baghdad of the west; its doctors were as learned as the doctors of Cordova, its musicians as skilful as the musicians of Seville. A wealthy and powerful Morocco could not exist without its influence being felt across the desert; the position of Timbuktu in reference to Morocco was precisely that of Meroe to Memphis or to Thebes. The Sahara, it is true, is much wider across from Morocco to Timbuktu than from Egypt to Ethiopia, but the introduction of camels brought the Atlas and the Niger near to one another. The Tuaricks, who had previously lived on horses, under whose bellies they tied water-bottles of leather when they went on a long journey, had been able to cross the desert only at certain seasons of the year; but now, with the aid of the camel, which they at once adopted and from which they bred the famous Mehara strain, they could cross the Sahara at its widest part in a few days. A regular trade was established between the two countries, and was conducted by the Berbers. Arab merchants, desirous of seeing with their own eyes the wondrous land of ivory and gold, took passage in the caravans, crossed the yellow seas, sprang from their camels upon the green shores of the Sudan, and kneeling on the banks of the Niger with their faces turned towards Mecca, dipped their hands in its waters and praised the name of the Lord. They journeyed from city to city and from court to court, and composed works of travel which were read with eager delight all over the Moslem world, from Spain to Hindustan.

The Arabs thronged to this newly discovered world. They built factories; they established schools; they converted dynasties. They covered the river with masted vessels; they built majestic temples with graceful minaret and swelling dome. Theological colleges and public libraries were founded; camels came across the desert laden with books; the negroes swarmed to the lectures of the mullahs; Plato and Aristotle were studied by the banks of the Niger, and the glories of Granada were reflected at Timbuktu. That city became the refuge of political fugitives and criminals from Morocco. In the sixteenth century the Emperor dispatched across the desert a company of harquebusiers who, with their strange, terrible weapons, everywhere triumphed like the soldiers of Cortes and Pizarro in Mexico and Peru. These musketeers made enormous conquests not for their master but for themselves. They established an oligarchy of their own; it was afterwards dethroned by the natives, but there yet exist men who, as Barth informs us, are called the descendants of the musketeers and who wear a distinctive dress. But that imperial expedition was the last exploit of the Moors. After the conquest of Granada by the Christians and of Algeria by the Turks, Morocco, encompassed by enemies, became a savage and isolated land; Timbuktu, its commercial dependent, fell into decay, and is now chiefly celebrated as a cathedral town.

The Arabs carried cotton and the art of its manufacture into the Sudan, which is one of the largest cotton-growing areas in the world. Its Manchester is Kano, which manufactures blue cloth and coloured plaids, clothes a vast negro population, and even exports its goods to the lands of the Mediterranean Sea. Denham and Clapperton, who first reached the lands of Haoussa and Bornu, were astonished to find among the negroes magnificent courts; regiments of cavalry, the horses caparisoned in silk for gala days and clad in coats of mail for war; long trains of camels laden with salt and natron and corn and cloth and cowrie shells--which form the currency--and kola nuts, which the Arabs call "the coffee of the negroes." They attended with wonder the gigantic fairs at which the cotton goods of Manchester, the red cloth of Saxony, double-barrelled guns, razors, tea and sugar, Nuremberg ware and writing-paper were exhibited for sale. They also found merchants who offered to cash their bills upon houses at Tripoli, and scholars acquainted with Avicenna, Averroes, and the Greek philosophers.

The Mohammedans in Central Africa

The Mohammedan religion was spread in Central Africa to a great extent by the travelling Arab merchants, who were welcomed everywhere at the negro or semi-negro courts, and who frequently converted the pagan kings by working miracles--that is to say, by means of events which accidentally followed their solemn prayers, such as the healing of a disease, rain in the midst of drought, or a victory in war. But the chief instrument of conversion was the school. It is much to the credit of the negroes that they keenly appreciate the advantages of education; they appear to possess an instinctive veneration and affection for the book. Wherever Mohammedans settled, the sons of chiefs were placed under their tuition. A Mohammedan quarter was established; it was governed by its own laws; its sheikh rivalled in power and finally surpassed the native kings. The machinery of the old pagan court might still go on; the negro chief might receive the magnificent title of sultan; he might be surrounded by albinos and dwarfs and big-headed men and buffoons; he might sit in a cage, or behind a curtain in a palace with seven gates, and receive the ceremonial visits of his nobles, who stripped off a garment at each gate and came into his presence naked, and cowered on the ground, and clapped their hands, and sprinkled their heads with dust, and then turned round and sat with their backs presented in reverence towards him, as if they were unable to bear the sight of his countenance shining like a well-blacked boot. But the Arab or Moorish sheikh would be in reality the king, deciding all questions of foreign policy, of peace and war, of laws and taxes and commercial regulations, holding a position resembling that of the Gothic generals who placed Libius Severus and

Augustulus upon the throne--of the mayors of the palace beside the Merovingian princes, of the Company's servants at the court of the great Mogul. And when the Mohammedans had become numerous, and a fitting season had arrived, the sheikh would point out a well-known Koran text and would proclaim war against the surrounding pagan kings. And so the movement which had been begun by the school would be continued by the sword.

It may, however, be doubted whether the Arab merchants alone would have spread Islam over the Niger plateau. On the east coast of Africa they have possessed settlements from time immemorial. Before the Greeks of Alexandria sailed into the Indian Ocean, before the Tyrian vessels, with Jewish supercargoes, passed through the straits of Bab-el-Mandeb, the Arabs of Yemen had established factories in Mozambique and on the opposite coast of Malabar, and had carried on a trade between the two lands, selling to the Indians ivory, ebony, slaves, bees-wax, and gold dust brought down in quills from the interior by the negroes, to whom they sold in return the sugar beads, and blue cotton goods of Hindustan. In the period of the caliphs these settlements were strengthened and increased, in consequence of civil war, by fugitive tribes from Oman and other parts of the Arabian peninsula. The emigrants made Africa their home; they built large towns which they surrounded with orchards of the orange-tree and plantations of the date; they introduced the culture of tobacco, sugar cane and cotton. They were loved and revered by the negroes; they made long journeys into the interior for the purposes of trade. Yet their religion has made no progress, and they do not attempt to convert the blacks. Their towns resemble those of the Europeans; they dwell apart from the natives, and above them.

The Mohammedans who entered the Niger regions were not only the Arab merchants but also the Berbers of the desert, who, driven by war or instigated by ambition, poured into the Sudan by tribes, seized lands and women, and formed mulatto nationalities. Of these the Fulahs are the most famous. They were originally natives of Northern Africa; having intermarried during many generations with the natives, they have often the appearance of pure negroes, but they always call themselves white men, however black their skins may seem to be. In the last century they were dispersed in small and puny tribes. Some wandered as gipsies selling wooden bowls; others were roaming shepherd clans, paying tribute to the native kings and suffering much ill-treatment. In other parts they lived a bandit life. Sometimes, but rarely, they resided in towns which they had conquered, pursued commerce, and tilled the soil. Yet in war they were far superior to the negroes: if only they could be united the most powerful kingdoms would be unable to withstand them. And finally their day arrived. A man of their own race returned from Mecca, a pilgrim and a prophet, gathered them like wolves beneath his standard, and poured them forth on the Sudan.

The pilgrimage to Mecca is incumbent only on those who can afford it, but hundreds of devout negroes every year put on their shrouds and beg their way across the continent to Massowah. There, taking out a few grains of gold dust cunningly concealed between the leaves of their Korans, they pay their passage across the Red Sea and tramp it from Jidda to Mecca, feeding as they go on the bodies of the camels that have been left to die, and whose meat is lawful if the throat is cut before the animal expires. As soon as the negroes--or Takrouri, as they are called--arrive in the Holy City they at once set to work, some as porters and some as carriers of water in leather skins; others manufacture baskets and mats of date leaves; others establish a market for firewood, which they collect in the neighbouring hills. They inhabit miserable huts or ruined houses in the quarter of the lower classes, where the sellers of charcoal dwell and where locusts are sold by the measure. Some of these poor and industrious creatures spread their mats in the cloisters of the great Mosque, and stay all the time beneath that sacred and hospitable roof. They are subject to the exclamatory fits and pious convulsions so common among the negroes of the Southern States. Often they may be seen prostrate on the pavement, beating their foreheads against the stones, weeping bitterly, and pouring forth the wildest ejaculations.

The Great Mosque at Mecca is a spacious square surrounded by a colonnade. In the midst of the quadrangle is the small building called the Caaba. It has no windows; its door, which is seldom opened, is coated with silver; its padlock, once of pure gold, is now of silver gilt. On its threshold are placed every night various small wax candles and perfuming pans filled with aloeswood and musk. The walls of the building are covered with a veil of black silk, tucked up on one side, so as to leave exposed the famous Black Stone which is niched in the wall outside. The veil is not fastened close to the building, so that the least breath of air causes it to wave in slow, undulating movements, hailed with prayer by the kneeling crowd around. They believe that it is caused by the wings of guardian angels who will transport the Caaba to paradise when the last trumpet sounds.

At a little distance from this building is the Zemzem well, and while some of the pilgrims are standing by its mouth waiting to be served, or walking round the Caaba, or stooping to kiss the stone, other scenes may be observed in the cloisters and the square; and, as in the Temple at Jerusalem, these are not all of the most edifying nature. Children are playing at games, or feeding the wild pigeons whom long immunity has rendered tame. Numerous schools are going on, the boys chanting in a loud voice, and the master's baton sometimes falling on their backs. In another corner a religious lecture is being delivered. Men of all nations are clustered in separate groups--the Persian heretics, with their caps mounting to heaven and their beards descending to the earth; the Tartar, with oblique eyes and rounded limbs and light silk handkerchief tied round his brow; Turks with shaven faces and in red caps; the lean Indian pauper, begging with a miserable whine; and one or two wealthy Hindu merchants not guiltless of dinners given to infidels, and of iced champagne. At the same time an active business is being done in sacred keepsakes--rosaries made of camel bone, bottles of Zemzem water, dust collected from behind the veil, tooth-sticks made of a fibrous root such as that which Mohammed himself was wont to use, and coarsely executed pictures of the Caaba. Mecca itself, like most cities frequented by strangers, whether pilgrims or mariners, is not an abode of righteousness and virtue. As the Tartars say of it, "The Torch is dark at its foot," and many a pilgrim might exclaim with the Arabian Ovid; "I set out in the hopes of lightening my sins, And returned, bringing home with me a fresh load of transgressions."

But the very wickedness of a holy city deepens real enthusiasm into severity and wrath. When Abd-ul-Wahhab saw taverns opened in Mecca itself, and the inhabitants alluring the pilgrims to every kind of vice; when he found that the sacred places were made a show, that the mosque was inhabited by guides and officials who were as greedy as beasts of prey, that wealth, not piety, was the chief object of consideration in a pilgrim, he felt as Luther felt at Rome. The disgust which was excited in his mind by the manners of the day was extended also to the doctrines that were in vogue. The prayers that were offered up to Mohammed and the saints resembled the prayers that were once offered up to the Daughters of Heaven, the intercessors of the ancient Arabs. The pilgrimages that were made to the tombs of holy men were the old journeys to the ancestral graves. The worship of one God, which Mohammed had been sent to restore, had again become obscured; the days of darkness had returned. He preached a Unitarian revival; he held up as his standard and his guide the Koran, and nothing but the Koran; he founded a puritan sect which is now a hundred years of age, and still remains an element of power and disturbance in the East.

Othman Dan Fodio, the Black Prophet, also went out of Mecca, his soul burning with zeal. He determined to reform the Sudan. He forbade, like Abd-ul-Wahhab, the smoking of tobacco, the wearing of ornaments and finery. But he had to contend with more gross abuses still. In many negro lands which professed Islam, palm wine and millet beer were largely consumed; the women did not veil their faces nor even their bosoms; immodest dances were performed to the profane music of the drum; learned men gained a livelihood by writing charms, the code of the Koran was often supplanted by the old customary laws. Dan Fodio sent letters to the great kings of Timbuktu, Haoussa, and Bornu, commanding them to reform their own lives and those of their subjects, or he would chastise them in the name of God. They received these instructions from an unknown man, as the King of Kings received the letter of Mohammed, and their fate resembled his. Dan Fodio united the Fulah tribes into an army which he inspired with his own spirit. Thirsting for plunder and paradise, the Fulahs swept over the Sudan; they marched into battle with shouts of frenzied joy, singing hymns and waving their green flags on which texts of the Koran were embroidered in letters of gold. The empire which they established at the beginning of this century is now crumbling away, but the fire is still burning on the frontiers. Wherever the Fulahs are settled in the neighbourhood of pagan tribes they are extending their power, and although the immediate effects are disastrous--villages being laid in ashes, men slaughtered by thousands, women and children sold as slaves--yet in the end these crusades are productive of good. The villages are converted into towns; a new land is brought within the sphere of commercial and religious intercourse, and is added to the Asiatic world.

The phenomenon of a religious Tamerlane has been repeated more than once in Central Africa. The last example was that of Oumar the Pilgrim, whose capital was Segou, and whose conquests extended from Timbuktu to Senegal, where he came into contact with French artillery and for ever lost his prestige as a prophet. But we are taught by the science of history that these military empires can never long endure. It is probable that Mohammedan Sudan will in time become a province of the Turks. Central Africa, as we have shown, received its civilisation not from Egypt but from the grand Morocco of the Middle Ages. Egypt has always lived with its back to Africa, its eyes and often its hands on Syria and Arabia. Abyssinia was not subdued by the caliphs because it was not coveted by them, and there was little communication between Egypt and the Sudan. Mohammed Ali was the first to re-establish the kingdom of the Pharaohs in Ethiopia, and to organise negro regiments. Since his time the Turkish power has been gradually spreading towards the interior, and the expedition of Baker Pasha, whatever may be its immediate result, is the harbinger of great events to come. Should the Turks be driven out of Europe, they would probably become the emperors of Africa, which in the interests of civilisation would be a fortunate occurrence. The Turkish government is undoubtedly defective in comparison with the governments of Europe, but it is perfection itself in comparison with the governments of Africa. If the Egyptians had been allowed to conquer Abyssinia there would have been no need of an Abyssinian expedition, and nothing but Egyptian occupation will put an end to the wars which are always being waged and always have been waged in that country between bandit chiefs. Those who are anxious that Abyssinian Christianity should be preserved need surely not be alarmed, for the Pope of Abyssinia is the Patriarch of Cairo, a Turkish subject, and the aboona or archbishop has always been an Egyptian. But the Turks no longer have it in their power to commit actions which Europeans would condemn. They now belong to the civilised system; they are subject to the law of opinion. Already they have been compelled by that mysterious power to suppress the slave-making wars which were formerly waged every year from Kordofan and Sennaar, and which are still being waged from the independent kingdoms of Darfur, Waday, Bagirmi, and Bornu. Wherever the Turks reign a European is allowed to travel; wherever a European travels a word is spoken on behalf of the oppressed. That word enters the newspapers, passes into a diplomatic remonstrance, becomes a firman, and a governor or commandant in some sequestered province of an Oriental empire suffers the penalty of his misdeeds. It should be the policy of European Powers to aid the destruction of all savage kingdoms, or at least never to interfere on their behalf.

It has now been shown that a vast region within the Dark Continent, the world beyond the sandy ocean, is governed by Asiatic laws and has attained an Asiatic civilisation. We must next pass to the Atlantic side, and study the effects which have been produced among the negroes by the intercourse of Europeans. It will be found that the transactions on the coast of Guinea belong not only to the biography of Africa but also to universal history, and that the domestication of the negro has indirectly assisted the material progress of Europe and the development of its morality. The programme of the next chapter will be as follows: The rise of Europe out of darkness; the discovery of Western Africa by the Portuguese; the institution of the slave-trade, and the history of that great republican and philanthropic movement which won its first victory in the abolition of the slave-trade in 1807, its last in the taking of Richmond in 1865.

Chapter III. Liberty

Ancient Europe

The history of Europe in ancient times is the history of those lands which adjoin the Mediterranean Sea. Beyond the Alps lay a vast expanse of marsh and forest, through which flowed the swift and gloomy Rhine. On the right side of that river dwelt the Germans; on its left, the Celtic Gauls. Both people, in manners and customs, resembled the Red Indians. They lived in round wigwams, with a hole at the top to let out the smoke. They hunted the white-maned bison and the brown bear, and trapped the beaver, which then built its lodges by the side of every stream. They passed their spare time in gambling, drunkenness, and torpor; while their squaws cut the firewood, cultivated their garden-plots of grain, tended the shaggy-headed cattle, and the hogs feeding on acorns and beech-mast, obedient to the horn of the mistress, but savage to strangers as a pack of wolves. At an early period, however, the Gauls came into contact with the Phoenicians and the Greeks; they served in the Carthaginian armies, and acquired a taste for trade; they learnt the cultivation of the vine, and some of the metallic arts; their priests, or learned men, employed the Greek characters in writing. But the Gauls had a mania for martial glory, and often attacked the peaceful Greek merchants of Marseilles. The Greeks at last called in the assistance of the Romans, who not only made war on the hostile tribes, but on the peaceful tribes as well. Thus began the conquest of Gaul. It was completed by Caesar, who used that country as an exercise ground for his soldiers, and prepared them, by a hundred battles, for the mighty combat in which Pompey was overthrown.

Military roads were made across the Alps, Roman colonies were dispatched into the newly conquered land, Italian farmers took up their abode in the native towns, and the chiefs were required to send their sons to school. Thus the Romans obtained hostages, and the Celts were pleased to see their boys neatly dressed in white garments edged with purple, displaying their proficiency on the waxen tablets and the counting board. In a few generations the Celts had disappeared. On the banks of the Rhone and the Seine magnificent cities arose, watered by aqueducts, surrounded by gardens, adorned with libraries, temples, and public schools. The inhabitants called themselves Romans, and spoke with patriotic fervour of the glorious days of the Republic.

Meanwhile the barbarians beyond the Rhine remained in the savage state. They often crossed the river to invade the land which had ripened into wealth before their eyes: but the frontier was guarded by a chain of camps; and the Germans, armed only with clumsy spears and wooden shields, could not break the line of Roman soldiers, who were dressed in steel, who were splendidly disciplined, and who had military engines. The Gauls had once been a warlike people; they now abandoned the use of arms. The empire insured them against invasion in return for the taxes which they paid.

But there came a time when the tribute of the provinces no longer returned to the provinces to be expended on the public buildings and the frontier garrisons and the military roads. The rivers of gold which had so long flowed into Rome at last dried up: the empire became poor, and yet its expenses remained the same. The Praetorian Guards had still to be paid; the mob of the capital had still to be rationed with bread, and bacon, and wine, and oil, and costly shows. Accordingly the provinces were made to suffer. Exorbitant taxes were imposed: the aldermen and civil councillors of towns were compelled to pay enormous fees in virtue of their office, and were forbidden to evade such expensive honours by enlisting in the army, or by taking holy orders. The rich were accused of crimes that their property might be seized: the crops in the fields were gathered by the police. A blight fell upon the land. Men would no longer labour, since the fruits of their toil might at any time be taken from them. Cornfield and meadow were again covered with brambles and weeds; the cities were deserted; grass grew in all the streets. The province of Gaul was taxed to death, and then abandoned by the Romans. The government could no longer afford to garrison the Rhine frontier: the legions were withdrawn, and the Germans entered.

The German Invasion

The invading armies were composed of free men, who, under their respective captains or heads of clans, had joined the standard of some noted warrior chief. The spoil of the army belonged to the army, and was divided according to stipulated rules. The king's share was large, but more than his share he might not have. When the Germans, instead of returning with their booty, remained upon the foreign soil, they partitioned the land in the same manner as they partitioned the cattle and the slaves, the gold crosses, the silver chalices; the vases, the tapestry, the fine linen, and the purple robes. An immense region was allotted to the king; other tracts of various sizes to the generals and captains (or chiefs and chieftains) according to the number of men whom they had brought into the field; and each private soldier received a piece of ground. But the army, although disbanded, was not extinct; its members remained under martial law the barons or generals were bound to obey the king when he summoned them to war; the soldiers to obey their ancient chiefs. Sometimes the king and the great barons gave lands to favourites and friends on similar conditions, and at a later period money was paid instead of military service, thus originating rent.

The nobles of Roman Gaul lived within the city except during the villeggiatura in the autumn. The German lords preferred the country, and either fortified the Roman villas or built new castles of their own. They surrounded themselves with a bodyguard of personal retainers; their prisoners of war were made to till the ground as serfs. And soon they reduced to much the same condition the German soldiers, and seized their humble lands. In that troubled age none could hold property except by means of the strong arm. Men found it difficult to preserve their lives, and often presented their bodies to some powerful lord in return for protection, in return for daily bread. The power of the king was nominal: sovereignty was broken and dispersed: Europe was divided among castles: and in each castle was a prince who owned no authority above his own, who held a high court of justice in his hall, issued laws to his estates, lived by the court fees, by taxes levied on passing caravans, and by ransoms for prisoners, sometimes obtained in fair war, sometimes by falling upon peaceful travellers. Dark deeds were done within those ivy-covered towers which now exist for the pleasure of poets and pilgrims of the picturesque. Often from turret chambers and grated windows arose the shrieks of violated maidens and the yells of tortured Jews. Yet castle life had also its brighter side. To cheer the solitude of the isolated house minstrels and poets and scholars were courted by the barons, and were offered a peaceful chamber and a place of honour at the board. In the towns of ancient Italy and Greece there was no family: the home did not exist. The women and children dwelt together in secluded chambers: the men lived a club life in the baths, the porticoes, and the gymnasiums. But the castle lord had no companions of his own rank except the members of his own family. On stormy days, when he could not hunt, he found a pleasure in dancing his little ones upon his knee, and in telling them tales of the wood and weald. Their tender fondlings, and their merry laughs, their half formed voices, which attempted to pronounce his name--all these were sweet to him. And by the love of those in whom he saw his own image mirrored, in whom his own childhood appeared to live again, he was drawn closer and closer to his wife. She became his counsellor and friend; she softened his rugged manners; she soothed his fierce wrath; she pleaded for the prisoners and captives, and the men condemned to die. And when he was absent, she became the sovereign lady of the house, ruled the vassals, sat in the judgment-seat, and often defended the castle in time of siege. A charge so august could not but elevate the female mind. Women became queens. The Lady was created. Within the castle was formed that grand manner of gentleness, mingled with hauteur, which art can never stimulate, and which ages of dignity can alone confer.

The barons dwelt apart from one another, and were often engaged in private war. Yet they had sons to educate and daughters to marry; and so a singular kind of society arose. The king's house or court, and the houses of the great barons, became academies to which the inferior barons sent their boys and girls to school. The young lady became the attendant of the Dame, and was instructed in the arts of playing on the virginals, of preparing simples, and of healing wounds; of spinning, sewing, and embroidery. The young gentleman was at first a page. He was taught to manage a horse with grace and skill, to use bow and sword, to sound the notes of venerie upon the horn, to carve at table, to ride full tilt against the quintaine with his lance in rest, to brittle a deer, to find his way through the forest by the stars in the sky and by the moss upon the trees. It was also his duty to wait upon the ladies, who tutored his youthful mind in other ways. He was trained to deport himself with elegance; he was nurtured in all the accomplishments of courtesy and love. He was encouraged to select a mistress among the dames or demoiselles; to adore her in his heart, to serve her with patience and fidelity, obeying her least commands; to be modest in her presence; to be silent and discreet. The reward of all this devotion was of no ethereal kind, but it was not quickly or easily bestowed; and vice almost ceases to be vice when it can only be gratified by means of long discipline in virtue. When the page had arrived at a certain age, he was clad in a brown frock; a sword was fastened to his side, and he obtained the title of Esquire. He attended his patron knight on military expeditions, until he was old enough to be admitted to the order. Among the ancient Germans of the forest, when a young man came of age, he was solemnly invested with shield and spear. The ceremony of knighthood at first was nothing more than this. Every man of gentle birth became a knight, and then took an oath to be true to God and to the ladies and to his plighted word; to be honourable in all his actions, to succour the oppressed. Thus, within those castle-colleges arose the sentiment of Honour, the institution of Chivalry, which, as an old poet wrote, made women chaste and men brave. The women were worshipped as goddesses, the men were revered as heroes. Each sex aspired to possess those qualities which the other sex approved. Women admire, above all things, courage and truth; and so the men became courageous and true. Men admire modesty, virtue, and refinement; and so the women became virtuous, and modest, and refined. A higher standard of propriety was required as time went on: the manners and customs of the Dark Ages became the vices of a later period; unchastity, which had once been regarded as the private wrong of the husband, was stigmatised as a sin against society; and society found a means of taking its revenge. At first the notorious woman was insulted to her face at tournament and banquet; or knights chalked an epithet upon her castle gates, and then rode on. In the next age she was shunned by her own sex: the discipline of social life was established as it exists at the present day. Though it might sometimes be relaxed in a vicious court, at least the ideal of right was preserved. But in the period of the Troubadours the fair sinners resembled the pirates of the Homeric age. Their pursuits were of a dangerous, but not of a dishonourable nature: they might sometimes lose their lives; they never lost their reputation.

The Castle

We must now descend from ladies and gentlemen to the people in the field, who are sometimes forgotten by historians. The castle was built on the summit of a hill, and a village of serfs was clustered round its foot. These poor peasants were often hardly treated by their lords. Often they raised their brown and horny hands and cursed the cruel castle which scowled upon them from above. Humbly they made obeisance, and bitterly they gnawed their lips as the baron rode down the narrow street on his great war-horse, which would always have its fill of corn, when they would starve, followed by his beef-fed varlets with faces red from beer, who gave them jeering looks, who called them by nicknames, who contemptuously caressed their daughters before their eyes. Yet it was not always thus: the lord was often a true nobleman, the parent of their village, the god-father of their children, the guardian of their happiness, the arbiter of their disputes. When there was sickness among them, the ladies of the castle often came down, bringing them soups and spiced morsels with their own white hands; and the castle was the home of the good chaplain, who told them of the happier world beyond the grave. It was there also that they enjoyed such pleasures as they had. Sometimes they were called up to the castle to feast on beef and beer in commemoration of a happy anniversary or a Christian feast. Sometimes their lord brought home a caravan of merchants whom he had captured on the road and while the strange guests were quaking for the safety of their bales, the people were being amused with the songs of the minstrels, and the tricks of the jugglers, and the antics of the dancing bear. And sometimes a tournament was held: the lords and ladies of the neighbourhood rode over to the castle; turf banks were set for the serfs and a gallery was erected for the ladies, above whom sat enthroned the one who was chosen as the Queen of Beauty and of Love. Then the heralds shouted, "Love of ladies, splintering of lances! stand forth, gallant knights; fair eyes look upon your deeds!" And the knights took up their position in two lines fronting one another, and sat motionless upon their horses like pillars of iron, with nothing to be seen but their flaming eyes. The trumpets flourished: "Laissez aller!" cried a voice; and the knights, with their long spears in rest, dashed furiously against each other, and then plied battle-axe and sword, to the great delight and contentment of the populace.

In times of war the castle was also the refuge of the poor, and the villagers fled behind its walls when the enemy drew near. They did not then reflect that it was the castle which had provoked the war; they viewed it only as a hospitable fortress which had saved their lives. It was therefore, in many cases, regarded by the people not only with awe and veneration, but also with a sentiment of filial love. It was associated with their pleasures and their security. But in course of time a rival arose to alienate the affections, or to strengthen the resentment of the castle serfs. It was the Town.

In the days of the Republic and in the first days of the Empire, all kinds of skilled labour were in the hands of slaves: in every palace, whatever was required for the household was manufactured on the premises. But before the occupation of the Germans, a free class of artisans had sprung up, in what manner is not precisely known; they were probably the descendants of emancipated slaves. This class, divided into guilds and corporations, continued to inhabit the towns: they manufactured armour and clothes they travelled as pedlars about the country, and thus acquired wealth, which they cautiously concealed, for they were in complete subservience to the castle lord. They could not leave their property by will, dispose of their daughters in marriage, or perform a single business transaction without the permission of their liege. But little by little their power increased. When war was being waged, it became needful to fortify the town; for the town was the baron's estate, and he did not wish his property to be destroyed. When once the burghers were armed and their town walled they were able to defy their lord. They obtained charters, sometimes by revolt, sometimes by purchase, which gave them the town to do with it as they pleased; to elect their own magistrates, to make their own laws, and to pay their liege lord a fixed rent by the year instead of being subjected to loans and benevolences, and loving contributions. The Roman Law, which had never quite died out, was now revived; the old municipal institutions of the Empire were restored. Unhappily the citizens often fought among themselves, and towns joined barons in destroying towns. Yet their influence rapidly increased, and the power of the castle was diminished. Whenever a town received privileges from its lord, other towns demanded that the same rights should be embodied in their charters, and rebelled if their request was refused. Trade and industry expanded; the products of burgher enterprise and skill were offered in the castle halls for sale. The lady was tempted with silk and velvet; the lord, with chains of gold, and Damascus blades, and suits of Milan steel; the children clamoured for the sweet white powder which was brought from the countries of the East. These new tastes and fancies impoverished the nobles. They reduced their establishments; and the discarded retainers, in no sweet temper, went over to the Town.

The Town

And there were others who went to the Town as well. In classical times the slaves were unable to rebel with any prospect of success. In the cities of Greece every citizen was a soldier: in Rome an enormous army served as the slave police. But in the scattered castle states of Europe, the serfs could rise against their lords, and often did so with effect. And then the Town was always a place of refuge: the runaway slave was there welcomed; his pursuers were duped or defied; the file was applied to his collar; his blue blouse was taken off; his hair was suffered to grow; he was made a burgher and a free man. Thus the serfs had often the power to rebel, and always the power to escape; in consequence of which they ceased to be serfs and became tenants. In our own times we have seen emancipation presented to slaves by a victorious party in the House of Commons, and by a victorious army in the United States. It has, therefore, been inferred that slavery in Europe was abolished in the same manner, and the honour of the movement has been bestowed upon the Church. But this is reading history upside down. The extinction of villeinage was not a donation but a conquest: it did not descend from the court and the castle; it ascended from the village and the town. The Church, however, may claim the merit of having mitigated slavery in its worst days, when its horrors were increased by the pride of conquest and the hostility of race. The clergy belonged to the conquered people, whom they protected from harsh usage to the best of their ability. They taught as the Moslem doctors also teach, and as even the pagan Africans believe, that it is a pious action to emancipate a slave. But there is no reason to suppose that they ever thought of abolishing slavery, and they could not have done so had they wished. Negro slavery was established by subjects of the Church in defiance of the Church. Religion has little power when it works against the stream, but it can give to streams a power which they otherwise would not possess, and it can unite their scattered waters into one majestic flood.

Rome was taken and sacked but never occupied by the barbarians. It still belonged to the Romans: it still preserved the traditions and the genius of empire. Whatever may have been the origin of British or Celtic Christianity, it is certain that the English were converted by the Papists; the first Archbishop of Canterbury was an Italian; his converts became missionaries, entered the vast forests of pagan Germany, and brought nations to the feet of Rome. The alliance of Pepin and the Roman See placed also the French clergy under the dominion of the Pope, who was acknowledged by Alcuin, the adherent of Charlemagne, to be the "Pontiff of God, vicar of the apostles, heir of the fathers, prince of the Church, guardian of the only dove without stain."

The Church

The ordinance of clerical celibacy increased the efficacy of the priesthood and the power of the Pope. The ranks of the clergy were recruited, generation after generation, from the most intelligent of the lay men in the lower classes, and from those among the upper classes who were more inclined to intellectual pursuits than to military life. These men, divided as they were from family connections, ceased to be Germans, Englishmen, or Frenchmen, and became catholic or universal-hearted men, patriots of religion, children of the Church. And those enthusiastic laymen who had adopted an ascetic isolated life, or had gathered together in voluntary associations; those hermits and monks, who might have been so dangerous to the Established Church, were welcomed as allies. No mean jealousy in the Roman Church divided the priest and the prophet, as among the ancient Jews; the mullah and the dervish, as in the East at the present time. The monks were allowed to preach, and to elect their own monastery priests; they were gradually formed into regular orders, and brought within the discipline of ecclesiastic law. The monks of the East, who could live on a handful of beans, passed their lives in weaving baskets, in prayer and meditation. But the monks of the West, who lived in a colder climate, required a different kind of food; and as at first they had no money, they could obtain it only by means of work.

They laboured in the fields in order to live and that which had arisen from necessity was continued as a part of the monastic discipline. There were also begging friars, who journeyed from land to land. These were the first travellers in Europe. Their sacred character preserved their lives from all robbers, whether noble or plebeian, and the same exemption was accorded to those who put on the pilgrim's garb. The smaller pilgrimage was that to Rome the greater that to the Holy Land, by which the palmers obtained remission of their sins, and also were shown by the monks of Egypt, Sinai, and Palestine, many interesting relics and vestiges of supernatural events. They were shown the barns which Joseph had built, vulgarly called the Pyramids; the bush which had burnt before Moses and was not consumed, and the cleft out of which he peeped at the "back parts" of Jehovah; the pillar of salt which was once Lot's wife, and which, though the sheep continually licked it out of shape, was continually restored to its pristine form; the ruins of the temple which Samson overthrew; the well where Jesus used to draw water for his mother when he was a little boy, and where she used to wash his clothes; the manger in which he was born, and the table on which he was circumcised; the caves in which his disciples concealed themselves during the crucifixion, and the cracks in the ground produced by the earthquake, which followed that event; the tree on which Judas hanged himself, and the house in which he resided, which was surrounded by the Jews with a wall that it might not be injured by the Christians.

It was not only the rich who undertook this pilgrimage; many a poor man begged his way to the Holy Land. When such a person was ready to depart, the village pastor clad him in a cloak of coarse black serge, with a broad hat upon his head, put a long staff in his hand, and hung round him a scarf and script. He was conducted to the borders of the parish in solemn procession, with cross and holy water the neighbours parted from him there with tears and benedictions. He returned with cockle-shells stitched in his hat, as a sign that he had been across the seas, and with a branch of palm tied on to his staff, as a sign that he had been to Jerusalem itself. He often brought also relics and beads; a bag of dust to hang at the bedside of the sick; a phial of oil from the lamp which hung over the Holy Sepulchre, and perhaps a splinter of the true cross.

When the Saracens conquered Palestine and Egypt, they did not destroy the memorials of Jesus, for they reverenced him as a prophet. Pious Moslems made also the pilgrimage to Jerusalem; and the Christians were surprised and edified to see the turbaned infidels removing their sandals like Moses on Mount Sinai, and prostrating themselves upon the pavement before the tomb. The caliphs were sufficiently enlightened to encourage and protect the foreign enthusiasts who filled the land with gold; and although the palmers were exempt from "passage" and "pontage" and other kinds of blackmail levied by the barons on lay travellers, they found it more easy and more safe to travel in Asia than in Europe. The passion for the pilgrimage to Palestine, which had gradually increased since the days of Helena and Jerome, burst forth as an epidemic at the close of the tenth century. The thousand years assigned in Revelation as the lifetime of the earth were about to expire. It was believed that Jesus would appear in Jerusalem, and there hold a grand assize: thousands bestowed their property upon the Church, and crowded to the Holy Land.

While they thus lived at Jerusalem and waited for the second coming, continually looking up at the sky and expecting it to open, there came instead a host of men with yellow faces and oblique slit-shaped eyes, who took the Holy City by assault, drove the Arabs out of Syria, killed many pilgrims, stripped them of all their money, and if they found none outside their bodies, probed them with daggers, or administered emetics in the hope of finding some within. When the pilgrims returned, they related their sufferings, and showed their scars. The anger of Christendom was aroused. A crusade was preached, and the enthusiasm which everywhere prevailed enabled the Church to exercise unusual powers. The Pope decreed that the men of the cross should be hindered by none. Creditor might not arrest; master might not detain. To those who joined the army of the Church, absolution was given; and paradise was promised in the Moslem style to those who died in the campaign. The tidings flew from castle to castle, and from town to town; there was not a land, however remote, which escaped the infection of the time. In the homely language of the monk of Malmesbury, "the Welshman left his hunting, the Scotch his fellowship with vermin, the Dane his drinking party, the Norwegian his raw fish." Europe was torn up from its foundations and hurled upon Asia. Society was dissolved. Monks, not waiting for the permission of their superiors, cast off their black gowns and put on the buff jerkin, the boots and the sword. The serf left his plough in the furrow, the shepherd left his flock in the field. Men servants and maid servants ran from the castle. Wives insisted upon going with their husbands, and if their husbands refused to take them, went with some one else. Murderers, robbers, and pirates declared that they would wash out their sins in pagan blood. In some cases, the poor rustic shod his oxen like horses, and placed his whole family in a cart, and whenever he came to a castle or a town, inquired whether that was Jerusalem. The barons sold or mortgaged their estates, indifferent about the future, hoping to win the wealth of Eastern princes with the sword. During two hundred years, the natives of Europe appeared to have no other object than to conquer or to keep possession of the Holy Land.

The Christian knights were at length driven out of Asia; in the meantime, Europe was transformed. The kings had taken no part in the first crusades; the estates of the barons had been purchased partly by them, and partly by the burghers. An alliance was made between Crown and Town. The sovereignty of the castle was destroyed. Judges appointed by the king travelled on circuit through the land; the Roman law, from being municipal became national; the barons became a nobility residing chiefly at the court; the middle class came into life. The burghers acknowledged no sovereign but the king: they officered their own trainbands; they collected their own taxes; they were represented in a national assembly at the capital. New tastes came into vogue; both mind and body were indulged with dainty foods. The man of talent, whatever his station, might hope to be ennobled; the honour of knighthood was reserved by the king, and bestowed upon civilians. The spices of the East, the sugar of Egypt and Spain, the silk of Greece and the islands were no longer occasional luxuries, but requirements of daily life. And since it was considered unworthy of a gentleman to trade, the profits of commerce were monopolised by the third estate. Education was required for mercantile pursuits; it was at first given by the priests who had previously taught laymen only to repeat the paternoster and the credo, and to pay tithes. Schools were opened in the towns, and universities became secular. The rich merchants took a pride in giving their sons the best education that money could obtain, and these young men were not always disposed to follow commercial pursuits. They adopted the study of the law, cultivated the fine arts, made experiments in natural philosophy, and were often sent by their parents to study in the land beyond the Alps, where they saw something which was in itself an education for the burgher mind--merchants dwelling in palaces, seated upon thrones, governing great cities, commanding fleets and armies, negotiating on equal terms with the proudest and most powerful monarchs of the North.

Italy, protected by its mountain barrier, had not been so frequently flooded by barbarians as the provinces of Gaul and Spain. The feudal system was there established in a milder form, and the cities retained more strength. Soon they were able to attack the castle lords, to make them pull down their towers, and to live like peaceable citizens within the walls. The Emperor had little power; Florence, Genoa, and Pisa grew into powerful city-states resembling those of Italy before the rise of ancient Rome, but possessing manufactures which, in the time of ancient Italy, had been confined to Egypt, China, and Hindustan.

Venice

The origin of Venice was different from that of its sister states. In the darkest days of Italy, when a horde of savage Huns, with scalps dangling from the trappings of their horses, poured over the land, some citizens of Padua and other adjoining towns took refuge in a cluster of islands in the lagoons which were formed at the mouths of the Adige and the Po. From Rialto, the chief of these islands, it was three miles to the mainland; a mile and a half to the sandy breakwater which divided the lagoons from the Adriatic. At high water the islands appeared to be at sea; but when the tide declined, they rose up from the midst of a dark green plain in which blue gashes were opened by the oar. But even at high water the lagoons were too shallow to be entered by ships--except through certain tortuous and secret channels; and even at low water they were too deep to be passed on foot. Here, then, the Venetians were secure from their foes, like the lake-dwellers of ancient times.

At first they were merely salt-boilers and fishermen, and were dependent on the mainland for the materials of life. There was no seaport in the neighbourhood to send its vessels for the salt which they prepared: they were forced to fetch everything that they required for themselves. They became seamen by necessity: they almost lived upon the water. As their means improved, and as their wants expanded, they bought fields and pastures on the mainland; they extended their commerce, and made long voyages. They learnt in the dockyards of Constantinople the art of building tall ships; they conquered the pirates of the Adriatic Sea. The princes of Syria, Egypt, Barbary, and Spain were all of them merchants, for commerce is an aristocratic occupation in the East. With them the Venetians opened up a trade. At first they had only timber and slaves to offer in exchange for the wondrous fabrics and rare spices of the East. In raw produce Europe is no match for Asia. The Venetians, therefore, were driven to invent; they manufactured furniture and woollen cloth, armour, and glass. It is evident, from the old names of the streets, that Venice formerly was one great workshop; it was also a great market city. The crowds of pilgrims resorting to Rome to visit the tombs of the martyrs, and to kiss the Pope's toe, had suggested to the Government the idea of fairs which were held within the city at stated times. The Venetians established a rival fair in honour of St. Mark, whose remains, revered even by the Moslems, had been smuggled out of Alexandria in a basket of pork. They took their materials, like Moliere, wherever they could find them--stole the corpse of a patriarch from Constantinople, and the bones of a saint from Milan. They made religion subservient to commerce: they declined to make commerce subservient to religion. The Pope forbade them to trade with infidels: but the infidel, trade was their life. Siamo Veneziani poi Cristiani, they replied. The Papal nuncios arrived in Venice, and excommunicated two hundred of the leading men. In return they were ordered to leave the town. The fleets of the Venetians, like the Phoenicians of old, sailed in all the European waters, from the wheat fields of the Crimea to the ice-creeks of the Baltic. In that sea the pirates were at length extinct; a number of cities along its shores were united in a league. Bruges in Flanders was the emporium of the Northern trade, and was supplied by Venetian vessels with the commodities of the South. The Venetians also travelled over Europe, and established their financial colonies in all great towns. The cash of Europe was in their hands; and the sign of three golden balls declared that Lombards lent money within.

During the period of the Crusades, their trade with the East was interrupted but it was exchanged for a commerce more profitable still. The Venetians in their galleys conveyed the armies to the Holy Land, and also supplied them with provisions. Besides the heavy sums which they exacted for such services, they made other stipulations. Whenever a town was taken by the Crusaders, a suburb or street was assigned to the Venetians; and when the Christians were expelled, the Moslems consented to continue the arrangement. In all the great Eastern cities, there was a Venetian quarter containing a chapel, a bath-house, and a factory ruled over by a magistrate or consul.

Constantinople, during the Crusades, had been taken by the Latins, with the assistance of the Venetians, and had been recovered by the Greeks, with the assistance of the Genoese. The Venetians were expelled from the Black Sea, but obtained the Alexandria trade. In the fifteenth century the Black Sea was ruined, for its caravan routes were stopped by the Turkish wars. Egypt, which was supplied by sea, monopolised the India trade, and the Venetians monopolised the trade of Egypt. Venice became the nutmeg and pepper shop of Europe: not a single dish could be seasoned, not a tankard of ale could be spiced, without adding to its gains. The wealth of that city soon became enormous; its power, south of the Alps, supreme.

Times had changed since those poor fugitives first crept in darkness and sorrow on the islands of the wild lagoon, and drove stakes into the sand, and spread the reeds of the ocean for their bed. Around them the dark lone waters, sighing, soughing, and the sea-bird's melancholy cry. Around them the dismal field of slime, the salt and sombre plain. On that cluster of islands had arisen a city of surpassing loveliness and splendour. Great ships lay at anchor in its marble streets; their yards brushed sculptured balconies, and the walls of palaces as they swept along. Branching off from the great thoroughfares, bustling with commerce, magnificent with pomp, were sweet and silent lanes of water, lined with summer palaces and with myrtle gardens, sloping downwards to the shore. In the fashionable quarter was a lake-like space--the Park of Venice--which every evening was covered with gondolas; and the gondoliers in those days were slaves from the East, Saracens or Negroes, who sang sadly as they rowed, the music of their homes--the camel-song of the Sahara, or the soft minor airs of the Sudan.

The government of Venice was a rigid aristocracy. Venice therefore has no Santa Croce; it can boast of few illustrious names. However, its Aldine Press and its poems in colour were not unworthy contributions to the revival of ancient learning and the creation of modern art. The famous wanderings of Marco Polo had also excited among learned Venetians a peculiar taste for the science of exploration. All over Europe they corresponded with scholars of congenial tastes, and urged those princes who had ships at their disposal to undertake voyages of enterprise and discovery. Among their correspondents there was one who carried out their ideas too well. Venice was not so much injured by the potentates who assembled at Cambrai as by a single man who lived in a lonely spot on the south-west coast of the Spanish peninsula.

Arab Spain

That country had been taken from the natives by the Carthaginians, from the Carthaginians by the Romans, from the Romans by the Goths, from the Goths by the Arabs and the Moors. It was the first province of the Holy Empire of the Caliphs to shake itself free, and to crown a monarch of its own. The Arabs raised Spain to a height of prosperity which it has never since attained; they covered the land with palaces, mosques, hospitals, and bridges; and with enormous aqueducts which, penetrating the sides of mountains, or sweeping on lofty arches across valleys, rivalled the monuments of ancient Rome. The Arabs imported various tropical fruits and vegetables, the culture of which has departed with them. They grew, prepared, and exported sugar. They discovered new mines of gold and silver, quicksilver and lead. They extensively manufactured silks, cottons, and merino woollen goods, which they despatched to Constantinople by sea, and which were thence diffused through the valley of the Danube over savage Christendom. When Italians began to navigate the Mediterranean, a line of ports was opened to them from Tarragona to Cadiz. The metropolis of this noble country was Cordova. It stood in the midst of a fertile plain washed by the waters of the Guadalquivir. It was encircled by suburban towns; there were ten miles of lighted streets. The great mosque was one of the wonders of the mediaeval world; its gates embossed with bronze; its myriads of lamps made out of Christian bells; and its thousand columns of variegated marble supporting a roof of richly carved and aromatic wood. At a time when books were so rare in Europe that the man who possessed one often gave it to a church, and placed it on the altar pro remedio animae suae, to obtain remission of his sins; at a time when three or four hundred parchment scrolls were considered a magnificent endowment for the richest monastery: when scarcely a priest in England could translate Latin into his mother tongue; and when even in Italy a monk who had picked up a smattering of mathematics was looked upon as a magician, here was a country in which every child was taught to read and write; in which every town possessed a public library; in which book collecting was a mania; in which cotton and afterwards linen paper was manufactured in enormous quantities; in which ladies earned distinction as poets and grammarians, and in which even the blind were often scholars; in which men of science were making chemical experiments, using astrolabes in the observatory, inventing flying machines, studying the astronomy and algebra of Hindustan.

When the Goths conquered Spain they were reconquered by the clergy, who established or revived the Roman Law. But to that excellent code they added some special enactments relating to pagans, heretics, and Jews. With nations as with individuals, the child is often the father of the man; intolerance, which ruined the Spain of Philip, was also its vice, in the Gothic days. On the other hand, the prosperity of Spain beneath the Arabs was owing to the tolerant spirit of that people. Never was a conquered nation so mercifully treated. The Christians were allowed by the Arab laws free exercise of their religion. They were employed at court; they held office; they served in the army. The caliph had a bodyguard of twelve thousand men; picked troops, splendidly equipped; and a third of these were Christians. But there were some ecclesiastics who taught their congregations that it was sinful to be tolerated. There were fanatics who, when they heard the cry of the muezzin, "There is no God but God, and Mohammed is the messenger of God," would sign the cross upon their foreheads and exclaim in a loud voice, "Keep not thou silence, O God, for lo! thine enemies make a tumult, and they that hate thee have lifted up the head"; and so they would rush into the mosque, and disturb the public worship, and announce that Mohammed was one of the false prophets whom Christ had foretold. And when such blasphemers were put to death, which often happened on the spot, there was an epidemic of martyr-suicide such as that which excited the wonder and disgust of the younger Pliny. And soon both the contumacy of the Christians and the evil passions of the Moslems, which that contumacy excited, were increased by causes from without. When Spain had first been conquered, a number of Gothic nobles, too proud to submit on any terms, retreated to the Asturias, taking with them the sacred relics from Toledo. They found a home in mountain ravines clothed with chestnut woods, and divided by savage torrents foaming and gnashing on the stones. Here the Christians established a kingdom, discovered the bones of a saint which attracted pilgrims from all parts of Europe, and were joined from time to time by foreign volunteers, and by the disaffected from the Moorish towns.

The Caliph of Cordova was a Commander of the Faithful: he united the spiritual and temporal powers in his own person: he was not the slave of Mamelukes or Turkish guards. But he had the right of naming his successor from a numerous progeny, and this custom gave rise, as usual, to seraglio intrigue and civil war. The empire broke up into petty states, which were engaged in continual feuds with one another. Thus the Christians were enabled to invade the Moslem territory with success. At first they made only plundering forays; next they took castles by surprise or by storm and garrisoned them strongly; and then they began slowly to advance upon the land. By the middle of the ninth century they had reached the Douro and the Ebro. By the close of the eleventh they had reached the Tagus under the banner of the Cid. In the thirteenth century the kingdom of Granada alone was left. But that kingdom lasted two hundred years. Its existence was preserved by causes similar to those which had given the Christians their success. Portugal, Arragon, Leon, and Castile were more jealous of one another than of the Moorish kingdom. Granada was unaggressive; and at the same time it belonged to the European family. There was a difference in language, religion, and domestic institutions between Moslem and Christian Spain; yet the manners and mode of thought in both countries were the same. The cavaliers of Granada were acknowledged by the Spaniards to be "gentlemen, though Moors." The Moslem knight cultivated the sciences of courtesy and music, fought only with the foe on equal terms, esteemed it a duty to side with the weak and to succour the distressed, mingled the name of his mistress with his Allah Akbar! as the Christians cried, Ma Dame et mon Dieu! wore in her remembrance an embroidered scarf or some other gage of love, mingled with her in the graceful dance of the Zambra, serenaded her by moonlight as she looked down from the balcony. Granada was defended by a cavalry of gallant knights, and by an infantry of sturdy mountaineers. But it came to its end at last. The marriage of Ferdinand and Isabella united all the crowns of Spain. After eight centuries of almost incessant war, after three thousand seven hundred battles, the long crusade was ended; Spain became once more a Christian land; and Boabdil, pausing on the Hill of Tears, looked down for the last time on the beautiful Alhambra, on the city nestling among rose gardens, and the dark cypress waving over Moslem tombs. His mother reproached him for weeping as a woman for the kingdom he had not defended as a man. He rode down to the sea and crossed over into Africa. But that country also was soon to be invaded by the Christians.

The Portuguese Discoveries

That part of the Peninsula which is called Portugal preserved its independence and its dialect from the encroachments of Castile. While the kingdom of Granada was yet alive, the Portuguese monarch, having driven the Moors from the banks of the Tagus, resolved to pursue them into Africa. He possessed an excellent crusade machinery, and naturally desired to apply it to some purpose. In Portugal were troops of military monks, who had sworn to fight with none but unbelievers. In Portugal were large revenues granted or bequeathed for that purpose alone. In Portugal the passion of chivalry was at its height; the throne was surrounded by knights panting for adventure. It is related that some ladies of the English court had been grossly insulted by certain cavaliers, and had been unable to find champions to redress their wrongs. An equal number of Portuguese knights at once took ship, sailed to London, flung down their gauntlets, overthrew their opponents in the lists, and returned to Lisbon having received from the injured ladies the tenderest proof of their gratitude and esteem.

It seems that already there had risen between Portugal and England that diplomatic friendship which has lasted to the present day. A commerce of wine for wool was established between the ports of the Tagus and the Thames; and with this commerce the pirates of Ceuta continually interfered. Ceuta was one of the pillars of Hercules: it sat opposite Gibraltar, and commanded the straits. The King of Portugal prepared a fleet; great war-galleys were built having batteries of mangonels or huge crossbows, with winding gear, stationed in the bow; great beams, like battering rams; swung aloft; and jars of quicklime and soft soap to fling in the faces of the enemy. The fleet sailed forth, rustling with flags, beating drums, and, blowing Saracen horns; the passage to Ceuta was happily made; the troops were landed, and the pirate city taken by assault.

Among those who distinguished themselves in this exploit was the Prince Henry, a younger son of the king. He was not only a brave knight, but also a distinguished scholar; his mind had been enriched by a study of the works of Cicero, Seneca, and Pliny, and by the Latin translations of the Greek geographers. He now stepped on that mysterious continent which had been closed to Christians for several hundred years. He questioned the prisoners respecting the interior. They described the rich and learned cities of Morocco: the Atlas mountains, shining with snow and the sandy desert on their southern side. It was there the ancients had supposed all life came to an end. But now the Prince received the astounding intelligence that beyond the Sahara was a land inhabited entirely by negroes; covered with fields of corn and cotton watered by majestic rivers, on the banks of which rose cities as large as Morocco, or Lisbon, or Seville. In that country were gold mines of prodigious wealth; it was also a granary of slaves. By land it could be reached in a week from Morocco by a courier mounted on the swift dromedary of the desert, which halted not by day or night. There were regular caravans or camel fleets, which passed to and fro at certain seasons of the year. The Black Country, as they called it, could also be reached by sea. If ships sailed along the desert shore towards the south, they would arrive at the mouths of wide rivers, which flowed down from the gold-bearing hills.

This conversation decided Prince Henry's career. To discover this new world beyond the desert became the object of his life. He was Grand Master of the Order of Christ, and had ample revenues at his disposal and he considered himself justified in expending them on this enterprise which would result in the conversion of many thousand pagans to the

Christian faith. He retired to a castle near Cape St. Vincent, where the sight of the ocean continually inflamed his thoughts. It was a cold, bleak headland, with a few juniper trees scattered here and there: all other vegetation had been withered by the spray. But Prince Henry was not alone. He invited learned men from all countries to reside with him. He established a court, in which weather-beaten pilots might discourse with German mathematicians and Italian cosmographers. He built an observatory, and founded a naval school. He collected a library, in which might be read the manuscript of Marco Polo, which his elder brother had brought from Venice; copies on vellum of the great work of Ptolemy; and copies also of Herodotus, Strabo, and other Greek writers, which were being rapidly translated into Latin under the auspices of the Pope at Rome. He had also a collection of maps and sea-charts engraved on marble or on metal tables, and painted upon parchment. At a little distance from the castle were the harbour and town of Sagres, from which the vessels of the Prince went forth with the cross of the order painted on their sails.

They sailed down the coast of the Sahara; on their right was a sea of darkness, on their left a land of fire. The gentlemen of the household who commanded the ships did not believe in the country of green trees beyond the ocean of sand. Instead of pushing rapidly along, they landed as soon as they detected any signs of the natives--the old people of Masinissa and Jugurtha--attacked them crying, Portugal! Portugal! and having taken a few prisoners returned home. In every expedition the commander made it a point of honour to go a little further than the preceding expedition. Several years thus passed, and the Black Country had not been found. The Canary Islands were already known to the Spaniards: but the Portuguese discovered Porto Santo and Madeira. A shipload of emigrants was despatched to the former island, and among the passengers was a female rabbit in an interesting situation. She was turned down with her young ones on the island, and, there being no checks to rabbit population, they increased with such rapidity that they devoured every green thing, and drove the colonists across into Madeira. In that island the colonists were more fortunate; instead of importing rabbits they introduced the vine from Cyprus, and the sugar cane from Sicily; and soon Madeira wine and sugar were articles of export from Lisbon to London and to other ports. In the meantime the expeditions to Africa became exceedingly unpopular. The priests declared that the holy money was being scandalously wasted on the dreams of a lonely madman. That castle on the Atlantic shore, which will ever be revered as a sacred place in the annals of mankind, was then regarded with abhorrence and contempt. The common people believed it to be the den of a magician, and crossed themselves in terror when they met in their walks a swarthy strong-featured man, with a round barret cap on his head, wrapped in a large mantle, and wearing black buskins with gilt spurs. Often they saw him standing on the brink of the cliff, gazing earnestly towards the sea, his eyes shaded by his hand. It was said that on fair nights he might be seen for hours and hours on the tower of Babel which he had built, holding a strange weapon in his hands, and turning it towards the different quarters of the sky.

There was an orthodox geography at that period founded upon statements in the Jewish writings, and in the Fathers of the Church. The earth was in the centre of the universe; the sun and the moon and the stars humbly revolving round it. Jerusalem was in the precise centre of the earth. In Eastern India was the Terrestrial Paradise, situated on high ground, and surrounded by a wall of fire, reaching to the sky. St. Augustine, Lactantius, and Cosmas Indicopleustes opposed the Antipodes as being contrary to Scripture; and there could not be people on the other side of the earth, for how would they be able to see the Son of God descending in his glory? It was also generally believed that there was a torrid zone, an impassable belt on both sides of the equator, which Providence had created for the lower animals, and in which no man could live. It was to this fiery land that the Prince kept sending vessel after vessel. The Portuguese did not see what would come of these expeditions except to make widows and orphans. "The Prince seems to think," said they, "that because he has discovered two desert islands he has conferred a great blessing upon us but we have enough uncultivated land without going across the seas for more. His own father, only a little while ago, gave land to a nobleman of Germany, on condition that he should people it with emigrants. But Dom Henry sends men out of Portugal instead of asking them in. Let us keep to the country that God has given us. It may be seen how much better suited those lands are for beasts than men by what happened with the rabbits. And even if there are in that unfound land as many people as the Prince pretends, we do not know what sort of people they are; and if they are like those in the Canaries who jump from rock to rock, and throw stones at Christian heads, of what use is it to conquer a land so barren, and a people so contemptible?"

However, an incident occurred which produced a revolution in popular and ecclesiastic feeling. The prisoners captured on the desert coast offered a ransom for their release and this ransom consisted of negro slaves and gold. The place where this metal first made its appearance was called the Golden River. It was not in reality a river but an arm of the sea, and the gold had been brought from the mines of Bambouk in the country of the negroes. Its discovery created an intense excitement: the priests acknowledged that it could not have been placed there for the use of the wild animals. Companies were formed and were licensed by the Crown, which assigned to the Prince a fifth part of the cargoes returned. He himself cared little for the gold but the discovery of this precious metal, of which India was proverbially the native land, suggested the idea that by following the coast of Africa the Indies might be reached by sea. Letters and maps which he received from his Venetian correspondents encouraged him in this belief, and he obtained without delay a Bull from the Pope granting to the Crown of Portugal all lands that its subjects might discover as far as India inclusive, with license to trade with infidels, and absolution for the souls of those that perished in these semi-commercial, semi-crusading expeditions.

The practice of piracy was now partly given up: the Portuguese, like the Phoenicians of old, traded in one place and kidnapped in another. The commodities which they brought home were gold dust, seal skins, and negroes. Yet still they did not reach the negro land, till at last a merchant of Lagos, one time an equerry in the Prince's service, knowing his old master had exploration at heart more than trade, determined to push on, without loitering on the desert coast. He was rewarded with the sight of trees growing on the banks of a great river, which Prince Henry and his cosmographers supposed to be the Nile. On one side were the brown men of the desert with long, tangled hair, lean, and fierce in expression, living on milk, wandering with their camels from place to place. On the other side were large, stout, comely men with hair like wool, skins black as soot, living in villages and cultivating fields of corn.

The Portuguese had now discovered the coast of Guinea, and they were obliged to give up their predatory practices. Instead of an open plain in which knights habited in armour and men dressed in quilted cotton jackets could fight almost with impunity against naked Moors, they entered rivers the banks of which were lined with impenetrable jungles. The negroes, perched in trees, shot down upon them from above, or attacked the ships' boats in mid-channel with their swift and light canoes. The Portuguese had no firelocks, and the crossbow bolt was a poor missile compared with the arrows which the negroes dipped in a poison so subtle that as soon as the wounded man drank he died, the blood bursting from his nose and ears. A system of barter was therefore established, and the negroes showed themselves disposed to trade. The Gold Coast was discovered: a fort and a chapel were built at Elmina, where a commandant was appointed to reside. This ancient settlement has just been ceded to the English by the Dutch. The ships carried out copper bracelets, brass basins, knives, rattles, looking-glasses, coloured silks, and woollen goods, green Rouen cloth, coral, figured velvet, and dainty napkins of Flanders embroidered with gold brocade, receiving chiefly gold dust in exchange. This trade was farmed out to a company for five years, on condition that the company should each year explore to a certain distance along the coast.

The excitement which followed the discovery of gold dust, and the institution of the House of Mines, gradually died away. The noble Prince Henry was no more. The men who went out to the coast were not of the class who devote their lives to the chivalry of enterprise. An official who had just returned from Elmina being presented to the king, His Majesty asked him how it was that although he had lived in Africa his face and hands were so white. The gentleman replied that he had worn a mask and gloves during the whole period of his absence in that sultry land; upon which the king told him what he thought he was fit for in words too vigorous to be translated. This same king, John the second, was a vigorous-minded man, and in him the ambition of Prince Henry was revived. He found in a chest belonging to the late king a series of letters from a Venetian gentleman giving much information about the India trade, and earnestly advising him to prosecute his explorations along the coast. The librarians of St. Mark had also sent maps in which the termination of the continent was marked. The king sent out new expeditions and fostered the science of nautical astronomy. A Jew named Zacuto and the celebrated Martin Behem improved the mariner's compass and modified the old Alexandrian astrolabe, so that it might be used at sea. Wandering knights from distant lands volunteered for these expeditions desiring to witness the tropical storms and the strange manners of the New World, as it was called.

Many skilful mariners and pilots visited Lisbon, were encouraged to remain, and became naturalised Portuguese. Among these was the glorious Christopher Columbus, who made more than one voyage to the Gold Coast, married a Portuguese lady, and lived for some time in the Azores. It was his conviction that the eastern coast of Asia could be reached by sailing due west across the ocean. It was his object not to discover a new land, but to reach by sea the country which Marco Polo had visited by land. He eventually sailed with letters to the Emperor of China in his pockets and came back from the West India Islands thinking that he had been to Japan. He made his proposals in the first place to the king, who referred it to a council of learned men. There were now two plans for sailing to India before the court: the one by following the African coast, the other by sailing west across the ocean. But expeditions of all kinds were at that time unpopular in Lisbon. The Guinea trade did not pay, and it was strenuously urged at the council that the West African Settlements should be abandoned. The friends of exploration were obliged to stand on the defensive. They could not carry the proposal of Columbus; it was all that they could do to save the African expeditions. But when Columbus had won for Castile the east coast of Asia (as was then supposed) the king perceived that if he wished to have an Indian empire he must set to work at once. He accordingly conducted the naval expeditions with such vigour that the Cape of Storms was discovered, was then called the Cape of Good Hope, and, was then doubled, though without immediate result, the sailors forcing their captain to return. The king also sent a gentleman, named Covilham, to visit the countries of the East by land. His instructions were to trace the Venetian trade in drugs and spices to its source, and to find out Prester John.

Covilham went to Alexandria in the pilgrim's garb, but instead of proceeding to the Holy Land, he passed on to Aden, and sailed round the Indian Ocean or the Green Sea, that Lake of Wonder with the precious ambergris floating on its waters and pearls strewed upon its bed, whitened with the cotton sails of the Arab vessels, of the Gujrat Indians, and even of the Chinese, whose four-masted junks were sometimes to be seen lying in the Indian harbours with great wooden anchors dangling from their bows. The east coast of Africa, as low down as Madagascar, or the Island of the Moon, was lined with large towns in which the Arabs resided as honoured strangers, or in which they ruled as kings. On this coast Covilham obtained in formation respecting the Cape. He then crossed over to the India shore; he sailed down the coast of Malabar from city to city, and from port to port. He was astounded and bewildered by what he saw: the activity and grandeur of the commerce; the magnificence of the courts; the half-naked kings blazing with jewels, saying their prayers on rosaries of precious stones, and using golden goblets as spittoons; the elephants with pictures drawn in bright colours on their ears, and with jugglers in towers on their backs; the enormous temples filled with lovely girls; the idols of gold with ruby eyes; the houses of red sandalwood; the scribes who wrote on palm leaves with iron pens; the pilots who took observations with instruments unknown to Europeans; the huge bundles of cinnamon or cassia in the warehouses of the Arab merchants; the pepper vines trailing over trees; and drugs, which were priceless in Europe, growing in the fields like corn.

He returned to Cairo, and there found two Jews, Rabbi Abraham and Joseph the Shoemaker, whom the king had sent to look after him. To them he gave a letter for the king, in which he wrote that the ships which sailed down the coast of Guinea might be sure of reaching the termination of the continent by keeping on to the south; and that when they arrived in the Eastern ocean, they must ask for Sofala and the Island of the Moon. Covilham himself did not return. He had accomplished one part of his mission; he had traced the Venetian commerce to its source; but he had now to find out Prester John.

A fable had arisen, in the Dark Ages, of a great Christian king in Central Asia; and when it was clearly ascertained that the Grand Khan was not a Christian, and that none of the Tartar princes could possibly be Christians, as they could not keep Lent, having no fish or vegetables in their country, it was hoped that Prester John, as the myth was called, might be found elsewhere. Certain pilgrims were met with at Jerusalem who were almost negroes in appearance. Their baptism was of three kinds of fire, of water, and of blood: they were sprinkled, they were circumcised, they were seared on the forehead with a red-hot iron in the form of a cross. Their king, they said, was a good Christian and a hater of the Moslems, and was descended from the Queen of Sheba. This swarthy king, the ancestor of Theodore, could be no other than Prester John; and Covilham felt it his duty to bear him the greetings of his master before he went home to enjoy that reputation which he had so gloriously earned, and to take a part in the great discoveries that were soon to be made.

But the king of Abyssinia wanted a tame white man. He gave his visitor wife and lands; he treated him with honour; but he would not let him go. This kind of complimentary captivity is a danger to which African travellers are always exposed. It is the glory and pride of a savage king to have a white man at his court. And so Covilham was detained, and he died in Abyssinia. But he lived to hear that Portugal had risen in a few years to be one of the great European powers, and that the flag he loved was waving above those castles and cities which he had been the first of his nation to behold. His letter arrived at the same time as the ship of Dias, who had doubled the Cape. The king determined that a final expedition should be sent, and that India should be reached by sea.

It was a fete day in Lisbon. The flags were flying on every tower; the fronts of the houses were clothed in gorgeous drapery, which swelled and floated in the wind; stages were erected on which mysteries were performed; bells were ringing, artillery boomed. Marble balconies were crowded with ladies and cavaliers, and out of upper windows peeped forth the faces of girls, who were kept in semi-Oriental seclusion. Presently the sound of trumpets could be heard; and then came in view a thousand friars, who chanted a litany, while behind them an immense crowd chanted back in response. At the head of this procession rode a gentleman richly dressed; he was followed by a hundred and forty-eight men in sailors' clothes, but bare-footed, and carrying tapers in their hands. On they went till they reached the quay where the boats, fastened to the shore, swayed to and fro with the movement of the tide, and strained at the rope as if striving to depart. The sailors knelt. A priest of venerable appearance stood before them, and made a general confession, and absolved them in the form of the Bull which Prince Henry had obtained. Then the wives and mothers embraced their loved ones whom they bewailed as men about to die. And all the people wept. And the children wept also, though they knew not why.

Thirty-two months passed, and again the water-side was crowded, and the guns fired, and the bells rang. Again Vasco da Gama marched in procession through the streets; and behind him walked, with feeble steps, but with triumph gleaming in their eyes, fifty-five men--the rest were gone. But in that procession were not only Portuguese, but also men with white turbans and brown faces; and sturdy blacks, who bore a chest which was shown by their straining muscles to be of enormous weight; and in his hand the Captain General held a letter which was written with a pen of iron on a golden leaf, and which addressed the king of Portugal and Guinea in these words: "Vasco da Gama, a gentleman of thy house, came to my country, of whose coming I was glad. In my country there is plenty of cinnamon, cloves, pepper, and precious stones. The things which I am desirous to have out of thy country are silver, gold, coral, and scarlet."

That night all the houses in Lisbon were illuminated; the gutters ran with wine; the skies, for miles round, were reddened with the light of bonfires. The king's men brought ten pounds of spices to each sailor's wife, to give away to her gossips. The sailors themselves were surrounded by crowds, who sat silent and open-mouthed, listening to the tales of the great waters, and the marvellous lands where they had been.

They told of the wonders of the Guinea coast, and of the men near the Cape, who rode on oxen and played sweet music on the flute; and of the birds which looked like geese, and brayed like donkeys, and did not know how to fly, but put up their wings like sails, and scudded along before the wind. They told how as they sailed on towards the south, the north star sank and sank, and grew fainter and fainter, until at last it disappeared; and they entered a new world, and sailed beneath strange skies; and how, when they had doubled the Cape, they again saw sails on the horizon, and the north star again rose to view. They told of the cities on the Eastern shore, and of their voyage across the Indian Ocean, and of that joyful morning when, through the grey mists of early dawn, they discerned the hills of Calicut.

And then they sank their voices, and their eyes grew grave and sad as they told of the horrors of the voyage; of the long, long nights off the stormy Cape when the wind roared, and the spray lashed through the rigging, and the waves foamed over the bulwarks, and the stones that were their cannon-shot crashed from side to side, and the ships like live creatures groaned and creaked, and hour after hour the sailors were forced to labour at the pumps till their bones ached, and their hands were numbed by cold. They told of treacherous pilots in the Mozambique, who plotted to run their ships ashore; and of the Indian pirates, the gipsies of the sea, who sent their spies on board. They told of that new and horrible disease which, when they had been long at sea, made their bodies turn putrid and the teeth drop from their jaws. And as they told of those things, and named the souls who had died at sea, there rose a cry of lamentation, and widows in new garments fled weeping from the crowd.

That night, the Venetian ambassador sat down and wrote to his masters that he had seen vessels enter Lisbon harbour laden with spices and with India drugs. His next letter informed them that a strong fleet was being prepared, and that Vasco da Gama intended to conquer India. The Venetians saw that they were ruined. They wrote to their ally, the Sultan of Egypt, and implored him to bestir himself. They gave him artillery to send to the India princes. They offered to open the Suez Canal at their own expense, that their ships might arrive in the Indian Ocean before the Portuguese. On the other hand, came the terrible Albuquerque, who told the Sultan to beware, or he would destroy Mecca and Medina, and turn the Nile into the Red Sea. The Indian Ocean became a Portuguese lake. There was scarcely a town upon its shores which had not been saluted by the Portuguese bombardiers. Not a vessel could cross its waters without a Portuguese passport. As a last resource, the Venetians offered to take the India produce off the king's hands, and to give him a fair price. This offer was declined, and Lisbon, instead of Venice, became the market-place of the India trade. The great cities on the Euphrates, the Tigris, and the Nile fell into decay; the caravan trade of Central Asia declined; the throne of commerce was transferred from the basin of the Mediterranean to the basin of the Atlantic; and the oceanic powers, though rigidly excluded from the commerce itself, were greatly benefited by the change. They had no longer to sail through the straits of Gibraltar; Lisbon was almost at their doors.

The achievements of the Portuguese were stupendous--for a time. They established a chain of forts all down the western coast of Africa, and up the east coast to the Red Sea; then round the Persian Gulf, down the coast of Malabar, up the coast of Coromandel, among the islands of the Archipelago, along the shores of Siam and Burma to Canton and Shanghai. With handfuls of men they defeated gigantic armies; with petty forts they governed empires. But from first to last they were murderers and robbers, without foresight, without compassion. Our eyes are at first blinded to their vices by the glory of their deeds; but as the light fades, their nakedness and horror are revealed. We read of Arabs who had received safe conducts, and who made no resistance, being sewed up in sails and cast into the sea, or being tortured in body and mind by hot bacon being dropped upon their flesh; of crocodiles being fed with live captives for the amusement of the soldiers, and being so well accustomed to be fed that whenever a whistle was given they raised their heads above the water. We read of the wretched natives taking refuge with the tiger of the jungle and the panther of the hills; of mothers being forced to pound their children to death in the rice mortars, and of other children being danced on the point of spears, which it was said was teaching the young cocks to crow. The generation of heroes passed away; the generation of favourites began. Courtiers accepted offices in the Indies with the view of extorting a fortune from the natives as rapidly as could be done. It was remarked that humanity and justice were virtues which were always left behind at the Cape of Good Hope by passengers for India. It was remarked that the money which they brought home was like excommunicated money, so quickly did it disappear. And as for those who were content to love their country and to serve their king, they made enemies of the others, and were ruined for their pains. Old soldiers might be seen in Lisbon wandering through the streets in rags, dying in the hospitals, and crouched before the palace which they had filled with gold. Men whose names are now worshipped by their countrymen were then despised. Minds which have won for themselves immortality were darkened by sorrow and disgrace. In the island of Macao, on the Chinese coast, there is a grove paved with soft green velvet paths, and roofed with a dome of leaves which even the rays of a tropical sun cannot pierce through. In the midst is a grotto of rocks, round which the roots of gigantic trees clamber and coil; and in that silent hermitage a poor exile sat and sang the glory of the land which had cast him forth. That exile was Camoens; that song was the Lusiad.

The vast possessions of the Spaniards and Portuguese were united under Philip the Second, who closed the port of Lisbon against the heretical and rebellious natives of the Netherlands. The Dutch were not a people to undertake long voyages out of curiosity, but when it became necessary for them in the way of business to explore unknown seas they did so with effect. Since they could not get cinnamon and ginger, nutmegs and cloves at Lisbon, they determined to seek them in the lands where they were grown. The English followed their example, and so did the French. There was for a long period incessant war within the tropics. At last things settled down. In the West and East Indies the Spaniards and Portuguese still possessed an extensive empire; but they no longer ruled alone. The Dutch, the English, and the French obtained settlements in North America and the West India Islands, in the peninsula of Hindustan, and the Indian Archipelago; and also on the coast of Guinea.

West Africa is divided by nature into pastoral regions, agricultural regions, and dense forest, mountains, or dismal swamps, where the natives remain in a savage and degraded state. The hills and fens are the slave preserves of Africa, and are hunted every year by the pastoral tribes, with whom war is a profession. The captives are bought by the agricultural tribes, and are made to labour in the fields. This indigenous slave-trade exists at the present time, and has existed during hundreds of years.

The Tuaricks or Tawny Moors inhabiting the Sahara on the borders of the Sudan, made frequent forays into that country for the purpose of obtaining slaves, exacted them as tribute from conquered chiefs, or sometimes bought them fairly with horses, salt, and woollen clothes. When Barbary was inhabited by rich and luxurious people, such as the Carthaginians, who on one occasion bought no less than five thousand negroes for their galleys, these slaves must have been obtained in prodigious numbers, for many die in the middle passage across the desert, a journey which kills even a great number of the camels that are employed. The negroes have at all times been highly prized as domestic and ornamental slaves, on account of their docility and their singular appearance. They were much used in ancient Egypt, as the monumental pictures show: they were articles of fashion both in Greece and Rome. Throughout the Middle Ages they were exported from the east coast to India and Persia, and were formed into regiments by the Caliphs of Baghdad. The Venetians bought them in Tripoli and Tunis, and sold them to the Moors of Spain. When the Moors were expelled, the trade still went on; negroes might still be seen in the markets of Seville. The Portuguese discovered the slave-land itself, and imported ten thousand negroes a year before the discovery of the New World. The Spaniards, who had often negro slaves in their possession, set some of them to dig in the mines at St. Domingo: it was found that a negro's work was as much as four Indians', and arrangements were made for importing them from Africa. When the Dutch, the English, and the French obtained plantations in America, they also required negro labour, and made settlements in Guinea in order to obtain it. Angola fed the Portuguese Brazil; Elmina fed the Dutch Manhattan; Cape Coast Castle fed Barbados, Jamaica, and Virginia; Senegal fed Louisiana and the French Antilles; even Denmark had an island or two in the West Indies, and a fort or two upon the Gold Coast. The Spaniards alone having no settlements in Guinea, were supplied by a contract or assiento; which at one time was enjoyed by the British Crown. We shall now enter into a more particular description of this trade, and of the coast on which it was carried on.

Sailing through the Straits of Gibraltar, on the left hand for some distance is the fertile country of Morocco watered by streams descending from the Atlas range. Then comes a sandy shore, on which breaks a savage surf; and when that is passed, a new scene comes to view. The ocean is discoloured; a peculiar smell is detected in the air; trees appear as if standing in the water; and small black specks, the canoes of fishermen, are observed passing to and fro.

The first region, Senegambia, still partakes of the desert character. With the exception of the palm and the gigantic Adansonia, the trees are for the most part stunted in appearance. The country is open, and is clothed with grass, where antelopes start up from their forms like hares. Here and there are clumps of trees, and long avenues mark the water courses, which are often dry, for there are only three months' rain. The interior abounds with gum-trees, especially on the borders of the desert. The people are Mohammedans, fight on horseback, and dwell in towns fortified with walls and hedges of the cactus. In this country the French are masters, and have laid the foundations of a military empire; an Algeria on a smaller scale.

But as we pass towards the south, the true character of the coast appears. A mountain wall runs parallel with the sea, and numberless rivers leap down the hill slopes, and flow towards the Atlantic through forest covered and alluvial lands, which they themselves have formed. These rivers are tidal, and as soon as the salt water begins to mingle with the fresh, their banks are lined with mangrove shrubberies, forming an intricate bower-work of stems, which may be seen at low water encrusted with oysters, thus said by sailors to grow on trees. The mountain range is sometimes visible as a blue outline in the distance; or the hills, which are shaped like an elephant's back, draw near the shore: or rugged spurs jut down with their rocks of torn and tilted granite to the sea. The shore is sculptured into curves; and all along the coast runs a narrow line of beach, sometimes dazzling white, sometimes orange yellow, and sometimes a deep cinnamon red.

This character of coast extends from Sierra Leone to the Volta, and includes the Ivory Coast, the Pepper Coast, and the Gold Coast. Then the country again flattens; the mountain range retires and gives place to a gigantic swamp, through which the Niger debouches by many mouths into the Bight of Benin, where, according to the old sailor adage, "few come out, though many go in." It is indeed the unhealthiest region of an unhealthy coast. A network of creeks and lagoons unite the various branches of the Niger, and the marshes are filled with groves of palm-oil trees, whose yellow bunches are as good as gold. But in the old day the famous red oil was only used as food, and the sinister name of the Slave Coast indicates the commodity which it then produced.

Again the hills approach the coast, and now they tower up as mountains. The Peak of Cameroons is situated on the Line; it is nearly as high as the Peak of Teneriffe; the flowers of Abyssinia adorn its upper sides, and on its lofty summit the smoke of the volcano steals mist-like across a sheet of snow.

A little lower down, the primeval forest of the Gorilla Country resembles that of the opposite Brazil; but is less gorgeous in its vegetation, less abundant in its life.

Farther yet to the south, and a brighter land appears. We now enter the Portuguese province of Angola. The land, far into the interior, is covered with farmhouses and coffee plantations, and smiling fields of maize. San Paolo de Loanda is still a great city, though the colony has decayed; though the convents have fallen into ruin, though oxen are stalled in the college of the Jesuits. Below Angola, to the Cape of Good Hope, is a waterless beach of sand. The west coast of Africa begins with a desert inhabited by Moors; it ends with a desert inhabited by Hottentots.

The Slave Trade

In the eighteenth century, a trifling trade was done in ivory and gold; but these were only accessories; the Guinea trade signified the trade in slaves. At first the Europeans kidnapped the negroes whom they met on the beach, or who came off to the ships in their canoes; but the "treacherous natives" made reprisals; the practice was, therefore, given up, and the trade was conducted upon equitable principles. It was found that honesty was the best policy, and that it was cheaper to buy men than to steal them. Besides the settlements which were made by Europeans, there were many native ports upon the Slave Coast, and of these Whydah, the seaport of Dahomey, was the most important. When a slave vessel entered the roads, it fired a gun, the people crowded down to the beach, the ship's boat landed through an ugly surf, and the skipper made his way to a large tree in the vicinity of the landing-place, where the governor of the town received him in state, and regaled him with trade-gin, by no means the most agreeable of all compounds. The capital was situated at a distance of sixty miles, and the captain would be carried there in a hammock, taking with him some handsome silks and other presents for the king. This monarch lived by hunting his neighbours and by selling them to Europeans. There was a regular war-season, and he went out once a year, sometimes in one direction, sometimes in another. Kings in Africa have frequently a bodyguard of women.

A certain king of Dahomey had developed this institution into female regiments. These women are nominally the king's wives; they are in reality old maids--the only specimens of the class upon the continent of Africa; they are excellent soldiers--hardy, savage, and courageous. In the siege of Abbeokuta, the other day, an Amazon climbed up the wall; her right arm was cut clean off, and as she fell back she pistolled a man with her left. When the king returned from his annual campaign, he sent to all the white men at Whydah, who received the special title of the "king's friends," and invited them up to witness his "customs" and to purchase his slaves, In the first place, the king murdered a number of his captives to send to his father as tokens of regard; and the traders were mortified to see good flesh and blood being wasted on religion. However, slaves were always in abundance. They were also obtained from the settlements upon the coast. The Portuguese Angola could alone be dignified with the name of colony. The Dutch, English, and French settlements were merely fortified factories, half castle, half shop, in which the agents lived, and in which the dry goods, rum, tobacco, trade powder and muskets, were stored. There were native traders, who received a quantity of such goods on trust, and travelled into the interior till they came to a war-town. They then ordered so many slaves; and laid down the goods. The chief ordered out the militia, made a night march, attacked a village just before the dawn, killed those who resisted, carried off the rest in irons manufactured at Birmingham, and handed them over to the trader; who drove them down to the coast. They were then warehoused in the fort dungeons, or in buildings called "barracoons" prepared for their reception; and as soon as a vessel was ready they were marked and shipped. On board they were packed on the lower deck like herrings in a cask. The cargo supposed that it also resembled herrings, in being exported as an article of food.

The slaves believed that all white men were cannibals; that the red caps of the trade were dyed in negro blood, and that the white soap was made of negro brains. So they often refused to eat; upon which their mouths were forced open with an instrument known in surgery as speculum oris, and used in cases of lockjaw; and by means of this ingenious contrivance they breakfasted and dined against their will. Exercise also being conducive to health, they were ordered to jump up and down in their fetters; and if they declined to do so, the application of the cat had the desired effect, and made them exercise not only their limbs, but also their lungs, and so promoted the circulation of the blood and the digestion of the horse-beans on which they were fed. Yet such was the obstinacy of these savage creatures, that many of them sulked themselves to death; and sometimes, when indulged with an airing on deck, the ungrateful wretches would jump overboard, and, as they sank, waved their hands in triumph at having made their escape. On reaching the West Indies they were put into regular schools of labour, and gradually broken in; and they then enjoyed the advantage of dwelling in a Christian land. But their temporal happiness was not increased. If a lady put her cook into the oven because the pie was overdone; if a planter soused a slave in the boiling sugar; if the runaway was hunted with bloodhounds, and then flogged to pieces and hung alive in chains; if the poor old worn-out slave was turned adrift to die, the West Indian laws did not interfere. The slave of a planter was "his money" it was only when a man killed another person's slave that he was punished; and then only by a fine. It may be said, without exaggeration, that dogs and horses now receive more protection in the British dominions than negroes received in the last century.

In order to understand how so great a moral revolution has been wrought we must return for a moment to the Middle Ages. We left the burgher class in alliance with the kings, possessing liberal charters, making their own laws, levying their own taxes, commanding their own troops. Their sons were not always merchants like themselves: they invaded the intellectual dominions of the priests: they became lawyers, artists, and physicians.

Then another change took place. Standing armies were invented, and the middle class were re-enslaved. Their municipal rights were taken from them; troops were stationed in their towns; the nobles collected round the king, who could now reward their loyalty with lucrative and honourable posts, the command of a regiment, or the administration of a province. Heavy taxes were imposed on the burghers and the peasants, and these supported the nobles and clergy who were exempt. Aristocracy and monarchy became fast friends, and the Crown was protected by the thunders of the Church.

The rebellion of the German monk established an idol of ink and paper, instead of an idol of painted wood or stone; the Protestant believed that it was his duty to study the Bible for himself, and so education was spread throughout the countries of the Reformed Religion. A desire for knowledge became general, and the academies of the Jesuits were founded in self-defence. The enlargement of the reading class gave the Book that power which the pulpit once enjoyed, and in the hands of Voltaire the Book began to preach. The fallacies of the Syrian religion were exposed: and with that religion fell the doctrine of passive obedience and divine right: the doctrine that unbelievers are the enemies of God: the doctrine that men who adopt a particular profession are invested with magical powers which stream into them from other men's finger ends: the doctrine that a barbarous legal code was issued viva voce by the Creator of the world. Such notions as these are still held by thousands in private life, but they no longer enter into the policy of states or dictate statutes of the realm.

Voltaire destroyed the authority of the Church and Rousseau prepared the way for the destruction of the Crown. He believed in a dream-land of the past which had never existed: he appealed to imaginary laws of Nature. Yet these errors were beneficial in their day. He taught men to yearn for an ideal state, which they with their own efforts might attain; he inspired them with the sentiment of Liberty, and with a reverence for the Law of Right. Virtuous principles, abstract ideas, the future Deities of men were now for the first time lifted up to be adored. A thousand hearts palpitated with excitement; a thousand pens were drawn; the people that slumbered in sorrow and captivity heard a voice bidding them arise; they strained, they struggled, and they burst their bonds. Jacques Bonhomme, who had hitherto gone on all fours, discovered to his surprise that he also was a biped; the world became more light; the horizon widened; a new epoch opened for the human race.

Abolition in Europe

The anti-slavery movement, which we shall now briefly sketch, is merely an episode in that great rebellion against authority which began in the night of the Middle Ages; which sometimes assumed the form of religious heresy, sometimes of serf revolt; which gradually established the municipal cities, and raised the slave to the position of the tenant; which gained great victories in the Protestant Reformation, the two English Revolutions, the American Revolution, and the French Revolution; which has destroyed the tyranny of governments in Europe, and which will in time destroy the tyranny of religious creeds.

In the middle of the eighteenth century negro slavery, although it had frequently been denounced in books, had not attracted the attention of the English people. To them it was something in the abstract, something which was done beyond the seas. But there rose an agitation which brought up its distant horrors in vivid pictures before the mind, and produced an outcry of anger and disgust.

It had been the custom of the Virginian or West Indian planter, when he left his tobacco or sugar estate for a holiday in England, to wear very broad hats and very wide trousers and to be accompanied by those slaves who used to bring him his coffee in the early morning, to brush away the blue-tailed fly from his siesta, and to mix him rum and water when required. The existence of such attendants was some what anomalous in this island, and friends would often observe with a knowing air it was lucky for him that Sambo was not up to English law. That law, indeed, was undefined. Slavery had existed in England and had died out of itself, in what manner and at what time no one could precisely say. It was, however, a popular impression that no man could be kept as a slave if he were once baptised. The planters enjoyed the same kind of reputation which the nabobs afterwards obtained: a yellow skin and a bad heart were at one time always associated with each other. The negroes were often encouraged to abscond, and to offer themselves before the font. They obtained as sponsors respectable well-to-do men, who declared that they would stand by their god-sons if it came to a case at law. The planters were in much distress, and in order to know the worst went to Messrs. York and Talbot, the Attorney and Solicitor General for the time being, and requested an opinion. The opinion of York and Talbot was this: that slaves breathing English air did not become free; that slaves on being baptised did not become free; and that their masters could force them back to the plantations when they pleased.

The planters, finding that the law was on their side, at once acted on their opinion. Advertisements appeared in the newspapers offering rewards for runaway slaves. Negroes might be seen being dragged along the streets in open day: they were bought and sold at the Poultry Compter, an old city jail. Free men of colour were no longer safe; kidnapping became a regular pursuit.

There was a young man named Granville Sharp, whose benevolent heart was touched to the quick by the abominable scenes which he had witnessed more than once. He could not believe that such was really English law. He examined the question for himself, and, after long search, discovered precedents which overthrew the opinion of the two great lawyers. He published a pamphlet in which he stated his case; and not content with writing, he also acted in the cause, aiding and abetting negroes to escape. On one occasion a Virginian had disposed of an unruly slave to a skipper bound for the West Indies. The vessel was lying in the river; the unfortunate negro was chained to the mast; when Granville Sharp climbed over the side with a writ of Habeas Corpus in his hand. James Somerset's body was given up, and with its panting, shuddering, hopeful, fearful soul inside, was produced before a Court of Justice that Lord Mansfield might decide to whom it belonged. The case was argued at three sittings, and excited much interest throughout the land. It ended in the liberation of the slave.

Several hundred negroes were at once bowed out by their masters into the street, and wandered about, sleeping in glass-houses; seated on the door-steps of their former homes, weeping, and cursing Granville Sharp. It was resolved to do something for them, and a grant of land was obtained from the native chiefs at the mouth of the Sierra Leone River: a company was formed; four hundred destitute negroes were sent out; and, as if there were no women in Africa, fifty "unfortunates" were sent out with them. The society of these ladies was not conducive to the moral or physical well-being of the emigrants, eighty-four of whom died before they sighted land, and eighty-six in the first four months after landing. The philanthropists thus produced a middle passage at which a slave trader would have been aghast. In a short time the white women were dead, and the Granvilles, as they are traditionally called upon the coast, adopted savage life. But the settlement was re-peopled from another source. In the American Revolutionary War, large numbers of negroes had flocked to the royal standard, attracted by the proclamations of the British generals. These runaway slaves were sent to Nova Scotia, where they soon began to complain; the climate was not to their taste, and they had not received the lands which had been promised them. They were then shipped off to Sierra Leone. They landed singing hymns, and pitched their tents on the site of the present town. The settlement was afterwards recruited with negroes in thousands out of slave ships; but the American element may yet be detected in the architecture of the native houses and in the speech of the inhabitants.

In the meantime the slave-trade was being actively discussed. Among those who felt most deeply on the question was Dr. Peckard, of St. John's College, Cambridge, who, being in 1785 Vice-Chancellor, gave as a subject for the Latin essay, "Anne liceat invitos in servitutem dare?" [Is it right to make men slaves against their will?]

Among the candidates was a certain bachelor of arts, Mr. Thomas Clarkson, who had gained the prize for the best Latin essay the year before, and was desirous of keeping up his reputation. He therefore took unusual pains to collect materials respecting the African slave-trade, to which he knew Dr. Peckard's question referred. He borrowed the papers of a deceased friend who had been in the trade, and conversed with officers who had been stationed in the West Indies. He read Benezet's Historical Account of Guinea, and was thence guided to the original authorities, which are contained in the large folios of Hakluyt and Purchas. These old voyages, written by men who were themselves slavers, contain admirable descriptions of native customs, and also detailed accounts of the way in which the man-trade was carried on. Clarkson possessed a vivid imagination and a tender heart: these narratives filled him with horror and alarm. The pleasure of research was swallowed up in the pain that was excited by the facts before him. It was one gloomy subject from morning to night. In the day-time he was uneasy; at night he had little rest. Sometimes he never closed his eyes from grief. It became not so much a trial for academical reputation as for the production of a work which might be useful to injured Africa. He always slept with a candle in the room that he might get up and put down thoughts which suddenly occurred to him. At last he finished his painful task, and obtained the prize. He went to Cambridge, and read his essay in the Senate House. On his journey back to London the subject continually engrossed his thoughts. "I became," he says, "very seriously affected upon the road. I stopped my horse occasionally, and dismounted and walked. I frequently tried to persuade myself, in these intervals, that the contents of my essay could not be true. Coming in sight of Wades Mill, in Hertfordshire, I sat down disconsolate on the turf by the roadside and held my horse. Here a thought came into my mind, that if the contents of the essay were true, it was time that some person should see these calamities to their end."

On arriving in London he heard for the first time of the labours of Granville Sharp and others. He determined to give up his intention of entering the Church, and to devote himself entirely to the destruction of the slave-trade. At this time a Committee was formed for the purpose of preparing the public mind for abolition. Granville Sharp, to whom more than to any other individual the abolition of the slave-trade is due, became the president, and Clarkson was deputed to collect evidence. He called on the leading men of the day and endeavoured to engage their sympathies in the cause. His modest, subdued demeanour, the sad, almost tearful expression of his face, which the painter of his portrait has fortunately seized, the earnestness and passion with which he depicted the atrocities of the slave-hunt in Africa and the miseries of the slave hold at sea, secured him attention and respect from all; and among those with whom he spoke was one whose fame is the purest and the best that parliamentary history records.

William Wilberforce was the son of a rich merchant at Hull, and inherited a large fortune. He went to Cambridge, and was afterwards elected member for his native city, an honour which cost him £8,000. He became a member of the fashionable clubs, and chiefly frequented Brooks', where he became a votary of faro till his winnings cured him of his taste for play. He soon obtained a reputation in the House and the salon. He had an easy flow of language, and a voice which was melody itself. He was a clever mimic and an accomplished musician. He possessed the rare arts of polished raillery and courteous repartee. Madame de Stael declared that he was the wittiest man in England. But presently he withdrew from her society and that of her friends, because it was brilliant and agreeable. He also took his name off all his clubs. He was travelling on the Continent with Pitt, who was his bosom friend, when a change came over him. In the days of his childhood he had been sent to reside with an aunt who was a great admirer of Whitfield's preaching, and kept up a friendly connection with the early Methodists. He was soon infected with her ideas, and "there was remarked in him a rare and pleasing character of piety in his twelfth year." This excited much consternation among the other members of his family. His mother at once came up to London and fetched him home. "If Billy turns Methodist," said his grandfather, "he shall not have a sixpence of mine." We are informed that theatrical diversions, card parties, and sumptuous suppers (at the fashionable hour of six in the evening) obliterated these impressions for a time. They were not, however, dead, for the perusal of Doddridge's "Rise and Progress" was sufficient to revive them. This amiable and excellent young man became the prey of a morbid superstition. Often in the midst of enjoyment his conscience told him he was not in the true sense of the word a Christian. "I laughed, I sang, I was apparently gay and happy, but the thought would steal across me, What madness is all this: to continue easy in a state in which a sudden call out of the world would consign me to everlasting misery, and that when eternal happiness is within my grasp?" The sinful worldling accordingly reformed. He declined Sunday visits; he got up earlier in the morning; he wrestled continually in prayer; he began to keep a common place book, serious and profane, and a Christian duty paper. He opened himself completely to Pitt, and said he believed the Spirit was in him. Mr. Pitt was apparently of a different opinion, for he tried to reason him out of his convictions. "The fact is," says Mr. Wilberforce, "he was so absorbed in politics that he had never given himself time for due reflection in religion. But amongst other things he declared to me that Bishop Butler's work raised in his mind more doubts than it had answered." Now if that was the character of Pitt's intellect we must venture to think that the more he reflected on religion the less he would have believed in it.

Superstition intensifies a man. It makes him more of what he was before. An evil-natured person who takes fright at hell-fire becomes the most malevolent of human beings. Nothing can more clearly prove the natural beauty of Wilberforce's character than the fact that he preserved it unimpaired in spite of his Methodistic principles. It would be unjust to deny that after he became a Methodist he became a wiser and a better man. His intellect was strengthened, his affections were sweetened, by a faith the usual tendency of which is to harden the heart and to soften the head. He endeavoured to control a human, and therefore sometimes irritable, temper; he laid down for himself the rule to manifest rather humility in himself than dissatisfaction at others; and so well did he succeed that a female friend observed, "If this is madness I hope that he will bite us all."

Yet there was a flaw in Wilberforce's brain, or he could never have supposed that a man might be sent to hell for playing the piano. He soon showed that in another age he might have been an excellent inquisitor; and inquisitors there were not less pure-hearted, not less benevolent in private life than Wilberforce himself. He desired to do something in public for the glory of God, and he believed it was his mission to reform the manners of the age. When a man of fashion was always a gambler, and when all the clubs in St. James' Street were hells; when speeches were often incoherent in the House after dinner; when comic songs were composed against Mr. Pitt, not because he had a mistress, but because he had none; when ladies called adultery "a little affair"; when the Prince of Wales was a young man about town, grazing on the middle classes, it cannot be questioned that, from the Royal Family downwards, there was room for improvement. The reader will perhaps feel curious to learn in what manner Mr. Wilberforce commenced his laudable but difficult crusade. He obtained a royal proclamation for the discouragement of vice and immorality; and letters from the secretaries of state to the lords-lieutenant, expressing his Majesty's pleasure, that they recommend it to the justices throughout their several counties to be active in the execution of the laws against immoralities. He also started a society, to assist in the enforcement of the proclamation, as a kind of amateur detective corps, to hunt up indecent and blasphemous publications. And that was what he called reforming the manners of the age!

Happily, the slave-trade question began to be discussed, and Mr. Wilberforce obtained a cause which was worthy of his noble nature. The miseries of Africa had long attracted his attention: even in his boyhood he had written on the subject for the daily journals. Lady Middleton, who had heard from an eye-witness of the horrors of slavery, had begged him to bring it before parliament. Mr. Pitt had also advised him to take up the question, and he had agreed to do so whenever an opportunity should occur. This happened before his acquaintance with Clarkson, to whom he said at their first interview that abolition was a question near his heart. A short time after, there was a dinner at Mr. Bennet Langton's, at which Sir Joshua Reynolds, Boswell, Windham, and himself were present. The conversation turned upon the African slave-trade, and Clarkson exhibited some specimens of cotton cloth manufactured by the natives in their own looms, the plant being grown in their own fields. All the guests expressed themselves on the side of abolition, and Mr. Wilberforce was asked if he would bring it forward in the House. He said that he would have no objection to do so when he was better prepared for it, providing no more proper person could be found.

The Committee now went to work in earnest, and held weekly meetings at Mr. Wilberforce's house. Clarkson was sent to Bristol and Liverpool, where he collected much information, though not without difficulty, and even, as he thought, danger of his life. A commission was appointed by the Lords of the Privy Council to collect evidence. It was stated by the Liverpool and planter party that not only the colonial prosperity, but the commercial existence of the nation was at stake; that the Guinea trade was a nursery for British seamen; that the slaves offered for sale were criminals and captives who would be eaten if they were not bought; that the middle passage was the happiest period of a negro's life; that the sleeping apartments on board were perfumed with frankincense; and that the slaves were encouraged to disport themselves on deck with the music and dances of their native land. On the other hand, the Committee proved from the muster rolls which Clarkson had examined that the Guinea trade was not the nursery of British seamen, but its grave; and they published a picture of an African slaver, copied from a vessel which was lying in the Mersey, and certain measurements were made, which, being put into feet and inches, justified the statement of a member in the House, that never was so much human suffering condensed into so small a space.

Lord Chancellor Thurlow and two other members of the Cabinet were opposed to abolition, and therefore Mr. Pitt could not make it a government measure; and so although it was called the battle between the giants and the pigmies; although Pitt, Fox, Burke, Sheridan, Windham, and Wilberforce, the greatest orators and statesmen of the day, were on one side, and the two members for Liverpool on the other, the brute votes went with the pigmies, and the bill was lost.

But now the nation was beginning to be moved. The Committee distributed books, and hired columns in the newspapers. They sealed their letters with a negro in chains kneeling, and the motto, "Am I not a man and a brother?" Wedgwood made cameos with the same design; ladies wore them in their bracelets or their hair-pins; gentlemen had them inlaid in gold on the lids of their snuff boxes. Cowper sent to the Committee the well-known poem, "Fleecy locks and black complexion"; the Committee printed it on the finest hot-pressed paper, folded it up in a small and neat form, gave it the appropriate title of "A subject for conversation at the tea-table," and cast it forth by thousands upon the land. It was set to music, and sung as a street ballad. People crowded at shop windows to see the picture of the ship in which the poor negroes were packed like herrings in a cask. A murmur arose, and grew louder and louder; three hundred thousand persons gave up drinking sugar in their tea; indignation meetings were held; and petitions were sent into Parliament by the ton. Everything seemed to show that the nation had begun to loathe the trade in flesh and blood, and would not be appeased till it was done away. And then came events which made the sweet words Liberty, Humanity, Equality, sound harsh and ungrateful to the ear: which caused those who spoke much of philanthropy, and eternal justice, to be avoided by their friends, and perhaps supervised by the police; which rendered negroes and emancipation a subject to be discussed only with sneers and shakings of the head. When the slave-trade question had first come up, Mr. Pitt proposed to the French Government that the two nations should unite in the cause of abolition. Now in France the peasantry themselves were slaves; and the negro trade had been bitterly attacked in books which had been burnt by the public executioner, and the authors of which had been excommunicated by the Pope. Mr. Pitt's proposal was at once declined by the coterie of the OEil de Boeuf. In the meantime it was discovered that the French nation was heavily in debt; there was a loss of nearly five million sterling every year; a fact by no means surprising, for the nobles and clergy paid no taxes; each branch of trade was an indolent monopoly; and poor Jacques Bonhomme bore the weight of the court and army on his back. Chancellors of the Exchequer one after, the other were appointed, and attempted in vain to grapple with the difficulty. As a last resource, the House of Commons was revived, that the debt of bankrupt despotism might be accepted by the nation. A Parliament was opened at Versailles; lawyers and merchants dressed in black walked in the same procession, and sat beneath the same roof with the haughty nobles, rustling with feathers, shining with gold, and wearing swords upon their thighs. But the commoners soon perceived that they had only been summoned to vote away the money of the nation; they were not to interfere with the laws. Their debates becoming offensive to the king, the hall in which they met was closed against them. They then gathered in a tennis court, called themselves the National Assembly, and took an oath that they would not dissolve until they had regenerated France. Troops were marched into Versailles; a coup d'etat was evidently in the wind. And then the Parisians arose; the army refused to fight against them; the Bastille was destroyed; the National Assembly took the place of the OEil de Boeuf: democracy became the Mayor of the Palace. A constitution was drawn up, and was accepted by the king. The nobility were deprived of their feudal rights; church property was resumed by the nation; taxes were imposed on the rich as well as on the poor; the peasantry went out shooting every Sunday; the country gentlemen fled from their chateaux to foreign courts, where wars began to brew.

Such was the state of affairs in France when Wilberforce suggested that Clarkson should be sent over to Paris to negotiate with the leading members of the National Assembly. There was in Paris a Society called the Friends of the Blacks; Condorcet and Brissot were among its conductors. Clarkson, therefore, was sanguine of success; but it was long before he could obtain a hearing. At last he was invited to dinner at the house of the Bishop of Chartres, that he might there meet Mirabeau and Seiyes, the Duc de Rochefoucauld, Pétion de Villeneuve, and Bergasse, and talk the matter over. But when the guests met, a much more interesting topic was in everybody's mouth. The king at that time lived at Versailles, a little town inhabited entirely by his servants and his bodyguards. The Parisians for some time had been uneasy; they feared that he would escape to Metz; and that civil war would then break out. There was a rumour of a bond signed by thousands of the aristocrats to fight on the king's side. The Guards had certainly been doubled at Versailles; and a Flanders regiment had marched into the town with two pieces of cannon. Officers appeared in the streets in strange uniforms, green faced with red; and they did not wear the tricolour cockade which had already been adopted by the French nation. And while thus uneasy looks were turned towards Versailles, an incident took place which heightened the alarm. On October 1st a banquet had been given by the Guards to the officers of the Flanders Regiment. The tables were spread in the court theatre: the boxes were filled with spectators. After the champagne was served, and the health of the royal family had been drunk, the wine and the shouting turned all heads; swords were drawn and waved naked in the air: the tricolour cockades were trampled under foot; the band struck up the tender and beautiful ballad, "O Richard! O my King! the world is all forsaking thee!"; the queen came in and walked round the tables, bowing, and bestowing her sweetest smiles; the bugles sounded the charge; the men from different regiments were brought in; all swore aloud they would protect the king, as if he was just then in danger of his life; and some young ensigns carried by assault certain boxes which expressed dissent at these proceedings. This was the subject of conversation at the dinner to which Clarkson was invited; and the next day the women of Paris marched upon Versailles; the king was taken to the Tuileries and the National Assembly became supreme--under favour of the mob.

After several weeks Clarkson at last received a definite reply. The Revolution, he was told, was of more importance than the abolition of the slave-trade. In Bordeaux, Marseilles, Rouen, Nantes, and Havre, there were many persons in favour of that trade. It would be said that abolition would be making a sacrifice to England. The British parliament had as yet done nothing, and people doubted the sincerity of Pitt. Mr. Clarkson asked whether, if the question were postponed to the next legislature, it would be more difficult to carry it then than now. "The question produced much conversation, but the answer was unanimous-- that people would daily more and more admire their constitution, and that by the constitution certain solid and fixed principles would be established, which would inevitably lead to the abolition of the slave-trade; and if the constitution were once fairly established, they would not regard the murmurs of any town or province."

Clarkson was not the only envoy who was defeated by the planter interest on French soil. In the flourishing colony of St. Domingo there were many mulatto planters, free and wealthy men, but subject to degrading disabilities. When they heard of the Revolution, they sent Oge to Paris with a large sum of money as a present to the National Assembly, and a petition for equal rights. The president received him and his companions with cordiality: he bid them take courage; the Assembly knew no distinction between black and white; all men were created free and equal. But soon the planters began to intrigue, the politicians to prevaricate, and to postpone. Oge's patience was at last worn out; he declared to Clarkson that he did not care whether their petition was granted them or not. "We can produce," he said, "as good soldiers on our estates as those in France. If we are once forced to desperate measures, it will be in vain to send thousands across the Atlantic to bring us back to our former state." He finally returned to St. Domingo, armed his slaves, was defeated and broken on the wheel. Then the slaves rose and massacred the whites, and the cause of abolition was tarnished by their crimes. In England the tide of feeling turned; a panic fell upon the land. The practical disciples of Rousseau had formed a club in Paris, the members of which met in a Jacobin church, whence they took their name. This club became a kind of caucus for the arrangement of elections, to decide the measures which should be brought forward in the National Assembly, and to preach unto all men the gospel of liberty, equality, and fraternity. It had four hundred daughter societies in France; it corresponded with thousands of secret societies abroad; it had missionaries in the army, spies in foreign lands. It desired to create a universal republic; it grew in power, in ambition, and in bravado; it cast at the feet of the kings of Europe the head of a king; it offered the friendship and aid of France to all people who would rise against their tyrants. Thomas Paine, who used to boast that he had created the American Revolution with his pamphlet, "Common Sense," now tried to create an English Revolution with his "Rights of Man." In the loyal towns his effigy, with a rope round its neck, was flogged with a cart whip, while the market-bell tolled, and the crowd sang the national anthem, with three cheers after each verse. In other towns, "No King! Liberty! Equality!" were scribbled on the walls. The soldiers were everywhere tampered with, and the king was mobbed. Pitt, the projector of Reform Bills, became a tyrant. Burke, the champion of the American Revolution, became a Tory.

It was not a time to speak of abolition, which was regarded as a revolutionary measure. And such in reality it was, though accidentally associated in England with religion and philanthropy, on account of the character of its leaders. It was pointed out that the atheist philosophers had all of them begun by sympathising with the negroes; one of Thomas Paine's first productions was an article against slavery. The Committee was declared to be a nest of Jacobins, their publications were denounced as poisonous. There was a time when the king had whispered at a levee, "How go on your black clients, Mr. Wilberforce?"

But now the philanthropist was in disgrace at court. At this time poor Clarkson's health gave way, and he was carried off the field. And then from Paris there came terrible news; the people were at last avenged. The long black night was followed by a blood-red dawn. The nobles who had fled to foreign courts had returned with foreign troops; the kings of

Europe had fallen on the new republic, the common enemy of all. The people feared that the old tyranny was about to be replaced, and by a foreign hand; they had now tasted liberty; they knew how sweet it was; they had learnt the joy of eating all the corn that they had sown; they had known what it was to have their own firelocks and their own swords, and to feel that they, the poor and hungry serfs, were the guardians of their native land. They had learnt to kiss the tricolour; to say Vive la nation! to look forward to a day when their boys, now growing up, might harangue from the Tribune, or sit upon the Bench, or grasp the field-marshal's baton. And should all this be undone? Should they be made to return to their boiled grass and their stinging nettle soup? Should the days of privilege and oppression be restored?

The nation arose and drove out the invaders. But there had been a panic, and it bore its fruits. What the Jacobins were to Pitt, the aristocrats were to Danton and Robespierre. Hundreds of royalists were guillotined, but then, thousands had plotted the overthrow of the Republic, thousands had intrigued that France might be a conquered land. Such at least was the popular belief; The massacres of September, the execution of the king and queen, were the result of fear. After which, it must be owned, there came a period when suspicion and slaughter had become a habit; when blood was shed to the sound of laughter; when heads, greeted with roars of recognition, were popped out of the little national sash-window, and tumbled into the sawdust, and then were displayed to the gallery in the windows, and to the pit upon the square. The mere brute energy which lay at the bottom of the social mass rose more and more towards the top; and at length the leaders of the people were hideous beings in red woollen caps, with scarcely an idea in their heads or a feeling in their hearts; ardent lovers of liberty, it is true, and zealots for the fatherland, scarcely taking enough from the treasury to fill their bellies and to clothe their backs (Marat, when killed, had elevenpence halfpenny in his possession), but mere senseless fanatics, who crushed that liberty which they tried to nurse; who governed only by the guillotine, which they considered a sovereign remedy for all political disorders; who killed all the great men whom the Republic had produced, and were finally guillotined themselves.

The death of Robespierre closed the Revolution; the last mob-rising was extinguished by the artillery of Bonaparte. The Jacobins fell into disrepute; there was a cry of "Down with the Jacoquins!"; stones were hurled in through their windows; the orators were hustled and beaten as they sallied forth, and the ladies who knitted in the gallery were chastised in a manner scarcely suited for adults. The age of revolutions for a time was past; Bonaparte became Dictator; Thomas Paine took to drink; the English reign of terror was dispelled; the abolitionists again raised their voices on behalf of the negro, and in 1807 the slave-trade was abolished. That traffic, however, was only abolished so far as English vessels and English markets were concerned, and Government now commenced a long series of negotiations with foreign powers. In course of time the other nations prohibited the slave-trade, and conceded to Great Britain the police control of the Guinea coast, and the right of search. A squadron of gunboats hovered round the mouths of rivers, or sent up boating expeditions, or cruised to and fro a little way out at sea, with a man always at the mast-head with a spy glass in his hand, scanning the horizon for a sail. When a sail was sighted, the gunboat got up steam, bore down upon the vessel, ordered her to heave to, sent men on board, and overhauled her papers. If they were not in order, or if slaves were on board, or even if the vessel was fitted up in such a way as to have the appearance of a slaver, she was taken as a prize; the sailors were landed at the first convenient spot; the slaver was sold, and the money thereby obtained, with a bounty on each captured slave, was divided among the officers and crew. The slaves were discharged at Sierra Leone, where they formed themselves into various townships according to their nationalities, spoke their own language, elected their own chiefs, and governed themselves privately by their own laws, opinion acting as the only method of coercion--a fact deserving to be noted by those who study savage man. However, this was only for a time. All these imported negroes were educated by the missionaries, and they now support their own church; the native languages and distinctions of nationality are gradually dying out; the descendants of naked slaves are many of them clergymen, artisans, shopkeepers, and merchants; they call themselves Englishmen, and such they feel themselves to be. However ludicrous it may seem to hear a negro boasting about Lord Nelson and Waterloo, and declaring that he must go home to England for his health, it shows that he possesses a kind of emulation, which, with proper guidance, will make him a true citizen of his adopted country, and leave him nothing of the African except his skin.

But the slave-trade was not extinguished by the "sentimental squadron." The slavers could make a profit if they lost four cargoes in every five; they could easily afford to use decoys. While the gunboat was giving chase to some old tub with fifty diseased and used-up slaves on board, a clipper with several hundreds in her holds would dash out from her hiding-place among the mangroves and scud across the open sea to Cuba and Brazil.

It was impossible to blockade a continent; but it was easy to inspect estates. The negroes were purchased as plantation hands; a contraband labourer was not a thing to be concealed. There were laws in Cuba and Brazil against negro importation, but these existed only for the benefit of the officials. The bribery practice was put an end to in Brazil about 1852; that great market was for ever closed. Slavers were ruined; African chiefs became destitute of rum and this branch of commerce began to look forlorn. Yet still Cuba cried, "More! Give me more!"; still the profits were so large that the squadron was defeated and the man-supply obtained. Half a million of money a year, and no small amount of men, did that one island cost Great Britain. Yet still it might be hoped that even Cuba would he filled full in time; that the public opinion of Europe would act upon Madrid; that in time it would imitate Brazil. But in 1861 there happened an event which made the Cubans turn their back on Spain, and look with longing eyes the other way; and a beautiful vision uprose before their minds. They dreamt of a New Empire to which Cuba would belong, and to which slavery in a state of medieval beauty would be restored. It was only a dream; it was quickly dispelled; they awoke to find Liberty standing at their doors; and there now she stands waiting for her time to come.

When Great Britain was teasing the colonies into resistance, it was often predicted that they would not unite. There was little community of feeling between the old Dutch families of New York, the Quakers of Pennsylvania, the yeomen of New England, who were descended from Roundheads, and the country gentlemen of Virginia, who were descended from Cavaliers. But when the king closed Boston Port, and the vessels mouldered in the docks, and the shops were closed, and the children of fishermen and sailors began to cry for bread, the colonies did unite with one heart and one hand to feed the hunger of the noble town; and then to besiege it for its own sake, and to drive the red coats back into their ships. Yet when the war was over, and the squirrel guns had again been hung upon the wall, and the fire of the conflict had died out, the old jealousy reappeared. A loose-jointed league was tried and came to nought. The nation existed; the nation was in debt; union could not be dispensed with. But each colony approached this Union as a free and sovereign state. If one colony had chosen to remain apart, the others would not have interfered; if one colony after entering the Union had chosen to withdraw, its right to do so would not have been denied. In European countries, republican or royal, the source of authority is the nation; all powers not formally transferred reside with the Assembly or the Crown. In America, however; it was precisely the reverse; all powers not delivered to the central government were retained by the contracting states.

Abolition in America

At the time of the Revolution, negro slavery existed in the colonies without exception. But it did not enter the economy of Northern life. Slavery will only pay when labour can be employed in gangs beneath an overseer, and where work can be found for a large number of men without cessation throughout the year. In the culture of rice, sugar, cotton, and tobacco, these conditions exist; but in corn-growing lands labour is scanty and dispersed, except at certain seasons of the year. Slaves in the North were not employed as field hands, but only as domestic servants in the houses of the rich. They could therefore be easily dispensed with; and it was proposed by the Northern delegates, when the Constitution was being prepared, that the African slave-trade should at once be abolished, and that certain measures should be taken, with a view to the gradual emancipation of the negro. Upon this question Virginia appears to have been divided. But Georgia and the Carolinas at once declared that they would not have the slave-trade abolished: they wanted more slaves; and unless this species of property were guaranteed, they would not enter the Union at all. They demanded that slavery should be recognised and protected by the Constitution. The Northerners at once gave in; they only requested that the words "slave" and "slavery" might not appear. To this the Southerners agreed, and the contract was delicately worded; but it was none the less stringent all the same. It was made a clause of the Constitution that the slave-trade should not be suppressed before the year 1808. It might then be made the subject of debate and legislation--not before. It was made a clause of the Constitution that, if the slaves of any state rebelled, the national troops should be employed against them. It was made a clause of the Constitution that, if a slave escaped to a free state, the authorities of that state should be obliged to give him up. And lastly, slave-owners were allowed to have votes in proportion to the number of their slaves. Such was the price which the Northerners paid for nationality--a price which their descendants found a hard and heavy one to pay. The fathers of the country ate sour grapes, and the children's teeth were set on edge.

But the Southerners had not finished yet. The colonies possessed, according to their charters, certain regions in the wilderness out west, and these they delivered to the nation. A special proviso was made, however, by South Carolina and by Georgia, that at no future time should slavery be forbidden in the territories which they gave up of their own free will and these territories in time became slave states. It is therefore evident that the South intended from the first to preserve, and also to extend slavery. It must be confessed that their policy was candid and consistent, and of a piece throughout. They refused to enter the Union unless their property was guaranteed; they threatened to withdraw from the Union whenever they thought that the guarantee was about to be evaded or withdrawn. The clauses contained in the Constitution were binding on the nation; but they might be revoked by means of a constitutional amendment, which could be passed by the consent of three-fourths of the states. Emigrants continually poured into the North; and these again streamed out towards the West. It was evident that in time new states would be formed, and that the original slave states would be left in a minority. These states were purely agricultural; they had no commerce; they had no manufactures. Indigo, rice, and tobacco were the products on which they lived; and the markets for these were in an ugly state. The East Indies had begun to compete with them in rice and indigo; the demand for tobacco did not increase. There was a general languor in the South; the young men did not know what to do. Slavery is a wasteful and costly institution, and requires large profits to keep it alive; it seemed on the point of dying in the South, when there came a voice across the Atlantic crying for cotton in loud and hungry tones; and the fortune of the South was made.

In the seventeenth century the town of Manchester was already known to fame. It was a seat of the woollen manufacture, which was first introduced from Flanders into England in the reign of Edward the Third. It bought yarn from the Irish, and sent it back to them as linen. It imported cotton from Cyprus and Smyrna, and worked it into fustians, vermilions, and dimities. In the middle of the eighteenth century the cotton industry had become important. In thousands of cottages surrounding Manchester might be heard the rattle of the loom and the humming of the one-thread wheel, which is now to be seen only in the opera of Marta. Invention, as usual, arose from necessity; the weavers could not get sufficient thread, and were entirely at the mercy of the spinners. Spinning machines were accordingly invented: the water frame, the spinning jenny, and the mule. And now the weavers had more thread than they could use, and the power loom was invented to preserve the equilibrium of supply and demand. Then steam was applied to machinery; the factory system was established; hundred-handed engines worked all the day: and yet more labourers were employed than had ever been employed before; the soft white wool was carded, spun, and woven in a trice; the cargoes from the East were speedily devoured; and now raw material was chiefly in demand. The American cotton was the best in the market; but the quantity received had hitherto been small. The picking out of the small black seeds was a long and tedious operation. A single person could not clean more than a pound a day. Here, then, was an opening for Yankee ingenuity; and Whitney invented his famous saw-gin, which tore out the seeds as quick as lightning with its iron teeth. Land and slaves abounded in the South; the demand from Manchester became more and more hungry--it has never yet been completely satisfied--and, under King Cotton, the South entered upon a new era of wealth, vigour, and prosperity as a slave plantation. The small holdings were unable to compete with the large estates on which the slaves were marshalled and drilled like convicts to their work; society in the South soon became composed of the planters, the slaves, and the mean whites who were too proud to work like niggers, and who led a kind of gipsy life.

While the intellect of the North was inventing machinery, opening new lands, and laying the foundations of a literature, the Southerners were devoted entirely to politics; and by means of their superior ability they ruled at Washington for many years, and almost monopolised the offices of state. When America commenced its national career there were two great sects of politicians; those who were in favour of the central power, and those who were in favour of state rights. In the course of time the national sentiment increased, and with it the authority of the President and Congress; but this centralising movement was resisted by a certain party of the North whose patriotism could not pass beyond the state house and the city hall. The Southerners were invariably provincial in their feelings; they did not consider themselves as belonging to a nation, but a league; they inherited the sentiments of aversion and distrust with which their fathers had entered the Union; threats and provisos were always on their lips. The executive, it was true, was in their hands, but the House of Representatives belonged to the North. In the Senate the states had equal powers, irrespective of size and population. In the Lower House the states were merely sections of the country; population was the standard of the voting power. The South had a smaller population than the North; the Southerners were therefore a natural minority, and only preserved their influence by allying themselves with the states' rights party in the North. The free states were divided: the slave states voted as one man.

In the North politics was a question of sentiment, and sentiments naturally differ. In the South politics was a matter of life and death; their bread depended on cotton; their cotton depended on slaves; their slaves depended on the balance of power. The history of the South within the Union is that of a people struggling for existence by means of political devices against the spirit of the nation and the spirit of the age. By annexation, purchase, and extension they kept pace with the North in its rush towards the West. Free states and slave states ran neck and neck towards the shores of the Pacific. The North obtained Vermont, Ohio, Indiana, Illinois, Maine, Michigan, Iowa, Wisconsin, and California. The South obtained Tennessee, Kentucky, Louisiana, Mississippi, Alabama, Missouri, Arkansas, Florida, and Texas. Whenever a territory became a state, the nation possessed the power of rejecting and therefore of modifying its constitution. The Northern politicians made an effort to prohibit slavery in all new states; the South as usual threatened to secede, and the Union which had been manufactured by a compromise was preserved by a compromise. It was agreed that a line should be drawn to the Pacific along the parallel 36° 30'; that all the states which should afterwards be made below the line should be slave-holding; and all that were made above it should be free. But this compromise was not, like the compromise of the constitution, binding on the nation, and only to be set aside by a constitutional amendment. It was simply a parliamentary measure, and as such could be repealed at any future session. However, it satisfied the South; the North had many things to think of; and all remained quiet for a time. But only for a time.

The mysterious principle which constitutes the law of progress produces similar phenomena in various countries at the same time, and it was such an active period of the human mind which produced about forty years ago a Parisian Revolution, the great Reform Bill, and the American agitation against slavery. There was a man in a Boston garret. He possessed some paper, pens and ink, and little else besides; and even these he could only use in a fashion of his own. He had not what is called a style; nor had he that rude power which can cast a glow on jagged sentences and uncouth words. This poor garretteer, a printer in his working hours, relied chiefly on his type for light and shade, and had much recourse to capital letters, italics and notes of exclamation, to sharpen his wit, and to strengthen his tirades. But he had a cause, and his heart was in that cause. When W. L. Garrison commenced his Liberator, the government of Georgia set a price upon his head, he was mobbed in his native city, and slavery was defended in Faneuil Hall itself, sacred to the memory of men who cared not to live unless they could be free. The truth was, that the Northerners disliked slavery, but nationality was dear to them and they believed that an attack upon the "domestic institution" of the South endangered the safety of the Union. But the abolitionists became a sect; they increased in numbers and in talent; they would admit of no compromise; they cared little for the country itself so long as it was stained. They denounced the constitution as a covenant with death, and an agreement with hell. No union with slave-holders! they cried. No union with midnight robbers and assassins! Hitherto the war between the two great sections of the country had been confined to politicians. The Southerners had sent their boys to Northern colleges and schools. Attended by a retinue of slaves they had passed the summer at Saratoga or Newport, and sometimes the winter at New York. But now their sons were insulted, their slaves decoyed from them by these new fanatics; and the South went North no more.

Abolition societies were everywhere formed, and envoys were sent into the slave states to distribute abolition tracts and to publish abolition journals, and to excite, if they could, a St. Domingo insurrection. The Northerners were shocked at these proceedings and protested angrily against them. But soon there was a revulsion of feeling in their minds, The wild beast temper arose in the South, and went forth lynching all it met. Northerners were flogged and even killed. Negroes were burnt alive. And so the meetings of abolitionists were no longer interrupted at the North; mayors and select-men no longer refused them the use of public halls. The sentiment of abolition was however not yet widely spread. There were few Northerners who preferred to give up the Union rather than live under a piebald constitution, or who considered it just to break a solemn compact in obedience to an abstract law. But there now arose a strong and resolute party who declared that slavery might stay where it was, but that it must go no farther. The South must be content with what it had. Not another yard of slave soil should be added to the Union. On the other hand, the South could not accept such terms. Slavery extension was necessary for their lives. More land they must have or they could not exist. There was waste land in abundance in the South; but it was dead. Their style of agriculture was precisely that which is pursued in Central Africa. They took a tract from the wilderness and planted it again and again with cotton and tobacco till it gave up the ghost, and would yield no more. They then moved on and took in another piece. Obliged to spend all their cash in buying prime slaves at two hundred pounds a piece, they could not afford to use manure or to rotate their crops; they could not afford to employ so costly a species of labour on anything less lucrative than sugar, cotton, and tobacco. Besides, if slavery were not to be extended they would be surrounded and hemmed in by free states; the old contract would be annulled. Already the South were in a minority. The free states and slave states might be equal in number; but they were not equal in population and prosperity. The Northerner who travelled down South was astonished to find that the cities of the maps were villages, and the villages clusters of log huts. Fields covered with weeds, and moss-grown ruins showed where farms once flourishing had been. He rode through vast forests and cypress swamps, where hundreds of mean whites lived like Red Indians, hunting and fishing for their daily bread, eating clay to keep themselves alive, prowling round plantations to obtain stolen food from the slaves. He saw plantations in which the labour was conducted with the terrible discipline of the prison and the hulks; and where as he galloped past the line of hoeing slaves, so close that he splashed them with mud, they hoed on, they toiled on, not daring to raise their eyes from the ground. From early dawn to dusky eve it was so with these poor wretches: no sound broke the silence of those fearful fields but the voice of the overseer and the cracking of the whip. And out far away in the lone western lands, by the side of dark rivers, among trees from which drooped down the dull grey Spanish moss, the planters went forth to hunt; there were well-known coverts where they were sure to find; and as the traveller rode through the dismal swamp he might perhaps have the fortune to see the game; a black animal on two legs running madly for its life, and behind it the sounding of a horn, and the voices of hounds in full cry--a chase more infernal than that of the Wild Huntsman who sweeps through the forest with his spectral crew.

But the end of all this was at hand. Kansas, a tract of rich prairie land, was about to become a territory, and would soon become a state. It was situated above the 36° 30' line, and therefore belonged to the North. But the Southerners coveted this Naboth's vineyard; their power at Washington was great just then; they determined to strike out the line which had been in the first place demanded by themselves. With much show of justice and reason they alleged that it was not fair to establish the domestic institutions of a country without consulting the inhabitants themselves. They proposed that, for the future, the question of slavery or free soil should be decided by a majority of votes among the settlers on the spot. This proposal became law, and then commenced a race for the soil. In Boston a political society was formed for the exportation to Kansas of Northern men. In the slave state. Missouri, blue lodges were formed for a similar purpose, and hundreds of squatters, dressed in flannel shirts, and huge boots up to their knees, and skin caps on their heads, bristling with revolvers and bowie knives, stepped across the Border. For the first time the people of the North and South met face to face. A guerrilla warfare soon broke out; the New Englanders were robbed and driven back; they were murdered, and their scalps paraded by Border ruffians upon poles. The whole country fell into a distracted state. The Southerners pursued their slaves into Boston itself, and dragged them back, according to the law. A mad abolitionist invaded Virginia with a handful of men, shot a few peaceful citizens, and was hanged. A time of terror fell upon the South; there was neither liberty of print nor liberty of speech; the majority reigned; and the man who spoke against it was lynched upon the spot. A Southerner assaulted and battered a Northerner on the floor of the Senate.

The North at last was thoroughly aroused. The people itself began to stir; a calm, patient, law-abiding race, slow to be moved, but when once moved, swerving never till the thing was done. A presidential election was at hand, and a Northerner was placed upon the throne. The South understood that this was not a casual reverse, which might be redeemed when the four years had passed away. It was to them a sign that the days of their power had for ever passed. The temper of the North was not to be mistaken. It had at last rebelled; it would suffer tyranny no more. Mr. Lincoln's terms were conciliatory in the extreme. Had the South been moderate in its demands, he would have been classed with those statesmen who added compromise to compromise, and so postponed the evil but inevitable day. He was not an abolitionist. He offered to give them any guarantee they pleased--a constitutional amendment if they desired it --that slavery as it stood should not be interfered with. He offered to bring in a more stringent law, by which their fugitive slaves should be restored. But on the matter of extension he was firm. The Southerners demanded that a line should again be drawn to the Pacific; that all south of that line should be made slave soil, and that slavery should be more clearly recognised by the central government, and more firmly guaranteed. These terms were not more extravagant than those which their fathers had obtained. But times had changed: the sentiment of nationality was now more fully formed; "Uncle Tom's Cabin" had been written; the American people were heartily ashamed of slavery; they refused to give it another lease. The ultimatum was declined; the South seceded, and the North flew to arms, not to emancipate the negro, but to preserve the existence of the nation. They would not indeed submit to slavery extension; they preferred disunion to such a disgrace. But they had no intention when they went to war of destroying slavery in the states where it existed; they even took pains to prove to the South that the war was not an anti-slavery crusade. The negroes were treated by the Northern generals not as men, but as contraband of war; even Butler in New Orleans did not emancipate the slaves; a general who issued a proclamation of that nature was reprimanded by the government, although he only followed the example of British generals in the Revolutionary war. But as the contest became more severe and more prolonged, and all hopes of reconciliation were at an end, slavery became identified with the South in the Northern mind, and was itself regarded as a foe. The astute and cautious statesman at the head of affairs perceived that the time had come; the constitution was suspended during the war; and so, in all legality and with due form, he set free in one day four million slaves.

It is impossible to view without compassion the misfortunes of men who merely followed in the footsteps of their fathers, and were in no sense more guilty than Washington and Jefferson, who remained slaveholders to their dying day. It was easy for Great Britain to pay twenty millions; it was easy for the Northern states to emancipate their slaves, who were few in number, and not necessary to their life. But it was impossible for the South to abandon slavery. The money of a planter was sunk in flesh and blood. Yet the Southern politicians must be blamed for their crazy ambition, and their blind ignorance of the world. Instead of preparing as the Cuban planters are preparing now for those changes which had been rendered inevitable by the progress of mankind, they supposed that it was in their power to defy the spirit of the age, and to establish an empire on the pattern of ancient Rome. They firmly believed that, because they could not exist without selling cotton, Great Britain could not exist without buying it from them; which is like a shopkeeper supposing he could ruin his customers by putting up his shutters.

It may console those who yet lament the lost cause if we picture for their benefit what the Southern empire would have been. There would have been an aristocracy of planters, herds of slaves, a servile press, a servile pulpit, and a rabble of mean whites formed into an army. Abolition societies would have been established in the North, to instigate slaves to rebel or run away; a cordon of posts with a system of passports would have been established in the South. Border raids would have been made by fanatics on the one side, and by desperadoes on the other. Sooner or later there must have been a war. Filibustering expeditions on Mexico and Cuba would have brought about a war with Spain, and perhaps with France. It was the avowed intention of the planters, when once their empire was established, to import labour from Africa; to re-open the trade as in the good old times. But this, Great Britain would certainly have not allowed; and thus, again, there would have been war. Even if the planters would have displayed a little common sense, which is exceedingly improbable, and so escaped extirpation from without, their system of culture would have eaten up their lands. But happily such hypotheses need no longer be discussed; a future of another kind is in reserve for the Southern states. America can now pursue with untarnished reputation her glorious career, and time will soften the memories of a conflict, the original guilt of which must be ascribed to the founders of the nation, or rather to the conditions by which those great men were mastered and controlled.

Materials of Human History

I have now accomplished the task which I set myself to do. I have shown to the best of my ability what kind of place in universal history Africa deserves to hold. I have shown that not only Egypt has assisted the development of man by educating Greece, Carthage by leading forth Rome to conquest, but that even the obscure Sudan, or land of the negroes, has also played its part in the drama of European life.

The slave-trade must be estimated as a war; though cruel and atrocious in itself, it has, like most wars, been of service to mankind. I shall leave it to others to trace cut in detail the influence of the negro in the human progress. It will be sufficient to observe that the grandeur of West Indian commerce in the last generation, and of the cotton manufacture at the present time, could not have been obtained without the assistance of the negro: and that the agitation on his behalf, which was commenced by Granville Sharp, has assisted much to expand the sympathies, and to educate the heart of the Anglo-Saxon people, who are somewhat inclined to pride of colour and prejudice of race. Respecting the prospects of the negro, it is difficult for me to form an opinion; but what I have seen of the Africans in their native and semi-civilised condition inclines me to take a hopeful view. The negroes are imitative in an extraordinary degree, and imitation is the first principle of progress. They are vain and ostentatious, ardent for praise, keenly sensitive of blame. Their natural wants, indeed, are few; they inherit the sober appetites of their fathers who lived on a few handfuls of rice a day; but it will, I believe, be found that when they enjoy the same inducements to work as other men, when they can hope to distinguish themselves in the Parliament, the pulpit, or in social life, they will become as we are, the slaves of an idea, and will work day and night to obtain something which they desire, but do not positively need. Whether the negroes are equal in average capacity to the white man, whether they will ever produce a man of genius, is an idle and unimportant question; they can at least gain their livelihood as labourers and artisans; they are therefore of service to their country; let them have fair play, and they will find their right place whatever it may be: As regards the social question, they will no doubt, like the Jews, intermarry always with their own race, and will thus remain apart. But it need not be feared that they will become hostile to those with whom they reside. Experience has shown that, whenever aliens are treated as citizens, they become citizens, whatever may be their religion or their race, It is a mistake to suppose that the civilised negro calls himself an African, and pines to return to his ancestral land. If he is born in the States, he calls himself an American he speaks with an American accent; he loves and he hates with an American heart.

It is a question frequently asked of African travellers, What is the future of that great continent? In the first place, with respect to the West Coast, there is little prospect of great changes taking place for many years to come. The commerce in palm oil is important, and will increase. Cotton will be received in large quantities from the Sudan. The East Coast of Africa, when its resources have been developed, will be a copy of the West Coast. It is not probable that European colonies will ever flourish in these golden but unwholesome lands. The educated negroes will in time monopolise the trade, for they can live at less expense than Europeans, and do not suffer from the climate. They may perhaps at some future day possess both coasts, and thence spread with Bible and musket into the interior. This prospect, however, is uncertain, and in any case exceedingly remote.

That part of Africa which lies above the parallel 10° North belongs to the Eastern Question. What ever may be the ultimate destiny of Egypt, Algeria, and Morocco, will be shared by the regions of the central Niger, from Haussa to Timbuctoo.

That part of the continent which lies below the parallel 20° South, already belongs in part, and will in time entirely belong to settlers of the Anglo-Saxon race. It resembles

Australia, not only in its position with respect to the Equator, but also in its natural productions. It is a land of wool and mines, without great navigable rivers, interspersed with sandy deserts, and enjoying a wholesome though sultry air. Whatever may be the future of Australia will also be the future of Southern Africa.

Between these two lines intervenes a region inhabited for the most part by pagan savages, thinly scattered over swamp and forest. This concealed continent, this unknown world, will at some far-off day, if my surmises prove correct, be invaded by three civilising streams; by the British negroes from the coasts by the Mohammedan negroes in robe and turban from the great empires of the Niger region; and by the farmers and graziers and miners of South Africa.

When, therefore, we speculate on the future of Africa, we can do no more than bring certain regions of that continent within the scope of two general questions; the future of our colonies, and the future of the East; and these lead us up to a greater question still, the future of the European race.

Upon this subject I shall offer a few remarks; and it is obvious that in order to form some conception of the future it is necessary to understand the present and the past. I shall therefore endeavour to ascertain what we have been and what we are. The monograph of Africa is ended. I shall make my sketch of history complete, adding new features, passing quickly over the parts that have been already drawn. I shall search out the origin of man, determine his actual condition, speculate upon his future destiny, and discuss the nature of his relations towards that unknown Power of whom he is the offspring and the slave. I shall examine this planet and its contents with the calm curiosity of one whose sentiments and passions, whose predilections and antipathies, whose hopes and fears, are not interested in the question. I shall investigate without prejudice; I shall state the results without reserve.

What are the materials of human history? What are the earliest records which throw light upon the origin of man? All written documents are things of yesterday, whether penned on prepared skins, papyrus rolls, or the soft inner bark of trees; whether stamped on terra-cotta tablets, carved on granite obelisks, or engraved on the smooth surface of upright rocks. Writing, even in its simplest picture form, is an art which can be invented only when a people have become mature.

The oldest books are therefore comparatively modern, and the traditions which they contain are either false or but little older than the books themselves. All travellers who have collected traditions among a wild people know how little that kind of evidence is worth. The savage exaggerates whenever he repeats, and in a few generations the legend is transformed.

The evidence of language is of more value. It enables us to trace back remotely divided nations to their common birth-place, and reveals the amount of culture, the domestic institutions, and the religious ideas which they possessed before they parted from one another. Yet languages soon die, or rather become metamorphosed in structure as well as in vocabulary; the oldest existing language can throw no light on the condition of primeval man.

The archives of the earth also offer us their testimony: the graves give up their dead, and teach us that man existed many thousand years ago, in company with monstrous animals that have long since passed away; and that those men were savages, using weapons and implements of stone, yet possessing even then a taste for ornament and art, wearing shell bracelets, and drawing rude figures upon horns and stones. The manners and ideas of such early tribes can best be inferred by a study of existing savages. The missionary who resides among such races as the Bushmen of Africa or the Botocudos of Brazil may be said to live in pre -historic times.

But as regards the origin of man, we have only one document to which we can refer; and that is the body of man himself. There, in unmistakable characters, are inscribed the annals of his early life. These hieroglyphics are not to be fully deciphered without a special preparation for the task: the alphabet of anatomy must first be mastered, and the student must be expert in the language of all living and fossil forms. One fact, however, can be submitted to the uninitiated eye, and it will be sufficient for the purpose. Look at a skeleton and you will see a little bone curled downwards between the legs, as if trying to hide itself away. That bone is a relic of pre-human days, and announces plainly whence our bodies come. We are all of us naked under our clothes, and we are of all us tailed under our skins. But when we descend to the man-like apes, we find that, with them as with us, the tail is effete and in disuse; and so we follow it downwards and downwards until we discover it in all its glory in the body of the fish; being there present, not as a relic or rudimentary organ, as in man and the apes; not a mere appendage, as in the fox; not a secondary instrument, a spare hand, as in certain monkeys, or a fly-flapper, as in the giraffe; but as a primary organ of the very first importance, endowing the fish with its locomotive powers. Again, we examine the body of the fish, and we find in it also rudimentary organs as useless and incongruous as the tail in man; and thus we descend step by step, until we arrive at the very bottom of the scale.

The method of development is still being actively discussed, but the fact is placed beyond a doubt. Since The Origin of Species appeared, philosophical naturalists no longer deny that the ancestors of man must he sought for in the lower kingdom. And, apart from the evidence which we carry with us in our own persons, which we read in the tail-bone of the skeleton, in the hair which was once the clothing of our bodies, in the nails which were once our weapons of defence, and in a hundred other facts which the scalpel and the microscope disclose; apart from the evidence of our own voices, our incoherent groans and cries, analogy alone would lead us to believe that mankind had been developed from the lowest forms of life. For what is the history of the individual man? He begins life as an ambiguous speck of matter which can in no way be distinguished from the original form of the lowest animal or plant. He next becomes a cell; his life is precisely that of the animalcule. Cells cluster round this primordial cell, and the man is so far advanced that he might be mistaken for an undeveloped oyster; he grows still more, and it is clear that he might even be a fish; he then passes into a stage which is common to all quadrupeds, and next assumes a form which can only belong to quadrupeds of the higher type. At last the hour of birth approaches; coiled within, the dark womb he sits, the image of an ape; a caricature and, a prophecy of the man that is to be. He is born, and for some time he walks only on all-fours; he utters only inarticulate sounds; and even in his boyhood his fondness for climbing trees would seem to be a relic of the old arboreal life. Since, therefore, every man has been himself in such a state that the most experienced observer could not with the aid of the best microscopes have declared whether he was going to be man or plant, man or animalcule, man or mollusc, man or lobster, man or fish, man or reptile, man or bird, man or quadruped, man or monkey; why should it appear strange that the whole race has also had its animalcule and its reptile days? But whether it appears strange or not, the public must endeavour to accustom its mind to the fact which is now firmly, established, and will never be overthrown.

Not only are the bodies, but also the minds of man constructed on the same pattern as those of the lower animals. To procure food; to obtain a mate; and to rear offspring; such is the real business of life with us as it is with them. If we look into ourselves we discover propensities which declare that our intellects have arisen from a lower form; could our minds be made visible we should find them tailed. And if we examine the minds of the lower animals, we find in them the rudiments of our talents and our virtues. As the beautiful yet imperfect human body has been slowly developed from the base and hideous creatures of the water and the earth, so the beautiful yet imperfect human mind has been slowly developed from the instincts of the lower animals. All that is elevated, all that is lovely in human nature has its origin in the lower kingdom. The philosophic spirit of inquiry may be traced to brute curiosity, and that to the habit of examining all things in search of food. Artistic genius is an expansion of monkey imitativeness. Loyalty and piety, the reverential virtues, are developed from filial love. Benevolence and magnanimity, the generous virtues, from parental love. The sense of decorum proceeds from the sense of cleanliness; and that from the instinct of sexual display. The delicate and ardent love which can become a religion of the heart, which can sanctify and soften a man's whole life; the affection which is so noble, and so pure, and so free from all sensual stain, is yet derived from that desire which impels the male animal to seek a mate; and the sexual timidity which makes the female flee from the male is finally transformed into that maiden modesty which not only preserves from vice, but which conceals beneath a chaste and honourable reticence the fiery love that burns within; which compels the true woman to pine in sorrow, and perhaps to languish into death, rather than betray a passion that is not returned.

There is a certain class of people who prefer to say that their fathers came down in the world through their own follies rather than to boast that they rose in the world through their own industry and talents. It is the same shabby-genteel sentiment, the same vanity of birth which makes men prefer to believe that they are degenerated angels, rather than elevated apes. In scientific investigations such whims and fancies must be set aside. It is the duty of the inquirer to ascertain the truth, and then to state it as decisively and as clearly as he can. People's prejudices must not be respected but destroyed. It may, however, be worth while to observe, for the comfort of weak souls, that in these new revelations of science human nature is not in any way degraded. A woman's body is not less lovely because it was once a hideous mass of flesh. A woman's modesty is not less noble because we discover that it was once a mere propensity, dictated, perhaps, by the fear of pain. The beauty of the mind is not less real than the beauty of the body, and we need not be discouraged because we ascertain that it has also passed through its embryonic stage. It is Nature's method to take something which is in itself paltry, repulsive, and grotesque, and thence to construct a masterpiece by means of general and gradual laws; those laws themselves being often vile and cruel. This method is applied not only to single individuals, but also to the whole animated world; not only to physical but also to mental forms. And when it is fully realised and understood that the genius of man has been developed along a line of unbroken descent from the simple tendencies which inhabited the primeval cell, and that in its later stages this development has been assisted by the efforts of man himself, what a glorious futurity will open to the human race! It may well be that our minds have not done growing, and that we may rise as high above our present state as that state is removed from the condition of the insect and the worm. For when we examine the human mind we do not find it perfect and mature; but in a transitional and amphibious condition. We live between two worlds; we soar in the atmosphere; we creep upon the soil; we have the aspirations of creators and the propensities of quadrupeds. There can be but one explanation of this fact. We are passing from the animal into a higher form; and the drama of this planet is in its second act. We shall now endeavour to place the first upon the stage, and, then passing through the second, shall proceed to speculate upon the third. The scene opens with the solar system. Time uncertain; say, a thousand million years ago.

Chapter IV. Intellect

Animal Period of the Earth

That region of the universe which is visible to mortal eyes has been named the solar system: it is composed of innumerable stars, and each star is a white hot sun, the centre and sovereign of a world. Our own sun is attended by a company of cold, dark globes, revolving round it in accordance with the law of gravitation; they also rotate like joints before the fire, turning first one side, and then the other, to the central light. The path that is traced by the outermost planet is the limit of the sun's domain, which is too extensive to be measured into miles. If a jockey mounted on a winner of the Derby had started when Moses was born, and had galloped ever since at full speed, he would be by this time about half the way across. Yet this world seems large to us, only because we are so small. It is merely a drop in the ocean of space. The stars which we see on a fine night are also suns as important as our own; and so vast is the distance which separates their worlds from ours, that a flash of lightning would be years upon the road. These various solar systems are not independent of one another they are members of the same community. They are sailing in order round a point to us unknown. Our own sun, drawing with it the planets in its course, is spinning furiously upon its axis, and dashing through space at four miles a second. And not only is the solar system an organ of one gigantic form; it has also grown to what it is, and may still be considered in its youth. As the body of a plant or animal arises from a fluid alike in all its parts, so this world of ours was once a floating fiery cloud, a nebula or mist, the molecules of which were kept asunder by excessive heat. But the universe is pervaded by movement and by change; there came a period when the heat declined, and when the atoms obeying their innate desires rushed to one another, and, concentrating, formed the sun, which at first almost filled the solar world. But as it cooled, and as it contracted, and as it rotated, and as it revolved, it became a sphere in the centre of the world; and it cast off pieces which became planets, satellites, attendant stars, and they also cast off pieces which became satellites to them. Thus the earth is the child, and the moon the grandchild of the sun. When our planet first came out into the world it was merely a solar fragment, a chip of the old star, and the other planets were in a similar condition. But these sunballs were separated from one another, and from their parent form, by oceans of ether, a kind of attenuated air, so cold that frost itself is fire in comparison. The sun burning always in this icy air is gradually cooling down; but it parts slowly with its heat on account of its enormous size. Our little earth cooled quickly, shrank in size--it had once extended to the moon--and finally went out. From a globe of glowing gas it became a ball of liquid fire, enveloped in a smoky cloud. When first we are able to restore its image and examine its construction, we find it composed of zones or layers in a molten state, arranged according to their weight;

and above it we find an atmosphere also divided into layers. Close over the surface vapour of salt was suspended in the air; next, a layer of dark, smoky, carbonic acid gas; next, oxygen and nitrogen, and vapour of water or common steam. Within the sphere, as it cooled and changed, chemical bodies sprang from one another, rushed to and fro, combined with terrible explosions; while in the variegated atmosphere above, gas-hurricanes arose and flung the elements into disorder. So sped the earth, roaring and flaming through the sky, leaving behind it a fiery track, sweeping round the sun in its oval course.

Year followed year, century followed century, epoch followed epoch. Then the globe began to cool upon its surface. Flakes of solid matter floated on the molten sea, which rose and fell in flaming tides towards a hidden and benighted moon. The flakes caked together, and covered the ball with a solid sheet, which was upraised and cracked by the tidal waves beneath, like thin ice upon the Arctic seas. In time it thickened and became firm, but subterranean storms often ripped it open in vast chasms, from which masses of liquid lava spouted in the air, and fell back upon the hissing crust. Everywhere heaps of ashes were thus formed, and the earth was seamed with scars and gaping wounds. When the burning heat of the air had abated, the salt was condensed, and fell like snow upon the earth, and covered it ten feet thick. The Atlantic and Pacific Oceans, lying overhead in the form of steam, descended in one great shower, and so the primeval sea was formed. It was dark, warm, and intensely salt; at first it overspread the surface of the globe; then volcanic islands were cast up; and as the earth cooled downwards to its core, it shrivelled into folds as an apple in the winter when its pulp dries up. These folds and wrinkles were mountain ranges, and continents appearing above the level of the sea. Our planet was then divided into land and water in the same proportions as exist at the present time. For though land is always changing into water, and water is always changing into land, their relative quantities remain the same. The air was black, night was eternal, illumined only by lightning and volcanoes; the earth was unconscious of the sun's existence; its heat was derived from the fire within, and was uniform from pole to pole. But the crust thickened; the inner heat could no longer be felt upon the surface; the atmosphere brightened a little, and the sun's rays penetrated to the earth. From the shape, the altitude, and the revolutions of our planet, resulted an unequal distribution of solar heat, and to this inequality the earth is indebted for the varied nature of its aspects and productions. Climate was created: winds arose in the air; currents in the deep; the sun sucked up the waters of the sea, leaving the salt behind; rain-clouds were formed, and fresh water bestowed upon the land. The underground fires assisted the planet's growth by transforming the soils into crystalline structures, and by raising the rocks thus altered to the surface; by producing volcanic eruptions, hot springs, and other fiery phenomena. But the chief architect and decorator of this planet was the sun. When the black veil of the earth was lifted, when the sunlight entered the turbid waters of the primeval sea, "an interesting event" took place. The earth became with young.

In water there are always floating about a multitude of specks which are usually minute fragments of the soil. But now appeared certain specks which, though they resembled the others, possessed certain properties of a very peculiar kind. First, they brought forth little specks, precise copies of themselves: they issued their own duplicates. And secondly, they performed in their own persons an elaborate chemical operation. Imbibing water and air, they manufactured those elements with the assistance of the solar rays, into the compounds of which their own bodies were composed, giving back to the water those components which they did not require. And then appeared other little specks which swallowed up the first, and manufactured them into the compounds more complex still, of which they, the second comers, were composed. The first were embryonic plants; the second were embryonic animals. They were both alike in appearance; both repeated themselves, or reproduced, in the same manner. The difference between them was this, that the plants could live on raw air and water, the animals could live only on those elements when prepared by sun light in the body of the plant. The office of vegetation upon the earth is therefore of a culinary nature, and the plant, when devoured, gives the animal that heat which is its life, just as coal (a cake of fossil vegetation) gives heat to the apartment in which it is consumed. But this heat, whether it lies hidden in the green and growing plant, or in its black and stony corpse, was at first acquired from the sun. Glorious Apollo is the parent of us all. Animal heat is solar heat; a blush is a stray sunbeam; Life is bottled sunshine, and Death the silent-footed butler who draws out the cork.

Origin and Early History of Man

Those dots of animated jelly, without definite form or figure, swimming unconsciously in the primeval sea, were the ancestors of man. The history of our race begins with them, and continues without an interruption to the present day; a splendid narrative, the materials of which it is for science to discover, the glories of which it is for poets to portray.

Owing to the action of surrounding forces, the outer parts of the original jelly-dot became harder and more solid than the parts within, and so it assumed the shape of the cell or sphere. Its food consisted of microscopic fragments of vegetable matter imbibed through its surface or outer rind, such portions as were not "made up" being expelled or excreted in the same manner as they were taken in. There was no difference of parts, except that the outside was solid and the inside soft. The creature's body was its hand, its stomach, and its mouth. When it had lived a certain time it burst and died, liberating, as it did so, a brood of cells which had slowly ripened within. But sometimes these new cells, instead of being detached when they were born, remained cohering to the parent cell, thus making the animal consist of several cells instead of only one. In the first case the process is termed reproduction; in the second case it is termed growth. But the two operations are in reality the same. Growth is coherent reproduction; reproduction is detached growth.

Time goes on. Our animal is now a cell-republic enclosed by a wrapper of solidified and altered cells. Next, in this wrapper a further change takes place. It protrudes into limbs; a gaping month appears. The limbs or tentacles grasp the food and put it within the mouth; other limbs sprout forth and carry their owner from place to place. In the meantime the cells within are also changed; their partitions are removed; the many-walled apartments are converted into galleries or tubes, along which the food is conveyed from one part of the body to another. These tubes are filled with blood, pumped backwards and forwards by the heart. The muscles which move the outer limbs are equipped with nerves, the movements of which are directed from centres in the spine and brain. The functions of life are thus divided, and each department has an organ of its own. The reproductive function is divided farther still. Two separate elements are formed; one prepares and ejects the sperm-cell which the other receives, and unites to the germ-cell. At a later period in the history of life this arrangement is supplanted by another, more complicated still. The two elements no longer co-exist in the same form, and thus reproduction can only be effected by means of co-operation between two distinct and independent individuals. How important a fact is this will presently appear.

These various inventions of Nature, so far as we have gone; the limbs of locomotion and prehension; the heart with its vessels; the brain with its nerves; and the separation of the sexes, all occurred in the marine period of the earth's life: in the dark deep sea womb.

Similar changes, but inferior in degree, occurred in the vegetable world. The shapeless specks became one-celled: they were next strung together like a chain of beads; they then grew into seaweed and aqueous plants, which floated about, and finally obtained a footing on the land. But they dwelt long ages on the earth before their sex appeared. There were no flowers in that primeval world, for the flower is a sign of love. Gigantic mosses and tree ferns clothed the earth, and reproduced themselves by scattering cells around.

Animals followed their prey, the plants, from the water to the land and became adapted for terrestrial life. At that period the atmosphere was thickened with carbonic acid gas, and was more pestilential than the Black Hole of Calcutta. Only reptiles, with sluggish and imperfect respiratory organs, could breathe in such an air. But that fatal gas was bread to the vegetable world, which took the carbon into its body, and thus the atmosphere was purified in time. The vast masses of carbon which the plants took out of the air in order to allow a higher class of animal to appear upon the stage, were buried in the earth, hardened into coal, and were brought in by the Author in the second act--now on.

The coal-matter being thus removed, the air was bright and pure; the sun glowed with radiance and force; the reptiles were converted into birds and quadrupeds of many kinds; insects rising from the land and from the water hummed and sparkled in the air; the forests were adorned with flowers, and cheered with song. And as the periods rolled on, the inhabitants of the earth became more complex in their structure, more symmetrical in form, and more advanced in mental power, till at last the future lord of the planet himself appeared upon the stage. The first act of the drama is here concluded: but the division is merely artificial; in Nature there is no entr'acte; no curtain falls. Her scenes resemble dissolving views; the lower animals pass into man by soft, slow, insensible gradations.

We must now consider the question, How and why have these marvellous changes taken place? How and why did the primeval jelly-dots assume the form of the cell or sphere?

It has been already shown that continual changes occurred in the primeval atmosphere and in the primeval sea. These changes acting upon animal life produced changes in its composition. For as animals are the result and expression of the conditions under which they are born, it is natural to suppose that when these conditions are changed, the animals should also change. When the conditions of life are abruptly altered and instantaneously transformed, the animals are of course destroyed; but when, as is usually the case, the changes are gradual, the animals are slowly modified into harmony with the neighbouring conditions. The primeval speck of life being acted upon by a variety of forces, became varied in its structure and as these forces varied from period to period, the organisms also varied. Complexity of parts results from complexity of environment. Multiformity of circumstance produces multiformity of species. The development of animal life from the homogeneous to the heterogeneous, from the simple to the complex, from uniformity to multiformity, is caused by the development of the earth itself from a monotonous water-covered globe with one aspect, one constitution, and one temperature to this varied earth on which we dwell, where each foot of land differs in some respect from the one beside it. The modifications on modifications of the animal are due to the modifications on modifications of the medium in which and on which it lived. And this operation of Nature is hastened and facilitated by a law which in itself is murderous and cruel. The earth is over-populated upon principle. Of the animals that are born, a few only can survive. There is not enough food for all; Nature scrambles what there is among the crowd. If any animal possesses an advantage, however slight, over those with whom he competes in this food-scramble or struggle for existence, he will certainly survive; and if he survives, then some one else, so gentle Nature orders it, must die. This law of competition becomes itself a force by developing slight variations along lines of utility into widely different and specific forms.

But how is it that animals of the higher type prevail? Why should species, with a tendency towards a complicated structure, generally triumph over simple forms? The reason appears to be this, that whenever a change takes place, it is almost invariably a change towards complexity. Now it is an ascertained law that animals are invigorated by a slight change; they are therefore improved by an approach towards complexity. Let us take the most mysterious of all progressive operations--the division of the sexes. The hermaphrodite can fertilise itself, but its organs are so arranged that it can be fertilised by another individual, the wind or the water acting as the go-between. The offspring of such separate unions are always more vigorous than the home-born progeny of the hermaphrodite. The latter are therefore killed off by means of the struggle for existence, and sexual union, at first the exception, becomes the rule. Just as a body of artisans can do more work and better work when each man devotes his whole life to a single department of the craft, so it is good for the animal that division of labour should be established in its structure; that instead of the creature being its own mouth, its own stomach, its own organ of excretion, reproduction, and locomotion, it should be divided into separate parts, one of which moves it, another part takes the food, another part chews, another part digests, another part prepares the blood, another part pumps the blood to and fro, another part reproduces the species, another part nourishes the young, while over all presides the brain.

But how is it that some animals have progressed while others have remained at the bottom of the scale, and others again have advanced only to a certain point? If all have grown out of such specks of animated jelly as are still to be found within the sea, how is it that some have remained throughout infinite periods of time unchanged; that others have remained in the form of the sponge, rooted upon rocks; that others, like the lobster, have never exchanged their jointed bodies for the more perfect skeleton of the fish; that some fish have taken to the land, and have been converted into reptiles, and then into birds or quadrupeds, while others have remained in the aqueous condition; and lastly, that one animal, namely Man, has contrived to distance all the others when, as it is acknowledged, they all started fair?

In reply, let me ask those who admit the development of all civilised people from the savage state--and that no geologist will now deny; --let me ask them how it is that Europeans have advanced (this involving a change in the structure of the brain), while others have remained in the savage state, others in the pastoral condition, others fixed at a certain point of culture, as the Hindus and the Chinese? The analogy is perfect, and the answer is in either case the same. Those forms remain stationary which are able to preserve their conditions of life unchanged. The savages of the primeval forest, when the game is exhausted in one region, migrate to another region where game exists. They remain therefore in the hunting state. The shepherds of the boundless plains, when one pasture is devoured by their flocks, migrate to another pasture where they find grass and water in abundance. But when, in a land like Egypt, the inhabitants are confined to a certain tract of land they are unable to evade the famine of food produced by the vicissitudes of nature and the law of population; they are compelled to invent in order to subsist; new modes of life, new powers, new desires, new sentiments arise; and the human animal is changed. Then a second period of immobility arrives; by means of despotism, caste, slavery, and infanticide, the status quo is preserved.

In the primeval sea the conditions of life were constantly changing, but its inmates could usually keep them constant by migration. For instance, let us imagine a species accustomed to dwell at the bottom of the sea, feeding on the vegetable matter and oxygen gas which come down by liquid diffusion from the waters of the surface. By elevation of the sea-bed, or by the deposit of sediment from rivers, that part of the sea which this species inhabits becomes gradually shallow and light. The animal would migrate into deep dark water, and would therefore undergo no change. But let us suppose that it is prevented from migrating by a wall of rocks. It would then be exposed to light, and to other novel forces, and it would either change or die.

Here progress is the result of absolute necessity, and such must always be the case. Animals which inhabit the waters have no innate desire to make acquaintance with the land; but it sometimes happens that they live in shallow places, where they are left uncovered at low water for a certain time, and so in the course of geological periods the species becomes amphibious in habit; and then the hard struggle for life in the water, with the abundance of food upon the land, leads them to adopt terrestrial life. There are creatures now existing of whom it is not easy to say whether they belong to the water or the land: there are fishes which walk about on shore, and climb trees: It is not difficult to imagine such animals as these deserting the water, and entirely living upon land.

But the development of life, in its varied aspects, must always remain incomprehensible to those who have not studied the noble science of geology, or who at least have not made themselves acquainted with its chief results. Unless the student understands what extraordinary transformation scenes have taken place upon the globe, all that is now land, having formerly been sea, and all that is now sea having formerly been land, not only once, but again, and again, and again; unless he understands that these changes have been produced by the same gradual, and apparently insignificant, causes as those which are now at work before our eyes; the sea gnawing away the cliff upon the shore; the river carrying soil to the sea; the glacier gliding down the mountain slope; the iceberg bearing huge boulders to mid ocean; the coralline insects building archipelagoes; the internal fires suddenly spouting forth stones and ashes, or slowly upheaving continents; unless he fully understands how deliberate is Nature's method, how prodigal she is of time, how irregular and capricious she is in all her operations--he will never cease to wonder that allied forms should be distributed in apparent disorder and confusion, instead of being arranged on a regular ascending scale. And, moreover, unless he understands how Nature, like the Sibyl, destroys her own books, he will never cease to wonder at missing links.

For it is not one missing link, but millions, that we require. It would however be just as reasonable to expect to find every book that ever was written; every clay tablet that ever was baked in the printing ovens of Chaldaea; every rock that was ever inscribed; every obelisk that was ever engraved, every temple wall that was ever painted with hieroglyphics, as to expect to find every fossil of importance. Where are the missing links in literature, and where are the primeval forms? Where are the ancient Sanskrit hymns that were written without ink on palm leaves with an iron pen? Where are the thousands of Hebrew bibles that were written before the tenth century A.D.? Where are the lost books of the Romans and the Greeks? We know that many manuscripts have been consumed in great fires; the fire of Alexandria in the time of Julius Caesar, which no doubt destroyed papyri that could never be replaced; the fire in the time of Omar; the fires lighted by Popes and reverend Fathers of the Church; and the fire of Constantinople during the Crusades, which robbed us for ever of Arian's history of the successors of Alexander; Ctesias' history of Persia, and his description of India; several books of Diodorus, Agatharcides, and Polybius; twenty orations of Demosthenes, and the Odes of Sappho. But the material of books, whether paper or parchment, bark, clay, or stone, is always of a perishable nature, and, under ordinary circumstances, is destroyed sooner or later by the action of the atmosphere. Were it not that books can be copied, what would remain to us of the literature of the past?

In a rainless country such as Egypt, which is a museum of Nature, a monumental land, not only painted and engraven records, but even paper scrolls of an immense antiquity, have been preserved. But if we add to these the rock inscriptions, the printed bricks, and inscribed cylinders of Western Asia, how scanty and fortuitous are the remains! Let us now remember that fossils cannot be copied; once destroyed, they are for ever lost. Is it wonderful, therefore, that so few should be left? Fires greater than those of Alexandria and Constantinople are ever burning beneath our feet; at this very moment a precious library may be in flames. Yet that is not the worst. The action of air and water is fatal to the archives of Nature, which it is not part of Nature's plan to preserve for our instruction. Those animals which have neither bones nor shells are at once destroyed; and those which possess a solid framework are only preserved under special and exceptional conditions. The marvel is not that we find so little, but that we find so much. The development of man from the lower animals is now an authenticated fact. We believe, therefore, that connecting links between man and some ape-like animal existed for the same reason that we believe the Second Decade of Livy existed. It is not impossible that the missing books of Livy may be, discovered at some future day beneath the Italian soil. It is not impossible that forms intermediate between man and his ape-like ancestors may be discovered in the unexplored strata of equatorial Africa, or the Indian Archipelago. But either event is improbable in the extreme; and the existence of such intermediate forms will be admitted by the historians of the next generation, whether they are found or not.

We shall now proceed to describe the rise and progress of the mental principle. The origin of mind is an inscrutable mystery, but so is the origin of matter. If we go back to the beginning we find a world of gas, the atoms of which were kept asunder by excessive heat. Where did those atoms come from? How were they made? What were they made for? In reply to these questions theology is garrulous, but science is dumb.

Mind is a property of matter. Matter is inhabited by mind. There can be no mind without matter; there can be no matter without mind. When the matter is simple in its composition, its mental tendencies are also simple; the atoms merely tend to approach one another and to cohere; and as matter under the influence of varied forces (evolved by the cooling o the world) becomes more varied in its composition, its mental tendencies become more and more numerous, more and more complex, more and more elevated, till at last they are developed into the desires and propensities of the animal, into the aspirations and emotions of the man. But the various tendencies which inhabit the human mind, and which devote it to ambition, to religion, or to love, are not in reality more wonderful than the tendency which impels two ships to approach each other in a calm. For what can be more wonderful than that which can never be explained? The difference between the mind of the ship and the mind of man is the difference between the acorn and the oak.

The simplest atoms are attracted to one another merely according to distance and weight. That is the law of gravitation. But the compound atoms, which are called elements, display a power of selection. A will unite itself to C in preference to B; and if D passes by, will divorce itself from C, and unite itself to D. Such compounds of a compound are still more complex in their forms, and more varied in their minds. Water, which is composed of two gases--oxygen and hydrogen--when hot, becomes a vapour; when cold, becomes a crystal. In the latter case it displays a structural capacity. Crystals assume particular forms according to the substances of which they are composed; they may be classed into species, and if their forms are injured by accident, they have the power of repairing their structure by imbibing matter from without. A live form is the result of matter subjected to certain complex forces, the chief of which is the chemical power of the sun. It is continually being injured by the wear and tear of its own activity; it is continually darning and stitching its own life. After a certain period of time it loses its self-mending power, and consequently dies. The crystal grows from without by simple accretions or putting on of coats. The plant or animal grows and re-grows from within by means of a chemical operation. Moreover, the crystal is merely an individual; the plant or animal is the member of a vast community; before it dies, and usually as it dies, it produces a repetition of itself. The mental forces which inhabit the primeval jelly-dot are more complex than those which inhabit the crystal; but those of the crystal are more complex than those of a gas, and those of a gas than those of the true elementary atoms which know only two forces--attraction and repulsion --the primeval "Pull and Push," which lie at the basis of all Nature's operations.

The absorption of food and the repetition of form in the animal are not at first to be distinguished from that chemical process which is termed growth. Then from this principle of growth, the root of the human flower, two separated instincts like twin seed-leaves arise. The first is the propensity to preserve self-life by seeking food; from this instinct of self-preservation our intellectual faculties have been derived. The second is the propensity to preserve the life of the species; and from this instinct of reproduction our moral faculties have been derived.

The animal at first absorbs its food and unites with its mate as blindly and as helplessly as the crystal shapes itself into its proper form, as oxygen combines with hydrogen, or as ships roll towards each other in a calm. How then can a line be drawn between the inorganic and the organic, the lifeless and the alive? The cell that vibrates in the water, and the crystal that forms in the frost, are each the result of certain forces over which they have no control. But as the body of the animal is developed in complexity, by the action of complex forces, certain grey lumps of matter make their appearance within its structure, and out of these rises a spirit which introduces the animal to himself, which makes him conscious of his own existence. He becomes aware that he is alive; that he has an appetite; and that other animals have an appetite for him. His mind, though feeble and contracted, is improved by experience. He devises stratagems to avoid his enemies, or to seize his prey.

At certain seasons he becomes conscious of his desire for a mate and that which, with his ancestors, was a blind tendency, an inherited part of growth, becomes with him a passion brightened by intelligence.

It is usually supposed that the transition of an ape-like animal into man is the most remarkable event in the history of animated forms. But this idea arises from human vanity and ignorance. The most remarkable event, after the origin of life, is certainly that to which we now allude; the first glimmering of consciousness and reason. Yet even here we can draw no dividing line. The animal becomes conscious that he desires food, and at certain periods, a mate; but the desires themselves are not new; they existed and they ruled him long before. When developed to a certain point, he begins to "take notice," as the nurses say; but his nature remains the same, However, this intelligence becomes in time itself a force, and gradually obtains to some extent the faculty of directing the forces by which the animal was once despotically ruled. By an effort of the human brain, for example, the reproductive force, or tendency, or instinct, can be obliterated and suppressed.

What we have to say, then, respecting the origin of our early ancestors is this: That when matter was subjected to a complicated play of forces, chief among which was solar influence, plants and animals came into life; and that when animals were subjected to an ever-increasing variety of forces, they became varied in their structure; and that when their structure had attained a certain measure of variety they became conscious of their own existence; and that then Nature endowed them with the faculty of preserving their lives and that of their species by means of their own conscious efforts. Next, it will be shown that the successful competitors in the struggle for existence not only obtained the food and females for which they strove, but also, by means of the efforts which they made in order to obtain them, raised themselves unconsciously in the animated scale. And lastly, we shall find that men who, in the savage state, are little better than the brutes, their lives being absorbed in the business of self-preservation and reproduction, are now in the civilised condition becoming conscious of the scheme of Nature, and are beginning to assist her by the methodical improvement of their mental powers.

The lower animals have a hard matter to earn their daily bread, and to preserve their children from starvation; and with them the course of true love does not by any means run smooth. Since only a few can succeed in the scramble for food, and not all can obtain mates, for polygamy frequently prevails, it follows as a matter of necessity that those animals which are the strongest, the swiftest, and the most intelligent will survive and leave offspring, and by the continued survival of the fittest the animated world improves from generation to generation, and rises in the scale. So far as strength and swiftness are concerned, limits are placed upon improvement. But there are no limits to the improvement of intelligence. We find in the lower kingdom muscular power in its perfection; but the brain is always imperfect, always young, always growing, always capable of being developed. In writing the history of animal progress we must therefore concentrate our attention upon the brain, and we shall find that the development of that organ is in great measure due to the influence of the affections.

Whether Nature has placed pain at the portals of love throughout the animal kingdom as she has at the portals of maternity, or whatever may be the cause, it is certain that the female flees from the male at the courting season, and that he captures her by means of his strength, swiftness, dexterity, or cunning, in the same manner as he obtains his prey. He is also obliged to fight duels in order to possess or to retain her, and thus his courage is developed. But at a later period in animal life a more peaceable kind of courtship comes into vogue. The females become queens. They select their husbands from a crowd of admirers, who strive to please them with their colours, their perfumes, or their music. The cavaliers, adorned in their bright wedding suits, which they wear only at the lovemaking season, display themselves before the dames. Others serenade them with vocal song, or by means of an apparatus fitted to the limbs, which corresponds to instrumental music. Rival troubadours will sing before their lady, as she sits in her leafy bower till one of them is compelled to yield from sheer exhaustion, and a feathered hero has been known to sing till he dropped down dead. At this period sexual timidity becomes a delicious coyness which arouses the ardour of the male. Thus love is born: it is brought forth by the association of ideas. The desire of an animal to satisfy a want grows into an affection beyond and independent of the want.

In the same manner the love of the young for its parents grows out of its liking for the food which the parents supply; and the love of parents for the young, though more obscure, may perhaps also be explained by association. The mother no doubt believes the offspring to be part of herself, as it was in fact but a short time before, and thus feels for it a kind of self-love. The affection of the offspring for the parents, and of parents for the offspring, and of spouses for each other, at first endures only for a season. But when the intelligence of the animals has risen to a certain point, their powers of memory are improved, they recognise their parents, their spouses, their young, long after the business of the nest is over, and consort together to renew their caresses and endearments. In this manner the flock is formed; it is based upon domestic love. And soon experience teaches them the advantages of union. They are the better able when in flocks to obtain food, and to defend themselves against their foes. They accordingly dwell together, and by means of their social habits their intelligence is quickened, their affections are enlarged. The members of animal societies possess in a marvellous degree the power of co-operation, the sentiment of fidelity to the herd. By briefly describing what the lower animals do, and what they feel, we shall show that they possess in a dispersed and elementary condition all the materials of which human nature is composed.

In their communities there is sometimes a regular form of government and a division into castes. They have their monarch, their labourers, and soldiers, who are sterile females like the Amazons of Dahomey. They have slaves which they capture by means of military expeditions, attacking the villages of their victims and carrying off the prisoners in their mouths. They afterwards make the slaves carry them. They have domestic animals which they milk. They form alliances with animals of a foreign species or nationality and admit them into the community when it can be profited thereby. They build houses or towns which are ingeniously constructed, and which, in proportion to the size of the architects, are greater than the Pyramids. They have clubhouses or salons which they decorate with flowers and bright shells. They march in regular order; when they feed they post sentries which utter alert cries from time to time, just as our sentries cry "All's well." They combine to execute punishment, expelling or killing an ill-conducted member of the tribe. As among savages, the sick and the weakly are usually killed: though sometimes they are kept alive by alms; even the blind being fed by charitable persons. They labour incessantly for the welfare of the community; they bear one another's burdens; they fight with indomitable courage for the fatherland, and endeavour to rescue a comrade even against overwhelming odds. The domestic virtues are strong among them. Their conjugal love is often intense and pure;

spouses have been known to pine to death when parted from each other. But if they have human virtues, they have also human vices; conjugal infidelity is known among them; and some animals appear to be profligate by nature. They are exceedingly jealous. They sport, and gamble, and frisk, and caress, and kiss each other, putting mouth to mouth. They shed tears. They utter musical sounds in tune. They are cleanly in their persons. They are ostentatious and vain, proud of their personal appearance, bestowing much time upon their toilet. They meditate and execute revenge, keeping in memory those who have offended them. They dream. They are capable of reflection and selection; they deliberate between two opposite desires. They are inquisitive and often fall victims to their passion for investigating every object which they have not seen before. They profit by experience; they die wiser than they were born, and though their stock of knowledge in great measure dies with them, their young ones acquire some of it by means of inheritance and imitation.

These remarkable mental powers were acquired by the lower animals partly through the struggle to obtain food, which sharpened their intelligence; and partly through the struggle to obtain the favours of the females, which developed their affections. In all cases, progress resulted from necessity. Races change only that they may not die; they are developed, so to speak, in self-defence. They have no inherent tendency to rise in the organic scale as plants grow to their flower, as animals grow to their prime. They have, however, a capacity for progress, and that is called forth by circumstances acting upon them from without. The law of growth in the lower kingdom is this, that all progress is preceded by calamity, that all improvement is based upon defect. This law affords us the clue to a phenomenon which at first is difficult to understand. That animal which has triumphed over all the rest was exceedingly defective in its physique. The race has not been to the swift, nor the battle to the strong. But the very defects of that animal's body made it exclusively rely upon its mind; and when the struggle for life became severe, the mind was improved by natural selection, and the animal was slowly developed into man.

Our ape-like ancestors were not unlike the existing gorilla, chimpanzee, and orang-utang. They lived in large herds and were prolific; polygamy was in vogue, and at the courting season love-duels were fought among the males. They chiefly inhabited the ground, but ascended the trees in search of fruit, and also built platforms of sticks and leaves, on which the females were confined, and which were occasionally used as sleeping-places, just as birds sometimes roost in old nests. These animals went on all fours, rising to the upright posture now and then, in order to see some object at a distance, but supporting that posture with difficulty, holding on to a branch with one hand. They were slow in their movements; their body was almost naked, so scantily was it clothed with hair; the males had but poorly developed tusks, or canine teeth; the ears were flattened from disuse, and had no longer the power of being raised; the tail as in all great apes had disappeared beneath the skin. This defenceless structure resulted from the favourable conditions under which, during many ages, these animals had lived. They inhabited a warm tropical land; they had few enemies, and abundant food; their physical powers had been enfeebled by disuse, But nothing is ever lost in nature. What had become of the force which had once been expended on agility and strength? It had passed into the brain.

The chimpanzee is not so large a creature or so strong as the gorilla; but, as I was informed by the natives in that country where the two species exist together, the chimpanzee is the more intelligent of the two. In the same manner our ape-like ancestors were inferior to the chimpanzee in strength and activity, and its superior in mental powers.

All gregarious animals have a language, by means of which they communicate with one another, Some times their language is that of touch: cut off the antennae of the ant, and it is dumb. With most animals the language is that of vocal sound, and its varied intonations of anger, joy, or grief may be distinguished even by the human ear. Animals have also their alarm-cries, their love-calls, and sweet murmuring plaintive sounds, which are uttered only by mothers as they fondle and nurse their young. The language of our progenitors consisted of vocal sounds, and also movements of the hands. The activity of mind and social affection developed in these animals through the Law of Compensation, made them fond of babbling and gesturing to one another, and thus their language was already of a complicated nature, when events occurred which developed it still more. Owing to causes remotely dependent on geological revolutions, dark days fell upon these creatures. Food became scanty; enemies surrounded them. The continual presence of danger, the habit of incessant combat, drew them more closely together. Their defects of activity and strength made them rely on one another for protection. Nothing now but their unexampled power of combination could save their lives. This power of combination was entirely dependent upon their language, which was developed and improved until at length it passed into a new stage. The first stage of language is that of intonation, in which the ideas are arranged on a chromatic scale. We still use this language in conversing with our dogs, who perfectly understand the difference between the curses, not loud but deep, which are vented on their heads, and the caressing sounds, which are usually uttered in falsetto; while we understand the growl, the whine, and the excited yelp of joy.

The new stage of language was that of imitation. Impelled partly by necessity, partly by social love, combined with mental activity, these animals began to notify events to one another by imitative sounds, gestures, and grimaces. For instance, when they wished to indicate the neighbourhood of a wild beast, they gave a low growl; they pointed in a certain direction; they shaped their features to resemble his; they crawled stealthily along with their belly crouched to the ground. To imitate water, they bubbled with their mouths; they grubbed with their hands and pretended to eat, to show that they had discovered roots. The pleasure and profit obtained from thus communicating their ideas to one another led them to invent conversation. Language passed into its third stage--the conventional or artificial. Certain objects were pointed out, and certain sounds were uttered, and it was agreed that those sounds should always signify the objects named. At first this conventional language consisted only of substantives; each word signified an object, and was a sentence in itself. Afterwards adjectives and verbs were introduced; and lastly words, which had at first been used for physical objects, were applied to the nomenclature of ideas.

Combination is a method of resistance; language is the instrument of combination. Language, therefore, may be considered the first weapon of our species, and was improved, as all weapons would be, by that long, never-ceasing war, the battle of existence. Our second weapon was the hand. With monkeys the hand is used as a foot, and the foot is used as a hand. But when the hand began to be used for throwing missiles, it was specialised more and more, and feet were required to do all the work of locomotion. This separation of the foot and hand is the last instance of the physiological division of labour; and when it was effected, the human frame became complete. The erect posture was assumed; that it is modern and unnatural is shown by the difficulty with which it is maintained for any length of time. The centre of gravity being thus shifted, certain alterations were produced in the physical appearance of the species; since that time, however, the human body has been but

291

slightly changed, the distinctions which exist between the races of men being unimportant and external. Such as they are, they have been produced by differences of climate and food acting indirectly upon the races throughout geological periods; and it is also possible that these distinctions of hair and skin were chiefly acquired at a time when man's intelligence being imperfectly developed, his physical organisation was more easily moulded by external conditions than was afterwards the case. For while with the lower animals the conditions by which they are surrounded can produce alterations throughout their whole structure, or in any part; with men, they can produce an alteration only in the brain. For instance, a quadruped inhabits a region which, owing to geological changes, is gradually assuming an Arctic character. In the course of some hundreds or thousands of centuries the species puts on a coat of warm fur, which is either white in colour, or which turns white at the snowy period of the year. But when man is exposed to similar conditions he builds a warm house and kills certain animals, that he may wear their skins. By these means he evades the changed conditions so far as his general structure is concerned. But his brain has been indirectly altered by the climate. Courage, industry, and ingenuity have been called forth by the struggle for existence; the brain is thereby enlarged, and the face assumes a more intelligent expression.

Of such episodes the ancient history of man was composed. He was ever contending with the forces of nature, with the wild beasts of the forest, and with the members of his own species outside his clan. In that long and varied struggle his intelligence was developed. His first invention, as might be supposed, was an improvement in the art of murder. The lower animals sharpen their claws and whet their tusks. It was merely an extension of this instinct which taught the primeval men to give point and edge to their sticks and stones; and out of this first invention the first great discovery was made. While men were patiently rubbing sticks to point them into arrows, a spark leapt forth and ignited the wood-dust which had been scraped from the sticks. Thus fire was found. By a series of accidents its uses were revealed. Its possessors cooked their food, and so were improved in health and vigour both of body and of mind. They altered the face of nature by burning down forests. By burning the withered grass they favoured the growth of the young crop, and thus attracted, in the prairie lands, thousands of wild animals to their fresh green pastures. With the assistance of fire they felled trees and hollowed logs into canoes. They hardened the points of stakes in the embers; and with their new weapons were able to attack the mammoth, thrusting their spears through his colossal throat. They made pots. They employed their new servant in agriculture and in metallurgy. They used it also as a weapon; they shot flaming arrows, or hurled fiery javelins against the foe. Above all, they prepared, by means of fire, the vegetable poison which they discovered in the woods; and this invention must have created a revolution in the art of ancient war. There is a custom in East Africa for the king to send fire to his vassals, who extinguish all the fires on their hearths, and re-light them from the brand which the envoy brings. It is possible that this may be a relic of tribe subjection to the original fire tribe: it is certain that the discovery of fire would give the tribes which possessed it an immense advantage over all the others. War was continually being waged among the primeval men, and tribes were continually driven, by battle or hunger, to seek new lands. As hunters they required vast areas on which to live, and so were speedily dispersed over the whole surface of the globe, and adopted various habits and vocations according to the localities in which they dwelt. But they took with them, from their common home, the elements of those pursuits. The first period of human history may be entitled forest-life. The forest was the womb of our species, as the ocean was that of all our kind. In the dusky twilight of the primeval woods the nations were obscurely born. While men were yet in the hunting stage, while they were yet mere animals of prey, they made those discoveries by means of which they were afterwards formed into three great families--the pastoral, the maritime, and the agricultural.

When a female animal is killed, the young one, fearing to be alone, often follows the hunter home; it is tamed for sport, and when it is discovered that animals can be made useful, domestication is methodically pursued. While men were yet in the forest they tamed only the dog to assist them in hunting, and perhaps the fowl as an article of food.

But when certain tribes, driven by enemies or by starvation from their old haunts, entered the prairie land, clad in skins or bark-cloth, taking with them their fire-sticks, and perhaps some blacksmith's tools, they adopted breeding as their chief pursuit, and subdued to their service the buffalo, the sheep, the goat, the camel, the horse, and the ass. At first these animals were merely used as meat; next, their milk-giving powers were developed, and so a daily food was obtained without killing the animal itself; then they were broken in to carry burdens, to assist their masters in the chase and in war; and clothes and houses were manufactured from their skins.

The forest tribes who settled on the banks of rivers learnt to swim and to make nets, fish-traps, rafts, and canoes. When they migrated they followed the river, and so were carried to the sea. Then the ocean became their fish-pond. They learnt to build large canoes, with mast and matting sails; they followed the fish far away; lost the land at night, or in a storm; discovered new shores, returned home, and again set out as colonists, with their wives and families, to the lands which they had found. By such means the various tribes were dispersed beyond the seas.

Thirdly, when the tribes were in the forest condition they lived partly upon roots and berries, partly upon game. The men hunted, and the women collected the vegetable food, upon which they subsisted exclusively during the absence of their husbands. When the habitations of a clan were fixed, it often happened that the supply of edible plants in the neighbourhood would be exhausted, and starvation suggested the idea of sowing and transplanting. Agriculture was probably a female invention; it was certainly at first a female occupation. The bush was burnt down to clear a place for the crop, and the women, being too idle to remove the ashes from the soil, cast the seed upon them. The ashes acting as manure, garden varieties of the eating plants appeared. Among the pastoral people, the seed-bearing grasses were also cultivated into large-grained corn. But as long as the tribes could migrate from one region to another, agriculture was merely a secondary occupation, and was left, for the most part, in female hands. It was when a tribe was imprisoned in a valley with mountains or deserts all around that agriculture became their main pursuit, as breeding was that of the shepherd wanderers, and fishing that of the people on the shore.

The pastoral tribes had a surplus supply of meat, milk, wool, and the rude products of the ancient loom. The marine tribes had salt and smoked fish. The agricultural tribes had garden-roots and grain. Here, then, a division of labour had arisen among the tribes; and if only they could be blended together, a complete nation would be formed. But the butcher tribes, the fishmonger tribes, and the baker tribes lived apart from one another; they were timid, ferocious, and distrustful; their languages were entirely distinct. They did not dare to communicate with one another, except to carry on dumb barter, as it is called. A certain tribe, for example, who desired salt approached the frontier of the sea-coast people, lighted a fire as a signal, and laid down some meat or flour. They then retired; the coast tribe came up, laid down salt, and also retired. The meat or flour tribe again went to the spot; and if the salt was sufficient, they took it away; if not, they left it untouched, to indicate that they required more; and so they chaffered a considerable time, each bid consisting of a promenade.

It is evident that such a system of trade might go on for ages without the respective tribes becoming better acquainted with each other. It is only by means of war and of religion that the tribes can be compressed into the nation. The shepherd tribes had a natural aptitude for war. They lived almost entirely on horseback; they attacked wild beasts in hand-to-hand conflict on the open plain, and they often fought with one another for a pasture or a well. They were attracted by the crops of the agricultural people, whom they conquered with facility. Usually they preferred their roaming life, and merely exacted a tribute of corn. But sometimes a people worsted in war, exiled from their pastures, wandering homeless through the sandy deserts, discovered a fruitful river plain, in which they settled down, giving up their nomad habits, but keeping their flocks and herds. They reduced the aborigines to slavery; made some of them labourers in the fields; others were appointed to tend the flocks; others were sent to the river or the coast to fish; others were taught the arts of the distaff and the loom; others were made to work as carpenters and smiths. The wives of the shepherd conquerors were no longer obliged to milk the cows and camels, and to weave clothes and tents; they became ladies, and were attended by domestic slaves. Their husbands became either military nobles or learned priests; the commander-in-chief or patriarch became the king. Foreign wars led to foreign commerce, and the priest developed the resources of the country. The simple fabrics of the old tent life were refined in texture and beautified with dyes; the potter's clay was converted into fine porcelain and glass, the blacksmith's shop became a manufactory of ornamented arms; ingenious machines were devised for the irrigation of the soil the arts and sciences were adopted by the government, and employed in the service of the state.

Here then we have a nation manufactured by means of war. Religion is afterwards useful as a means of keeping the conquered people in subjection; but in this case it plays only a secondary part. In another class of nationalities, however, religion operates as the prime agent.

When the human herd first wandered through the gloomy and gigantic forest, sleeping on reed platforms in the trees, or burrowing in holes, there was no government but that of force. The strongest man was the leader, and ceased to be the leader when he ceased to be the strongest. But as the minds of men became developed, the ruler was elected by the members of the clan, who combined to depose him if he exceeded his rightful powers; and chiefs were chosen not only for their strength, but also sometimes for their beauty, and sometimes on account of their intelligence. These chiefs possessed but little power; they merely expressed and executed the voice of the majority. But when it was believed that the soul was immortal, or, in other words, that there were ghosts; when it was believed that the bodies of men were merely garments, and that the true inmates were spirits, whom death stripped bare of flesh and blood, but whom death was powerless to kill; when it was believed that these souls or ghosts dwelt among the graves, haunted their old homes, hovered round the scenes in which they had passed their lives, and even took a part in human affairs, a theory arose that the ghost of the departed chief was still the ruler of the clan, and that in his spiritual state he could inflict terrible punishments on those by whom he was offended, and could also bestow upon them good fortune in hunting, in harvests, and in war. So then homage and gifts were rendered to him at his grave. A child of his house became the master of the clan, and professed to receive the commands of the deceased. For the first time the chiefs were able to exercise power without employing force; but this power had also its limits.

In the first place the chief feared he would be punished by the ghost if he injured the people over whom he ruled, and there were always prophets or seers who could see visions and dream dreams when the mind of the people was excited against the chief. By means therefore of religion, which at first consisted only in the fear of ghosts, the government of the clan was improved; savage liberty or licence was restrained; the young trembled before the old, whom previously they had eaten as soon as they were useless. Religion was also of service in uniting separated clans. In the forest, food was scanty; as soon as a clan expanded it was forced to divide, and the separated part pursued an orbit of its own. Savage dialects change almost day by day; the old people can always speak a language which their grandchildren do not understand, and so, in the course of a single generation, the two clans become foreigners and foes to one another. But when ghost-worship had been established, the members of the divided clans resorted to the holy graves at certain seasons of the year to unite with the members of the parent clan in sacrificing to the ancestral shades; the season of the pilgrimage was made a Truce of God; a fair was held, at which trade and competitive amusements were carried on. Yet still the clans or tribes had little connection with one another, excepting at that single period of the year. It was for war to continue the work which religion had begun. Some times the tribes uniting invaded a foreign country, and founded an empire of the kind which has already been described; then the army became a nation, and the camp a town. In other cases the tribes, being weaker than their neighbours, were compelled for their mutual protection to draw together into towns, and to fortify themselves with walls.

In its original condition the town was a federation. Each family was a little kingdom in itself, inhabiting a fortified cluster of dwellings, having its own domestic religion, governed by its own laws. The paterfamilias was king and priest; he could put to death any member of his family. There was little distinction between the wives, the sons, and the daughters, on the one hand, and the slaves, the oxen, and the sheep on the other. These family fathers assembled in council, and passed laws for their mutual convenience and protection. Yet these laws were not national; they resembled treaties between foreign states; and two houses would frequently go to war and fight pitched battles in the streets without any interference from the commonwealth at large. If the town progressed in power and intelligence, the advantages of centralisation were perceived by all; the fathers were induced to emancipate their children, and to delegate their royal power to a senate or a king; each man was responsible for his own actions, and for them alone; individualism was established. This important revolution, which, as we have elsewhere shown, tends to produce the religious theory of rewards and punishments in a future state, was itself in part produced by the influence and teaching of the priests.

Besides the worship of the ancestral shades the ancient people adored the great deities of nature who governed the woods and the waters, the earth and the sky. When men died, it was supposed that they had been killed by the gods; it was therefore believed that those who lived to a good old age were special favourites of the divine beings. Many people asked them by what means they had obtained the good graces of the gods. With savages nothing is done gratis; the old men were paid for their advice; and in course of time the oracle system was established. The old men consulted the gods they at first advised, they next commanded what gifts should be offered on the altar. They collected taxes, they issued orders on the divine behalf. In the city of federated families the priests formed a section entirely apart; they belonged not to this house, or to that house, but to all; it was to their interest that the families should be at peace; that a national religion should be established; that the household gods or ancestral ghosts should be degraded, that the despotism of the hearth should be destroyed. They acted as peacemakers and arbitrators of disputes. They united the tribes in the national sacrifice and the solemn dance. They preached the power and grandeur of the gods. They became the tutors of the people; they rendered splendid service to mankind. We are accustomed to look only at the dark side of those ancient faiths; their frivolous and sanguinary laws, their abominable offerings, their grotesque rites. Yet even the pure and lofty religions of Confucius and Zoroaster; of Moses, and Jesus, and Mohammed; of the Brahmins and the Buddhists, have not done so much for man as those barbarous religions of the early days. They established a tyranny, and tyranny was useful in the childhood of mankind. The chiefs could only enact those laws which were indispensable for the life of the community. But the priests were supposed to utter the commands of invisible beings whose strange tempers could clearly be read in the violent outbreaks and changing aspects of the sky. The more irrational the laws of the priests appeared, the more evident it was that they were not of man. Terror generated piety; wild savages were tamed into obedience; they became the slaves of the unseen; they humbled themselves before the priests, and implicitly followed their commands that they might escape sickness, calamity, and sudden death; their minds were subjected to a useful discipline; they acquired the habit of self-denial, which like all habits can become a pleasure to the mind, and can be transmitted as a tendency or instinct from generation to generation. They were ordered to abstain from certain kinds of food; to abstain from fishing and working in the fields on days sacred to the gods of the waters and the earth; they were taught to give with generosity not only in fear, but also in thanksgiving. Even the human sacrifices which they made were sometimes acts of filial piety and of tender love. They gave up the slaves whom they valued most to attend their fathers in the under-world; or sent their souls as presents to the gods.

But the chief benefit which religion conferred upon mankind, whether in ancient or in modern times, was undoubtedly the oath. The priests taught that if a promise was made in the name of the gods, and that promise was broken, the gods would kill those who took their name in vain. Such is the true meaning of the Third Commandment. Before that time treaties of peace and contracts of every kind in which mutual confidence was required could only be effected by the interchange of hostages. But now by means of this purely theological device a verbal form became itself a sacred pledge: men could at all times confide in one another; and foreign tribes met freely together beneath the shelter of this useful superstition which yet survives in our courts of law. In those days, however, the oath required no law of perjury to sustain its terrors: as Xenophon wrote, "He who breaks an oath defies the gods"; and it was believed that the gods never failed sooner or later to take their revenge.

The priests, in order to increase their power, studied the properties of plants, the movements of the stars; they cultivated music and the imitative arts; reserving their knowledge to their own caste, they soon surpassed in mental capacity the people whom they ruled. And being more intelligent, they became also more moral, for the conscience is an organ of the mind; it is strengthened and refined by the education of the intellect. They learnt from Nature that there is unity in all her parts; hence they believed that one god or man-like being had made the heavens and the earth. At first this god was a despotic tithe-taker like themselves; but as their own minds became more noble, and more pure; as they began to feel towards the people a sentiment of paternity and love, so God, the reflected image of their minds, rose into a majestic and benignant being, and this idea reacted on their minds, as the imagination of the artist is inspired by the masterpiece which he himself has wrought. And, as the Venus of Milo and the Apollo Belvedere have been endowed by man with a beauty more exquisite than can be found on earth; a beauty that may well be termed divine; so the God who is worshipped by elevated minds is a mental form endowed with power, love, and virtue in perfection. The Venus and the Apollo are ideals of the body; God is an ideal of the mind. Both are made by men; both are superhuman in their beauty; both are human in their form. To worship the image made of stone is to worship the work of the human hand. To worship the image made of ideas is to worship the work of the human brain. God-worship, therefore, is idolatry; but in the early ages of mankind how fruitful of good was that error, how ennobling was that chimera of the brain! For when the priests had sufficiently progressed in the wisdom of morality to discover that men should act to others, as they would have others act to them; and that they should never do in thought what they would not do in deed; then these priests, the shepherds of the people, desired to punish those who did evil, and to reward those who did good to their fellow-men; and thus, always transferring their ideas to the imaginary being whom they had created, and whom they adored, they believed and they taught that God punished the guilty, that God rewarded the good; and when they perceived that men are not requited in this world according to their deeds, they believed and they taught that this brief life is merely a preparation for another world; and that the souls or ghosts will be condemned to eternal misery, or exalted to everlasting bliss, according to the lives which they have led within the garment of the flesh.

This belief, though not less erroneous than that on which the terrors of the oath were based; this belief, though not less a delusion than the faith in ghosts, of which, in fact, it is merely an extension; this belief, though it will some day become pernicious to intellectual and moral life, and has already plundered mankind of thousands and thousands of valuable minds, exiling earnest and ardent beings from the mainstream of humanity, entombing them in hermitage or cell, teaching them to despise the gifts of the intellect which nature has bestowed, teaching them to waste the precious years in barren contemplations and in selfish prayers; this belief has yet undoubtedly assisted the progress of the human race. In ancient life it exalted the imagination, it purified the heart, it encouraged to virtue, it deterred from crime. At the present day a tender sympathy for the unfortunate, a jealous care for the principles of freedom, a severe public opinion, and a law difficult to escape are the safeguards of society but there have been periods in the history of man when the fear of hell was the only restriction on the pleasure of the rulers; when the hope of heaven was the only consolation in the misery of the ruled.

The doctrine of rewards and punishments in a future state is comparatively modern; the authors of the Iliad, the authors of the Pentateuch, had no conception of a heaven or a hell; they knew only Hades or Scheol, where men dwelt as shadows, without pain, without joy; where the wicked ceased from troubling and the weary were at rest. The sublime conception of a single God was slowly and painfully attained by a few civilised people in ancient times. The idea that God is a being of virtue and of love has not been attained even in the present day except by a cultivated few. Such is the frailty of the human heart that men, even when they strive to imagine a perfect being, stain him with their passions, and raise up an idol which is defective as a moral form. The God of this country is called a God of love; but it is said that he punishes the crimes and even the errors of a short and troubled life with torture which will have no end. It is not even a man which theologians create; for no man is quite without pity; no man, however cruel he might be, could bear to gaze for ever on the horrors of the fire and the rack; no man could listen for ever to voices shrieking with pain, and ever crying out for mercy and forgiveness. And if such is the character of the Christian God, if such is the idea which is worshipped by compassionate and cultivated men, what are we to expect in a barbarous age? The God of Job was a sultan of the skies, who, for a kind of wager, allowed a faithful servant to be tortured, like that man who performed vivisection on a favourite dog which licked his hand throughout the operation. The Jehovah of the Pentateuch was a murderer and bandit; he rejoiced in offerings of human flesh The gods of Homer were lascivious and depraved. The gods of savages are merely savage chiefs.

God, therefore, is an image of the mind, and that image is ennobled and purified from generation to generation, as the mind becomes more noble and more pure. Europeans believe in eternal punishment, partly because it has been taught them in their childhood and because they have never considered what it means; partly because their imaginations are sluggish, and they are unable to realise its cruelty; and partly also, it must be feared, because they have still the spirit of revenge and persecution in their hearts. The author of Job created God in the image of an Oriental king, and in the East it is believed that all men by nature belong to the king, and that he can do no wrong.

The Bedouins of the desert abhorred incontinence as a deadly sin; but brigandage and murder were not by them considered crimes. In the Homeric period, piracy was a profession, and vices were the customs of the land. The character of a god is that of the people who have made him. When, therefore, I expose the crimes of Jehovah, I expose the defective morality of Israel; and when I criticise the God of modern Europe, I criticise the defective intellects of Europeans. The reader must endeavour to bear this in mind, for, though he may think that his idea of the creator is actually the Creator, that belief is not shared by me.

We shall now return to the forest and investigate the origin of intellect; we shall first explain how the aptitude for science and for art arose; and next how man first became gifted with the moral sense.

The desire to obtain food induces the animal to examine everything of novel appearance which comes within its range of observation. The habit is inherited and becomes an instinct, irrespective of utility. This instinct is curiosity, which in many animals is so urgent a desire that they will encounter danger rather than forego the examination of any object which is new and strange. This propensity is inherited by man, and again passes through a period of utility. When fire is first discovered, experiments are made on all kinds of plants, with the view of ascertaining what their qualities may be. The remarkable knowledge of herbs which savages possess; their skill in preparing decoctions which can act as medicines or as poisons, which can attract or repel wild animals, is not the result of instinct but of experience; and, as with the lower animals, the habit of food-seeking is developed into curiosity, so the habit of searching for edibles, medicine, and poison becomes the experimental spirit, the passion of inquiry which animates the lifetime of the scientific man, and which makes him, even in his last hours, observe his own symptoms with interest, and take notes on death as it draws near. It has been said that genius is curiosity. That instinct is at least an element of genius; it is the chief stimulant of labour; it keeps the mind alive.

The artistic spirit is, in the same manner, developed from the imitative instinct, the origin of which is more obscure than that of the inquisitive propensity. However, its purpose is clear enough; the young animal learns from its parent, by means of imitation, to feed, to arrange its toilet with beak or tongue, and to perform all the other offices of life. The hen, for instance, when she discovers food, pecks the ground, not to eat, but to show her chickens how to eat, and they follow her example. The young birds do not sing entirely by instinct, they receive lessons from their parents. The instinct of imitation, so essential to the young, remains more or less with the adult, and outlives its original intent. Animals imitate one another, and with the monkeys this propensity becomes a mania. It is inherited by men, with whom even yet it is half an instinct, as is shown by the fact that all persons, and especially the young, reflect, in spite of their own efforts, the accent and the demeanour of those with whom they live. This instinct, when adroitly managed, is a means of education; it is, in fact, the first principle of progress. The Red Indians are not imitative, and they have now nearly been destroyed; the negroes imitate like monkeys, and what is the result? They are preachers, traders, clerks, and artisans, all over the world, and there is no reason to suppose that they will remain always in the imitative stage. With respect to individuals it is the same. Paradoxical as it may appear, it is only the imitative mind which can attain originality, the artist must learn to copy before he can create. Mozart began by imitating Bach; Beethoven began by copying Mozart. Moliere mimicked the Greek dramatists before he learnt to draw from the world. The many-sided character of Goethe's mind, which has made him a marvel among men, was based upon his imitative instincts; it has been said that he was like a chameleon, taking the hue of the ground on which he fed. What, in fact, is emulation but a noble form of imitativeness? Michaelangelo saw a man modelling in clay in the garden of Lorenzo, and was seized with the desire to become a sculptor; and most men who have chosen their own vocation could trace its origin in the same way to some imitative impulse.

Among the primeval men this instinct, together with wonder and the taste for beauty, explains the origin of art: The tendency to reproduce with the hand whatever pleases and astonishes the mind, undoubtedly begins at an early period in the history of man; pictures were drawn in the period of the mammoth; I once saw a boy from a wild bush tribe look at a ship with astonishment and then draw it on the sand with a stick. It frequently happens in savage life, that a man is seized with a passion for representing objects, and such a Giotto is always invited, and perhaps, paid, to decorate walls and doors. With this wall-painting the fine arts began. Next the outlines were engraved with a knife, making a figure in relief. Next came a statue with the back adhering to the wall, and lastly the sculptured figure was entirely detached. In the same manner painting was also separated from the wall; and mural painting was developed into another form of art. By means of a series of pictures a story was told; the picture-writing was converted into hieroglyphics, and thence into a system of alphabetical signs. Thus the statue, the picture, and the book are all descended from such figures as those which savages scrawl with charcoal on their hut walls, and which seldom bear much resemblance to the thing portrayed. The genius of art and the genius of science are developed by means of priesthoods and religion but when a certain point has been attained, they must be divorced from religion, or they will cease to progress.

And now, finally, with respect to music. There is a science of music; but music is not a science. Nor is it an imitative art. It is a language.

Words at first were rather sung than spoken, and sentences were rhythmical. The conversation of the primeval men was conducted in verse and song; at a later period they invented prose; they used a method of speech which was less pleasing to the ear, but better suited for the communication of ideas. Poetry and music ceased to be speech, and became an art, as pantomime, which once was a part of speech, is now an art exhibited upon the stage. Poetry and music at first were one; the bard was a minstrel, the minstrel was a bard. The same man was composer, poet, vocalist, and instrumentalist, and instrument-maker. He wrote the music and the air; as he sang he accompanied himself upon the harp, and he also made the harp. When writing came into vogue the arts of the poet and the musician were divided, and music again was divided into the vocal and the instrumental, and finally instrument-making became a distinct occupation, to which fact may partly be ascribed the superiority of modern music to that of ancient times.

The human language of speech bears the same relation to the human language of song as the varied bark of the civilised dog to its sonorous howl. There seems little in common between the lady who sings at the piano and the dog who chimes in with jaws opened and nose upraised; yet each is making use of the primitive language of its race the wild dog can only howl, the wild woman can only sing.

Gestures with us are still used as ornaments of speech, and some savage languages are yet in so imperfect a condition that gestures are requisite to elucidate the words. Gestures are relics of the primeval language, and so are musical sounds. With the dog of the savage there is much howl in its bark: its voice is in a transitional condition. The peasants of all countries sing in their talk, and savages resemble the people in the opera. Their conversation is of a "libretto" character; it glitters with hyperbole and metaphor, and they frequently speak in recitative, chanting or intoning, and ending every sentence in a musically sounded O! Often also in the midst of conversation, if a man happens to become excited, he will sing instead of speaking what he has to say; the other also replies in song, while the company around, as if touched by a musical wave, murmur a chorus in perfect unison, clapping their hands, undulating their bodies, and perhaps breaking forth into a dance.

Just as the articulate or conventional speech has been developed into rich and varied tongues, by means of which abstract ideas and delicate emotions can be expressed in appropriate terms, so the inarticulate or musical speech, the true, the primitive language of our race, has been developed with the aid of instruments into a rich and varied language of sound in which poems can be composed. When we listen to the sublime and mournful sonatas of Beethoven, when we listen to the tender melodies of Bellini, we fall into a trance; the brain burns and swells; its doors fly open; the mind sweeps forth into an unknown world where all is dim, dusky, unutterably vast; gigantic ideas pass before us; we attempt to seize them, to make them our own, but they vanish like shadows in our arms. And then, as the music becomes soft and low, the mind returns and nestles to the heart; the senses are steeped in languor; the eyes fill with tears; the memories of the past take form; and a voluptuous sadness permeates the soul, sweet as the sorrow of romantic youth when the real bitterness of life was yet unknown.

What, then, is the secret of this power in music? And why should certain sounds from wood and wire thus touch our very heart strings to their tune? It is the voice of Nature which the great composers combine into harmony and melody; let us follow it downwards and downwards in her deep bosom, and there we discover music, the speech of passion, of sentiment, of emotion, and of love; there we discover the divine language in its elements; the sigh, the gasp, the melancholy moan, the plaintive note of supplication, the caressing murmur of maternal love, the cry of challenge or of triumph, the song of the lover as he serenades his mate.

The spirit of science arises from the habit of seeking food; the spirit of art arises from the habit of imitation, by which the young animal first learns to feed; the spirit of music arises from primeval speech, by means of which males and females are attracted to each other. But the true origin of these instincts cannot be ascertained: it is impossible to account for primary phenomena. There are some who appear to suppose that this world is a stage-play, and that if we pry into it too far, we shall discover ropes and pulleys behind the scenes, and that so agreeable illusions will be spoiled. But the great masters of modern science are precisely those whom Nature inspires with most reverence and awe. For as their minds are wafted by their wisdom into untravelled worlds, they find new fields of knowledge expanding to the view; the firmament ever expands, the abyss deepens, the horizon recedes. The proximate Why may be discovered; the ultimate Why is unrevealed. Let us take, for instance, a single law. A slight change invigorates the animal; and so the offspring of the pair survive the offspring of the single individual. Hence the separation of the sexes, desire, affection, family love, combination, gregariousness, clan-love, the Golden Rule, nationality, patriotism, and the religion of humanity, with all those complex sentiments and emotions which arise from the fact that one animal is dependent on another for the completion of its wants. But why should a slight change invigorate the animal? And if that question could be answered; we should find another why behind. Even when science shall be so far advanced that all the faculties and feelings of men will be traced with the precision of a mathematical demonstration to their latent condition in the fiery cloud of the beginning, the luminous haze, the nebula of the sublime Laplace: even then the origin and purpose of creation, the How and the Why, will remain unsolved. Give me the elementary atoms, the philosopher will exclaim; give me the primeval gas and the law of gravitation, and I will show you how man was evolved, body and soul, just as easily as I can explain the egg being hatched into a chick. But, then, where did the egg come from? Who made the atoms and endowed them with the impulse of attraction? Why was it so ordered that reason should be born of refrigeration, and that a piece of white-hot star should cool into a habitable world, and then be sunned into an intellectual salon, as the earth will some day be? All that we are doing, and all that we can do, is to investigate secondary laws; but from these investigations will proceed discoveries by which human nature will be elevated, purified, and finally transformed.

The ideas and sentiments, the faculties and the emotions, should be divided into two classes; those which we have in common with the lower animals, and which therefore we have derived from them; and those which have been acquired in the human state. Filial, parental, and conjugal affection, fellow-feeling and devotion to the welfare of the community, are virtues which exist in every gregarious association. These qualities, therefore, were possessed by the progenitors of man before the development of language, before the separation of the foot and the hand. Reproduction was once a part of growth:

301

animals, therefore, desire to perpetuate their species from a natural and innate tendency inherited from their hermaphrodite and animalcule days. But owing to the separation of the sexes, this instinct cannot be appeased except by means of co-operation. In order that offspring may be produced, two animals must enter into partnership; and in order that offspring may be reared, this partnership must be continued for a considerable time. All living creatures of the higher grade are memorials of conjugal affection and parental care; they are born with a tendency to love, for it is owing to love that they exist. Those animals that are deficient in conjugal desire or parental love produce or bring up no offspring, and are blotted out of the book of Nature. That parents and children should consort together is natural enough; and the family is multiplied into the herd. At first the sympathy by which the herd is united is founded only on the pleasures of the breeding season and the duties of the nest. It is based entirely on domestic life. But this sympathy is extended and intensified by the struggle for existence; herd contends against herd, community against community; that herd which best combines will undoubtedly survive; and that herd in which sympathy is most developed will most efficiently combine. Here, then, one herd destroys another, not only by means of teeth and claws, but also by means of sympathy and love. The affections, therefore, are weapons, and are developed according to the Darwinian Law. Love is as cruel as the shark's jaw, as terrible as the serpent's fang. The moral sense is founded on sympathy, and sympathy is founded on self-preservation. With all gregarious animals, including men, self-preservation is dependent on the preservation of the herd. And so, in order that each may prosper, they must all combine with affection and fidelity, or they will be exterminated by their rivals.

In the first period of the human herd, co-operation was merely instinctive, as it is in a herd of dog-faced baboons. But when the intelligence of man was sufficiently developed, they realised the fact that the welfare of each individual depended on the welfare of the clan, and that the welfare of the clan depended on the welfare of each efficient individual. They then endeavoured to support by laws the interests of the association; and though, owing to their defective understandings, they allowed, and even enjoined, many customs injurious to their own welfare, yet, on the whole, they lived well and wisely within the circle of their clan. It will now be seen that the moral laws by which we are guided are all due to the law of self-preservation. It was considered wicked and wrong to assault, to rob, to deceive, or in any way to ill-treat or offend an able-bodied member of the clan; for, if he were killed or disabled, his services were lost to the clan, and if he were made discontented he might desert to another corporation. But these vices were wrong, merely because they were injurious; even murder in the abstract was not regarded by them as a sin. They killed their sickly children, and dined upon their superannuated parents without remorse; for the community was profited by their removal. This feeling of fidelity to the clan, though, no doubt, often supported by arguments addressed to the reason, was not with them a matter of calculation. It was rooted in their hearts; it was a true instinct inherited from animal and ancient days; it was with them an idea of duty, obedience to which was prompted by an impulse, neglect of which was punished by remorse. In all fables there is some fact; and the legends of the noble savage possess this element of truth, that savages within their own communion do live according to the Golden Rule, and would, in fact, be destroyed by their enemies if they did not. But they are not in reality good men. They have no conscience outside their clan. Their virtue after all is only a kind of honour among thieves. They resemble those illustrious criminals who were excellent husbands and fathers, and whose biographies cannot be read without a shudder. Yet it is from these people that our minds and our morals are descended. The history of morals is the extension of the reciprocal or selfish virtues from the clan to the tribe, from the tribe to the nation, from the nation to all communities living under the same government, civil or religious, then to people of the same colour, and finally to all mankind.

In the primitive period, the males contended at the courting season for the possession of the females; polygamy prevailed, and thus the strongest and most courageous males were the fathers of all the children that were born; the males of the second class died "old maids." The weakly members of the herd were also unable to obtain their share of food. But when the period of brute force was succeeded by the period of law, it was found that the men of sickly frames were often the most intelligent, and that they could make themselves useful to the clan by inventing weapons and traps, or at least by manufacturing them.

In return for their sedentary labour, they were given food; and as they were too weak to obtain wives by force, females also were given them; the system of love-duels was abolished; the women belonged to the community, and were divided fairly, like the food. The existence of the clan depended on the number of its fighting men, and therefore on the number of children that were born. The birth of a male child was a matter of rejoicing: the mother was honoured as a public benefactress. Then breeding began to be studied as an art; young persons were methodically paired. It was observed that children inherit the qualities and inclinations of their parents, and so the brave and the intelligent were selected to be sires.

If food was scarce and if children were difficult to rear, the new-born infants were carefully examined, and those that did not promise well were killed. Promiscuous intercourse on the part of the females was found to result in sterility, and was forbidden. Cohabitation during the suckling period, which lasted at least three years, was supposed to injure the mother's milk, on which the savage baby is entirely dependent; and during that period the woman was set apart. Premature unions among children were forbidden, and sometimes prevented by infibulation, but savages seldom seem to be aware that for the young to marry as soon as the age of puberty has been attained is injurious to the womb and to the offspring. The ancient Germans, however, had excellent laws upon this subject.

Finally the breeders made a discovery from which has resulted one of the most universal of moral laws, and one which of all laws has been the least frequently infringed. Clans made war on foreign clans not only for game preserves, and fish waters, and root, and berry grounds, but also for the purpose of making female prisoners. A bachelor was expected to catch a wild wife for his own benefit, and for that of the community. He accordingly prowled round the village of the enemy, and when an eligible person came down to the brook to fill her pitcher, or went into the bush to gather sticks, he burst forth from his ambush, knocked her down with his club, and carried her off in triumph to his own people. It was observed that the foreign wives produced more children, and stronger children, than the home-born wives, and, also that the nearer the blood-relationship between husband and wife, the more weakly and the less frequent were the offspring. On this account a law was passed forbidding marriage between those who were closely related to one another; sometimes even it was forbidden to marry within the tribe at all; and all wives were obtained from foreign tribes by means of capture or exchange. These laws relating to marriage, enacted by the elders, and issued as orders of the gods, were at first obeyed by the young merely out of fear; but in the second generation they were ingrained on the minds of children, and were taken under the protection of the conscience.

When the clans or families first leagued together in order to form a town, the conscience of each man was confined to his own circle. He left it at home when he went out into the town. He considered it laudable to cheat his fellow townsmen in a bargain, or to tell them clever lies. If he committed a murder or a theft, his conscience uttered no reproach. But each father was responsible for the crimes of the members of his clan; he might inflict what punishment he chose on the actual offender; but he himself was the culprit in the eyes of the law, and was condemned to pay the fine. If the municipal government was not fully formed, the injured family took its own revenge; it did not seek for the thief or murderer himself; the individual did not exist; all the family to them were one. No man, therefore, could break a law without exposing his revered father and all the members of his family to expense, and even to danger of their lives. No savage dares to be unpopular at home; the weight of opprobrium is more than any man can bear. His happiness depends on the approbation of those with whom he lives; there is no world for him outside his clan. The town laws were, therefore, respected by each man for the sake of his family, and then by a well-known mental process they came to be respected for themselves, and were brought under the moral law which was written on the heart. Men ceased to be clansmen; they became citizens. They next learnt to cherish and protect those foreigners who came to trade and who thus conferred a benefit upon the town; and at last the great discovery was made. Offences against the Golden Rule are wrong in themselves, and displeasing to the gods. It is wicked for a man to do that which he would not wish a man to do to him; it is wrong for a man to do that to a woman which he would not wish done to his sister or his wife. Murder, theft, falsehood, and fraud, the infliction of physical or mental pain, all these from time immemorial had been regarded as crimes between clansmen and clansmen; they were now regarded as crimes between man and man. And here we come to a singular fact. The more men are sunk in brutality the less frequently they sin against their conscience; and as men become more virtuous, they also become more sinful. With the primeval man the conscience is an instinct; it is never disobeyed. With the savage the conscience demands little; that little it demands under pain of death; it is, therefore, seldom disobeyed. The savage seldom does that which he feels to be wrong. But he does not feel it wrong to commit incest, to eat "grandfather soup," to kill a sickly child like a kitten, to murder any one who lives outside his village. In the next period, the matrimonial and religious laws which have proceeded from the science of breeding and the fear of ghosts place a frequent restraint upon his actions. He now begins to break the moral law; he begins a career of sin; yet he is, on the whole, a better man.

We finally arrive at the civilised man; he has refined sentiments and a cultivated intellect; and now scarcely a day passes in which he does not offend against his conscience. His life is passed in self-reproach. He censures himself for an hour that he has wasted; for an unkind word that he has said; for an impure thought which he has allowed to settle for a moment on his mind. Such lighter sins do not indeed trouble ordinary men, and there are few at present whose conscience reproaches them for sins against the intellect. But the lives of all modern men are tormented with desires which may not be satisfied; with propensities which must be quelled. The virtues of man have originated in necessity; but necessity developed the vices as well. It was essential for the preservation of the clan that its members should love one another, and live according to the Golden Rule; men, therefore, are born with an instinct of virtue.

But it was also essential for the existence of the clan that its members should be murderers and thieves, crafty and ferocious; fraudulent and cruel. These qualities, therefore, are transmitted by inheritance. But as the circle of the clan widens, these qualities are rarely useful to their possessors, and finally are stigmatised as criminal propensities. But because their origin was natural and necessary, their guilt is not lessened an iota. All men are born with these propensities; all know that they are evil; all can suppress them if they please. There are some, indeed, who appear to be criminals by nature; who do not feel it wrong to prey upon mankind. These are cases of reversion; they are savages or wild beasts; they are the enemies of society, and deserve the prison, to which sooner or later they are sure to come. But it is rare indeed that these savage instincts resist a kind and judicious education; they may all be stifled in the nursery. Life is full of hope and consolation; we observe that crime is on the decrease, and that men are becoming more humane. The virtues as well as the vices are inherited; in every succeeding generation the old ferocious impulses of our race will become fainter and fainter, and at length they will finally die away.

There is one moral sentiment which cannot be ascribed to the law of gregarious preservation, and which is therefore of too much importance to be entirely passed over, though it cannot here be treated in detail. The sense of decorum which is outraged at the exposure of the legs in Europe is as artificial as that which is shocked at the exhibition of the female face in the East: if the young lady of London thinks that the absence of underclothing in the Arab peasant girl "looks rather odd," on the other hand no Arab lady could look at her portrait in an evening dress without a feeling of discomfort and surprise. Yet although the minor details of nudity are entirely conventional; although complete nudity prevails in some parts of Africa, where yet a petticoat grows on every tree, and where the people are by no means indifferent to their personal appearance, for they spend half their lives upon their coiffure; although in most savage countries the unmarried girl is never permitted to wear clothes; although decoration is everywhere antecedent to dress, still the traveller does find that a sentiment of decency, though not universal, is at least very common among savage people.

Self-interest here affords an explanation, but not in the human state; we must trace back the sentiment to its remote and secret source in the animal kingdom. Propriety grows out of cleanliness through the association of ideas. Cleanliness is a virtue of the lower animals, and is equivalent to decoration; it is nourished by vanity, which proceeds from the love of sexual display, and that from the desire to obtain a mate; and so here we do arrive at utility after all. It is a part of animal cleanliness to deposit apart, and even to hide, whatever is uncleanly; and men, going farther still, conceal whatever is a cause of the uncleanly. The Tuaricks of the desert give this as their reason for bandaging the mouth; it has, they say, the disgusting office of chewing the food, and is therefore not fit to be seen. The custom probably originated as a precaution against the poisonous wind and the sandy air; yet the explanation of the people themselves, though incorrect, is not without its value in affording a clue to the operations of the savage mind. But the sense of decorum must not be used by writers on Mind to distinguish man from the lower animals, for savages exist who are as innocent of shame and decorum as the beasts and birds.

There is in women a peculiar timidity, which is due to nature alone, and which has grown out of the mysterious terror attendant on the functions of reproductive life. But the other qualities, physical or mental, which we prize in women are the result of matrimonial selection. At first the female was a chattel common to all, or belonging exclusively to one, who was by brute force the despot of the herd. When property was divided and secured by law, the women became the slaves of their husbands, hewing the wood, drawing the water, working in the fields; while the men sewed and washed the clothes, looked after the house, and idled at the toilet, oiling their hair, and adorning it with flowers, arranging the chignon or the wig of vegetable fibre, filing their teeth, boring their ears, putting studs into their cheeks, staining their gums, tattooing fanciful designs upon their skins, tying strings on their arms to give them a rounded form, bathing their bodies in warm water, rubbing them with lime-juice and oil, perfuming them with the powdered bark of an aromatic tree. Decoration among the females was not allowed. It was then considered unwomanly to engage in any but what are now regarded as masculine occupations. Wives were selected only for their strength. They were hard, coarse, ill-favoured creatures, as inferior to the men in beauty as the females are to the males almost throughout the animal kingdom. But when prisoners of war were tamed and broken in, the women ceased to be drudges, and became the ornaments of life. Poor men select their domestic animals for utility: rich men select them for appearance. In the same manner, when husbands became rich they chose wives according to their looks. At first the hair of women was no longer than that of men, probably not so long. But long hair is universally admired. False hair is in use all over the world, from the Eskimos of the Arctic circle to the negroes of Gaboon. By the continued selection of long-haired wives the flowing tresses of the sex have been produced. In the same manner the elegance of the female form, its softness of complexion, its gracefulness of curve are not less our creation than the symmetry and speed of the racehorse, the magnificence of garden flowers, and the flavour of orchard fruits. Even the reserved demeanour of women, their refined sentiments, their native modesty, their sublime unselfishness, and power of self-control are partly due to us.

The wife was at first a domestic animal like a dog or a horse. She could not be used without the consent of the proprietor; but he was always willing to let her out for hire. Among savages it is usually the duty of the host to lend a wife to his stranger guest, and if the loan is declined the husband considers himself insulted. Adultery is merely a question of debt. The law of debt is terribly severe: the body of the insolvent belongs to the creditor to sell or to kill. But no other feelings are involved in the question. The injured husband is merely a creditor, and is always pleased that the debt has been incurred. Petitioner and co-respondent may often be seen smoking a friendly pipe together after the case has been proved and the money has been paid. However, as the intelligence expands and the sentiments become more refined, marriage is hallowed by religion; adultery is regarded as a shame to the husband, and a sin against the gods; and a new feeling-- Jealousy--enters for the first time the heart of man. The husband desires to monopolise his wife, body and soul. He intercepts her glances; he attempts to penetrate into her thoughts. He covers her with clothes; he hides even her face from the public gaze. His jealousy, not only anxious for the future, is extended over the, past. Thus women from their earliest childhood are subjected by the selfishness of man to severe but salutary laws. Chastity becomes the rule of female life. At first it is preserved by force alone. Male slaves are appointed to guard the women who, except sometimes from momentary pique, never betray one another, and are allied against the men.

But as the minds of men are gradually elevated and refined through the culture of the intellect, there rises within them a sentiment which is unknown in savage life. They conceive a contempt for those pleasures which they share with the lowest of mankind, and even with the brutes. They feel that this instinct is degrading: they strive to resist it; they endeavour to be pure. But that instinct is strong with the accumulated power of innumerable generations; and the noble desire is weak and newly born: it can seldom be sustained except by the hopes and fears of religion, or by the nobler teaching of philosophy. But in women this new virtue is assisted by laws and customs which were established, long before, by the selfishness of men. Here, then, the abhorrence of the impure, the sense of duty, the fear of punishment, all unite and form a moral law which women themselves enforce, becoming the guardians of their own honour, and treating as a traitor to her sex the woman who betrays her trust. For her the most compassionate have no mercy: she has broken those laws of honour on which society is founded. It is forbidden to receive her; it is an insult to women to allude to her existence, to pronounce her name. She is condemned without inquiry, as the officer is condemned who has shown cowardice before the foe. For the life of women is a battlefield: virtue is their courage, and peace of mind is their reward. It is certainly an extraordinary fact that women should be subjected to a severe social discipline, from which men are almost entirely exempt. As we have shown, it is explained by history; it is due to the ancient subjection of woman to the man. But it is not the women who are to be pitied: it is they who alone are free; for by that discipline they are preserved from the tyranny of vice. It would be well for men if they also were ruled by a severe opinion. The passions are always foes, but it is only when they have been encouraged that they are able to become masters; it is only when they have allied themselves with habit that their terrible power becomes known. They resemble wild beasts which men feed and cherish until they are themselves devoured by their playmates. What miseries they cause, how many intellects they paralyse, how many families they ruin, how many innocent hearts they break asunder, how many lives they poison, how many young corpses they carry to the tomb! What fate can be more wretched than that of the man who resigns himself to them?

As to the beautiful mind of Mendelssohn every sound, whatever it might be--the bubbling of a brook, the rustling of the wind among the trees, the voice of a bird, even the grating of a wheel--inspired a musical idea, so--how melancholy is the contrast!--so--how deep is the descent!--so to the mind that is steeped in sensuality every sight, every sound, calls up an impure association. The voluptuary dreads to be alone; his mind is a monster that exhibits foul pictures to his eyes: his memories are temptations: he struggles, he resists, but it is all in vain: the habits which once might so easily have been broken are now harder than adamant, are now stronger than steel: his life is passed between desire and remorse: when the desire is quenched he is tortured by his conscience: he soothes it with a promise; and then the desire comes again. He sinks lower and lower until indulgence gives him no pleasure: and yet abstinence cannot be endured. To stimulate his jaded senses he enters strange and tortuous paths which lead him to that awful borderland where all is darkness, all is horror, where vice lies close to crime. Yet there was a time when that man was as guileless as a girl: he began by learning vice from the example of his companions, just as he learnt to smoke. Had his education been more severe: had the earliest inclinations been checked by the fear of ruin and disgrace, he would not have acquired the most dangerous of all habits. That men should be subjected to the same discipline as women is therefore to be wished for: and although the day is far distant, there can be no doubt that it will come: and the future historian of morals will record with surprise that in the nineteenth-century society countenanced vices in men which it punished in women with banishment for life.

Since men are in a transitional condition; since Nature ordains that the existence of the race can only be preserved by means of gross appetites inherited from our ancestors, the animals, it is obvious that men should refine them so far as they are able. Thus the brute business of eating and drinking is made in civilised life the opportunity of social intercourse; the family, divided by the duties of the day, then assemble and converse: men of talent are drawn together and interchange ideas. Many a poem, many an invention, many a great enterprise, has been born at the table; loves and friendships have originated there. In the same manner the passions are sanctified by marriage. Blended with the pure affections, their coarseness disappears: their violence is appeased: they become the ministers of conjugal and parental love.

If we place exceptions aside, and look at men in the mass, we find that, like the animals, they are actively employed from morning to night in obtaining food for themselves and for their families. But when they have satisfied their actual wants, they do not, like the animals, rest at their ease: they continue their labour. Let us take the life of an ordinary man. He adopts an occupation at first in order to get his bread; and then that he may marry and have children; and these also he has to feed. But that is not all. He soon desires to rise in his profession, or to acquire such skill in his craft that he may he praised by his superiors and by his companions. He desires to make money that he may improve his social position. And lastly, he begins to love his occupation for itself, whatever it may be: the poor labourer has this feeling as well as the poet or the artist. When the pleasures of money and fame have been exhausted: when nothing remains on earth that can bribe the mind to turn from its accustomed path, it is labour itself that is the joy; and aged men who have neither desires, nor illusions, who are separated from the world, and who are drawing near to the grave, who believe that with life all is ended, and that for them there is no hereafter, yet continue to work with indefatigable zeal. This noble condition of the mind which thus makes for itself a heaven upon earth can be attained by those who have courage and resolution. It is merely the effect of habit: labour is painful to all at first; but if the student perseveres he will find it more and more easy, until at last he will find it necessary, to his life. The toils which once were so hard to endure are now sought and cherished for themselves: the mind becomes uneasy when its chains are taken off.

The love of esteem is the second stimulant of labour; it follows the period of necessity; it precedes the period of habit. It is founded on that feeling of sympathy which unites the primeval herd, and which is necessary to its life. The man who distinguishes himself in battle; the man who brings home a deer, or a fish, or a store of honey, or a bundle of roots is praised by his comrades; so he is encouraged to fresh exertions, and so the emulation of others is excited. The actions of savages are entirely directed by the desire to exist, and by the desire to obtain the praises of their fellows. All African travellers have suffered from the rapacity of chiefs, and yet those same chiefs are the most open-handed of men. They plunder and beg from the white man his cloth, in order to give it away; and they give it away in order to obtain praise. A savage gentleman is always surrounded by a host of clients, who come every morning to give him the salutation, who chant his praises and devour him alive. The art of song had its origin in flattery. Mendicant minstrels wander from town to town, and from chief to chief, singing the praises of their patrons and satirising those who have not been generous towards them. In Africa the accusation of parsimony is a more bitter taunt than the accusation of cowardice. Commerce first commenced in necessity. The inland people required salt; the coast people required vegetables to eat with their fish. But soon the desire of esteem induced men to contrive, and labour, and imperil their lives in order to obtain ornaments or articles of clothing which came from abroad. In Central Africa it is more fashionable to wear a dirty rag of Manchester cloth, such as we use for a duster, than their own beautiful aprons of woven grass. An African chief will often commission a trader to buy him a handsome saddle, or some curious article of furniture, on condition that he will not supply it to any one else, just as connoisseurs will pay a higher price for a work of art when the mould has been broken.

Both in civilised and in savage life the selfish desires of man are few, and are quickly satisfied. Enormous sums are lavished upon cookery and wines, but more from ostentation than from true gourmanderie. The love of display, or the more noble desire to give pleasure to their friends, has much to do with the enthusiasm of those who spend fortunes on works of art and objects of virtue; and there are few amusements which can be enjoyed alone. Nihil est homini amicum sine homine amico. All the actions of men may therefore be traced first to the desire of preserving life and continuing their species; secondly to the desire of esteem; and thirdly to the effects of habit. In the religious conduct of man there is nothing which cannot be thus explained. First, men sacrifice and pray in order to escape sickness and death; or if they are a little more advanced, that they may not be punished in a future state. Secondly, they desire to win the esteem and affections of the gods; they are ambitious of obtaining a heavenly reputation. And lastly, prayer and praise, discipline and self-denial, become habits, and give pleasure to the mind. The rough hair shirt, the hard bed, the cold cell, the meagre food, the long vigil, the midnight prayer, are delights to the mind that is inured to suffer; and as other men rejoice that they have found something which can yield them pleasure, so the ascetic rejoices that he has found something which can yield him pain.

Summary of Universal History

In the preceding sketch, which is taken from the writings of others, I have told how a hot cloud vibrating in space, cooled into a sun rotating on its axis, and revolving round a point, to us unknown; and how this sun cast off a piece, which went out like a coal that leaps from the fire, and sailed round the sun a cinder wrapped in smoke; and how, as it cooled, strange forces worked within it, varied phenomena appeared upon its surface; it was covered with a salt sea; the smoke cleared off; the sunlight played upon the water; gelatinous plants and animals appeared at first simple in their forms, becoming more complex as the forces which acted on them increased in complexity; the earth wrinkled up; the mountains and continents appeared; rain-water ascended from the sea, and descended from the sky; lakes and rivers were created; the land was covered with ferns, and gigantic mosses, and grasses tall as trees; enormous reptiles crawled upon the earth, frogs as large as elephants, which croaked like thunder; and the air, which was still poisonous and cloudy, was cleared by the plants feeding on the coaly gas; the sun shone brightly; sex was invented; love was born; flowers bloomed forth, and birds sang; mammoths and mastodons revelled upon the infinity of pastures the world became populous; the struggle for life became severe; animals congregated together; male struggled against male for spouses, herd struggled against herd for subsistence; a nation of apes, possessing peculiar intelligence and sociability, were exposed to peculiar dangers; as a means of resistance, they combined more closely; as they combined more closely, their language was improved; as a means of resistance, they threw missiles with their hands; thus using their hands, they walked chiefly with their feet; the apes became almost man, half walking, half crawling through the grim forests, jabbering and gesticulating in an imitative manner, fighting furiously for their females at the rutting season, their matted hair begrimed with dirt and blood, fighting with all nature, even with their own kind, but remaining true to their own herd; using the hand more and more as a weapon and a tool, becoming more and more erect; expressing objects by conventional sounds or words; delighting more and more to interchange ideas; sharpening stones and pointing sticks, heading javelins with bone and horn, inventing snares and traps; then fire was discovered, and, by a series of accidents, its various uses were revealed; the arts of agriculture, domestication, and river navigation were acquired: the tribes migrating from the forests were scattered over the world; their canoes of hollow trees skimmed the tepid waters of the Indian Ocean; their coracles of skin dashed through the icy waves of the Arctic seas; in valleys between mountains, or in fertile river plains, they nurtured seed-bearing grasses into grain; over pastoral mountains, or sandy deserts, or broad grassy steppes, they wandered with their flocks and herds; these shepherd tribes poured down on the plains, subdued the inhabitants and reduced them to serfdom; thus the nation was established, and consisted at first of two great classes--the rulers and the ruled.

The period thus rapidly described, which begins with the animal globules preying on the plant globules in the primeval sea, and which ends with the conquest by the carnivorous shepherds of the vegetable eaters in the river plains, may be termed the Period of War. Throughout that period mind was developed by necessity. The lower animals merely strive to live, to procure females, and to rear their young. It is so ordered by Nature, that by so striving to live they develop their physical structure; they obtain faint glimmerings of reason; they think and deliberate, they sympathise and love; they become Man. In the same way the primeval men have no other object than to keep the clan alive. It is so ordered by Nature, that, in striving to preserve the existence of the clan, they not only acquire the arts of agriculture, domestication, and navigation; they not only discover fire, and its uses in cooking, in war, and in metallurgy; they not only detect the hidden properties of plants, and apply them to save their own lives from disease, and to destroy their enemies in battle; they not only learn to manipulate Nature, and to distribute water by machinery; but they also, by means of the long life-battle, are developed into moral beings: they live according to the Golden Rule, in order that they may exist, or, in other words, they do exist because they live according to the Golden Rule. They have within them innate affections, which are as truly weapons as the tiger's teeth and the serpent's fang; which belong, therefore, to the Period of War. Their first laws, both social and religious, are enacted only as war measures. The laws relating to marriage and property are intended to increase the fertility and power of the clan; the laws relating to religion are intended to preserve the clan from the fury of the gods, against whom, at an earlier period, they actually went to war. But out of this feeling of sympathy, which arose in necessity, arises a secondary sentiment, the love of esteem; and hence wars, which at first were waged merely in self-defence, or to win food-grounds and females necessary for the subsistence and perpetuation of the clan, are now waged for superfluities, power, and the love of glory; commerce, which was founded in necessity, is continued for the acquisition of ornaments and luxuries; science, which at first was a means of life, provides wealth, and is pursued for fame; music and design, which were originally instincts of the hand and voice, are developed into arts. It is therefore natural for man to endeavour to better himself in life, that he may obtain the admiration of his comrades. He desires to increase his means or to win renown in the professions and the arts. Thus man presses upon man, and the whole mass rises in knowledge, in power, and in wealth. But owing to the division of classes resulting from war, and also from the natural inequality of man, the greater part of the human population could not obey their instinctive aspirations; they were condemned to remain stationary and inert. By means of caste, slavery, the system of privileged classes, and monopolies, the people were forbidden to raise themselves in life; they were doomed to die as they were born. But that they might not be altogether without hope, they were taught by their rulers that they would be rewarded with honour and happiness in a future state. The Egyptian fellah received the good tidings that there was no caste after death; the Christian serf was consoled with the text, that the poor would inherit the kingdom of heaven. This long and gloomy period of the human race may be entitled Religion. History is confined to the upper classes. All the discoveries, and inventions, and exploits of ancient times are due to the efforts of an aristocracy; not only the Persians and Hindus, but also the Greeks and the Romans, were merely small societies of gentlemen reigning over a multitude of slaves. The virtues of the lower classes were loyalty, piety, obedience.

The third period is that of Liberty: it belongs only to Europe and to modern times. A middle class of intelligence and wealth arises between the aristocracy and the plebeians. They contend with the monopolies of caste and birth; they demand power for themselves; they espouse the cause of their poorer brethren; they will not admit that equality in heaven is a valid reason for inequality on earth; they deny that the aristocracy of priests know more of divine matters than other men; they interpret the sacred books for themselves, and translate them into the vulgar tongue; they separate religion from temporal government, and reduce it to a system of metaphysics and morality. It is in this period that we are at present. Loyalty to the king has been transformed into patriotism; and piety, or the worship of God, will give way, to the reverence of law and the love of mankind. Thus the mind will be elevated, the affections deepened and enlarged; morality, ceasing to be entangled with theology, will be applied exclusively to virtue.

It is difficult to find a title for the fourth period, as we have as yet no word which expresses at the same time the utmost development of mind and the utmost development of morals. I have chosen the word Intellect, because by the education of the intellect the moral sense is of necessity improved. In this last period the destiny of Man will be fulfilled. He was not sent upon the earth to prepare himself for existence in another world; he was sent upon earth that he might beautify it as a dwelling, and subdue it to his use; that he might exalt his intellectual and moral powers until he had attained perfection, and had raised himself to that ideal which he now expresses by the name of God, but which, however sublime it may appear to our weak and imperfect minds, is far below the splendour and majesty of that power by whom the universe was made.

We shall now leave the darkness of the primeval times, and enter the theatre of history. The Old World is a huge body, with its head buried in eternal snows; with the Atlantic on its left, the Pacific on its right, the Indian Ocean between its legs. The left limb is sound and whole; its foot is the Cape of Good Hope. The right limb has been broken and scattered by the sea; Australia and the Archipelago are detached; Asia has been amputated at the thigh. The lower extremities of this Old World are covered for the most part with thorny thickets and with fiery plains. The original natives were miserable creatures, living chiefly on insects and shells, berries and roots; casting the boomerang and the bone-pointed dart; abject, naked, brutish, and forlorn. We pass up the body in its ancient state; through the marsh of Central Africa, with its woolly-haired blacks upon the left, and through the jungles of India, with its straight-haired blacks upon the right; through the sandy wastes of the Sahara, and the broad Asiatic tablelands; through the forest of Central Europe, the Russian steppes, and the Siberian plains, until we arrive at the frozen shores of the open Polar Sea. The land is covered with fields of snow, on which white bears may be seen in flocks like sheep. Ice mountains tower in the air, and, as the summer approaches, glide into the ocean and sail towards the south, The sky is brightened by a rosy flame, which utters a crisp and crackling sound. All else is silent, Nature is benumbed. The signs of human habitations are rare; sometimes a tribe of Esquimaux may be perceived, dwelling in snow huts, enveloped in furs, driving sledges with teams of dogs, tending their herds of reindeer on the moss-grounds, or dashing over the cold waters in their canoes to hunt the walrus and the seal.

This gloomy region, where the year is divided into one day and one night, lies entirely outside the stream of history. We descend through the land of the pine to the land of the oak and beech. Huge woods and dismal fens covered Europe in the olden time; by the banks of dark and sullen rivers the beavers built their villages; the bears and the wolves were the aristocracy of Europe; men paid them tribute in flesh and blood. A people, apparently of Tartar origin, had already streamed into this continent from Asia; but the true aborigines were not extinct; they inhabited huts built on piles in the lakes of Switzerland; they herded together in mountain caves. They were armed only with stone weapons; but they cultivated certain kinds of grain, and had tamed the reindeer, the ox, the boar, and the dog. In ancient history Europe has no place. Even the lands to the south of the Alps were inhabited by savages at a time when Asia was in a civilised condition.

It is therefore Asia that we must first survey; it is there that the history of books and monuments begins. The Tigris and Euphrates rise in a tableland adjoining the Black Sea, and flow into the Persian Gulf. On the right is a desert extending to the Nile; on the left, a chain of hills. A shepherd people descended from the plateau, occupied the land between the rivers, the plains between the Tigris and the hills, and the alluvial regions at the lower course of the Euphrates. They wandered over the Arabian desert with their flocks and herds, settled in Canaan and Yemen, crossed over into Africa, extended along its northern shores as far as the Atlantic, overspread the Sahara, and made border wars upon the Sudan. In the course of many centuries the various branches of this people diverged from one another. In Barbary and Sahara they were called Berbers; in the valley of the Nile, Egyptians; Arabs, in the desert and in Yemen; Canaanites, in Palestine; Assyrians, in Mesopotamia and the upper regions of the Tigris; Chaldeans or Babylonians, in the lower course of the Euphrates. The Canaanites, the Arabs of Yemen, and the Berbers of Algeria adopted agricultural habits and lived in towns; the Berbers of Sahara, the Bedouins of the Syro-Arabian desert and of the waste regions in Assyria, remained a pastoral and wandering people. But in Chaldea and in Egypt the colonists were placed under peculiar conditions. Famines impelled the shepherds to make war on other tribes; famines impelled the Chaldeans and Egyptians to contend with the Euphrates and the Nile, to domesticate the waters, to store them in reservoirs, and to distribute them, as required, upon the fields. It is not improbable that the Egyptians were men of Babylonia driven by war or by exile into the African deserts; that they were composed of two noble classes, the priests and the military men; that they took with them some knowledge of the arts and sciences, which they afterwards developed into the peculiar Egyptian type; that they found the valley inhabited by a negro race, fishing in papyrus canoes, living chiefly on the lotus root, and perhaps growing doura corn; that they reduced those negroes to slavery, divided them into castes, allowed them to retain in each district the form of animal worship peculiar to the respective tribes, making such worship emblematical, and blending it with their own exalted creed; and finally, that they married the native women, which would thus account for the dash of the "tar-brush" plainly to be read by the practised eye in the portraits, though not in the conventional faces of the monuments. On the other hand it may be held that Egypt was colonised by a Berber tribe; that its civilisation was entirely indigenous; that the distinction of classes arose from natural selection, and was afterwards petrified by law, and that the negro traits in the Egyptian physiognomy were due to the importation of Ethiopian girls, who have always been favourites in the harems of the East. But whichever of these hypotheses may be true, the essential point is this, that civilisation commenced in the application of mechanics to the cultivation of the fields, and that this science could only have been invented under pressure of necessity.

Let us now pass beyond the Tigris and climb up the hills which bound it on the left. We find ourselves on the steppes of Central Asia, in some parts lying waste in salt and sandy plains, in others clothed with fields of waving grass. Over these broad regions roamed the Turks or Tartars, living on mares' milk, dwelling in houses upon wheels. Beyond the steppes towards the east is another chain of hills, and beyond them lies the Great Plain of China, watered by two majestic rivers, the Yang-tse Kiang and the Hoang Ho. The people of the steppes and the mountains poured down upon this country, subdued the savage aborigines, covered the land with rice fields, irrigated by canals, and established many kingdoms which were afterwards blended into one harmonious and civilised empire.

To the right hand of the Tartar steppes, as you travel towards China, is a lofty tableland, the region of the sources of the Oxus and Jaxartes. Thence descended a people who called themselves the Aryas, or "the noble"; they differed much in appearance from the slit-eyed, smooth-faced, and fleshy-limbed Mongols; and little in appearance, but widely in language, from the people of the tableland of the Tigris and Euphrates. They poured forth in successive streams over Persia, Asia Minor, Greece, Italy, and the whole of Europe from the Danube and the Rhine to the shores of the Atlantic. They also descended on the Punjab, or country of the Indus, where they established their first colony, and thence spread to the region of the Ganges, and over the Deccan. They intermarried much with the native women, but divided the men into servile castes, and kept them in subjection partly by means of an armed aristocracy, partly by means of religious terror.

These then are the elemental lands; China, India, Babylonia, and Egypt. In these countries civilisation was invented; history begins with them. The Egyptians manufactured linen goods, and beautiful glass wares, and drew gold, ivory, and slaves from the Sudan. Babylonia manufactured tapestry and carpets. These people were known to one another only by their products; the wandering Bedouins carried the trade between the Euphrates and the Nile. A caravan route was also opened between Babylon and India via Bokhara or Balkh and Samarkand. India possessed much wealth in precious stones, but the true resources of that country were its vegetable products and the skilful manufactures of the natives. India, to use their own expression, sells grass for gold. From one kind of plant they extracted a beautiful blue dye: from another they boiled a juice, which cooled into a crystal, delicate and luscious to the taste; from another they obtained a kind of wool, which they spun, wove, bleached, glazed, and dyed into fabrics transparent as the gossamer, bright as the plumage of the jungle birds. And India was also the half-way station between China, Ceylon, and the Spice Islands on the one hand: and of the countries of Western Asia on the other. It was enriched not only by its own industry and produce, but by the transit trade as well.

At an early epoch in history, the Chinese became a great navigating people; they discovered America, at least so they say; they freighted their junks with cargoes of the shining fibre, and with musk in porcelain jars; they coasted along the shores of the Pacific, established colonies in Burmah and Siam, developed the spice trade of the Indian Archipelago and the resources of Ceylon, sailed up the shores of Malabar, entered the Persian Gulf, and even coasted as far as Aden and the Red Sea. It was probably from them that the Banians of Gujrat and the Arabs of Yemen acquired the arts of shipbuilding and navigation. The Indian Ocean became a basin of commerce; it was whitened by cotton sails. The Phoenicians explored the desolate waters of the Mediterranean Sea; with the bright red cloth, and the blue bugles, and the speckled beads, they tempted the savages of Italy and Greece to trade; they discovered the silver mines of Spain; they sailed forth through the Straits of Gibraltar, they braved the storms of the Atlantic, opened the tin trade of Cornwall, established the amber diggings of the Baltic. Thus a long thread of commerce was stretched across the Old World from England and Germany to China and Japan. Yet, still the great countries in the central region dwelt in haughty isolation, knowing foreign lands only by their products until the wide conquests and the superb administration of the Persians made them members of the same community. China alone remained outside. Egypt, Babylonia, and India were united by royal roads with half-way stations in Palestine and Bokhara, and with seaports in Phoenicia, and on the western coast of Asia Minor That country is a tableland belted on all sides by mountains; but beneath the wall of hills on the western side is a fruitful strip of coast, the estuary land of four rivers which flow into the Mediterranean parallel to one another. That coast is Ionia; and opposite to Ionia lies Greece.

The tableland was occupied by an Aryan or Arya nation, from whom bands of emigrants went forth in two directions. The Dorians crossed the Hellespont, and, passing through Thrace, settled in the hill cantons of Northern Greece, and thence spread over the lower parts of the peninsula. The Ionians descended to the fruitful western coast, and thence migrated into Attica, which afterwards sent back colonies to its ancient birth-place. These two people spoke the same language, and were of the same descent; but their characters differed as widely as the cold and barren mountains from the soft and smiling plains. The Dorians were rude in their manners, and laconic in their speech, barbarous in their virtues, morose in their joys. The Ionians lived among holidays, they could do nothing without dance and song. The Dorians founded Sparta, a republic which was in reality a camp, consisting of soldiers fed by slaves. The girls were educated to be viragoes; the boys to bear torture, like the Red Indians, with a smile. The wives were breeding-machines, belonging to the state; a council of elders examined the new-born children, and selected only the finer specimens, in order to keep up the good old Spartan breed. They had no commerce and no arts; they were as filthy in their persons as they were narrow in their minds. But the Athenians were the true Greeks, as they exist at the present day; intellectual, vivacious, inquisitive, shrewd, artistic, patriotic, and dishonest; ready to die for their country, or to defraud it. The Greeks received the first rudiments of knowledge from

Phoenicia; the alphabet was circulated throughout the country by means of the Olympian fairs; colonies were sent forth all round the Mediterranean; and those of Ionia and the Delta of the Nile obtained partial access to the arts and sciences of Babylon and Memphis.

The Persian wars developed the genius of the Greeks. The Persian conquests opened to them the University of Egypt. The immense area of the Greek world, extending from the Crimea to the straits of Gibraltar, for at one time the Greeks had cities in Morocco; the variety of ideas which they thus gathered, and which they interchanged at the great festival, where every kind of talent was honoured and rewarded the spirit of noble rivalry, which made city contend with city, and citizen with citizen, in order to obtain an Olympian reputation; the complete freedom from theology in art; the tastes and manners of the land; the adoration of beauty; the nudity of the gymnasium: all these sufficiently explain the unexampled progress of the nation, and the origin of that progress, as in all other cases, is to be found in physical geography. Greece was divided into natural cantons; each state was a fortress; while Egypt, Assyria, India, and China were wide and open plains, which cavalry could sweep, and which peasants with their sickles could not defend. But the rivalry of the Greeks among themselves, so useful to the development of mental life, prevented them from combining into one great nation; and Alexander, although he was a Greek by descent, for he had the right of contending at the Olympian games, conquered the East with an army of barbarians, his Greek troops being merely a contingent.

But the kingdoms of Asia and Egypt were Greek, and in Alexandria the foundations of science were laid. The astrolabes which had been invented by the Egyptians were improved by the Greeks and afterwards by the Arabs, were adapted to purposes of navigation by the Portuguese, and were developed to the sextant of the nineteenth century. The Egyptians had invented the blow-pipe, the crucible, and the alembic; the Alexandrines commenced or continued the pursuit of alchemy, which the Arabs also preserved, and which has since grown into the science of Lavoisier and Faraday. Hippocrates separated medicine from theology; his successors dissected and experimented at Alexandria, learning something no doubt from the Egyptian school; the Arabs followed in a servile manner the medicine of the Greeks, and the modern Europeans obtained from the Canon of Avicenna the first elements of a science which has made much progress, but which is yet in its infancy, and which will some day transform us into new beings. The mathematical studies of the Alexandrines were also serviceable to mankind, and the work of one of their professors is a text-book in this country; they discovered the Precession of the Equinoxes; and the work which they did in Conic Sections enabled Kepler to discover the true laws of the planetary motions. But Alexandria did not possess that liberty which is the true source of continued progress. With slaves below and with despots above, the mind was starved in its roots, and stifled in its bud, dried and ticketed in a museum. The land itself had begun to languish and decay, when a new power arose in the West.

The foot of Italy was lined with Greek towns, and these had spread culture through the peninsula, among a people of a kindred race. They dwelt in cities, with municipal governments, public buildings, and national schools. One Italian city, founded by desperadoes, adopted a career of war; but the brigands were also industrious farmers and wise politicians; they conciliated the cities whom they conquered. Rome became a supreme republic, ruling a number of minor republics, whose municipal prerogatives were left undisturbed, who paid no tribute save military service. The wild Gauls of Lombardy were subdued. The Greeks on the coast were the only foreigners who retained their freedom in the land. They called over Pyrrhus to protect them from the Romans; but the legion conquered the phalanx, the broadsword vanquished the Macedonian spear. The Asiatic Carthaginians were masters of the sea; half Sicily belonged to them; they were, therefore, neighbours of the Romans. They had already menaced the cities of the southern coast; the Romans were already jealous and distrustful; they had now a Monroe doctrine concerning the peninsula: an opportunity occurred, and they stepped out into the world. The first Punic War gave them Sicily, the second Punic War gave them Spain, the third Punic War gave them Africa.

Rome also extended her power towards the East. She did not invade, she did not conquer, she did not ask for presents and taxes, she merely offered her friendship and protection. She made war, it is true, but only on behalf of her allies. And so kingdom after kingdom, province after province, fell into her vast and patient arms. She became at first the arbiter and afterwards the mistress of the world. Her legions halted only on the banks of the Euphrates, and on the shores of the Sahara, where a wild waste of sand and a sea-horizon appeared to proclaim that life was at an end. She entered the unknown world beyond the Alps, established a chain of forts along the banks of the Danube and the Rhine from the Black Sea to the Baltic, covered France with noble cities, and made York a Roman town. The Latin language was planted in all the countries which this people conquered, except in those where Alexander had preceded them. The empire was therefore divided by language into the Greek and Latin world. Greece, Asia Minor, Syria, and Egypt belonged to the Greek world: Italy, Africa, Spain, and Gaul belonged to the Latin world. But the Roman law was everywhere in force, though not to the extinction of the native laws. In Egypt, for instance, the Romans revived some of the wise enactments of the Pharaohs which had been abrogated by the Ptolemies. The old courts of injustice were swept away. Tribunals were established which resembled those of the English in India. Men of all races, and of all religions, came before a judge of a foreign race, who sat high above their schisms and dissensions, who looked down upon them all with impartial contempt, and who reverenced the law which was entrusted to his care. But the provinces were forced to support not only a court but a city. As London is the market of England, to which the best of all things find their way, so Rome was the market of the Mediterranean world; but there was this difference between the two, that in Rome the articles were not paid for. Money, indeed, might be given, but it was money which had not been earned, and which therefore would come to its end at last.

Rome lived upon its principal till ruin stared it in the face. Industry is the only true source of wealth, and there was no industry in Rome. By day the Ostia road was crowded with carts and muleteers, carrying to the great city the silks and spices of the East, the marble of Asia Minor, the timber of the Atlas, the grain of Africa and Egypt; and the carts brought nothing out but loads of dung. That was their return cargo. London turns dirt into gold. Rome turned gold into dirt. And how, it may be asked, was the money spent? The answer is not difficult to give. Rome kept open house. It gave a dinner party every day; the emperor and his favourites dined upon nightingales and flamingo tongues, on oysters from Britain, and on fishes from the Black Sea; the guards received their rations; and bacon, wine, oil, and loaves were served out gratis to the people. Sometimes entertainments were given in which a collection of animals as costly as that in Regent's Park was killed for the amusement of the people. Constantine transferred the capital to Constantinople; and now two dinners were given every day. Egypt found the bread for one, and Africa found it for the other. The governors became satraps, the peasantry became serfs, the merchants and landowners were robbed and ruined, the empire stopped payment, the legions of the frontier marched on the metropolis, the dikes were deserted, and then came the deluge.

The empire had been already divided. There was an empire of the West, or the Latin world; there was an empire of the East, or the Greek world. The first was overrun by the Germans, the second by the Arabs. But Constantinople remained unconquered throughout the Dark Ages; and Rome, though taken and sacked, was never occupied by the barbarians. In these two great cities the languages and laws of the classical times were preserved; and from Rome religion was diffused throughout Europe; to Rome a spiritual empire was restored.

The condition of the Roman world at one time bore a curious resemblance to that of China. In each of these great empires, separated by a continent, the principal feature was that of peace. Vast populations dwelt harmoniously together, and were governed by admirable laws. The frontiers of each were threatened by barbarians. The Chinese built a wall along the outskirts of the steppes; the Romans built a wall along the Danube and the Rhine. In China, a man dressed in yellow received divine honours; in Rome, a man dressed in purple received divine honours; in each country the religion was the religion of the state, and the emperor was the representative of God. In each country, also, a religious revolution occurred. A young Indian prince, named Sakya Muni, afflicted by the miseries of human life which he beheld, cast aside his wealth and his royal destiny, became a recluse, and devoted his life to the study of religion. After long years of reading and reflection he took the name of Buddha, or "the Awakened." He declared that the soul after death migrates into another form, according to its deeds and according to its thoughts. This was the philosophy of the Brahmins. But he also proclaimed that all existence is passion, misery, and pain, and that by subduing the evil emotions of the heart the soul will hereafter finally obtain the calm of non-existence, the peaceful Nirvana, the unalloyed, the unclouded Not to Be.

A religion so cheerless, a philosophy so sorrowful, could never have succeeded with the masses of mankind if presented only as a system of metaphysics. Buddhism owed its success to its catholic spirit and its beautiful morality. The men who laboured in the fields had always been taught that the Brahmins were the aristocracy of heaven, and would be as high above them in a future state as they were upon the earth. The holy books which God had revealed were not for them, the poor dark-skinned labourers, to read; burning oil poured into their ears was the punishment by law for so impious an act. And now came a man who told them that those books had not been revealed at all, and that God was no respecter of persons; that the happiness of men in a future state depended, not upon their birth, but upon their actions and their thoughts. Buddhism triumphed for a time in Hindustan, but its success was greatest among the stranger natives in the north-west provinces, the Indo-Scythians and the Greeks. Then came a period of patriotic feeling; the Brahmins preached a war of independence; the new religion was associated with the foreigners, and both were driven out together. But Buddhism became the religion of Ceylon, Burmah, and Siam, and finally entered the Chinese Empire. It suffered and survived bloody persecutions. It became a licensed religion, and spread into the steppes of Tartary among those barbarians by whom China was destined to be conquered. The religion of the Buddhists was transformed; its founder was worshipped as a god; there was a doctrine of the incarnation; they had their own holy books, which they declared to have been revealed; they established convents and nunneries, splendid temples, adorned with images, and served by priests with shaven heads, who repeated prayers upon rosaries, and who taught that happiness in a future state could best be obtained by long prayers and by liberal presents to the Church.

At the period of the importation of Buddhism into China, a similar event occurred in the Roman world. It was the pagan theory that each country was governed by its own gods. The proper religion for each man, said an oracle of Delphi, is the religion of his fatherland. Yet these gods were cosmopolitan; they punished or rewarded foreigners. Imilkon, having offended the Greek gods in the Sicilian wars, made atonement to them when he returned to Carthage: he offered sacrifices in the Phoenician temples, but according to the milder ceremonies of the Greeks. The Philistines sent back the ark with a propitiatory present to Jehovah. Alexander, in Asia Minor, offered sacrifices to the gods of the enemy. The Romans, when they besieged a town, called upon its tutelary god by name, and offered him bribes to give up the town. Rome waged war against the world, but not against the gods; she did not dethrone them in their own countries; she offered them the freedom of the city. Men of all races came to live in Rome; they were allowed to worship their own gods; the religions of the empire were regularly licensed; Egyptian temples and Syrian chapels sprang up in all directions. But though the Romans considered it right that Egyptians should worship Isis, and that Alexandrines should worship Serapis, they justly considered it a kind of treason for Romans to desert their tutelary gods. For this reason, foreign religions were sometimes proscribed. It was also required from the subjects of the empire that they should offer homage to the gods of Rome, and to the genius or spirit of the emperor; not to the man, but to the soul that dwelled within. The Jews alone were exempt from these regulations. It was believed that they were a peculiar people, or rather that they had a peculiar god. While the other potentates of the celestial world lived in harmony together, Jehovah was a sullen and solitary being, who separated his people from the rest of mankind, forbade them to eat or drink with those who were not of their own race, and threatened to punish them if they worshipped any gods but him. On this account the Roman government, partly to preserve the lives of their subjects, and partly out of fear for themselves, believing that Jehovah like the other gods, had always an epidemic at his command, treated the Jews with exceptional indulgence.

These people were scattered over all the world; they had their Ghetto or Petticoat Lane in every great city of the empire; their religion, so superior to that of the pagans, had attracted much attention from the Gentiles. Ovid, in his "Art of Love," counsels the dandy who seeks a mistress to frequent the theatre, or Temple of Isis, or the synagogue on the Sabbath day. But the Jews in Rome, like the Jews in London, did not attempt to make proselytes, and received them with reluctance and distrust. Their sublime faith, divested of its Asiatic customs, was offered to the Romans some Jewish heretics called Christians or Nazarenes.

A young man named Joshua or Jesus, a carpenter by trade, believed that the world belonged to the devil, and that God would shortly take it from him, and that he the Christ or Anointed would be appointed by God to judge the souls of men, and to reign over them on earth. In politics he was a leveller and communist, in morals he was a monk; he believed that only the poor and the despised would inherit the kingdom of God. All men who had riches or reputations would follow their dethroned master into everlasting pain. He attacked the church-going, sabbatarian ever-praying Pharisees; he declared that piety was worthless if it were praised on earth. It was his belief that earthly happiness was a gift from Satan, and should therefore be refused. If a man was poor in this world, that was good; he would be rich in the world to come. If he were miserable and despised, he had reason to rejoice; he was out of favour with the ruler of this world, namely Satan, and therefore he would be favoured by the new dynasty. On the other hand, if a man were happy, rich, esteemed, and applauded, he was for ever lost. He might have acquired his riches by industry; he might have acquired his reputation by benevolence, honesty, and devotion; but that did not matter; he had received his reward. So Christ taught that men should sell all that they had and give to the poor; that they should renounce all family ties; that they should let to-morrow take care of itself; that they should not trouble about clothes: did, not God adorn the flowers of the fields? He would take care of them also if they would fold their hands together and have faith, and abstain from the impiety of providing for the future. The principles of Jesus were not conducive to the welfare of society; he was put to death by the authorities; his disciples established a commune; Greek Jews were converted by them, and carried the new doctrines over all the world. The Christians in Rome were at first a class of men resembling the Quakers. They called one another brother and sister; they adopted a peculiar garb, and peculiar forms of speech; the Church was at first composed of women, slaves, and illiterate artisans but it soon became the religion of the people in the towns. All were converted excepting the rustics (pagani) and the intellectual free-thinkers, who formed the aristocracy. Christianity was at first a republican religion; it proclaimed the equality of souls; the bishops were the representatives of God, and the bishops were chosen by the people. But when the emperor adopted Christianity and made it a religion of the state, it became a part of imperial government, and the parable of Dives was forgotten. The religion of the Christians was transformed; its founder was worshipped as a god; there was a doctrine of the incarnation; they had their own holy books, which they declared to have been revealed; they established convents, and nunneries, and splendid temples, adorned with images, and served by priests with shaven heads, who repeated prayers upon rosaries, and who taught that happiness in a future state could best be obtained by long prayers and by liberal presents to the Church. In the Eastern or Greek world, Christianity in no way assisted civilisation, but in the Latin world it softened the fury of the conquerors, it aided the amalgamation of the races. The Christian priests were reverenced by the barbarians, and these priests belonged to the conquered people.

The Church, it is true, was divided by a schism; Ulphilas, the apostle of The Goths, was an Arian; the dispute which had arisen in a lecture-room at Alexandria, between a bishop and a presbyter, was continued on a hundred battlefields. But the Franks were Catholics, and the Franks became supreme. The Arians were worsted in the conflict of swords as they had formerly been worsted in the conflict of words. The Empire of the West was restored by Charlemagne, who spread Christianity among the Saxons by the sword, and confirmed the spiritual supremacy of Rome. He died, and his dominions were partitioned among kings who were royal only in the name. Europe was divided into castle-states. Savage isolation, irresponsible power: such was the order of the age. Yet still there was a sovereign whom all acknowledged, and whom all to a certain extent obeyed. That sovereign was the Pope of Rome. The men who wore his livery might travel throughout Europe in safety, welcome alike at cottage and castle, paying for their board and lodging with their prayers. If there is a Great Being who listens with pleasure to the prayers of men, it must have been in the Dark Ages that he looked down upon the earth with most satisfaction. That period may be called The Age of the Rosary. From the Shetland Islands to the shores of China, prayers were being strung, and voices were being sonorously raised. The Christian repeated his Paternosters and his credos on beads of holy clay from Palestine; the Persian at Teheran, the negro at Timbuctoo; the Afghan at Kabul, repeated the ninety-nine names of God on beads made of camel bones from Mecca. The Indian prince by the waters of the Ganges muttered his devotions on a rosary of precious stones. The pious Buddhist in Ceylon, and in Ava, and in Pekin, had the beads ever between his fingers, and a prayer ever between his lips.

By means of these great and cosmopolitan religions, all of which possessed their sacred books, all of which enjoined a pure morality, all of which united vast masses of men of different and even hostile nationalities beneath the same religious laws, beneath the same sceptre of an unseen king; all of which prescribed pilgrimage and travel as a pious work, the circulation of life in the human body was promoted; men congregated together at Rome, Jerusalem, Mecca, and Benares. Their minds and morals were expanded. Religious enthusiasm united the scattered princes of Europe into one great army, and poured it on the East. The dukes and counts and barons were ruined; the castle system was extinguished: and the castle serfs of necessity were free. The kings allied themselves with the free and fortified cities, who lent troops to the crown, but who officered those troops themselves; who paid taxes to the crown, but who voted those taxes in constitutional assemblies, and had the power to withhold them if they pleased. Those towns now became not only abodes of industry and commerce, but of learning and the arts. In Italy the ancient culture had been revived. In Italy the towns of the Western Empire had never quite lost their municipal prerogatives. New towns had also arisen, founded in despair and nurtured by calamity. These towns had opened a trade with Constantinople, a great commercial city in which the Arabs had a quarter and a mosque. The Italians were thus led forth into a trade with the Mohammedans, which was interrupted for a time by the Crusades only to be afterwards resumed with redoubled vigour and success. For then new markets were opened for the spices of the East. Pepper became a requisite of European life; and pepper could be obtained from the Italians alone. The Indian trade was not monopolised by a single man, as it was in the lands of the East. It was distributed among an immense population. Wealth produced elegance, leisure, and refinement. There came into existence a large and active-minded class, craving for excitement, and desirous of new things. They hungered and thirsted after knowledge; they were not content with the sterile science of the priests. And when it was discovered that the world of the ancients lay buried in their soil, they were seized with a mania resembling that of treasure-seekers in the East, or of the gold-hunters in the New World.

The elements of the Renaissance were preserved partly in Rome and the cities of the West, partly in Constantinople, and partly in the East. The Arabs, when they conquered Alexandria, had adopted the physical science of the Greeks, and had added to it the algebra and arithmetic of India. Plato and Aristotle, Galen and Hippocrates, Ptolemy and Euclid, had been translated by the Eastern Christians into Syriac, and thence into the Arabic. But the Arabs had not translated a single Greek historian or poet. These were to be found at Constantinople, where the Greek of the ancients was still spoken in its purity at the court and in the convents though not by the people of the streets. The Greeks also had preserved the arts of their forefathers; though destitute of genius, they at least retained the art of laying on colours, of modelling in clay, and of sculpturing in stone. The great towns of Italy, desirous to emulate the beauties of St. Sophia, employed Greeks to build them cathedrals, and to paint frescoes on their convent walls, and to make them statues for their streets. These Greek strangers established academies of art; and soon the masters were surpassed by their pupils. The Italians disdained to reproduce the figures of the Greek school, with their meagre hands, and sharp pointed feet, and staring eyes. Free institutions made their influence felt even in the arts; the empire of authority was shaken off. The fine arts spread beyond the Alps; they were first adopted and nurtured by the Church, afterwards by the Town. Oil-painting was invented in the North. Masterpieces of the ancients were discovered in the South. Then the artists ceased to paint Madonnas, and children, and saints, and crucifixions. They were touched with the breath of antiquity; they widened their field; their hands were inspired by poetical ideas. It is a significant fact that a Pope should himself conceive the project of pulling down the ancient Basilica of St. Peter, every stone of which was consecrated by a memory, and of erecting in its stead a church on the model of a pagan temple.

The Pope was also urged to set on foot a crusade; not to rescue the sepulchre from the hands of the infidels, but in the hope that the lost writings of the Greeks and Romans might be discovered in the East. For now had arrived the book-hunting age. In the depth of the Dark Ages there had always been ecclesiastics who drew the fire of their genius from the immortal works of the pagan writers. There were also monks who had a passion for translating the writings of the Greeks into Latin; who went to Constantinople and returned with chests full of books, and who, if Greek manuscripts could not otherwise be procured, travelled into Arab Spain, settled at Cordova, and translated the Greek from the Arabic version, together with the works of Averroes and Avicenna. The Greeks, frequently visiting Italy, were invited to give lectures on their literature, and lessons in their language. The revival of Greek was commenced by Boccacio, who copied out Homer with his own hand; and a Greek academy was established at Florence. Petrarch revived the literature of Rome he devoted his life to Cicero and Virgil; he wrote the epitaph of Laura on the margin of the Aeneid; he died with his head pillowed on a book. The Roman law was also revived; as Greeks lectured on literature in Italy, so Italians lectured on law beyond the Alps.

And now began the search for the lost. Pilgrims of the antique wandered through Europe, ransacking convents for the treasures of the past. At this time whatever taste for learning had once existed among the monks appears to have died away. The pilgrims were directed to look in lofts, where rats burrowed under heaps of parchment; or to sift heaps of rubbish lying in the cellar. In such receptacles were found many of those works which are yet read by thousands with delight, and which are endeared to us all by the associations of our boyhood. It was thus that Quintilian was discovered, and, to use the language of the time, was delivered from his long imprisonment in the dungeons of the barbarians. Lucretius was disinterred in Germany; a fragment of Petronius in Britain. Cosmo de' Medici imported books in all languages from all parts of the world. A copyist became Pope, founded the Library of the Vatican, and ordered the translation of the Greek historians and philosophers into Latin. A great reading public now existed; the invention of printing, which a hundred years before would have been useless, spread like fire over Europe, and reduced, by four-fifths, the price of books. The writings of the classical geographers inspired Prince Henry and Columbus. The New World was discovered; the sea-route to India was found. Cairo and Baghdad, the great broker cities between India and Europe, were ruined. As the Indian Ocean, at first the centre of the world, had yielded to the Mediterranean, so now the basin of the Mediterranean was deserted, and the Atlantic became supreme. Italy decayed; Spain and Portugal succeeded to the throne. But those countries were ruined by religious bigotry and commercial monopolies. The trade of Portugal did not belong to the country, but to the court. The trade of Spain was also a monopoly shared between the Crown and certain cities of Castile. The Dutch, the English, and the French obtained free access to the tropical world, and bought the spices of the East with the silver of Peru. And then the great movement for Liberty commenced. All people of the Teutonic race; the Germans, the Swiss, the Dutch, the English and the Scotch, the Danes and the Swedes, cast off the yoke of the Italian supremacy, and some of the superstitions of the Italian creed.

But now a new kind of servitude arose. The kings reduced the burghers of Europe to subjection. The constitutional monarchies of the Middle Ages disappeared. In England alone, owing to its insular position, a standing army was not required for the protection of the land. In England, therefore, the encroachments of the Crown were resisted with success. Two revolutions established the sovereignty of an elected parliament, and saved England from the fate of France. For in that land tyranny had struck its roots far down into the soil, and could not be torn up without the whole land being rent in twain. In Spain, despotism might rule in safety over ignorance; but the French had eaten of the Tree of Knowledge, and they demanded to eat of the Tree of Life. A bread riot became a rebellion; the rebellion became a revolution. Maddened by resistance, frenzied with fear, they made their revolution a massacre. Yet, in spite of mummeries and murders, and irreligious persecutions; in spite of follies perpetrated in the name of Reason, and cruelties committed in the name of Humanity, that revolution regenerated France, and planted principles which spread over the continent of Europe, and which are now bearing fruit in Italy and Spain. With the nineteenth century, a new era of history begins.

Such then is the plain unvarnished story of the human race. We have traced the stream of history to its source in the dark forest; we have followed it downwards through the steppes of the shepherds and the valleys of the great priest peoples; we have swept swiftly along, past pyramids and pagodas, and the brick-piles of Babylon; past the temples of Ionia, and the amphitheatres of Rome; past castles and cathedrals lying opposite to mosques with graceful minaret and swelling dome; and so, onwards and onwards, till towns rise on both sides of the stream; towns sternly walled with sentinels before the gates; so, onwards and onwards, till the stream widens and is covered with ships large as palaces, and towering with sail; till the banks are lined with gardens and villas; and huge cities, no longer walled, hum with industry, and becloud the air; and deserts or barren hills are no longer to be seen; and the banks recede and open out like arms, and the earth-shores dissolve, and we faintly discern the glassy glimmering of the boundless sea. We shall descend to the mouth of the river, we shall explore the unknown waters which lie beyond the present, we shall survey the course which man has yet to run. But before we attempt to navigate the future, let us return for a moment to the past; let us endeavour to ascertain the laws which direct the movements of the stream, and let us visit the ruins which are scattered on its banks.

The progress of the human race is caused by the mental efforts which are made at first from necessity to preserve life, and secondly from the desire to obtain distinction. In a healthy nation, each class presses into the class which lies above it; the blood flows upwards, and so the whole mass, by the united movements of its single atoms, rises in the scale. The progress of a nation is the sum-total of the progress of the individuals composing it. If certain parts of the body politic are stifled in their growth by means of artificial laws, it is evident that the growth of the whole will be arrested; for the growth of each part is dependent on the growth of all. It is usual to speak of Greece as a free country; and so it was in comparison with Asia. But more than half its inhabitants were slaves; labour was degraded; whatever could be done by thought alone, and by delicate movements of the hands, was carried to perfection; but in physical science the Greeks did little, because little could be done without instruments, and instruments can seldom be invented except by free and intelligent artisans. So the upper part of the Greek body grew; the lower part remained in a base and brutal state, discharging the offices of life, but without beauty and without strength. The face was that of Hyperion; the legs were shrivelled and hideous as those of a satyr. In Asia human laws have been still more fatal to the human progress. In China there is no slavery, and there is no caste; the poorest man may be exalted to the highest station; not birth but ability is the criterion of distinction; appointments are open to the nation, and are awarded by means of competitive examinations. But the Chinese are schoolboys who never grow up; generals and statesmen who incur the displeasure of the Crown are horsed and flagellated in the Eton style, a bamboo being used instead of a birch. The patriarchal system of the steppes has been transferred to the imperial plain. Just as a Chinese town is merely a Tartar camp encircled by earthen walls; just as a Chinese house is merely a Tartar tent, supported by wooden posts and cased with brick, so it is with the government, domestic and official, of that country. Every one is the slave of his father, as it was in the old tent-life; every father is the slave of an official who stands in the place of the old clan chief; and all are slaves of the emperor, who is the viceroy of God. In China, therefore, senility is supreme; nothing is respectable unless it has existed at least a thousand years; foreigners are barbarians, and property is insecure.

In this one phrase the whole history of Asia is contained. In the despotic lands of the East, the peasant who grows more corn than he requires is at once an object of attention to the police; he is reported to the governor, and a charge is laid against him, in order that his grain may be seized. He not only loses the fruit of his toil, but he also receives the bastinado. In the same manner, if a merchant, by means of his enterprise, industry, and talents, amasses a large fortune; he also is arrested and is put to death, that his estate may escheat to the Crown. As the Chinese say, "The elephant is killed for his ivory." This, then, is the secret of Asiatic apathy, and not the heat of the climate, or the inherent qualities of race. Civilised Asia has been always enthralled, because standing armies have always been required to resist the attacks of those warlike barbarians who cover the deserts of Arabia and Tartary, the highlands of Ethiopia and Kabul. Asia, therefore, soon takes a secondary place, and Europe becomes the centre of the human growth. Yet it should not be forgotten that Asia was civilised when Europe was a forest and a swamp. Asia taught Europe its A B C; Asia taught Europe to cipher and to draw; Asia taught Europe the language of the skies, how to calculate eclipses, how to follow the courses of the stars, how to measure time by means of an instrument which recorded with its shadow the station of the sun; how to solve mathematical problems; how to philosophise with abstract ideas. Let us not forget the school in which we learnt to spell, and those venerable halls in which we acquired the rudiments of science and of art.

The savage worships the shades of his ancestors chiefly from selfish fear; the Asiatic follows, from blind prejudice, the wisdom of the ancients, and rejects with contempt all knowledge which was unknown to them. Yet within these superstitions a beautiful sentiment lies concealed. We ought, indeed, to reverence the men of the past, who, by their labours and their inventions, have made us what we are. This great and glorious city in which we dwell, this mighty London, the metropolis of the earth; these streets flowing with eager-minded life, and gleaming with prodigious wealth; these forests of masts, these dark buildings, turning refuse into gold, and giving bread to many thousand mouths; these harnessed elements which whirl us along beneath the ground, and which soon will convey us through the air; these spacious halls, adorned with all that can exalt the imagination or fascinate the sense; these temples of melody; these galleries, exhibiting excavated worlds; these walls covered with books in which dwell the souls of the immortal dead, which, when they are opened, transport us by a magic spell to lands which are vanished and passed away, or to spheres created by the poet's art; which make us walk with Plato beneath the plane trees, or descend with Dante into the dolorous abyss--to whom do we owe all these? First, to the poor savages, forgotten and despised, who, by rubbing sticks together, discovered fire, who first tamed the timid fawn, and first made the experiment of putting seeds into the ground. And, secondly, we owe them to those enterprising warriors who established nationality, and to those priests who devoted their lifetime to the culture of their minds.

There is a land where the air is always tranquil, where Nature wears always the same bright yet lifeless smile; and there, as in a vast museum, are preserved the colossal achievements of the past. Let us enter the sad and silent river; let us wander on its dusky shores. Buried cities are beneath our feet; the ground on which we tread is the pavement of a tomb. See the Pyramids towering to the sky; with men, like insects, crawling round their base; and the Sphinx, couched in vast repose, with a ruined temple between its paws. Since those great monuments were raised, the very heavens have been changed. When the architects of Egypt began their work, there was another polar star in the northern sky, and the Southern Cross shone upon the Baltic shores. How glorious are the memories of those ancient men, whose names are forgotten, for they lived and laboured in the distant and unwritten past. Too great to be known, they sit on the height of centuries and look down on fame. The boat expands its white and pointed wings; the sailors chaunt a plaintive song; the waters bubble around us as we glide past the tombs and temples of the by-gone days. The men are dead, and the gods are dead. Nought but their memories remain. Where now is Osiris, who came down upon earth out of love for men, who was killed by the malice of the Evil One, who rose again from the grave, and became the Judge of the dead? Where now is Isis the mother, with the child Horus on her lap? They are dead; they are gone to the land of the shades. To-morrow, Jehovah, you and your son shall be with them!

Men die, and the ideas which they call gods die too; yet death is not destruction, but only a kind of change. Those strange ethereal secretions of the brain, those wondrously distilled thoughts of ours--do they ever really die? They are embodied into words; and from these words, spoken or written, new thoughts are born within the brains of those who listen or who read. There was a town named Heliopolis; it had a college garden, and a willow hanging over the Fountain of the Sun; and there the professors lectured and discoursed on the Triune God, and the creation of the world, and, the Serpent Evil, and the Tree of Life; and on chaos and darkness, and the shining stars; and there the stone quadrant was pointed to the heavens; and there the laboratory furnace glowed. And in that college two foreign students were received, and went forth learned in its lore. The first created a nation in the Egyptian style; the second created a system of ideas; and, strange to say, on Egyptian soil the two were reunited: the philosophy of Moses was joined in Alexandria to the philosophy of Plato, not only by the Jews, but also by the Christians; not only in Philo Judaeus, but also in the Gospel of St. John.

Over the bright blue waters, under the soft and tender sky, with the purple sails outspread and roses twining round the mast, with lute and flute resounding from the prow, and red wine poured upon the sea, and thanksgiving to the gods, we enter the Piraeus, and salute with our flag the temple on the hill. Vessels sweep past us, outward bound, laden with statues and paintings, for such are the manufactures of Athens, where the milestones are masterpieces, and the streetwalkers poets and philosophers. Imagine the transports of the young provincial who went to Athens to commence a career of ambition, to make himself a name! What raptures he must have felt as he passed through that City of the Violet Crown with Homer in his bosom, and hopes of another united Greece within his heart! What a banquet of delights, what varied treasures of the mind were spread before him there! He listened first to a speech of Pericles on political affairs, and then to a lecture by Anaxagoras. He was taken to the studio of Phidias and of Polygnotus: he went to a theatre built of Persian masts to see a new tragedy by Sophocles or Euripides, and finished the evening at Aspasia's establishment, with odes of Sappho, and ballads of Anacreon, and sweet-eyed musicians, and intellectual Heterae.

So great are the achievements of the Greeks, so deep is the debt which we owe to them, that criticism appears ungrateful or obtuse. It is scarcely possible to indicate the vices and defects of this people without seeming guilty of insensibility or affectation. It is curious to observe how grave and sober minds accustomed to gather evidence with care, and to utter decisions with impartiality, cease to be judicial when Greece is brought before them. She unveils her beauty, and they can only admire: they are unable to condemn. Those who devote themselves to the study of the Greeks become nationalised in their literature, and patriots of their domain. It is indeed impossible to read their works without being impressed by their purity, their calmness, their exquisite symmetry and finish resembling that which is bestowed upon a painting or a statue. But it is not only in the Greek writings that the Greek spirit is contained: it has entered the modern European mind it permeates the world of thought; it inspires the ideas of those who have never read the Greek authors, and who perhaps regard them with disdain. We do not see the foundations of our minds: they are buried in the past. The great books and the great discoveries of modern times are based upon the works of Homer, Plato, Aristotle, and their disciples. All that we owe to Rome we owe to Greece as well, for Italy was a child of Greece. The cities on the southern coast bestowed on the rude natives the elements of culture, and when Rome became famous it was colonised by Grecian philosophers and artists.

To Rome we are indebted for those laws from which our jurisprudence is descended, and to Rome we are indebted for something else besides. We shall not now pause on the Rome, of the Republic, when every citizen was a soldier, and worked in the fields with his own hands; when every temple was the monument of a victory, and every statue the memorial of a hero; when door-posts were adorned with the trophies of war, and halls with the waxen images of ancestors; when the Romans were simple, religious, and severe, and the vices of luxury were yet unknown, and banquets were plain and sociable repasts, where the guests in turn sang old ballads while the piper played. Nor shall we pause on the Rome of Augustus, when East and West were united in peace and with equal rights before the law; when the tyranny of petty princedoms, and the chicanery of Grecian courts of law, and the blood-feuds of families had been destroyed; and the empire was calm and not yet becalmed, and rested a moment between tumult and decay. We shall pass on to a Rome more great and more sublime; a Rome which ruled Europe, but not by arms; a Rome which had no mercenary legions, no Praetorian Guards, and which yet received the tribute of kings, and whose legates exercised the power of proconsuls. In this Rome a man clad in the purple of the Caesars and crowned with the tiara of the Pontifex sent forth his soldiers armed with the crucifix, and they brought nations captive to his feet. Rome became a city of God: she put on a spiritual crown. She cried to the kings, Give! and gold was poured into her exchequers; she condemned a man who had defied her, and he had no longer a place among mankind; she proclaimed a Truce of God, and the swords of robber knights were sheathed; she preached a crusade, and Europe was hurled into Asia. She lowered the pride of the haughty, and she exalted the heart of the poor; she softened the rage of the mighty, she consoled the despair of the oppressed. She fed the hungry, and she clothed the naked; she took children to her arms and signed them with the Cross; she administered the sacraments to dying lips, and laid the cold body in the peaceful grave. Her first word was to welcome, and her last word to forgive.

In the Dark Ages the European States were almost entirely severed from one another; it was the Roman Church alone which gave them one sentiment in common, and which united them within her fold. In those days of violence and confusion, in those days of desolation and despair, when a stranger was a thing which, like a leper or a madman, any one might kill, when every gentleman was a highway robber, when the only kind of lawsuit was a duel, hundreds of men dressed in gowns of coarse dark stuff, with cords round their waists and bare feet, travelled with impunity from castle to castle, preaching a doctrine of peace and good will, holding up an emblem of humility and sorrow, receiving confessions, pronouncing penance or absolutions, soothing the agonies of a wounded conscience, awakening terror in the hardened mind. Parish churches were built: the baron and his vassals chanted together the Kyrie Eleison, and bowed their heads together when the bell sounded and the Host was raised. Here and there in the sombre forest a band of those holy men encamped, and cut down the trees and erected a building which was not only a house of prayer, but also a kind of model farm. The monks worked in the fields, and had their carpenters' and their blacksmiths' shops. They copied out books in a fair hand: they painted Madonnas for their chapel: they composed music for their choir: they illuminated missals: they studied Arabic and Greek: they read Cicero and Virgil: they preserved the Roman Law.

Bright, indeed, yet scanty are these gleams. In the long night of the Dark Ages we look upon the earth, and only the convent and the castle appear to be alive. In the convent the sound of honourable labour mingles with the sound of prayer and praise. In the castle sits the baron with his children on his lap, and his wife, leaning on his shoulder: the troubadour sings, and the page and demoiselle exchange a glance of love. The castle is the home of music and chivalry and family affection. The convent is the home of religion and of art. But the people cower in their wooden huts, half starved, half frozen, and wolves sniff at them through the chinks in the walls. The convent prays, and the castle sings: the cottage hungers, and groans, and dies. Such is the dark night: here and there a star in the heaven: here and there a torch upon the earth: all else is cloud and bitter wind. But now, behold the light glowing in the East: it brightens, it broadens, the day is at hand! The sun is rising, and will set no more: the castle and the convent disappear: the world is illumined: freedom is restored. Italy is a garden, and its blue sea shines with sails. New worlds are discovered, new arts are invented: the merchants enrich Europe, and their sons set her free. In a hall at

Westminster, in a redoubt at Bunker Hill, in a tennis court at Versailles, great victories are won, and liberty at last descends even to the poor French peasant growing grey in his furrow, even to the negro picking cotton in the fields. Yet after all, how little has been done! The sun shines as yet only on a corner of the earth: Asia and Africa are buried in the night. And even here in this island, where liberty was born, where wealth is sustained by enterprise and industry, and war comes seldom, and charity abounds, there are yet dark places where the sunlight never enters, and where hope has never been: where day follows day in never-changing toil, and where life leads only to the prison, or the work house, or the grave. Yet a day will come when the whole earth will be as civilised as Europe: a day will come when these dark spots will pass away.

If we compare the present with the past, if we trace events at all epochs to their causes, if we examine the elements of human growth, we find that Nature has raised us to what we are, not by fixed laws, but by provisional expedients, and that the principle which in one age effected the advancement of a nation, in the next age retarded the mental movement, or even destroyed it altogether. War, despotism, slavery, and superstition are now injurious to the progress of Europe, but they were once the agents by which progress was produced. By means of war the animated life was slowly raised upward in the scale, and quadrupeds passed into man. By means of war the human intelligence was brightened, and the affections were made intense; weapons and tools were invented; foreign wives were captured, and the marriages of blood relations were forbidden; prisoners were tamed, and the women set free; prisoners were exchanged, accompanied with presents; thus commerce was established, and thus, by means of war, men were first brought into amicable relations with one another. By war the tribes were dispersed all over the world, and adopted various pursuits according to the conditions by which they were surrounded. By war the tribes were compressed into the nation. It was war which founded the Chinese Empire. It was war which had locked Babylonia, and Egypt, and India. It was war which developed the genius of Greece. It was war which planted the Greek language in Asia, and so rendered possible the spread of Christianity. It was war which united the world in peace from the Cheviot Hills to the Danube and the Euphrates. It was war which saved Europe from the quietude of China. It was war which made Mecca the centre of the East. It was war which united the barons in the Crusades, and which destroyed the feudal system.

Even in recent times the action of war has been useful in condensing scattered elements of nationality, and in liberating subject populations. United Italy was formed directly or indirectly by the war of 1859, 1866, and 1870. The last war realised the dreams of German poets, and united the Teutonic nations more closely than the shrewdest statesmen could have conceived to be possible a few years ago. That same war, so calamitous for France, will yet regenerate that great country, and make her more prosperous than she has ever been. The American War emancipated four million men, and decided for ever the question as to whether the Union was a nationality or a league. But the Crimean War was injurious to civilisation; it retarded a useful and inevitable event. Turkey will some day be covered with cornfields; Constantinople will some day be a manufacturing town; but a generation has been lost. Statesmen and journalists will learn in time that whatever is conquered for civilisation is conquered for all. To preserve the Balance of Power was an excellent policy in the Middle Ages, when war was the only pursuit of a gentleman, and when conquest was the only ambition of kings. It is now suited only for the highlands of Abyssinia. The jealousy with which 'true Britons' regard the Russian success in Central Asia is surely a very miserable feeling. That a vast region of the earth should be opened, that robbery and rapine and slave-making raids should be suppressed, that waste-lands should be cultivated, that new stores of wealth should be discovered, that new markets should be established for the products of European industry, our own among the rest, that Russia should adjoin England in Asia as she adjoins Germany in Europe--what a lamentable occurrence, what an ominous event! In Central Africa it often happens that between two barbarous and distrustful nations there is a wide neutral ground, inhabited by wild beasts, which prey upon the flocks and herds on either side. Such is the policy which maintains the existence of barbarous kingdoms between two civilised frontiers.

The great Turkish and Chinese Empires, the lands of Morocco, Abyssinia, and Tibet, will be eventually filled with free, industrious, and educated populations. But those people will never begin to advance until their property is rendered secure, until they enjoy the rights of man; and these they will never obtain except by means of European conquest. In British India the peasant reaps the rice which he has sown; and the merchant has no need to hide his gold beneath the ground. The young men of the new generation are looking forward to the time when the civil appointments of their country will he held by them. The Indian Mutiny was a mutiny only, and not a rebellion; the industrial and mercantile classes were on the English side. There is a sickly school of politicians who declare that all countries belong to their inhabitants, and that to take them is a crime. If any country in Asia did belong to its inhabitants, there might be some force in this objection. But Asia is possessed by a few kings and by their soldiers; these rulers are usually foreigners; the masses of the people are invariably slaves. The conquest of Asia by European Powers is therefore in reality emancipation, and is the first step towards the establishment of Oriental nationality. It is needless to say that Europe will never engage in crusades to liberate servile populations; but the pride and ignorance of military despots will provoke foreign wars, which will prove fatal to their rule. Thus war will, for long years yet to come, be required to prepare the way for freedom and progress in the East; and in Europe itself, it is not probable that war will ever absolutely cease until science discovers some destroying force, so simple in its administration, so horrible in its effects, that all art, all gallantry, will be at an end, and battles will be massacres which the feelings of mankind will be unable to endure.

A second expedient of Nature is religion. Men believe in the existence of beings who can punish and reward them in this life or in the next, who are the true rulers of the world, and who have deputed certain men, called priests, to collect tribute and to pass laws on their behalf. By means of these erroneous ideas, a system of government is formed to which kings themselves are subjected; the moral nature of man is improved, the sciences and arts are developed, distinct and hostile races are united. But error, like war, is only provisional. In Europe, religion no longer exists as a political power, but it will probably yet render service to civilisation in assisting to Europeanise the barbarous nations whom events will in time bring under our control.

A third expedient of Nature is inequality of conditions. Sloth is the natural state of man; prolonged and monotonous labour is hard for him to bear. The savage can follow a trail through the forest, or can lie in ambush for days at a time; this pertinacity and patience are native to his mind; they belong to the animals from whom he is descended: but the cultivation of the soil is a new kind of labour, and it is only followed from compulsion. It is probable that when domestic slavery was invented, a great service was rendered to mankind, and it has already been shown that when prisoners of war were tamed and broken in, women were set free, and became beautiful, long-haired, low-voiced, sweet-eyed creatures, delicate in form, modest in demeanour, and refined in soul. It was also by means of slavery that a system of superfluous labour was established; for women, when slaves, are made only to labour for the essentials of life. It was by means of slavery that leisure was created, that the priests were enabled to make experiments, and to cultivate the arts, that the great public buildings of the ancient lands were raised. It was slavery which arrested the progress of Greece; but it was also slavery which enabled all the free men of a Greek town to be sculptors, poets, and philosophers. Slavery is now happily extinct, and can never be revived under the sanction of civilised authority. But a European Government, ought perhaps to introduce compulsory labour among the barbarous races that acknowledge its sovereignty and occupy its land. Children are ruled and schooled by force, and it is not an empty metaphor to say that savages are children. If they were made to work, not for the benefit of others, but for their own; if the rewards of their labour were bestowed, not on their masters, but on themselves, the habit of work would become with them a second nature, as it is with us, and they would learn to require luxuries which industry only could obtain. A man is not a slave in being compelled to work against his will, but in being compelled to work without hope and without reward. Enforced labour is undoubtedly a hardship, but it is one which at present belongs to the lot of man, and is indispensable to progress.

The Future of Human Race

Mankind grows because men desire to better themselves in life, and this desire proceeds from the inequality of conditions. A time will undoubtedly arrive when all men and women will be equal, and when the love of money, which is now the root of all industry, and which therefore is now the root of all good, will cease to animate the human mind. But changes so prodigious can only be effected in prodigious periods of time. Human nature cannot be transformed by a coup d'etat, as the Comtists and Communists imagine. It is a complete delusion to suppose that wealth can be equalised and happiness impartially distributed by any process of law, Act of Parliament, or revolutionary measure. It is easy to compose a pathetic scene in a novel, or a loud article in a magazine by contrasting Dives lunching on turtle at Birch's with Lazarus feeding on garbage in a cellar. But the poor man loses nothing, because another man is rich. The Communist might as well denounce one man for enjoying excellent health, while another man is a victim to consumption. Wealth, like health, is in the air; if a man makes a fortune he draws money from Nature and gives it to the general stock. Every millionaire enriches the community. It is undoubtedly the duty of the government to mitigate so far as lies within its power, the miseries which result from overpopulation. But as long as men continue unequal in patience, industry, talent, and sobriety, so long there will be rich men and poor men--men who roll in their carriages, and men who die in the streets. If all the property of this country were divided, things would soon return to their actual condition, unless some scheme could also be devised for changing human nature; and as for the system of the Commune, which makes it impossible for a man to rise or to fall, it is merely the old caste system revived; if it could be put into force, all industry would be disheartened, emulation would cease, mankind would go to sleep.

It is not, however, strange that superficial writers should suppose that the evils of social life can be altered by changes in government and law. In the lands of the East, in the Spain and Portugal of the sixteenth century, in the France of the eighteenth century, in the American Colonies, and in England itself, whole classes were at one time plunged by misgovernment into suffering of body and apathy of mind. But a government can confer few benefits upon a people except by destroying its own laws. The great reforms which followed the publication of "The Wealth of Nations" may all be summed up in the word Repeal. Commerce was regulated in former times by a number of paternal laws, which have since been happily withdrawn. The government still pays with our money a number of gentlemen to give us information respecting a future state, and still requires that in certain business transactions a document shall be drawn up with mysterious rites in a mediaeval jargon; but, placing aside hereditary evils which, on account of vested interests, it is impossible at once to remove, it may fairly be asserted that the government of this country is as nearly perfect as any government can be. Power rests upon public opinion, and is so beautifully poised that it can be overthrown and replaced without the business of the state being interrupted for a day. If the Executive is condemned by the nation, the press acts with irresistible force upon the Commons; a vote of censure is passed and the rulers of a great empire abdicate their thrones. The House of Lords is also an admirable Upper Chamber; for if it were filled with ambitious men elected by the people it would enter into conflict with the Commons. And as for the Royal Image it costs little and is useful as an emblem. The government of England possesses at the same time the freedom which is only found in a republic, and the loyalty which is only felt towards a monarch.

Some writers believe that this monarchy is injurious to the public and argue as follows: There are no paupers in America, and America is a republic. There are many paupers in England, and England is a monarchy. Therefore England should imitate America. It may astonish these writers to learn that America is in reality more of a monarchy than England. Buckingham Palace is a private dwelling; but the White House, though it has none of the pomp, has all the power of a Court. The king of America has more to give away than any king of Great Britain since the time of Charles the Second. He has the power to discharge of his own good pleasure and mere motion every ambassador, every consul, every head of department, every government employee, down to the clerk on two hundred dollars a year, and to fill their places with his own friends. In America the opinion of the public can with difficulty act upon the government. The press has no dignity, and very little power. Practices occur in the House of Representatives which have been unknown in England since the days of Walpole. If the prosperity of a country depended on its government, America would be less prosperous than England. But in point of fact America is the happiest country in the world. There is not a man in the vast land which lies between the oceans who, however humble his occupation may be, does not hope to make a fortune before he dies. The whole nation is possessed with the spirit which may be observed in Fleet Street and Cheapside; the boys sharp-eyed and curious, the men hastening eagerly along, even the women walking as if they had an object in view. There are in America no dull-eyed heavy-footed labourers, who slouch to and fro from their cottage to their work, from their work to the beer-house, without a higher hope in life than a sixpence from the squire when they open a gate. There are no girls of the milliner class who prefer being the mistresses of gentlemen to marrying men of their own station with a Cockney accent and red hands. The upper classes in America have not that exquisite refinement which exists in the highest circles of society in Europe. But if we take the whole people through and through, we find them the most civilised nation on the earth. They, preserve in a degree hitherto without example the dignity of human nature unimpaired. Their nobleness of character results from prosperity; and their prosperity is due to the nature of their land. Those who are unable to earn a living in the east, have only to move towards the west.

This then is the reason that the English race in America is more happy, more enlightened, and more thriving, than it is in the motherland. Politically speaking, the emigrant gains nothing; he is as free in England as he is in America; but he leaves a land where labour is depreciated, and goes to a land where labour is in demand. That England may become as prosperous as America, it must be placed under American conditions; that is to say, food must be cheap, labour must be dear, emigration must be easy. It is not by universal suffrage, it is not by any Act of Parliament that these conditions can be created. It is Science alone which can Americanise England; it is Science alone which can ameliorate the condition of the human race.

When Man first wandered in the dark forest, he was Nature's serf; he offered tribute and prayer to the winds, and the lightning, and the rain, to the cave-lion, which seized his burrow for its lair, to the mammoth, which devoured his scanty crops. But as time passed on, he ventured, to rebel; he made stone his servant; he discovered fire and vegetable poison; he domesticated iron; he slew the wild beasts or subdued them; he made them feed him and give him clothes. He became a chief surrounded by his slaves; the fire lay beside him with dull red eye and yellow tongue waiting his instructions to prepare his dinner, or to make him poison, or to go with him to the war, and fly on the houses of the enemy, hissing, roaring, and consuming all. The trees of the forest were his flock, he slaughtered them at his convenience; the earth brought forth at his command. He struck iron upon wood or stone and hewed out the fancies of his brain; he plucked shells, and flowers, and the bright red berries, and twined them in his hair; he cut the pebble to a sparkling gem, he made the dull clay a transparent stone. The river which once he had worshipped as a god, or which he had vainly attacked with sword and spear, he now conquered to his will. He made the winds grind his corn and carry him across the waters; he made the stars serve him as a guide. He obtained from salt and wood and sulphur a destroying force. He drew from fire, and water, the awful power which produces the volcano, and made it do the work of human hands. He made the sun paint his portraits, and gave the lightning a situation in the post-office.

Thus Man has taken into his service, and modified to his use, the animals, the plants, the earths and the stones, the waters and the winds, and the more complex forces of heat, electricity, sunlight, magnetism, with chemical powers of many kinds. By means of his inventions and discoveries, by means of the arts and trades, and by means of the industry resulting from them, he has raised himself from the condition of a serf to the condition of a lord. His triumph, indeed, is incomplete; his kingdom is not yet come. The Prince of Darkness is still triumphant in many regions of the world; epidemics still rage, death is yet victorious. But the God of Light, the Spirit of Knowledge, the Divine Intellect, is gradually spreading over the planet and upwards to the skies. The beautiful legend will yet come true; Ormuzd will vanquish Ahriman; Satan will be overcome; Virtue will descend from heaven, surrounded by her angels, and reign over the hearts of men. Earth, which is now a purgatory, will be made a paradise, not by idle prayers and supplications, but by the efforts of man himself, and by means of mental achievements analogous to those which have raised him to his present state. Those inventions and discoveries which have made him, by the grace of God, king of the animals, lord of the elements, and sovereign of steam and electricity, were all of them founded on experiment and observation. We can conquer Nature only by obeying her laws, and in order to obey her laws we must first learn what they are. When we have ascertained, by means of Science, the method of Nature's operations, we shall be able to take her place and to perform them for ourselves. When we understand the laws which regulate the complex phenomena of life, we shall be able to predict the future as we are already able to predict comets and eclipses and the planetary movements.

Three inventions which perhaps may be long delayed, but which possibly are near at hand, will give to this overcrowded island the prosperous conditions of the United States. The first is the discovery of a motive force which will take the place of steam, with its cumbrous fuel of oil or coal; secondly, the invention of aerial locomotion which will transport labour at a trifling cost of money and of time to any part of the planet, and which, by annihilating distance, will speedily extinguish national distinctions; and thirdly, the manufacture of flesh and flour from the elements by a chemical process in the laboratory, similar to that which is now performed within the bodies of the animals and plants. Food will then be manufactured in unlimited quantities at a trifling expense; and our enlightened posterity will look back upon us who eat oxen and sheep just as we look back upon cannibals. Hunger and starvation will then be unknown, and the best part of the human life will no longer be wasted in the tedious process of cultivating the fields. Population will mightily increase, and the earth will be a garden. Governments will be conducted with the quietude and regularity of club committees. The interest which is now felt in politics will be transferred to science; the latest news from the laboratory of the chemist, or the observatory of the astronomer, or the experimenting room of the biologist will be eagerly discussed. Poetry and the fine arts will take that place in the heart which religion now holds. Luxuries will be cheapened and made common to all; none will be rich, and none poor. Not only will Man subdue the forces of evil that are without; he will also subdue those that are within. He will repress the base instincts and propensities which he has inherited from the animals below; he will obey the laws that are written on his heart; he will worship the divinity within him. As our conscience forbids us to commit actions which the conscience of the savage allows, so the moral sense of our successors will stigmatise as crimes those offences against the intellect which are sanctioned by ourselves. Idleness and stupidity will be regarded with abhorrence. Women will become the companions of men, and the tutors of their children. The whole world will be united by the same sentiment which united the primeval clan, and which made its members think, feel, and act as one. Men will look upon this star as their fatherland; its progress will be their ambition; the gratitude of others their reward. These bodies which now we: wear belong to the lower animals; our minds have already outgrown them; already we look upon them with contempt. A time will come when Science will transform them by means which we cannot conjecture, and which, even if explained to us, we could not now under stand, just as the savage cannot understand electricity, magnetism, steam. Disease will be extirpated; the causes of decay will be removed; immortality will be invented. And then, the earth being small, mankind will migrate into space, and will cross the airless Saharas which separate planet from planet, and sun from sun. The earth will become a Holy Land which will be visited by pilgrims from all the quarters of the universe. Finally, men will master the forces of Nature; they will become themselves architects of systems, manufacturers of worlds.

Man then will be perfect; he will then be a creator; he will therefore be what the vulgar worship as a god. But even then, he will in reality be no nearer than he is at present to the First Cause, the Inscrutable Mystery, the GOD. There is but a difference in degree between the chemist who to-day arranges forces in his laboratory so that they produce a gas, and the creator who arranges forces so that they produce a world; between the gardener who plants a seed, and the creator who plants a nebula. It is a question for us now to consider whether we have any personal relations towards the Supreme Power; whether there exists another world in which we shall be requited according to our actions. Not only is this a grand problem of philosophy; it is of all questions the most practical for us, the one in which our interests are most vitally concerned. This life is short; and its pleasures are poor; when we have obtained what we desire, it is nearly time to die. If it can be shown that, by living in a certain manner, eternal happiness may be obtained, then clearly no one except a fool or a madman would refuse to live in such a manner. We shall therefore examine the current theory respecting the nature of the Creator, the design of Creation; and the future destiny of Man. But before we proceed to this inquiry, we must first state that we intend to separate theology from morality. Whatever may be the nature of the Deity, and whether there is a future life or not, the great moral laws can be in no way changed. God is a purely scientific question. Whether he is personal or impersonal, definable or undefinable, our duties and responsibilities remain the same. The existence of a heaven and a hell can affect our calculations, but, cannot affect our moral liabilities.

The Religion of Reason and Love

The popular theory is this:--the world was made by a Great Being; he created man in his own image; and therefore his mind is analogous to that of man. But while our minds are imperfect, troubled by passions, stained with sin, and limited in power, his mind is perfect in beauty, perfect in power, perfect in love. He is omnipotent and omnipresent. He loves men whom he has made, but he sorrows over their transgressions. He has placed them on earth as a means of probation; those who have sinned and repent, those who are contrite and humble, he will forgive, and on them he will bestow everlasting happiness. Those who are wicked, and stubborn, and hard of heart, those who deny and resist his authority, he will punish according to his justice. This reward is bestowed, this punishment is inflicted on the soul, a spirit which dwells within the body during life. It is something entirely distinct from the intellect or mind. The soul of the poorest creature in the streets and the souls of the greatest philosopher or poet are equal before the Creator; he is no respecter of person; souls are measured only by their sins. But the sins of the ignorant will be forgiven; the sins of the more enlightened will be more severely judged.

Now this appears a very reasonable theory as long as we do not examine it closely, and as long as we do not carry out its propositions to their full extent. But when we do so, we find that it conducts us to absurdity, as we shall very quickly prove.

The souls of idiots not being responsible for their sins will go to heaven; the souls of such men as Goethe and Rousseau are in danger of hell-fire. Therefore it is better to be born an idiot than to be born a Goethe or a Rousseau; and that is altogether absurd.

It is asserted that the doctrine of the immortality of the soul, and of happiness in a future state, gives us a solution of that distressing problem, the misery of the innocent on earth. But in reality it does nothing of the kind, It does not explain the origin of evil, and it does not justify the existence of evil. A poor helpless infant is thrust into the world by a higher force; it has done no one any harm, yet it is tortured in the most dreadful manner; it is nourished in vice, and crime, and disease; it is allowed to suffer a certain time and then it is murdered. It is all very well to say that afterwards it was taken to everlasting bliss; but why was it not taken there direct? If a man has a child and beats that child for no reason whatever, is it any palliation of the crime to say that he afterwards gave it cake and wine?

This brings us to the character of the Creator. We must beg to observe again that we describe, not the actual Creator, but the popular idea of the Creator. It is said that the Supreme Power has a mind; this we deny, and to show that our reasons for denying it are good, we shall proceed to criticise this imaginary mind.

In the first place, we shall state as an incontrovertible maxim in morality that a god has no right to create men except for their own good. This may appear to the reader an extraordinary statement; but had he lived in France at the time of Louis XIV, he would also have thought it an extraordinary statement that kings existed for the good of the people and not people for the good of kings. When the Duke of Burgundy first propounded that axiom, St. Simon, by no means a servile courtier, and an enlightened man for his age, was "delighted with the benevolence of the saying, but startled by its novelty and terrified by its boldness." Our proposition may appear very strange, but it certainly cannot be refuted; for if it is said that the Creator is so great that he is placed above our laws of morality, then what is that but placing Might above Right? And if the maxim be admitted as correct, then how can the phenomena of life be justified?

It is said that the Creator is omnipotent, and also that he is benevolent. But one proposition contradicts the other. It is said that he is perfect in power, and that he is also perfect in purity. We shall show that he cannot possibly be both.

The conduct of a father towards his child appears to be cruel, but it is not cruel in reality. He beats the child, but he does it for the child's own good; he is not omnipotent; he is therefore obliged to choose between two evils. But the Creator is omnipotent; he therefore chooses cruelty as a means of education or development; he therefore has a preference for cruelty or he would not choose it; he is therefore fond of cruelty or he would not prefer it; he is therefore cruel, which is absurd.

Again, either sin entered the world against the will of the Creator, in which case he is not omnipotent, or it entered with his permission, in which case it is his agent, in which case he selects sin, in which case he has a preference for sin, in which case he is fond of sin, in which case he is sinful, which is an absurdity again.

The good in this world predominates over the bad; the good is ever increasing, the bad is ever diminishing. But if God is Love why is there any bad at all? Is the world like a novel in which the villains are put in to make it more dramatic, and in which virtue only triumphs in the third volume? It is certain that the feelings of the created have in no way been considered. If indeed there were a judgment-day it would be for man to appear at the bar not as criminal but as an accuser. What has he done that he should be subjected to a life of torture and temptation? God might have made us all happy, and he has made us all miserable. Is that benevolence? God might have made us all pure, and he has made us all sinful. Is that the perfection of morality? If I believed in the existence of this man-created God, of this divine Nebuchadnezzar, I would say, "You can make me live in your world, O Creator, but you cannot make me admire it; you can load me with chains, but you cannot make me flatter you; you can send me to hell-fire, but you can not obtain my esteem. And if you condemn me, you condemn yourself. If I have committed sins, you invented them, which is worse. If the watch you have made does not go well, whose fault is that? Is it rational to damn the wheels and the springs?"

But it is when we open the Book of Nature, that book inscribed in blood and tears; it is when we study the laws regulating life, the laws productive of development, that we see plainly how illusive is this theory that God is Love. In all things there is cruel, profligate, and abandoned waste. Of all the animals that are born a few only can survive; and it is owing to this law that development takes place. The law of Murder is the law of Growth. Life is one long tragedy; creation is one great crime. And not only is there waste in animal and human life, there is also waste in moral life. The instinct of love is planted in the human breast, and that which to some is a solace is to others a torture. How many hearts yearning for affection are blighted in solitude and coldness! How many women seated by their lonely firesides are musing of the days that might have been! How many eyes when they meet these words which remind them of their sorrows will be filled with tears! O cold, cruel, miserable life, how long are your pains, how brief are your delights! What are joys but pretty children that grow into regrets? What is happiness but a passing dream in which we seem to be asleep, and which we know only to have been when it is past? Pain, grief, disease, and death--are these the inventions of a loving God? That no animal shall rise to excellence except by being fatal to the life of others--is this the law of a kind Creator? It is useless to say that pain has its benevolence, that massacre has its mercy. Why is it so ordained that bad should be the raw material of good? Pain is not less pain because it is useful; murder is not less murder because it is conducive to development. Here is blood upon the hand still, and all the perfumes of Arabia will not sweeten it.

To this then we are brought with the much-belauded theory of a semi-human Providence, an anthropoid Deity, a Constructive Mind, a Deus Paleyensis, a God created in the image of a watchmaker. What then are we to infer? Why, simply this, that the current theory is false; that all attempts to define the Creator bring us only to ridiculous conclusions; that the Supreme Power is not a Mind, but something higher than a Mind; not a Force, but something higher than a Force; not a Being, but something higher than a Being; something for which we have no words, something for which we have no ideas. We are to infer that Man is not made in the image of his Maker, and that Man can no more understand his Maker than the beetles and the worms can understand him. As men in the days of ignorance endeavoured to discover perpetual motion and the philosopher's stone, so now they endeavour to define God. But in time also they will learn that the nature of the Deity is beyond the powers of the human intellect to solve. The universe is anonymous; it is published under secondary laws; these at least we are able to investigate, and in these perhaps we may find a partial solution of the great problem. The origin of evil cannot be explained, for we cannot explain the origin of matter. But a careful and unprejudiced study of Nature reveals an interesting fact and one that will be of value to mankind.

The earth resembles a picture, of which we, like insects which crawl upon its surface, can form but a faint and incoherent idea. We see here and there a glorious flash of colour; we have a dim conception that there is union in all its parts; yet to us, because we are so near, the tints appear to be blurred and confused. But let us expand our wings and flutter off into the air; let us fly some distance backwards into Space until we have reached the right point of view. And now the colours blend and harmonise together, and we see that the picture represents One Man.

The body of a human individual is composed of cell-like bodies which are called "physiological units." Each cell or atom has its own individuality; it grows, it is nurtured, it brings forth young, and it dies. It is in fact an animalcule. It has its own body and its own mind. As the atoms are to the human unit, so the human units are to the human whole. There is only One Man upon the earth; what we call men are not individuals but components; what we call, death is merely the bursting of a cell; wars and epidemics are merely inflammatory phenomena incident on certain stages of growth. There is no such thing as a ghost or soul; the intellects of men resemble those instincts which inhabit the corpuscules, and which are dispersed when the corpuscule dies. Yet they are not lost, they are preserved within the body and enter other forms. Men therefore have no connection with Nature, except through the organism to which they belong. Nature does not recognise their individual existence. But each atom is conscious of its life; each atom can improve itself in beauty and in strength; each atom can therefore, in an infinitesimal degree, assist the development of the Human Mind. If we take the life of a single atom, that is to say of a single man, or if we look only at a single group, all appears to be cruelty and confusion; but when we survey mankind as One, we find it becoming more and more noble, more and more divine, slowly ripening towards perfection. We belong to the minutiae of Nature, we are in her sight, as the rain-drop in the sky; whether a man lives, or whether he dies, is as much a matter of indifference to Nature as whether a rain-drop falls upon the field and feeds a blade of grass, or falls upon a stone and is dried to death. She does not supervise these small details. This discovery is by no means flattering, but it enlarges our idea of the scheme of creation. That universe must indeed be great in which human beings are so small!

The following facts result from our investigations: Supernatural Christianity is false. God-worship is idolatry. Prayer is useless. The soul is not immortal. There are no rewards and there are no punishments in a future state.

It now remains to be considered whether it is right to say so. It will doubtless be supposed that I shall make use of the plea that a writer is always justified in publishing the truth, or what he conscientiously believes to be the truth, and that if it does harm he is not to blame. But I shall at once acknowledge that truth is only a means towards an end--the welfare of the human race. If it can be shown that by speaking the truth an injury is inflicted on mankind, then a stubborn adherence to truth becomes merely a Pharisee virtue, a spiritual pride. But in moral life Truth, though not infallible, is our safest guide, and those who maintain that it should be repressed must be prepared to bring forward irrefutable arguments in favour of their cause. If so much as the shadow of a doubt remains, their client, Falsehood, is non-suited, and Truth remains in possession of the conscience. Let us now hear what the special pleaders have to say. The advocates for Christianity versus Truth will speak first, and I shall reply; and then the advocates for Deism will state their case. What they will endeavour to prove is this, that even admitting the truth of my propositions, it is an immoral action to give them to the world. On the other hand, I undertake to show that the destruction of Christianity is essential to the interests of civilisation; and also that man will never attain his full powers as a moral being until he has ceased to believe in a personal God and in the immortality of the soul.

"Christianity, we allow, is human in its origin, erroneous in its theories, delusive in its threats and its rewards," say the advocates for Christianity. "Jesus Christ was a man with all the faults and imperfections of the prophetic character. The Bible is simply a collection of Jewish writings. The miracles in the Old Testament deserve no more attention from historians than the miracles in Homer. The miracles in the gospels are like the miracles in Plutarch's Lives; they do not lessen the value of the biography, and the value of the biography does not lessen the absurdity of the miracles. So far we go with you. But we assert that this religion with all its errors has rendered inestimable services to civilisation, and that it is so inseparably associated in the minds of men with purity of life, and the precepts of morality, that it is impossible to attack Christianity without also attacking all that is good, all that is pure, all that is lovely in human nature. When you travelled in Africa did you not join in the sacrifices of the pagans? Did you not always speak with respect of their wood spirits and their water spirits, and their gods of the water and the sky? And did you not take off your shoes when you entered the mosque, and did you not, when they gave you the religious blessing, return the religious reply? And since you could be so tolerant to savages, surely you are bound to be more tolerant still to those who belong to your own race, to those who possess a nobler religion, and whose minds can be made by a careless word to suffer the most exquisite pain. Yet you attack Christianity, and you attack it in the wrong way. You ought, in the interests of your own cause, to write in such a manner that minds might be gradually trained to reflection and decoyed to doubt. It is not only heartless and inhuman, it is also unwise, it is also unscientific, to say things which will shock and disgust those who are beginning to inquire, and it is bad taste to jest on subjects which if not sacred in themselves are held sacred in the, eyes of many thoughtful and cultivated men. You ought to adopt a tone of reluctance and to demonstrate, as it were against your will, the errors of the popular religion. Believers at least have a right to demand that if you discuss these questions upon which their hopes of eternal happiness are based, you will do so with gravity and decorum."

To this I reply that the religion of the Africans, whether pagan or Moslem, is suited to their intellects, and is therefore a true religion; and the same may be said of Christianity among uneducated people. But Christianity is not in accordance with the cultivated mind; it can only be accepted or rather retained by suppressing doubts, and by denouncing inquiry as sinful. It is therefore a superstition, and ought to be destroyed. With respect to the services which it once rendered to civilisation, I cheerfully acknowledge them, but the same argument might once have been advanced in favour of the oracle at Delphi, without which there would have been no Greek culture, and therefore no Christianity. The question is not whether Christianity assisted the civilisation of our ancestors, but whether it is now assisting our own. I am firmly persuaded that whatever is injurious to the intellect is also injurious to moral life; and on this conviction I base my conduct with respect to Christianity. That religion is pernicious to the intellect; it demands that the reason shall be sacrificed upon the altar; it orders civilised men to believe in the legends of a savage race. It places a hideous image, covered with dirt and blood, in the Holy of Holies; it rends the sacred Veil of Truth in twain, It teaches that the Creator of the Universe, that sublime, that inscrutable power, exhibited his back to Moses, and ordered Hosea to commit adultery, and Ezekiel to eat dung. There is no need to say anything more. Such a religion is blasphemous and foul. Let those admire it who are able. I, for my part, feel it my duty to set free from its chains as many as I can. Upon this point my conscience speaks clearly, and it shall be obeyed. With respect to manner and means, I shall use the arguments and the style best suited for my purpose. There has been enough of writing by implication and by innuendo; I do not believe in its utility, and I do not approve of its disguise. There should be no deceit in matters of religion. In my future assaults on Christianity I shall use the clearest language that I am able to command.

Ridicule is a destructive instrument, and it is my intention to destroy. If a man is cutting down a tree, it is useless asking him not to strike so hard. But because I make use of ridicule, it does not follow that I am writing merely for amusement; and because I tear up a belief by the roots, it does not follow that I am indifferent to the pain which I inflict. Great revolutions cannot be accomplished without much anguish and some evil being caused. Did not the Roman women suffer when the Christians came and robbed them of their gods, and raised their minds, through pain and sorrow, to a higher faith? The religion which I teach is as high above Christianity as that religion was superior to the idolatry of Rome. And when, the relative civilisations of the two ages are compared, this fetish of ink and paper, this Syrian book is, in truth, not less an idol than those statues which obtained the adoration of the Italians and the Greeks. The statues were beautiful as statues; the book is admirable as a book; but the statues did not come down from heaven; the book was not a magical composition; it bears the marks not only of human genius, but also of human depravity and superstition.

As for the advocates of Deism they acknowledge that Christianity is unsuited to the mental condition of the age; they acknowledge that the Bible ought to be attacked as Xenophanes attacked Homer; they acknowledge that the fables of a god impregnating a woman, of a god living on the earth, are relics of pagan superstition; they acknowledge that the doctrine of eternal punishment is incompatible with justice, and is therefore incompatible with God. But they declare that Christianity should not be destroyed but reformed; that its barbarous elements should be expelled, and that then, as a pure God-worship, it should be offered to the world. "It is true", they say, "that God is an idol, an image made of human ideas which, to superior beings, would appear as coarse and vile for such a purpose as the wood and the stone of the savage appear to us. But this idolatry is conducive to the morality of man. That exquisite form which he raises in his mind, and before which he prostrates him self in prayer, that God of purity and love, becomes his ideal and example. As the Greek women placed statues of Apollo and Narcissus in their chambers that the beauty of the marble form might enter their wombs through the windows of their eyes, so by ever contemplating perfection the mind is ennobled, and the actions born of it are divine. And surely it is a sweet and consoling faith that there is above us a great and benignant Being who, when the sorrows of this life are past, will take us to himself. How can it injure men to believe that the righteous will he rewarded and that the wicked will be punished in a future state? What good can be done by destroying a belief so full of solace for the sorrowful, so full of promise for the virtuous, so full of terror for the workers of iniquity? You do not deny that 'much anguish and some evil will be caused' by the destruction of this belief; and what have you to show on the other side? What will you place in the balance? Consider what a dreadful thing it is to take even from a single human being the hopes of a future life.

"All men cannot be philosophers; all cannot resign themselves with fortitude and calm to the death-warrant of the soul. Annihilation has perhaps more terrors for the mind than eternal punishment itself. O, make not the heart an orphan, cast it not naked and weeping on the world! Take it not away from its father, kill not its hopes of an eternal home! There are mothers whose children have gone before them to the grave, poor miserable women whose beauty is faded, who have none to care for them on earth, whose only happiness is in the hope that when their life is ended they will be joined again to those whom they have lost. And will you take that hope away? There are men who have passed their whole lives in discipline and self-restraint that they may be rewarded in a future state; will you tell them that they have lived under an illusion, that they would have done better to laugh, and to feast, and to say 'Let us make merry, for to-morrow we shall die'? There are men whom the fear of punishment in a future life deters from vice and perhaps from crime. Will you dare to spread a doctrine which unlooses all restraints, and leaves men to the fury of their passions? It is true that we are not demoralised by this belief in the impersonality of God and the extinction of the soul; but it would be a dangerous belief for those who are exposed to strong temptations, and whose minds have not been raised by culture to the religion of dignity and self-control."

In the first place, I admit that the worship and contemplation of a man-like but ideal Being must have, through the law of imitation, an ennobling effect on the mind of the idolater, but only so long as the belief in such a Being harmonises with the intellect. It has been shown that this theory of a benignant God is contradicted by the laws of Nature. We must judge of the tree by its fruits; we must judge of the maker by that which he has made. The Author of the world invented not only the good but also the evil in the world; he invented cruelty; he invented sin. If he invented sin how can he be otherwise than sinful? And if he invented cruelty how can he be otherwise than cruel? From this inexorable logic we can only escape by giving up the hypothesis of a personal Creator. Those who believe in a God of Love must close their eyes to the phenomena of life, or garble the universe to suit their theory. This, it is needless to say, is injurious to the intellect; whatever is injurious to the intellect is injurious to morality; and, therefore, the belief in a God of Love is injurious to morality. God-worship must be classed with those provisional expedients, Famine, War, Slavery, the Inequality of Conditions, the Desire of Gain, which Nature employs for the development of man, and which she throws aside when they have served her turn, as a carpenter changes his tools at the various stages of his work.

The abolition of this ancient and elevated faith; the dethronement of God; the extinction of piety as a personal feeling; the destruction of an Image made of golden thoughts in the exquisite form of an Ideal Man, and tenderly enshrined in the human heart--these appear to be evils, and such undoubtedly they are. But the conduct of life is a choice of evils. We can do nothing that is exclusively and absolutely good. Le genre humain n'est pas place entre le bien et le mal, mais entre le mal et le pire. No useful inventions can be introduced without some branch of industry being killed and hundreds of worthy men being cast, without an occupation, on the world. All mental revolutions are attended by catastrophe. The mummeries and massacres of the German Reformation, though known only to scholars, were scarcely less horrible than those of Paris in 1793, and both periods illustrate the same law. I have facts in my possession which would enable me to show that the abolition of the slave-trade, that immortal and glorious event, caused the death of many thousand slaves, who were therefore actually killed by Sharp, Clarkson, Wilberforce, and their adherents. But by means of abolition millions of lives have since been saved. The first generation suffered; prisoners were captured to be sold, and the market having been suppressed, were killed. This was undoubtedly an evil. But then the slave-making wars came to an end, and there was peace. In the same manner I maintain that even should the present generation be injured by the abolition of existing faiths, yet abolition would be justified. Succeeding generations would breathe an atmosphere of truth instead of being reared in an atmosphere of falsehood, and we who are so deeply indebted to our ancestors have incurred obligations towards our posterity. Let us therefore purify the air, and if the light kills a few sickly plants which have become acclimatised to impurity and darkness, we must console ourselves with the reflection that in Nature it is always so, and that of two evils we have chosen that which is the least.

But the dangers of the Truth are not so great as is commonly supposed. It is often said that if the fears of hell-fire were suddenly removed men would abandon themselves without restraint to their propensities and appetites; that recklessness and despair would take possession of the human race, and society would be dissolved. But I believe that the fears of hell-fire have scarcely any power upon earth at all, and that when they do act upon the human mind it is to make it pious, not to make it good. A metaphysical theory cannot restrain the fury of the passions: as well attempt to bind a lion with a cobweb. Prevention of crime it is well known depends not on the severity but on the certainty of retribution. Just as a criminal is often acquitted by the jury because the penalties of the law are disproportioned to the magnitude of the offence, so the diabolic laws which inflict an eternal punishment for transitory sins have been tempered by a system of free pardons which deprive them of any efficiency they might have once possessed. What would be the use of laws against murder if the condemned criminal could obtain his liberty by apologising to the Queen? Yet such is the Christian system, which, though in one sense beautiful on account of its mercy, is also immoral on account of its indulgence. The supposition that the terrors of hell-fire are essential or even conducive to good morals is contradicted by the facts of history. In the Dark Ages there was not a man or a woman, from Scotland to Naples, who doubted that sinners were sent to hell. The religion which they had was the same as ours, with this exception, that everyone believed in it. The state of Europe in that pious epoch need not be described.

Society is not maintained by the conjectures of theology, but by those moral sentiments, those gregarious virtues, which elevated men above the animals, which are now instinctive in our natures, and to which intellectual culture is propitious. For, as we become more and more enlightened, we perceive more and more clearly that it is with the whole human population as it was with the primeval clan; the welfare of every individual is dependent on the welfare of the community, and the welfare of the community depends on the welfare of every individual. Our conscience teaches us it is right, our reason teaches us it is useful, that men should live according to the Golden Rule. This conduct of life is therefore enjoined upon every man by his own instincts, and also by the voice of popular opinion. Those cannot be happy who are detested and despised by their fellow-men; and as for those, the outlaws of society, who, like domestic animals run wild, herd together in secret places, and, faithful only to their own gang, make war upon mankind, the Law, which is seldom evaded, the Law, which never forgives, chases them from den to den, and makes their lives as full of misery as they are full of crime.

The current religion is indirectly adverse to morals, because it is adverse to the freedom of the intellect. But it is also directly adverse to morals by inventing spurious and bastard virtues. One fact must be familiar to all those who have any experience of human nature--a sincerely religious man is often an exceedingly bad man. Piety and vice frequently live together in the same dwelling, occupying different chambers, but remaining always on the most amicable terms. Nor is there anything remarkable in this. Religion is merely loyalty: it is just as irrational to expect a man to be virtuous because he goes to church, as it would be to expect him to be virtuous because he went to court. His king, it is true, forbids immorality and fraud. But the chief virtues required are of the lickspittle denomination-- what is called "a humble and a contrite heart." When a Christian sins as a man, he makes compensation as a courtier. When he has injured a fellow-creature, he goes to church with more regularity, he offers up more prayers, he reads a great number of chapters in the Bible, and so he believes that he has cleared off the sins that are laid to his account. This, then, is the immorality of religion as it now exists. It creates artificial virtues and sets them off against actual vices. Children are taught to do this and that, not because it is good, but to please the king. When Christians are informed that not only our physical but our moral actions are governed by unchangeable law, and that the evil treatment of the mind, like the evil treatment of the body, is punished by a loss of happiness and health, they cry out against a doctrine which is so just and so severe. They are like the young Roman nobles who complained when the Tarquins were expelled, saying, that a king was a human being, that he could be angry and forgive, that there was room for favour and kindness, but that the law was a deaf and inexorable thing--leges rem surdam inexorabilem esse; that it allowed of no relaxation and indulgence--nihil laxa-menti nec veniae habere, and that it was a dangerous thing for weak and erring men to live by their integrity alone --periculosum esse in tot humanis erroribus sola innocentia vivere. Christians believe themselves to be the aristocracy of heaven upon earth; they are admitted to the spiritual court, while millions of men in foreign lands have never been presented. They bow their knees and say that they are miserable sinners, and their hearts rankle with abominable pride. Poor infatuated fools! Their servility is real, and their insolence is real, but their king is a phantom and their palace is a dream.

Even with Christians of comparatively blameless lives their religion is injurious. It causes a waste of moral force. There are passionate desires of virtue, yearnings for the good, which descend from time to time like a holy spirit upon all cultivated minds, and from which, strange as it may seem, not even free-thinkers are excluded. When such an impulse animates the godless man he expends it in the service of mankind; the Christian wastes it on the air; he fasts, he watches, and he prays. And what is the object of all his petitions and salaams? He will tell you that he is trying to save his soul. But the strangest feature in the case is this. He not only thinks that it is prudent and wise on his part to improve his prospects of happiness in a future state; he considers it the noblest of all virtues. But there is no great merit in taking care of one's own interests whether it be in this world or the next. The man who leads a truly religious life in order to go to heaven is not more to be admired than the man who leads a regular and industrious life in order to make a fortune in the city; and the man who endeavours to secure a celestial inheritance by going to church, and by reading chapters in the Bible, and by having family prayers, and by saying grace in falsetto with eyes hypocritically closed, is not above the level of those who fawn and flatter at Oriental courts in order to obtain a monopoly or an appointment.

The old proverb holds good in religious as in ordinary life, that self-preservation is the first law of Nature. As long as men believe that there is a god or king who will listen to their prayers and who will change his mind at their request; as long as they believe that they can obtain a mansion in the heavenly Belgravia, so long they will place the duties of the courtier above the duties of the man, so long they will believe that flattery is pleasing to the Most

High, so long they will believe that they can offend against the law and escape the penalties of the law, so long they will believe that acts of devotion may be balanced against acts of immorality, so long they will make selfishness a virtue, and salvation of the soul a higher principle of conduct than social love. But when the faith in a personal god is extinguished; when prayer and praise are no longer to be heard; when the belief is universal that with the body dies the soul, then the false morals of theology will no longer lead the human mind astray. Piety and virtue will become identical. The desire to do good which arose in necessity, which was developed by the hopes of a heavenly reward, is now an instinct of the human race. Those hopes and illusions served as the scaffolding, and may now safely be removed.

There will always be enthusiasts for virtue as there are now, men who adorn and purify their souls before the mirror of their conscience, and who strive to attain an ideal excellence in their actions and their thoughts. If from such men as these the hope of immortality is taken, will their natures be transformed? Will they who are almost angels turn straightway into beasts? Will the sober become drunkards? Will the chaste become sensual? Will the honest become fraudulent? Will the industrious become idle? Will the righteous love that which they have learnt to loathe? Will they who have won by hard struggles the sober happiness of virtue return to the miseries of vice by which few men have not at one time or another been enthralled? No; they will pass through some hours of affliction; they will bear another illusion to the grave; not the first that they have buried, not the first they have bewailed. And then, no longer able to hope for themselves, they will hope for the future of the human race: unable to believe in an eared God who listens to human supplications they will coin the gold of their hearts into useful actions instead of burning it as incense before an imaginary throne.

We do not wish to extirpate religion from the life of man; we wish him to have a religion which will harmonise with his intellect, and which inquiry will strengthen, not destroy. We wish, in fact, to give him a religion, for now there are many who have none. We teach that there is a God, but not a God of the anthropoid variety, not a God who is gratified by compliments in prose and verse, and whose attributes can be catalogued by theologians. God is so great that he cannot be defined by us. God is so great that he does not deign to have personal relations with us human atoms that are called men. Those who desire to worship their Creator must worship him through mankind. Such it is plain is the scheme of Nature. We are placed under secondary laws, and these we must obey. To develop to the utmost our genius and our love, that is the only true religion. To do that which deserves to be written, to write that which deserves to be read, to tend the sick, to comfort the sorrowful, to animate the weary, to keep the temple of the body pure, to cherish the divinity within us, to be faithful to the intellect, to educate those powers which have been entrusted to our charge and to employ them in the service of humanity, that is all that we can do. Then our elements shall be dispersed and all is at an end. All is at an end for the unit, all is at an end for the atom, all is at an end for the speck of flesh and blood with the little spark of instinct which it calls its mind, but all is not at an end for the actual Man, the true Being, the glorious One. We teach that the soul is immortal; we teach that there is a future life; we teach that there is a Heaven in the ages far away; but not for us single corpuscles, not for us dots of animated jelly, but for the One of whom we are the elements, and who, though we perish, never dies, but grows from period to period and by the united efforts of single molecules called men, or of those cell-groups called nations, is raised towards the Divine power which he will finally attain. Our religion therefore is Virtue, our Hope is placed in the happiness of our posterity; our Faith is the Perfectibility of Man.

A day will come when the European God of the nineteenth century will be classed with the gods of Olympus and the Nile; when surplices and sacramental plate will be exhibited in museums; when nurses will relate to children the legends of the Christian mythology as they now tell them fairy tales. A day will come when the current belief in property after death (for is not existence property, and the dearest property of all?) will be accounted a strange and selfish idea, just as we smile at the savage chief who believes that his gentility will be continued in the world beneath the ground, and that he will there be attended by his concubines and slaves. A day will come when mankind will be as the Family of the Forest, which lived faithfully within itself according to the Golden Rule in order that it might not die. But Love not Fear will unite the human race. The world will become a heavenly Commune to which men will bring the inmost treasures of their hearts, in which they will reserve for themselves not even a hope, not even the shadow of a joy, but will give up all for all mankind. With one faith, with one desire, they will labour together in the Sacred Cause--the extinction of disease, the extinction of sin, the perfection of genius, the perfection of love, the invention of immortality, the exploration of the infinite, and the conquest of creation.

You blessed ones who shall inherit that future age of which we can only dream; you pure and radiant beings who shall succeed us on the earth; when you turn back your eyes on us poor savages, grubbing in the ground for our daily bread, eating flesh and blood, dwelling in vile bodies which degrade us every day to a level with the beasts, tortured by pains, and by animal propensities, buried in gloomy superstitions, ignorant of Nature which yet holds us in her bonds; when you read of us in books, when you think of what we are, and compare us with yourselves, remember that it is to us you owe the foundation of your happiness and grandeur, to us who now in our libraries and laboratories and star-towers and dissecting-rooms and work-shops are preparing the materials of the human growth. And as for ourselves, if we are sometimes inclined to regret that our lot is cast in these unhappy days, let us remember how much more fortunate we are than those who lived before us a few centuries ago. The working man enjoys more luxuries to-day than did the King of England in the Anglo-Saxon times; and at his command are intellectual delights, which but a little while ago the most learned in the land could not obtain. All this we owe to the labours of other men. Let us therefore remember them with gratitude; let us follow their glorious example by adding something new to the knowledge of mankind; let us pay to the future the debt which we owe to the past.

All men indeed cannot be poets, inventors, or philanthropists; but all men can join in that gigantic and god-like work, the progress of creation. Whoever improves his own nature improves the universe of which he is a part. He who strives to subdue his evil passions--vile remnants of the old four-footed life--and who cultivates the social affections: he who endeavours to better his condition, and to make his children wiser and happier than himself; whatever may be his motives, he will not have lived in vain. But if he act thus not from mere prudence, not in the vain hope of being rewarded in another world, but from a pure sense of duty, as a citizen of Nature, as a patriot of the planet on which he dwells, then our philosophy which once appeared to him so cold and cheerless will become a religion of the heart, and will elevate him to the skies; the virtues which were once for him mere abstract terms will become endowed with life, and will hover round him like guardian angels, conversing with him in his solitude, consoling him in his afflictions, teaching him how to live, and how to die. But this condition is not to be easily attained; as the saints and prophets were often forced to practise long vigils and fastings and prayers before their ecstasies would fall upon them and their visions would appear, so Virtue in its purest and most exalted form can only be acquired by means of severe and long-continued culture of the mind. Persons with feeble and untrained intellects may live according to their conscience; but the conscience itself will be defective. To cultivate the intellect is therefore a religious duty; and when this truth is fairly recognised by men, the religion which teaches that the intellect should be distrusted, and that it should be subservient to faith, will inevitably fall.

We have written much about inventions and discoveries and transformations of human nature which cannot possibly take place for ages yet to come, because we think it good that the bright though distant future should be ever present in the eyes of man. But we shall now consider the existing generation, and we shall point out the work which must be accomplished, and in which all enlightened men should take a part. Christianity must be destroyed. The civilised world has outgrown that religion, and is now in the condition of the Roman Empire in the pagan days. A cold-hearted infidelity above, a sordid superstition below, a school of Plutarchs who endeavour to reconcile the fables of a barbarous people with the facts of science and the lofty conceptions of philosophy; a multitude of augurs who sometimes smile when they meet, but who more often feel inclined to sigh, for they are mostly serious and worthy men. Entering the Church in their youth, before their minds were formed, they discover too late what it is that they adore, and since they cannot tell the truth, and let their wives and children starve, they are forced to lead a life which is a lie. What a state of society is this in which "free-thinker" is a term of abuse, and in which doubt is regarded as a sin! Men have a Bluebeard's chamber in their minds which they dare not open; they have a faith which they dare not examine lest they should be forced to cast it from them in contempt. Worship is a convention, churches are bonnet shows, places of assignation, shabby-genteel salons where the parochial "at home" is given, and respectable tradesmen exhibit their daughters in the wooden stalls. O wondrous, awful, and divine religion! You elevate our hearts from the cares of common life, you transport us into the unseen world, you bear us upwards to that sublime temple of the skies where dwells the Veiled God, whom mortal eye can never view, whom mortal mind can never comprehend. How art thou fallen! How art thou degraded! But it will be only for a time. We are now in the dreary desert which separates two ages of Belief. A new era is at hand.

It is incorrect to say "theology is not a progressive science." The worship of ancestral ghosts, the worship of pagan deities, the worship of a single god, are successive periods of progress in the science of Divinity. And in the history of that science, as in the history of all others, a curious fact may be observed. Those who overthrow an established system are compelled to attack its founders, and to show that their method was unsound, that their reasoning was fallacious, that their experiments were incomplete. And yet the men who create the revolution are made in the likeness of the men whose doctrines they subvert. The system of Ptolemy was supplanted by the system of Copernicus, yet Copernicus was the Ptolemy of the sixteenth century. In the same manner, we who assail the Christian faith are the true successors of the early Christians, above whom we are raised by the progress, of eighteen hundred years. As they preached against gods that were made of stone, so we preach against gods that are made of ideas. As they were called atheists and blasphemers so are we. And is our task more difficult than theirs? We have not, it is true, the same stimulants to offer. We cannot threaten that the world is about to be destroyed; we cannot bribe our converts with a heaven, we cannot make them tremble with a hell. But though our religion appears too pure, too unselfish for mankind, it is not really so, for we live in a noble and enlightened age. At the time of the Romans and the Greeks the Christian faith was the highest to which the common people could attain. A faith such as that of the Stoics and the Sadducees could only be embraced by cultivated minds, and culture was then confined to a chosen few. But now knowledge, freedom, and prosperity are covering the earth; for three centuries past, human virtue has been steadily increasing, and mankind is prepared to receive a higher faith. But in order to build we must first destroy. Not only the Syrian superstition must be attacked, but also the belief in a personal God, which engenders a slavish and oriental condition of the mind; and the belief in a posthumous reward which engenders a selfish and solitary condition of the heart. These beliefs are, therefore, injurious to human nature. They lower its dignity; they arrest its development; they isolate its affections.

We shall not deny that many beautiful sentiments are often mingled with the faith in a personal Deity, and with the hopes of happiness in a future state; yet we maintain that, however refined they may appear, they are selfish at the core, and that if removed they will be replaced by sentiments of a nobler and a purer kind. They cannot be removed without some disturbance and distress; yet the sorrows thus caused are salutary and sublime. The supreme and mysterious Power by whom the universe has been created, and by whom it has been appointed to run its course under fixed and invariable law; that awful One to whom it is profanity to pray, of whom it is idle and irreverent to argue and debate, of whom we should never presume to think save with humility and awe; that Unknown God has ordained that mankind should be elevated by misfortune, and that happiness should grow out of misery and pain.

I give to universal history a strange but true title--The Martyrdom of Man. In each generation the human race has been tortured that their children might profit by their woes. Our own prosperity is founded on the agonies of the past. Is it therefore unjust that we also should suffer for the benefit of those who are to come? Famine, pestilence, and war are no longer essential for the advancement of the human race. But a season of mental anguish is at hand, and through this we must pass in order that our posterity may rise. The soul must be sacrificed; the hope in immortality must die. A sweet and charming illusion must be taken from the human race, as youth and beauty vanish never to return.

THE OUTCAST

Introduction

MANY readers of The Martyrdom of Man must have speculated upon the character and the fate of the other books written by the same hand. It seems on the face of it incredible that a work which, on its first appearance in 1872, won its way to popular favor in spite of total neglect or unbridled condemnation by the newspapers and reviews, and in spite of its slashing onslaughts upon accepted opinions, should stand quite alone. No favorable review of this disturbing volume appeared until 1906, yet edition after edition bore witness to a steady demand. Even upon the post-war generation, to whom the successes of the Victorian age mean less than nothing, Winwood Reade's vision of the world has cast its spell. Within ten years fully one hundred thousand copies have passed into circulation. No shadow of mortality has yet fallen upon its pages. Is there nothing else among his writings that yet lives?

If this question had to be answered without qualification in the negative, an adequate explanation might be given on two grounds. Winwood Reade died young, at the age of thirty-six -- an age when, in the comparatively slow-maturing period during which he lived, achievement might be expected to have only begun. Moreover, his earlier writings were written in fiction form, to which his powers were not well adapted. In choosing the vehicle of fiction Winwood Reade was probably inspired by the example of his famous uncle, Charles Reade, who was fresh risen to fame at the time when Winwood was at Oxford. Before he was twenty-one Winwood published a short novel, 'Charlotte and Myra,' following this a year later with a three-decker 'Liberty Hall, Oxon,' in which the lives of undergraduates were portrayed. Both were failures, and the disappointment over these early ventures may have had something to do with their author's decision, in 1862, to visit Africa as an explorer. It was in Africa, during a series of adventurous journeys, followed by experiences as 'The Times' correspondent during the Ashanti War, that he gathered much of the material woven later into 'The Martyrdom of Man.' During 1865 another novel appeared -- 'See-Saw,' a story dealing with Roman Catholicism in Italy and Protestantism in England -- but it was no more fortunate than its predecessors. In his 'African Sketch Book' Reade confessed that "my books are literary insects, doomed to a trifling and ephemeral existence, to buzz and hum for a season -- and to die."

The books in which he recorded his African adventures were somewhat more fortunate, though they failed to bring him his due recognition as an intrepid explorer. According to Mr. F. Legge, "the cause which chiefly contributed to the public neglect of his results was the extraordinary form in which he thought fit to publish them. They did not appear at all until three years after his return to England, and then only in the form of a journal kept while in the bush for the perusal of a lady whom he addresses as 'Dear

Margaret,' and for whom he seems to have had a deep and tender affection." Further, although this work, the 'African Sketch Book,' contained much solid information on anthropological matters and several good maps, it "was stuffed with tales of savage life which are avowedly, like the illustrations with which it abounds, drawn from the imagination merely."

Only in 'The Martyrdom of Man,' in an earlier work 'The Veil of Isis' (1861) recounting the history of the Druids, and in 'The Story of the Ashanti Campaign,' which amplifies his contributions to The Times, does Winwood Reade make a definite departure from the fictional model at which he first tried his hand. It is significant, therefore, that in his last book, 'The Outcast,' he returns to this model and uses it as a vehicle for the expression of his deepest thoughts on the problems of life -- or, rather, the problem of life.

'The Outcast' was written during his last illness. His strength had been undermined during his earlier journeys in Africa, and the dysentery and fever contracted in the Ashanti campaign broke down his last defenses. Death was near, and in the nearness of death he penned his brief and eloquent confession of faith. It was published in 1875 -- the year of his, death -- and within that year it had passed into a third edition.

Since then 'The Outcast' has not, until now, been reprinted. But it has not been forgotten. Copies have been treasured by their possessors and passed to trusted and discerning friends. The passage of time has proved that although the book cannot rival 'The Martyrdom of Man' in magnitude or brilliance, and although the treatment recalls the conventions of an age that seems almost archaic, it has the touch of greatness and the universal appeal that defy time and change. Each generation as it emerges to the stage of conscious reflection confronts anew the ancient puzzle of the existence of evil. Each of us must, in our own way, settle our account with a universe which involves the martyrdom of man. Here, through the medium of a story which is really a philosophical essay, Winwood Reade discusses more than one solution, from the bankrupt evasion of suicide to the illusory prospect of compensation in another world where the errors of omniscience shall be made good. His own solution is finally offered -- a solution based on the frank acceptance of facts of life, sinister and cheerful alike, and culminates in the faith that man may, by the exercise of reason and goodwill, become the master of a happier destiny. He finds joy and fulfillment in a religion of service: "To labor and love without hope of requital or reward, what religion could be more pure and more sublime?"

A few days after Winwood Reade's death, Charles Reade wrote that he had died "heir to considerable estates which he did not live long enough to inherit, and gifted with genius which he had no time to mature." While this is a just estimate, we may console ourselves with the though that during his short span Winwood Reade lived intensely, thought deeply, and gave expression to his zeal for intellectual honesty and his fervor for human betterment in two volumes which still illumine the mind and touch the heart.

Letter I

MY DEAR FRANK, -- I welcome you back to your native land, and take it for granted that you and Ellen are tired enough of travelling. Life in a strange country is always artificial -- it seems to me like being at a play -- and constant change becomes monotonous after a time. I hear from Ellen that she intends to stop in London a week before joining you at home; and I shall reserve till then my latest budget of news about the tenants, and the harvest, and the pets, and the penny readings, &c. just now I can think of little else but the tragedy at Dr. Scott's, some account of which no doubt you have seen in the papers. But I will tell you the whole story.

Arthur Elliott was the only son of a wealthy landed proprietor, one of my nearest neighbors, and a brother magistrate. Arthur had a most amiable nature, and was tenderly loved, not only by his parents, but by all who knew him intimately. His attainments were remarkable, as I can testify; for we read much together. He was an excellent classical scholar, but his favorite study was that of metaphysics, from which he was led to the study of natural science. Religion was the poetry and passion of his life; and, though of a different belief, it afforded me pleasure to hear him discourse on the grandeur and benevolence of God. Sometimes when we were together in a deep green wood on a sultry summer afternoon; or sometimes walking at night beneath the glorious starlit sky; or sometimes when reading the dialogues of Plato, some divine thought rose from the book like an immortal spirit from the grave, and passed into his soul; then the tears would stream from his eyes, and falling on his knees he would utter praises or prayers in words of surpassing eloquence, and with a voice of the sweetest melody. And often -- how well I remember it now -- often at such times his gestures grew wild and almost furious, his utterance was choked, and a strange bubbling sound came from his mouth. Dr. Scott, who was present on one of these occasions, watched him I thought, with an air of anxiety; and I heard that he advised the Elliotts to take away their son from his books and send him abroad with a travelling tutor. But Arthur disliked the idea of leaving home, and his parents did not urge him to go, believing that the danger was imaginary. So he remained, and things went on as before.

One day he came to me in trouble. He had been reading the great work of Malthus -- the 'Essay on Population' -- and said that it made him doubt the goodness of God. I replied with the usual common-place remarks; he listened to me attentively, then sighed, shook his head, and went away. A little while afterwards he read 'The Origin of Species,' which had just come out, and which proves that the Law of Population is the chief agent by which Evolution has been produced. From that time he began to show symptoms of insanity -- which disease, it is thought, he inherited from one of his progenitors. He dressed always in black, and said that he was in mourning for mankind. The works of Malthus and <u>Darwin</u>, bound in somber covers, were placed on a table in his room; the first was lettered outside 'The Book of Doubt,' and the second 'The Book of Despair.' He took long solitary walks in the most secluded parts of the estate, and was sometimes seen gesticulating to the heavens, sometimes seated by the wayside plucking grass and casting it from him with a strange, tremulous movement of the hands. It was in vain that his good parents and the rector attempted to soothe his troubled mind with the hopes and consolations of a future life. He said that a wrong was always a wrong, and that no reward could atone for unmerited punishment. It was then I thought it right to express my own opinions on the subject of theology. But, though Arthur could cease to love and revere, he could not cease to believe. I have often observed that men of powerful intellect, especially those of the poetic constitution, find it almost impossible to shake off the faith which has been taught them in their childhood. In Arthur's case the boldest spirit of inquiry and a remorseless power of induction were allied to a rigid habit of belief. If he could have closed his eyes, in common with so many inquirers, to the barbarous element in nature, or simply dismissed it from his mind after a brief period of discomfort, he might have continued to believe in the God of his imagination and preserved his happiness. If, on the other hand, unable to escape from positive fact, he could have given up, or doubted ever so little, the dogma of a Personal Creator, he would, I believe, have finally found repose. As it was, he fell into a most deplorable condition. His God had never been an abstraction, but a Father and a Friend; and now, by ever brooding on the subject, by ever directing his thoughts towards this Imaginary Person, he actually felt its presence, as the hermit in the desert after months of contemplation, as the cenobite in the solitary cell. With him, however, it was not love and devotion, it was anger and hatred, which kindled the dangerous fire in the brain, inspired the vision, and forced him to commune with the shadow of his mind.

He spent much of his time with me, and at last I wearied of his complaints. I told him that it was useless to repine against the Inexorable; that after all there was more good than evil in the world if we went the right way to find it; and that if he sympathized so much with the miseries of men he should try to mitigate them, instead of pouring forth idle lamentations. He looked at me sadly, and embraced me, resting his head upon my shoulder; he never spoke of his troubles again, and I often repented of my harshness. But not long afterwards we all thought that he was saved. He became betrothed to a lovely and charming girl, Miss Lilian Moore, who was visiting at the rectory. She seemed to possess some tranquillizing power; her eyes, were calm and deep, and goodness was written in every feature of her face. She saw that Arthur required occupation, and asked him to compose some stories to amuse her. He complied, and wrote a number of tales, in which the trees, and flowers, and rocks, and animals were his characters and heroes. These stories were fanciful, quaint, and humorous; and several being published in the magazines, attracted notice from the press. Arthur received more than one flattering offer from London publishing firms, and began to show himself ambitious of literary fame. He had now quite recovered his health and happiness; he saw Lilian every day; but ah, Frank, how shall I tell you, the dear girl caught an infectious fever from nursing a sick child in the village, and died. Arthur went to the funeral, but sat a little way off on the tombstone plucking the grass and casting it from him with the strange movement of the hands I mentioned before. As the service was ended the clock struck twelve. He got up and said, "The wedding will be late!" and approached the grave which had just been filled up. Then he flung himself upon it with fearful shrieks and curses against the supposed Author of the world. When people attempted to lead him away he dashed them to the ground with superhuman strength. Yet even in this fearful attack of mania he seemed to recognize his father, and only shrank back from the aged hands carousingly placed upon his arm. He was taken to Dr. Scott's private asylum, which was but a little way from the church, and in a few days ceased to be violent, asked for his papers and books, and, having obtained them studied from morning to night. He appeared perfectly quiet and contented; but every night, when the church clock struck twelve, he opened the window of his room, which was on the ground floor, murmured the name of Lilian, folded his arms upon his breast, as if he had embraced her, and kissed the air. Then, with the connivance of his servant, he sprang out of the window and walked to the churchyard, followed by the man, who at least never let him go out of his sight. All the while he conversed (as if with Lilian) in the most animated manner, and, having reached the grave, made movements with his hands as if covering her up; after which he said "Good-night" in a cheerful voice and returned. These promenades were, of course, discovered in time. Arthur was carefully watched, the servant was dismissed, the windows were barred. Nothing else could have been done, yet there is too much reason to fear that this restraint proved injurious. When the hour of midnight drew near he became uneasy and restless; and when prevented from going to the window be fell into a state of dejection. He no longer slept well, and was often troubled with visions and dreams. One morning, when he awoke, he sat up in bed, and laughed till the tears ran out of his eyes. He sent for the doctor, and told him he had "found it all out," and, when asked to explain what he meant, replied that it was an original idea -- a most important discovery -- and that he should send it to a magazine. "If I told you what it was," he continued, "you would keep me here all my life, and pass off my idea on a deluded public as your own." The doctor, to humor him, replied that he was incapable of such malpractice. "Ah, well!" replied Arthur, "at ordinary times, and in ordinary cases, no doubt you are an honest man; but here the temptation would be too strong. Still, I don't mind telling you my title. It's 'A New Thing under the Moon.'" He then burst out laughing again, and rubbed his hands together with glee. In the afternoon he became violent, said he should "throw up his part," and tried to spring out of the window, dashing himself against the bars. He was placed in a padded room. The next day he was quiet as usual, and asked for paper and ink; but as the doctor wished to get him to sleep, of which he stood in much need, this request was refused. At first he seemed angry, then shrugged his shoulders and smiled. It was afterwards found that he had a note-book and pencil in his pocket. At ten o'clock p.m. he appeared drowsy, but said that he could not sleep with people in the room; and Dr. Scott told the attendants to go outside, but to look in from time to time. In an hour or so he seemed to fall into a sleep, which was probably assumed, and the vigilance of the watchers was relaxed. But in the grey hour of the dawn they heard a struggle in the room and a choked kind of cry. They pushed the door, but it had been secured from within by a small piece of wood wedged in underneath. They forced it open at last, and the body of the unfortunate young man was found hanging from the window bar. Life was extinct. On the table was a note-book in which he had been writing. Dr. Scott has just sent it over, and advises me to read it; so in my next letter I may give you an account of its contents. Such, dear son-in-law, is the sad history of Arthur Elliott.

Letter II

MY DEAR FRANK, -- I enclose you a copy of Elliott's last production, written in a state of insanity, just before he committed suicide. It will reach you, I hope, before. Ellen's return, as I suppose you would not wish her to see it. You make it a rule, I know, not to discuss theology with women, and I am much of your opinion. When Ellen was a girl I carefully attended to the culture of her mind, and encouraged her to read works of philosophy and science. But, though I saw that she possessed a vigorous intellect, I did not dare to carry her beyond the limits of Theism. I feared that for her my faith would be but a system of cold and comfortless philosophy, and that if at some future time, in adversity or suffering, a religion became necessary to her, she would run no slight risk of falling into Superstition. I saved her from that danger by teaching her to believe in a God, compared with whom the God of the Bible is a very indifferent character. But I need not say that my God, though a nobler conception, is just as much a creature of fiction as the other. They are both made by human heads, as idols are made by human hands; only, while the people of the churches and the chapels worship an idol of brass, I gave my daughter an idol of gold. I formed her a God of the purest and noblest ideas, and she still believes it to be real. Of course, some day or other she may discover the deception; and were she to read the enclosed manuscript, she would, I think, cease to believe in the Divine benevolence, and next would begin to suspect that the Being called God is as much a fabulous creature as Jupiter, Mars, or Apollo. And then comes the great question, "Would she be able to accept our religion, which demands such an utter abnegation of self? Would she even understand it?" I fear that she would lapse into that state of skepticism and indifference which, in a woman at least, is more odious and harmful than superstition.

I therefore advise you not to show her this manuscript. But read it yourself without delay, for you will be able to enjoy it. It will not make you tremble in your shoes. You have climbed above theology, as the Alpine mountaineer above the clouds.

A New Thing Under The Moon

The habit of reading in bed is delightful, but the books used for that purpose should be carefully selected. It was most imprudent of me to read, and at Dr. Scott's of all places in the world, the 'Confessions of an Opium-Eater' just after three chapters of Butler's Analogy. I might have known that it would give me mental indigestion. Needless to say that I had a dream, and such a dream! or rather such a series of dreams! Yet, though I spent a bad night, it is some consolation to reflect it was so ordained for the good of mankind. I am willing indeed to admit that the system of Cosmogony set forth in my dream may possibly not be true, and I shall not claim for it the name of Revelation as other dreamers have done; I merely assert that my theory of Cause and Creation is the best that has ever been propounded. It explains all the facts of history and nature, is in harmony with science, and is supported by analogy. Above all, it is quite original; nothing like it has ever been imagined before; and, though Solomon wisely observes that there is no new thing under the Sun, there may be a new thing under the Moon; and dreams are exceptions to every rule. However, my readers shall judge for themselves

I dreamt, first of all, I was standing, as it seemed to me, in Space, and I had a curious kind of impression that the Infinite was not too large, but just the right size for a person of my dimensions. I observed something in the distance of a dark and shadowy appearance, in form like a promontory, of which I could plainly perceive the extremity or point, but not the base and middle parts, although, as the point was exactly opposite my range of vision, and was turned away from me, it was clear that the bulk of the promontory must be situated between me and the extremity in question. This puzzled me much, and after staring some time I closed my left eye in order to see more distinctly. Then up shot a huge wall to the left of my right and still open eye. If you look at your nose with both eyes open, and then look at it with one eye shut, you will understand what I mean. I had, in fact, been surveying the tip of my own nose, which was distant many thousand miles from the middle of my face. I glanced at my shoulders, but they extended indefinitely into space; I could not see either of my hands, they were too far off; and when I lifted one up it seemed like a huge flesh-colored mountain sailing towards me through the air, and threatening to crush me if I did not pull it back. Then I thought what a dreadful thing it was to have such a nose, and a body which could be measured only by means of a trigonometrical survey. A cold perspiration broke out on my forehead, and I calculated that each drop was about the size of the Atlantic Ocean. This woke me with a start. I sat up in bed, felt my nose, and then, cursing all opium-eaters, lay down and fell asleep again.

I next dreamt that I was seated in an amphitheater or circus, in the midst of a large audience. I was conscious that I had the same body as before, and that all the persons present were equally enormous; yet I could see the ends of my shoulders, and my nose did not seem to be long; the reason of which I suppose to be this -- that in my previous dream I was in a transitional state; my body had become that of the Demigods, whose kingdom I had entered, while my eyesight remained in the human condition. But now my vision had also been enlarged, and I soon found that it possessed extraordinary powers.

The arena of the circus must have been many millions of miles in extent, and was a bottomless pit of pure ether, traversed by a bright shining ball, round which sailed a number of dark little beads attending its course. Now I fancied I had seen them somewhere before. I looked at them again more attentively, -- there could be no doubt at all about the matter, -- it was the Solar System.

My mind was still that of a mortal; so, instead of looking down on our little universe with the calm curiosity of a superior being, I had the injured feeling of an inhabitant, and rose to go, saying, "It is only an ornery after all."

However, I observed that the eyes of the spectators were all turned in the direction of the Earth; so I looked at it too; and then, oh, wonder of wonders what did I behold!

I could see the whole globe, and everything upon it, even worlds of animalcule too minute to be distinguished with the best microscopes; even the waves of light, invisible to mortals, which break upon the surface of the Earth like the waves of the sea upon the shore. I could see every man woman, and child, and study their actions without effort or confusion. I could view, at the same time, numberless dramas of domestic life which were being performed within the dramas of the nations; while these were only parts of the great drama of the Earth. It is, of course, difficult to explain how so many different objects could be at the same time gathered by the eye, transmitted to the brain, and assimilated by the intellect. It would be difficult to explain to a maggot how the eye of a man can take in a landscape at a glance. Yet these powers of vision will not seem excessive when the size of the eye is taken into consideration. I should say that the pupil of a demigod's eye is about double the sun's diameter, and no doubt, if dissected, would be found to contain lenses of extraordinary structure. But I have merely to record facts and am not called upon to offer explanations.

The pleasure I derived at first from looking at the Earth was soon marred by the fearful tragedies which I saw everywhere enacted. It was nearly all blood and tears; and, unable to gaze any longer on the torture of my kind, I rose to leave the theater. At the same time one of the audience went out, followed by a titter from the crowd, and I recognized in him the likeness of an historical personage; or, rather, the historical personage was a likeness of him. Then I understood that this earth-life of ours is only a satirical play, that our great men are caricatures of famous demigods, their vicissitudes and actions, ingenious lampoons. And is this all? thought I to myself. Are we with our proud aspirations only as puppets in a show? Are love, ambition, and religious sentiment -- the tremulous passion, the desire of fame, the divine yearnings of the soul -- are these but as the jerkings of a wire cunningly contrived? Are the terrible combats of life as gladiator- games to make the demigods a holiday? Ah, then it is sad! and yet do not men as it is often martyr their lives to make a noise in the world and gain the plaudits of a human audience? And should not we who aspire to greatness rejoice that we play before the Immortals, and may hope to achieve celestial fame? Thus I tried to console my suffering heart; but alas! it was in vain. I had a hope -- one last hope -- and now it was destroyed. For I saw that the dead cannot be united, since we are but as shadows that vanish away. All is lost, all is done; farewell for ever, Lilian: farewell, my only love, for evermore.

I fled into Space. But I found that the senses of hearing and smell were endowed with powers not less marvelous than those of the sight. Though now far away, I could smell the Earth, which gave forth a carrion stench not only from its body but its soul. Each vice had its horrible odor. It is true that each virtue had its fragrance as well, and sometimes, though rarely, a breath of perfume floated through the air. And now strange sounds arose. I heard the humming of the Earth as it spun, and the roaring of the fire in its innermost depths. I heard the whispers of conscience and the chidings of remorse, the sighs of unrequited love, the cries of many agonies. At the same time I heard the audience hooting and shouting, Off! off! Shame! Apologize! Where is the Lord Chamberlain? But in the midst of this turmoil the cries of anguish were hushed, a sweet balmy smell was diffused through space, the voices of the earth rose in a strain of enchanting melody, and thunders of applause seemed to indicate that the drama was concluded. Then I woke up and found my cheeks all wet with tears which I had shed.

My servant, who is very attentive -- perhaps a little over- attentive -- has taken my lamp away, but there is a splendid moon, and I am writing near the window by its light. I do not understand why, the day after my dream, they put me into this room, which is not so large as my own, and furnished in very bad taste, the walls being stuffed like a first-class carriage on a railway. Where are my books? What mean those sentinel footsteps outside, the door stealthily opened, and the cold grey eyes which search into my soul? Ha! ha! ha! Look at those little black imps dancing in the moonlight on the floor! Patter, patter, patter! pit-a-pat, pit-a- pat! Ah! Lilian, my dear, you should not come out at night in that thin white shroud, and it's no use your coming here any more. The windows are barred, and I can't take you home to the quiet churchyard and put you to bed in your cozy little grave. We can meet no more by the light of the moon. Besides, it is but a play; we should only be amusing the people up there. Oh! cruel Author, why did you kill her? -- in the first act, too; very inartistic. At least I don't know. As this life is a penny-gaff sort of performance, it was more effective to do it when she was young, for if she was old and ugly no one would care. But who could see her die then with the beauty of girlhood still blushing upon her, and her death caught nursing the poor sick child; who could see her die then without being smitten to the heart? It must have brought down the house. Weep, ye gods, weep your oceanic tears, and wait your sighs in gentle gales to mourn poor Lilian. And her lover lying on the grave, digging at the ground with his nails and teeth, seized, bound hand and foot, and then brought here. Oh, no doubt it was a fine stroke of art -- most charmingly devised. Well, it's a hard world, and we cannot all be kings and queens; to one is the part of the villain -- he is hissed; to another the maiden in distress; and poor Mad Tom must be played too.

I kept myself awake, for I feared another dream; but the odors of the earth lingered in my nostrils, and its horrible cries still sounded in my ears. After all, I thought it was best to sleep if I could. Luckily, the last number of the 'Quarterly Review' happened to be in the room, and I knew that Dr. Scott recommends this publication in cases of sleeplessness and nervous excitement. The article I selected was a perfect soporific -- an essay on the Darwinian Theory, and before I had finished the preamble it had sent me to sleep. But on that fatal night even the 'Quarterly Review' could not prevent me from dreaming; and, in fact, I dreamt of a review, for my third dream took me to a Demigod club where I found the following critique in a periodical lying on the table. I wrote it from memory as soon as I awoke.

The Review

The custom of creating worlds, and of peopling them with animated beings who reflect the vices or follies of the day, or offer an example of ideal virtues and moral excellence, has of late become popular in art; and, though it may be a fashion which, like others of its kind, will soon pass away, it is in the meantime for us, who are critics and censors, to pass judgment on all such works as succeed in obtaining the attention of the public. The anonymous drama which has just been performed is said to be a first attempt; and this we should have inferred from internal evidence. For, though the work is by no means deficient in power, and contains some original ideas, there is a want of symmetry in form and of finish in detail, a prodigal waste of raw material, a roughness of style and execution which bear the stamp of inexperience. However, as will be shown, it is chiefly on moral grounds that we think this production ought to be condemned.

The work is simple in conception and modest in design. We have not here, as in some ambitious compositions, a number of inhabited worlds contributing each its part to the story. One system only is placed upon the stage, and the action is confined to one planet of that system.

At first the world was presented to our view as a fiery cloud. It became compressed to a Sun, which advanced through Space, rotating on its axis, and cast off certain pieces from itself like tyres from a wheel. These cooled into planetary bodies, and one of them, called by its inhabitants 'The Earth,' was the scene of the drama which we shall now endeavor to describe. We observed with unmixed pleasure the gradual growth of the planet from a cinder enveloped in cloud to a globe covered with water; the sun-rays causing the origin of life; the floating animalcules and one-celled plants; the rise of the land from the deep, and its naked skin being clothed with a green mantle of palm and fern vegetation. Monstrous reptiles and ungainly quadrupeds inhabited the primeval marshes of the earth; and at night the croaking of enormous frogs rose like thunder in the air. But as time flowed on the face of the earth assumed a more gentle and benignant expression; flowers blossomed in the forest, and the voices of singing birds were heard; the quadrupeds became less gigantic in size, but more graceful and varied in their forms; and finally Men appeared upon the scene, roaming in herds through the forest, clambering the trees, jabbering semi-articulate sounds. But, as language formed upon their lips, the erect posture was assumed, the fore-foot was used as a hand, weapons were invented, fire was discovered, caverns in the rock, burrows in the ground, and platforms on the trees were exchanged for huts surrounded by gardens. Wild animals were tamed, the seed-bearing grasses were cultured into grain, canoes glided on the waters, commerce became the rival of war, which, once incessant, was now occasional. The tribes were united into nations, the nations into empires, great cities flourished on the banks of rivers and by harbors on the sea-shore; classes were divided, the arts and sciences arose. At first these were kept as state secrets, and often perished with the state. At first wealth, culture, and power belonged exclusively to the dominant caste, while the masses labored in subjection. But by means of useful inventions knowledge was widely diffused, and the passion for liberty entered the bosom of the people. One nation after another shook itself free from the tyranny of kings and the tyranny of priests. When class restrictions were removed all could hope by honest labor to better their condition, and all striving for their own ends assisted the onward movement of the world. At a later period the social equality of men extinguished personal ambition, and the Welfare of the Race was the aim of those who labored for distinction. Fame could be obtained only by adding something to the knowledge or the happiness of men. Finally war ceased; the malignant forces of Nature were subdued, vice and disease were eradicated, the earth became a pleasure garden, and men learnt to bear without repining a painless death in extreme old age.

We suppose that the moral purpose of this drama is to teach the doctrine of Improvement, and to illustrate that tendency to Progress which pervades the universe. The evolution of mind from matter, by means of natural law, shows the innate power of that tendency or force, and the efforts by which Man achieves his own comparative perfection are no doubt intended as a protest against that habit of quiescence and content which is perhaps the natural failing of Immortals. We think that the satire on theology is wholesome and just. Nothing could be more ludicrous than to see these ephemeral beings, these creatures of a moment, building little houses in honor of the First Cause and glibly explaining mysteries which we do not profess to understand. This may serve as a warning to certain presumptuous philosophers who fabricate theories respecting the Supreme; for how can we know that we are not in the same relative position to beings of a higher race as those pygmies we create to ourselves? At least it is certain that our intellects, great as they are, or great as we think them to be, are unable to explain primary phenomena or to solve the problems of Cause, Existence, and Futurity. So far then we go with our author; and in numberless ways he has justly derided the follies of our race. We can afford to forgive him for creating human reviewers to parody our profession, the more so as coarse caricature fails of its effect; but we must object to the introduction of personal portraits; it was settled long ago as a dogma in art that mere copies should have no place in a creation. This, however, is not a defect on which we shall dwell, for, though in itself serious enough, it is light and trivial when compared with the faults it is now our duty to expose.

In the first place, it is most degrading that these men who are made in our image, who in their exterior form and mental faculties partly resemble ourselves, should be suffered to retain both in body and mind so much of the lower animals. The Creator may, perhaps, reply that he laid down the law of gradual transition, and that all traces of the beast in man could not be expelled except by departing from the law. But since he transformed, by gradual transition, the muzzle or snout to the lips of beauty radiant with smiles, the hairy paw to the skilful and delicate hand, he might surely have found some way to obliterate by change the instincts and actions of which we complain. No one can deny that he is ingenious enough when he chooses; the shark's jaw and the serpent's fang are models of dexterous contrivance, though we do not envy him these inventions. In any case, the difficulty is one of his own making, and if he could have devised no other plan he should have modified his law of evolution. It might have been less philosophical, but it would have been more decent; and we must own that we prefer an error in art to an outrage on decorum.

Secondly, the development of matter to mind, of quadruped to man, of savage to civilized nations, is laudable enough as an idea; but how has it been carried out? As regards the first stage of the progress we have only to praise and admire; but how has progress been produced in the animated world? We are almost ashamed to explain a law which, in its recklessness of life and prodigality of pain, almost amounts to a crime. In cold forethought the Creator so disposed the forces of nature that more animated beings were born than could possibly obtain subsistence on the earth. This caused a struggle for existence, a desperate and universal war; the best and improved animals were alone able to survive, and so in time Evolution was produced. We shall not deny that there is a kind of perverted ingenuity in the composition of this law; but the waste of life is not less clumsy than it is cruel. By means of this same struggle for existence, man was raised from the bestial state and his early discoveries were made. Afterwards, ambition of fame, and later still more noble motives came into force, but that was towards the conclusion of the drama. At first, every step in the human progress was won by conflict, and every invention resulted from calamity. The most odious vices and crimes were at one time useful to humanity, while war, tyranny, and superstition assisted the development of man.

Evil unhappily exists, and we do not condemn its employment in art. We are not in favor of those impossible dramas in which only the virtues are displayed. But we do condemn this confusion of evil and good, and maintain that nothing can be more immoral than to make crime the assistant of progress and vice the seed of which virtue is the fruit.

Again, Death is a useful and perhaps indispensable appliance in works of this kind, but so potent a means of exciting sympathy should be employed with moderation. Now what do we find here? The law of evolution is the law of death. Massacre is incessant; flowers, animals, and men die at every moment; the earth is a vast slaughter-house, and the ocean reddened with blood. Nor, incredible as it may seem, is that the worst. With a talent for torture which rouses our wonder only next to our disgust, the Creator has smitten the animated world, even to the insects, with numerous painful and lingering diseases, while the intellect is also afflicted with maladies peculiar to itself. The affections which at first would appear to afford some meager consolation in the martyrdom of man are themselves too often the cause of mental pain and incurable despair. What can be said for such a world? What kind of defence or excuse can there be for its Creator? It is true that he made men himself, but that does not justify his cruelty. The Supreme has endowed us with the power of producing and destroying animated forms, but so terrible a gift should not be abused. We should never forget that though these little creatures live only for a moment, they are yet sentient beings, and their torments while they last are real and intense. Who could view that melancholy Earth and those writhing masses of humanity, who could hear those agonizing cries without a shudder of pain and a glow of honest indignation against the Author of such woes and wrongs? Many of the audience withdrew, while others hooted the Creator, and at one time we thought his planet would be damned. But, all's well that ends well is the easy maxim of a pleasure-seeking world, and the public, fickle and easily impressed, applauded the virtuous finale and forgot the horrors that had gone before. We were unable to do so, and declare that it seemed to us a most cruel and immoral exhibition. That is what we have to say. We know nothing of the author, but if we should meet him at a future time shall be happy to hear what he can say to exonerate himself. We do not wish to be too hard upon a young beginner whose talents cannot be disputed, and we trust that this critique, which is not unkindly meant in spite of its severity, will induce him to reform. When next he produces a world let it be one which we can take our wives and daughters to see, which will excite in the audience none but the nobler sentiments, and which also, we must add, will give us a more favorable impression of the personal character of its Creator.

Letter III

So, Ellen, you have been into Bluebeard's chamber; you have read the manuscript; and these ravings of a lunatic have made you doubt the existence of a Personal God. You suspect that I doubt it too. My dear, you are wrong; I disbelieve it. There is no doubt in my mind about the matter.

Oh, Daughter of Eve, an apple from the Tree of Knowledge was hidden in a drawer; then came the serpent Curiosity; and now, having eaten, you are banished from the Eden of belief. You wish me to tell you the whole truth, or what I believe to be the truth. Well, it can do you no harm in the present condition of your mind and may do you good -- though as to that I am not very sanguine. But I will not merely expound my religious opinions; I will describe their birth and growth in my mind. I will tell you the story of my life.

Ah! the story of my life. ... Apart from all matters of religion it will deeply, too deeply, interest you. I fear, my darling, it will give you much pain; yet it is right that you should hear it; and you will be inclined more than ever, I believe, to pity and succor the unfortunate when you learn in what misery your childhood was passed.

You tell me that sometimes when you approach anything that is dead, a strange and horrible scene rises like a picture to your mind. You see a bare and squalid room -- the walls blackened with dirt, the broken window-panes stuffed with rags. On the floor a woman with long yellow hair; beside her a man on his knees dressed in a ragged black coat; behind him some men and women of coarse and evil countenance, yet grave and sad, whispering together.

You shall now learn what was this scene which your memory has faithfully though fitfully retained. You shall learn how your father was an outcast, reduced to the extremity of sorrow, to the brink of despair; how his misfortunes resembled, but exceeded, those of the unhappy Elliott, and how narrowly he escaped a similar fate.

Letter IV

IN the last century an East India nabob named Mordaunt returned to England with an immense fortune, said to have been obtained in no very creditable manner from the treasury of a Rajah in Bengal at whose court he was Resident. My father, his only son, inherited several landed estates and a large sum of money in the funds. He was sent to Eton and Christchurch, at which latter place of education he chiefly distinguished himself as an athlete; he also rode hard across country, was a noted skittle-player, and had gained much academic fame by successfully bruising with bargees. But all this came to an end before he left the university, for he went to hear a noted field-preacher, intending to create a disturbance, and was converted on the spot. He gave up his old habits and companions, read hard for his degree, went into orders, and took the living of Harborne-in-the-Moors, which was in his own presentation. Such is the account of his youth, which I received from the excellent Bishop of T----, who was his contemporary. There was nothing in my father's appearance to show that he had ever been inclined to dissipation, or even to innocent pleasure. His features were inexpressibly severe; his eyes were cold and hard, and overhung with thick, bushy eyebrows; his lips were thin and Closely compressed. His strength was great, as I, when a boy, knew to my cost; and even his hands had a stern aspect, being broad and powerful, the spaces between the knuckles covered with long, black hairs. He did not send me to school, but taught me Greek, Latin, mathematics, and divinity himself; and seldom, I believe, has any apprentice been more harshly treated by his master. However, I ought to remind you that I was born in a flogging, cudgelling age, and that humanity to schoolboys is a virtue of recent growth. Moreover, my father was not indulgent to himself, and no paid tutor, however conscientious, would have toiled as he did with me. His day's work was almost incredible. He rose at daybreak, and read Hebrew and theology till breakfast: if it was winter, he laid and lighted his own fire. The forenoon and afternoon he devoted to me, except at two intervals which I spent in amusement, he in attending to the duties of his parish. He allowed me to pass the evenings with my mother while he corrected my exercises, and studied the lessons of the next day in Homer, Aristotle, Virgil, or Tacitus, comparing the various readings and referring to the German commentators and critics as if he were preparing an exhaustive treatise on the subject. His religion was of the lowest Calvinistic type, but at least it was sincere. He allowed himself no pleasures of any kind, and though less strict with my mother and myself, we lived in a very frugal manner. After his death I was informed by the family lawyer that he spent immense sums in anonymous donations for religious and charitable purposes. My mother died in the belief that he was a miser and had never done a benevolent action in his life,, He thought it right to conceal from her this giving of alms, and perhaps also he loved her more than he allowed her to suppose. But he did not make her very happy. Ah, what would have been my life without her! How often she caught me in her arms as I fled from the chamber of torture and kissed my bruised and bleeding hands! How often she soothed my wounded spirit with words of the tenderest love, and persuaded me to endure with patience the trials of my childish life! I did not then know that she suffered more than myself. She was ardent and romantic, fond of intellectual society, and not indifferent to admiration, possessed of remarkable beauty and many elegant accomplishments. But Harborne was a lone and sequestered village in the moors, and my father objected to social pleasures; so we received no visitors.

She had a heart which pined for affection; and he was a man of stone. She once told me that my birth had saved her from absolute despair: thenceforth she had something to live for, something to love. Often, as she pressed me to her bosom, she would gaze into my face with a timid, searching, craving look; and when with some cold words I tried to shake myself free, her deep, dark eyes would fill with tears. So it was also in your case, dear Ellen, and so no doubt you have found it with your little girl. Children cannot love us as we love them; and when they become old enough to return our affection, they leave us to marry or to make their way in the world. Happily it is good for us to love as it is good for us to labor, even when the reward is slight and inadequate.

My mother was a sad invalid, being afflicted with a pulmonary complaint which required constant attendance. The parish doctor saw her nearly every day, and received a fixed fee or salary per annum. Herbert Chalmers, whose name is yet remembered in science, was a student of promise and repute who had taken the cure of bodies in the parish of Harborne, partly for the sake of daily bread, and partly to study that particular phase of the profession. He had not been there more than a year when his friends obtained him a lucrative appointment. He thanked them and declined it, saying he was not ambitious and preferred living in the country. Now as the duties of a parish doctor combine in themselves all that is most unpleasant in the life of an apothecary's apprentice and the checkered existence of a post-boy, namely the rolling and pinching of innumerable pills, and long night-rides in the hardest of weather, his friends thought him out of his wits; but they could not change his resolution. Some time afterwards a relation died and left him a fortune. He built a mansion with a laboratory, hot- houses, and rooms suitable for collections and experiments, engaged a medical assistant, and devoted his time to scientific researches on the physiology and chemistry of the vegetable kingdom. But he still remained the doctor of the parish and attended all difficult cases himself. He reversed the usual order of things, for when he left a poor patient he slipped a guinea into his hand: that was the good doctor's idea of being humorous. His skill and unremitting care certainly prolonged my dear mother's life, though it could not save her from death at the early age of forty-three.

I had always been told from my boyhood that I was to be a clergyman; my father and mother both wished it, and I had no desire for any other profession. My college life was quite uneventful. I joined no set, indulged in none of the popular amusements, such as boating or cricket; and, living for the most part in my rooms, made neither enemies nor friends. I took a first class in Great Go, and the Bishop of T----, who ordained me, wrote a most kind letter to congratulate my father on the good examination I had passed in divinity. I preached my first sermon in Harborne Church; and though no one was there but our tenants and servants, my parents and the doctor, I did not dare raise my eyes from the book, and felt myself blushing two or three times as I read out some eloquent passages which I had composed in a state of exaltation, but which now seemed rather too fine for the occasion. However, my mother was delighted with this maiden composition, and felt very proud that I was ordained.

On Sundays, Dr. Chalmers always dined with us in the middle of the day; and that same afternoon we were strolling together in the garden -- my mother, the doctor and I -- when she said, "Well, doctor, you have not quite wasted your life in this dismal place; for you have made me live long enough to enjoy one day of perfect happiness." He made some reply which I do not remember, and then she said, "But tell me, dear doctor, I do not understand; why do you stay here when you might go to London and become the intimate friend of Davy, and Buckland, and the other great men with whom you correspond?" He answered, "That is my secret; and female curiosity cannot always be indulged." "Well, then, tell me.something else," she said. "Is it true you are going to be married? " He smiled and shook his head, and replied that it was not true. He was now forty- six years of age, and his day was gone. "Oh, doctor," she said, "you mustn't say that. Have you forgotten I am forty-three? Is my day gone too? " She drew herself up and looked very beautiful. Then she said, "You are still young enough, why do you not marry? Are you a woman hater? "Again he smiled, but this time I thought rather sadly, and said he was far from being that. "And do you not find it very lonely living in that great house by yourself? "Yes," he said, "it is very lonely." "And do you not sometimes feel unhappy?" "Yes, sometimes I feel very unhappy indeed." "And you do not think that if you were to marry ...?" "I cannot," he replied, "Is it for the same reason that prevented you from taking that appointment?" "Yes," he replied in a sharp voice, "it is the same reason." "Will you not tell me what it is?" (He shook his head.) "Ah, my dear friend, it would be better. You have something on your mind; will you not trust it to me? You have saved my life again and again; will you not let me prove my gratitude? Oh, disburden your heart, I beseech you. Edward, dear, leave us alone."

"No, sir," said he with emphasis, "do not go away." My mother thought that he was angry, and laid her hand upon his arm. I saw his lips turn pale, but he said in a firm voice, "Ellen Mordaunt, I thank you for your sympathy, but I cannot tell you this secret of my life, it would make you unhappy, and would give me no relief, but quite the contrary." He then shook hands with us both, and saying he was wanted at home, walked quickly towards the garden gate.

My mother looked after him, her eyes wide open with astonishment. I said there was a skeleton in every house. "Oh!" she cried, "Edward, what do you mean? He cannot have done anything wrong; that is impossible."

I did not reply, and we walked up and down the gravel walk. My mother seemed buried in thought. Suddenly she gave an exclamation and put her hand to her heart. She turned round and went a few steps as if to overtake the doctor, who had just reached the gate and paused there to look at us as he passed through. "Are you in pain, mother?" said I; "let me run after Dr. Chalmers?" "No," she cried earnestly, "do not call him back;" and seizing my hand she pressed it with convulsive force. I remained silent and lost in wonder, as she had been a moment before.

Then she said in her own quiet voice, "It was only a passing spasm, and Dr. Chalmers has other patients to attend. It is getting rather cold; I think we had better go in."

We went indoors, and my mother, complaining of a headache, retired to her room. The next morning I was awoke by the sun-beams streaming through the window. It was a fine spring morning, the birds in the garden were singing merrily. I felt in glorious health; the blood seemed to dance in my veins. Hitherto I had known no serious cares, and the troubles of childhood were past. A bright calm life was before me, and as I reflected on my happy condition my heart was filled with the love of God and with gratitude for his goodness.

One of the servants came in, gave me a letter, and hastened from the room. The letter was from my father. I have it before me now, yellow and crumpled and stained -- written more than thirty years ago -- yet still I weep as I read it.

"My son, I cannot see you to-day. It has pleased the Lord to chasten us with a heavy and sore affliction. Last night when I went to bed at a late hour your mother was asleep, but seemed to be dreaming. She turned from side to side, and was whispering something under her breath. I stooped down and listened, and heard her say the doctor's name. Then I feared that she was ill. Still sleeping, she flung her arms round my neck and awoke. When she saw me she gave a scream and shrank to the farther side of the bed. 'Wife,' I said, 'you have a fever; your face is flushed, and your hands are burning hot.; I will send James for the doctor at once.' I moved towards the bell, but she sprang from the bed and exclaimed, 'It is nothing, I am quite well, indeed I am; you must not send for him. Oh, do not send for him!' I saw that she was delirious, and rang the bell in spite of her feeble efforts to prevent me. Then she gave a great cry; the blood rushed from her lips and she fell to the floor. When I raised her in my arms she was dead."

Letter V

I REMAINED three months at home, and my father was very gentle and kind. One Sunday, as we stood side by side in the churchyard looking at the grave, he put his hand on my shoulder and said, "You were a good son to her." I noticed that his sermons were more humane, his mien and manners less austere; and I heard the coachman (an old servant) declare that "master was quite a changed man." But before I left home his old severity seemed to be returning.

The Bishop of T---- gave me a small living at Stilbroke in ----shire. The rectory being out of repair, I was invited by Mr. Jameson, apparently the squire, for his letter was dated Stilbroke Court, to stay at his house until my own was habitable. I accepted this invitation. A talkative neighbor on the coach told me that Mr. Jameson was a London tradesman retired from business, who about ten years ago had bought the manor of Stilbroke and set up as a country gentleman. "But," added my informant with a grin, and sinking his voice to a whisper, "the gentry don't call upon him, and he's not in the commission of the peace." He then went on to inform me that Mr. Jameson had one son, a lieutenant or captain in the Guards, and one daughter, who was lady of the house, her mother being dead. He said, "You'll find the bishop there spending the day; he's come down to consecrate a church." My companion then proceeded to elicit from me as much information respecting myself as I felt disposed to give him, and got down at a village near Stilbroke. I supposed he was a lawyer, or land agent, or something of that kind. I found Stilbroke Court a fine specimen of the old English manor-house, and Mr. Jameson, who came out of doors to welcome me, certainly seemed at first sight a fine specimen of the old English country gentleman. He wore a blue coat with brass buttons and a buff- colored waistcoat, and a snowy neck-cloth swathed round his throat. He had also a full-blooded, country-looking complexion; but when he spoke there was beneath a false accent of rusticity, a certain intonation which savored of the counter. I also observed in our first interview that he spoke with much hesitation, and made long stops between every phrase, the reason being, as I was afterwards able to infer, that on account of the bishop's presence he was leaving out the expletives with which he usually garnished his discourse. For when he first came down to Stilbroke, supposing that every country gentleman swore, he assiduously practiced the habit; and by the time he had discovered his mistake, the habit was acquired and could not be shaken off.

I felt some little trepidation when I found myself in the same room with the bishop. But Dr. Lambton came forward to meet me, and shook me warmly by the hand. Mr. Jameson asked me what I would have to eat, and resting his hands in a peculiar manner on the table, described the various dainties before him as if they were articles he wanted to sell. He was ... that is ... very glad to see me. Hoped I had a pleasant journey. Heard that the roads were ... extremely bad and heavy after the rain. Then I heard him mutter to himself, "Damn the damns, can't keep them down."

The bishop took me out for a walk in the grounds after lunch. He talked about my father and his own college days, described Oxford as it was in the last generation, gave me many practical hints respecting my parochial duties, and made me promise I would write to him as a friend if ever I required his advice.

He was to go away that afternoon, and we now saw the carriage driving round the sweep. Bidding me good-bye, he hastened to the house, and I walked along the gravel path, darkened by rain, to the end of the garden, where I found a little iron gate opening into a wood. But it was not an ordinary wood, being planted with many foreign trees, and bright with crimson rhododendrons. In other parts of the wilderness," as it was called, nature was left undisturbed; tiny little pathlets marked the "runs" of hares, and in thick patches of bramble were their "forms." The beech-mast of last year, brown twigs and dry leaves littered the ground, which was carpeted with moss and ribbed with the roots of trees. One charming little dell that I discovered was filled with blue-bells, more beautiful in color, I thought, than the flowers of the Himalaya shrub.

Brought up as I had been amidst desolate moors, it gave me an exquisite pleasure to walk in the shade of trees, to inhale their delicate fragrance, to view their dark pillar-like trunks and fair edifice of foliage. I stood on the brink of the dell and gazed down on the flowers like a blue lake lying in its depths. A few others of these wild hyacinths were growing singly or in clusters on the sides of the dell mingled with young ferns of the tenderest green, and one flower was growing at my feet. I had almost stepped upon it. A little way off, the sunlight descending through a window in the leafy roof flowed through the wood like a silvery stream, while around me the trunks of trees were flecked with patches of light. I heard a chirrup overhead and saw a squirrel leaping nimbly from branch to branch, running home to its young in the dusk, Sometimes the wind rustled faintly in the branches overhead and cast down raindrops shining like pearls as they fell. I was softened by these sweet influences. A tender melancholy stole upon me. A memory never long absent returned to my heart which was its home. Mine eyes streaming with tears fell on the hyacinth growing at my feet. I stooped down and caressed it with my hand. "Oh, delicate flower," I said, "your life is short enough and I will not pluck it from you; but if I could plant you in a garden where death and decay were unknown, then I would gather you at once. Thus God gathers beautiful souls; he loves them and takes them to himself. Dear mother, I weep not for you, but for myself; I know that you are happy, it is I -- it is I who am forlorn."

I put my hand in my bosom and drew forth a locket, and pressed it to my lips. Mother, I said, send a ray of your love for me into some woman's heart that resembles your own, and so brighten my solitary life.

Then I lifted up my eyes and saw standing beside me a young lady of surpassing loveliness. She wore a white muslin dress of the kind which my mother used to wear; and from under her broad garden hat, long tresses of golden hair fell upon her shoulders. Her face had a grave and gentle expression which I know not how to describe, her complexion was pale, her eyes of a soft and liquid blue. Such was your mother when I first looked upon her. She was then only seventeen, the purest, the most affectionate of women, and one of the most unfortunate.

I rose and bowed; she shook hands as if we were friends. "Papa," she said, "sent me to call you."

We went towards the house; she made room for me in the narrow path to walk by her side. I furtively wiped the tears from my eyes. She blushed and said, "I fear, Mr. Mordaunt, that you are in much trouble?"

"My mother is dead," I replied; "and she was my only friend."

"Your only friend," she said timidly; "and your father?"

"I cannot love him," I answered, "so much as I wish;" and I gave a sigh. She sighed too. "Our parents," she said, "are our best friends, but sometimes ---" Then she checked herself and said, "Have you a sister?" "Ah, no," I replied, "if I had a sister then I should be happy, for I would make her live with me here."

"And what," she said a little more gaily, "what would you make your sister do -- besides keeping house?"

"I would make her go with me to visit the poor and the sick -- to tell you the truth, I am rather afraid of them -- and she would teach me what to do. And then there would be someone who cared for me. It is hard to be alone in the world."

She did not reply. Her father took me over the village and gave me an account of my parish, prosing and swearing dreadfully. The next morning Miss Jameson came to me in the garden, followed by a maid carrying a covered basket on her arm. "Would you like," she said, "to be introduced to some of your parishioners?" I assented, of course, and enjoyed my second visit to the village more than the first. Margaret and I soon became intimate friends, and indeed almost like brother and sister. I stayed a month in the house, and when I went to live at the rectory our companionship was not interrupted. We were together all the day; and I almost reproached myself for being so happy a few months after my mother's death.

But about the middle of August the house was filled with guests, and Margaret's time was so taken up that we seldom saw each other alone. At the end of the month her brother came down with the Honorable William Fitzclarence, his friend. Captain Jameson was a sodden-faced dissolute-looking young man, with a carefully cultivated lisp and a vulgar laugh. He never pronounced the letter "r" except by inadvertence, and never replied to a question without screwing an eye-glass into his orbit, and surveying the other person through it with an air of mild astonishment, as if he had never seen him before. In short, he had taken the part of the dandy as his father had taken that of the country gentleman. In each case the impersonation was clever, which is all that can be said. Fitzclarence was a character. The heir to a peerage and a vast fortune, he was what was then called a "Philosophical Radical." He sat at the feet of James Mill, dined tete-a-tete with the famous Jeremy, and wrote for the 'Westminster Review.' He was one of the agitators for Reform, and was also reputed to be a violent hater of the Bible and the Church, a second Tom Paine. In those days a Radical aristocrat was almost unknown, and I really think he was the first of the species. The popular theory was that his head was turned, and certainly his manners were singular and his language often extravagant. As soon as he became excited in conversation he wriggled and writhed in his chair, and when he finished what he had to say, snapped his jaws sharply together like a dog at a fly. Though he disapproved of the game-laws he had a passion for shooting, and having quarrelled with all his relations, was induced by the fame of the Stilbroke turnip-fields to accept young Jameson's invitation. The other guests were mostly City people, and among them was an heiress to whom Mr. Jameson anxiously directed the attention of his son; for he was not enormously rich, and the captain was enormously extravagant.

One day when I was dining at the house the conversation turned at dessert, after the ladies had left the table, upon the recent discoveries in geology, which revealed the earth's antiquity and the creation of fish, reptiles, and quadrupeds in epochs separated by vast intervals of time. Fitzclarence expounded the matter with much lucidity, and each guest was apparently drawing his own conclusions for himself when Captain Jameson blurted out:

"Then the world was not made in six days. after all."

There was a dead silence, and all eyes were turned upon me. I said that the geologists must be mistaken if such was their theory, because it was clearly stated in the Bible that God had made the world in six days.

"Well then, Mr. Mordaunt," said Fitzclarence, "you do not agree with those of your brethren who declare that the six days in question were not actual days, but geological periods?

"How can they say that," I replied, "when each day is described as having an evening and morning, and when it is also said that God 'blessed the seventh day and sanctified it'?"

"Nothing," answered Fitzclarence, "could be proved more completely and concisely. We may, therefore, take it for granted that the six days of Genesis are not geological periods? "He looked at me with a questioning air. I bowed and smiled, and was going to change the conversation, when he said: "But now, if it were proved as an actual fact, beyond the shadow of a doubt, by the same kind of evidence as that which proves that the earth revolves round the sun -- supposing, I say, it could be proved that the world was not made in six days, but that thousands and thousands of years intervened between, for example, the fish and birds of the fifth day, and man who was created on the sixth, what may I ask would you say then? "

"My dear sir," I replied, "you might as well ask what I would say if it could be proved that a circle is square."

But supposing it could be proved -- please to answer for my argument's sake -- what then?"

"Then," I replied, "of course it would be proved that the Bible was not inspired."

"Good," said Fitzclarence, rising from the table. "Well now, I will tell you this. It has been proved," And he walked out of the room.

Mr. Jameson poured forth a volley of oaths at his son for having set Fitz upon his hobby. The next day Fitzclarence wrote me a letter apologizing for his rudeness and begging me not to think of what he had said. The advice was kindly meant, but quite unnecessary; what he said seemed to me incredible, and it soon passed away from my mind. Not so, however, with the man. I observed that he gave up shooting and passed all the day at the house. Mr. Jameson, who knew my father to be rich, had always encouraged my visits, but now his manner was changed, and whenever we had any business to discuss, he was careful to make the appointment at the rectory. An infallible instinct warned me that Fitzclarence was my rival, and a gossiping servant confirmed it. My rival, I say, for now I discovered that I loved Margaret. So long as we were constantly together I was contented with her friendship; the days passed happily; I did not attempt to analyze my feelings; I did not reflect on the future. But, as soon as we were separated, my affection forced back upon itself became craving and intense. Unable to see her or speak with her as before, she became the constant companion of my thoughts. And now came the fear that I should lose her altogether. From my library window I could see into the Stilbroke grounds. Every day, at the same hour, they walked together on the terrarel he speaking with animated gestures, she listening with attention -- no doubt with admiration. He was a noted orator, how could she resist his eloquence? Besides, he was heir to a peerage and her father was a tradesman.

Soon it was all over the village that they were engaged. A farmer told me the news, and declared Mr. Jameson himself had hinted as much to him, saying that before very long they'd hear wedding bells. Strange as it may seem, from that time I became more easy in my mind. It was a relief to be out of suspense, and now my duty lay clear before me; silence, self-conquest, resignation. I even smiled at the thought that perhaps I might have to marry them. At this time I read for the first time the 'Imitation of Jesus Christ,' and became enamored of the spiritual life. I resolved to place my happiness no more in earthly pleasures and human affections, but to seek only the divine love by purification of the soul, and fasting, and prayer, and exclusion of mundane thoughts. I resolved to banish Margaret from my mind and memory; when her vision forced itself upon me, I took up the 'Imitation' or the Bible. In the solitude of the night I found it hard to abstain from thinking of her, and I kept a taper burning opposite the bed to remind me of my resolution. I tied myself down in the chair to be prevented from going to the window at the time when she walked upon the terrace. In church I forbade myself to glance at the pew where she sat. My whole time was passed in idle devotion and selfish cares for the well-being of my soul. I almost ceased to visit my parishioners, and yearned to seclude myself wholly from the world.

A few months more and my ruin would have been complete. I should have become a mere God-fawning devotee. But this was not to be. Mr. Jameson called upon me one morning and said: "Come, parson, I say, you have dropped us. Won't you call over to-day and have a bit of lunch?"

I declined. "Ah," said he, "I know what it is. You don't like that infidel fellow; but he's gone away, and young Hopeful's gone with him. They had one day at the pheasants, that's all."

"What," said I, "Mr. Fitzclarence gone away! but, I thought ---"

"Ah, yes, you thought, and so did a good many more. But I'd never let my girl marry a damned infidel."

"Oh, please, Mr. Jameson, do not swear," said I.

"I am not swearing," said he. "I use the word ecclesiastically, just as you might in the pulpit; though it's enough to make anybody swear the way those fellows go on with their cursed atheism. Well, they'll find out their mistake some day. But you'll come, won't you? Let me tell Margaret you will."

I looked up at him. His little keen eyes were diving into mine. "My daughter," he said with emphasis, "will be very glad to see you; very glad to see you."

"I will come," said I. He went out, and I heard him chuckle as he went down stairs. There was little attempt at disguise in his words or his manner. Margaret was mine! At this thought the blood rushed from my heart and flamed on my pale ascetic face. I tore the hair shirt from my bosom. I dashed Thomas a Kempis on the flames. I knelt down and prayed. I jumped up and danced, exclaiming, "She is mine! She refused him for me! "As rivers, released from their bonds of ice, pour down swift torrents from the hills, so the natural feelings of my heart, so long held down by frozen piety, coursed swiftly through my frame and made me drunk with excitement and joy. However, I calmed down, and felt rather foolish as I took the 'Imitation,' all charred and smoking, from the fire. I remembered that, after all, nothing was certain as yet; and soon I became just as anxious as I had before been confident. It wanted an hour of the time, but I could not wait any longer and went up to the house. She was in the drawing-room alone. As I entered at the door I felt a strange faintness and fluttering within me. In a few minutes my fate would be decided. Her look reassured me, and the gentle pressure of her hand and the tone in which she said, "It is so long since I have seen you."

We conversed for some time. I feared to speak, and yet for my own peace of mind I knew it must be done that day, and that hour. At last I said with a bantering air, "Margaret, I hear that you have had an offer of marriage?" "Yes," she said with a smile, "and poor papa was so disappointed." "And why did you not marry him?" I asked. She blushed and turned her head aside. I took her hand in mine. "Tell me, dear Margaret," I whispered. She looked up, and told me with her eyes. Then I clasped her in my arms; I strained her to my breast; I pressed my lips to hers and fondled her long golden hair. Oh, raptures of a first and innocent love, who can describe them? What power have words to express the deep inner feelings of the heart? I can only tell you I was happy -- that is all.

Letter VI

My father approved of the match and promised me a liberal allowance. The marriage was to take place in a twelvemonth. Captain Jameson did not deign to give us his blessing, being deeply offended with his sister for her refusal of Fitzclarence, for he preferred a brother-in-law with a handle to his name. His father's sentiments were not dissimilar, but he took the trouble to conceal them, having come to the conclusion that it would be foolish to refuse the heir to a large fortune because the heir to a still larger fortune and a peerage had been lost. So he was always loud and boisterous with me to show his cordiality. One day, at luncheon, he winked and said, "The bishop has a good opinion of you, Master Ned, a deuced good opinion of you."

I said I was glad to hear that I was so honored. No prelate was more loved in his diocese or more distinguished on the bench.

"Cannot you remember what he said, dear papa? asked Margaret, blushing with pleasure.

"I should rather think I could," he replied. "'Mr. Jameson,' said my Lord, 'Mr. Jameson,' said he, 'our young friend did well at college, damned well, and, by Jove, he'll do the right thing by your parish.'"

"Oh, papa!" exclaimed Margaret, "he could not have said that."

"Well, my dear," said her father, somewhat confused, "I don't mean to say he used those very words, but that was the general sense."

A servant came in with the letters of the afternoon post. Mr. Jameson's face fell as he examined the blue envelopes. "Ah!" muttered he, "I know what these are well enough. Reform -- reform is all the cry. I wish they could pass a bill for reforming extravagant sons."

"You know, dearest Edward," said Margaret, as we walked to the rectory together, "Robert spends a great deal of money -- papa would send him into the Guards -- and we have heard that he gambles at Crockford's. And he is so dreadfully conceited; he would not even look at Miss Brown when she was here. His wife, he says, must have three things -- birth, beauty, and money (or blunt, as he calls it). Now, as he has neither of the three to offer in return ---"

"But your father is rich?" said I. Margaret shook her head. "Papa," she said, "was in such a hurry to be a country gentleman that he gave up his business too soon, and though he is an excellent manager, and spends very little money on himself, he does not seem able to refuse Robert anything. The rents of the farms on the estate just cover our expenses down here, and I fear that papa's other money is going very fast. When he asked me to marry Fitzclarence, he said, 'My girl, you must not marry a poor man, for if at any future time you should want money, God only knows whether I should be able to assist you.'"

Dear Margaret, thought I, as I went up to my library, when we are married you will not need any money from your father. None of these sordid cares shall trouble your life.

I sat down in my arm-chair and abandoned myself to reverie. I had now found in love -- chaste, secure, requited love -- that calm of mind which I had sought in monkish devotion. No passion disturbed me; no disquietude alarmed me; no sad experience made me doubt my future happiness. I knew not the dangers of life. I pictured myself the rector of a large parish, and Margaret the queen of our world, distributing her bounty to the poor, alleviating their miserable lot. Often we had planned and plotted together how we could do good. And I saw her seated by my side after the labors of the day, and rosy-cheeked children clambered on my knees. And the love of my children unborn filled my heart, and I revelled in anticipated joys.

While thus I was wrapped in sweet meditation, I observed lying on the table before me a large brown-paper parcel which must have come down by the London coach that afternoon. I found that it contained Lyell's 'Principles of Geology,' and some other works upon that science. I supposed these were sent by the disappointed rival, and with no good intent; and as I turned over the books a letter dropped out. It was without an envelope, and as follows: --

DEAR YOUTH, -- Here are the books you ask for, viz. the grand work of Lyell, and the orthodox attempts at a reply. Why on earth do you want them? Are you going to study these problems? If so, it would be better than some of your other occupations. I hear that you go very often to the top of St. James' Street. Ah, beware!

"Impossible to accept your invitation. I only go to Reform dinners nowadays. I talk, think, dream of nothing else. All is going on well: we are certain to succeed.

"Lastly, oblige me, once for all, by not writing as you do about a certain young lady. I admire her, I esteem her, I love her; it was my fault that she could not love me; but it eases my vanity to know that there was a prior attachment. -- FITZ."

It was now evident that the books came from the captain, who had mislaid the letter in the parcel. I thought I could best disappoint his benevolent intentions by reading them carefully through; in fact, I had intended to order from London the latest works upon geology, as I considered it my duty to study the enemy's arguments in order to be able to refute them. I began to read the 'Principles' at once, and was soon captivated by the beauty of the style, the modesty of the author, and the wondrous world he opened to my view. There was not an allusion to theology in the book, which I read all through like a novel, with no sensation but that of enjoyment. But when I remembered afterwards the duration of time and absence of catastrophe on which it insisted, I was seriously troubled, and I read it again, now well on my guard, and in a hostile attitude of mind. But I could discern no flaw in the reasoning, and could only venture to hope that the facts were not to be relied on. Having spent a week upon the 'Principles,' taking many notes, and honestly forcing my brain to receive ideas it did not like (which I found at first very difficult), I took from the parcel an orthodox work which was then of much repute in the religious world. This book settled the matter in my mind: it was not unfairly written, admitted the facts which science had established, and tried to reconcile them with the Mosaic account of the creation. It was most ingenious -- a perfect specimen of special pleading -- but nevertheless could only deceive those who wished to be deceived: no doubt the author was among that number; I do not question his sincerity. There was also a pamphlet in the parcel, written by a clergyman, who allowed that the first chapter of Genesis could not be accepted as literal truth, but argued that it was of no consequence, as the Bible was intended to teach us religion, not to teach us geology. For me it was enough that there was one mistake in the Bible; that proved it could not have been written by God.

The next six months I devoted to biblical studies. I read the Bible all through, with no commentary but that of common sense, and the scales fell from my eyes. Never did I more keenly appreciate the beauties of the book as a literary production; but I found proofs in every page that it was written by men, and by men immersed in superstition. I passed many unhappy hours, for old beliefs are not torn up without a pang; but my chief feeling was one of burning shame, that I could ever have credited the many profane and ridiculous fables contained in the Bible. It seemed to me an awful blasphemy to assert that the great God of heaven clothed himself in the body of a man, and I prayed him to forgive me for having believed it. My conception of the Creator was ennobled, my devotion was increased, a pure and sublime Theism reconciled me to the loss of some illusions. Thus I did not suffer as much as might have been anticipated.

But I was a clergyman. I was the priest of what I now believed to be a pagan religion, and received money to teach what I knew to be false. I felt it incumbent upon me at once to leave the Church and to enter some other profession. Mr. Watson, the rector of the neighboring parish, frequently visited Stilbroke Court; his wife was a friend of Margaret's, and he, I knew, was a man of temperate views, who would patiently hear what I had to say and advise me how to carry out my resolution.

Letter VII

MR. WATSON had a large family, as was shown by the number of small caps and coats hanging up in the hall. I was ushered into an apartment which, like a desert island, bore no traces of human habitation. Everything remained as it had come from the hands of the upholsterer. The atmosphere was damp and cold, as if no fire had ever been lighted in the polished grate. The chairs and sofas looked as if they were in a shop-window; the gorgeous books on the central table had perhaps never been opened, certainly never been read. All feudal castles contained a dungeon in which malefactors were cast; and in many old-fashioned houses a desert chamber is set apart for the reception of guests. I did not like to sit down for fear I should crease something, and did not dare to walk about for fear of soiling the carpet; as it was, I could see a bootmark which the lady of the house would view with no less horror than Robinson Crusoe the footprint in the sand. I therefore remained in a most uncomfortable attitude, while the door was constantly opened by small children who peeped in and made faces at me, and then shut it with a bang and a shout of exultation. At last the rustle of a silk dress announced that the change of toilet was completed, and Mrs. Watson came into the room, round which she glanced with an air of evident pride. She begged me to sit down; but I said I was anxious to see Mr. Watson at once, so she led the way into his study, having made me promise that I would take a dish of tea before I went home. Soon afterwards I heard, not without satisfaction, the sound of manual punishment, accompanied by shouts which were not of a gleeful character.

Mr. Watson was seated in his study, reading Paley's 'Natural Theology' and smoking a long clay pipe. When I had explained the object of my visit, he did not seem surprised, but asked me a number of questions which showed that he was well acquainted with works of science and philosophy. Having received my replies, he reflected a little, and then said, laying down his pipe, "I see you have thought out this matter for yourself and have not taken it at second-hand. It would be useless for me to try and move you out of your position. I shall therefore place myself in that position; I shall admit (for argument's sake, you understand) that you have found out the truth. We shall, therefore, discuss what is best for you to do."

"Surely," I said, "there can be no doubt about that. I ought to act according to the truth."

"You think it is your duty to withdraw from the Church?"

"Most certainly," I answered, "and I have come here to ask your advice as to how to proceed in this difficult matter. I do not wish to cause scandal or to give unnecessary pain. But remaining in the Church is out of the question altogether."

"Gently, gently," he replied; "allow me to ask you what are your circumstances? What have you to live upon when you are married?"

"I inherit a sum of money from my mother, the interest of which is 150 pounds a year. That is my own. Besides that, my father has promised me a liberal allowance, and then there is the money I shall make."

"Perhaps your father may refuse to give you an allowance when he finds that you have left the Church. Is that quite impossible?"

A little reflection forced me to admit that it was not quite impossible; but, on the contrary, rather probable than otherwise. "However," said I, "that matters little; I am young, I will enter another profession, I will make my way in the world."

"You are not then aware," said Mr. Watson, that clergymen are forbidden by law to enter any other profession?" [This law has since been repealed.]

"Then," said I, nothing daunted, "I will get work from publishers and editors. I shall easily get on."

"Excuse me," he replied; "I have lived some years in London and have written for the press. Hundreds of indigent clergymen, many of whom are fine scholars, seek in vain for employment of that kind. The supply far exceeds the demand. No; look at the future fairly in the face and don't stir up a vague mist of hopes and illusions. If you leave the Church you cannot marry Margaret."

I was stupefied. Strange to say, I had never thought of this.

Mr. Watson did not interrupt my meditations, but quietly filled another pipe and began to smoke again. I said, "What do you advise?"

"I think," said he in a kind voice, "that I can show you are not bound by the moral law to give up the Church."

"Ah, sir," said I, "duty speaks to me clearly enough, though I have not, I feel it, the strength to obey its commands. I cannot part from Margaret. But I know that I ought."

"All moralists are agreed," he replied, "that the welfare of mankind is the test of the Right. The virtues so called are virtues because they contribute to human happiness. If they become injurious they cease to be virtues. Now life is so constituted that no positive dogma, no undeviating rule can be laid down for the guidance of conduct. In a broad sense, we may say it is for the welfare of mankind that everyone should speak the truth, but there are many exceptions to the rule. No one would hesitate to tell a lie in order to save the life of an innocent man. Here, as often happens, there is a choice between two evils, and the lesser evil is selected. It is wrong to tell a lie, but it is more wrong to participate in murder. Or, if you please, we may put it another way. Here is a choice between two virtues. It is good to tell the truth, but far better to save an innocent life from destruction, while the struggle it costs the good man to lie adds to the nobleness of the deed.

"Having thus proved, as, I think you will allow, that there can be a case in which falsehood is a virtue, I will take a case which, from what I know of the clergy, happens, I imagine, very often. A parson with a wife and family of children entirely dependent upon him ceases to believe in the doctrines of the Anglican Church. His first impulse is to obey the voice of his conscience, and to leave the Church, but a little reflection warns him that if he did so his wife and children would starve. He chooses the lesser of two evils. He becomes, if you will, a hypocrite" -- (here the pipe fell and broke into splinters on the hearth) --" that he may not violate the sacred duties of the husband and the father.

"And now, my dear Edward (if you will allow me so to call you), which, in your case, is the greater evil, and which is the less? If you were a man living alone and bound by no ties to another human heart; if your leaving the Church would only involve loss of money and social position, I would say, Be honest, be free! live on bread and water, work with your hands, break stones upon the road, rather than be untrue. But you are not alone; a life is entwined round yours like the ivy round that larch over there on the lawn. Margaret loves you. And consider how much harm you will do to others if you proclaim yourself an infidel; consider how much good you may do if you remain in the Church. You need never preach a doctrinal sermon; in the New Testament you will find maxims of the purest morality and precepts of the tenderest love. Let these be your texts. What does it matter, after all, if your parishioners believe in some fabulous legends of the East and some Greek definitions of the Undefinable? These are only intellectual errors. You are not surely like those theologians who maintain that an incorrect theory of the Universe involves eternal perdition. You believe in a life of future rewards and punishments, and it is in your power, as a clergyman, to convert men and women from a life of brutality and vice. Outside the Church you could do little; but, clothed with its authority, how much sin you might destroy, how much misery you might alleviate! Let this be your atonement, and it will not be refused -- it will not be refused."

The good man's eyes were filled with tears, and he said as he pressed my hand: "Let us not speak of this again unless it is necessary for you. It is a painful subject for me."

We are easily won over by arguments to that which we secretly wish. That same evening I wrote to inform Mr. Watson that I had determined to take his advice, and, as he desired, would not allude to the matter again, I read no theological books, increased my devotional exercises, and spent the greater part of the day with the sick and the poor. Practicing the strictest economy, I was able to give away in charity all the money I received from the Church. Thus I quieted my conscience for a time -- but only for a time. It was not with me a question of the moral law and of the duty of man to man. I was deeply, fervidly religious; and when I knelt down by my bedside at night to confess myself to God, when I reviewed my conduct of the day, I could not believe that it was pleasing in his sight. I felt myself a traitor to him -- a coward, who paid outward allegiance to a false God and worshipped the true God in secret as if it were a sin. I felt that I was doing wrong. My conscience spoke in no uncertain voice. I could only sigh and weep, and pray God to have mercy on my weakness and forgive Me.

But I knew my own guilt in which I persevered, and I knew that I did not deserve to be forgiven. And in time there came upon me in these nightly prayers -- often prolonged till the dawn -- a conviction that God had turned his face away. For when I offered up my supplications, no response came back to my heart; that wondrous feeling of relief and consolation, the reflex action of the soul which rewards those who pray with intensity and faith, ceased to exist for me, and I rose from my knees unrefreshed. Yet when I thought of proclaiming the truth, of parting for ever from my love, I cried, "It is impossible!"

Now I began to suffer the most horrible torments. As I lay in bed unable to sleep, I saw lights dancing in the room and shadows passing to and fro; I heard groans and sobs, mingled with bursts of smothered laughter. One night I beheld my mother and Margaret in heaven, whilst I was borne past them by demons, and a voice cried aloud, "They believed in the false, but they were sincere. To you the truth was revealed and you hid it in your heart."

The Sunday I dreaded as a day of doom. The tolling of the bell seemed to summon me to the tortures of the rack. Often, when I was reading the lessons, I felt an almost uncontrollable impulse to throw down the Book and proclaim it a lie. Often, as I was preaching, voices whispered in my ear all kinds of blasphemous things, and sometimes I thought that I had repeated them, and, stopping short, would question the faces of the congregation to see if it were so. Ah, terrible days! even now it would give me pain to enter that church. I see it before me as if it were only yesterday -- the white-washed walls, with texts in many-colored letters -- the plain, open pews, and the people ranged in long rows -- the window of crimson glass, and the sun-rays lying like blood streaks on the floor.

Margaret saw that I was ill and begged me to go to the seaside. She thought I had overworked myself among the poor; and, indeed, my labors were prodigious -- but they had been a kind of relief. I did not take her advice, for I felt that I must make an end. Mr. Watson's arguments might be perfectly just, but in every great crisis of the mind it is feeling, not reason, that decides. Convinced that if I continued my life of falsehood and silence I should forfeit my eternal happiness, I resolved to seek security -- even at the cost of Margaret. Again and again I sought her to tell the sad news, but when I came within the charm of her presence, I felt as if I could suffer anything, even the torments of the damned, rather than relinquish her love. Then, again, when I returned to my house, haunted by demons, I cursed my cowardice and swore that next time should be the last. But my confession was wrung from me by an accident.

One evening, Margaret and I strolled out after dinner to the wilderness. We went to the hyacinth dell; the flowers were as beautiful as ever; it was the same time of year. We stood on the spot where then we had met. I told her I thought at first she was an angel from my mother in heaven; and she said with a blush that she loved me from the first because I looked so pale and sad; pity made her take me to her heart. We spoke yet more of the past and revived tender memories; for a brief space I forgot the troubles that menaced our life.

We saw Margaret's maid tripping down the path which led from the village to the house. She held a letter in her hand, and said that as she was passing the post-office a gentleman's groom rode up and inquired the way to the rectory. When she found that he had a letter for me she took charge of it, thinking I would like to see it at once.

Margaret took the letter from her hand. "Oh, thank you, Jane," she said, "it is important indeed!" And she showed me the episcopal seal. Jane smiled and curtseyed and went on to the house.

I opened the letter, and we read it together. The bishop had heard of my labors, and was glad to say it was now in his power to give me a wider field. He offered me a parish in the county town with a salary of 800 pounds a year.

Margaret clapped her hands. "Oh," she said, "this is the high- road to fortune. You will be as great as you are good."

Then she stopped and looked at me in wonder.

"I cannot take it," I said; "I am an infidel."

She started back in horror, clasping her hands. She thought that I was mad.

"I have long concealed it from you," I said. "It is all over now. Dear Margaret, we must part -- for ever."

She turned ashy pale and trembled all over.

"O Thou Divine Ruler," I cried, "eternal Spirit of Truth, for thee I have wounded this heart that I love more than all that is on earth. Give her strength to bear this affliction."

She sank on my breast and flung her arms round my neck. "Edward," she said, as she raised her haggard face towards mine, "Edward, I cannot give you up. I am still your betrothed. I will be your wife for better for worse, rich or poor, sinner or saint -- what do I care? Without you I shall die."

"My child," I said, "the Almighty God has sent us here for a few short and unhappy years, not to do that which is pleasant, but that which is good, and to prepare for the life beyond the grave. You must not disobey your father; and he will never consent to our marriage. From this day I cease to be a clergyman."

"You do not love me," she cried.

"I do not love you, Margaret! Look at these sunken cheeks, these hollow eyes, these emaciated hands. Love and religion, love and honor have daily contended within me; see, have I not suffered?"

"And love has lost! love has lost!" she cried, and clung to me with her despairing arms. Not a tear dimmed her eyes, which were filled with and woe. "Edward," she whispered, "let us be silent; let us keep this dangerous secret for a time' Ah, I have a way. You are too ill to take a large parish. You are forced to travel for your health; but before you go we shall be married. Then we will live abroad for a long, long time; and then --"

"O God!" I cried in a loud voice, "preserve me!"

Her head drooped upon her bosom.

"Preserve us," I said, "from sin and hypocrisy."

She drew back and folded her trembling hands, pallid from violent emotion. "Command me," she said, "and I obey."

"Dear love," I said, "let us suffer on earth that we may be united hereafter, to part no more."

"Then, life, pass quickly," she said; "and come death, to make us meet again."

"As a perishable day," I said, "life will pass, and death will soon come to herald in the dawn."

I pressed her to my heart. The shades of evening descended, and the voices of the wilderness were hushed. The pale moon arose; the hours passed by. Twice, thrice, the great bell rang from the house; again and again we said farewell, again and again we flew back to each other's arms. At length we saw torches gleaming through the trees. One last kiss and she ran down the path to the house. I returned to the spot where first we had met, and gathered some flowers and put them in my breast.

Letter VIII

WHEN I returned home, I told the servants that particular business called me to London at once, and that I might perhaps not return for some little time. The whole night I was engaged in writing letters: to Margaret a long farewell; to Mr. Jamesod, a short note explaining my departure. I wrote to my father, gave my reasons for quitting the Church, and promised to write again as soon as I had a fixed address. I sent my cheque book to Mr. Watson, and begged him to pay the tradesmen, servants, &c., and to send my personal effects to an address which I would afterwards communicate. I also asked him to permit his curate to take my duty till someone should be sent by the bishop in my place. Having packed a small valise, which I carried in my hand, I walked down into the village a little before day break and posted the letters. Then I waited for the coach. The grey streaks of dawn were beginning to flushing into pink, the birds were twitter and to shake the dew from their plumage, laboring men were going to their work, when the horn sounded and the horses' hoofs rang sharply on the road. In a few minutes more I was borne swiftly away, looking back on a vanishing scene and lamenting the joys that were gone.

I took lodgings for a week at a market-town twenty miles from Stilbroke, on the London road. Thence I wrote two letters to the Bishop of T----; the first was a formal resignation of my living; in the other, which I marked "Private," I thanked him for his great kindness, and related at length the process of thought which had led to the change of my belief.

He wrote back the kindest letter possible, and told me how he himself, when at my age, had also passed through a period of skeptical gloom and had all but given up his profession. However, his doubts soon passed away and never returned to trouble him again. He advised me to travel on the Continent for a year, and before the twelvemonth was ended he had little doubt that I should have returned to my belief. In the meantime my interests should not suffer; he should consider my absence as sick leave; for he was sure that my brain was over-worked and that this attack of infidelity resulted from physical disease.

Return to my belief! As well might a river return to its source. My reply was respectfully, gratefully expressed; but it was conclusive.

This correspondence being ended, and Mr. Watson having sent me my clothes and books, nothing detained me in the town; and now I felt a yearning for home. I remembered what Margaret had said, that "our parents are our best friends." I remembered my father's kindness when last I was at Harborne, and the promptness with which he had consented to my marriage. I believed that, in spite of his cold exterior, he really loved me tenderly; and it was my duty to consult him before I began my new life. I thought of going to London; but if he wished me to stay with him I would obey.

As soon as I had made up my mind to go home, I felt too impatient to wait for a reply, and wrote word to say that I was coming by the next day's coach.

Harborne was not on the coaching road; and I alighted as usual at a wayside inn, about five miles from the village. The ostler took down my luggage and greeted me in the accents of the north, which sounded home-like to my ears. Presently I saw the dog-cart in the distance, and James drove up to the door. The horse had his water and hay, James had his beer, and I was just stepping up when he suddenly said, "Beg pardon, Master Eddard, I nearly forgot this here; "and he took a handkerchief out of his hat, and a letter out of the handkerchief. I read it with one foot still upon the step. It was from my father, who said that he could not receive in his house a hardened infidel; and that if I came in spite of his letter, he would turn me out in the presence of the servants.

I ordered the ostler to take out the luggage and carry it indoors. James became red in the face. "Bain't you coming home, sir?" said he. "No, James," said I; "my father and I have a quarrel it seems; but I daresay we shall make it up by and by." He touched his hat and slowly drove off. I inquired if a coach would again pass the house that day. They said that none would pass either way till the next morning at eight o'clock. I ordered a bed and some dinner, and then going up to my room locked the door.

I tried to eat something at dinner, for I knew that I had need of bodily strength; but it was impossible. The sight of food disgusted me. Feeling restless and excited, I went out of doors and walked quickly along a familiar path. A strong wind was blowing from the north; and across the moon sailed the clouds, tinged by its tawny halo and pierced by its cold white rays. Around me lay the moors like a wide black sea. On, on I walked, wailing aloud. At length I could give vent to my grief. Nobody could hear me. O miserable man! two sorrows had stricken me at once. I had lost my love; I had lost my home. I was an OUTCAST; alone and desolate. Then my blood boiled and my tears dried up; and I cursed my hard- hearted father who had put me to shame that day.

Lights twinkled in the distance. Harborne was before me. I skirted the village and climbed a steep hill lying on the left. The sky was now covered with clouds, and the wind was boisterous. A storm was coming up.

The church loomed before me mistily on the summit of the hill. I found that the gate was not locked, and entered the graveyard. Above the grass mounds and small stone slabs, a white obelisk rose; I fell on my knees before it, as before an altar, and prayed to God. I summoned the spirit of my mother from the past, and she to my memory vividly returned. Again I saw her face so loving and resigned; again I heard her sweet sad voice. And as I thought of the long years she had passed with a loveless man in a lonely house, and what she must have suffered, and how she had endured, I repented of my own poor rage and resolved that her life should be my example, and that never would I cherish an unkind thought against my father any more. For what pleasure had I left but that of being good?

The black night deepened, and still I remained kneeling by the tomb. But now the storm, which had long been gathering, burst forth; in a few minutes I was drenched to the skin, and the moist wind penetrated to my bones. I tried to shelter myself beneath the yew, but it creaked, and groaned, and swayed to and fro as if about to be torn from its roots. Then I crouched under the wall and fell into a stupefied sleep.

When I awoke, the storm had ceased, the sky had cleared, the moon, dull and red, was near the horizon. I knew that the dawn must be near, and that I must go back to the inn.

But my limbs were cramped, I could scarcely stir, and my whole body was racked with pain. I dragged myself along on my hands and knees, and this movement partly restored my circulation. But to walk five miles! It seemed hardly possible. Yet done it must be, somehow or another.

At that moment I heard the sound of wheels. A man driving a gig stopped at the churchyard gate, and, having fastened the horses' reins to the post, walked slowly to my mother's tomb.

He bared his head and stood with his arms folded on his breast, gazing intently on the grave. Then he said in a low voice, Ellen! and turned to go away. I cried out his name and staggered towards him. He bore me in his arms to the gate, put me beside him in the gig, and drove at full gallop to his house. Having given me some brandy, he called two men and made them rub me with flesh- gloves from head to foot. But the next day I was delirious with fever.

Letter IX

AN overworked brain, a troubled heart, days of incessant anxiety, and nights without sleep were the true elements of my illness, and exposure to the storm but its proximate cause. Sooner or later it must have come; and I was fortunate in being cast like a waif by the winds into the house of Dr. Chalmers. He restored me to health; but I was in bed some weeks, and my convalescence was slow, though not tedious. For many it is a happy time, that period which lies between sickness and health. It has its own delicate enjoyments, such as the singing of a bird, the scent of a flower, the prospect of the blue sky, the mere sensation of being in the bright open air. The brain soon becomes weary, but a calm and soothing sleep at once relieves its fatigue. The selfishness of suffering is past; gratitude and love, which too often cease with convalescence, then at least animate even the coldest dispositions.

I used to sit for hours in an easy-chair watching the doctor as he performed chemical experiments, or made microscopic observations. When I had regained my health, I began the study of physical science; and in six months had made considerable progress, not only in the literature, but also in the practice, if I may use the expression, of astronomy, chemistry, botany, geology, and comparative anatomy.

But could Dr. Chalmers teach me all this? Was he a universal genius? The fact is that his house was a College of the Sciences. Since I had left home he had taken to live with him, besides his medical assistant, three scientific men whom he called his Professors. They were an astronomer, a geologist, and a comparative anatomist -- all men of mature years who, having given up their lives to pure science, had found it difficult to live. Dr. Chalmers had plucked them out of poverty and had given them a home, only stipulating in return that they should work, and regularly publish the results of their researches. They were all delighted when I was presented to them as a pupil, and spared no pains to make me a proficient, each in turn privately assuring me that his science was the most important and the most interesting. I spent an hour or two with each of them every day.

The Anatomist inhabited a room built over the stables. On a large marble table usually lay some quaint-looking animal which he was dissecting; and round the room were arranged, in systematic order, the skeletons of the animal kingdom, culminating in a chimpanzee and a man, standing side by side, their arms affectionately interlocked. The Anatomist told me that his parents, who were poor, had sent him to Guy's Hospital. He had passed a good examination and had taken his diploma; but a visit to the Museum of the College of Surgeons sent him out of his senses; from that time he could think of nothing else but comparative anatomy; and Dr. Chalmers saved him from starvation.

The Geologist resided in a fine library, furnished with works on his science in English, German, and French, and colored maps and diagrams hung from the walls. He had a large cabinet filled with specimens of rocks, and of precious minerals in nests of cotton wool; and promised that when I had mastered these and read up the text-books he would give me lessons in field geology, and show me nature at work, and take me where I could study the "dip" of strata, and "faults," and other phenomena, which could be but imperfectly learnt from books. The Geologist had once been a laborer, and had taught himself to read and write. The finding of some fossils in a quarry "set him on to geology," which he studied after his day's work was done; and the rector of the parish, having a taste for the science, obtained him a situation in a small country museum. There he educated himself and continued his favorite pursuit; and there he was found by Dr. Chalmers, who offered him bed and board, and all his time to himself, and as much pocket-money as he might require.

The Astronomer had been an optician. He studied the sun and the moon and the stars from a tower at the end of the garden, with a small chamber at the top almost filled by an enormous telescope. The roof of the observatory was a dome in which was a fissure or window-like opening. The telescope being pointed towards that part of the sky which was to be the field of observation, a crank was turned, and the dome, which rested on cannon-balls in grooves, turned round till the window came opposite the telescope. On a table were papers covered with abstruse mathematical calculations.

The Professors met at dinner in the evening, and I found their conversation delightful and instructive. After dinner they went to the Common-room, as it was called, where they read the papers and the scientific periodicals. To these they contributed, but each Professor was also preparing a book, the labor of years, and the summary of a life's investigations. The Volcanoes of the Moon -- the Natural Arrangement of Fossils -- the Homologies of the Animal Kingdom, were the titles of these forthcoming works. Dr. Chalmers had already published a book on the chemistry of plants. He maintained that it was the duty of every student in science, history, and all other provinces of knowledge, to place on record in a permanent and accessible form the result of his research and experience. To amass knowledge, and to take it to the grave, was to be a miser of that which was to mankind more precious than gold. Such a person, however learned he might be, was utterly useless to his species; and the modesty which shrank from publication was in most cases an excessive vanity resembling disease.

He advised me to continue my general studies for some months more and then to select one science. He had little doubt that I would fix upon geology, in which case some knowledge of botany and comparative anatomy would be indispensable; and therefore my present work would not be thrown away.

I followed his advice and utilized my opportunities. But you must not think that Margaret was forgotten. If the virulence of my grief had abated, the dull aching pain yet remained. I told Dr. Chalmers how the ardor of the spiritual life had once enabled me to drive Margaret from my mind, and I asked him if he thought that devotion to science would have a similar effect.

"Why," said he, "do you wish to forget her? I should say, rather hallow and preserve her memory, place her image on the altar of your heart; believe that she is the witness and judge of your actions and your thoughts; then your life will be noble and pure. Love without hope, then your love will be to you as a religion, for none so nearly approaches the love that is divine."

These words, extravagant as they may seem, touched me deeply, for I knew that he had given up his life to a hopeless love which he had kept during long years chained down within his breast, as in a dungeon, and had fed it only with the bread of affliction and the water of tears.

However, I must proceed more quickly with my narrative. It was tacitly settled between the doctor and myself that I was always to stay at his house, and he also projected visits to London, geological excursions, and so forth. One day as I was passing through a shrubbery near the stable-yard (which overlooked the road), I heard James, who was in the dog-cart, talking with one of the doctor's grooms, and as they spoke very loud I soon discovered that my father was the subject of the conversation. He was like a mad dog, James said, when he heard that I was living with the doctor. He had taken the latter to task, James being present, and "had got as good as he gave, with sommat to spare; and he was that furious he'd ride over the moors and leap the stone walls rather than pass the doctor's house." This seemed to afford satisfaction to the servants, for my father was not universally beloved; but it was a sad blow for me. I felt that I must go. When I announced this resolution to my friend, he said I owed my father no duty since he had cast me off, I replied that still he was my father. He had brought me up, I had lived upon his bread, he had loved me so far as was in him to love, he had sacrificed to me many long hours, and had placed all his hopes in my gaining glory, or at least doing my duty in the Church. Those hopes I had shattered; the last half of his life I had embittered. It could not be helped; it was not my fault; but still so it was, and at least I ought not to cause him unnecessary pain. It would cost me much to go away, for I was very happy there; but my conscience left me no choice.

"Do you love your father?" inquired the doctor.

I answered without hesitation, "No."

"I," he said, "made a sacrifice for one whom I loved. But you can sacrifice yourself for one whom you do not love, and yet you say you are not a Christian."

"Because I have ceased to be a Christian," I replied, "that is to say, because I have ceased to believe in the Divinity of Christ, is that a reason for me to reject what is good in the teaching of a good man?"

Dr. Chalmers was much depressed by this determination; he loved me for myself, and not only for myself. Often I had observed his eyes fixed sadly and fondly on my face, in which he saw the features of one who was no more. However, in a few days something occurred which gave another channel to his thoughts.

He received a letter from my father, to the following effect: It was all over the country, that on the night of my arrival he (my father) had discovered in a secret drawer a packet of letters from Dr. Chalmers to my mother. Having read these letters, he showed them to me, and turned me out of doors; and I, of course, was adopted by the doctor. My father said that this mischievous tale would be kept alive so long as I remained where I was; he made no appeal to me, whom he looked upon as "lost," but if Dr. Chalmers cared for the reputation of a lady who could no longer defend herself, he would prove it by sending me away. He must see for himself that this abominable scandal had arisen wholly and solely from the fact of my being harbored in his house.

Dr. Chalmers at first declared that the story was a trick, but that I could not allow, for I knew that my father would never tell a lie. A few inquiries made through a trustworthy servant brought ample confirmation of the fact. It made a sad impression on the doctor's mind. "For a quarter of a century," he said, "I have lived with these people, and there is not one amongst them who has not received a personal kindness at my hands. She also was good to them all, and this is how they speak of us. Oh, poor human nature -- poor human nature!"

He resolved to leave Harborne and never to see it again. Having placed the establishment under the charge of his housekeeper till he could make some permanent arrangements for the Professors, he went with me up to London. He declared that he would travel and explore the wild countries of the world, and seek in savage life that gratitude of which civilized men merely possess a shadowy remnant -- the relic of primitive times. I may as well say at once that he was not very successful. At Mozambique he bought and set free a negro slave who stole his gold watch and decamped with a slave-hunting expedition into the interior. In Patagonia he rescued a wife from being half-murdered by her giant of a husband -- in return for which she assisted with a hearty good-will her lord and master to belabor him. Lastly, he took up his abode in Brazil with a tribe of Bush Indians, who, having begged from him all that he had in his possession, stripped him of his clothes and turned him out of their camp as an idle vagabond who knew nothing of hunting or fishing and was not able to pay for his keep.

Letter X

BEFORE Dr. Chalmers left England he saw me embarked in my new profession -- if such it can be called. He begged me to accept from him a small annuity, but I said my 150 pounds a year was almost sufficient for my wants, and the rest I ought to earn for myself. He then introduced me to his publishers, Jansen and Haines, in Paternoster Row. This firm, now extinct, was famous in its day for the publication of the classics; of original scientific works; of translations from the German; of lexicons, encyclopedias, annotated catalogues, and so forth. Now, my father had taught me German, on account of its value in "dogmatik," and the doctor had made me take it up again on account of its value in geology. French, and a little Italian, I had learnt from my mother. I had a general smattering of science, while the prima classes before my name in the University Calendar incontestably proved my classical learning and made a profound impression on the firm. Having first tested my capacity for work, they set me on their Paternoster Cyclopedia, which was rather out of date, to correct its errors and insert the latest additions to knowledge. As change of work is a species of repose, I was also employed to enlarge and improve a Greek lexicon which they had published for "the use of colleges and schools." I agreed to produce a stated quantity of "copy" per week, and they to pay me the sum of 3 pounds for the same. Thus I had now 300 pounds a year and was perfectly content. I took lodgings near the British Museum, in the reading-room of which my days were passed. It was not the magnificent hall I once took you to see -- the paradise of learned loungers and spectacled flirts -- but a dingy apartment frequented by none but genuine students.

At first I was obliged to work very hard and had not an hour to myself; but when I had hit upon a system, and learnt the art of reference, I was able to complete my appointed task at the Museum, and could study in the evening for my own pleasure and improvement. I must own that often I felt my existence lonely and monotonous. The days followed one another, and all, except Sundays, were the same. One evening, as I sat by my fire, I said to myself, "What a poor life is this, drudging from morning to night just to earn food, and lodgings, and clothes! You have no one to care for you, no one to converse with, no friend, not even an acquaintance. You say 'Good morning' to your landlady at the lodgings, and you make some remark about the weather to the man who takes charge of your umbrella at the Museum. You go once a week to Paternoster Row, hand your roll of manuscript across the counter, and receive three sovereigns in an envelope. Such are the social pleasures you enjoy; there is no place for you in the human family; years will pass, and your life will not change, and at length you will become an old man, and, unloved, unpitied, will go down with sorrow to the grave."

Then I felt sick at heart, and the tears rose to my eyes, and I thought of the happiness I had lost. "Oh! Margaret, dear Margaret!" I cried, "do you still remember? do you still lament? Do you weep for me as I weep for you? Does a vision haunt you sleeping and awake -- by night a dream, by day a memory?

"Past are the joys of love, the thirsty kisses, and the long embrace; past are the hours of chaste converse and tender confidence; past are the hopes that once were all assured. None but Margaret can be my wife, and she for me is dead and buried in the grave. I must go through life solitary and alone; no pretty children will clamber on my knee. Alone -- alone -- alone. O God, my Father, and my Friend, you have poured love into my heart, and my nature is affectionate. Must I be lonely and childless? Is that, indeed, my destiny? Then, I pray you, assist me to bear life with patience to the end."

At that moment the servant brought in a copy of Mrs. Carter's 'Epictetus' which I had ordered at a book-shop that day as I was coming home. I opened it at hazard and began to read; and soon, as if by a magic spell, my pains were charmed away, my mind was filled with serene and elevated thoughts. Ah, what a divine gift is that which, by scattering some ink drops on paper, can, after two thousand years, still give solace to hearts in sickness and adversity! It is said that the ancient Egyptians placed over their public library this inscription, The medicine of the soul; and in all such melancholy hours as that I have described, I used to take up a great writer of the past or present time, and in half an hour my troubles were forgotten. It was this antidote to sorrow, and also my discipline of daily work, which saved me from brooding on my woes. I do not think that I loved Margaret less than she loved me; but I certainly suffered less, as I was soon to learn.

One day I met Mr. Jameson in New Oxford Street. To my surprise his face brightened up when he saw me, and he said, "Ah, here you are! I've been looking for you everywhere."

"Looking for me, Mr. Jameson," I repeated.

"Well, no," said he, "not exactly that; but I've been in London some time (Stilbroke is let), and I've been always expecting to see you in the theater saloons, or larking about at the Finish, or some of those places."

"And pray, sir," I asked, "why should you expect to find me in such scenes of dissipation?"

"Why, ain't you an infidel?" he said. "And don't they always knock about town? But there, I didn't mean to offend you. Why, you're as red as a turkey-cock! Is there any place handy where we can have a quiet bit of chat?"

I took him to my lodgings, which were small but comfortable. "Well," said he, "this is a snug little crib; and the Governor ain't cut up rough after all?

I explained to him what my circumstances were, and said that, "Thank God, I had as much money as I wanted."

"Thank God!" said he. "Then you do believe there's a God, after all?

"Certainly, I do."

"Well, then, you believe in the Bible too?

"No," said I; "not all of it."

"My dear fellow," he said, "you contradict yourself; for how can you believe in God and not believe in God's Word? But, then, never mind -- that's not the point -- that's not the point."

He walked up and down the room, muttering according to his wont when excited or disturbed. "Three hundred a year isn't much -- but it's bread -- it's bread. Will your father disinherit you, Mr. Edward, do you think?"

"That, I should say, was certain," I replied.

He went on, walking backwards and forwards, saying, "Bad, sir, bad; but it must be done; there's no choice -- no choice."

I was much puzzled by this strange behavior, and the questions he asked, and his evident anxiety as he waited for my answers. Something rose within me, too vague to be called hope; a kind of expectation. Finally, Mr. Jameson put on his gloves and said, "I want to see you on particular business; will you call at ----'s Private Hotel in Half-Moon Street, at nine o'clock this evening."

I went there at nine o'clock, and was shown into a large, dimly-lighted drawing-room. A young woman came and advanced hastily towards me. It was Margaret's maid. "Please to sit down," said she, pointing to the sofa near which I was standing. "Jane," I said, "tell me ----" "Sit down, sir," said she. I sat down. "It is all right," she said with emphasis, "and Miss Margaret will be down directly." My head swam round and fell back on the pillow of the sofa. "So I thought," muttered the girl. "No, Jane," I said, "I have not fainted, but it was very near." "Bear up, sir," she said, "and be calm. Do not agitate my mistress; she is still very ill ----"

"What has happened?" I asked. "What has happened!" she said bitterly. "Why, what else could have happened! When you ran off like a thief in the night, Miss Margaret took ill; and since that day she has never laughed nor cried; and she never said a word, but just pined and pined away. And then the doctor and Mrs. Watson told her father that he must find you for her again or she would die. And he promised he would, and that made her hearten up a little. Oh! sir, be kind to her, for she's the best young lady in the world, and she's going to send me away because you can't afford her a maid; and my old mother's got only my wages to live on, or I'd serve her gladly for nothing. O dear!"

I put a sovereign into her hand and said, "There, Jane, give that to your mother, or buy something pretty for yourself; and you must not mind leaving your mistress, for you will get married yourself before very long, I dare say."

This vulgar panacea for the woes of the lower classes seldom fails of its effect; and Jane wiped her eyes, smiled, dropped me a curtsey, and saying, "I wish you all happiness, sir, and many of them," went out of the room.

I waited. The moments seemed hours, and she did not come. The lamp burned dimly and cast vague shadows on the ceiling overhead. The fire crackled in the grate; the furniture creaked; hasty footsteps passed along the street; Piccadilly murmured in the distance. Why did she not come? Presentiments assailed me. Her father had changed his mind; she had fallen ill. A misfortune had happened. I cast myself in a chair by the fire and resigned myself to melancholy thoughts. Then suddenly something quivered through me like a flame. I felt that she was standing by my side.

But was this my beautiful Margaret? Pale and hollow were her cheeks, and the dress hung loosely on her wasted form. She looked at me sadly with her sweet blue eyes. I drew her towards me and kissed her pale and trembling lips. I took her on my knees and laid her head upon my breast. Thus she remained -- sometimes uttering a sigh, sometimes nestling her head more closely to my bosom, as one who had been long weary and would sleep. Two hours glided by; the girl came in to take her to bed. I rose and said, "To-morrow." No other word passed between us in this meeting sad as a farewell.

Letter XI

AND this same sadness at first underlay our married life. I was perfectly content so far as my own lot was concerned; for me our marriage was all pure gain; I did my work as usual, and then, instead of the gloomy parlor of my bachelor days, I returned to a love-bright home. But it pained me to see that my wife was not happy; and yet how could it be otherwise? This was not the life of which we had spoken in the days of our betrothal; this lodging-house parlor and bedroom; this solitude and separation, I at the museum, she in utter loneliness. This it was which troubled her, not our poverty. She did not care for books, and was not a musician: she had no intellectual resources, and could not amuse herself when she was alone. As the wife of a curate she would have been in her proper sphere. She loved the sick and the poor, and all old people and children. She loved all who were helpless and in want, and spent much of her time by cottage bedsides, and by the arm-chairs of the aged placed out in the sun. But in London none of these kindly occupations came within her life; and she had no gossip with female acquaintances, none of those little gregarious pleasures which women think more of than men perhaps can understand. Then her health was shattered, and often I saw her looking mournfully on her thin neck and emaciated arms. Once only I alluded to her illness. She blushed, and hid her bead in my breast, and said that "only women knew how to love." Then she burst into tears. But save on this occasion I never saw her give way to sadness. I inferred rather than perceived the sorrow at her heart, for in my presence she was cheerful and vivacious. I gave up my book-hours, and read only now and then at odd moments: my evenings belonged to Margaret, and were spent in playing at chess, draughts, &c., or in conversation.

When you were born, my dear child, we found our lodgings rather small, for a baby takes up a good deal of room. But we determined not to increase our expenses, for we had no expectations from my father (who had not answered the letter in which I informed him of my marriage), nor from hers. The Guardsman continued his extravagance, till at last Mr. Jameson summoned up courage to declare that he should not have another farthing unless he sold out. Captain Jameson asked his father what a damned tradesman like him meant talking that way to an officer in Her Majesty's Guards, but finally the matter was compromised by his exchanging into a cavalry regiment.

I must now beg you to suppose that four years had elapsed since our marriage. I was engaged by Jansen and Haines in compiling notices of the "obscure names" in a Classical Dictionary, which was intended to supersede Lempriere, at that time alone in the field. Margaret was also engaged on a work of education. The arrival of Miss Ellen Mordaunt into our social circle was a most fortunate event: my dear wife had now all that she wished for; she was never lonely, being never alone; and was perfectly happy and contented. She often said if our life had few pleasures it had also few cares: and that if we were rich we should always be anxious and fretful about some trifle or another. And we had one very great pleasure. Every summer we spent a fortnight at Limmerleigh, on the East Coast. A lawyer from that little town, with his wife and daughter, once took the drawing-room floor in the house where we lodged, and we happened to make their acquaintance. They saw that Margaret was in delicate health, and suggested a trip to the seaside, and placed their house at our disposal for a fortnight, saying they should be glad to have someone there who would take care of the furniture, garden, &c. This same arrangement was repeated the next year and the next: the Irvines always went away for two or three weeks in the summer, and then we took our holiday.

One Sunday, Margaret came to me with her eyes cast down, and said, blushing a little, that she had a favor to ask: would I go to church with her that morning? I said that I would go to church with her as often as she pleased, and we always went together after that. Dear Margaret! she had secret hopes that I might be converted, and used to glance anxiously at me when the preacher alluded to infidelity. She was much perplexed by my long and fervent devotions in the morning and the evening; for she could not understand how one could worship God and yet not be a Christian. But we never discussed matters of religion.

Well, as I said, we had been four years married, and Margaret was happy. Then came the great calamity. Captain Jameson had soon obtained an evil reputation in his regiment. The passion for gambling of the last generation was already in its decline; and a man was looked upon with disfavor who carried dice in his pocket and held out a pack of cards like a pistol to everyone who called upon him at his quarters. Moreover, ugly stories got afloat; the colonel warned young cornets against him, and he withdrew from the Guards' club, not, it was said, without pressure from within. In fact, Captain Jameson was not only a thoroughly unscrupulous gambler, but also "tout" or agent to a famous West-End usurer, into whose toils he decayed many a young officer, receiving a commission on his ruin. This commission was so small, and the destruction of future prospects and happiness so great, that it was really like burning down a friend's house to roast an apple. But what did he care? He was one of those men who are quite insensible to the suffering they cause, and are never troubled with qualms of any kind either before or after an event. However, his career was suddenly brought to a close, and he involved others in his fall. A young subaltern was heavily in debt and wished to raise a large sum of money. His father was immensely rich, and Jameson having reported the case by letter to his principal, received his instructions. He told Lieutenant Smith (as I will call him) that he could have the 8000 pounds whenever he pleased; his note of hand would be sufficient; but, as it was pure speculation on the part of the people in London, it would have to be paid for accordingly. This, of course, the man of great expectations did not mind in the least, and asked Captain Jameson to go up to town and arrange the "transaction," giving him the note of hand and full authority to act on his behalf. Captain Jameson obtained the 8000 pounds and his commission, went to Crockford's to gamble with the latter, and lost it, and then lost the eight thousand pounds. Lieutenant Smith wisely wrote to his father, and confessed all, in consequence of which Captain Jameson shortly afterward wrote to his father and informed him that unless 8000 pounds were produced within a few days, the matter would go to the C.C.C. In other words, he would be charged with felony, arrested, tried, and no doubt transported for the same.

Mr. Jameson's late foreman, and the family lawyer, and myself held council together. It was found that Stilbroke had been sold; that Mr. Jameson no longer possessed eight thousand pounds, that the sale of his son's commission was not a sufficient addition, and that to make up that sum it would be necessary for me to contribute my stock of money in the funds. I did not hesitate for a moment; my wife's family was mine, and the sacrifice was made. A few days afterwards, the Jamesons, father and son, the foreman and I met together at the lawyer's in Lincoln's Inn Fields. It had been made a stipulation with the captain that he should emigrate, and measures had been taken to prevent him from evading this arrangement. The lawyer read out the accounts. "Then there is nothing left over?" said the foreman. "Only this twenty-pound note which will pay for Captain Jameson's passage to Australia and buy him a rope when he gets there," said the lawyer. "Or perhaps the colony will save him that expense."

Captain Jameson took the money and retired. Mr. Jameson looked from one to another with a bewildered air. "Did you say there was nothing left, Mr. Lawyer; nothing left of all that money I earned? I worked hard for it, gentlemen. I was up early and late. I never wasted an hour. I was honest in all my dealings. Yes, yes; poor Bob has spent it all." Then he looked round at us again. "How," said he, "am I to live?"

I was, of course, prepared with an answer to this question, and had taken a bedroom for him at home. But the foreman said, "Come, my dear, kind old master; come and live with me." Then he turned to me and said, "Excuse me, sir, for taking your place; but you have done enough." He rose and went out, and my poor father-in-law tottered after him, holding his hand. He died in a few months; and Captain Jameson was shot in a gambling-house in Sydney, soon after his arrival, for something equivalent to what is called "welching" on the Turf.

It would have been better, perhaps, to have kept our money and left him to his fate; and yet, I am sure, we acted on the right principle. For he might have reformed; he might have become an honest, hard-working man, and even acquired a fortune. In novels, the air of australia has a wonderfully restorative effect on the characters of emigrants; and sometimes, no doubt, it is so in real life. Margaret said that he had great natural ability, and he must have had some qualities to make him the friend of Fitzclarence. But the passion for play quickly depraves a man; what are the pleasures of society or culture to those who have sat knee-deep in cards, and played night and day without intermission? Gambling is the most dangerous of vices, because its excitements are incomparable, and are followed by no reaction; it ruins, but it does not satiate.

We now lived from hand to mouth, but I was not alarmed; and there seemed no reason for alarm. Thousands of married persons were in a position not less precarious; it was, in fact, the ordinary lot. I was earning 150 pounds a year, and knew I could get copying and translating to do, for such work had been offered to me by other readers at the Museum. And, in fact, before long I was fully employed. But the work was miserably paid and was often required in haste. My evenings were no longer devoted to Margaret. I had to write -- write -- write from morning to midnight, or even to the following dawn. Thus, by immense efforts, I was able to make two pounds a week. When job-work was slack I tried my hand at literary composition, and wrote about twenty essays on social and literary subjects, which I dropped into Editor's boxes; but none of them ever appeared in print, so I confined myself to the manual labor of the scribe. We were still fifty pounds short of our previous income, and Margaret had to practice the mean little arts of economy, the saving and hashing the scraps of one meal for another, and so forth. I hate extravagance and waste; but it seems to me that this kind of thrift is apt to make the mind sordid and money paramount. "My dear," said I to her one day, "there are two kinds of poverty. When we had 300 pounds a year, if we had taken a house, we should have found it difficult to make both ends meet. But you were content with these bachelor lodgings and money never troubled us. In one sense of the word we were poor; but, as a matter of fact, we lived easily on a small scale. Well, now we are poor; our regular expenses are too much for our income, and so we have to scrape and stint in little matters, and think of pennies at every hour of the day. We have lost 50 pounds a year, and ought to reduce our expenses by living in a more humble way. At first we may find it hard to give up those little comforts to which we have been long accustomed; but habit will soon make us happy without them, and there will be an end to all this petty trouble and anxiety."

Margaret had grown fond of our dingy rooms and was sorry to leave them. It was there we had spent our honeymoon, and there you were born. However, she assented at once, as she did to all that I proposed; but a misfortune postponed our departure, and then rendered it no longer a question of choice and free-will. Alas! I had said there were two kinds of poverty. We had soon to learn by terrible experience that there were other kinds, the horrors of which may not be, cannot be, fully described. A part only of the truth I shall unfold.

Letter XII

As I told you, I read and wrote all day, and the greater part of the night as well. My night-work was mostly copying, and I made the mistake of writing on white paper, which is very trying to the eyes; I was also employed for some time copying manuscripts in a private library, and this work taxed my eyesight severely. I found that when I woke up in the morning, my eyelids were glued together, and a young doctor, whose acquaintance I had made at the reading-room, observing them to be watery and bloodshot, advised me to give them rest for a month. But how could I pass a month without doing any work, unless we could pass it without eating any food? I hoped for the best and worked on as before; and the consequences may be imagined. The next time I caught cold it flew to my eyes, inflammation set in, and a few days afterwards I was sightless.

My employers were exceedingly kind. They sent me ten pounds on account and begged me not to be anxious. I always did my work honestly and well, and they would not lose me on any account. They would find a substitute while I was ill, and as soon as I had recovered my health, there was my place ready for me. Unluckily, I twice returned to my work too soon (money was so needful to us), and twice I relapsed. This caused the firm much inconvenience and threw my eyes into a bad state. The disease assumed a chronic form, and a great oculist whom I consulted, said that time, rest, country air, nourishing food, and attention to the general health were the only medicines he could recommend.

Margaret had a good deal of jewellery, chiefly presents from her father. This we were now forced to sell, and obtained what we thought a considerable sum. We felt quite confident, that before it was spent my health would be restored, and went to live near Hempstead Heath where we found board and lodging at a very reasonable rate. But my eyes became worse, and, returning to London, we took a bedroom near the hospital at Charing Cross, for which I had procured an out-patient's ticket. There my case received every attention; but, as the oculist had predicted, medicines did me no good. Our money being now nearly at an end, we migrated to the neighborhood of Islington, where we took a garret at four shillings a week. We spent little money, but none came in; and, slowly, slowly our store decreased, till at last it was finished altogether. Hitherto, my dearest wife had alleviated the sorrows of my blindness by reading to me from my favorite books, but now they had to go too. I got very little for them, but we lived on the money two weeks.

"Dear Edward," said my wife, "you must let me write to your father, or our poor little Elly will starve." I gave my consent, of course, and she wrote; but no answer was received. We made inquiries about Dr. Chalmers. He had gone on a canoe voyage up the Amazon and had not been heard of for a year.

On my left hand I wore a gold ring, which my mother had made me promise always to wear in memory of her; but I thought that our destitution released me from this promise to the dead. However, I would not sell it; I would only pawn it, and within a year's time I should surely be able to redeem it.

One evening at dusk I went out and walked backwards and forwards before several pawnbroker's shops; but they were all too public -- too near the crowded thoroughfare. At last I saw some way off, down a narrow side-street the three golden balls branching out from the wall of a house. This I thought was the place for me; so taking off my green shade, for fear of being conspicuous, and looking anxiously around me, though I only knew two or three persons in London, I slipped in at the door, which was invitingly ajar. I found inside three small doors, which opened into cells or private boxes with partitions on either side, so that those who stood before the counter could not see one another.

The shop-man was talking in a jocular manner to a woman in the box on my left; and having tied up her bundle of linen, put it on a shelf, pinned a ticket to it, and handed her the duplicate, he wished her good-day, and came to me. I handed him the ring, and he took it to the light, examined it carefully, and offered to advance me two pounds. I said that would do very well, as I only wanted the money for a few days. As I made this very foolish speech a tall thin young man in the box on my right stretched himself half over the counter and looked round into my box with a derisive expression on his face. The next evening I saw him talking to some girls before a public-house, with his white hat cocked on one side and a cigar in his mouth. There, thought I is a Captain Jameson of low degree, and perhaps he too has ruined his relations.

I learnt before long to go to the pawnbrokers without shame, and even to bargain with the shop-man. Little by little everything went -- our boxes, our clothes -- nearly all we had except what we wore. For the first time we were in debt; we owed a week's rent. The landlady came to us, and said "she saw we couldn't pay the rent, and she wouldn't demand it. But she'd got an old lodger come back who wanted our room, and so out we must go. There was his portmantle down-stairs, and him waiting in her parlor, We must foot it at once."

The little we had was soon made into a bundle, which I tied to a stick, as I had seen tramps do in the country. Your mother took you in her arms, and so we went out into the street.

It was the month of November. A fine drizzly rain filled the air, and covered the pavement with a layer of damp in which the gaslights were reflected. We walked eastward, keeping close to the houses on the right-hand side, for the street was thronged with men going home from the City. What a heartless crowd it seemed to us poor exiles of happiness, outcasts from humanity. There was scarcely a woman among them. They had pale resolute faces, and walked as fast as they were able, looking neither to the right nor to the left. Weary of being jolted and pushed, we sank under a doorway and watched them go by. An elderly man, poorly but neatly dressed, noticed us as he passed; he went on a few steps, paused, hesitated, then returned, put a penny in my hand, and went quickly away. We bought a roll, which we divided into three equal parts. It was the first time we had eaten that day.

The street grew empty, as it seemed, of a sudden, and we continued our journey. We made you walk a little now and then, and carried you by turns. Margaret insisted on this, though scarcely able to bear your weight. For a long time past she had been in failing health, and I knew she must be feeling very ill; but she said not a word in complaint. Sometimes she gently pressed my hand; sometimes I put my arm round her waist and gave her a kiss. Our love was greater than our misery.

We were now in the heart of the City, and it resembled a city of the dead. The streets that in day teemed with human beings were silent and deserted.

In the midst of these vast solitudes we felt like travellers lost in a wilderness of stone. We sat down and rested for a while. Then Margaret said, "Dear Edward, my courage faints. Will you pray with me?"

"No, Margaret," I answered, "I pray no more, God is hard-hearted."

"Edward! Edward!" she cried with a gesture of affright, "do not put such thoughts into my heart; they come there often, and I drive them away. Oh! my dear husband, make me good; help me to place my trust in God, and to love him, and to ---

Her words ended in sobs.

I embraced her and knelt on the cold stones. But I did it only of my love for her. I was sullen and rebellious. She knelt also, and prayed aloud with the sleeping child in her arms.

A policeman came up while thus we were engaged and told us to move on. I laughed a mocking laugh to myself. Yet my wife, was cheered by this hasty prayer and her eyes brightened up. When we had gone a little way she stopped and said, "Edward, it is useless to walk about like this; we can sleep in the workhouse, and that is better than being out of doors."

I had thought of this and feared to propose it, but it was no time for sentiment and pride. I saw a man coming towards us, and when he drew near it was plain that he belonged to the class who could give poor vagrants information and advice. He wore a fur cap on his head and a white comforter round his throat; he slouched along with his hands in the pockets of his corduroy trousers and was whistling a tune. I asked him if he could direct us to the nearest workhouse, where we might sleep. "Well," said he, "you won't get much sleep in them institutions. Why won't you go to a model lodging-house? It's only a penny a night, and every luxury of the season." I replied that we had not so much as a penny. "God strike me dead!" said he, catching up my hand, and feeling the tips of my fingers; "you're gentlefolk, too, by your hand". "We were," said I, "a long time ago." "I dare say now," said he in a coaxing voice, "as you were a clerk or something of that?" "Yes," said I, "not exactly a clerk, but doing the same kind of work." "And when your eyes went bad," he said, glancing at my green shade, "they gave you the sack?" I nodded. "And then you spouted all you'd got, except what's there in your bundle, and I don't think it's much, and you got behind hand with your rent, and they turned you out into the streets?"

I told him he had guessed right.

"Guessed I" said this man learned in misery, "it ain't guessing at all. Can't I see it before me just as plain as a play-bill on the wall? Now come along with me, and I'll give you a night's lodging and a bit of hot supper into the bargain. I'm flush, for I've just done a good bit of work. Don't trouble, sir; I'll carry the young'un."

"I suppose," said I, "that you are a skilled working-man."

Yes," he replied, "there ain't a skilleder man than me in my own line -- bar one. I began life as a policeman, but I saw the error of my ways, and left off making war on my fellow-creatures what never done me any harm."

I asked several other questions, and he returned answers which I did not always understand, and which seemed intended chiefly for his own amusement, as he chuckled to himself after he had made them. He took us beyond the Bank, into a part of London where I had never been before. I saw to my astonishment a great wide street lined on both sides of the way with innumerable trays or trucks of fruit, fish, and other edibles, each truck being lighted by a candle in a glass shade. The pavement was crowded with people, all of the lower class, and the bustle was extraordinary. Our companion told us that this was the Whitechapel Road, and seeing that Margaret and I were both very weak, he bought us a penny cup of coffee. This gave us new strength, and we were able to keep up with him, though he walked very quickly, glancing from side to side and sometimes looking back over his shoulder. He said that it was against his principles, as a respectable working man, to dawdle in the streets; then he had such a large acquaintance in the Force, he feared he might perhaps be detained if he met any of them.

"Lor' bless you," said he, "they wouldn't let me go. I might tell 'em I'd got particular business, or that my old mother was anxious if I stopped out late, or that I was taking home friends to supper -- they wouldn't listen to a word. They're so wary pressing in their invitations, are my old pals, they won't take no refusal, not at any price whatever." He now left the Whitechapel Road, and, turning to the right, plunged us into a perfect labyrinth of by-streets and alleys. Some of these streets were deserted like those in the City, and we passed two large buildings, each of which perfumed the air for a considerable distance; the first was a sugar bakery, the second a brewery, which last our guide sniffed with much satisfaction. One street we entered was devoted to festivity. Nearly every house was brilliantly lighted, and from half-open doors proceeded the sounds of harp and fiddle and thumping of feet; or laughter, clamor, and song. Women without any bonnets strolled to and fro, and half-drunken sailors rollicked merrily along. Not far from this street we came to another, in which the houses were all more or less dilapidated, and most of them seemed to be empty. The man told us we were "nearly there," and, giving a long shrill whistle, stopped to listen as if for a reply. Two whistles responded from the bottom of the street. He then pushed quickly on, passed under an arch into a small court, and, knocking at the door of a house within, called for a light. An old woman opened the door with a farthing dip in her hand, and the man having chucked her under the chin, and asked her if she felt pretty bobbish, led us up to a room on the second floor. It was a poor bare room enough, the walls blackened with dirt, the broken window-panes stuffed with rags; but it was a sweet refuge to us that night after our weary wanderings. Our host told us the old woman was his mother, and we mustn't mind her being cross, she being a real good sort all the same. He went out and talked with her some time. At first her voice sounded keen and shrill, but it softened down, and she came in with a mattress and blanket, which she laid on the floor, then served us some sausages, with potatoes backed in their skins.

After we had supped, our host came in and sat with us, smoking a short clay pipe. I was now able to study his appearance. On his right hand was a fresh red scar which he tried to keep covered with his left. It seemed like the bite of a dog. The expression of his face was not prepossessing. His look was kind, but it was askant, and there was something cunning in his smile. When he paid us little acts of attention, such as arranging the mattress, or making up the fire, it was done, so I thought, in an underhanded kind of way. However, I stopped myself in the midst of these reflections, which were not very grateful, and thanked him warmly for having saved us from the miseries of the street. He mumbled something about a workhouse being no place for her -- pointing at my wife with his thumb.

I observed a heap of tools in the Corner of the room, and made some remark about them. He at once became vivacious and talkative as he was in the street, and his eyes twinkled in a most singular manner as he spoke. "You see," said he, "I'm in the patent lock and key line. Now, here is a little inwention of my own." He showed me a leaden hammer capped with leather. "What d'ye think it's for? I'll tell you. Gentlemen often loses the keys of their patent safes, and then they send to the shop and ask for a man to open 'em. Of course they don't send the safe, 'cos it's full of gold and bank-notes. Well, it's no good trying to pick a patent lock; so the safe has to be opened by force with a wedge and a hammer. Now, I needn't tell you, gentlemen don't like a noise being made in their house like a blacksmith's shop; it wakes up the baby, sets the dogs barking, and alarms the neighborhood. So I inments this leather cap hammer, and it drives the wedge in without making any noise."

"I suppose you have taken out a patent?" said I.

"Well, no," said he, "I ain't done that -- not ex-act-ly. But it's been the means of putting money in my pocket all the same. There's Jem Black what works with me, he goes to the Hall of Science and cultiwates his mind; and he says to me, 'Thomas, that's a beautiful inwention; Thomas, I'm proud of you; Thomas, you're a benefactor of our specie.'"

He now left us to ourselves, taking the tools with him, and in the morning gave us a breakfast of tea, and bacon, and eggs. In the midst of the meal a man rushed into the room and whispered something in his ear. I heard the word "peached." Our host sprang up, wrung me by the hand, and hastened out followed by his friend. In the afternoon the old woman came in. She was crying. She said, "We should never see her son any more." I asked her why. She only shook her head and covered her face with her apron, and rocked herself to and fro. After a time she went out.

A sergeant of police came in with two constables and searched the room. I now began to understand, and asked if the man who lived there had been taken up. The sergeant looked at me with some surprise and said, "Yes; burglary with violence."

The old woman left the house, and no one disturbed us in our occupation of the room. We lived chiefly on dry bread, which I begged from servants and at bakers' shops. I never begged for money, at Margaret's earnest request. Thus we were kept from actual starvation; but my poor wife became weaker and weaker every day. Then came a hard frost. We had no fire, and when I felt the keen air streaming in at the window, I knew that it would kill her. She lay with her eyes fixed upon me, trembling and shivering, yet pressing you to her bosom, chafing your hands and bare feet, while you cried in a weak, plaintive voice, "Poor Elly! so hungry, so cold!

Oh, Edward," she said, "if I could only have some tea; I think it would save me."

I went first to a large coal-yard, and picked up the pieces which were lying in the street near the gate, and put them in a cloth I had brought with me for that purpose. A gentleman who was coming out of the yard stopped and said, "Are you so poor that you can't afford to buy coals this terrible weather?"

"I cannot even buy food," I answered; "and my wife is dying."

"You have a gentleman's voice," said he.

"I was once a clergyman."

"I have known many cases of this kind," he replied, "and excuse my saying so; the cause has been always the same -- drink."

"In my case," said I, "it was something you may think worse -- Infidelity. Then followed sickness from overwork, doubtless a judgment you would call it. These eyes failed me, and they fail me still, or I should be at work."

"Well," said he, "I dare say I can find you something to do which won't try your eyes. Meet me here to-morrow at the same hour, and in the meantime take this for immediate necessities." He gave me a five-pound note and stepped into a brougham, which was out of sight before I had recovered from my astonishment. It causes me a pang even now when I think of that broken appointment. Why it was broken he never could know, and must have supposed I was drinking the money. Perhaps (who can tell?) it may have set him against being charitable any more.

I went to a grocer's and changed the note. I almost feared he would say it was a bad one, for the luck seemed too great to be true. I bought some tea and some coals and wood, and borrowed a tea-pot and mug from the people in the house. Margaret seemed to be asleep. I would not wake her till the tea was quite ready; then I would put the mattress close down by the fire; and when she had finished her tea, I would go to the cook-shop and buy her some good strong soup.

Her eyes opened; I sat down beside her on the floor, and told her the good news. She smiled; then her face changed in a curious manner; she put up her lips to be kissed like a child before it goes to sleep, and expired.

I sat there without moving. The dusky shadows were falling on the floor when a hand was placed upon my shoulder. I looked round. It was a City Missionary whom I had often seen passing from house to house; but he had never been to my room before. "My brother," he said, "you are in affliction."

I started to my feet. "There has been murder done here," I cried.

"What," said he, turning pale, "do you suspect ----"

"God has murdered her," I said. "The God who made her, the God whom she loved and faithfully obeyed."

He looked softly into my furious eyes and said, Do you think, then, that she is dead? No, dear friend, she is but released from this poor tenement of clay, and now lives with God in paradise."

"And could not," I cried, "could not this benevolent God make her happy in another world without inflicting these horrible tortures upon her? Look at that body, once so beautiful, battered and beaten by its maker. And it is not only her body he has wounded. If her soul could be made visible, it would show the marks of many a cruel and savage blow."

"Oh, silence these angry thoughts," he said, "and be resigned to the will of God. For he is our sovereign and our Lord; it is he who has made us and not we ourselves; we are his people, and the sheep of his pasture. My friend, let me implore you to humble your heart and kneel with me before the throne."

"What," I cried, with anger redoubled, "pray to that monster, that demon, that fiend! Think you that I, like a grovelling hound, will lick the hand that strikes without mercy and without provocation? Think you I am as the base Oriental slave, who presses the bowstring to his lips and to his brow? Think you that I fear his malignant rage? Hear me, bloodthirsty tyrant of the skies, you have power, and can rack me with everlasting pains. But I curse you, I defy you ... murderer ... fiend ... "

The foam fell from my mouth on my hands. I saw the missionary running from the room. Then I swooned and fell senseless to the ground.

When I came to myself I was still alone. I went to the window and looked out. Snow was falling heavily, and already the roofs of the houses were white. I listened to the roar of the streets. I pondered on my misery; and I thought of the black river which I had once crossed on such a night. The bridge was lonely I remembered. Few people passed by, and their footsteps could be heard from afar. But again fierce wrath rose within me; and I cried with a loud voice, "God, you shall not conquer me; I will fight out my life to its natural end."

Then a tiny little hand was put into mine, and a little voice said in a pleading tone, "Papa, why do you talk so angry and loud? you will wake up mamma. And you never look at Elly to-day. Poor Elly! so hungry, so cold!"

Then I was stricken with shame and self-disgust. I had let my poor child starve whilst I was ranting idly at the clouds.

I took out a handful of coins. "O thou vile dross!" I cried, "thou canst not give true happiness, yet without thee is misery and death. See, Elly, here is some money to play with, and I will go out and buy you something nice."

Your eyes sparkled -- we all love money by instinct -- and you took the silver in your lap. I knelt down beside the inanimate body, and asked it in a whisper to forgive me, for I felt that with my foolish rage I had profaned the presence of the dead. Presently you ran to me with a frightened face and pushed the money into my hands.

A number of men and women were standing behind me, looking sadly on the corpse. Then they led me away to another room. Thieves and prostitutes did the last offices of love for the body of my poor Margaret.

Letter XIII

WHEN I awoke from sleep -- a sleep, as I thought, of many dreams -- I was in the room where Margaret had died. But her body was not there. The sun was shining brightly, the window was open, and the air that came in was balmy and warm. I sat up and looked out; there was no snow on the ground; flowers were blooming in a box on the sill, and a lark was singing in a cage fastened to the wall outside.

This I could not understand; besides, I was lying in a bed placed under the window. How had it come there? I glanced round the room. It was furnished. There was a plain deal table and several rush-bottomed chairs, and cups and saucers, dishes and plates in shelves, and a kitchen dresser; and signs of cooking in the grate. I lay back in bed and tried to collect my thoughts.

The door opened, and two young women came in.

"If you please," said I.

"Hark, Sal, he speaks!" said one of them. "Lord! I feel 'most afraid."

"Oh, you fool! said the other; and coming towards me she drew a chair up to the bedside. Well, sir?" she cried.

"Where is the -- Where is Margaret?" I asked.

"She was buried long ago," said the girl.

"Long ago! it was only last night that it happened. How can you talk to me like that?

"Hush, hush," she said, in a soft soothing voice; "listen to me while I tell you. That was three months gone by, and all that time you've been very ill. Then it was winter -- cold, snowy winter. Don't you remember? And now it is the spring. Feel the warm air coming in at the window; hear the lark singing, smell the sweet flowers, see the blue sky.,)

Then those were not dreams after all, those days and nights that had followed one another, those faces I had seen, those voices I had heard.

"Where is she buried?" I asked.

She held up her finger. "You must not speak of that or your illness will come back."

"Tell me then, who are you?" I said, "and who is that girl over there?"

"We belong to him as brought you here. She is my sister, and we live in this and in another room. But now you're well you shall have this one to yourself."

"I believe," said I, "that you have saved my life." Her eyes became full of tenderness. "Yes," she said, "I have saved your life." Then she put her hand in her pocket. "The parson gave me this for you as soon as you got well."

It was a New Testament. "But I cannot read," said I. "Try it," said she, smiling. I opened and read without difficulty; my sight was restored! One malady had destroyed the other. I uttered an exclamation of delight. At the same moment the other girl who had gone out of the room a few moments before, brought you in, very nicely dressed, and your golden hair carefully combed out. "Kiss your papa, Elly," said the girl named Sarah, "he knows you now." Then, as she turned to go, she said, "If you think you owe me anything, please do not fret yourself ill, and ask me no questions about myself or my sister."

In a few days I was able to walk about, and tried to obtain some employment. But my appearance did not recommend me, for I was in rags, and my toes protruded from my boots. However, I called upon a law-stationer who was attracted rather than repelled by my evident poverty. This worthy man, as his shopman afterwards informed me, employed by preference persons in a state of utter destitution, as he usually found them not only grateful for his kindness, but also willing to work on very moderate terms. Having inspected my calligraphy (I had learned to write clerk's hand), he feared it would not do, but just as I was going from the shop, called me back and offered to pay me so much a folio -- half the regulation price -- which I accepted gladly enough. I wrote to Jansen and Haines, and said that my eyesight being now perfectly restored, I hoped they would allow me to resume my connection with the firm. I gave the law-stationer's as an address, and the publishers replied by return of post, that they had made arrangements with another gentleman in respect to the Classical Dictionary, but as soon as they had an opportunity, they would gladly avail themselves of my valuable services, and would lose no time in communicating with me.

No one would tell me where Margaret was buried, for they feared it might cause a relapse if I went to her grave. And I never found it out, for we changed our name when we went to live at the thief's house. Margaret was buried under the name we had assumed, and I could not remember it after my illness. On the day of my recovery, I told Sarah that my name was Mordaunt, and this trifling circumstance shaped out my future destiny by giving a clue to those who were in search.

I will tell you a strange thing. My illness caused by the passion of grief had swallowed up and absorbed that grief to itself. I did not mourn for Margaret, and almost rejoiced that she was taken from a life so full of suffering and pain. Now, the object of my life was to save you from such trials as she had undergone. I would work hard, and restore you to that position in which your parents had been born.

The day after I received the letter from Jansen and Haines, as I was standing near the door of the house, three whistles sounded, or rather shrieked, in the street outside. At once there was great commotion in the court. Several men dashed into their houses, and then emerging through the skylights, ran nimbly over the roofs. Those who were not frightened were inquisitive, and crowded to the windows and doors. The cause of all this stir was a middle-aged man with a fresh-colored face and yellowish whiskers streaked with grey. As he came into the court an old man (who had probably retired from business) went up to him and said, "Is anybody wanted?

"No," said the other; "private inquiry." Then be glanced at my face, and gave me a letter addressed Edward Mordaunt, Esq. "That is for you, sir, I think," said he.

This letter was from my father's lawyer, who informed me that Mr. Mordaunt was travelling abroad when my wife's letter was written: he replied to it when he came back, and as we had changed our address, his reply was returned by the Dead Letter Post Office. Mr.

Mordaunt had then instructed him (the lawyer) to find out where I was, but all inquiries had failed, till at last a detective had heard of a person named Mordaunt living in the thieves' quarter, Whitechapel, and ascertained that the person in question was a gentleman by birth and answered to my description. Mr. Mordaunt, on receiving this information, was grieved, but not surprised to find that my infidel opinions had led me to adopt a career of crime, and that, having defied the laws of God, I should now set myself in opposition to the laws of man. In order to save a soul from perdition he was willing to adopt his grandchild, on the understanding that I made no attempt to see her again; and so long as I adhered to this condition be would pay me an annuity equal to that which I had squandered.

I said that I would consider the matter, and send a reply in a few days. I felt it was my duty to think of nothing else but your own welfare and happiness. I should endeavor to silence my affection for you since that affection would be a vice if it persuaded me to sacrifice your future. In my hands was your fate; what a terrible responsibility! If I could earn for myself a respectable position you would, I thought, have a happier childhood, and grow up a better woman than if educated by that austere old man. But was it in my power to escape from this kennel of crime? That morning the state of my eyes had given me cause for alarm, and in my weak state of health overwork might soon set them wrong again. Breathing a pestiferous air, living on insufficient food, it was not likely that I should regain my full strength, and without it I was doomed to remain in my prison- house. Before I went free I had debts to pay -- debts which would never be claimed and could never be forgotten. After much thought I came to this determination. The next morning I would call upon the publishers, and tell them how I was situated, and ask them for pity's sake to give me a helping hand, not in the way of charity, but of employment. If they refused, then you should go; and though I feared your life would not be a happy one, at least you would not be brought up in a den of thieves.

I obtained on hire a suit of black clothes, which, though threadbare and worm-eaten, were better than the rags I usually wore.

As I stooped down to kiss you before I left the house, I could not refrain from tears. "Oh, my beloved child," I said, "they will take you from me and I shall never see you again. They will tell you that I am a wicked man, and teach you to hate and despise me. My darling, it is hard to give you up; but I must -- I must -- if it is for your good."

The tears rolled down my cheeks, and you took out your little handkerchief and wiped them away. I put on my hat. Then you said you would go too, and without waiting for an answer put on your things and thrust your hand into mine. "And why," thought I, "should I not take her? It may be our last day together." So off we went, through alleys and by-ways, into the Whitechapel Road, and past the Bank towards St. Paul's. It was a bright sunny morning, and the streets, I thought, were even more crowded than usual. Many a hard-featured man of business turned back to look at the pretty child perched upon my arm, her blue eyes bright with excitement, her hair shining like gold in the sun. I entered the well-known shop in Paternoster Row, and said I wished to see Mr. Haines on particular business. The clerk gave a start of recognition, then coldly said he feared Mr. Haines was out, but would go and see. My heart sank. Perhaps I might not be able to obtain an interview.

At that moment I saw the Bishop of T--- at the other end of the shop, turning over the pages of a new book. I felt my lips quiver. You observed it, and said in a clear shrill voice, "Do not cry again, dear papa, do not cry again." The bishop looked up from his book, and then bending over the counter asked a question of the clerk. I heard the words, "poor scholar ... used to do work for the firm." The bishop came towards me with a face full of benevolence and compassion. When our eyes met he cried, "What! Do I see Mr. Mordaunt?"

"Yes, my lord," I replied, "I am that unfortunate man."

He took me by the hand, and, pressing it kindly in his, led me to the chair where he had been seated; but the clerk, with an obsequious bow, showed us into an office like an old-fashioned pew; a kind of box with wooden sides and a railing round the top; inside, a desk and two stools. I told the good bishop all that had happened since I left Stilbroke. He listened attentively to my narrative, and said, "Wait here a little while, and I will see Mr. Haines: I am sure he will give you something to do." Then, having paused for a moment, he said, "Understand, Mr. Mordaunt, I do not sympathies with your opinions; they are most hateful to me; but your distress ----" He put his hand to his heart, and said, "it has gone in here." He stooped down and kissed you, and hurried from the office. That was the last time we met, for in after-days he always avoided me, and I did not force myself upon him; but often I have gone to the House of Lords to have the pleasure of looking on the face of my dear benefactor.

In a quarter of an hour I was called up to Mr. Haines' room. He appeared rather confused, but I did not think him to blame for his answer to my last letter. A publisher's is a house of business, not a charitable institution. "Mr. Mordaunt," he said, his Lordship has just asked me to provide you with some literary work, and I am happy to say that it is in my power to do so. We have been commissioned by a client of ours, who is something of a connoisseur in the classics, to bring out an edition of Thucydides, with critical notes. He wishes it put into good hands, and the bishop assures us that you have the requisite scholarship; besides, we know that you took a first-class at Oxford, a fact which speaks for itself. The editor is to receive three hundred pounds, and here" (handing me a cheque) "is a hundred in advance. But we make this stipulation, that you go into the country for the full space of three months and take a complete rest, that your system may recover its tone. It is easy to see that you are still far from being well, and if you begin work too soon we shall have the old trouble over again. So we make this condition on behalf of the ---, of our client. At the end of three months we shall expect you to return and prepare the work for the following book-season. And now I wish you a pleasant holiday, and shall be glad to hear how you are getting on whenever you are able to write me a line."

It was, of course, easy enough to understand whence came this shower of gold; but I did not trouble the bishop with a letter of thanks. I thought that the best way of showing my gratitude was to follow his instructions, and to edit the work in such a manner as to give him satisfaction.

Having cashed the cheque, I went back with you to the court in Whitechapel. Sarah was seated by the fire in my room cooking our dinner. I told her I was going, and had come back with Ellen to wish her good-bye. At the same time I gave her some money to repay her for what she had spent during my illness, and also wrote down an address to which she could apply whenever she was in need of any more. She took the notes with an air of indifference and thrust them into the bosom of her dress.

"Sarah," said I, "you saved me from death, and now I can save you from something as bad. Will you come with me and take care of Elly, and be a good girl?"

Her eyes brightened for a moment. Then she turned to the fire. "No," said she, "I mustn't leave Jem; it's only me keeps him from the drink."

She would not speak another word or even shake hands; and when you kissed her she turned her head impatiently aside.

Ah! who can understand a woman's heart? Who could tell by that cold set face what feelings were surging in her bosom? I have not said much about this girl, for there was bad in her as well as good, as many a robbed, half-murdered sailor had discovered to his cost; and I knew that any attempt to reclaim her would probably fail. But I also knew she would never do you any harm; that I could judge of from the past.

I have not described her character in full; nor have I described in full the horrible life of that White-chapel court. But I have shown -- for it was my duty in justice and gratitude to show -- that even in that sink of iniquity, even amongst those degraded and ferocious beings there were hearts full of compassion and eager to soccer the distressed.

That same afternoon I bought from the clothes-man a suit of the most gentlemanly garments he possessed; they had rather a marine aspect, but that did not so much matter, as we were going to the seaside. I redeemed my mother's ring and some trifles that had belonged to Margaret, and bought back some of my books (dear old companions and friends) which had not been disposed of I also had you dressed out like a fine little lady, and started for Limmerleigh that same afternoon.

Thus ended the days of my adversity.

Letter XIV

MY first month at Limmerleigh was spent in a state of unalloyed delight. To see innocent faces, to breathe the fresh air, was pleasure enough for one who had been imprisoned so long in a den of crime, a dungeon of disease. My strength was rapidly restored, and new blood flowed through my veins, as sap in dry trees when the winter is past. But my brain having recovered its vigor, forced me to remember and reflect. I was in the midst of scenes hallowed and endeared by the memory of Margaret. I thought of all her virtues, her piety, and love. I had never known her to be angry or cold, and she bore the most terrible calamities with cheerfulness and courage. When I came home to our hideous garret in Whitechapel, I found the same affectionate welcome as in the days of our prosperity; and when I gave her the scraps of dry bread which I had begged, she took them joyfully and jestingly, as if it were a feast. She once said that she thought Jesus and his disciples must have lived like ourselves, because it was in the Lord's Prayer, "Give us this day our daily bread;" and this fancy invested for her with a halo of romance our miserable lives. Her trust in God seldom wavered, but seemed to be strengthened by affliction, and the more she suffered the more she loved. My nature was not so submissive, and though now the spirit of foolish and impotent wrath had passed away -- though now the old habit of devotion was knocking at the door of my heart -- though now I longed to worship God, it was necessary first I should be able to revere him. I considered that if he were omnipotent, the death of Margaret was a crime; but from this painful conclusion I took refuge in a theory I had seen somewhere suggested, that God was perfectly benevolent, and had made the world as well as he was able, but that his power was contracted and controlled by the evil nature of the material with which he had to deal. This gave me comfort for a time, but I soon saw through the fallacy. For since men have been upon the earth they have made it better; and therefore, before they came upon the earth, God could have made it better had he pleased. If not, man is more powerful than God, which is contrary to reason.

But the opposite theory brought me to an equally ludicrous dilemma. For no man, if endowed with miraculous power, his moral nature being left unchanged, would be guilty of making a world in which murder is as the mainspring to a watch. Therefore man is more good than God, which again is absurd.

I now began to suspect that our conception of God was entirely erroneous. For what is the definition of God? A Perfect Mind. And what is Mind? It is a product of the earth, a created thing, existing within the lower animals in a rudimentary condition, and in truth not less human than the body. Mind cannot create, it can only arrange and dispose, as Shelley remarked long ago. Even a perfect mind could not create a grain of sand. We suppose that

God is a mind, or has a mind, because mind is the highest species of force with which we are acquainted; and if we must define God, it is the best definition of which the human intellect is capable. But is it for man to define God? Is it probable that we who are but as animalcules crawling on a speck of matter floating in space -- an infinitesimal fraction of the Universe -- is it probable that we should be able to form from our minds a correct image of the Creator?

At this time I happened to read the well-known passage in Bacon's 'Advancement of Learning' -- " Certain it is that God worketh nothing in nature except by second causes"; and this set me thinking on all that I had read in scientific works about natural law governing physical phenomena; and thence I was taken on to the conclusion that all moral phenomena and events are also subject to fixed and invariable law; that God has no personal relations with the earth; and that his entity or being is higher than a perfect mind, and far beyond human comprehension. But perhaps some clue might be obtained to the intentions of God in regard to ourselves by a careful study of the natural laws which govern the earth, as these laws, which for brevity's sake I shall sometimes call Nature, may fairly be considered the expression of his Will.

My friends, the Irvines, had left Limmerleigh, and their villa was for sale. One day I entered the garden, where I had passed so many delightful hours. It was now quite neglected. The lawn was strewed with brown and yellow leaves; the shrubberies were ragged and wild; weeds covered the gravel paths and the well-known flower-beds, which once were splendid with color and delicious with perfume. Everything bore the impress of decay. I went to Margaret's favorite rose-bush; it was dead! Alas! thought I, the same cruel law pervades the whole animated kingdom. Trees and flowers, insects and birds, the fish of the sea, the beasts of the earth -- all must die, as men die, after a life of combat and pain.

Then I considered this fact from another point of view. Was it not strange that Man, who is God's "noblest work," should be subject to the same law as the lower animals, to the same law even as the flower? Was it not strange that Nature should treat the greatest men with the same unconcern as the meanest creatures of the soil, slaying wit a breath of pestilence a genius over his noble work, as she sweeps away with a breath of wind a spider spinning in its web? The injustice of this law, and its imperfection, troubled me exceedingly. After much thought I found the solution of the problem; but it was a sad discovery.

We are not sent upon the earth to pass through an ordeal, and to be rewarded or punished in another world, after death, according to our actions. We are sent upon the earth for the sake of the earth. In common with the atoms of water and air, we are part of the material with which the Creator, through secondary laws, carries out his scheme, whatever it may be. Those laws are evil and imperfect to us as they are to the insects and the flowers, but they were not arranged for our approval and convenience, and are no doubt perfect as regards the purpose for which they were designed.

This made me very sad. I reasoned with myself that it was but a theory; yet I felt it was the truth, and it forced itself upon me in spite of the aversion it provoked. I was humbled and mortified. So then we were merely as slaves, merely as lower animals, merely as potters' clay! And where now was the hope of a life beyond the grave? It is the best argument in favor of a future life that man deserves compensation for unmerited suffering; but if man is only raw material that hope falls to the ground. Then again the spirit of science spoke within me. "It is probable that in death the mind is decomposed (nothing is ever destroyed), and that its elements are recombined into other forms of mental life, so that though the individual intellect perishes, nothing is lost to the race. If this supposition be correct, great men bequeath not only their works but their minds to Humanity."

One soft June night I went out and sat on a cliff overhanging the seashore. The voices of the hay-reapers working by moonlight mingled with the sound of the waves breaking on the beach. On the west, dark pine woods lined the horizon; on the east lay the grey ocean; above was a cloudless sky, shining with innumerable stars, each Star a sun, the center and sovereign of a system. My head swam as, gazing upwards, I beheld worlds lying as thickly together as leaves in a forest -- at least so it seemed; we know that in reality vast distances divide them. Oh, prodigious universe! I sighed. And oh, poor, vain, ignorant man, that could believe all these were made for him. Low indeed is our true condition in this wondrous galaxy of worlds. We call ourselves God's "noblest work," but perhaps there are in those distant orbs, or rather in the planets by which they are attended, beings who would look upon us as we look upon the ants and the bees; to whom our highest efforts of mind would seem but as curious instincts or faint gleams of rudimentary intelligence.

At that moment a gun was fired from the sea; the reapers came running to the brink of the cliff; and a great ship passed, gliding through the waters against wind and tide, its chimney of flame casting sparks into the air. It was the first steamer I had seen, and I rejoiced at this triumph of Art over Nature. Ha! ha! thought I, if man is small in relation to the Universe, he is great in relation to the Earth. He abbreviates distance and time, and brings the nations together. He covers the wilderness with cities, and cornfields, and gardens. He modifies climate and dispels disease. In every generation he makes the world happier and better than it was before.

I sprang to my feet and walked quickly to and fro. My brain was in a whirl. I saw the light again, the blessed light of hope and joy. "If we," I exclaimed, "are fellow-slaves with the humblest creatures of the earth, and even with the elements, we are also fellow-workers with God, and assistants of his inscrutable designs. For it is plain that one part of the Divine Scheme is the progress of the earth from a lair of wild beasts and savages to a paradise of happiness and virtue, and that Man has been selected to represent the good, to extinguish the evil; to be the Ormuzd that shall conquer Ahriman; to master by the powers of his intellect those laws of which he is now the subject and the slave."

And I believed that when Man fully understood and realized his mission, a new religion would animate his life. It would be a religious duty to battle with the evil in Nature and to labor for the glory of the planet, since for that purpose men were placed by God upon the earth. The intellect would be carefully trained; idleness and ignorance would be stigmatized as sins. The social affections would be developed to the fullest extent, and all men would abandon the hopes of personal immortality as a selfish craving at variance with the general welfare of the race. Having cast aside these personal desires, they would labor for posterity, and look forward with chivalrous delight to the bliss that others would enjoy.

Then I cast aside all thought for the future fate of my own soul. To labor and love without hope of requital or reward, what religion could be more pure and more sublime? Hitherto I had looked on the Earth as a strange country, and life as the journey of a traveller. But now the Earth became my fatherland, and all mankind my fellow-countrymen. I kissed the grass and flowers growing on the brink of the cliff; I sang to the waters, and the winds, and the beasts, and the birds, saying, "Together we accomplish the work of the Creator." And then -- smile at me Ellen if you will -- I felt a rapture of love for the whole human race. I resolved to preach the New Gospel far and wide, and proclaim the glorious mission of mankind.

This dream of prophecy did not last beyond the night. However, I had discovered a religion for myself; never since have I been distressed by the problems of existence; and I then laid down a rule of life to which I have always rigidly adhered.

My time at Limmerleigh being now at an end, I returned to London and worked at the Thucydides, which was received with much favor at both Universities. Henceforth I was a known man, and Mr. Haines, who was alone in the firm, and advanced in years, offered me a situation, with a fair prospect of becoming junior partner. Then Dr. Chalmers returned from the uttermost ends of the earth, took up his abode in town, and made me live with him. He published his notes on the Flora of the countries he had visited, and was made a Fellow of the Royal Society. He gave Sunday evening receptions, at which I had the pleasure of meeting nearly all the great men of science, and many distinguished authors and artists. All urged him to prepare his Narrative for publication; but he had begun to travel too late in life; the book was beyond his strength; and the dear noble-hearted man died in my arms only three years after his return.

Shortly afterwards my father also died. He left the bulk of his fortune to various Christian missions for the conversion of India, as some compensation to the natives of that country for the exactions and oppressions of his father, the Nabob, when Resident at the court of Goruckpore. My name was not mentioned in the will; but the Hollywood estate was entailed, and therefore came into my hands. Had I known this, Margaret's life would have been saved; but I did not even know that there was such an estate in existence. I was informed by James, whom I now took into my service (or rather I gave him a pension), that my father's health, in spite of his iron constitution, had quite broken down of late years. Something seemed to be preying on his mind, and ten years before his death he left Harborne altogether. I believe that he loved me in his heart, and suffered like another Brutus. But what else could he have done? He acted rightly according to his barbarous Calvinistic creed. In his eyes I was a servant of Satan; and he refused me admission to his house, as he believed that God would refuse me admission to heaven when I died. Such is Faith! It is not only opposed to Reason, but to Charity; and with an unnatural piety can tear the fibers of a father's heart and leave him wounded to languish and to die. It was the perfection of his belief that led to so much misery.

If I were a young man endowed with literary powers, and about to begin my career, I should adopt as the work of my life the Diffusion of Doubt; for doubt dissipates superstition and softens the rancor of religious life. Without doubt there can be no tolerance, and the history of tolerance is the history of doubt. The skepticism spread by Voltaire humanized the dogmas of the Roman Church; and we ourselves are passing through a silent, gradual, but momentous doubting revolution. What is it that has made the clergymen of all denominations in these later days so temperate in their views, so considerate for the opinions of others? It is Doubt arising from discoveries in science, and from numberless works in which religious topics have been treated with freedom of spirit. Certainly there has been a wonderful change within the last twenty years. When I lived with Dr. Chalmers in London, men spoke of these matters under their breath, but now ladies discuss them freely enough: and I have heard a clergyman of the Church of England say things in the pulpit which in my younger days very few laymen would have dared to say at a dinner- party. Yet in spite of all this progress much religious persecution goes on, and bigotry abounds. The diffusion of Doubt is the only remedy for these evils; and though the hacking and hewing of old beliefs must cause much suffering, it is better that a thousand should suffer rather than that one crime of intolerance should be committed.

I now withdrew from the firm and adopted the pleasant life of the country gentleman, retaining, however, the habits of the scholar. I had determined when I left Limmerleigh never to pass a day without doing a kind action; and also to contribute something every day to the general knowledge of mankind. Having no special talents, I was at first puzzled what to do. However, I thought it might be of use if I translated into popular English some of the great writers of antiquity. This, as you know, has been my daily task for many years, and the works already published attest my industry.

And now a last word about my religion. It has been with me very many years. We are no longer strangers to each other. It has given me peace. It has made me content. It has taught me to value and enjoy life, yet not to dread annihilation.

I believe in God the Incomprehensible, whose nature man can never ascertain. To adore this extraordinary power would be irrational; nor do I allow myself to speculate upon the mystery; for it is wrong to waste the powers of the brain, which might otherwise be usefully employed, in reflecting on problems which cannot be solved.

I continue to gather knowledge, and shall do so to my last hour. I endeavor to be good, and rigidly watch my temper and my thoughts. I seek the happiness of others. I will own that often in these twenty-five years I have sighed for my old belief, when to me God was semi-human and man was semi-divine; and after death, life began, and happiness never ceased; and my mother, my Margaret, would be joined to me again. And also sometimes my heart has rebelled against the fate of the human race, doomed to work like the coral insects of the sea. But I learnt how to stifle such repinings and regrets; and now I have attained the perfection of unselfishness as regards the disposition of my soul. Last year, when I was given up by the doctors and expected to die every hour, I had no desire whatever to begin a new state of existence; and it even seemed ludicrous to me, the idea of my feeble imperfect mind being transplanted to another world. It was, I thought, just and natural that I should go back to the Earth whence I came.

I have little more to say. I think you will admit, my dear Ellen, that one may cease to believe in a Personal God and in the Immortality of the Soul, and yet not cease to be a good and even a religious man; indeed, I think I have proved something more -- namely, that this Religion of Unselfishness, for those who are able to embrace it, is far more ennobling than any religion which holds out the hope of celestial rewards. It may be that precisely on account of its unselfishness and purity it can make but few converts in the present condition of the human mind; and certainly long ages must elapse before it can become the Religion of the World. But I believe that year by year the power of this religion will increase, and that more and more, as time goes on, it will give rest to troubled hearts, as it did to mine at Limmerleigh.

Lastly, there is one thing you ought to understand. I disbelieve in a future life; and this disbelief amounts to a positive conviction. But I may be mistaken, It is impossible to know. The doctrine or theory of a future life is not contrary to reason like that of a Personal Creator. We can show it to be most improbable; but on the other hand we must allow that it is a possible contingency.

Well now, you might say, "Suppose that a good man, converted by your arguments, gave, up the belief in his own immortality, loved others, labored for others, strove to purify his heart, but took no heed for his own soul, and died believing in annihilation and there should be a future life after all -- what then? "Why, then he would be perfectly prepared for the life which he did not anticipate. For this is a beautiful quality of our religion. We disbelieve in future rewards, and so eradicate all selfish longings from our hearts; but if, contrary to our expectations, there should be a future life with rewards, none will be able to rank with ourselves. For what life is so highly deserving of reward as that which is spent in doing good without the hope or desire of reward?

Also from Benediction Books …
Wandering Between Two Worlds: Essays on Faith and Art
Anita Mathias
Benediction Books, 2007
152 pages
ISBN: 0955373700

Available from www.amazon.com, www.amazon.co.uk

In these wide-ranging lyrical essays, Anita Mathias writes, in lush, lovely prose, of her naughty Catholic childhood in Jamshedpur, India; her large, eccentric family in Mangalore, a sea-coast town converted by the Portuguese in the sixteenth century; her rebellion and atheism as a teenager in her Himalayan boarding school, run by German missionary nuns, St. Mary's Convent, Nainital; and her abrupt religious conversion after which she entered Mother Teresa's convent in Calcutta as a novice. Later rich, elegant essays explore the dualities of her life as a writer, mother, and Christian in the United States-- Domesticity and Art, Writing and Prayer, and the experience of being "an alien and stranger" as an immigrant in America, sensing the need for roots.

About the Author

Anita Mathias is the author of *Wandering Between Two Worlds: Essays on Faith and Art.* She has a B.A. and M.A. in English from Somerville College, Oxford University, and an M.A. in Creative Writing from the Ohio State University, USA. Anita won a National Endowment of the Arts fellowship in Creative Nonfiction in 1997. She lives in Oxford, England with her husband, Roy, and her daughters, Zoe and Irene.

Visit Anita at http://www.anitamathias.com.

The Church Thad Had Too Much
Anita Mathias
Benediction Books, 2010
52 pages
ISBN: 9781849026567

Available from www.amazon.com, www.amazon.co.uk

The Church That Had Too Much was very well-intentioned. She wanted to love
God, she wanted to love people, but she was both hampered by her muchness and
the abundance of her possessions, and beset by ambition, power struggles and
snobbery. Read about the surprising way The Church That Had Too Much began
to resolve her problems in this deceptively simple and enchanting fable.

About the Author

Anita Mathias is the author of *Wandering Between Two Worlds: Essays on Faith
and Art.* She has a B.A. and M.A. in English from Somerville College, Oxford
University, and an M.A. in Creative Writing from the Ohio State University, USA.
Anita won a National Endowment of the Arts fellowship in Creative Nonfiction in
1997. She lives in Oxford, England with her husband, Roy, and her daughters,
Zoe and Irene.

Visit Anita at http://www.anitamathias.com

Francesco, Artist of Florence: The Man Who Gave Too Much
Anita Mathias
Benediction Books, 2014
52 pages (full colour)
ISBN: 978-1781394175

In this lavishly illustrated book by Anita Mathias, Francesco, artist of Florence, creates magic in pietre dure, inlaying precious stones in marble in life-like "paintings." While he works, placing lapis lazuli birds on clocks, and jade dragonflies on vases, he is purely happy. However, he must sell his art to support his family. Francesco, who is incorrigibly soft-hearted, cannot stand up to his haggling customers. He ends up almost giving away an exquisite jewellery box to Signora Farnese's bambina, who stands, captivated, gazing at a jade parrot nibbling a cherry. Signora Stallardi uses her daughter's wedding to cajole him into discounting his rainbowed marriage chest. His old friend Girolamo bullies him into letting him have the opulent table he hoped to sell to the Medici almost at cost. Carrara is raising the price of marble; the price of gems keeps rising. His wife is in despair. Francesco fears ruin.

* * *

Sitting in the church of Santa Maria Novella at Mass, very worried, Francesco hears the words of Christ. The lilies of the field and the birds of the air do not worry, yet their Heavenly Father looks after them. As He will look after us. He resolves not to worry. And as he repeats the prayer the Saviour taught us, Francesco resolves to forgive the friends and neighbours who repeatedly put their own interests above his. But can he forgive himself for his own weakness, as he waits for the eternal city of gold whose walls are made of jasper, whose gates are made of pearls, and whose foundations are sapphire, emerald, ruby and amethyst? There time and money shall be no more, the lion shall live with the lamb, and we shall dwell trustfully together. Francesco leaves Santa Maria Novella, resolving to trust the One who told him to live like the lilies and the birds, deciding to forgive those who haggled him into bad bargains--while making a little resolution for the future